INTRODUCTION TO

GLOBAL

POLITICS

INTRODUCTION TO
GLOBAL
POLITICS

Steven L. Lamy
University of Southern California

John Baylis
Swansea University

Steve Smith
University of Exeter

Patricia Owens
Queen Mary, University of London

New York Oxford
OXFORD UNIVERSITY PRESS
2011

Oxford University Press, Inc., publishes works that further Oxford University's
objective of excellence in research, scholarship, and education.

Oxford New York

Auckland   Cape Town   Dar es Salaam   Hong Kong   Karachi
Kuala Lumpur   Madrid   Melbourne   Mexico City   Nairobi
New Delhi   Shanghai   Taipei   Toronto

With offices in

Argentina   Austria   Brazil   Chile   Czech Republic   France   Greece
Guatemala   Hungary   Italy   Japan   Poland   Portugal   Singapore
South Korea   Switzerland   Thailand   Turkey   Ukraine   Vietnam

Published by Oxford University Press, Inc.
198 Madison Avenue, New York, New York 10016
http://www.oup.com

Oxford is a registered trademark of Oxford University Press

Library of Congress Cataloging-in-Publication Data

Introduction to global politics / Steven L. Lamy ... [et al.].
        p. cm.
    ISBN 978-0-19-538527-4
    1. Geopolitics. 2. World politics. 3. International relations. I. Lamy,
Steven L.
    JC319.I66 2011
    327—dc22

                                    2010019214

Printing number: 9 8 7 6 5 4 3 2 1

Printed in the United States of America
on acid-free paper

Brief Contents

Contents

CHAPTER 4: Alternative Approaches   92

Stephen Hobden, Patricia Owens, Steve Smith, Richard Wyn Jones, and Steven L. Lamy

PART III: **GLOBAL ACTORS**

CHAPTER 5: States and Foreign Policy   116

Steven L. Lamy

CHAPTER 6: Global and Regional Governance   158

Devon Curtis, Christian Reus-Smit, Paul Taylor, and Steven L. Lamy

CHAPTER 7: Transnational Actors   194

Peter Willetts and Steven L. Lamy

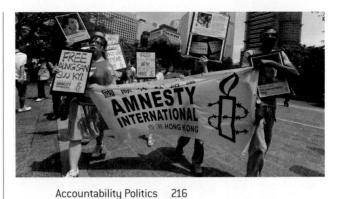

PART IV: **GLOBAL ISSUES: SECURITY**

CHAPTER 8: International Security and Military Power   222

John Baylis, Darryl Howlett, and Steven L. Lamy

Preface

TODAY THE WORLD IS SMALLER and yet more complex. We live in a time when international news is instantaneous; when the Internet can open windows into the lives of people around the globe—and new economies; when distant countries are seeking new ways to cooperate with each other (or not); when questions of global climate change, human trafficking, and nuclear proliferation seem to affect everyone from Georgia, USA, to the nation-state of Georgia; and when we as citizens of the world can travel to foreign lands in no time flat. And yet it seems a small idea to say our world is merely "shrinking."

Because our lives have become more tightly interconnected with the lives of everyone else on the planet, everything has also become much more complex.

Isolation is no longer a viable option, for societies or for individuals, nor is deviance or defiance. Our everyday decisions—even private decisions about what food to eat, what clothes to wear, what books to read, or what movies to see—affect the quality of life of everyone around us and of billions of people in distant countries. At the same time, decisions made around the world affect our daily life. As Dr. Martin Luther King Jr. put it, in 1967, "Before you finish eating breakfast this morning, you've depended on more than half the world. This is the way our universe is structured. We aren't going to have peace on earth until we recognize this basic fact of the interrelated structure of all reality."

However, to understand where we are today—and where we are going tomorrow—it is important to see where we've been and to study the overarching arguments that attempt to explain world events. And so *Introduction to Global Politics* has been written with this increasingly interdependent world in mind, with a singularly global approach that also teaches an appreciation for a variety of worldviews.

One World...

Perhaps the word "globalization" has become so overplayed in the various media of today that it has not retained much of its original force. And yet, there is no other unifying topic more important than globalization, no other trend worth our attention—not only for those who study world politics but for those who increasingly describe themselves as citizens of the world. So what does it mean to have a new textbook that takes a global view of world politics?

When we say our approach is "global" we really mean two things: First, this textbook brings together **academics from around the world**. No other textbook draws from such a diversity of thought from around the globe. Indeed, it can be said that scholars of world politics are by nature contentious: if there are two of us in a room, there will be at least three arguments. Yet all of us teach international relations courses, and all of us agree that to be an effective and productive citizen it is critical to have a basic understanding of how this world works and the important global challenges that we face as members of a global community. Students need to be exposed to the diversity of thinking in our field, but they should come to appreciate these common elements as well.

Second, we also discuss in some detail the **critical actors in global politics**. We explore the role of individual nation-states and international institutions like the United Nations, the European Union, and the critically important economic institutions like the World Bank Group and the World Trade Organization. We carefully assess how different groups and individuals shaped these global institutions, holding different views on how best to govern this world of independent nation-states now numbering nearly two hundred. Generally these views reflect the theoretical debates in the field of international relations. We also explore the growing number and significance of nonstate actors, both multinational corporations like Nike and McDonalds and nongovernmental organizations (NGOs) like Oxfam and Doctors Without Borders. The entire world saw how important these actors are as we experienced two significant events: the global economic crisis in 2008–2009 and the 2010 earthquake that resulted in the devastation of Haiti. The field is changing as the world changes. And yet, until now, no textbook has provided such in-depth coverage of these important nonstate actors. As you will see, with *Introduction to Global Politics* we hope to improve on the standard conversation; to bring the introductory course more in line with today's research; to ask (and try to answer) the kind of questions most relevant for students of world politics today.

...Many Worldviews

Of course it is simply not enough to know about current events. Students also need to develop a deeper understanding of these events—of the contending explanations surrounding the events and issues we hear about in the news every day. These explanations—or theoretical arguments—frame our understanding of this complex world, often acting as intellectual lenses that filter what is important and what is ignored. Theory matters because we all use it—whether we know it or not—to decide our priorities and to act on our decisions. As the economist Ken Boulding suggested in his book *The Image* (1956), we do not react to reality, we react to our *image of reality*, and theories and beliefs that we embrace help to shape that image. Students of this textbook will be introduced to the mainstream theoretical traditions of *realism* and *liberalism* (Chapter 3) and the more relevant alternative theories of constructivism, Marxism, and feminism (Chapter 4) that are usually left out of other texts. Our goal is to introduce students to all relevant voices so they can make an informed choice about how best to both explain and understand the world in which we live. We aim to demystify important theories so that they may illuminate the actors and issues we discuss, rather than cloud them in further mystery. In short, we hope each student will read these pages and develop a more informed worldview.

The Structure of the Book

Introduction to Global Politics is divided into five distinct parts, offering an unbiased, flexible arrangement of foundational topics, important actors, and timely issues.

The first two parts are foundational, covering the basic **histories and theories** a student should know to be an effective citizen in this global society. The third part then proceeds to introduce the main **actors on the world stage**—from states, to intergovernmental organizations, to transnational actors and nongovernmental agencies. Instructors can mix and match these beginning chapters as needed, selecting some chapters for class review and others for background, so that the larger, more exciting issues of the day can receive faster—and more informed—attention. After all, the field of international relations began as a response to the scourge of WWI; thus, one might argue that ours is practical discipline, with war and inequality being the two most challenging issues we face. In that vein, our final two parts of the textbook focus on those issues of crucial importance to the security and prosperity of the people in the world. We discuss war, terrorism, and human rights and human security in our section on global security. In fact, it is worth noting that the **human rights and security** chapter (Chapter 10) is unique among introductory textbooks; we chose these related topics for a complete coverage not only because they are "hot topics" but also because most textbooks today lack serious, integrated treatment of these very serious, inextricably linked topics. Then, in the last section of the book we focus on the **global economy**, with an emphasis on trade, development, and environmental sustainability. Each chapter provides essential information about the issue area and presents case studies and worldview questions that encourage students to think about these issues from contending perspectives—which brings us to our next point, regarding this textbook's pedagogy.

Pedagogy

To aid students with the development of their own, more well-informed worldview, we have supplied several active teaching strategies, outside of the main text, within every chapter. These boxed essays and other textual or visual elements bring into sharp relief some of the unique themes of this book:

- **Global Perspectives**—Each one of these feature essays opens a window onto another part of the world, showing how other countries and world organizations perceive and manage global politics.
- **Theory in Practice**—These features examine real-world scenarios using a variety of theoretical lenses, demonstrating the explanatory power of theories in global politics.
- **Case Studies**—For a more in-depth analysis of a subject, students can turn to these boxed essays that delve into world events.
- **What's Your Worldview?**—These short, critical-thinking questions in every chapter challenge students to develop their own, more well-informed ideas about global actors and issues.

In fact, every part of this textbook has been developed with today's college student in mind; it includes a number of integrated study aids—such as a **running glossary, review questions**, and annotated lists of **further readings** and **online resources**—all of which help students read and retain important information while extending the learning experience. Two **opposing quotations** frame every chapter at the beginning, setting up two sides of one possible debate for students to consider while reading. And then, at the end of every chapter, rather than simply summarizing the contents for students—which can lead to spoon-feeding—we have provided a **conclusion** that requires students to analyze the various topics and themes of the chapter a bit more critically, placing everything they have learned into the broader context of the adjacent chapters. Instructors around the globe agree: students need to acquire strong critical-thinking skills; they need to learn how to make connections among real-world events they hear about in the news and the ideas they learn about in class—and so it is with these goals in mind that the authors and editors have built this new introductory textbook.

One last point with regard to pedagogy: the art program has been carefully selected to support critical thinking as well; not only do we present a number of maps that offer unique global perspectives on historic events and modern world trends, but we have also incorporated extensive **data graphics** and **compelling photographs** to engage the reader visually. The captions of many of these images include questions for further thought—once again connecting the reader back to the core content of the course, with an interesting prompt or relevant point. At the same time, the design of each page has been carefully considered so that the interior is focused and clean, fresh and inviting—easy to read, difficult to forget.

Supplements

Oxford University Press offers instructors and students a comprehensive ancillary package for qualified adopters of *Introduction to Global Politics*.

Companion Website at www.oup.com/he/lamy

- For instructors, this site includes the teaching tools described below, available for immediate download. Contact your local OUP sales representative for access.
- For students, the companion website includes a number of study tools, including learning objectives, key-concept summaries, quizzes and essay questions, Web activities, and Web links.

Instructor's Resource Manual with Test Item File

- The Instructor's Resource Manual includes chapter objectives, a detailed chapter outline, lecture suggestions and activities, discussion questions, video resources, and Web resources. Available in print, on the Instructor's Resource CD, or as a download from the Web at **www.oup.com/us/lamy**.
- The Test Item File includes over 1,400 test items, including multiple-choice, short-answer, and essay questions. Questions are identified as factual, conceptual, or applied, and correct answers are keyed to the text pages where the concepts are presented. Available in print format or on the Instructor's Resource CD.

PowerPoint-Based Slides

Each chapter slide deck includes a succinct chapter outline and incorporates relevant chapter graphics. Available on the Instructor's Resource CD or as a download from the Web.

Computerized Test Bank

Employing the popular Diploma test authoring and management tool, this system is designed for both novice and advanced users. Diploma enables instructors to create and edit questions, create quizzes and tests with an easy-to-use drag-and-drop tool, publish quizzes and tests to online courses, and print quizzes and tests for paper-based assessments. Available on the Instructor's Resource CD.

Instructor's Resource CD

This resource puts all of your teaching tools in one place. This CD includes the Instructor's Resource Manual with Tests, the Computerized Test Bank, the PowerPoint-based slides, and the graphics from the text.

Please contact your Oxford University Press sales representative for more information at (800) 280-0208.

Packaging Options

Adopters of *Introduction to Global Politics* can package **ANY** Oxford University Press book with the text for a 20 percent savings off the total package price. See our many trade and scholarly offerings at **www.oup.com**, then contact your local OUP sales representative to request a package ISBN. In addition, the following items can be packaged with the text for free:

> **Oxford Pocket World Atlas, Sixth Edition:** This full-color atlas is a handy reference for international relations/global politics students.
>
> **Very Short Introduction Series:** These very brief texts offer succinct introductions to a variety of topics. Titles include *Terrorism* by Townshend, *Globalization,* Second Edition, by Steger, and *Global Warming* by Maslin, among others.

Acknowledgments

The authors wish to thank all members of Oxford University Press, in particular Jennifer Carpenter, executive editor, for her tireless sponsorship of this complex project, for her guidance, enthusiasm, and insights; Frederick Speers, development editor, for his diplomatic coordination of this book's many authors and elements and for his contribution to the book's vision overall; and Thomas Pold and Maegan Sherlock, editorial assistants, who worked efficiently behind the scenes to arrange reviews, prepare manuscripts, and secure permissions. Managing editor Lisa Grzan managed the project with style and grace; Teresa Nemeth, copyeditor, provided the right amount of polish; and last but not least, art director Paula Schlosser is responsible for the book's fresh, inviting look. Beyond the individual authors and editors of this edition, there are many others who contributed to its shape and its success. We owe a debt of gratitude to the following people:

Expert Reviewer and Supplements Author

John Masker, Temple University

Reviewers

Ali R. Abootalebi
University of Wisconsin, Eau Claire—Eau Claire, Wisconsin

Linda S. Adams
Baylor University—Waco, Texas

Klint Alexander
Vanderbilt University—Nashville, Tennessee

Youngshik D. Bong
American University—Washington, DC

Marijke Breuning
University of North Texas—Denton, Texas

Alison Brysk
University of California, Irvine—Irvine, California

Jeanie Bukowski
Bradley University—Peoria, Illinois

Manochehr Dorraj
Texas Christian University—Fort Worth, Texas

John S. Duffield
Georgia State University—Atlanta, Georgia

Michelle Frasher-Rae
Ohio University—Athens, Ohio

Brian Frederking
McKendree University—Lebanon, Illinois

Matthew Fuhrmann
University of South Carolina—Columbia, South Carolina

David M. Goldberg
College of DuPage—Glen Ellyn, Illinois

Jeannie Grussendorf
Georgia State University—Atlanta, Georgia

James R. Hedtke
Cabrini College—Radnor, Pennsylvania

Jeanne Hey
Miami University—Oxford, Ohio

Jeneen Hobby
Cleveland State University—Cleveland, Ohio

Arend A. Holtslag
University of Massachusetts, Lowell—Lowell, Massachusetts

Christopher Housenick
American University—Washington, DC

Aida A. Hozic
University of Florida—Gainesville, Florida

Maorong Jiang
Creighton University—Omaha, Nebraska

Michael D. Kanner
University of Colorado at Boulder—Boulder, Colorado

Aaron Karp
Old Dominion University—Norfolk, Virginia

Joyce P. Kaufman
Whittier College—Whittier, California

Bernd Kaussler
James Madison University—Harrisonburg, Virginia

Howard Lehman
University of Utah—Salt Lake City, Utah

Steven Lobell
University of Utah—Salt Lake City, Utah

Domenic Maffei
Caldwell College—Caldwell, New Jersey

Mary K. Meyer McAleese
Eckerd College—St. Petersburg, Florida

Mark J. Mullenbach
University of Central Arkansas—Conway, Arkansas

William W. Newmann
Virginia Commonwealth University—Richmond, Virginia

Miroslav Nincic
University of California, Davis—Davis, California

Michael Nojeim
Prairie View A & M University—Prairie View, Texas

Richard Nolan
University of Florida—Gainesville, Florida

Asli Peker
New York University—New York, New York

Meg Rincker
Purdue University Calumet—Hammond, Illinois

Brigitte H. Schulz
Trinity College—Hartford, Connecticut

Shalendra D. Sharma
University of San Francisco—San Francisco, California

David Skidmore
Drake University—Des Moines, Iowa

Michael Struett
North Carolina State University—Raleigh, North Carolina

James Larry Taulbee
Emory University—Atlanta, Georgia

Faedah Totah
Virginia Commonwealth University—Richmond, Virginia

John Tuman
University of Nevada, Las Vegas—Las Vegas, Nevada

Brian R. Urlacher
University of North Dakota—Grand Forks, North Dakota

Thomas J. Volgy
University of Arizona—Tucson, Arizona

Kimberly Weir
Northern Kentucky University—Highland Heights, Kentucky

Yi Yang
James Madison University—Harrisonburg, Virginia

The book would not have been the same without the assistance and insight from these outstanding scholars and teachers. Meanwhile, any errors you may find in the book remain our own. We welcome your feedback and thank you for your support.

Steven L. Lamy
John Baylis
Steve Smith
Patricia Owen

About the Authors

Amitav Acharya is Professor of International Relations at American University. He has been Professor of Global Governance at the University of Bristol, UK, Professor of International Relations at Nanyang Technological University, Singapore, Professor of Political Science at York University, Toronto, and a Fellow of the John F. Kennedy School of Government at Harvard University. He is author of *Promoting Human Security: Ethnical, Normative and Educational Frameworks in South-East Asia* (UNESCO 2007) and recent articles dealing with international relations theory, norm diffusion, comparative regionalism, and Asian security in *International Organization, World Politics, International Security*, and *International Studies Quarterly*.

David Armstrong is Emeritus Professor of International Relations at the University of Exeter. His books include *Revolutionary Diplomacy* (California University Press 1977), *The Rise of the International Organization* (Macmillan 1981), *Revolution and World Order* (Clarendon Press 1993), *International Law and International Relations* (co-authored with Theo Farrell and Hélène Lambert; Cambridge University Press 2007), and *Routledge Handbook of International Law* (editor; Routledge 2009).

John Baylis was formerly Professor of Politics and International Relations and Pro-Vice-Chancellor of Swansea University. He is the author of more than twenty books, the most recent of which are *The Globalization of World Politics: An Introduction to International Relations* (5th ed. with Steve Smith and Patricia Owens, OUP 2010), *Strategy in the Contemporary World: An Introduction to Strategic Studies* (3rd ed. with James Wirtz and Colin S. Gray, OUP 2010), and *The United States and Europe: Beyond the Neo-Conservative Divide* (edited with John Roper, Routledge 2006).

Alex J. Bellamy is Professor of International Relations and Executive Director of the Asia-Pacific Centre for the Responsibility to Protect at The University of Queensland, Australia. His books include *Understanding Peacekeeping* (with Paul D. Williams, 2nd edition, 2010), *The Responsibility to Protect: The Global Effort to End Mass Atrocities* (Polity, 2009), and *Just Wars: From Cicero to Iraq* (Polity, 2007). He is currently writing *Massacres and Morality: Mass Atrocities in an Age of Non-Combatant Immunity* (Oxford), and a book on the Responsibility to Protect (with Sara E. Davies).

Chris Brown is Professor of International Relations at the London School of Economics and Political Science and the author of *International Relations Theory: New Normative Approaches* (Columbia 1992), *Understanding International Relations* (Palgrave Macmillan 1997; 4th ed. 2009), *Sovereignty, Rights and Justice* (Palgrave 2002), *Practical Judgement in International Political Theory* (Routledge 2010), as well as numerous book chapters and journal articles in the field of international political theory. He edited *Political Restructuring in Europe: Ethical Perspectives* (Routledge 1994) and co-edited (with Terry Nardin and N. J. Rengger) *International Relations in Political Thought: Texts from the Greeks to the First World War* (Cambridge 2002). A former Chair of the British International Studies Association (1998/99), he was Head of the Department of International Relations from 2004 to 2007 and is currently Vice-Chair of the Academic Board at LSE.

Professor **Michael Cox** holds a Chair in International Relations at the London School of Economics and Political Science, where he is also Co-director of IDEAS-a Centre for Strategy and Diplomacy. He is the author and editor of several books on US foreign policy, world politics, and the international theory of E. H. Carr, including the definitive edition of his *The Twenty Years' Crisis*, published in 2001. His latest books include *US Foreign Policy* (edited with Doug Stokes; Oxford 2008), *Soft Power and US Foreign Policy: Theoretical, Historical and Contemporary Perspectives* (edited with Inderjeet Parmar; Routledge 2010), and *The Global 1989* (edited with George Lawson and Chris Armbruster; Cambridge, forthcoming).

Devon Curtis is Lecturer in the Department of Politics and International Studies at the University of Cambridge and a Fellow of Emmanuel College. Her main research interests and publications deal with power-sharing and governance arrangements following conflict, UN peacebuilding, the "transformation" of rebel movements to political parties in Africa, and critical perspectives on conflict, peacebuilding, and development.

Tim Dunne is Dean of the new College of Social Science and International Studies at the University of Exeter. He has written and edited nine books. His most recent is the second edition of *International Relations Theories: Discipline* *and Diversity* (co-edited with Steve Smith and Milja Kurki; Oxford 2010). He is an editor of the *European Journal of International Relations*.

Stephen Hobden is Senior Lecturer in International Politics at the University of East London, where he teaches courses on international relations theory, US foreign policy, and China's growing international role. He is currently working on a research project, together with his colleague Erika Cudworth, on complexity theory and international relations.

Darryl Howlett is Senior Lecturer in the Division of Politics and International Relations at the University of Southampton. His most recent publications include (with Jeffrey S. Lantis) "Strategic Culture," in *Strategy in the Contemporary World* (John Baylis, James Wirtz, Colin S. Gray, editors; 3rd ed., Oxford University Press 2010) and "Cyber Security and the Critical National Infrastructure," in *Homeland Security in the UK* (Paul Wilkinson, editor; Routledge 2007).

James D. Kiras is Associate Professor at the School of Advanced Air and Space Studies, Maxwell Air Force Base, Alabama, where he teaches on the subjects of irregular warfare and military theory. He is also Senior Fellow of the Strategic Studies Division at the Joint Special Operations University, Hurlburt Field, Florida, and worked for a number of years in the defense policy and consulting world. Dr. Kiras publishes and lectures on subjects including special operations, irregular warfare, and suicide bombing. His most recent book, co-authored with other contributors, is *Understanding Modern Warfare* (Cambridge University Press 2008). Dr. Kiras's first book was entitled *Special Operations and Strategy: From World War II to the War on Terrorism* (Routledge 2006).

Steven L. Lamy is Professor of International Relations in the School of International Relations at the University of Southern California. He is also the Vice Dean for Academic Programs in the College of Letters, Arts and Sciences. His latest research focuses on religion and international relations and is funded by a grant from the Luce Foundation. A book of foreign policy case studies will be published next year.

Anthony McGrew is Professor of International Relations and Head of the School of Social Sciences, Southampton University, UK.

Patricia Owens is Senior Lecturer at Queen Mary, University of London. She has held research positions at Princeton, UC–Berkeley, USC, UCLA, and Oxford and is the author of *Between War and Politics: International Relations and the Thought of Hannah Arendt* (Oxford 2007).

Christian Reus-Smit is Professor of International Relations at the European University Institute, Florence. He is author of *American Power and World Order* (Polity Press 2004) and *The Moral Purpose of the State* (Princeton University Press 1999), co-author of *Theories of International Relations* (Palgrave 2001, 2005, 2009), editor of *The Politics of International Law* (Cambridge University Press 2004), and co-editor of *The Oxford Handbook of International Relations* (Oxford University Press 2008), *Resolving International Crises of Legitimacy* (special issue, *International Politics* 2007), and *Between Sovereignty and Global Governance* (Macmillan 1998). Between 2001 and 2010 he was Head of the Department of International Relations at the Australian National University.

Brian C. Schmidt is Associate Professor of Political Science at Carleton University, Ottawa, Canada. He is the author of *The Political Discourse of Anarchy: A Disciplinary History of International Relations* (SUNY 1998) and *Imperialism and Internationalism in the Discipline of International Relations*, co-edited with David Long (SUNY 2005).

Len Scott is Professor of International Politics at Aberystwyth University, where he is Dean of Social Sciences. He is also Director of the Centre for Intelligence and International Security Studies. His recent publications include (with R. Gerald Hughes and Peter Jackson, eds.) *Exploring Intelligence Archives: Enquiries into the Secret State* (Routledge 2008) and *The Cuban Missile Crisis and the Threat of Nuclear War* (Continuum 2007).

Professor **Steve Smith** is Vice Chancellor of the University of Exeter and Professor of International Relations. He has written or edited fifteen books. His most widely read work is *Explaining and Understanding International Relations* (co-authored with the late Professor Martin Hollis). He was the editor of the prestigious Cambridge University Press / British International Studies Association series from 1986 to 2005. In 2003–2004 he was President of the International Studies Association. In 1999 he received the Susan Strange Award of the International Studies Association for the person who has most challenged the received wisdom in the profession. He is an Academician of the Social Sciences (AcSS).

Paul Taylor is Emeritus Professor of International Relations at the London School of Economics. Most recently he has published *The End of European Integration: Anti-Europeanism Examined* (Routledge 2008), *International Organization in the Age of Globalization* (Continuum 2003; paperback version June 2005), and *The Careless State: Wealth and Welfare in Britain Today* (Bloomsbury 2010).

The late **Caroline Thomas** was Deputy Vice-Chancellor and Professor of Global Politics at the University of Southampton. She specialized in North-South relations and published widely on the global politics of security, development, environment, and health.

John Vogler is Professor of International Relations in the School of Politics, International Relations and Environment (SPIRE) at Keele University, UK. He is a member of the ESRC Centre for Climate Change Economics and Policy. His books include *The Global Commons: Environmental and Technological Governance* (John Wiley 2000) and, with Charlotte Bretherton, *The European Union as a Global Actor* (Routledge 2006). He has also edited, with Mark Imber, *The Environment and International Relations* (Routledge 1996) and with Alan Russell, *The International Politics of Biotechnology* (Manchester University Press 2000).

Nicholas J. Wheeler is Professor in the Department of International Politics at Aberystwyth University. His publications include *The Security Dilemma: Fear, Cooperation, and Trust in World Politics* (with Ken Booth; Palgrave Macmillan 2008), *National Interest Versus Solidarity: Particular and Universal Ethics in International Life* (edited with Jean-Marc Coicaud; United Nations University Press 2008), and *The British Origins of Nuclear Strategy 1945–55* (with Ian Clark; Oxford University Press). He has also written widely on humanitarian intervention and is the author of *Saving Strangers: Humanitarian Intervention in International Society* (Oxford University Press 2000). He is currently researching a book provisionally entitled *Building Trust in a World of Nuclear Powers* as part of a three-year ESRC/AHRC Fellowship under Research Councils UK's "Global Uncertainties: Security for All in a Changing World" program on "The Challenges to Trust-Building in Nuclear Worlds." He is Director of the David Davies Memorial Institute of International Studies at Aberystwyth University, a Trustee of the Welsh Centre of International Affairs, and a member of the United Nations Association of the UK's Policy Advisory Committee.

Peter Willetts is Visiting Professor of Global Politics at City University, London. He has written extensively on international organizations, particularly on the Nonaligned Movement. He was a pioneer in studying the impact of NGOs on global politics, editing two early books on the subject, *Pressure Groups in the Global System* (Pinter and St. Martins 1982) and *"The Conscience of the World": The Influence of Non-Governmental Organisations in the UN System* (Hurst and Brookings 1996). His latest work, *NGOs in Global Politics* (Routledge, forthcoming), merges his long-standing arguments for an issue-based pluralist approach with empirical work on the expansion of the role of NGOs in diplomacy, international law, and global communications to produce a constructivist interpretation of the contribution of NGOs to global governance.

Ngaire Woods is Professor of International Political Economy and Director of the Global Economic Governance Programme at Oxford University. Her recent books include *Networks of Influence: Developing Countries in a Networked Global Order* (with Leonardo Martinez-Diaz, Oxford University Press, 2009), *The Politics of Global Regulation* (with Walter Mattli, Oxford University Press, 2009), *The Globalizers: the IMF, the World Bank and their Borrowers* (Cornell University Press, 2006), *Exporting Good Governance: Temptations and Challenges in Canada's Aid Program* (with Jennifer Welsh, Laurier University Press, 2007), and *Making Self-Regulation Effective in Developing Countries* (with Dana Brown, Oxford University Press, 2007). She has previously published *The Political Economy of Globalization* (Macmillan, 2000), *Inequality, Globalization and World Politics* (with Andrew Hurrell: Oxford University Press, 1999), *Explaining International Relations since 1945* (Oxford University Press, 1986), and numerous articles on international institutions, globalization, and governance. Ngaire Woods has served as an Advisor to the IMF Board, the UNDP's Human Development Report, and the Commonwealth Heads of Government.

Richard Wyn Jones is Director of the Wales Governance Centre at Cardiff University. He has written extensively on Welsh politics, devolution, nationalism, and security studies. His book, *Security, Strategy and Critical Theory* (Rienner 1999) is an important work in the area of critical theory.

MAPS

OF THE WORLD

1 **2** **3** **4** **5** **6** **7** **8** **9**

A

Beaufort Sea · Parry Is. · Queen Elizabeth Islands · Devon I. · Ellesmere I. · GREENLAND (KALAALLIT NUNAAT) (Denmark)

Bering Strait · ALASKA (U.S.A.) · Banks I. · Victoria I. · Baffin Bay · Baffin I. · Davis Strait · Jan Mayen (Norway) · Norwe Se

B

Anchorage · Fairbanks · Great Bear L. · Yellowknife · Great Slave L. · Hudson Bay · Iqaluit · Nuuk · Denmark Strait · Reykjavík · ICELAND · Faroe Is. (Den.)

Gulf of Alaska · Kodiak I. · Edmonton · Calgary · CANADA · Churchill · Québec · Newfoundland · St. John's · UNITED KINGDOM · Glasgow · Dublin · IRELAND · LONDON · Amst · Bru

Queen Charlotte Is. · Vancouver · Vancouver I. · Seattle · Portland · Winnipeg · Winnipeg · Minneapolis-St. Paul · Ottawa · Montréal · Halifax · NORTH · Bordeaux · Ly · FRA

UNITED STATES · Milwaukee · Detroit · TORONTO · Boston · NEW YORK · PHILADELPHIA · Washington D.C. · Baltimore · ATLANTIC · Azores (Port.) · PORTUGAL · MADRID · Barc · SPAIN

C

PACIFIC · Sacramento · Salt Lake City · Denver · Kansas City · CHICAGO · Cincinnati · Pittsburgh · St. Louis · Lisbon · Tangier

SAN FRANCISCO · Las Vegas · Memphis · Atlanta · Madeira (Port.) · Casablanca · MOROCCO · Marrakesh

LOS ANGELES · Phoenix · Dallas-Ft. Worth · OCEAN · Bermuda (U.K.) · Rabat · MOROCCO

San Diego · El Paso · Houston · New Orleans · Jacksonville · Canary Is. (Sp.) · El Aaiún · ALGE

Tropic of Cancer · Guadalupe (Mex.) · Ciudad Juárez · Rio Grande · San Antonio · Orlando · Tampa-St. Petersburg · MIAMI · WESTERN SAHARA

Honolulu · Oahu · HAWAII (U.S.A.) · Monterrey · Gulf of Mexico · Havana · Nassau · BAHAMAS · Nouakchott · MAURITANIA · MALI

Hawai'i · Revilla Gigedo Is. (Mex.) · MEXICO · León · Guadalajara · CUBA · Turks & Caicos Is. (U.K.) · CAPE VERDE IS. · Dakar · SENEGAL · Tombouctou

OCEAN · MÉXICO · Puebla · Cayman Is. (U.K.) · Port-au-Prince · DOMINICAN REP. · PUERTO RICO (U.S.A.) · Praia · GAMBIA · BISSAU · GUINEA-BISSAU · Bamako · Ouagadougou · BURKINA FASO

D

GUATEMALA · BELIZE · JAMAICA · HAITI · Santo Domingo · Virgin Is. (U.S.A.-U.K.) · ANTIGUA & BARBUDA · GUADELOUPE (Fr.) · DOMINICA · CONAKRY · Freetown · SIERRA LEONE · Yamoussoukro · GHANA

Guatemala · HONDURAS · Tegucigalpa · NETH. ANTILLES · ST. KITTS & NEVIS · MARTINIQUE (Fr.) · GUINEA · IVORY COAST · Abidjan · Accra

San Salvador · SALVADOR · NICARAGUA · Kingston · ST. VINCENT · ST. LUCIA · BARBADOS · Monrovia · LIBERIA

Clipperton I. (Fr.) · Managua · Barranquilla · GRENADA · TRINIDAD & TOBAGO · Gulf of Guinea · SÃO & PR

COSTA RICA · PANAMÁ · San José · Panamá · Caracas · Georgetown

Palmyra Is. (U.S.A.) · Kiritimati · Medellín · VENEZUELA · Paramaribo · Cayenne

Equator · Jarvis I. (U.S.A.) · BOGOTÁ · COLOMBIA · GUYANA · SURINAME · FRENCH GUIANA (Fr.)

KIRIBATI · Starbuck I. · Cali · Orinoco

Galapagos (Ecuador) · Quito · ECUADOR · Guayaquil · Japurá · Amazon · Belém · Fortaleza · Fernando de Noronha (Brazil)

E

Penrhyn Is. · Manihiki · Marquesas Is. · FRENCH · Manaus · Madeira · Natal · Recife

AMER. SAMOA (U.S.A.) · Society Is. · Tuamotu Is. · PERU · Callao · LIMA · BRAZIL · SOUTH

Niue (N.Z.) · Cook Is. (N.Z.) · Tahiti · BOLIVIA · Brasília · Salvador · Ascension I. (U.K.)

Tropic of Capricorn · Tubai Is. · POLYNESIA · Ducie I. · Pitcairn I. (U.K.) · Arequipa · La Paz · Sucre · BELO HORIZONTE · ATLANTIC · St. Helena (U.K.)

Rapa · Sala-y-Gómez (Chile) · Easter I. (Chile) · Antofagasta · PARAGUAY · Asunción · RIO DE JANEIRO · Trindade (Brazil)

San Felix (Chile) · San Ambrosio (Chile) · San Miguel de Tucumán · Curitiba · SÃO PAULO · OCEAN

F

Valparaíso · Córdoba · Paraná · Pôrto Alegre · Rio Grande

SANTIAGO · Rosario · URUGUAY · Tristan da Cunha (U.K.)

Talcahuano · BUENOS AIRES · Montevideo · Bahía Blanca

CHILE · ARGENTINA · Chiloé I.

G

Falkland Is. (U.K.) · South Georgia (U.K.)

Punta Arenas · Tierra del Fuego · Scotia Sea · South Sandwich Is. (U.K.)

C. Horn · Drake Passage · South Orkney Is.

South Shetland Is.

Bellingshausen Sea · Weddell Sea · Ant

Amundsen Sea

Antarctic Circle

H

150°W · 120°W · 90°W · 60°W · 30°W · Gree Me

Projection: Winkel III

West from Greenwi

90 · 160 · 140 · 120 · 100 · 80 · 60 · 40 · 20

1:47 000 000

1:42 000 000

Projection: Azimuthal Equidistant · West from Greenwich · East from Greenwich · COPYRIGHT PHILIP'S

● Dakar   Capital Cities

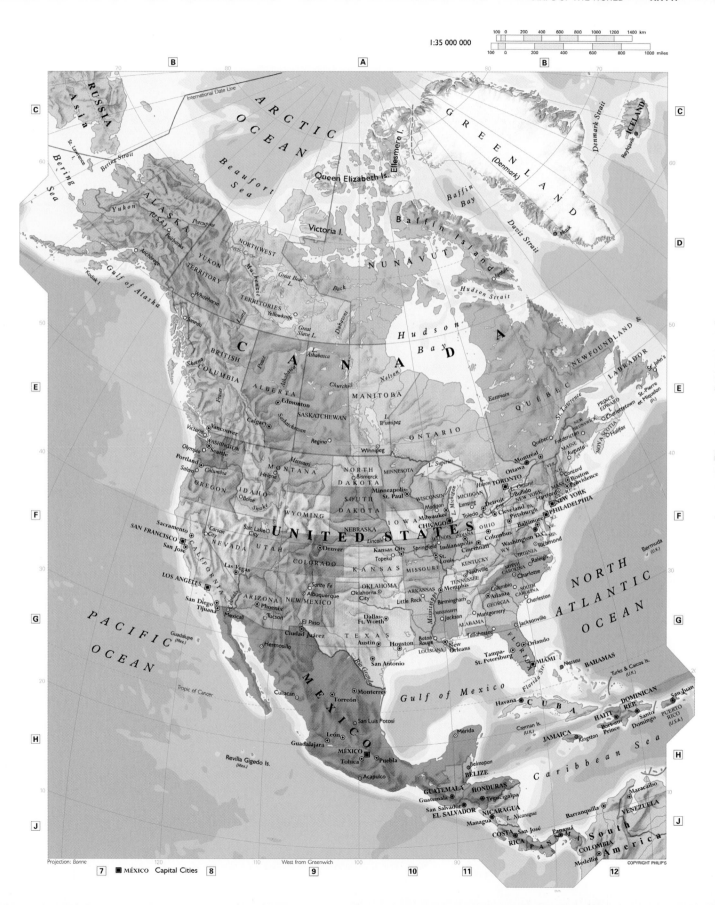

1:35 000 000

Projection: *Bonne*

7 ■ **MÉXICO** Capital Cities **8**

1:35 000 000

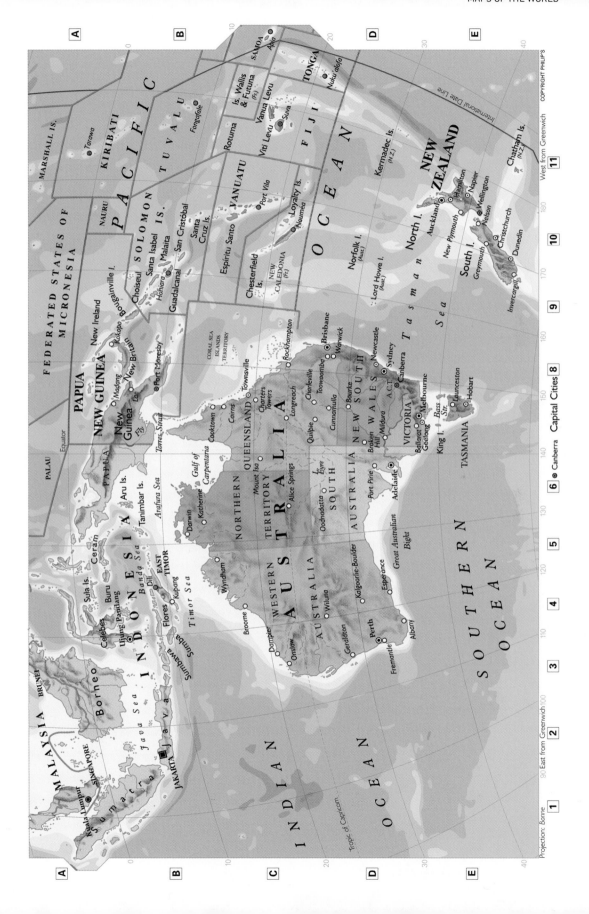

Projection: Bonne

6 ⊚ Canberra   Capital Cities 8

PART ONE

Foundations

I n this part of the book, we want to provide you with a historical context within which to make sense of globalization. We have two main aims: **first**, we want to introduce you to **the main aspects of globalization**, beginning in Chapter 1, and we will do this by giving you a more chronologically concentrated chapter. Then, in Chapter 2, we start with **an overview of international society**

from the Peace of Westphalia in 1648 through to the beginning of the twenty-first century. We think that you need to have some basic understanding of the main developments in **the history of world politics**, as well as some kind of context for thinking about the contemporary period of world history. We want this chapter to give you a lot of historical information that will be of interest in its own right, but our **second** aim is to draw to your attention the main themes of international history so that you can develop a deeper understanding of the issues, both theoretical and empirical, that are dealt with in the remaining four parts of this book. We think that an overview of international history gives you a context within which to begin thinking about globalization: is it a new phenomenon that fundamentally changes the main patterns of international history, or are there precedents for it that make it seem less revolutionary?

CHAPTER 1

Introduction
to Global Politics

> I am a citizen of the world.
>
> —*Diogenes*

> I am not a citizen of the world . . . I am not even aware that there is a world such that one could be a citizen of it. No one has ever offered me citizenship, or described the naturalization process, or enlisted me in the world's institutional structures, or given me an account of its decision procedures . . . or provided me with a list of the benefits and obligations of citizenship, or shown me the world's calendar and the common celebrations and commemorations of its citizens.
>
> —*Michael Walzer*

To many Americans the world changed on September 11, 2001. The entire world watched the hijacked planes fly into the World Trade Center towers, on their television sets, trying to make sense of the horror as it played out in what we call "real time." This was what we call a "defining event" that people will remember for years. It defines an era and defines United States foreign policy, now focused on the global war on terrorism. But how many of us can remember where we were when we first heard of the subprime mortgage crisis? Was it the summer of 2007, when analysts warned of the impending collapse? Maybe you know people who lost their homes to foreclosure? Or maybe it was in the autumn of 2008, as major banks around the world vanished overnight and the Bush administration struggled to stem the hemorrhage of money in the United States? This slowly unfolding global economic crisis threatens to do more damage to the world's financial system than the destruction of the World Trade Center, yet few of us can explain what is occurring.

How we react to momentous events like the September 11 attacks and the global financial collapse of 2008–2009 is linked to how we identify ourselves. Are you a citizen of the world, like Diogenes, or a citizen of a specific place, like Michael Walzer? You might be surprised to know how connected you are to the world. Look at the labels in your clothing. The tag says "Made in someplace," but have you

Eight years after the attacks of
September 11, 2001, people gathered
to remember that day.

3

ever wondered how the pieces of, for example, your sneakers got to the factory where they were assembled? Or how the shoes traveled from that factory in Asia to the store in California, Kansas, or Vermont where you purchased them? Have you ever asked yourself who made your sneakers? How does that person live? How do others in the world view the United States? Do you have a passport and have you traveled internationally? Do you have a Web-capable cell phone, and are you constantly plugged in to Internet applications like Facebook? Have you signed up for news alerts from news agencies? Do you also read the international news from foreign sources such as the BBC or Al Jazeera?

All of us have connections to the world that we are not aware of. Other connections we make, like joining a political group or sorority on campus, are more personal and immediate. Yet both types of connections—known and unknown—help shape our identities as individuals in the wider world. The purpose of this book is to help you to understand the world of politics that provides those connections. Along the way you will see how interdependent we all are and how our way of life is shaped by forces of globalization. This chapter presents an overview of the textbook—the main actors and topics that we will examine. It also introduces the theories that will guide us in our study of world politics.

Introduction

September 11, 2001 The day when Islamic terrorists in the United States hijacked four aircraft—two of which destroyed the World Trade Center in New York, one partially destroyed the Pentagon, and a fourth crash-landed in a field in Pennsylvania (see also "9/11").

The events of **September 11, 2001** (hereafter 9/11), probably more than any other single event, brought home just how globalized the contemporary world is. The subsequent war in Afghanistan (2001–2002) and the particularly controversial invasion of Iraq in 2003, followed by insurgency and civil war, are further clear examples of what it means to call the current era globalized—they involved international coalitions and transnational violent networks in conflicts that linked events in seemingly unrelated parts of the world. Let us look at how aspects of the 9/11 attacks illustrate the impact of globalization.

First, 9/11 was an event taking place in one country, the United States, but immediately observed throughout the world: the television pictures of the second plane crashing into the World Trade Center are probably the most widely seen images in television history. Thus, 9/11 was a world event, which had far more of an effect than represented by the simple number of deaths involved (about three thousand died in the four attacks that day; on an average day thirty thousand children throughout the world die of malnutrition and preventable diseases, though not often of course in front of the gaze of the television cameras).

Second, the attacks were carried out by nineteen individuals in the name of an until-then shadowy organization known as Al Qaeda. This organization was not a state or formal international body but a loose coalition of committed men based, it is claimed, in over fifty countries. This was a truly globalized network and not just a traditional organization.

Third, the attacks were coordinated by using some of the most powerful technologies of the globalized world, namely, mobile phones, international bank accounts, and the Internet. Moreover, the key personnel traveled regularly between continents, using yet another symbol of globalization, mass air travel.

Fourth, the reactions to the events throughout the world were intense, instantaneous, and very mixed: in some Arab and Muslim countries there was jubilation that the West generally, and the United States specifically, had been hit; in many other countries there was profound shock and an immediate empathy with the United States.

Fifth, although the attacks were on buildings in the United States, these were not ordinary buildings; while the Pentagon is the symbol of the United States' military power and hegemony, the World Trade Center was (as the name implies) an icon of the world financial network and the triumph of capitalism led by the United States and other Western countries.

Sixth, it is worth noting that although these were attacks on the United States, many individuals of other nationalities were killed; it is estimated that citizens from about ninety countries were killed in the attacks on the World Trade Center.

Finally, though there is a lot of disagreement over why Osama bin Laden ordered the attacks, the main reasons seem to have concerned events in yet other parts of the world: bin Laden himself cited the plight of the Palestinians, as well as the continued support of the United States for the current Saudi regime and the presence of US advisers on that country's "holy" soil. Therefore, though there are many indicators that the world has become increasingly globalized over the last thirty years, in many ways 9/11 is the best symbol.

Still, globalization can also be seen as one of the causes of the 9/11 attacks. In many parts of the world dominated by traditional cultures and religious communities, fundamentalists see globalization as a Western process bringing popular culture and Western ideas that undermine their core values and beliefs. This "Westoxification" pushed and promoted by globalization is the enemy, and the United States is the leader of this noxious process. Many fundamentalist communities are trying to control, manage, and, if possible, stop the process of globalization. This is possible in totalitarian societies, but it is becoming more difficult as the Internet and global communications spread around the world.

Generally, people care most about what is going on at home or in their local communities. We usually elect people to office who promise to provide jobs, fix roads, offer loans for housing, build good schools, and provide quality health care. These promises may get candidates votes, but people in office soon learn that many of the promises cannot be fulfilled without considering the dynamics of the global economy. Leaders are now realizing that in order to provide for their citizens they must manage the processes of globalization, and this is not a task one country can do alone. Not since the energy crisis of the early 1970s has the world experienced the costs of global interdependence and the vulnerabilities created by globalization. We all became aware of the breadth and depth of globalization with the economic crisis of 2008 and 2009. The costs of this global financial crisis are unemployment, home foreclosures, bank failures, a collapse in the stock markets around the world, and a general anger and dissatisfaction with political leaders for failing to anticipate these problems and respond before the near collapse. Governments must prove that they can regulate global finance and manage the processes of globalization. World leaders have met in a number of settings, including G-20 meetings in London and in the United States. These leaders are now hoping that government spending might stimulate demand and that they can work together to regulate global finance. Further, they hope to direct more funds to countries in the developing world and reform the global institutions that must monitor and manage the forces of globalization. Slowly, people throughout the world are realizing that their own well-being or quality of life is directly tied to the well-being of others in distant lands.

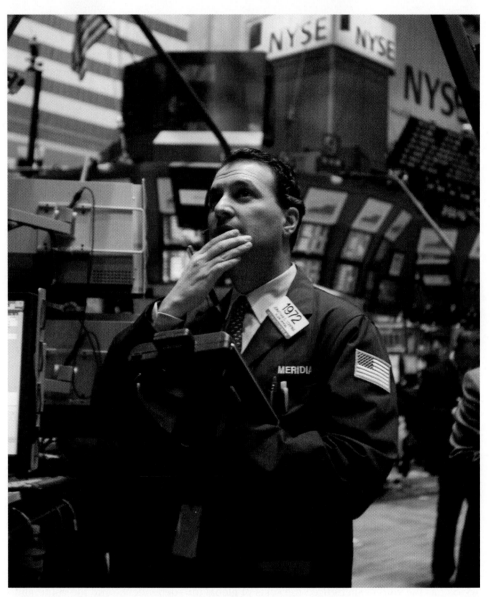

A trader in the New York Stock Exchange considers his options. Has the global economic collapse of 2008–2009 impacted lives more than the 9/11/2001 attacks?

Again, the aim of this book is to provide an overview of global politics in this globalized world. Let us start, though, with a few words about the title. It is not accidental. First, we want to introduce you to global politics, as distinct from international politics or international relations. Second, many think that the contemporary, post–Cold War world is markedly different from previous periods because of the effects of globalization. We think that it is especially difficult to explain global politics in such an era because globalization is a particularly controversial term. There is considerable dispute over just what it means to talk of this being an era of globalization and whether that means that the main features of global politics are any different from those of previous eras. In this introduction we want to explain how we propose to deal with the concept of globalization, and we offer you some arguments for and against seeing it as an important new development in global politics.

Before turning to look at globalization, in order to set the scene for the chapters that follow, we want to do two things. We will first say something about the various terms used to describe international relations, world politics, and global politics, and then we will spend some time looking at the main ways in which global politics has been explained.

International Relations and Global Politics

Why does the main title of this book refer to **global politics** rather than to international politics or **international relations**? These are the traditional names used to describe the kinds of interactions and processes that are the concern of this text. Indeed, you could look at the table of contents of many other introductory books and find a similar listing of main topics, yet often these books would have either "international relations" or "international politics" in their main title. Furthermore, the discipline that studies these issues is nearly always called "international relations" or "international politics." Our reason for choosing the phrase "global politics" is that we think it is more inclusive than either of the alternative terms. With this phrase, we mean to highlight our interest in the politics and political patterns in the world, and not only those between nation-states (as the term "international politics" implies). Thus, we are interested in relations among organizations that may or may not be states—such as, for example, multinational companies, terrorist groups, or **nongovernmental organizations (NGOs)**; these are all known as **transnational actors**. Similarly, the term "international relations" may be too exclusive. Of course, it does represent a widening of our concern from simply the political relations between nation-states, but it still restricts our focus to *inter*-national relations, whereas we think that relations between, say, cities or provinces and other **governments** or international organizations can be equally important. So we prefer to characterize the relations we are interested in as those of "world" politics—or, more specifically, given the powerful influences of globalization, "global" politics. However, we do not want such fine distinctions regarding word choice to force you, the reader, to define politics too narrowly. You will see this issue arising time and time again in the chapters that follow, since many academics want to define politics very widely. One obvious example concerns the relationship between politics and economics; there is clearly an overlap, and a lot of bargaining power goes to the person who can persuade others that the existing distribution of resources is "simply" economic rather than a political issue. So, we want you to think about politics very broadly for the time being. Several features of the contemporary world that you may not have previously thought of as "political" will be described as such in the chapters that follow. Our focus is with the patterns of political relations, defined broadly, that characterize the contemporary world.

Global Actors

After we review the foundational and theoretical aspects of global politics in Chapters 2, 3, and 4, we will take a look at a number of important actors on the world stage. Most specialists in international relations believe that states (nation-states or countries) are the most important actors in world politics—and so we begin our discussion with Chapter 5, "States and Foreign Policy." Nation-states or states are the primary actors in the study of global or world politics. States engage in diplomatic relations, sign the treaties that create the legal foundation for world politics, and go to war.

global politics The politics of global social relations in which the pursuit of power, interests, order, and justice transcends regions and continents.

international relations In a traditional sense, this is the study of the interactions of states in the international system. It was initially considered a part of diplomatic history or political science. Today, departments of international relations include concentrations in international security, political economy, foreign policy, human rights, global governance, and environmental issues. The field now includes the study of other actors, including corporations and NGOs, and a wide variety of issues, such as culture, identity, and ethics.

nongovernmental organization (NGO) An organization, usually a grassroots one, with policy goals, but not governmental in makeup. An NGO is any group of people relating to each other regularly in some formal manner and engaging in collective action, provided the activities are noncommercial and nonviolent and are not on behalf of a government.

transnational actor Any nongovernmental actor, such as a multinational corporation or one country's religious humanitarian organization, that has relations with any actor from another country or with an international organization.

governments The people and agencies that have the power and legitimate authority to determine who gets what, when, where, and how within a given territory.

World leaders like Italian prime minister Silvio Berlusconi and Russian president Dmitry Medvedev were quick to embrace Barack Obama at the Group of 20 Economic Summit. How much political change can one person bring to a country's foreign policy?

nonstate actor Any participant in global politics that is neither acting in the name of government nor created and served by government. NGOs, terrorist networks, global crime syndicates, and multinational corporations are examples.

multinational corporations or enterprises (MNCs/MNEs) A business or firm with administration, production, distribution, and marketing located in countries around the world. Such a business moves money, goods, services, and technology around the world depending upon where the firm can make the most profit.

nation A community of people who share a common sense of identity, which may be derived from language, culture, or ethnicity; this community may be a minority within a single country or live in more than one country.

state A legal territorial entity composed of a stable population and a government; it possesses a monopoly over the legitimate use of force; its sovereignty is recognized by other states in the international system.

Increasingly, however, **nonstate actors** are playing important roles in world politics. These can be supranational organizations that are composed of states. The United Nations (Chapter 6) is the most famous actor in this category; others include the European Union, the Organization of American States (OAS), the Shanghai Cooperation Organization, and the African Union. **Multinational corporations (MNCs)** have also become important players in world politics. These large business organizations can have their headquarters in one country, their design staff in another, and their production facilities in several other countries. MNCs are important in many ways but perhaps most significantly because a factory can provide vital jobs in a developing country. Starting in Chapter 7 we'll provide an in-depth look at these and other nonstate actors, including a discussion of nongovernmental organizations, or NGOs, which have increased in numbers and influence in world politics. NGOs like Oxfam or World Vision provide expertise for policy makers and provide programs and resources to address global problems like poverty and global health issues. To clarify the difference, some authors call MNCs for-profit nonstate actors and NGOs not-for-profit nonstate actors. However, in order to lay the groundwork for that future discussion, let's take a moment now to look more closely at the definitions—and debates—involving states and nation-states, as well as consider the problems of the traditional state-centered approach to studying global politics.

Like many of the terms used in this book, the terms "state" and "nation-state" can be somewhat confusing to newcomers to the field. The two parts of the term "nation-state" derived from different sources. **"Nation"** derived from the idea that a group of people sharing the same geographic space, the same language, the same culture, and the same history also shared a common identity. As most political scientists use the term, "nation" is meant to convey a group identity that is bigger than a family group or tribal unit. **"State"** has its origins in the Latin language and the legal system of the Roman Empire. In political science, "state" is a particularly divisive term, because, as we will see in Chapters 3 and 4, academics disagree about what the term means. At a minimum, political scientists agree that the "state" is the highest-level political structure that makes authoritative decisions within a territorially based political unit. What makes the term confusing for many students in the United States is that the country comprises subunits that are called "states." When "nation" and "state" are combined in the pair "nation-state," we have a term that describes a political unit within which people share an identity. It is important to note that *the state is not always coincidental with a nation*. While the "state" for many political scientists is a set of governing institutions, "nation" refers to the people who share a history, language, religion, or other cultural attributes. The Flemish in Belgium, the Welsh in the United Kingdom, and the Iroquois of the United States and Canada are examples of nations found within states. Most states, even when called "nation-states," actually comprise several nations. As we will see elsewhere in this book, many problems in the modern international system result from nations with historical rivalry that are forced to live within the borders of one state.

The concepts of state and sovereignty are critical to understand if you are a student of international relations, a diplomat, or a political leader. The **nation-state**—sometimes called "country" or simply "state"—is the primary unit of analysis in the study of international relations. As we will learn next, in Chapter 2, the Peace of Westphalia in 1648 recognized the state as supreme and the sovereign power within its boundaries. The Westphalian ideal of sovereignty emphasizes the principle of the inviolability of the borders of a state. Furthermore, all states agreed with the idea that it was not acceptable to intervene in the internal affairs of other states. **Sovereignty** is a complex and contested concept in international relations; basically, it suggests that within a given territory the leaders of a state have absolute and final political authority. However, international relations scholar Manuel Castells (2005) has suggested that the modern nation-state might be adversely affected by globalization in four ways; indeed, all our political institutions are facing the same four crises:

1. States cannot effectively manage global problems unilaterally and thus suffer a *crisis of efficiency*.
2. Policy makers are not always representative of their citizens' interests, and as policy making becomes more global, decisions are made further away from citizens. This is a *crisis of legitimacy*.
3. Citizens are being pulled toward their cultural identity and toward identity and affiliation with NGOs and other civil-society actors. A variety of forces pull them away from citizen identity and have created a *crisis of identity*.
4. Globalization has increased inequality in many states and created a *crisis of equity*.

Castells argues that nation-states must create collaborative networks with NGOs and other nonstate actors to respond effectively to these crises. The nation-state will survive, but states might be forced to share sovereignty with other global actors in order to provide for their citizens, meet their obligations, and face the issues in the world today.

Global Issues

While we define politics broadly, we can also group the global issues that we will study into two main categories: security and economy. Our purpose is to use these issues to demonstrate the connections between state and nonstate actors in the international system. In this textbook we have subdivided Part Four, "Global Security," into three chapters, each

nation-state A political community in which the state claims legitimacy on the grounds that it represents the nation.

sovereignty The condition of a state having control and authority over its own territory and being free from any higher legal authority. It is related to, but distinct from, the condition of a government being free from any external political constraints.

WHAT'S YOUR WORLDVIEW ?

Are you a member of a nation? If you are a US citizen, do you identify first as "American," or perhaps as "Texan" or "Floridian"? Do you identify with a particular ethnic community? Are you a member of an NGO, like Amnesty International or Greenpeace International? How do these connections affect your responsibilities as a citizen of a nation-state?

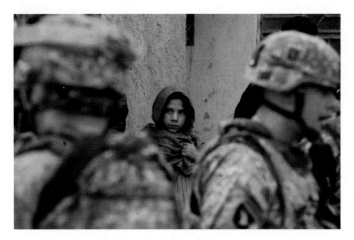

Troops from the US and other NATO states deployed to Afghanistan in 2001 to defeat Al Qaeda and the Taliban government, which gave sanctuary to the group. Nine years later the fighting continues.

examining a vital issue-area of the field. First, we consider international security and military power, the traditional responsibility of countries, that is, to provide for the physical security of the state's territory. Second, we examine terrorism, including the various groups that employ this method and the ways in which countries have responded to the threats. Chapter 10 rounds out this part of the book by discussing an emerging issue-area of world politics: human rights and human security.

Part Five, "Global Political Economy," presents four chapters that examine the intersections of world politics and economics—including trade, finance, poverty, development, and environmental issues. Each of these topics overlaps the others, and it's important not to read these chapters merely in a straightforward fashion but also to review the information from previous chapters as you progress through your coursework. Although we have neatly divided these issues for ease of reading, we do not mean to reduce them in their importance or complexity; indeed, throughout, we'll also examine how security issues and economic issues are inextricably linked.

Theories of Global Politics

The basic problem facing anyone who tries to understand contemporary global politics is that there is so much material to look at; it is difficult to know which things matter and which do not. Where on earth would you start if you wanted to explain the most important

Aid from international agencies like the World Food Program can help to provide immediate relief for starving people. In the long term, prolonged aid can undermine local agricultural production.

political processes? How, for example, would you explain 9/11 attacks on the US, or the 2003 war in Iraq? Why did Al Qaeda attack the United States? Why did President Bush and Prime Minister Tony Blair authorize the attack on Saddam Hussein's Iraq? Why did President Obama change the military strategy for Afghanistan? Where in the world did the 2008 economic crisis "originate"? Where will it "end"—and when? What policies will global leaders develop to respond to this economic crisis? There are very different answers to questions such as these, and there seems no easy way of arriving at a definitive answer to them. Was the invasion of Iraq motivated by a concern with human rights, with our dependency on oil, with unfinished business from the first Gulf War in 1991, with **imperialism**, with the "war against terrorism"? Whether they are aware of it or not, whenever individuals are faced with such a problem, they have to resort to **theories** to understand the problem and to develop effective responses to the problem.

A theory is not simply some grand formal model with hypotheses and assumptions. Rather, *a theory is a kind of simplifying device that allows you to decide which facts matter and which do not.* A good analogy is sunglasses with different colored lenses; put on the red pair and the world looks red, put on the yellow pair and it looks yellow. The world is not any different, it just looks different. And so it is with theories. Shortly we are going to summarize the main theoretical views that have dominated the study of global politics, so we will get an idea of which "colors" they paint the world. But before we do so, please note that the authors of this book do not think that theory is merely an option. It is not as if you can say that you do not want to bother with a theory, and instead all you want to do is to look at the "facts." We believe that this is impossible, since the only way you can decide which of the millions of possible facts to look at is by adhering to some simplifying device that tells you which ones matter the most. We think of theory as such a simplifying device.

You may not even be aware of your theory. It may just be the view of the world that you have inherited from family, a group of friends, or the media. It may just seem common sense to you and not at all anything complicated like a theory. But we fervently believe that all that is happening in such a case is that your theoretical assumptions are implicit rather than explicit, and we prefer to be as explicit as possible when it comes to thinking about world politics.

People have tried to make sense of world politics for centuries, and especially since the separate academic discipline of international politics was formed in 1919, when the Department of International Politics was set up at the University of Wales, Aberystwyth. Interestingly, the man who set up that department, a Welsh industrialist called David Davies, saw its purpose as being to help prevent war. By studying international politics scientifically, many scholars believed they could find the causes of the world's main political problems and put forward solutions to help politicians solve them. After the end of the First World War, the discipline was marked by such a commitment to change the world. This is known as a **normative** position, with the task of academic study being one of making the world a better place. Its opponents characterized this normative position as overly **idealistic**, in that it had a view of how the world

Theories of international relations can be like a pair of sunglasses. What tint do your glasses have?

imperialism The practice of foreign conquest and rule in the context of global relations of hierarchy and subordination. It can lead to the establishment of an empire.

theory A proposed explanation of an event or behavior of an actor in the real world. Definitions range from "an unproven assumption" to "a working hypothesis that proposes an explanation for an action or behavior." In international relations we have intuitive theories, empirical theories, and normative theories.

normative theory Systematic analyses of the ethical, moral, and political principles that either govern or ought to govern the organization or conduct of global politics. The belief that theories should be concerned with what ought to be, rather than merely diagnosing what is.

idealism Referred to by realists as utopianism since it underestimates the logic of power politics and the constraints this imposes on political action. Idealism as a substantive theory of international relations is generally associated with the claim that it is possible to create a world of peace. Some idealists seek to apply liberal thinking in domestic politics to international relations—in other words, to institutionalize the rule of law.

realism The theoretical approach that analyzes all international relations as the relation of states engaged in the pursuit of power. Realists see the international system as anarchic or without a common power, and they believe conflict is endemic in the international system.

liberalism According to Michael Doyle (1997, 207), liberalism includes the following four claims. First, all citizens are juridically equal and have equal rights to education, access to a free press, and religious toleration. Second, the legislative assembly of the state possesses only the authority invested in it by the people, whose basic rights it is not permitted to abuse. Third, a key dimension of the liberty of the individual is the right to own property, including productive forces. Fourth, liberalism contends that the most effective system of economic exchange is one that is largely market driven and not one that is subordinate to bureaucratic regulation and control.

Marxism A theory critical of the status quo or dominant paradigm. It is a critique of the capitalist political economy from the view of the revolutionary proletariat, or workers. The relations of production, or the relationship between workers and owners, is the determining factor in political relations. Marxists believe that those who own the means of production also control the political system. In capitalist systems, workers are exploited and thus alienated from both the economic and political systems. Marxists' ideal is a stateless and classless society.

Each year people gather in Hiroshima, Japan, near the damaged building that was the aim point of the first atomic bomb used in wartime. How have nuclear weapons revolutionized warfare?

ought to be and focused on means of preventing war and even making war and violence obsolete. It was during the years between WWI and WWII that **idealism** was embraced by a number of antiwar organizations. In its place its opponents preferred an approach they called **realism**, which, rather unsurprisingly, stressed seeing the world as it really is rather than how we would like it to be. And, the "real" world as seen by realists is not a very pleasant place; human beings are at best self-interest oriented and probably much worse. Notions such as the perfectibility of human beings and the possibility of an improvement of world politics seem far-fetched. This debate between idealism and realism has continued to the present day, but it is fair to say that realism has tended to have the upper hand. This is mainly because it appears to accord more with common sense than does idealism, especially when the media bombard us daily with images of how awful humans can be to one another.

Having said this, we would like you to think about whether such a realist view is as neutral as it is commonsensical. After all, if we teach global politics to generations of students and tell them that people are selfish, then doesn't that become common sense? And don't they, when they go off into the media or to work for government departments, or the military, or even when they talk to their children over the dinner table, simply repeat what they have been taught and, if in positions of power, act accordingly? We will leave you to think about this. For now, we would like to keep the issue open and simply point out that we are not convinced that realism is as objective or nonnormative as it is portrayed as being.

International Relations Theories and Globalization

It is true that realism has been the dominant way of explaining world politics in the last nearly one hundred years. It is not, however, the only way—and in Chapters 3 and 4 of this book we will examine realism and its four main rivals as theories of world politics, **liberalism**, **Marxism**, and alternative theories like **constructivism** and **feminism**. These theoretical perspectives have tended to be the main theories used to understand world politics, with constructivism becoming increasingly influential since the mid-1990s. In the 1980s it became common to talk of an **interparadigm debate** among realism, liberalism, Marxism, and constructivism; that is to say that the four major theories (designated **paradigms** by the influential philosopher of natural science Thomas Kuhn) were in competition and that the "truth" about world politics lay in the debate between them. At first glance each seems to be particularly good at explaining certain aspects of world politics, and an obvious temptation would be to try to combine them into some overall account. But this is not the easy option it may seem. The four theories are not so much different views of the same world but rather *four views of different worlds*. Let us examine this claim more closely.

While it is clear that each of the four broad theoretical traditions focuses on different aspects of world politics (realism on the power relations between states, liberalism on a much wider set of interactions between states and nonstate actors, Marxist theory on the patterns of the world economy, and constructivism on the ways in which we can develop different social structures and processes), each is saying more than this. Each view claims that it is picking out the most important features of world politics and that it offers a better account than the rival theories. Thus, the four approaches are really in competition with one another; and while you can certainly choose among them, it is not so easy to add bits from one to the others. For example, if you are a Marxist theorist, you think that state behavior is ultimately determined by class forces: forces that the realist does not think affect state behavior. Similarly, constructivism suggests that actors do not face a world that is fixed but rather one that they can in principle change—in direct contrast to the core beliefs of realists and Marxists alike. In other words, these four theories are really versions of what world politics is like rather than partial pictures of it. They do not agree on what world politics is fundamentally all about.

We do not think that any one of these theories has all the answers when it comes to explaining world politics in an era of globalization. In fact, each sees globalization differently. We do not want to tell you which theory seems best, since the purpose of this book is to give you a variety of conceptual lenses. By the end of the book we hope you will work out which of these theories (if any) best explains globalization. Part Two outlines the theories in more detail. We also introduce you to a set of other theories, such as feminism, that many believe

constructivism An approach to international politics that concerns itself with the centrality of ideas and human consciousness. As constructivists have examined world politics they have been broadly interested in how the structure constructs the actors' identities and interests, how their interactions are organized and constrained by that structure, and how their very interaction serves to either reproduce or transform that structure.

feminism A political project to understand so as to change women's inequality, liberation, or oppression. For some, the aim is to move beyond gender, so that it no longer matters; for others, to validate women's interests, experiences, and choices; for others, to work for more equal and inclusive social relations overall. Feminist theories tend to be critical of the biases of the discipline. Many focus their research on the areas where women are excluded from the analysis of major international issues and concerns.

interparadigm debate This is the debate between the two main theoretical approaches in the field of global politics: realism versus liberalism. Some present this debate as one between neorealism and neoliberalism. Critics argue that this is no real debate because the two theoretical approaches share many assumptions.

paradigm A model, or example. In the case of international relations theory, the term is a rough synonym for "academic perspective." A paradigm provides the essential basis for a theory. It presents a comprehensive framework for

In addition to UPC barcodes that provide a unique identification for products, "CE" means Conformité Européenne and signifies that an item meets the health, environmental, and safety requirements of the European Union. Is it a good thing to apply European standards to goods made in China?

the identification of factors that are referenced in the construction of theory. It tells us what is real and significant in a given area. Research questions fall within the paradigm. It provides a means of selecting what will be the object of theory.

are crucial in explaining globalization but that have not yet been dominant in the discipline of international relations. However, we want to reinforce here our earlier comment that theories do not portray "the" truth. In other words, the theories we have mentioned will see globalization differently because they have an a priori view of what is most important in world politics. Therefore, the option is not available of simply answering the tempting question of which theory has the "truest" or "correct" view of globalization.

How We Study Global Politics

As curious individuals we are all interested in understanding the nature of global politics and the behavior of different actors in this global society. Two of the more traditional ways of doing research are the historical and social scientific approaches. A less traditional method of understanding the world is the constructivist approach.

Historians arrive at an understanding of why actions are taken by states, or why events happen, after a careful review of public documents, memoirs, and interviews with key actors. Their goal is to understand a particular decision or event and create a thorough description or narrative that helps us understand decisions that were made by key actors during that event. The goal is not to understand all wars or all actions by states but to create a history of a particular war or a very thorough description of a country's decision to take a certain policy position.

The intellectual interests of social scientists are slightly different. Social scientists want to bring the precision and certainty of the natural sciences to the social world. Un-

---

Global Production and the iPod CASE STUDY

Take just one component of the iPod Nano: the central microchip provided by the US company PortalPlayer. The core technology of the chip is licensed from the British firm ARM and is modified by PortalPlayer's programmers in California, Washington State, and Hyderabad in India. PortalPlayer then works with microchip design companies in California that send the finished design to a foundry in Taiwan (China) that produces wafers (thin metal disks) imprinted with thousands of chips. The capital costs of these foundries can be more than $2.5 million. These wafers are then cut up into individual disks and sent elsewhere in Taiwan to be tested. The chips are then encased in plastic and readied for assembly by Siliconware in Taiwan and Amkor in the Republic of Korea. The finished microchip is then warehoused in Hong Kong (China) before being transported to mainland China where the iPod is assembled.

Working conditions and wages in China are low relative to Western standards. Many workers live in dormitories and work long hours. It is suggested that overtime is compulsory. Nevertheless, wages are higher than the average of the region in which the assembly plants are located and allow for substantial transfers to rural areas, helping to reduce rural poverty. PortalPlayer was only established in 1999 but had revenues in excess of $225 million in 2005. PortalPlayer's chief executive officer has argued that the outsourcing to countries such as India and Taiwan (China) of "non-critical aspects of your business" has been crucial to the development of the firm and its innovation: "It allows you to become nimbler and spend R&D dollars on core strengths."

Since 2003, soon after the iPod was launched, the share price of Apple, the company that produces and sells the iPod, has risen from just over $6 to over $60. Those who own shares in Apple have benefited from the globalization of the iPod.

C. Joseph, "The iPod's Incredible Journey," Mail on Sunday, July 15, 2006; "Meet the iPod's 'Intel,'" Business Trends 32 (April 2006) (World Bank (2006), Global Economic Prospects 2007: Managing the Next Wave of Globalization [Washington, DC: World Bank]: 118).

comfortable with the subjectivity and ambiguity of many historical accounts, social scientists develop hypotheses based on dependent ("Y") and independent ("X") variables (such as "if X, then Y"), then test and confirm these hypotheses or revise and refine them until they are accurate. They seek to explain international relations behavior, predict what others may do in similar situations, and develop a list of policy options or prescriptions for relevant policy makers. Research, then, is the search for the independent variable. For example, how do we explain a nation-state's allocation of development assistance? We know the amount of development assistance (dependent variable), but we now must find the independent variable that might explain this allocation. Independent variables reside in one of four levels:

- *Individual/Human Dimension*: This level explores the range of variables that can affect leaders' policy choices and implementation strategies. Current research reveals that individuals matter, particularly in the midst of crises, when decisions require secrecy and/or involve only a few actors, or when time is of the essence. The influence of individuals increases when they have a great deal of latitude to make decisions and when they have expertise in foreign policy.

- *Domestic Sources or National Attributes*: Factors at this level include a state's history, traditions, and political, economic, cultural, and social structures, as well as military power, economic wealth, and demographics, and more permanent elements like geographic location and resource base.

- *Systemic Factors*: The anarchic nature of international relations may be the most important factor at this level. However, the individual and collective actions states have taken to cope with anarchy via treaties, alliances, and trade conventions—formal contracts created by states in an attempt to provide order—also constitute significant systemic factors. More informal constraints based on traditions, common goals, and shared norms shape state behavior as well. For example, most states respect the sovereignty of all states and follow the rule of international law because they expect others to do the same. This notion of reciprocity is the primary incentive for states to support a rule-based international system. Finally, distribution of power in the system (e.g., bipolar, multipolar) and the nature of order (e.g., balance of power, collective security) are also important systemic factors.

- *Global Factors*: Often confused with system-level factors, global-level variables challenge notions of boundaries and sovereignty. They derive from decisions made or actions taken by individuals, states, or nonstate actors, but they are seldom traceable to the actions of any one state or even a group of states. A technological innovation—e.g., the Internet and the information revolution—that diffuses through the system affecting all, but not belonging to any single actor, is an obvious example. The movement of capital by multinational banks, the broadcasts of CNN, and the revolutionary ideas of religious fundamentalists all represent global factors that shape policy behavior. Natural conditions such as environmental degradation, pandemics (AIDS, SARS, and the flu), and weather patterns also impact foreign policy.

What is exciting about research in our field is that there is always disagreement about which variables explain the most. The strength of any one argument is based on the quality of the empirical evidence collected to support the hypothesis being tested. Since we are not lab scientists, we cannot conduct experiments with control groups to test our propositions. Instead, we look to the work of historians, public-policy records,

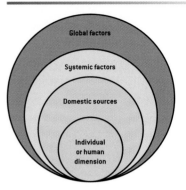

Levels of Analysis. In the study of global politics, there are four levels of analysis. Some scholars would say there are only three levels—but the authors of this book make a distinction between *systemic* (or international) factors and *global* factors. What is the argument for this distinction?

government documents, interviews, budgets, and journalist accounts to gather evidence to confirm or reject hypotheses.

The level chosen as a source for an independent variable depends on the situation you wish to examine, the availability of data or evidence, your research skills and interests, and, finally, your creativity and imagination. Each level is like a drawer in a toolbox; the analytical approaches or variables at each level are the tools that the researcher uses to develop and explore the explanatory power of three kinds of hypotheses: (1) causal hypotheses: if it rains, it will flood; (2) relational hypotheses: if it rains, flooding in certain geological and geographical areas will worsen; and (3) impact hypotheses: if it rains more than "n" amount, the flooding will be particularly severe.

Both Thucydides and Immanuel Kant indirectly discussed levels of analysis in their efforts to explain state behavior. Thucydides focused on the explanatory potential of power capabilities and even suggested that the distribution of power in the international system influenced a state's behavior. Kant referred to the first three levels of analysis when he suggested that nation-states could avoid war by eliminating standing armies, managing the self-interests of rival leaders, and finding ways to provide order in the international system.

Constructivists question the underlying assumptions supporting social scientific and historical approaches to understanding international relations. Instead, these scholars postulate that there is no single historical narrative. Rather, the interests of specific actors shape the story, and it is their control of that story that gives them power. No perspective offers the truth, because words, meanings, symbols, and identities are subjective and are used by individuals, groups, and society to gain and maintain power.

Further, constructivists argue that all of us interpret events and global conditions according to our beliefs, interests, values, and goals. We are not free to do anything we want in any given situation; instead, we are handed a menu reflective of dominant interests and goals of powerful groups within a state or in the international system.

These three research approaches help us explain and understand the decisions made by relevant individuals or decision makers in global politics. We will learn in Chapter 5 that foreign policy decisions are shaped by factors or variables that can be found in the levels of analysis framework.

The Origins of Globalization

The focus of this book is globalization, and as we have already said, our concern is with offering an overview of world politics in a globalized era. By **globalization** we simply mean *the process of increasing interconnectedness between societies such that events in one part of the world more and more have effects on peoples and societies far away.*

A globalized world is one in which political, economic, cultural, and social events become more and more interconnected, and also one in which they have more impact. In other words, societies are affected more and more extensively and more and more deeply by events of other societies. These events can conveniently be divided into three types: social, economic, and political. In each case, the world seems to be shrinking, and people are increasingly aware of this. The World Wide Web is but the most graphic example, since it allows you to sit at home and have instant communication with websites around the world. Electronic mail has also transformed communications in a way that the authors of this book would not have envisaged fifteen years ago. But these are only the most obvious examples. Others include worldwide television communications, global newspa-

globalization A historical process involving a fundamental shift or transformation in the spatial scale of human social organization that links distant communities and expands the reach of power relations across regions and continents.

pers, global production of goods (see the Case Study in this chapter), international NGOs such as Amnesty International or Greenpeace, global social movements like the International Campaign Against Landmines or the One Campaign aimed at eliminating global poverty, global franchises such as McDonald's and Ikea, the global economy (go and look in your nearest supermarket and work out the number of countries' products represented there), and global risks such as pollution, global warming, and the AIDS epidemic. There are, of course, many other examples, but you get the picture. It is this pattern of events that seems to have changed the nature of world politics from what it was just a few years ago. The important point is not just that the world has changed but that the changes are qualitative and not merely quantitative; a strong case can be made that a new world political system has emerged as a result of globalization.

Having said this, we want to point out that globalization is not some entirely new phenomenon in world history. Indeed, as we will examine later on, many argue that it is merely a new name for a long-term feature. While we leave it to you to judge whether in its current manifestation it represents a new phase in world history or merely a continuation of processes that have been around for a long time, we do want to note that there have been several precursors to globalization; and so, looking beyond this quick history of globalization that follows, in Chapter 2 we will also present more detailed examples of previous international orders.

Dimensions of Globalization

Our final task in this introductory chapter is to offer a summary of the main arguments for and against globalization as a distinct new phase in world politics. We do not expect you to decide where you stand on the issue at this stage, but we think that we have to give you some of the main arguments so that you can keep them in mind as you read the rest of this book. The main arguments in favor of globalization comprising a new era of world politics are the following:

1. *The pace of economic transformation is so great that it has created a new world politics.* States are no longer closed units; they cannot fully control their own economies. The world economy is more interdependent than ever, with trade and finances ever expanding.

2. *Communications have fundamentally revolutionized the way we deal with the rest of the world.* Now, events on one side of the world can be immediately observed on the other side. Electronic communications are also converging and thus altering our notions of the social groups we work with and live in.

3. *There is now, more than ever before, a global culture,* so that most urban areas resemble one another. The urban world shares a common culture, much of it emanating from Hollywood.

4. *The world is becoming more homogeneous in some material and ideational areas.* Differences in political and economic thinking between peoples are diminishing. The desire for democracy is universal, and many want a car, a house, and a television.

5. *Time and space seem to be collapsing.* Our old ideas of geography and chronology are undermined by the speed of modern communications and media.

6. *A* **global polity** *is emerging,* with transnational social and political movements and the beginnings of a transfer of allegiance from the state to substate, transnational, and international bodies. Global governance has become an important part of managing globalization.

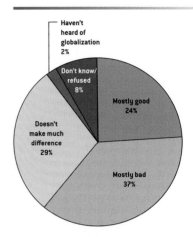

Haven't heard of globalization 2%

Don't know/ refused 8%

Mostly good 24%

Doesn't make much difference 29%

Mostly bad 37%

Opinions on Globalization. In 2008, Americans were asked the following question: "Based on what you know or may have heard, do you think the globalization of the world economy is mostly good for the United States, mostly bad for the United States, or doesn't make much difference?" What would be *your* response to this question? *Source: Pew Social Trends Poll, January, 2008.*

global polity The collective structures and processes by which "interests are articulated and aggregated, decisions are made, values allocated and policies conducted through international or transnational political processes" (Ougaard 2004, 5).

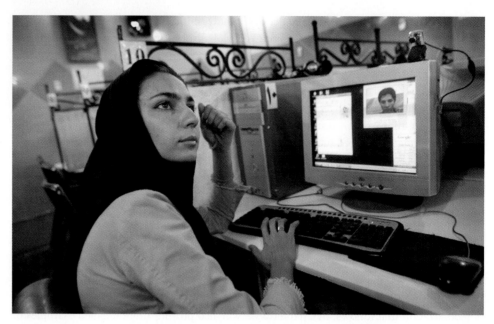

Internet cafés can be found around the world, creating global virtual communities. Should governments have the right to limit access to information about political dissidents?

cosmopolitan culture A pattern of relations within which people share the same goals and aspirations, generally to improve that culture for all members.

risk culture A pattern of relations within which people share the same perils.

7. *A* **cosmopolitan culture** *is developing.* People are beginning to "think globally and act locally."

8. *A* **risk culture** *is emerging.* People realize both that the main risks that face them are global (such as pollution and AIDS) and that states are unable to deal with the problems without some form of cooperation.

However, just as there are powerful reasons for seeing globalization as a new stage in world politics, often allied to the view that globalization is progressive—that is to say, that it improves the lives of people—there are also arguments that suggest the opposite. Some of the main ones are given below.

1. One obvious objection to the globalization thesis is that it is *merely a buzzword to denote the latest phase of capitalism.* In a very powerful critique of globalization theory, Hirst and Thompson (1996) argue that one effect of the globalization thesis is that it makes it appear as if national governments are powerless in the face of global trends. This ends up paralyzing governmental attempts to subject global economic forces to control and regulation. Believing that most globalization theory lacks historical depth, they point out that it paints the current situation as *more unique than it is*, and also as more firmly entrenched than it might in fact be. Current trends may well be reversible. They conclude that the more extreme versions of globalization are "a myth," and they support this claim with five main conclusions from their study of the contemporary world economy (1996, 2–3): First, the present internationalized economy is not unique in history. In some respects, they say, it is less open than the international economy was between 1870 and 1914. Second, they find that genuinely transnational companies are relatively rare; most are national companies trading internationally. There is no trend toward the development of international companies. Third, there is no shift of finance and capital from the developed to the underdeveloped worlds. Direct investment is highly concentrated among the countries of the developed world. Fourth, the world economy is not global; rather, trade, investment, and financial flows are concentrated in and between three blocs—Europe, North America, and Asia. Finally, they argue that this group of three blocs could, if they coordinated policies, regulate global economic markets and forces. Note that Hirst and Thompson are only looking at economic theories of globalization, and many of the main accounts deal with factors such as communications and culture more than economics. Nonetheless, theirs is a very powerful critique of one of the main planks of the more extreme globalization thesis, with their central criticism that seeing the global economy as something beyond our control both misleads us and prevents us from developing policies to control the national economy.

2. Another obvious objection is that globalization is very *uneven in its effects*. At times it sounds very much like a Western theory applicable only to a small part of humankind. To pretend that even a small minority of the world's population can connect to the World Wide Web is clearly an exaggeration, when in reality most people on the planet have probably never made a telephone call in their lives. In other words, globalization only applies to the developed world. We are in danger of overestimating globalization's extent and depth.

3. A related objection is that globalization may well be *simply the latest stage of Western imperialism*. It is the old modernization theory (a controversial theory that suggests nation-states move naturally from traditional societies that are rural and agricultural to modern societies that are complex, urban, and industrial) in a new guise. The forces that are being globalized are conveniently those found in the Western world. What about non-Western values? Where do they fit into this emerging global world? The worry is that they do not fit in at all, and what is being celebrated in globalization is the triumph of a Western worldview, at the expense of the worldviews of other cultures.

4. Critics have also noted that there are *people who have much to lose* as the world becomes more globalized. This is because it represents the success of liberal capitalism in an economically divided world. Perhaps one outcome is that globalization allows the more efficient exploitation of less well-off states, and all in the name of openness. The technologies accompanying globalization are technologies that automatically benefit the richest economies in the world and allow their interests to override local ones. So, not only is globalization imperialist, it is also exploitative.

5. We also need to make the straightforward point that *not all globalized forces are necessarily good ones*. Globalization makes it easier for drug cartels and terrorists to operate, and the World Wide Web's anarchy raises crucial questions of censorship and preventing access to certain kinds of material.

6. Turning to the so-called **global governance** aspects of globalization, the main worry here is about *responsibility*. To whom are the transnational social movements responsible and democratically accountable? If Microsoft or Shell becomes more and more

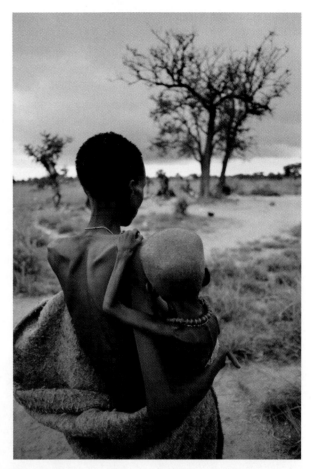

Globalization has not ended famine and poverty. Do prosperous countries have an obligation to help people in other lands?

global governance
Involves the regulation and coordination of transnational issue areas by nation-states, international and regional organizations, and private agencies through the establishment of international regimes. These regimes may focus on problem-solving or the simple enforcement of rules and regulations.

cosmopolitan democracy
A condition in which international organizations, transnational corporations, and global markets are accountable to the peoples of the world.

paradox An absurd or self-contradictory statement.

powerful in the world, does this not raise the issue of how accountable it is to democratic control? David Held has made a strong case for the development of what he calls **cosmopolitan democracy** (1995), but this cosmopolitan democracy has clearly defined legal and democratic features. The worry is precisely that most of the emerging powerful actors in a globalized world are not accountable. This argument also applies to seemingly "good" global actors such as Oxfam and the World Wildlife Fund.

7. Finally, *there seems to be a* **paradox** *at the heart of the globalization thesis*. On the one hand, globalization is usually portrayed as the triumph of Western, market-led values. But how do we then explain the tremendous economic success that some national economies have had in the globalized world? Consider the so-called Tigers of Asia, countries such as Singapore, Taiwan, Malaysia, and Korea, which have enjoyed some of the highest growth rates in the international economy but subscribe to very different views of the role of the state in managing the economy, the place of individual rights and privileges and political rights and freedoms. The paradox, then, will be if these countries can continue to modernize so successfully without adopting many Western values. If they can, then what does this do to one of the main themes of globalization, namely, the argument that globalization represents the spreading across the globe of a set of values? If these countries do continue

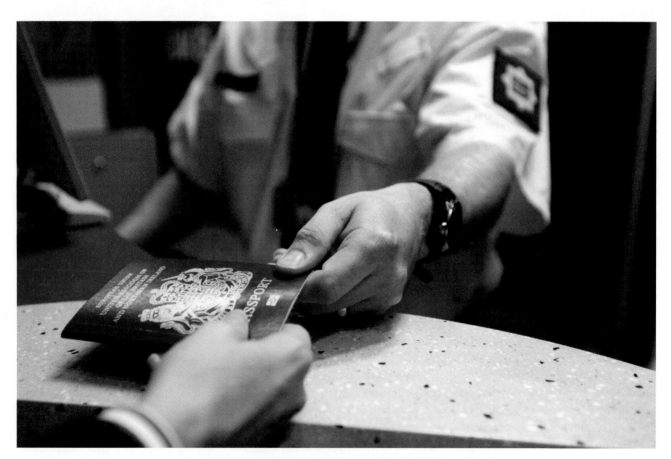

For many people, globalization means travel for business and the movement of goods and services. Should international border checkpoints become obsolete?

to follow their own roads toward economic and social modernization, then we must anticipate future disputes between Western and Non-western values over issues like human rights, gender, and religion.

We hope that these arguments for and against the dominant way of representing globalization will cause you to think deeply about the utility of the concept in explaining contemporary world politics. The chapters that follow do not take a common stance *for* or *against* globalization. We will end by posing some questions that we would like you to keep in mind as you read the remaining chapters:

- Is globalization a *new* phenomenon in world politics?
- Which theory discussed above—and more in Part Two of this textbook—best explains the effects of globalization?
- Is globalization a positive or a negative development?
- Does globalization make the state obsolete?
- Does globalization make the world more or less democratic?
- Is globalization merely Western imperialism in a new guise?
- Does globalization make war more or less likely?
- Last but not least, what will *your* role be in world politics? How will you choose to indentify yourself and participate locally, nationally, and globally?

Conclusion

We hope that this introduction and the chapters that follow help you to answer these questions and that this book as a whole provides you with a good overview of the politics of the contemporary world. We leave you to decide whether or not globalization is a new phase in world politics and whether it is a positive or a negative development.

Returning to 9/11 and its aftermath, we think it important to conclude this chapter by stressing that globalization clearly is a very complex phenomenon that is contradictory and difficult to comprehend. Just as the Internet is for most of us a liberating force, so was it the way in which those who planned the 9/11 attacks communicated. Similarly, television can bring live stories right into our living rooms so that we understand more about the world. But on 9/11, television was also a means of communicating a very specific message about the vulnerability of the United States and ultimately a way of constructing the categories within which we reacted. Finally, maybe the most fundamental lesson of 9/11 is that not all people in the world share a view of globalization as a progressive force in world politics. Those who undertook the attacks were rejecting, in part, the globalization-as-Westernization project. *Globalization is therefore not one thing.*

How we think about it will reflect not merely the theories we accept but our own positions in this globalized world. In this sense, the ultimate paradox of 9/11 is that the answers to questions such as what it was, what it meant, and how to respond to it may themselves be ultimately dependent on the social, cultural, economic, and political spaces we occupy in a globalized world. In other words, world politics suddenly becomes very personal: how does your economic position, your ethnicity, your gender, your culture, or your religion determine what globalization means to you?

Contributors to Chapter 1: John Baylis, Anthony McGrew, Patricia Owens, Steve Smith, and Steven L. Lamy.

REVIEW QUESTIONS

1. Is globalization a new phenomenon in world politics?
2. What are the ways in which you are linked to globalization?
3. How do ideas about globalization shape our understanding of the trend?
4. How can different levels of analysis lead to different explanations of the impact of globalization on global politics?
5. Why do theories matter?
6. International relations began as a problem-solving discipline in response to WWI. What are the global problems that now define our field of study?

FURTHER READING

There are several good introductory guides to globalization. The following provide a comprehensive discussion:

Enloe, C. (2007), *Globalization and Militarism: Feminists Make the Link* (Lanham, MD: Rowman & Littlefield), is a good analysis from a leading feminist of the connections between globalization and various forms of violence.

Held, D., et al. (1999), *Global Transformations* (Cambridge: Polity Press). See also Held, D., and McGrew, A. (eds.) (2003), *The Global Transformations Reader*, 2nd ed. (Cambridge: Polity Press).

McGrew, A., and Lewis, P. (1992), *Global Politics* (Cambridge: Polity Press), is a good collection of essays about global politics and contains some very relevant chapters on the relationship between the three theories discussed above and globalization.

Ojeili, C. el-, and Hayden, P. (2006), *Critical Theories of Globalization* (London: Palgrave Macmillan).

Rosenau, J. N., and Czempiel, E.-O. (1992), *Governance Without Government* (Cambridge: Cambridge University Press), is a good collection of essays dealing with the political aspects of globalization.

Scholte, J. A. (2000), *Globalization: A Critical Introduction* (London: Macmillan), offers an excellent overview.

Excellent critiques of the globalization thesis:

Held, D., and McGrew, A. (2002), *Globalization/Anti-globalization* (Cambridge: Polity Press).

Kaldor, M. (2003) has written a powerful account of the relationship between globalization and international civil society in her *Global Civil Society: An Answer to War* (Cambridge: Polity Press).

Stiglitz, J. (2003), *Globalization and Its Discontents* (London: Penguin) and (2006) *Making Globalization Work* (New York: W. W. Norton).

INTERNET RESOURCES

Asian Development Bank
http://www.adb.org/
   The web site of the leading multilateral lending agency aimed at improving economic conditions in that continent.

Canadian International Council
http://www.canadianinternationalcouncil.org/
   A foreign policy analysis web site offering research articles on a range of topics.

G-8 Information Centre
http://www.g7.utoronto.ca/
   The information clearing house of the organization of the eight largest capitalist economies.

International Atomic Energy Agency
http://www.iaea.or.at/
   A United Nations-linked organization whose mission is to encourage the peaceful dissemination of nuclear technology. Since 1991 it has increasingly played a role in inspecting nuclear weapons programs.

International Monetary Fund
www.imf.org
   Part of the Bretton Woods system, this multilateral organization helps to manage the global economy.

Multinational Monitor

http://multinationalmonitor.org/monitor.html

A nongovernmental organization that provides news and information about MNCs and TNCs.

One World Online

http://us.oneworld.net/

A social networking site that links not-for-profit organizations with news and information.

United Nations Research Institute for Social Development

http://www.unrisd.org/

A UN clearinghouse for information about social economic matters.

Women in International Security

http://wiis.georgetown.edu/

A site that seeks to build links among women who do research in international security matters.

World Trade Organization

http://www.wto.org

The prime multilateral organization that sets the "rules of the game" in international trade.

For more information, quizzes, case studies, and other study tools, please visit us at **www.oup.com/us/lamy**

CHAPTER

The History
of Global Politics

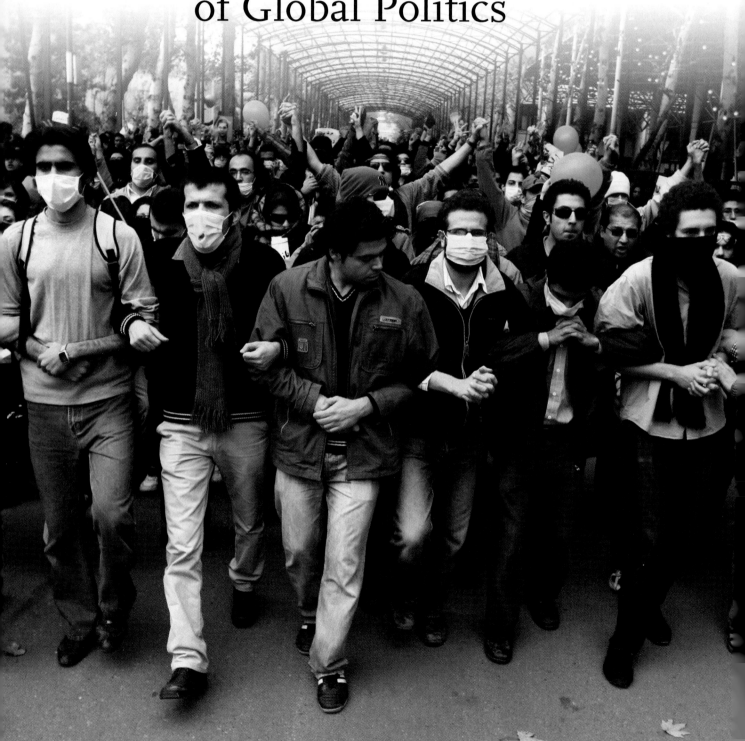

Those who cannot learn from history are doomed to repeat it.
—*George Santayana*

We learn from history that we learn nothing from history.
—*G. B. Shaw*

If we were to write a brief list of world events in 2009, it might include the following: the North Korean government conducting a long-range missile test and restarting its nuclear weapons program; concerns over the elections and ongoing violence in Iran and its unwillingness to give up its nuclear program; increasing violence in Afghanistan, and the United States announcing an increase in its troops there; pirates—living with impunity in the failed state of Somalia—cruising the Indian Ocean and, armed with antitank rockets, hijacking ships; and US president Barack Obama winning the Nobel Peace Prize. Add to our list the cycle of violence in Israel and Palestine showing no sign of abating and the economic crisis contributing to the poverty and misery of hundreds of millions of people who have no food, shelter, or health care. Sometimes it's difficult to imagine how things might ever improve; other times it's easy to get caught up in the moment, when something significant or strange occurs on the world stage. Yet each of the current events and enduring conditions listed here stems from a deeper world history, and knowing about these histories takes us a step closer to understanding global politics—past, present, and future.

Perhaps, despite our pessimistic list for 2009, the international system has actually moved in a positive direction. After all, countries that were enemies in 1944—including France, Germany, and Great Britain—are today working together to bring economic prosperity to the world as members of the European Union. The accumulation of human history—political change, economic progress, medical breakthroughs, the lives of ordinary people—are part of the fabric of struggle and cooperation, strife and comity. Our goal in this chapter is to demonstrate, briefly, how the international system and in some ways the global

Dissatisfied with what they believed was electoral fraud, university students in Iran stage protest demonstrations in 2009. Should Western democracies have intervened to support the prodemocracy marchers?

society has evolved during the last four hundred years. It is not possible to cover all of international history in one chapter. Therefore, our attention will be primarily on significant political events. In other chapters, we will discuss social and economic trends.

Introduction

The history of international relations did not begin in 1648, but it's a good place to begin our story. Kingdoms, empires, city-states, and nation-states have for centuries interacted in the same kinds of patterns that continued after the end of the Thirty Years' War (1618–1648). In China, Africa, India, and ancient Greece, political units of various sizes had engaged in economic relations, exchanged ambassadors, and fought wars. We choose to begin the study of history with 1648 because an event during that year represents a major dividing line in the history of Europe. After 1648 we can see the developing template for the international system, now referred to as the "globalized system," that is a theme of this book: Western European arrangements for governance, human rights, and economics that form the basis for the contemporary world. In this chapter we will discuss wars and political upheavals. It is a sweeping tale, covering the French Revolution; two world wars; the end of European colonization of Africa and Asia; the Cold War and the changes in the international political system that followed its end; and the September 11, 2001, attacks. Our goal is to provide some background, or context, for you to understand the topics that we examine in depth in Chapters 8 through 14.

The End of the Thirty Years' War

When Martin Luther nailed his Ninety-five Theses to the door of the cathedral in Wittenburg, Germany, in 1517, he launched more than the **Protestant Reformation**. For the next century, monarchs across Europe found in religion a reason to begin wars allegedly in defense of either Catholicism or Protestantism. For over a century of war and upheaval, religion provided the justification for conflicts that, most historians agree, were actually about politics and economics. The **Thirty Years' War** (1618–1648) was the last of these religious conflicts in Europe and ostensibly began over a disagreement about the right of political leaders to choose the state religion of their territories. The opponents—including at various times Denmark, France, Austria, Sweden, Spain, and the principalities of the Holy Roman Empire—conducted most of their operations in Germany, killing tens of thousands of soldiers and civilians and devastating cities and farmland.

Many analysts regard the **Peace of Westphalia** that ended the war in 1648 as the key event ushering in the contemporary international system. Political leaders, aware that the fighting had solved nothing and brought only widespread destruction, codified in the accord the right of the more than three hundred German states that constituted the Holy Roman Empire to conduct their own diplomatic relations—a very clear acknowledgement of their **sovereignty**. They were also to enjoy "an exact and reciprocal Equality": the first formal acceptance of **sovereign equality** for a significant number of states. More generally, the peace may be seen as encapsulating the very idea of a society of states. The participants of the conference, including ambassadors from the Netherlands, Spain, Sweden, France, Austria, and several of the larger German principalities, very clearly and explicitly took over from the papacy the right to confer international legitimacy on individual rulers and states and to insist that states observe religious toleration in their internal policies

Protestant Reformation A social movement in reaction to the widespread perception that the Catholic Church had become corrupt and had lost its moral compass.

Thirty Years' War The last of the great wars in Europe nominally for religion. Some historians believe that political leaders cynically used religious differences as an excuse to extend their kingdoms.

Peace of Westphalia, 1648 The treaties of Osnabrück and Münster, which together form the Peace of Westphalia, ended the Thirty Years' War and were crucial in delimiting the political rights and authority of European monarchs.

sovereignty The condition of a state having control and authority over its own territory and being free from any higher legal authority. It is related to, but distinct from, the condition of a government being free from any external political constraints.

sovereign equality The idea that all countries have the same rights, including the right of noninterference in their internal affairs.

(Armstrong 1993, 30–38). The balance of power was formally incorporated in the **Peace of Utrecht**, which ended the War of the Spanish Succession (1701–1714), when a "just equilibrium of power" was formally declared to be the "best and most solid basis of mutual friendship and durable harmony."

The period from 1648 to 1776 saw the international society that had been taking shape over the previous two hundred years come to fruition. Wars were frequent, if lacking the ideological intensity that religion brought to the Thirty Years' War. Some states, notably the Ottoman Empire, slowly declined; others, such as Britain and Russia, rose. Hundreds of ministates still existed, but it was the interaction among no more than ten key players that determined the course of events. Yet despite constant change and many wars, eighteenth- and nineteenth-century European writers were unanimous in their view that Europe in its entirety constituted a kind of "republic." Some pointed to religious and cultural similarities in seeking to explain this phenomenon, but the central elements that all agreed on were a determination by all states to preserve their freedom, a mutual recognition of each other's right to an independent existence, and above all a reliance on the balance of power. Diplomacy and international law were seen as the other two key institutions of international society, so long as the latter was based clearly on state consent.

Revolutionary Wars

Against this background of a polite, nominally rule-based European international society, the American and French revolutions (1776 and 1789, respectively) had profound consequences. In the case of the United States, one consequence was its eventual emergence as a global superpower in the twentieth century; the consequences of the French Revolution were more immediate. First, the revolutionary insistence that sovereignty was vested in "the nation" rather than in the rulers—especially dynastic imperial rulers like the Habsburgs—gave a crucial impetus to the idea of **national self-determination**. This principle would increasingly dominate international politics in the nineteenth and twentieth centuries and endanger imperial systems that were seen as denying the rights of **nations** (people defined by linguistic, ethnic, and cultural bonds) to become sovereign states themselves.

The second consequence of the French Revolution stemmed from the response of the main European powers. After the defeat of Napoleon in 1815, the leading states increasingly set themselves apart from the smaller ones as a kind of "great powers' club." This system, known as the **Concert of Europe**, lasted until World War I. It was characterized by regular meetings of the club that had the aims of maintaining the European balance of power drawn up at the end of the Napoleonic Wars and reaching collective decisions on various potentially divisive issues. The leading dynastic powers, Austria and Russia, wanted the concert to give itself the formal right to intervene against any revolution. This was strongly resisted by Britain, which was the least threatened by revolution, on the grounds that such a move would violate the key principle of nonintervention. However, the concert unquestionably marked a shift away from the free-for-all and highly decentralized system of eighteenth-century international society toward a more managed, hierarchical system. This affected all three of the key institutional underpinnings of the Westphalian international society: the balance of power, diplomacy, and international law.

In 1814 the powers had already formally declared their intention to create a "system of real and permanent balance of power in Europe," and in 1815 during the **Congress of Vienna** they carefully redrew the map of Europe to implement this system. The main

Peace of Utrecht, 1713 The agreement that ended the War of the Spanish Succession and helped to consolidate the link between sovereign authority and territorial boundaries in Europe. This treaty refined the territorial scope of sovereign rights of states.

national self-determination The right or desire of distinct national groups to become states and to rule themselves.

nation A community of people who share a common sense of identity, which may be derived from language, culture, or ethnicity; this community may be a minority within a single country or live in more than one country.

Concert of Europe Five great powers (Austria, Britain, France, Prussia, and Russia) created an informal institution and agreed on "rules of the game," including controlling revolutionary forces, managing the balance of power, and accepting interventions to keep current leaders in power. This system kept the peace in Europe from 1815 until WWI.

Congress of Vienna A meeting of major European leaders (1814–1815) that redrew the political map of Europe after the end of the Napoleonic Wars. The congress was an attempt to restore a conservative political order in the continent.

In 1789, opponents of the French monarchy planted "Trees of Liberty" to symbolize the spreading roots of the new democratic government.

diplomatic development was the greatly increased use of conferences to consider and sometimes settle matters of general interest. In a few technical areas, such as international postal services, telegraphy, and sanitation, permanent international organizations were set up. In international law, the powers sought to draft "a procedure of international legitimation of change" (Clark 1980, 91), especially in the area of territorial change. There were attempts by the great powers collectively to guarantee various treaties, such as those defining the status of Switzerland, Belgium, and Luxembourg. A great many treaties laid down rules governing various technical and economic issues, as well as a few humanitarian ones, notably slavery and the treatment of those wounded in war. It should be noted, however, that while the concert did help to bring some measure of peace and order to Europe, it was also one of the mechanisms whereby the European powers legitimized their increasing domination of Asia and Africa. For example, the **Congress of Berlin** of 1885 helped to prevent a major war over rival European claims in Africa, but it also set out the rules governing "new acts of occupation." Pious sentiments about bringing the "benefits of civilization" to Africa meant little.

Developments external and internal to the European Congress system brought about its demise. Externally, after the American Civil War the United States began to become a world power. Two events indicate this changing status. First, President Teddy Roosevelt brokered the Treaty of Portsmouth, New Hampshire, that ended the Russo-Japanese War in 1905. Second, Roosevelt sent the new American battle fleet, called the Great White Fleet for its paint scheme, around the world in a cruise that lasted from December 1907 to February 1909. The United States also intervened in Morocco and China, seeking equal access to regions where the Europeans already had influence.

Meanwhile, a critical internal change to the European concert system was the hardening of the Great Powers, as they were called, into two rival blocs after the Franco-Prussian

Congress of Berlin A meeting of the European states that had an interest in colonizing Africa. The Berlin conference redrew the existing political map of Africa, with a goal to avoid conflict between the Europeans in Africa.

War of 1870–1871. Prior to this the balance-of-power mentality meant that the major countries would realign themselves as necessary to keep any one power from becoming dominant. However, Bismarck's creation of the German Empire in 1871 caused a major imbalance in the system. Bismarck's alliance system was flexible and complex, and it maintained order among European states. With Bismarck out of power, less-skilled leaders let the alliance rules and protocols lapse. France refocused on Europe and less on Africa, and the German kaiser let the Russians ally with Great Britain. One result of this was the carnage of the First World War.

World Wars: Modern and Total

Wars on a global scale caused another shock to international society. Although separated by twenty years, the first and second world wars have some similarities beyond mere geography. Changes in military technology shaped the ways in which the combatants fought: machine guns, airplanes, and submarines all influenced operations. Both wars also featured controversies over the treatment of civilians. Indiscriminate bombing of cities occurred during both wars and reached its nadir with the British and American firebomb air raids on Germany and Japan. Yet one major distinction between the two world wars is worth noting here: the Nazi death camps were at the time without parallel in human history. Unfortunately, genocide and ethnic cleansing have continued to plague the international system.

For the victorious Allies, the question of how the First World War began became a question of how far the Germans and their allies should be held responsible. At the Versailles Palace outside Paris, the victors imposed a statement of German war guilt in Article 231 of the final settlement, primarily to justify the reparations they demanded. Debates among historians about the war's origins focused on political, military, and systemic factors. Some suggested that responsibility for the war was diffuse, as its origins lay in complex dynamics of the respective alliances and their military imperatives. One of the more influential postwar interpretations, however, came from the West German historian Fritz Fischer, who, in his 1967 book *Germany's Aims in the First World War*, argued that German aggression, motivated by the internal political needs of an autocratic elite, was responsible for the war.

> **WHAT'S YOUR WORLDVIEW**
>
> *Who or what factors were to blame for the start of WWI?*

However complex or contested the origins of the war were in retrospect, the motivations of those who fought were more explicable. The masses of the belligerent states shared nationalist beliefs and patriotic values. As they marched off to fight, most thought the war would be short, victorious, and, in many cases, glorious. The reality of the European battlefield and the advent of **trench warfare** determined otherwise. Defensive military technologies, symbolized by the machine gun, triumphed over the tactics and strategy of attrition, though by November 1918 the Allied offensive finally achieved the rapid advances that helped bring an end to the fighting. It was total war in the sense that whole societies and economies were mobilized: men were conscripted into armies and women went to work in factories. The western and eastern fronts remained the crucibles of the fighting, though conflict spread to various parts of the globe. Japan, for example, went to war in 1914 as an ally of Britain.

Most importantly, in response to German aggression on the high seas and domestic public opinion that supported the Allies, the United States entered the war in 1917 under President Woodrow Wilson. His vision of international society and world

trench warfare From 1914 to 1918 the two sides in the war dug elaborate defensive fortifications in the ground. Because of the power of weapons like machine guns and rapid-fire cannons, trenches often gave the advantage in battle to the defenders.

Map 2.1 Wars 1914–1945.

The two world wars were responsible for perhaps more than 80 million deaths. The First World War was essentially a European territorial dispute, which, because of extensive European empires, spread as far afield as Africa and Southeast Asia. The Second World War also started as a European conflict but spread to the Pacific when Japan seized territory. In the interwar period, disputes broke out over territory in South American and East Asia, but elsewhere the reluctance of the colonial powers to become embroiled in territorial disputes maintained an uneasy peace.

1 Wars 1914–45

- First World War 1914–18
- Second World War 1939–45
- Other major international war
- Major civil war

Poland v Russia 1919–20
Poland v Lithuania 1920
White Russians v Bolsheviks 1917–20
Greece v Turkey 1919–22
1915–18
1941–43
Republicans v Nationalists 1936–39
Libya v Italy 1920–32
Italy v Ethiopia 1935
1914–18
1914–18
1914–15
Paraguay v Bolivia 1932–35
1914
1914
1910–20
1914
1942
1937–45
1945
Japan v China 1931, 1933, 1937–45
Communists v Nationalists 1931–36
1942–45
1942–45
1942–45
1942–45
1914
1914

order, articulated in his **Fourteen Points**, would drive the agenda of the Paris Peace Conference in 1919. The overthrow of the tsar in February 1917 by what became known as the Provisional Government, and the seizure of power by the Bolsheviks in November 1917, soon led Russia's new leaders to negotiate withdrawal from the war. Germany no longer fought on two fronts but soon faced a new threat, as the resources of the United States were mobilized. With the failure of its last great military offensive in the west in 1918, and with an increasingly effective British naval blockade, Germany agreed to an **armistice**.

The **Peace Treaty of Versailles** failed to tackle what was for some the central problem of European security after 1870: a united and frustrated Germany. The treaty precipitated German revenge by creating new states out of former German and Austrian territories and devising contested borders. For some scholars, 1914–1945 represented two acts in a single play, or a thirty-year war. E. H. Carr saw the period from 1919 to 1939 as a twenty-year crisis. The crisis, Carr stated, was caused by an unrealistic and utopian peace treaty that did not address the real causes of the war and would never be supported by the victors. Economic factors were also crucial. The effects of the Great Depression, triggered in part by the Wall Street crash of 1929, weakened the forces of liberal democracy in many areas and strengthened the appeal of communist, fascist, and Nazi parties. It should be noted that from 1873 to 1914 the world economy changed dramatically. Most notably this included the rise of the US and German economies and the decline of Britain. At this time Japan was beginning to industrialize and India and China were beginning a rapid pace of economic development. What was most significant was the increase in global trade and financial transactions. This growing interdependence of national economies did not result in free trade; instead, protectionist policies increased.

WWI destroyed production facilities in Europe. Britain and France demanded reparations from Germany to pay for their reconstruction. Both the United States and Japan benefited from the war in terms of boosting their production levels. The Great Depression of 1930 and 1931 was not caused by the war. However, the change in the international political system helped bring about the collapse of the trade, finance, and economic management systems.

The effect on German society was particularly significant. All modernized states suffered mass unemployment, but in Germany, inflation was acute. Economic and political instability provided the ground in which support for the Nazis took root. By 1933, Adolf Hitler had achieved power, and the transformation of the German state began. There remain debates about how far Hitler's ambitions were carefully thought through and how much he seized opportunities. A. J. P. Taylor provided a controversial analysis in his 1961 book *Origins of the Second World War*, in which he argued that Hitler was no different from other German political leaders. What was different about Germany this time was the particular philosophy of Nazism and ideas of racial supremacy and imperial expansion. British and French attempts to negotiate with Hitler culminated in the Munich agreement of 1938. Hitler's territorial claims over the Sudetenland in Czechoslovakia were accepted

After a rapid German advance into France in August 1914, troops on both sides created extensive networks of defensive trenches. Millions of combatants died.

Fourteen Points President Woodrow Wilson's vision of international society, first articulated in January 1918, included the principle of self-determination, the conduct of diplomacy on an open (not secret) basis, and the establishment of an association of nation-states to provide guarantees of independence and territorial integrity. Wilson's ideas exerted an important influence on the Paris Peace Conference, though the principle of self-determination was only selectively pursued when it came to American colonial interests.

armistice A cease-fire agreement between enemies in wartime. In the case of World War I, the armistice began at 11:00 a.m., on November 11, 1918.

Peace Treaty of Versailles, 1919 The Treaty of Versailles formally ended the First World War (1914–1918). The treaty established the League of Nations, specified the rights and obligations of the victorious and defeated powers (including the notorious regime of reparations on Germany), and created the "Mandate" system under which "advanced nation-states" were given legal tutelage over colonial peoples.

appeasement A policy of making concessions to a revanchist (or otherwise territorially acquisitive) state in the hope that settlement of more modest claims will assuage that state's expansionist appetites. Appeasement remains most (in)famously associated with British prime minister Neville Chamberlain's acquiescence to Hitler's incursions into Austria and then Czechoslovakia, culminating in the Munich Agreement of September 1938. Since then, appeasement has generally been seen as synonymous with a craven collapse before the demands of dictators—encouraging, not disarming, their aggressive designs.

blitzkrieg The German term for "lightning war." This was an offensive strategy that used the combination of mechanized forces— especially tanks—and aircraft as mobile artillery to exploit breaches in an enemy's front line. The irony was that in 1940 the French army had more tanks than the German army. The French tanks, however, were spread among units along the front line, while the German commanders concentrated their tanks in a few units.

Holocaust The term used to describe the attempts by the Nazis to murder the Jewish population of Europe. Some 6 million Jewish people were killed in concentration camps, along with a further

During the economic collapse of the Great Depression, meteorological factors made the situation worse. The "Dust Bowls" of the American plains forced farmers off their land and into cities.

as the price for peace, but within months Germany had seized the rest of Czechoslovakia and was preparing for war on Poland. Recent debates about **appeasement** have focused on whether there were realistic alternatives to negotiation, given the lack of military preparedness with which to confront Hitler.

By 1939, the defensive military technologies of the Great War gave way to armored warfare and air power, as the German **blitzkrieg** brought speedy victories over Poland and in the west. Hitler was also drawn into the Balkans and North Africa, in support of his Italian ally, Mussolini. With the invasion of the Soviet Union in June 1941, the scale of fighting and scope of Hitler's aims were apparent. Massive early victories on the eastern front gave way to winter stalemate and the mobilization of Soviet peoples and armies. German treatment of civilian populations and Soviet prisoners of war reflected Nazi ideas of racial supremacy and resulted in the deaths of millions. German anti-Semitism and the development of concentration camps gained new momentum after a decision on the "Final Solution of the Jewish Question" in 1942. The term "**Holocaust**" entered the political lexicon of the twentieth century, as the Nazis attempted the **genocide** of the Jewish people and other minorities, such as the Roma, in Europe.

By 1941, German submarines and American warships were in an undeclared war. The imposition of American economic sanctions on Japan precipitated Japanese military preparations for a surprise attack on the US fleet at Pearl Harbor on December 7, 1941. When Germany and Italy declared war on America in support of their Japanese ally, Roosevelt decided to assign priority to the European over the Pacific theater of war. After a combined strategic bombing offensive with the British against German cities, the Allies launched a second front in France, for which the Soviets had been pressing.

Defeat of Germany in May 1945 came before the atomic bomb was ready. In an effort to shorten the war, avoid an invasion of Japan, and push the Japanese government to surrender, the United States dropped the first atomic bomb on Hiroshima on August 6, 1945, and the second on Nagasaki on August 9, 1945. The United States was the first and only state to use these weapons of mass destruction in war. The destruction of the two Japanese cities remains a controversy. Aside from moral objections to attacking civilian populations, their destruction generated fierce debate, particularly among American historians, about why the bomb was dropped.

When the Second World War ended, the United States and the Soviet Union remained as the two dominant countries in world politics. For some people in the United States, their homeland largely untouched by the destruction of the war, the country seemed poised to take its proper position as world leader. For the leaders of the Soviet Union, the world looked ready for the expansion of the Soviet style of rule. In the next section we examine the process of decolonization of Western European holdings. This process provided both countries, soon to be called superpowers, many opportunities to expand their influence. American hegemony in the world economy ran from 1938 to 1973. (See also Chapter 12.) The United States was willing to commit resources to stabilize the world economy and build global political structures to manage trade, development, and financial affairs.

A single atomic bomb wrought unprecedented damage on Hiroshima, Japan, killing as many as 100,000 civilians. Was the United States justified in dropping that bomb?

Legacies and Consequences of European Colonialism

The effects of the Second World War helped to cause the demise of European imperialism in the twentieth century. More than marking an end of Western European dominance in world politics, the end of imperialism seemed to be the death knell for the European style of managing international relations. This change took place against the background of the Cold War, which we will discuss in the next section; but it's important first to appreciate the context of decolonization because it reflected, and contributed to, the decreasing importance of Europe as the arbiter of world affairs.

The belief that national self-determination should be a guiding principle in international politics had early marked a transformation of attitudes and values; during the age of imperialism, political status accrued to imperial powers. However, after 1945, imperialism became a term of disgrace. Colonialism of the past and the new United Nations Charter were increasingly recognized as incompatible, though independence was often slow and sometimes marked by prolonged and armed struggle, especially in many African states. The Cold War also often complicated and hindered the transition to independence. Various factors influenced the process of decolonization: the attitude of the colonial power; the ideology and strategy of the anti-imperialist forces; and the role of external powers. Political, economic, and military factors played various roles in shaping the transfer of power. Different imperial powers and newly emerging independent states had different experiences of withdrawal from empire.

There was no one pattern of decolonization in Africa and Asia, and the paths to independence reflected attitudes of colonial powers, the nature of local nationalist or revolutionary movements, and in some cases the involvement of external states, including the Cold War protagonists. Ethnic and racial factors were also an ingredient in many cases. How far these divisions were created or exacerbated by the imperial powers is an important question in examining the political stability of the newly independent states. Equally important is how capable the new political leaderships in these societies were in tackling their political and economic problems.

million that included Soviet prisoners, Roma, Poles, communists, homosexuals, and the physically or mentally disabled.

genocide Deliberate and systematic extermination of an ethnic, national, tribal, or religious group.

Table 2.1
Principal Acts of European Decolonization, 1945–1980

Country	Colonial State	Year of Independence
India	Britain	1947
Pakistan	Britain	1947
Burma (Myanmar)	Britain	1948
Sri Lanka	Britain	1948
Indonesia	Netherlands	1949
Cambodia	France	1953
Indochina (Vietnam and Laos)	France	1954
Ghana	Britain	1957
Malaya (Malaysia)	Britain	1957
French African colonies*	France	1960
Congo (Zaire)	Belgium	1960
Nigeria	Britain	1960
Sierra Leone	Britain	1961
Tanganyika (Tanzania)	Britain	1961
Uganda	Britain	1962
Algeria	France	1962
Rwanda	Belgium	1962
Kenya	Britain	1963
Guinea-Bissau	Portugal	1974
Mozambique	Portugal	1975
Cape Verde	Portugal	1975
São Tomé	Portugal	1975
Angola	Portugal	1975
Zimbabwe	Britain	1980

*Including Cameroon, Central African Republic, Chad, Gabon, Ivory Coast, Madagascar, Mali, Mauritania, Niger, Senegal, and Upper Volta.

In Asia, the relationship between nationalism and revolutionary Marxism was a potent force. In Malaya, the British defeated a communist insurgent movement (1948–1960). In Indochina (1946–1954), the French failed to do likewise. For the Vietnamese, resentment toward centuries of foreign oppression—Chinese, Japanese, and French—soon focused on a new imperialist adversary, the United States. For leaders in Washington, early reluctance to support European imperialism gave way to incremental and covert commitments, and then, from 1965, open military and political support of the newly created state of South Vietnam. American leaders and a very influential anticommunist interest community spoke of a domino theory, in which if one state fell to communism, the next would be at risk. Chinese and Soviet support provided additional Cold War contexts. Washington failed, however, to coordinate limited war objectives with an effective political strategy and, once victory was no longer possible, sought to disengage through "peace with honor."

2 WARS SINCE 1945

- ✦ Major international war
- ✦ Minor international war
- ✦ Major civil war
- ✦ Minor civil war
- ✦ Long-running terrorist campaign

*Map labels (read on the map):*

N v S Vietnam 1959–74
USA v N Vietnam 1954–75
Vietnam v France 1946–54
Cambodia 1975–77, 1990
Korea 1950–53
Bangladesh 1971
China 1945–49
see inset
Malaya 1948–60
Indonesia 1965–68
India 1947–49
Afghanistan 1978–
Iran 1978–80
Iran v Iraq 1980–88
Iraq v Kuwait, USA 1990–91
Lebanon 1975–92
Arab nations v Israel 1947–49, 1956, 1967, 1973
Sri Lanka 1980–
Eritrea v Ethiopia 1963–93
see inset below
Somalia 1989–
Rwanda 1993–
Zaire 1960, 1992, 1997–
Mozambique v Portugal 1965–74
Zimbabwe 1965–80
Chechenia 1994–96
Sudan 1954–72, 1984–
1962–65, 1922
Nigeria (Biafra) 1967–70
Angola v Portugal 1961
Angola 1975–
Namibia 1975–89
see inset
Algeria v France 1954–62
Guinea-Bissau 1963–74
Liberia 1989–
Former Yugoslavia 1991–95
Greece 1946–48
UK (IRA) 1969–98
Spain (ETA) 1970
El Salvador 1972–92
Colombia 1948–69, 1976–

Map 2.2 Wars Since 1945.

As European colonial control was largely destroyed between 1945 and 1970, new nation-states were created. One result was an increase in localized wars, largely arising from boundary disputes, and in civil wars caused by conflicts between different ethnic groups or between those with conflicting religious or political beliefs. An estimated 25–30 million people died in these wars, two-thirds of whom were civilians.

The Tet (Vietnamese New Year) offensive of the Vietcong guerrillas in 1968 marked a decisive moment, convincing many Americans that the war would not be won, though it was not until 1973 that American forces finally withdrew, two years before South Vietnam was defeated. Many wars in Asia and Africa started as colonial wars and quickly became proxy wars in the Cold War struggle between the superpowers.

The global trend toward decolonization was a key development in the twentieth century, though one frequently offset by local circumstances. Yet while imperialism withered, other forms of domination or **hegemony** took shape. Simply stated, hegemony means a state has the means and the will to shape and govern the international system. Both the United States and the Soviet Union were vying for global hegemony during the Cold War. The notion of hegemony has been used as criticism of the behavior of the superpowers, most notably with Soviet hegemony in Eastern Europe and American hegemony in Central America. For both countries this struggle for dominance, regardless of the term used, was the central element of the period we discuss in the next section, the Cold War.

Cold War

The rise of the United States as a global power after 1945 was of paramount importance in international politics. Its conflict with the Soviet Union provided one of the crucial dynamics in world affairs—one that affected, directly or indirectly, every part of the world. In the West, historians have debated with vigor and acrimony which country was responsible for the collapse of the wartime alliance between Moscow and Washington. The rise of the USSR as a global power after 1945 is equally crucial in this period. Relations between Moscow and its Eastern European "allies," with the People's Republic of China (PRC), and with revolutionary forces in the third world have been vital issues in world politics, as well as key factors in Soviet-American affairs.

If one feature of the Cold War was its **bipolar** structure, another was its highly divided character born out of profoundly opposing views about the best way of organizing society: the Western system of market capitalism or the Eastern Bloc's centrally planned economies.

Yet for all its intensity the Cold War was very much a managed conflict in which both sides recognized the limits of what they could do. Certainly, policy makers in East and West appeared to accept in private—if not in public—that their rival had legitimate security concerns. The Cold War was thus fought within a framework of informal rules. This in part helps explain why it remained "cold"—at least in terms of general war between the United States and the Soviet Union, since millions of people died during the period 1945 to 1990 in what have been called "brushfire" or "proxy" wars in Africa and Asia. Indeed, how and why the Cold War remained "cold" has been the subject of much academic debate. Few, however, would dispute the fact that whatever else may have divided the two superpowers—ideology, economics, and the struggle for global influence—they were in full agreement about one thing: the overriding need to prevent a nuclear war that neither could win without destroying the world and themselves. This, in the end, is why the superpowers acted with such caution for the greater part of the Cold War era. In fact, given the very real fear of outright nuclear war, the shared aim of the two superpowers was not to destroy the other—though a few on both sides occasionally talked in such terms—but rather to contain the other's ambitions while avoiding anything that might lead to dangerous escalation (only once, in 1962, with the Cuban missile crisis, did the two superpowers come close to a nuclear exchange). This, in turn, helps explain another important feature of the Cold War: its stalemated and hence seemingly permanent character.

hegemony A system regulated by a dominant leader, or political (and/or economic) domination of a region. It also means power and control exercised by a leading state over other states.

bipolar A term to describe an international political order in which two states dominate all others. It is often used to describe the nature of the international system when the two superpowers, the USSR and the US, were dominant powers during the Cold War.

Truman Doctrine Statement made by US president Harry Truman in March 1947 that it "must be the policy of the United States to support free people who are resisting attempted subjugation by armed minorities or by outside pressures." Intended to persuade Congress to support limited aid to Turkey and Greece, the doctrine came to underpin the policy of containment and American economic and political support for its allies.

Some historians date the origins of the Cold War to the Russian Revolution of 1917, while most focus on events between 1945 and 1950. Whether the Cold War was inevitable, whether it was the consequence of mistakes and misperceptions, or whether it reflected the response of courageous Western leaders to aggressive Soviet intent are central questions in debates about the origins and dynamics of the Cold War. Until 1989, these debates have drawn from Western archives and sources and reflect Western assumptions and perceptions. With the end of the Cold War, greater evidence has emerged of Soviet and US motivations and understanding.

Onset of the Cold War

The start of the Cold War in Europe reflected failure to implement the principles agreed upon at the 1945 wartime conferences of Yalta and Potsdam. The futures of Germany and various Central and Eastern European countries, notably Poland, were issues of growing tension between the former wartime allies. Reconciling principles of national self-determination with national security was a formidable task. In the West, there was growing feeling that Soviet policy toward Eastern Europe was guided not by historic concern with security but by ideological expansion. In March 1947, the Truman administration sought to justify limited aid to Turkey and Greece with rhetoric designed to arouse awareness of Soviet ambitions and a declaration that America would support those threatened by Soviet subversion or expansion. The **Truman Doctrine** and the associated policy of **containment** expressed the self-image of the United States as inherently defensive and were underpinned by the **Marshall Plan** for European economic recovery, proclaimed in June 1947, which was essential to the economic rebuilding of Western Europe. In Eastern Europe, democratic socialist and other anticommunist forces were undermined and eliminated as Marxist-Leninist regimes, loyal to Moscow, were installed. The only exception was in Yugoslavia, where the Marxist leader, Marshal Tito,

> **WHAT'S YOUR WORLDVIEW**
>
> *The United States and the USSR fought many proxy wars across the globe. One writer lists some fifty-eight wars from 1945 to 1989 (Holsti 1991). Roughly 52 percent of the current armed conflicts began during the Cold War. Given these statistics, is it correct to call the period 1945 to 1989 a "Cold War"? Cold War historian John Lewis Gaddis has called this period the "Long Peace": Is this an accurate description of the Cold War period of tension and conflict?*

containment American political strategy for resisting perceived Soviet expansion, first publicly espoused by an American diplomat, George Kennan, in 1947 and aimed at limiting Soviet expansion in Europe. Containment became a powerful factor in American policy toward the Soviet Union for the next forty years and a self-image of Western policy makers. However, Kennan's view of containment did not include the aggressive militarization that brought the world closer to the brink of nuclear destruction.

Marshall Plan Officially known as the European Recovery Program, it was a program of financial and other economic aid for Europe after WWII. Proposed by Secretary of State George Marshall in 1948, it was offered to all European states, including the Soviet Union, and these funds played a critical role in European recovery.

Table 2.2
Cold War Crises

Years	Crisis	Key Actors
1948–1949	Berlin	USSR/US/UK
1950–1953	Korean Conflict	North Korea/South Korea/US/People's Republic of China
1954–1955	Taiwan Strait	US/People's Republic of China
1961	Berlin	USSR/US/NATO
1962	Cuba	USSR/US/Cuba
1973	Arab-Israeli War	Egypt/Israel/Syria/Jordan/US/USSR
1975	Angola	US/ USSR/Cuba/China/South Africa
1979–1992	Afghanistan	USSR/US/Saudi Arabia/Pakistan
1979–1990	Nicaragua-El Salvador	US/USSR/Cuba

consolidated his position while maintaining independence from Moscow. Subsequently, Tito's Yugoslavia was to play an important role in the third world Nonaligned Movement.

The first major confrontation of the Cold War took place over Berlin in 1948. During the Yalta and Potsdam conferences, Germany and Berlin were divided among the four victorious powers: the United States, the Soviet Union, Great Britain, and France. The former German capital was left deep in the heart of the Soviet zone of occupation (East Berlin), and in June 1948 Stalin sought to resolve its status by severing road and rail communications. West Berlin's population and political autonomy were kept alive by a massive airlift. Stalin ended the blockade in May 1949. The crisis saw the deployment of American long-range bombers in Britain, officially described as "atomic capable," though none were actually armed with nuclear weapons. US military deployment was followed by political commitment enshrined in the **North Atlantic Treaty Organization (NATO)** treaty signed in April 1949. The key article of the treaty—that an attack on one member would be treated as an attack on all—accorded with the principle of collective self-defense enshrined in Article 51 of the UN Charter. In practice, the cornerstone of the alliance was the commitment of the United States to defend Western Europe. In reality, this soon meant the willingness of the United States to use nuclear weapons to deter Soviet "aggression." For the Soviet Union "political encirclement" soon entailed a growing military, and specifically nuclear, threat.

While the origins of the Cold War were in Europe, events and conflicts in Asia and elsewhere were also crucial. In 1949, the thirty-year-long Chinese civil war ended in victory for the communists under Mao Zedong. This had a major impact on Asian affairs and on perceptions in both Moscow and Washington. In June 1950, the North Korean attack on South Korea was interpreted as part of a general communist strategy and as a test case for American resolve and the will of the United Nations to withstand aggression. The resulting American and UN commitment, followed in October 1950 by Chinese involvement, led to a war lasting three years, in which over 3 million people died before prewar borders were restored. North and South Korea themselves remained locked in seemingly perpetual hostility, even after the end of the Cold War.

Conflict, Confrontation, and Compromise

One consequence of the Korean War was the buildup of American forces in Western Europe, lest communist aggression in Asia distract from the real intent in Europe. The idea that communism was a monolithic political entity controlled from Moscow became an enduring American fixation, not shared in London and elsewhere. Western Europeans nevertheless depended on the United States for military security, and this dependence deepened as the Cold War confrontation in Europe was consolidated. The rearmament of the Federal Republic of Germany in 1954 precipitated the creation of the **Warsaw Pact** in 1955. The military buildup continued apace, with unprecedented concentrations of conventional and, moreover, nuclear forces. By the 1960s, there were some seven thousand nuclear weapons in Western Europe alone. NATO deployed nuclear weapons to offset Soviet conventional superiority, while Soviet short-range or "theater nuclear" forces in Europe compensated for overall American nuclear superiority.

The death of Stalin in March of 1953 portended significant consequences for the USSR at home and abroad. Stalin's eventual successor, Nikita Khrushchev, strove to modernize Soviet society, and in the process, he helped unleash reformist forces in Eastern Europe. While Poland was controlled, the situation in Hungary threatened Soviet hege-

North Atlantic Treaty Organization (NATO) Organization established by treaty in April 1949 comprising twelve (later sixteen) countries from Western Europe and North America. The most important aspect of the NATO alliance was the American commitment to the defense of Western Europe. Today NATO has twenty-eight member states.

Warsaw Pact The Warsaw Pact was created in May 1955 in response to West Germany's rearmament and entry into NATO. It comprised the USSR and seven communist states (though Albania withdrew support in 1961). The organization was officially dissolved in July 1991.

Although some scholars assert the atomic bomb revolutionized warfare, by 1951 the United States was still using conventional bombs during the Korean War. Had warfare changed?

mony, and in 1956 the intervention of the Red Army brought bloodshed to the streets of Budapest and international condemnation on Moscow. Soviet intervention coincided with an attack on Egypt by Britain, France, and Israel, precipitated by Colonel Nasser's nationalization of the Suez Canal in a manner that displeased Britain, the former colonial occupier. The French took part in the attack because Nasser's government was providing support to anti-French rebels in Algeria. The British government's actions provoked fierce domestic and international criticism and the most serious rift in the "special relationship" between Britain and the United States. President Eisenhower was strongly opposed to the actions of the US allies, and in the face of what were effectively US economic sanctions (a threat to cut off American oil exports to Britain), the British abandoned the operation, as well as their support for the French and Israelis.

Khrushchev's policy toward the West mixed a search for political coexistence with the pursuit of ideological confrontation. Soviet support for movements of national liberation aroused fears in the West of a global communist challenge. American commitment to **liberal democracy** and national self-determination was often subordinated to Cold War

liberal democracy States with democratic or representative governments and capitalist economies that are promoters of multilateralism and free trade. Domestic interests, values, and institutions shape foreign policy.

perspectives, as well as to US economic and political interests. The Cold War saw the growth of large permanent intelligence organizations, whose roles ranged from estimating intentions and capabilities of adversaries to covert intervention in the affairs of other states. Crises over Berlin in 1961 and Cuba in 1962 marked the most dangerous moments of the Cold War. In both, there was a risk of direct military confrontation and, certainly in October 1962, the possibility of nuclear war. How close the world came to Armageddon during the Cuban missile crisis and exactly why peace was preserved remain matters of debate among historians and surviving officials.

The events of 1962 were followed by a more stable period of coexistence and competition. Nuclear arsenals, nevertheless, continued to grow. Whether this is best characterized as an **arms race**, or whether internal political and bureaucratic pressures drove the growth of nuclear arsenals, is open to interpretation. For Washington, commitments to NATO allies also provided pressures and opportunities to develop and deploy their own shorter-range ("tactical" and "theater") nuclear weapons. The global nuclear dimension increased with the emergence of other nuclear-weapon states: Britain in 1952, France in 1960, and China in 1964. Growing concern at the spread, or proliferation, of nuclear weapons led to the negotiation of the Nuclear Nonproliferation Treaty (NPT) in 1968, wherein states that had nuclear weapons committed themselves to halt the arms race, while those who did not possess them promised not to develop them. Despite successes of the NPT, by 1990 several states had developed or were developing nuclear weapons, notably Israel, India, Pakistan, and apartheid South Africa. (South Africa later gave up its nuclear weapons program and remains the only state to do so.)

The Rise and Fall of Détente

At the same time that America's commitment in Vietnam was deepening, Soviet-Chinese relations were deteriorating. Indeed, by 1969 the People's Republic of China and the Soviet Union had fought a minor border war over a territorial dispute. Despite (or because of) these tensions, the foundations for what became known as **détente** were laid between the Soviet Union and the United States and for what became known as **rapprochement** between China and the United States. Both terms, long a part of the language of diplomacy, refer to the processes by which countries seek to improve their relations. Détente in Europe had its origins in the **Ostpolitik** of the German chancellor Willy Brandt and resulted in agreements that recognized the peculiar status of Berlin and the sovereignty of East Germany. For his efforts, which finally bore fruit with the end of the Cold War in 1989, Brandt won the Nobel Peace Prize. Soviet-American détente had its roots in mutual recognition of the need to avoid nuclear crises and in the economic and military incentives in avoiding an unconstrained arms race. Both Washington and Moscow also looked toward Beijing when making their bilateral calculations.

In the West, détente was associated with the political leadership of President Richard Nixon and his adviser Henry Kissinger, who were also instrumental in Sino-American rapprochement. This new phase in Soviet-American relations did not mark an end to political conflict, as each side pursued political goals, some of which were increasingly incompatible with the aspirations of the other superpower. Both sides supported friendly regimes and movements and subverted adversaries. All this came as various political upheavals were taking place in the Third World (see Table 2.1). The question of how far the superpowers could control their friends, and how far they were entangled by their commitments, was underlined in 1973 when the Arab-Israeli war embroiled both the United

arms race This is a central concept in realist thought. As states build up their military to address real or perceived threats to their national security, they may create insecurity in other states. These states, in turn, develop their military capacities and thus begin an arms race. This never-ending pursuit of security creates the condition we know as a security dilemma.

détente Relaxation of tension between East and West; Soviet–American détente lasted from the late 1960s to the late 1970s and was characterized by negotiations and nuclear arms control agreements.

rapprochement Reestablishment of more friendly relations between the People's Republic of China and the United States in the early 1970s.

Ostpolitik The West German government's "Eastern Policy" of the mid- to late 1960s, designed to develop relations between West Germany and members of the Warsaw Pact.

States and the Soviet Union in what became a potentially dangerous confrontation. Getting the superpowers involved in the war—whether by design or serendipity—helped create the political conditions for Egyptian-Israeli rapprochement. Diplomatic and strategic relations were transformed as Egypt switched its allegiance from Moscow to Washington. In the short term, Egypt was isolated in the Arab world. For Israel, fear of a war of annihilation fought on two fronts was lifted. Yet continuing political violence and terrorism, and the enduring enmity between Israel and other Arab states, proved insurmountable obstacles to a more permanent regional settlement.

In Washington, Soviet support for revolutionary movements in the third world was seen as evidence of duplicity. Some American politicians and academics claim that Moscow's support for revolutionary forces in Ethiopia in 1975 killed détente. Others cite the Soviet role in Angola in 1978. Furthermore, the perception that the USSR was using arms control agreements to gain military advantage was linked to Soviet behavior in the third world. Growing Soviet military superiority was reflected in growing Soviet influence, it was argued. Critics claimed the SALT (Strategic Arms Limitation Talks) process enabled the Soviets to deploy multiple independently targetable warheads on their large **Intercontinental Ballistic Missiles (ICBMs)**, threatening key American forces. America faced a "window of vulnerability," critics of détente claimed. The view from Moscow was different, reflecting different assumptions about the scope and purpose of détente and the nature of nuclear deterrence. Other events were also seen to weaken American influence. The overthrow of the shah of Iran in 1979 resulted in the loss of an important Western ally in the region, though the ensuing militant Islamic government was hostile to both superpowers.

December 1979 marked a point of transition in East-West affairs. NATO agreed to deploy land-based Cruise and Pershing II missiles in Europe if negotiations with the Soviets did not reduce what NATO saw as a serious imbalance. Later in the month, Soviet armed forces intervened in Afghanistan to support their revolutionary allies. The USSR was bitterly condemned in the West and in the third world for its actions and soon became committed to a protracted and bloody struggle that many compared to the American war in Vietnam. In Washington, President Carter, who had sought to control arms and reduce tensions with the USSR, hardened his view of the Soviet Union. The first reaction was the Carter Doctrine, which clearly stated that any Soviet attack on countries in the Persian Gulf would be seen as a direct attack on US vital interests. Another result was the Carter administration's decision to boycott the 1980 Summer Olympics in Moscow. Nevertheless, Republicans increasingly used foreign and defense policy to attack the Carter presidency. Perceptions of American weakness abroad permeated domestic politics, and in 1980, Ronald Reagan was elected President. He was committed to a more confrontational approach with the Soviets on arms control, third world conflicts, and East-West relations in general.

From Détente to a Second Cold War

In the West, critics of détente and arms control, some of whom would later advise the George W. Bush presidential administration, argued in the 1970s and 1980s that the Soviets were acquiring nuclear superiority. Some suggested that the United States should pursue policies and strategies based on the idea that victory in nuclear war was possible. The election of Ronald Reagan in 1980 was a watershed in Soviet-American relations. Ronald Reagan had made it clear during the election campaign that the United States

Intercontinental Ballistic Missiles (ICBMs) Weapons system the USA and USSR developed to threaten each other with destruction. The thirty- to forty-minute flight times of the missiles created a situation that is sometimes called "Mutually Assured Destruction (MAD)" or "the Balance of Terror."

would take a tough stance in its relations with the Soviet Union. In two monumental speeches delivered in March 1983, Reagan stated that the Soviet Union was the "focus of evil in the modern world" and he coined the phrase "evil empire" to describe the USSR. In the second speech, he outlined his idea for a strategic defense against Soviet missiles. One issue that Reagan inherited, and which loomed large in the breakdown of relations between East and West, was nuclear missiles in Europe. NATO's decision to deploy land-based missiles capable of striking Soviet territory precipitated a period of great tension in relations between NATO and the USSR and political friction within NATO.

Reagan's own incautious public remarks reinforced perceptions that he was as ill-informed as he was dangerous in matters nuclear, though key arms policies were consistent with those of his predecessor, Jimmy Carter. On arms control, Reagan was disinterested in agreements that would freeze the status quo for the sake of getting agreement, and Soviet and American negotiators proved unable to make progress in talks on long-range and intermediate-range weapons. One particular idea had significant consequences for arms control and for Washington's relations with its allies and its adversaries. The **Strategic Defense Initiative (SDI)**, quickly dubbed "Star Wars," after the new movie, was a research program designed to explore the feasibility of space-based defenses against ballistic missiles. The Soviets appeared to take SDI very seriously and claimed that Reagan's real purpose was to regain the nuclear monopoly of the 1950s. The technological advances claimed by SDI proponents did not materialize, however, and the program was eventually reduced and marginalized, although never fully eliminated from the United States defense budget.

The resulting period of tension and confrontation between the superpowers has been described as the second cold war or the end of détente and compared to the early period of confrontation and tension between 1946 and 1953. In Western Europe and the Soviet Union, there was real fear of nuclear war. Much of this was a reaction to the rhetoric and policies of the Reagan administration. American statements on nuclear weapons and military intervention in Grenada in 1983, and an air raid against Libya in 1986, were seen as evidence of a new belligerence. Reagan's policy toward Central America, and support for the rebel contras in Nicaragua, were sources of controversy within the United States and internationally. In 1986, the International Court of Justice (ICJ) found the United States guilty of violating international law by sowing sea mines in Nicaraguan harbors. The Reagan administration ignored this ruling, claiming the ICJ lacked jurisdiction in this situation.

The Reagan administration's use of military power was nonetheless limited: rhetoric and perception were at variance with reality. Some operations ended in humiliating failure, notably in Lebanon in 1983 after a truck bomb attack on the United States Marine barracks in Beirut. Nevertheless, there is evidence that the Soviet leadership took very seriously the words (and deeds) of the Reagan administration and believed that Washington was planning a nuclear first strike. In 1983, Soviet air defenses shot down a South Korean civilian airliner in Soviet airspace. The American reaction, and the imminent deployment of US nuclear missiles in Europe, created a climate of great tension in East-West relations.

Throughout the early 1980s, the Soviets were handicapped by a succession of aging political leaders (Brezhnev, Andropov, and Chernenko), whose ill health further inhibited Soviet responses to the American challenge and the American threat. This changed dramatically after Mikhail Gorbachev became general secretary of the Soviet Communist Party

Strategic Defense Initiative (SDI) A controversial strategic policy advocated by some conservative politicians and nuclear physicists such as Edward Teller, who helped to create the hydrogen bomb. SDI was embraced by the Reagan administration. The plan called for a defensive missile shield that would make Soviet offensive missiles ineffective by destroying them in flight. This defensive posture was to replace the US strategy of mutually assured destruction. Reagan wanted to make nuclear weapons impotent and obsolete. The plan is often derisively called "Star Wars," after the movies that were popular at the time.

in 1985, a position that gave him control over the state. Gorbachev's "new thinking" in foreign policy, and his domestic reforms, created a revolution, both in the USSR's foreign relations and within Soviet society. At home, **glasnost** (or openness) and **perestroika** (or restructuring) unleashed nationalist and other forces that, to Gorbachev's dismay, were to destroy the Union of Soviet Socialist Republics.

Gorbachev paved the way for agreements on nuclear and conventional forces that helped ease the tensions that had characterized the early 1980s. In 1987, he traveled to Washington to sign the Intermediate Nuclear Forces (INF) Treaty, banning intermediate-range nuclear missiles, including Cruise and Pershing II. This agreement was heralded as a triumph for the Soviet leader, but NATO leaders, including Margaret Thatcher and Ronald Reagan, argued that it was vindication of the policies pursued by NATO since 1979. The INF Treaty was concluded more quickly than a new agreement on cutting strategic nuclear weapons, in part because of continuing Soviet opposition to SDI. And it was Reagan's successor, George H. W. Bush, who concluded a **Strategic Arms Reductions Treaty (START)** agreement that reduced long-range nuclear weapons (though only back to the level they had been in the early 1980s). Gorbachev used agreements on nuclear weapons as a means of building trust and demonstrated the serious and radical nature of his purpose. However, despite similar radical agreements on conventional forces in Europe (culminating in the Paris agreement of 1990), the end of the Cold War marked success in nuclear arms control rather than nuclear disarmament. The histories of the Cold War and of the atomic bomb are very closely connected, but while the Cold War is now over, nuclear weapons are still very much in existence. We will discuss the issues surrounding nuclear weapons in Chapter 8.

glasnost Policy of greater openness pursued by Soviet leader Mikhail Gorbachev from 1985, involving greater toleration of internal dissent and criticism.

perestroika Gorbachev's policy of restructuring, pursued in tandem with glasnost and intended to modernize the Soviet political and economic system.

Strategic Arms Reductions Treaty (START) Negotiations began in 1982 and progressed at a very slow pace over eight years. The US and the USSR debated these issues in twelve rounds of formal negotiations, thirteen foreign ministers' meetings, and six summit conferences. In May 1990, George H. W. Bush and Gorbachev agreed to a framework for arms reduction. A treaty was signed in Moscow in July 1991. This treaty reversed a forty-five-year-old strategic nuclear arms race. The treaty broke new ground because it called for a reduction of nuclear arms rather than just a limit on the growth of these weapons.

The Brandenburg Gate in Berlin was the scene of joyful dancing in 1989 when the Communist government of East Germany permitted the destruction of the Berlin Wall. Has life improved since the end of the Cold War?

From the Cold War to the War on Terror

The first major global conflict after the Cold War ended was the 1990 Iraqi invasion of neighboring Kuwait. After some attempts to find an Arab solution, the United States led a comprehensive multilateral diplomatic and military effort to punish Saddam Hussein for his actions and to signal to the world that this kind of violation of international law would not stand. The war to liberate Kuwait lasted just forty-two days, and an international coalition of diplomats and military forces helped define the "New World Order" that President George H. W. Bush had talked about since taking office in 1989. The United States wisely included the Soviet Union in its plans and effectively used the UN Security Council to pass more than twelve resolutions condemning the actions of Iraq. What the first President Bush created was a US-led global coalition that was supported by all five permanent members of the Security Council—a first since the establishment of the UN. The majority of the world was behind this action. The invasion of Kuwait was illegal under international law and the major powers were willing to work together to protect and promote a "rule-based system."

So it was, once again, in 1989 when the last of the "great wars" of the twentieth century—the Cold War—finally wound down. The world in 1990 was full of promise (especially for the victors) but full of potential risk as well. It was also one replete with the sources of further conflict. In fact, looking back now from the perspective of the post-9/11 world, it would appear as if the years following the end of the Cold War were but a mere interregnum. This New World Order, as US president George H. W. Bush called it, existed briefly between two eras: one defined by an ongoing struggle between two competing secular ideologies and another shaped by an emerging clash between two conceptions of civilization itself.

The Cold War divided the world for over forty years, threatened humanity with near destruction, and led to the death of at least 25 million people, mostly in that highly contested zone that came to be referred to during the Cold War as the third world. Yet in spite of these dangers and costs, the Cold War in its central core areas still managed to create a degree of stability that the world had not experienced since the early part of the twentieth century. For this reason, many came to view the bipolar order after 1947 as something that was not merely the expression of a given international reality but something that was desirable and defensible too. Indeed, as we will see in Chapter 3, some realists seemed to celebrate the superpower relationship on the grounds that a world in which there were two balancing powers, each limiting the actions of the other, was likely to be a far more stable world than one in which there were several competing states.

One can thus imagine the enormous shock waves produced by what happened in Eastern Europe in 1989. The world at the time was already undergoing dramatic changes, mainly the result of radical new policies introduced by Soviet leader Mikhail Gorbachev. Many people, of course, hoped

United Nations Charter (1945) The charter of the United Nations is the legal regime that created the United Nations as the world's only "supranational" organization. The charter defines the structure of the United Nations, the powers of its constitutive agencies, and the rights and obligations of sovereign states party to the charter. Among other things, the charter is the key legal document limiting the use of force to instances of self-defense and collective peace enforcement endorsed by the United Nations Security Council.

WHAT'S YOUR WORLDVIEW ?

With the end of the Cold War, many analysts talked optimistically about a "peace dividend"—that is, a chance to shift spending from military to social programs like education, health, and job training. However, in the 1990s the US did not cut military spending and shift funding to domestic priorities. Why do you think this happened? Do you think US leaders feared a return of an authoritarian Soviet state, or did they anticipate the need for a strong military to support their hegemonic position?

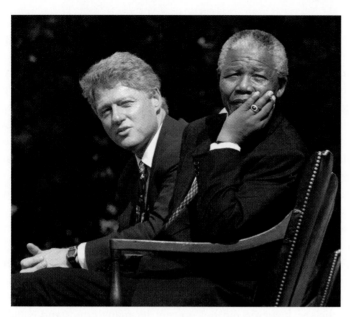

A clear sign that the world had changed was this meeting between US president Bill Clinton and Nelson Mandela. After almost thirty years in prison for his opposition to the apartheid South African government, Mandela became president of the country.

that Gorbachev's several reforms would make the world a safer and more humane place. Hardly anybody, though, seriously anticipated the collapse of communism and the destruction of the Berlin Wall. Moreover, few believed that this revolutionary process could be achieved peacefully. Nor had policy makers planned for it, and the intelligence agencies in the West had completely missed the signs of change in the Soviet bloc. It was all rather surprising if not disturbing for those who had thought that this superpower rivalry would never end without some nuclear confrontation. Now world leaders had to remake the world and find ways to integrate former enemies back into the West.

The tasks they confronted certainly seemed very great, ranging from the institutional one of devising new tasks for bodies such as NATO, the **United Nations**, and the **European Union** to the more economic challenge of facilitating the transition in countries that had had little experience running **market democracies**. Some wondered whether a US-led Atlantic Alliance could survive in an environment where there was no longer a well-defined threat. Certainly, many questioned the need for high military spending, arguing that if the world was now becoming a safer and more integrated place, what then was the purpose of spending billions on weapons?

Globalization: Challenging the International Order?

If the Cold War period was marked by a clear and sharp divide between opposing socioeconomic systems operating by radically different standards, then the post–Cold War order could readily be characterized as one in which many states were compelled to play by a single set of rules within an increasingly competitive world economy. The term most frequently used to describe this new order was **globalization**, a notion that had barely been used before 1989 but now came be to employed ever more regularly to define an apparently new system of international relations.

European Union (EU) The EU was formally created in 1992 following the signing of the Maastricht Treaty. However, the origins of the EU can be traced back to 1951 and the creation of the European Coal and Steel Community, followed in 1957 with a broader customs union (the Treaty of Rome, 1958). Originally a grouping of six countries in 1957, "Europe" grew by adding new members in 1973, 1981, and 1986. Since the fall of the planned economies in Eastern Europe in 1989, Europe has grown and now includes twenty-seven member states.

market democracies See "liberal democracies."

globalization A historical process involving a fundamental shift or transformation in the spatial scale of human social organization that links distant communities and expands the reach of power relations across regions and continents.

anarchy A system operating in the absence of any central government. It does not imply chaos but, in realist theory, the absence of political authority.

capitalism A system of production in which human labor and its products are commodities that are bought and sold in the marketplace.

Globalization, however, seemed to mean different things to different theorists. Thus for one school, the hyperglobalists, it was assumed to be undermining borders and states—quite literally abolishing the Westphalian system, which had begun to crystallize over 330 years ago, as we read about at the beginning of this chapter. Thomas Friedman (2000) argued that globalization has changed world politics forever, giving individuals more tools to influence markets and governments and create networks that challenge the power of states. Others—the skeptics—took a less cataclysmic view. Globalization, they agreed, was providing a different context within which international relations was now being played out. But it would be absurd to conclude that it was doing away with the state or destroying the underlying logic of **anarchy**. Anthony Giddens (2000) reminded us that globalization might pull power away from the state, but it might also empower local groups who want to defend their position in this global society. Some writers were even skeptical of whether there was anything especially novel about globalization. **Capitalism** after all had always been a global system. Since the sixteenth century, interdependence had been one of capitalism's more obvious features. So why assume that there was much new about the phenomenon simply because academics and publicists talked about it with greater frequency?

Such skepticism, however, did not prevent its many critics and equally influential defenders from engaging in an extended and at times heated debate about the impact of globalization on global inequality, climate change, and the more general distribution of power in the international system. It also made very little difference as to what governments tended to say and do. Globalization, they insisted with increasing regularity, was a simple fact of economic life. There was no escaping its logic. The only thing one could do (using the oft-repeated words of President Clinton) was to "compete not retreat." Moreover, if one did not do so, the future for one's own people, and by implication one's state, was bleak. UK prime minister Tony Blair agreed and even appeared to use the menace of globalization as a means of attacking those in Europe who would defend old economic ways. In a world of global competition, Blair observed, there was really very little choice. Europe had to either reform or decline. There was no other way.

But if there was little meeting of minds among politicians and academics, there was little doubt of the impact globalization was having on the world economy, and in particular on those three central core areas of it located in North America, Europe, and East Asia. Here, at least, the theoretical debate about the novelty, existence, and the meaning of the phenomenon was being resolved, as this very special triad of economic power (over 80 percent of the world's total) experienced reasonable growth, increased economic interdependence, and massive wealth creation. No doubt the process created great national uncertainty as firms became ever more internationalized. For example, with the creation of high-speed information technologies, a firm, whether large or small, could have its management offices in one country, its design staff in another, and its production facilities in a third. Many US corporations, encouraged by federal tax code, led the way in this process. There was also something distinctly unethical about an apparently unregulated economic process that literally made billions for the few (especially those in the financial sector) while generating insecurity for the many. However, this was a price well worth paying— or so its defenders inferred—if there was to be any semblance of economic progress. In a world where extreme competition ruled and money moved at the flick of a switch, there was only one thing worse than being part of this runaway system—and that was not being part of it.

From Superpower to Hyperpower—US Primacy

If a one-world economy operating under the same set of highly competitive rules was at least one consequence of the end of the Cold War, another was a major resurgence of American self-confidence in a new international system where it seemed to have no serious rival. This was not only a development that few had foretold (in the 1970s and 1980s many analysts believed that the United States was in decline); it was one that many had thought impossible (most realists in fact believed that after the Cold War the world would become genuinely multipolar). It was also a situation many feared, on the grounds that an America with no obvious peer competitor would act more assertively and with less restraint. That aside, all of the most obvious indicators by the late 1990s—military, economic, and cultural—seemed to point to only one conclusion: that as a result of the Soviet collapse, followed in short order by the economic crisis in Japan and Europe's manifest failure to manage the conflict in the former Yugoslavia, the United States by the turn of the century had been transformed from a mere superpower (its designation hitherto) to what the French foreign minister Hubert Vedrine in 1998 termed a **"hyperpower."**

hyperpower A term meant to describe the situation of the United States after the Cold War ended. With the Soviet Union's military might greatly diminished and China having primarily only regional power-projecting capability, the United States was unchallenged in the world.

International security specialists call the attack in 2000 by Al Qaeda members on the USS Cole using a motorboat containing a large bomb an example of asymmetrical warfare. Why did the leaders of the United States and other Western democracies ignore the growing threat of Islamic militants prior to September 11, 2001?

Former secretary of state Madeline Albright may have also agreed, in her own way, with this assessment, although she used more diplomatic language—she called the United States "the indispensable power" in global politics.

This claim to unilateral privilege was linked to a particularly bleak view of the world shared by many, though not all, US policy makers. The Cold War may have been over, they agreed: America may have emerged triumphant. But this was no reason to be complacent. To repeat a phrase often used at the time, although the "dragon" in the form of the USSR had been slain, there were still many "vipers and snakes" lurking in the long grass. Among the three most dangerous and pernicious of these were various "rogue states" (Iran, Iraq, North Korea, Libya, and Cuba), the constant threat of nuclear proliferation (made all the more likely by the disintegration of the USSR and the unfolding nuclear arms race between Pakistan and India), and the threat of religious fundamentalists and ideological extremists (all the more virulent now because of the fallout from the last great battlefield of the Cold War in Afghanistan). Indeed, long before 9/11, the dangers posed by radical Islamism were very well known to US intelligence, beginning with the bombing of the US Marine barracks in Beirut, Lebanon, in October 1983 that caused the deaths of almost three hundred American personnel. The devastating bombing of the World Trade Center in 1993 and the US embassies in Tanzania and Kenya five years later, as well as the audacious attack on the USS *Cole* in 2000, all pointed to a new form of **terrorism** that could be neither deterred nor easily defeated by conventional means.

Yet in spite of these several threats, there was no clear indication that the United States was eager during the 1990s to project its power with any serious purpose. The United States may have possessed vast capabilities, but there appeared to be no real desire, in a post–Cold War environment, to expend American blood and treasure in foreign adventures. The desire sank even further following the debacle in Somalia in 1993: the death of eighteen US soldiers there created its own kind of syndrome that made any more US forays abroad extremely unlikely. The United States after the Cold War was thus a most curious hegemon. On the one hand, its power seemed to be unrivalled (and was); on the other, it seemed to have very little idea about how to use this power other than to bomb the occasional "rogue" state when deemed necessary (as in former Yugoslavia), while supporting diplomatic solutions to most problems when need be (as in the cases of the Middle East and North Korea). The end of the Cold War and the disappearance of the Soviet threat may have rendered the international system more secure and the United States more powerful, but it also made the United States a very reluctant warrior. In a very important sense the United States during the 1990s remained a superpower without a mission.

terrorism The use of violence by nonstate groups or, in some cases, states to inspire fear, by attacking civilians and/or symbolic targets, and eliminating opposition groups. This is done for purposes such as drawing widespread attention to a grievance, provoking a severe response, or wearing down an opponent's moral resolve, to effect political change.

Europe in the New World System

If for the United States the most pressing post–Cold War problem was how to develop a coherent global policy in a world where there was no single major threat to its interests, then for Europeans the main issue was how to manage the new enlarged space that had been created as a result of the events in 1989. Indeed, while more triumphant Americans would continue to proclaim that it was they who had actually won the Cold War in Europe, it was Europeans who were the real beneficiaries of what had taken place in the late 1980s. There were sound reasons for thinking this way. A continent that had once been divided was now whole again. Germany had been peacefully united. The states of Eastern Europe had achieved one of the most important of international rights: the

Global Perspective

Perception, Continuity, and Change After January 20, 2009

The study of international relations depends to a great extent on perception. How we think about the world often determines what we think is important. This habit of mind helps to explain how political leaders and opinion makers in the United States were unprepared for the two key events of the late twentieth century: the collapse of the Soviet Union and the rise of militant Islamic fundamentalism. The signs of the two events were in plain sight, if you knew what to look for.

In the case of Islamic fundamentalism, certainly if you lived in a country with a large Muslim population, you would have been aware of the growing appeal of fundamentalist strains of Islam. The Wahabi sect in Saudi Arabia, for instance, forms the basis for society there. Egypt has had problems with violence linked to the Muslim Brotherhood since the time of British colonization. Indeed, the Brotherhood is often blamed for the assassination of President Anwar Sadat. In Afghanistan, the United States itself helped to arm Islamic fundamentalists in their war against the Soviet invasion during the 1980s. The trend was visible every day in public as people rejected European styles of dress: more men grew beards, and more women adopted the clothing styles the fundamentalists preferred.

If North American and European leaders were not ready for the impact of Islamic fundamentalism, how unprepared are people in the rest of the world for trends that will result from the election of Barack Obama as president of the United States? Will there be continuity or change? If we start with what the Bush administration called the "global war on terror," we can see that some things now are the same, and some are not. For example, in the early months of 2009 the Obama administration continued to use Predator drone aircraft to attack people suspected of being Islamic militants in the tribal areas in Pakistan along the Afghanistan border. Pakistani officials objected to such attacks during the Bush years, but President Obama clearly decided that the raids must continue. A major apparent change in US policy could be seen in the fund-raising efforts to rebuild Palestinian homes in Gaza. Moreover, as the United States increased the number of its troops in Afghanistan to fight the resurgent Taliban, officials in Washington also quietly expressed their dissatisfaction with the actions of the Karzai government there. Both were major changes from the policy of the Bush administration.

For people outside Western Europe and the United States it is difficult to assess what the appearance of continuity or change in the foreign policy of the United States means. One source of this difficulty is the perception popular in the developing world that the United States is the global hegemonic oppressor. People have been socialized by family members, schools, and political officials to blame the United States for all their sufferings. This is a perception that may not be based in fact, and it could be as incorrect as the perception that all Muslims are terrorists, or that Islamic fundamentalism did not pose a threat to Europe and the United States. Perceptions and images are often more powerful than reality.

The Nobel Peace Prize Committee members chose US president Barack Obama as their honoree in 2009. What must be done to fulfill the promise that the committee saw in the election of Mr. Obama?

Number of Wars in Progress Since 1950. Based on what you have read in this chapter, what accounts for these trends—for the increases, spikes, and decreases? *Source: University of Hamburg,* Vital Signs *2006–2007, Harborn and Wallensteen (2007, 62).*

right of self-determination. The threat of war with potentially devastating consequences for Europe had been eliminated. Naturally, the transition from one order to another was not going to happen without certain costs, borne most notably by those who would now have to face up to life under competitive capitalism. Nor was the collapse of communism in some countries an entirely bloodless affair, as events in former Yugoslavia (1990–1999) revealed only too tragically. With that said, a post–Cold War Europe still had much to look forward to.

While many in Europe debated the region's future, policy makers themselves were confronted with the more concrete issue of how to bring the "East" back into the "West," a process that went under the general heading of enlargement. In terms of policy outcome, the strategy scored some notable successes. Indeed, by 2007 the European Union had grown to become twenty-seven members, and NATO one less at twenty-six, with most of the new members coming from the former Soviet bloc. The two bodies also changed their clublike character in the process, much to the consternation of some people in the original member states, who found the entrants from the former Soviet bloc to be as much trouble as asset. In fact, according to critics—both politicians and academics—enlargement had proceeded so rapidly that the essential core meaning of both organizations had been lost. The EU, it was now argued by some, had been so keen to enlarge that it had lost the will to integrate. NATO meanwhile could no longer be regarded as a serious military organization with an integrated command structure. One significant aspect of this was the "out of area" problem that limited NATO activities to Europe itself. This would change after September 11, 2001. Still, it was difficult not to be impressed by the capacity of NATO and the EU in their new roles. These institutions had helped shape part of Europe during the Cold War and were now being employed to help manage the relatively successful (though never easy) transition from one kind of European order to another. For those who had earlier disparaged the part institutions might play in preventing anarchy in Europe, the important roles played by the EU and NATO seemed to prove that institutions were essential.

Europe, it was generally recognized, remained what it had effectively been since the end of the Second World War: a work in progress. The problem was that nobody could quite agree when—if ever—this work would be completed, and where—if anywhere—the European Union would end. Some analysts remained remarkably upbeat. The EU's capacity for dealing with the consequences of the end of the Cold War, its successful introduction of a single currency (the euro, in January 2002), and its ability to bring in new members all pointed to one obvious conclusion: the EU's future was assured. A few even speculated that the new twenty-first century would itself be European rather than American. Many, however, were more skeptical. After a decade-long period of expansion and experimentation, Europe, they believed, had reached a dead end. It was more divided than united over basic constitutional ends, and it faced several challenges—economic, cultural, and political—to which there seemed to be no easy answers. Indeed, according to some commentators, European leaders not only confronted older issues that remained unsolved, they also faced a host of new ones (for example, Turkish membership of the EU, how to integrate its 13 million Muslim citizens, and rising economic competition from China) to which they had no ready-made solutions. Europe, by the beginning of the twenty-first century, may have been well aware of where it was coming from, but it had no blueprint for where it wanted to go to. In some ways, Europe had "lost the plot."

Boris Yeltsin, then Russian Republic president, toured the United States in 1986 and received a warm reception from US president Ronald Reagan. Why has their goal of global nuclear disarmament remained distant?

Russia: From Yeltsin to Putin

One of the many problems facing the new Europe after the Cold War was how to define its relationship with postcommunist Russia, a country confronting several degrees of stress after 1991 as it began to transform itself from a Marxist superpower with a planned economy to a democratic country that was liberal and market oriented. As even the most confident of Europeans accepted, none of this was going to be easy for a state that had had the same system for nearly three-quarters of a century. And so it proved during the 1990s, an especially painful decade during which Russia lost its ability to effectively challenge the United States and was instead a declining power with diminishing economic and ideological assets. Nor was there much in the way of economic compensation. On the contrary, as a result of its speedy adoption of Western-style privatization, Russia experienced something close to a 1930s-style economic depression, with industrial production plummeting, living standards sinking, and whole regions once devoted to Cold War military production experiencing free fall.

oligarchs A term from ancient Greece to describe a political system in which a few people control a state.

President Boris Yeltsin's foreign policy, meanwhile, did little to reassure many Russians. Indeed, his decision to get close to Russia's old capitalist enemies gave the distinct impression that he was selling out to the West. This made him a hero to many outside Russia. However, to many ordinary Russians it seemed as if he (like his predecessor Gorbachev) was conceding everything and getting very little in return. Nationalists and old communists, still present in significant numbers, were especially scathing. Yeltsin and his team, they argued, had not only given away Russia's assets at "discount prices" to a new class of **oligarchs**, but he was also trying to turn Russia into a Western dependency. In short, he was not standing up for Russia's national interest.

Whether his successor Vladimir Putin, a former official in the KGB, had a clear vision for Russia when he took over the presidency matters less than the fact that, having assumed office, he began to stake out very different positions. These included a greater authoritarianism and nationalism at home, a much clearer recognition that the interests of Russia and those of the West would not always be one and the same, and what turned into a persistent drive to bring the Russian economy—and Russia's huge natural resources—back under state control. This did not lead to a turning back of the clock to Soviet times. What it did mean, though, was that the West's leaders could no longer regard the country as a potential strategic partner. Certainly, Western governments could not assume that Russia would forever be in a state of decline. The West must instead confront a state with almost unlimited supplies of oil and gas and with a leadership determined to defend Russia's interests and to restore Russia to a position of global leadership.

Still, the West had less to fear now than it had during the Cold War proper. Economic reform had made Russia dependent on the West (though some Western countries, like Germany, were dependent on Russia for their energy requirements). Furthermore, the official political ideology did not in any way challenge Western institutions or values. The world had changed forever since 1991. Nor was Russia the power it had once been, during Soviet times. Indeed, not only was it unable to prevent some of its former republics from either signing up to former enemy institutions like NATO or moving more openly into the Western camp, by 2007 it was effectively encircled by the three Baltic republics to the northwest, an increasingly pro-Western Ukraine to the south, and Georgia in the Caucasus. Adding to its potential woes was the fact that many of its more loyal, regional allies ran highly repressive and potentially unstable governments: Belorussia, Turkmenistan, and Azerbaijan, for example.

Meanwhile, in Chechnya, Russia faced an insurgency beginning in 1994 that not only revealed deep weaknesses in the Russian military but brought down Western outrage on its head—perhaps not to the point of causing a rupture, but certainly enough to sour relations. Many in the United States and a few in Europe were compelled to conclude that while Russia may have changed in several positive ways since the collapse of the USSR in 1991, at the end of the day it still remained historic Russia with an authoritarian outlook, a disregard for human rights, and an inclination toward empire. A new future may have beckoned, but the heavy hand of the past continued to influence relations between Russia and the West.

East Asia: Primed for Rivalry?

If perceived lessons from history continue to play a crucial role in shaping modern Western images of post-Soviet Russia, then the past also plays a part in defining the international relations of East Asia—and a most bloody past it has been. The time following the Second World War was punctuated by several devastating wars (in China, Korea, and Vietnam), revolutionary insurgencies (in the Philippines, Malaya, and Indonesia), authoritarian rule (nearly everywhere), and revolutionary extremism (most tragically in Cambodia). The contrast with the postwar European experience could not have been more pronounced. In fact, scholars of international relations have been much taken with the comparison, pointing out that whereas Europe managed to form a new liberal security community during the Cold War, East Asia did not. In part this was the result of the formation of the EU and the creation of NATO (organizations that had no equivalents in Asia). But it was also because Germany managed to effect a serious reconciliation with its immediate neighbors while Japan (for largely internal reasons) did not. The end of the Cold War in Europe transformed the continent dramatically, but this was much less true in East Asia, where powerful communist parties continued to rule—in China, North Korea, and Vietnam—

Due to its nuclear-weapon and space-launch programs, the government of the Democratic People's Republic of Korea presents a new threat to international peace. What can world leaders do to reduce the threat from Kim Jong-Il's leadership?

and at least two outstanding territorial disputes (one less important one between Japan and Russia and a potentially far more dangerous one between China and Taiwan) continued to threaten the security of the region.

For all these reasons, East Asia, far from being primed for peace, was still ripe for new rivalries. Europe's very bloody past between 1914 and 1945, went the argument, could easily turn into Asia's future. This was not a view shared by every commentator, however. In fact, as events unfolded, this uncompromisingly tough-minded realist perspective came under sustained criticism. Critics did not deny the possibility of future disturbances: how could they, given Korean division, North Korea's nuclear weapons program, and China's claim to Taiwan? But several factors did suggest that the region was not quite the powder keg some thought it to be.

The first and most important factor was the great economic success experienced by the region itself. The sources of this have been much debated, with some people suggesting that the underlying reasons were cultural, others that it was directly economic (cheap labor plus plentiful capital), and a few that it was the by-product of the application of a non-liberal model of development employing the strong state to drive through rapid economic development from above. Some have also argued that the United States played a crucial role

WHAT'S YOUR WORLDVIEW ?

Both China and India are gaining power and influence in global affairs. Both countries are members of the G-20 and both have strong economies that were not devastated by the recent economic crisis. These two states are also increasing their military spending, including the expansion of their naval power. Some experts argue that this is only the beginning of a shift of global power toward Asia. What do you think? Is this a real challenge to other major powers or just a rebalancing of the world?

gross domestic product (GDP) The sum of all economic activity that takes place within a country.

Association of Southeast Asian Nations (ASEAN) A geopolitical and economic organization of several countries located in Southeast Asia. Initially formed as a display of solidarity against communism, it has since redefined its aims and broadened to include the acceleration of economic growth and the promotion of regional peace. By 2005 the ASEAN countries had a combined GDP of about $884 billion.

soft power Influence and authority deriving from the attraction that a country's political, social, and economic ideas, beliefs, and practices have for people living in other countries.

by opening its market to East Asian goods while providing the region with critical security on the cheap. Whatever the cause, or combination of causes, the simple fact remains that East Asia by the end of the twentieth century had become the third-largest powerhouse in the global economy, accounting for nearly 25 percent of world **gross domestic product (GDP)**.

Second, though many states in East Asia may have had powerful memories of past conflicts, these were beginning to be overridden in the 1990s by a growth in regional trade and investment. Indeed, though East Asia carried much historical baggage (some of this deliberately exploited by political elites in search of legitimacy), economic pressures and material self-interest appeared to be driving countries in the region together rather than apart. The process of East Asian economic integration was not quick—**ASEAN, the Association of Southeast Asian Nations**, was only formed in 1967. Nor was integration accompanied by the formation of anything like the European Union. However, once regionalism began to take off during the 1990s, it showed no signs of slowing down.

A third reason for optimism lay with Japan. Here, in spite of an apparent inability to unambiguously apologize for past misdeeds and atrocities—a failure that cost it dearly in terms of **soft power** (see Chapter 5) influence in the region—its policies could hardly be characterized as disturbing. On the contrary, having adopted its famous peace constitution in the 1950s and renounced the possibility of ever acquiring nuclear weapons (Japan was one the strongest upholders of the original 1968 Nonproliferation Treaty), Japan demonstrated no interest in upsetting its neighbors by acting in anything other than a benign manner. Furthermore, by spreading its considerable largesse in the form of aid and large-scale investment, it went some of the way in fostering better international relations in the region. Even its old rival China was a significant beneficiary, and by 2003 over five thousand Japanese companies were operating on the Chinese mainland.

This leads us, then, to China itself. Much has been written about "rising China," especially by analysts who argue—in classical realist fashion—that when new powerful states emerge onto the international stage, they are bound to disturb the existing balance of power. China looks benign now, they agree. It will look different in a few years' time—once it has risen. Again, though, there may be more cause for guarded optimism than pessimism, largely because China itself has adopted policies (both economic and military) whose purpose clearly is to reassure its neighbors that it can rise peacefully and thus effectively prove the realists wrong. It has also translated policy into action by supporting regional integration, exporting its considerable capital to other countries in East Asia, and working as a responsible party rather than a spoiler inside regional multilateral institutions. Certainly, such policies are beginning to bear fruit, with once-skeptical neighbors—even possibly Japan—increasingly viewing China as a benevolent instrument of development rather than a threat.

In the end, however, all strategic roads in China (and in East Asia as a whole) lead to the one state whose presence in the region remains critical: the United States of America. Though theoretically opposed to a unipolar world in which there is only one significant global player, the new Chinese leadership has pursued a most cautious policy toward the United States. No doubt some Americans will continue to be wary of a state run by the Communist Party, whose human rights record can hardly be described as exemplary. However, so long as China continues to act in a cooperative fashion, there is a good chance that relations will continue to prosper. There is no guaranteeing the long-term outcome.

With growth rates around 10 percent per year, with its apparently insatiable demand for overseas raw materials, and with enormous dollar reserves at its disposal, China has already changed the terms of the debate about the future of international politics. Of course it remains to be seen what effects the global economic collapse of 2008–2009 will have on China; and for some time to come, China may well remain what one observer has called a "colossus with feet of clay," overly dependent on foreign investment and still militarily light years behind the United States. But even such a colossus presents a set of challenges that simply did not exist in the much simpler days of the Cold War. Indeed, one of the great ironies of international history may be that China as a rising capitalist power playing by the rules of the market may turn out to be more of a problem for the West than China the communist power, in those far-off days when it denounced the imperialists across the ocean and called on Asians to drive Americans out of the region.

The War on Terror: From 9/11 to Iraq

While the end of the Cold War marked one of the great turning points of the late twentieth century, 9/11 was a reminder that the international order that had come into being as a result was not one that found ready acceptance everywhere. Bin Laden was no doubt motivated by far more than a dislike for globalization and American primacy. As many analysts have pointed out, bin Laden's vision was one that pointed back to a golden age of Islam rather than forward to something modern. That said, his chosen method of attacking the United States using four planes, his use of video to communicate with followers, his employment of the global financial system to fund operations, and his primary goal of driving the United States out of the Middle East could hardly be described as medieval. US policy makers certainly did not regard him as some odd throwback to earlier times. Indeed, the fact that he threatened to use the most modern and dangerous weapons—namely, weapons of mass destruction—to achieve his objectives made him a very modern threat, one that could not be dealt with by the kind of traditional means developed during the Cold War. As the administration of George W. Bush constantly reiterated, this new danger meant that old strategies, such as containment and deterrence, were no longer relevant. If this was the beginning of a "new global war on terrorism," as some seemed to argue at the time, then it was one unlikely to be fought using policies and methods learned between 1947 and 1989.

The very peculiar character of this new nonstate threat, led by a man whose various pronouncements owed more to holy texts than to anything else, made it difficult for some in the West to understand the true character of radical Islamic movements and their use of terrorist tactics. A few, in fact, believed that the threat was more speculative than serious, more functionally useful for the United States in its quest for global preeminence than actually genuine. Furthermore, as the controversial "war on terror" unfolded—first in Afghanistan and then in other parts of the world—a few critics of a more radical persuasion began to wonder where the real danger actually lay. Indeed, as the United States began to flex its military muscle and widened the war on terror to include Iraq, and Iran, some began to turn their critical attention away from the original threat posed by radical Islamic terrorism and toward the United States itself. In this way the original target of 9/11—the United States—was transformed from the early status of victim into the imperial source of most of the world's growing problems.

The various controversies surrounding the Bush administration's responses to international terrorism should not, however, obscure one simple fact: the impact that 9/11

On the deck of a US aircraft carrier in May 2003, President George W. Bush proclaimed victory in Iraq. Peace and stability has still not come to Iraq. Was this proclamation of victory premature?

had on both the United States and US foreign policy more generally. Most obviously, the new threat environment provided the United States with a fixed point of reference around which to organize its international affairs; and organize it did, in the shape of building close relations with those many states—Russia, India, Pakistan, and China perhaps being the more important—that were now prepared to join it in waging a global war against terror. After the 9/11 attacks, the Bush administration officials felt compelled to act in a far more assertive fashion abroad. Indeed, some of Bush's more conservative supporters believed that one of the reasons for the attack on the United States in the first place was that it had not been assertive enough in the 1990s. Finally, in what some saw as a near revolution in US foreign policy, policy makers in the Bush Administration seemed to abandon the defense of the status quo in the Middle East. The events of 9/11, they argued, had changed the original formula whereby the United States turned a blind eye to autocratic regimes that existed in the region, in exchange for cheap oil and stability. US dependency on these two commodities was no longer enough, said the neoconservatives in government, in the news media, and in academia, to justify the United States doing deals with states like Saudi Arabia that produced the dangerous ideologies that had inspired those who had flown the planes on 9/11, or who directly or indirectly had given (and were still giving) aid and comfort to terrorists around the world.

In this way the intellectual ground was prepared for the war against Iraq in 2003. The war, though, remains something of a conundrum. After all, Iraq had not been involved in 9/11; the regime itself was secular; and it shared the same goal as the United States in at least one respect—that of seeking to contain the geopolitical ambitions of Islamic Iran. For all these reasons, different analysts have identified rather different factors to explain the war, ranging from the ideological influence exercised by the neoconservatives on President Bush, America's close relationship with Israel, and America's desire to control Iraq's oil. No doubt all these things fed into the final decision (see the Case Study in this chapter). However, one is still left with more questions than easy answers, with possibly the most credible answer being the less conspiratorial one that the United States went to war partly because it thought it would win fairly easily, partly because it got its intelligence wrong, and partly because some political leaders thought—rather unwisely—that building a new regime in Iraq would be just as easy as getting rid of the old one.

The Iraq War and Its Origins

International relations, as a field, has always been concerned with the origins of wars. Long-term changes in the balance of power, fear of encirclement, imperial ambition—not to mention misperception and ideology—have all been employed at one time or another to explain why states engage in military action. The Iraq War presents a useful, and possibly difficult, test case for various theories of war origins. Several competing explanations have been advanced so far to explain the US decision to go to war against Iraq in 2003. These include, among others, the official argument that Iraq represented a serious and potentially rising threat to a critically important region; the more materialist thesis that the United States was determined to secure direct control of Iraq's massive reserves of oil; and the popular claim that the war was the product of pressures arising from within the United States itself—here identified as the Israel lobby, the ideologically inclined neo-conservatives, and their various supporters on the Christian right. The student of world politics, however, is still left with a number of unanswered questions. First, would the war have happened without the quite unexpected election of George W. Bush in late 2000? In other words, did the president make a huge difference to the decision taken? Second, could Bush have then led the United States into war without the profound shock created by the equally unexpected attack of 9/11? Considered this way, wasn't the war largely the by-product of fear and insecurity? Third, what role did British prime minister Tony Blair play? Indeed, was this a war made possible by an alliance with a middle power? Fourth, would it have been feasible at all if various American writers and policy makers had not thought the United States so powerful that it could more or less do anything in the world? To what extent, in other words, did the notion of the "unipolar moment" contribute to the final decision to go to war? Furthermore, were the intellectual grounds for the war not also laid by those during the post–Cold War period who thought it wise to promote democracy and encouraged others to intervene in the internal affairs of sovereign states for humanitarian purposes? Finally, to what extent could one argue that the Iraq War was in the US national interest; and if it was, then why did so many realists oppose the war?

During the 2007 surge in US forces in Iraq to counter the increase in antigovernment and religiously linked sectarian attacks, American troops were often caught in a crossfire. Did the increase in troops succeed?

Whatever the original calculations made by those who planned this war, it was by 2009 clear that this "war of choice" was a strategic blunder that neither delivered stable democracy to Iraq nor inspired others in the region to undertake serious political reform. It has also had the doubly dangerous consequence of disturbing the whole of the Middle East, while making it possible for Iran to gain even greater influence in the region than it had before. In fact, by undermining the old regime in Iraq, the United States has effectively created a vacuum into which an increasingly self-confident Iranian regime has marched. Finally, as a result of their action in Iraq, the United States and its allies have provided radical Islamists around the world with a rallying point that they appear to have exploited with some skill. The bombings of transit systems in London (2005) and Madrid

(2004) were no doubt the result of many factors; however, few now believe they were entirely unconnected to what had been happening in the Middle East since 2003.

With or without Iraq, however, the West would still be confronted by a challenge in the form of violent radical Islam, a movement that not only feeds off Western blunders and policies (especially American ones in the Middle East) but is based on a set of cultural values, state practices, and historical grievances that make it almost impossible to deal with effectively—without compromising what it means to be part of the West. Herein, though, lay another problem: how precisely to define this conflict.

It was certainly fashionable to characterize it as one between two different "civilizations" (a term originally made popular by the American writer Samuel Huntington in 1993). Nevertheless, there was something distinctly uncompromising about a conflict between those on the one side who supported democracy, **pluralism**, individualism, and a separation between state and church, and those on the other who preached intolerance and supported **theocracy** while calling for armed struggle and **jihad** against the unbeliever. Not that these views were shared by all Muslims. Indeed, these radical views were roundly condemned by the overwhelming majority of Muslim clerics and followers of Islam. Still, as the antagonism unfolded, there seemed to be enough disaffected people in enough societies—including Western ones—to make this aggressive ideology an occasional but potent threat. The way the world in general, and the West in particular, chose to deal with it was likely to determine the shape of international relations for many years to come.

Conclusion

In this chapter we have seen some of the trends and events that created the contemporary globalized system. War (both "hot" and "cold"), revolutions, colonization and its collapse—each had a role in the evolution of international society. The irony might be found in this fact: religion played a role in both 1648 and 2001. The signatories of the Peace of Westphalia wanted to remove religion from European international politics. Members of Al Qaeda want to bring religion back into global politics.

The Peace of Westphalia in the seventeenth century created an international system in Europe that many people at the time believed would make for more orderly politics on the continent. In the same way, the end of the Cold War in the twentieth century seemed to promise a more peaceful world. But as we have seen in this chapter, these hopes went unfulfilled. The effects of revolutions, wars, and European imperialism have revealed the hollow nature of the European international system. Moreover, during the Cold War—while much of the attention of politicians and academics in the developed world was focused on the US-USSR confrontation—other wars, economic trends, and social movements around the world were too often ignored. As a result, the euphoria in Western Europe and the United States that followed the end of the Soviet Union soon gave way to new set of challenges and threats. And many of the "new" challenges were actually quite old, such as the persistence of poverty in underdeveloped nations. We'll explore these issues in depth later in Parts Three (Global Actors) and Four (Global Issues). But first, in Part Two, we will examine theories that we can use to approach these issues more thoughtfully, helping us better understand and explain our ever-changing political world.

Contributors to Chapter 2: David Armstrong, Michael Cox, Len Scott, and Steven L. Lamy.

pluralism The political theory of pluralism holds that political power and influence in society does not belong just to the citizens, nor to elite groups in various sectors of society, but is distributed among a wide number of groups in the society. It can also mean a recognition of ethnic, racial, and cultural diversity.

theocracy A state based on religion.

jihad In Arabic, *jihad* simply means "struggle." Jihad can refer to a purely internal struggle to be a better Muslim, or a struggle to make society more closely align with the teachings of the Koran.

REVIEW QUESTIONS

1. Why has an originally European society of states become the general norm around the world?
2. How did the French Revolution change European politics?
3. Was nineteenth-century European international society merely a means of legitimizing imperialism?
4. How did the method by which European colonies in Africa and Asia gained their independence determine their postindependence internal politics?
5. Why did the United States become involved in wars in Asia after 1950? Illustrate your answer by reference to either the Korean or the Vietnam war.
6. How have scholars of international relations attempted to explain the end of the Cold War?
7. Why did liberal theorists assume the world would become a more stable place after the end of the Cold War, and why did realists disagree with them?
8. If the United States won the Cold War, why did it have such problems defining a grand strategy for itself after 1989 and before 9/11?
9. Has globalization since the Cold War changed the basic character of world politics?
10. How successfully has Europe adapted to the challenges facing it since the end of the Cold War?
11. How has the "war on terror" changed international politics?

FURTHER READING

Bisley, N. (2006), *Rethinking Globalization* (Basingstoke: Palgrave). The single best volume on the subject.

Booth, K., and Dunne, T. (eds.) (2002), *Worlds in Collision* (Basingstoke: Palgrave). This is a collection of short, well-written essays on the world after 9/11.

Burstein, D., and de Keijzer, A. (1998), *Big Dragon: The Future of China* (New York: Simon & Schuster). In spite of the title, this is a relatively balanced account of China.

Cox, M., Ikenberry, G. J., and Inoguchi, T. (eds.) (2000), *American Democracy Promotion: Impulses, Strategies, and Impacts* (Oxford: Oxford University Press). This book looks at a critically important and neglected facet of US foreign policy.

Held, D., et al. (2005), *Debating Globalization* (Cambridge: Polity Press). A useful collection of opposing views.

Kaldor, M. (1999), *New and Old Wars: Organized Violence in a Global Era* (Cambridge: Polity Press). This book explains why millions have died in "small" wars since the end of the Cold War.

Leonard, M. (2005), *Why Europe Will Run the Twenty-first Century* (London: Fourth Estate). A now unfashionably optimistic perspective on the future of Europe.

Mann, J. (2004), *Rise of the Vulcans: The History of Bush's War Cabinet* (New York: Viking Press). An indispensable background on how the Bush administration viewed the world at large after 2001.

O'Meara, P., Mehlinger, H. D., and Krain, M. (eds.) (2000), *Globalization and the Challenges of a New Century* (Bloomington, IN: Indiana University Press). This is a very useful collection of many well-known essays about global order and disorder.

Ruthven, M. (2002), *A Fury for God: The Islamist Attack on America* (London: Granta Books). This is a fine analysis of the ideology of radical Islamism.

Sifry, M. L., and Cerf, C. (eds.) (2003), *The Iraq Reader* (New York: Touchstone Books). The best collection on the debate to go to war.

Video Suggestions

Crucial Turning Points of World War II (Reader's Digest, 1997)

Empires: Napoleon (PBS, 2000)

The French Revolution (History Channel, 2005)

Paths of Glory, Stanley Kubric (MGM Home Entertainment, ca. 1999)

Race for the Superbomb (PBS, 1999)

The Target for Tonight (Classic Pictures Entertainment, 2004)

War and Peace in the Nuclear Age (Boston: WGBH-TV, 1988)

White Light/Black Rain: The Destruction of Hiroshima and Nagasaki (HBO, 2007)

Witness: Voices from the Holocaust (Stories to Remember, 1999)

Woodrow Wilson: American Idealist (History Channel, 2007)

INTERNET RESOURCES

Cold War International History Project: the Woodrow Wilson International Center for Scholars

http://wwics.si.edu/index.cfm?topic_id=1409&fuseaction=
topics.home

The on-line resource center for Cold War research from a leading USA institute.

Intelligence Resource Program

http://www.fas.org/irp/

The federation of American scientists site contains fascinating material on most aspects of collection, analysis, and uses of information that states collect on each other.

Resources page for web site of Professor Vincent Ferraro, Mount Holyoke College, South Hadley, MA

http://www.mtholyoke.edu/acad/intrel/feros-pg.
htm#documents

A definitive collection of material on all aspects of US foreign policy, plus links to information about foreign governments, research institutes, TNCs, and NGOs of all kinds.

United States Holocaust Memorial Museum

http://www.ushmm.org/

The on-line collections of the museum offer a chance for people to remember the horrors of the Holocaust.

For more information, quizzes, case studies, and other study tools, please visit us at **www.oup.com/us/lamy**

PART TWO

Theories of World Politics

I n this part of the book, we introduce you to the main theories that try to explain world politics. We have two main aims: **first**, we want you to be able to grasp the primary themes of the theories that have been most influential. To this end, we have included in this section chapters on the leading theoretical perspectives on world politics: **realism** and **liberalism** in Chapter 3; and **Marxism**, **constructivism**, and **feminism** in Chapter 4. Of these, realism has been by far the most influential theory, but, as we mentioned in the introduction, it has also attracted fierce criticism for being an ideology masquerading as an objective theory. Most of the history of international relations theory has seen a dispute between realism and its liberal and Marxist rivals, with the debate between realism and liberalism being the most long-standing and well-developed. The discussion

of realism and liberalism is followed by a chapter on the primary alternative theories of international relations: Marxism, constructivism, and feminism. So, by the end of this part, we hope that you will be able to understand the main themes of the various theories and be able to assess their comparative strengths and weaknesses. Our **second** aim is to give you the overview of theory that you need

in order to be able to assess the significance of globalization for world politics. We hope that, after reading these chapters, you will be in a better position to see how these theories of world politics might interpret globalization and other global conditions and issues in different ways. You should be able to decide for yourself which interpretation you find most convincing. You will then be better able to sort through evidence you find in the remaining sections of the book in order to determine whether globalization marks a new distinct stage in world politics, requiring new theories, or whether it is simply a fad or fashion that might alter the surface of world politics but not its underlying features.

CHAPTER 3

Realism and Liberalism

"A nation's survival is its first and ultimate responsibility; it cannot be compromised or put to risk."

—*Henry Kissinger*

"Though it be true that democratic government will make wars less likely, it will not eliminate all causes of conflict between nations, and if the enormous sacrifices of this war are not to be made in vain, not merely must democracy triumph in individual states, but in the society of states as well.

—*Woodrow Wilson*

In early May 2009, North Korea test fired six missiles after detonating a nuclear device several days before. South Korean spy satellites captured images that showed the North Koreans moving missiles to launch pads close to the demilitarized zone. One of the suspected missiles is the type that is capable of reaching US territory.

Secretary of Defense Robert Gates, attending a regional security conference in Singapore, stated that these nuclear tests and missile launches were a direct threat to US national security. He was adamant in stating that the United States would not accept North Korea as a nuclear state. The United States does not fear a North Korean attack but worries that North Korea will sell its technology to terrorist networks or other rogue states. The North Korean government is in direct violation of international rules and has rejected attempts by the International Atomic Energy Agency (IAEA)—the international agency in charge of controlling the proliferation of nuclear arms—to inspect their nuclear sites and prevent the production of weapons-grade nuclear material.

From the realist perspective, negotiations and diplomacy have costs as well as benefits. Realists believe one must always negotiate from strength and be prepared to act with force or the threat of force when dealing with rogue states that have no intention of following international rules. Realists claim that the basic flaw of liberal thinking

After North Korea tested a nuclear weapon in May 2009, the South Korean demonstrators shown here demanded a strong response from their government. Why did South Korea, the United States, and other countries continue to seek a diplomatic settlement with North Korea?

is that North Korea can be talked out of these weapons. The power, prestige, and influence of the United States and liberal institutions like the IAEA are being undermined by North Korea. Realists argue that the major powers must put pressure on North Korea by choking off its ability to export and import weapons and military equipment, cut off all access to financial resources, and pressure China to rein in its North Korean ally. Liberal thinkers still hold out hope for arms-control talks and the promise that North Korean leaders will want to end their intransigence and join the international community of nation-states. As we will learn in this chapter, both realism and liberalism are effective theories by which we can more closely examine interactions among states.

Introduction

In Chapter 1, we asked you to consider your personal worldview, or perspective on international events, which can result from your citizenship, personal identity, and other factors. In this chapter we begin to present the concept of **theory**. By theory we mean a set of propositions that help us to understand events. Like pairs of sunglasses that can block different amounts of sunlight, a theory can limit what we see or, like magnifying glasses, help us to see things better.

theory A proposed explanation of an event or behavior of an actor in the real world. Definitions range from "an unproven assumption" to "a working hypothesis that proposes an explanation for an action or behavior." In international relations we have intuitive theories, empirical theories, and normative theories.

Theories of international relations can help us to understand international relations in many ways. As we will see in this chapter, the theories called realism and liberalism have an impact on the ways in which political leaders view and understand the world. We do not mean that a leader one day announces, "I am a realist," or, "I am a liberal," and then follows a recipe for foreign policy. Instead, we believe that theories can help us to look at actions and be able to describe and to explain events. Theories can also help us to predict future actions on the basis of what has occurred in the past. But we must keep in mind that the theories that we use—like sunglasses—might also restrict what we think.

Realism and liberalism are the focus of this chapter. Both have become important in the study of international relations at universities around the world. Yet both have their limitations as well. The basis for both theories is a very different understanding about human nature, the goal of a state's policy, and the nature of the international system.

What Is Realism?

Over the centuries, various world leaders have sought to create international rules in order to make life more stable and predictable by decreasing outbreaks of violent aggression. As you will recall from Chapter 2, key European nations signed two treaties that we now know as the Peace of Westphalia (1648), which established a principle that still governs international relations: sovereignty. Signatories agreed that only a legitimate government could exercise control over its citizens and territory, could act independently and flexibly in its relations with other states, and could craft its own strategies and policies aimed at securing perceived national interests. By inference, no state could interfere in the domestic affairs of any other state. Of course, the principle of sovereignty applied more to the continent of Europe and less to societies anywhere else on earth; nevertheless, sovereignty was—and still is today—a critically important concept.

By declaring some regions of the world to be sovereign and agreeing that sovereign states could not legally interfere with the internal business of other sovereign states, political leaders *thought* they had solved the problem of foreign wars. However, this attempt to eliminate war failed early and often: within a year of the Peace of Westphalia, England invaded Ireland; within four years, the English and the Dutch were at war; within six years, Russia and Poland were at war; and so it went.

With this reality in mind, it is relatively easy to understand why the earliest perspective on international relations, referred to as **realism**, is based on the following three assumptions:

- States are the only actors in international relations that matter.
- A policy maker's primary responsibility is to create and maintain national power at all costs.
- No central authority stands above the state.

The world perceived by realists is lawless, competitive, and uncertain. In fact, one influential philosopher who helped to define realism, Thomas Hobbes, published this pessimistic observation about life in his political treatise *Leviathan*: "The life of man is solitary, poor, nasty, brutish and short." The only way to avoid misery and anarchy, according to Hobbes, was to have a strong ruler of a strong state impose order and provide protection from external attack (Hobbes 1651).

> **realism** The theoretical approach that analyzes all international relations as the relation of states engaged in the pursuit of power. Realists see the international system as anarchic, or without a common power, and they believe conflict is endemic in the international system.

> **WHAT'S YOUR WORLDVIEW**
>
> *Do you think that Hobbes's pessimism about life applies to our society in the twenty-first century? Have we advanced at all since the seventeenth century?*

The Essential Realism

In later sections we will see how realism can be regarded as a broad theoretical umbrella, covering a variety of perspectives, each with its own leading authors and texts. Despite the numerous denominations, keep in mind that, essentially, all realists subscribe to the following three S's: *statism*, *survival*, and *self-help*. Let's discuss these three essential elements in more detail and also examine some of realism's shortcomings.

Realists assert that the most important national interest is defense of the homeland. In this picture Secretary Gates stands before an F-22 fighter jet (or "The Raptor").

Statism

For realists, the state is the main actor and sovereignty is its distinguishing trait. The meaning of the sovereign state is inextricably bound up with the use of force. In terms of its internal dimension, to illustrate this relationship between violence and the state we need to look no further than Max Weber's famous definition of the state as "the monopoly of the legitimate use of physical force within a given territory" (M. J. Smith 1986, 23). Within this territorial space, **sovereignty** means that the state has supreme authority to make and enforce laws. This is the basis of the unwritten contract between individuals and the state. According to Hobbes, for example, we trade our liberty in return for a guarantee of security. Once security has been established, **civil society** can begin. But in the absence of security, people are in the state of nature, where there can be no business, no art, no culture, no society. The first move, then, for the realist is to organize power domestically. Only after power has been organized can community begin.

Realist international theory assumes that, domestically, the problem of order and security is solved. However, in the real world—in the relations among independent sovereign states—insecurities, dangers, and threats to the very existence of the state loom large. Realists largely explain this on the basis that the very condition for order and security—namely, the existence of a sovereign world government—is missing from the international realm.

Realists claim that in this condition of anarchy, states compete with other states for power and security. The nature of the competition is viewed in zero-sum terms; in other words, more for one state means less for another. This competitive logic of power politics makes agreement on universal principles difficult, apart from the principle of nonintervention in the internal affairs of other sovereign states. But realists suspend even this principle—as we saw in the previous chapter, designed in seventeenth-century Europe to facilitate coexistence—and argue that in practice nonintervention does not apply in relations between great powers and their regional neighbors. As evidenced by the most recent behavior of the United States in Afghanistan and Iraq, modern hegemonic states are able to influence events far beyond their borders, overturning the nonintervention principle on the grounds of national security and international order.

Given that the first move of the state is to organize power domestically and maintain law and order, and the second is to accumulate power internationally, it is self-evidently important to consider in more depth what realists mean by their ubiquitous fusion of politics with power. It is one thing to say that international politics is a struggle for power, but this merely begs the question of what realists mean by power. Hans Morgenthau offers the following definition of power: "Man's control over the minds and actions of other men" ([1948] 1955, 26). There are two important points that realists make about the elusive concept of power. First, power is a relational concept; one does not exercise power in a vacuum but in relation to another entity. Second, power is a relative concept; calculations need to be made not only about one's own power capabilities but about the power that other states possess. Yet the task of accurately assessing the power of states is infinitely complex. Too often, power calculations are reduced to counting the number of troops, tanks, aircraft, and naval ships a country possesses in the often mistaken belief that this translates into the ability to get other actors to do something they would not otherwise do.

Survival

The second principle that unites realists is the assertion that in international politics the preeminent goal is survival. Although there is an ambiguity in the works of the realists as

sovereignty The condition of a state having control and authority over its own territory and being free from any higher legal authority. It is related to, but distinct from, the condition of a government being free from any external political constraints.

civil society [1] The totality of all individuals and groups in a society who are not acting as participants in any government institutions, or [2] all individuals and groups who are neither participants in government nor acting in the interests of commercial companies.

to whether the accumulation of power is an end in itself, one would think that there is no dissenting from the argument that the ultimate concern of states is for security. Survival is held to be a precondition for attaining all other goals, whether these involve conquest or merely independence. According to Kenneth Waltz, "beyond the survival motive, the aims of states may be endlessly varied" (1979, 91). Yet, as we will see in a later section of this chapter, a recent controversy among structural realists has arisen over the question of whether states are in fact principally *security* or *power* maximizers.

Niccolo Machiavelli tried to make a science out of his reflections on state survival. His short and engaging book, *The Prince*, was written with the explicit intention of codifying a set of maxims that would enable leaders to maintain their hold on power. In important respects, we find two related Machiavellian themes recurring in the writings of modern realists, both of which derive from the idea that the realm of international politics requires different moral and political rules from those that apply in domestic politics. The task of understanding what realists believe is the true nature of international politics, and the need to protect the state at all costs (even if this may mean the sacrifice of one's own citizens), places a heavy burden on the shoulders of state leaders. In the words of Henry Kissinger, the academic realist who became secretary of state during the Nixon presidency, "a nation's survival is its first and ultimate responsibility; it cannot be compromised or put to risk" (1977, 204). Their guide must be an **ethic of responsibility**: the careful weighing up of consequences; the realization that individual acts of an immoral kind might have to be taken for the greater good.

Think, for instance, of the ways in which governments frequently suspend the legal and political rights of suspected terrorists in view of the threat they pose to national security. For example, the United States altered its long-standing treaty obligations against torture and imprisoned what Bush administration officials called "enemy combatants" in the US Navy base at Guantánamo Bay. An ethic of responsibility is frequently used as a justification for breaking the laws of war, as in the case of the British nighttime firebombing raids on Nazi Germany or the United States' decision to drop nuclear bombs on Hiroshima and Nagasaki in 1945. The principal difficulty with the realist formulation of an "ethics of responsibility" is that, while instructing leaders to consider the consequences of their actions, it does not provide a guide for how state leaders should weigh the consequences (M. J. Smith 1986, 51).

Not only does realism provide an alternative moral code for state leaders, proponents claim, it also suggests a wider objection to the whole enterprise of bringing ethics into international politics. Starting from the assumption that each state has its own particular values and beliefs, realists argue that the state is the supreme good and there can be no community beyond borders. This moral relativism has generated a substantial body of criticism, particularly from liberal theorists who endorse the notion of universal human rights.

ethic of responsibility For historical realists, an ethic of responsibility represents the limits of ethics in international politics; it involves the weighing up of consequences and the realization that positive outcomes may result from amoral actions.

Self-Help

Kenneth Waltz's *Theory of International Politics* (1979) brought to the realist tradition a deeper understanding of the international system itself. Unlike many other realists, Waltz argued that international politics is not unique because of the regularity of war and conflict, since this is also familiar in domestic politics. The key difference between domestic and international orders lies in their structure. In the domestic polity, citizens usually do not have to defend themselves. In the international system, there is no higher authority, no global police officer, to prevent and counter the use of force. Security can therefore only be realized through self-help. In an anarchic structure, "self-help is necessarily the principle of action" (Waltz 1979, 111). But in the course of providing for one's own security, the state in question will automatically be fueling the insecurity of other states.

security dilemma In an anarchic international system, one with no common central power, when one state seeks to improve its security it creates insecurity in other states.

The term given to this spiral of insecurity is the **security dilemma**. According to Nick Wheeler and Ken Booth, security dilemmas exist "when the military preparations of one state create an irresolvable uncertainty in the mind of another as to whether those preparations are for 'defensive' purposes only (to enhance its security in an uncertain world) or whether they are for offensive purposes (to change the status quo to its advantage)" (1992, 30). This scenario suggests that one state's quest for security is often another state's source of insecurity. States find it very difficult to trust one another and often view the intentions of others in a negative light. Thus the military preparations of one state are likely to be matched by neighboring states. The irony is that at the end of the day, states often feel no more secure than before they undertook measures to enhance their own security. Thus insecurity becomes a self-fulfilling prophecy.

In a self-help system, structural realists argue that the balance of power will emerge even in the absence of a conscious policy to maintain it (i.e., prudent statecraft). Waltz argues that balances of power result irrespective of the intentions of any particular state. In an **anarchic system** populated by states with leaders who seek to perpetuate themselves, alliances will be formed that seek to check and balance the power against threatening states. Classical realists, however, are more likely to emphasize the crucial role state leaders and diplomats play in maintaining the balance of power. In other words, the balance of power is not natural or inevitable; the leaders of states construct it.

anarchic system A realist description of the international system that suggests there is no common power or central governing structure.

There is a lively debate among the various kinds of realists concerning the stability of a balance-of-power system. This is especially the case today, as many argue that the balance of power has been replaced by an unbalanced unipolar order. It is questionable whether other countries will actively attempt to balance against the United States,

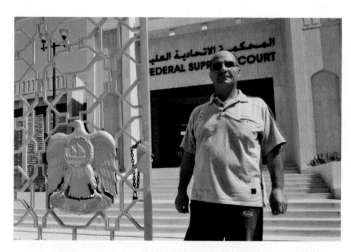

After September 11, 2001, courts around the world have confronted terrorism cases with evidence allegedly obtained by torture. Should Mohammed Hamdan's (shown here) brother Naji—an American citizen—go free because of potentially tainted evidence introduced in his trial in Abu Dhabi?

as structural realism might predict. Certainly the Obama administration has pledged to return to the United States' past policy of seeking multilateral cooperation and to end the unilateralism of its predecessor. But whether it is the contrived balance of the Concert of Europe in the early nineteenth century or the more fortuitous balance of the Cold War, balances of power are broken—either through war or peaceful change—and new balances emerge. What the perennial collapsing of the balance of power demonstrates is that states are at best able to mitigate the worst consequences of the security dilemma but are not able to escape it. The reason for this terminal condition, say realists, is the absence of trust in international relations.

Historically, realists have illustrated the lack of trust among states by reference to the parable of the "stag hunt." In *Man, the State and War*, Kenneth Waltz revisits Rousseau's parable:

> Assume that five men who have acquired a rudimentary ability to speak and to understand each other happen to come together at a time when all of them suffer from hunger. The hunger of each will be satisfied by the fifth part of a stag, so they "agree" to cooperate in a project to trap one. But also the hunger of any one of them will be satisfied by a hare, so, as a hare comes within reach, one of them grabs it. The defector obtains the means of satisfying his hunger but in doing so permits the stag to escape. His immediate interest prevails over consideration for his fellows. (1959, 167–8)

Waltz argues that the metaphor of the stag hunt provides a basis for understanding the problem of coordinating the interests of the individual versus the interests of the common good and the payoff between short-term interests and long-term interests. In the self-help system of international politics, the logic of self-interest mitigates against the provision of collective goods, such as "security" or "free trade." In the case of the latter, according to the theory of comparative advantage, all states would be wealthier in a world that allowed freedom of goods and services across borders. But individual states, or groups of states like the European Union, can increase their wealth by pursuing protectionist policies providing other states do not respond in kind. Of course, the logical outcome is for the remaining states to become protectionist, international trade to collapse, and a subsequent world recession to reduce the wealth of each state. Thus the question is not whether all will be better off through cooperation, but rather who will likely gain more than another. It is because of this concern with relative-gains issues that realists argue that cooperation is difficult to achieve in a self-help system.

One Realism, or Many?

So far in this chapter we have treated the realist lens as if it were a unified set of beliefs and propositions; it is, however, not at all that way, as both the model's supporters and critics have pointed out. The belief that there is not one realism but many leads logically to a delineation of different types of realism. The simplest distinction we can make is to differentiate realism into three historical periods. While these different periods suggest a neat historical sequence, they are problematic insofar as they close down the important question about divergence within each historical phase. Rather than opt for the neat but intellectually unsatisfactory system of historical periodization, we outline below our own representation of realisms that makes important connections with existing categories deployed by other thinkers in the field. A summary of the varieties of realism outlined below is contained in Table 3.1.

> **WHAT'S YOUR WORLDVIEW**
>
> *States, say realists, will cooperate if they see the possibility of mutual gains. Reciprocity, the idea that if you follow the rules then others will, also encourages cooperation. Do you think there are limits to cooperation? What factors work against cooperation in addressing global problems like climate change and poverty?*

Global Perspective

Russia and Realism

The year 2009 began quite cold for millions of people in Europe. Western Europeans shivered while the governments of Russia and Ukraine squabbled over the price of natural gas that Gazprom, the Russian state monopoly, charged Ukraine for its supply of this prime heating fuel. Because Ukrainian prime minister Yulia Timoshenko's government refused to meet Russia's price, Gazprom closed the valves on all the pipelines routed through that country and, by extension, on all of its Western European customers.

On the face of it, this crisis was a simple business dispute about supply and demand. Russian-owned Gazprom actually offered its product to Ukraine for less than it charged its other European customers—under the late-2008 proposal from Gazprom, Ukraine would pay $250 for each 1,000 cubic meters of gas, while other Europeans had to pay more than $500 for the same amount. Timoshenko's government complained that this was an unjustified increase. Gazprom's reaction to this rejection was a counteroffer of $418 per unit.

Realist theory provides a clear explanation for this dispute: both countries are former Soviet republics and this dispute is part of the end of that empire. Nationalists in both Moscow and Kyiv, goes this argument, were using the price of natural gas in an attempt to satisfy domestic political pressures in a game of international power politics. For many Russians, the implosion of the USSR was a humiliation. Instead of being the leaders of the country, Russians were forced to negotiate with other nationalities such as the Chechens, with whom Russia fought two wars in the 1990s, and the Ukrainians. By shutting off the heat for millions in Europe, Russia could show that it still mattered in international politics. For Ukrainians, supplies of natural gas were yet another unwanted example of how Russians were trying to continue their hated hegemony over the former Soviet republics. By standing up to the Russian giant, Ukraine's leaders were asserting the Ukrainian nationalist agenda.

In the end, Russia won. The terms of the new ten-year contract promised to supply Ukraine gas at a starting

Control over a state's vital resources is another tenet of realism. In that case, would you agree with the actions of Russian Federation prime minister Vladimir Putin in the Gazprom case?

price of $360 per 1000 cubic meters for the first quarter of 2009. For many Russians, this is a satisfying result. Fifteen years ago, as the program of economic shock therapy faltered, Russians leaders had to ask the IMF and World Bank for loans in exchange for radical restructuring of the economy. One ultranationalist politician called it a humiliation and "paying for the sausages." With its vital natural gas, Russia now held the cards, and it was the European leaders who had to ask for help.

Classical Realism

The classical-realist lineage begins with Thucydides' representation of power politics as a law of human behavior. The classical realists argued that the drive for power and the will to dominate are the fundamental aspects of human nature. The behavior of the state as a self-seeking egoist is understood to be merely a reflection of the characteristics of the

Table 3.1

A Taxonomy of Realisms

Type of Realism	Key Thinkers	Key Texts	"Big Idea"
Classical Realism (Human Nature)	Thucydides (ca. 430–406 BCE)	*The Peloponnesian War*	International politics is driven by an endless struggle for power that has its roots in human nature. Justice, law, and society either have no place or are circumscribed.
	Machiavelli (1532)	*The Prince*	Political realism recognizes that principles are subordinated to policies; the ultimate skill of the state leader is to accept, and adapt to, the changing power-political configurations in world politics.
	Morgenthau (1948)	*Politics Among Nations*	Politics is governed by laws that are created by human nature. The mechanism we use to understand international politics is the concept of interests, defined in terms of power.
Structural Realism (International System)	Rousseau (ca. 1750)	*The State of War*	It is not human nature but the anarchical system that fosters fear, jealousy, suspicion, and insecurity.
	Waltz (1979)	*Theory of International Politics*	Anarchy causes logic of self-help, in which states seek to maximize their security. The most stable distribution of power in the system is bipolarity.
	Mearsheimer (2001)	*Tragedy of Great Power Politics*	The anarchical, self-help system compels states to maximize their relative power position.
Neoclassical Realism	Zakaria (1998)	*From Wealth to Power*	The systemic account of world politics provided by structural realism is incomplete. It needs to be supplemented with better accounts of unit-level variables such as how power is perceived and how leadership is exercised.

people that comprise the state. Therefore, it is human nature that explains why international politics is necessarily power politics. This reduction of realism to a condition of human nature is one that frequently reappears in the leading works of the doctrine, most famously in the work of the most famous proponent of postwar realism, Hans J. Morgenthau. Classical realists argue that it is from the nature of man that the essential features of international politics, such as competition, fear, and war, can be explained. The important point for Morgenthau is, first, to recognize that these laws exist and, second, to devise the most appropriate policies that are consistent with the basic fact that human beings are flawed creatures. For both Thucydides and Morgenthau, the essential continuity of the power-seeking behavior of states is rooted in the biological drives of human beings.

Another distinguishing characteristic of classical realism is its adherents' belief in the primordial character of power and ethics. Classical realism is fundamentally about the struggle for belonging, a struggle that is often violent. Patriotic virtue is required in order for communities to survive in this historic battle between good and evil, a virtue that long predates the emergence of sovereignty-based notions of community in the mid-seventeenth century. Classical realists therefore differ from contemporary realists in the sense that they engaged with moral philosophy and sought to reconstruct an understanding of virtue in light of practice and historical circumstance.

Thucydides was the historian of the Peloponnesian War, a conflict between two great powers in the ancient Greek world, Athens and Sparta. Though he was a disgraced general on the losing side, Thucydides' work has been admired by subsequent generations of realists for its insights into many of the perennial issues of international politics. One of the significant episodes of the war between Athens and Sparta is known as the "Melian dialogue" and provides a fascinating illustration of a number of key realist principles. The Case Study in this chapter reconstructs Thucydides' version of the dialogue between the Melians and the Athenian leaders who arrived on the island of Melos to assert their right of conquest over the islanders. In short, what the Athenians are asserting over the Melians is the logic of power politics and the duty of a hegemon to maintain order. Because of their vastly superior military force, they are able to present a fait accompli to the Melians: either submit peacefully or be exterminated. Citing their neutrality in the war, the Melians for their part try to buck the logic of power politics, appealing in turn with arguments grounded in justice, God, and their lack of support for the Spartans. As the dialogue makes clear, although at a military disadvantage and bound to lose, the Melians chose to fight. Their defeat became the basis for a maxim of realism: "The strong do what they have the power to do and the weak accept what they have to accept."

How is a leader supposed to act in a world animated by such malevolent forces? The answer given by Machiavelli is that all obligations and treaties with other states must be disregarded if the security of the community is under threat. Moreover, imperial expansion is legitimate, as it is a means of gaining greater security. Other classical realists, however, advocate a more temperate understanding of moral conduct. Mid-twentieth-century realists such as Butterfield, Carr, Morgenthau, and Wolfers believed that wise leadership and the pursuit of the national interest in ways that are compatible with international order could mitigate anarchy. Taking their lead from Thucydides, they recognized that acting purely on the basis of power and self-interest without any consideration of moral and ethical principles frequently results in self-defeating policies. After all, as Thucydides showed, Athens suffered an epic defeat while following the realist tenet of self-interest.

Structural Realism, or Neorealism

Structural realists, sometimes called "neorealists," concur that international politics is essentially a struggle for power, but they do not endorse the classical-realist assumption that this is a result of human nature. Instead, structural realists attribute security competition and interstate conflict to the lack of an overarching authority above states and the relative distribution of power in the international system. Kenneth Waltz, the best-known structural realist, defined the structure of the international system in terms of three elements—organizing principle, differentiation of units, and distribution of capabilities. He identifies two different organizing principles: anarchy, which corresponds to the decentralized realm of international politics, and hierarchy, which is the basis of domestic order. He argues that the units of the international system are functionally similar sovereign states, hence unit-level variation is irrelevant in explaining international outcomes. It is the third tier, the distribution of capabilities across units, that is, according to Waltz, of fundamental importance to understanding crucial international outcomes. According to structural realists, the relative distribution of power in the international system is the key independent variable to understanding important international outcomes such as war and

Multipolar system

Bipolar

Unipolar (Hegemony)

Power, Politics, and Polarity. Which of these power arrangements best represents the world today? What about the world of the early twentieth century? Nineteenth century? How does theory help us understand these global power dynamics?

The Melian Dialogue—Realism and the Preparation for War

A short excerpt from the dialogue appears below (Thucydides 1954/1972, 401–407). Note that the symbol [...] indicates one or more line breaks from the original text.

ATHENIANS. Then we on our side will use no fine phrases saying, for example, that we have a right to our empire because we defeated the Persians. [. . .] you know as well as we do that, when these matters are discussed by practical people, the standard of justice depends on the equality of power to compel and that in fact the strong do what they have the power to do and the weak accept what they have to accept.

MELIANS. ...you should not destroy a principle that is to the general good of all men—namely, that in the case of all who fall into danger there should be such a thing as fair play and just dealing...

ATHENIANS. This is no fair fight, with honor on one side and shame on the other. It is rather a question of saving your lives and not resisting those who are far too strong for you.

MELIANS. It is difficult... for us to oppose your power and fortune... Nevertheless we trust that the gods will give us fortune as good as yours...

ATHENIANS. Our opinion of the gods and our knowledge of men lead us to conclude that it is a general and necessary law of nature to rule whatever one can. This is not a law that we made ourselves, nor were we the first to act upon it when it was made. We found it already in existence, and we shall leave it to exist forever among those who come after us. We are merely acting in accordance with it, and we know that you or anybody else with the same power as ours would be acting in precisely the same way. [. . .] You seem to forget that if one follows one's self-interest one wants to be safe, whereas the path of justice and honor involves one in danger. [. . .] This is the safe rule—to stand up to one's equals, to behave with deference to one's superiors, and to treat one's inferiors with moderation.

MELIANS. Our decision, Athenians, is just the same as it was at first. We are not prepared to give up in a short moment the liberty which our city has enjoyed from its foundation for 700 years.

ATHENIANS. . . . you seem to us . . . to see uncertainties as realities, simply because you would like them to be so.

peace, alliance politics, and the balance of power. Many structural realists are interested in providing a rank-ordering of states so as to be able to differentiate and count the number of great powers that exist at any particular point in time. The number of great powers, in turn, determines the structure of the international system. For example, during the Cold War from 1945 to 1989 there were two great powers—the United States and the Soviet Union—that constituted the bipolar international system.

How does the international distribution of power impact the behavior of states, particularly their power-seeking behavior? In the most general sense, Waltz argues that states, especially the great powers, have to be sensitive to the capabilities of other states. The possibility that any state may use force to advance its interests results in all states being worried about their survival. According to Waltz, power is a means to the end of security. In a significant passage, Waltz writes, "because power is a possibly useful means, sensible statesmen try to have an appropriate amount of it." He adds, "in crucial situations, however, the ultimate concern of states is not for power but for security" (Waltz 1989, 40). In other words, rather than being power maximizers, states, according to Waltz, are *security* maximizers. Waltz argues that power maximization often proves to be dysfunctional because it triggers a counterbalancing coalition of states.

WHAT'S YOUR WORLDVIEW

In our global system with new technologies, relatively easy opportunities for travel, and transnational networks willing to use weapons of mass destruction to challenge nation-states, can any state guarantee security for its citizens?

offensive realism A structural theory of realism that views states as security maximizers.

A different account of the power dynamics that operate in the anarchic system is provided by John Mearsheimer's theory of **offensive realism**, which is another variant of structural realism. While sharing many of the basic assumptions of Waltz's structural-realist theory, frequently termed "defensive realism," Mearsheimer differs from Waltz when it comes to describing the behavior of states. Most fundamentally, "offensive realism parts company with defensive realism over the question of how much power states want" (Mearsheimer 2001, 21). According to Mearsheimer, the structure of the international system compels states to maximize their relative power position. Under anarchy, he agrees that self-help is the basic principle of action. Yet he also argues that not only do all states possess some offensive military capability, but there is a great deal of uncertainty about the intentions of other states. Consequently, Mearsheimer concludes that there are no satisfied or status quo states; rather, all states are continuously searching for opportunities to gain power at the expense of other states. Contrary to Waltz, Mearsheimer argues that states recognize that the best path to peace is to accumulate more power than anyone else. Indeed, the ideal position, although one that Mearsheimer argues is impossible to achieve, is to be the global hegemon of the international system. Yet because Mearsheimer believes that global hegemony is impossible, he concludes that the world is condemned to perpetual great-power competition.

Contemporary Realist Challenges to Structural Realism

While offensive realism makes an important contribution to realism, some contemporary realists are skeptical of the notion that the international distribution of power alone can explain the behavior of states. Since the end of the Cold War, a group of scholars have attempted to move beyond the parsimonious—economical or frugal—assumptions of structural realism and incorporated a number of additional factors located at the individual and national level into their explanation of international politics. While systemic factors are recognized to be an important influence on the behavior of states, so are factors such as the perceptions of state leaders, state-society relationships, and the motivations of states (we will learn more about the various levels of analysis—*individual, national, systemic*, and *global*—in Chapter 5). This group of **neoclassical realist** scholars is attempting to build a bridge between international structural factors and unit-level factors, which many classical realists of the 1930s and 1940s emphasized (Rose 1998). According to Stephen Walt, the causal logic of neoclassical realism "places domestic politics as an intervening variable between the distribution of power and foreign policy behavior" (Walt 2002, 211).

neoclassical realism A version of realism that combines both structural factors such as the distribution of power and unit-level factors such as the interests of states.

One important intervening variable is leaders themselves, namely, how they perceive the international distribution of power. There is no objective, independent reading of the distribution of power: rather, what matters is how state leaders derive an understanding of the distribution of power. While structural realists assume that all states have a similar set of interests, neoclassical realists such as Randall Schweller (1996) argue that historically this is not the case. He argues, with respect to Waltz, that the assumption that all states have an interest in security results in neorealism exhibiting a profoundly status quo bias. Schweller returns to the writings of realists such as Morgenthau and Kissinger to remind us of the key distinction that they made between status quo and states seeking system change. Neoclassical realists would argue that the fact that Germany was a revisionist state in the 1930s and a status quo state since the end of the Second World War is of fundamental importance to understanding its role in the international system. Not only do states differ in terms of their interests, but they also differ in terms of their ability to

The People's Republic of China has the world's largest army. Here we see a ceremonial display of the country's military strength. Should people in other countries view that as a threat?

extract and direct resources from the societies that they rule. Fareed Zakaria (1998) introduces the intervening variable of state strength into his theory of state-centered realism. State strength is defined as the ability of a state to mobilize and direct the resources at its disposal in the pursuit of particular interests. Neoclassical realists argue that different types of states possess different capacities to translate the various elements of national power into state power. Thus, contrary to Waltz, all states cannot be treated as "like units" with similar goals, interests and values.

Given the varieties of realism that exist, it is hardly surprising that the overall coherence of the realist tradition of inquiry has been questioned. The answer to the question of "coherence" is, of course, contingent on how strict the criteria are for judging the continuities that underpin a particular theory. It is perhaps a mistake to understand traditions as a single stream of thought, handed down in a neatly wrapped package from one generation of realists to another. Instead, it is preferable to think of living traditions like realism as the embodiment of both continuities and conflicts. Despite the different strands running through the tradition, there is a sense in which all realists share a common set of propositions.

In the next section we will examine liberalism, another tradition within the field of international relations theory. We will see that realism and liberalism share certain assumptions about the international systems but disagree strongly about others.

> ### WHAT'S YOUR WORLDVIEW
>
> *Which of the assumptions of realism make the most sense to you? Do you think most world leaders embrace a realist worldview?*

What Is Liberalism?

The leaders of the victorious states in the First World War—the United States, the United Kingdom, and France—realized that national interactions needed to change substantially to avoid a second devastating war. They decided to adapt the underlying principles of the political and economic liberalism they had been practicing domestically since the seventeenth and eighteenth centuries to international relations. Liberal thought is grounded in the political and economic philosophies articulated by several scholars—Immanuel Kant, John Locke, Jean-Jacques Rousseau, whose ideas also inform realist thinking, and Adam Smith, among others—who viewed the world from a very different perspective than Thucydides and Hobbes. These liberal thinkers argued that human nature is good, not evil; that states can thrive best in a world governed by morality and law; and that reason and rationality will compel states to cooperate to achieve mutually held goals in peace. Envisioning a world where compliance with the principles of liberalism would facilitate more harmonious relationships among global actors, the United States, the United Kingdom, and France sought to recast the rules of international relations as they drafted the 1919 Treaty of Versailles at the end of World War I and then the charter for the League of Nations.

Just as realism derives from the observations and interpretations of political "realities," so does liberalism. The seeds of a liberal perspective had been sown in the wake of the fifteenth century's so-called Age of Discovery, which fostered the rampant expansion of global commerce as states, explorer entrepreneurs, and trading companies became involved in the business of exchanging goods and services. Commerce across political and cultural boundaries was never just a simple matter of private individuals swapping one commodity for another (otherwise known as *barter*) or for money. To engage in commerce, these pioneer global traders had to negotiate the terms of trade—that is, how much of one commodity was worth how much of another, or how much money; they had to abide by new and different cultural norms and legal systems; and they had to bargain with political leaders to gain and maintain market access. In other words, trade formed linkages that transcended political, social, cultural, and economic boundaries.

As trade expanded to include the exchange of a wider variety of commodities from all over the world, so did the linkages. Over time, a complex web of connections evolved, along with the multitude of formal and informal agreements needed to facilitate commerce. As economic and social interactions crossed political boundaries with increasing frequency, trade and immigration patterns rendered realist guidelines decreasingly useful to policy makers. It was no longer so easy to engage in unilateral actions without experiencing economic repercussions, as World War I had emphatically demonstrated.

In the end, however, realism prevailed. Its logic, combined with the physical realities of the world, led to its continued domination of global and foreign policy making. The major world powers of the twentieth century were not willing to abandon unilateralism. The United States never ratified the treaty creating the League of Nations, France sought revenge over Germany, and the United Kingdom sought to limit the power of the League. Then, one by one, Germany, Japan, and Italy violated Versailles Treaty covenants with impunity. No country was able *and* willing to provide the leadership that might have prevented renewed belligerence; Japan, Germany, and Italy sought to regain lost power by acquiring resources and invading other states, in a style reminiscent of Athens and Sparta, through aggression. President Woodrow Wilson, the leader of liberal thinking at the end of the war, naively believed that France and the UK would give up their territorial ambitions because they were dependent on US economic support.

The world was soon consumed by war again. World War II, like its predecessor, committed combatant and noncombatant alike to the national cause of winning. When it finally ended in 1945, Europe and Japan lay in smoldering ruins and the nuclear age had dawned. In a desperate effort to end the war, and to signal to others evidence of its military might, the United States dropped atomic bombs on Hiroshima and Nagasaki, Japan, triggering a profound and fundamental change in international and human relations. Now, no country was safe from war. Leaders and citizens alike feared the possible consequences of combat, whether over resources such as territory or economic markets or over political ideas and values. The introduction of **weapons of mass destruction**—biological, chemical, or nuclear weapons capable of nearly unfathomable lethality and incapable of discriminating between combatants and civilians—meant that future conflicts might lead to the extinction of the human race.

As the Second World War came to an end, key decision makers in the United States experienced their own transformation: They now recognized that the United States needed to be an active player on the world scene; they also saw that the United States had the financial and military power to enforce a new world order based on its political and economic visions. Moreover, they realized that, in a world where sovereignty remained the reigning principle, decisions affecting two or more states required the participation of all affected stakeholders and the backing of the rule of law. Embedded in this **multilateralist** approach to global governance is a principle of political liberalism, namely that the "governed" (in this case, states) should have a say in the development of those rules, norms, and principles by which they will be governed. And so, as they endeavored to avoid an even more calamitous World War III, the political leaders of the United States and its allies created a whole host of international governmental organizations (IGOs) to manage global relations in key political and economic arenas. The mandates of these IGOs were informed by **liberal internationalism**, a combination of

- democratic values (political liberalism),
- free-trade markets (economic liberalism),
- multilateral cooperation (multilateralism), and
- a rule-based international society that respects sovereignty and human rights.

We will discuss these principles further as we define the boundaries of liberal thinking and begin to understand how neoliberalism—and radical liberalism—have since evolved their own set of arguments from the liberal tradition.

Defining Liberalism

In essence, liberalism argues for human rights, parliamentary democracy, and free trade—while also maintaining that all such goals must begin *within a state*. The early European liberals thought that reforms within one's own country would be the first step in a long process, a process that could eventually extend to world affairs. While the belief in the possibility of progress is one identifier of a liberal approach to politics (Clark 1989, 49–66), there are other general propositions that define the broad tradition of liberalism.

Perhaps the appropriate way to begin this discussion is with a four-dimensional definition (Doyle 1997, 207). First, all citizens are equal before the law and possess certain basic rights to education, access to a free press, and religious toleration. Second, the legislative assembly of the state possesses only the authority invested in it by the people, whose basic rights it may not abuse. Third, a key dimension of the liberty of the individual is the right to own property, including productive forces. Fourth, liberalism contends that the most effective system of economic exchange is one that is largely market driven and not one that is subordinate to bureaucratic regulation and control, either domestically or

weapons of mass destruction A category defined by the United Nations in 1948 to include "atomic explosive weapons, radioactive material weapons, lethal chemical and biological weapons, and any weapons developed in the future which have characteristics comparable in destructive effects to those of the atomic bomb or other weapons mentioned above."

multilateralism The process by which states work together to solve a common problem.

liberal internationalism A perspective that seeks to transform international relations to emphasize peace, individual freedom, and prosperity, and to replicate domestic models of liberal democracy at the international level.

internationally. When these propositions are taken together, we see a stark contrast between liberal values of individualism, tolerance, freedom, and constitutionalism and realism's conservatism, which places a higher value on order and authority and is willing to sacrifice the liberty of the individual for the stability of the community.

Although in the past many writers have tended to view liberalism as a theory of domestic government, what is becoming increasingly apparent is the explicit connection between liberalism as a *domestic* political and economic theory and liberalism as an *international* theory. Properly conceived, liberal thought on a global scale embodies a domestic political and economic system *operating at the international level*. Like individuals, states have different characteristics—some are bellicose and war-prone, others are tolerant and peaceful: in short, the identity of the state determines its outward orientation. Liberals see a further parallel between individuals and sovereign states. Although the character of states may differ, all states in a global society are accorded certain "natural" rights, such as the generalized right to nonintervention in their domestic affairs. We see this in the "one-state, one-vote" principle in the UN General Assembly (see Chapter 6 for more on the UN). On another level, the domestic analogy refers to the extension of ideas that originated inside liberal states to the international realm, such as the coordinating role played by institutions and the centrality of the rule of law to the idea of a just order. In a sense, liberal thinkers seek to create an international system that embodies the values and structures of liberal democratic governments. Liberals concede that we have far to go before this goal can be reached. Historically, liberals have agreed with realists that war is a recurring feature of the anarchic states system. But unlike realists, they do not identify **anarchy** as the cause of war. How, then, do liberals explain war? As Table 3.2 demonstrates, certain strands of liberalism see the causes of war located in **imperialism**, others in the failure of the balance of power, and still others in the problem of undemocratic regimes. And can we prevent war through collective security, commerce, or world government? While it can be productive to think about the various strands of liberal thought and their differing pre-

anarchy A system operating in the absence of any central government. It does not imply chaos but, in realist theory, the absence of political authority.

imperialism The practice of foreign conquest and rule in the context of global relations of hierarchy and subordination. It can lead to the establishment of an empire.

Table 3.2
A Taxonomy of Liberalism: Levels of Analysis

Images of Liberalism	Public Figure/Period	Causes of Conflict	Determinants of Peace
First image (human nature)	Richard Cobden (mid-19th century)	Interventions by governments domestically and internationally disturbing the natural order.	Individual liberty, free trade, prosperity, interdependence.
Second image (the state)	Woodrow Wilson (early 20th century)	Undemocratic nature of international politics, especially foreign policy and the balance of power.	National self-determination; open governments responsive to public opinion; collective security.
Third image (the structure of the system)	I. Kant (18th century)	The balance of power system.	A world government, with powers to mediate and enforce decisions.

scriptions (Doyle 1997, 205–300), given the limited space permitted to deal with a broad and complex tradition, the emphasis below will be on the core concepts of international liberalism and the way these relate to the goals of order and justice on a global scale.

Unlike what we learned about realism, liberalism is at its heart a doctrine of change and belief in progress. As can be seen from a critical appraisal of the fourfold definition presented above, liberalism pulls in two directions: its commitment to freedom in the economic and social spheres leans in the direction of a minimalist role for governing institutions, while the democratic political culture required for basic freedoms to be safeguarded requires robust and interventionist institutions. This has variously been interpreted as a tension between different liberal goals and more broadly as a sign of rival and incompatible conceptions of liberalism. Should a liberal polity—no matter what the size or scale—preserve the right of individuals to retain property and privilege, or should liberalism elevate equality over liberty so that resources are redistributed from the strong to the weak? When we are looking at politics on a global scale, it is clear that inequalities are far greater while at the same time our institutional capacity to do something about them is that much less. As writers on globalization remind us, the intensification of global flows in trade, resources, and people has weakened the state's capacity to govern. Closing this gap requires nothing short of a radical reconfiguration of the relationship between territoriality and governance.

> ### WHAT'S YOUR WORLDVIEW ?
>
> *Liberal internationalism emerged as a dominant perspective after the two world wars. After these conflicts, most states wanted to return to a rule-based system that promotes democracy and free trade. Yet, historically, this view does not last. What are some possible reasons for the failure of liberal-internationalism thinking to prevail?*

The Essential Liberalism

Immanuel Kant and Jeremy Bentham were two of the leading liberals of the **Enlightenment**. Both were reacting to the barbarity of international relations, or what Kant graphically described as "the lawless state of savagery," at a time when domestic politics was at the cusp of a new age of rights, citizenship, and constitutionalism. Their abhorrence of the lawless savagery led them individually to elaborate plans for "perpetual peace." Although written over two centuries ago, these manifestos contain the seeds of core liberal ideas, in particular the belief that reason could deliver freedom and justice in international relations. For Kant the imperative to achieve perpetual peace required the transformation of individual consciousness, republican constitutionalism, and a federal contract between states to abolish war (rather than to regulate it, as earlier international lawyers had argued). This federation can be likened to a permanent peace treaty, rather than a "superstate" actor or world government. Kant's conditions for world peace, and Woodrow Wilson's for peace after WWI that were clearly influenced by Kant's ideas, are presented in Table 3.2.

Kant's claim that liberal states are peaceful in their international relations with other liberal states was revived in the 1980s. In a much-cited article, Michael Doyle argued that liberal states have created a "separate peace" (1986, 1151). According to Doyle, there are two elements to the Kantian legacy: restraint among liberal states and "international imprudence" in relations with nonliberal states.

Although the empirical evidence seems to support the **democratic peace thesis**, it is important to bear in mind the limitations of the argument. In the first instance, for the theory to be compelling, believers in the thesis need to provide an explanation as to why war has become unthinkable between liberal states. Kant had argued that if the decision to use force was taken by the people, rather than by the prince, then the frequency of conflicts would be drastically reduced. Democratic or liberal states tend not to go to war with

Enlightenment Associated with rationalist thinkers of the eighteenth century. Key ideas (which some would argue remain mottoes for our age) include secularism, progress, reason, science, knowledge, and freedom. The motto of the Enlightenment is *"Sapere aude!"* (Have courage to know!) (Kant 1991, 54).

democratic peace thesis A central plank of liberal-internationalist thought, the democratic-peace thesis makes two claims: first, liberal polities exhibit restraint in their relations with other liberal polities (the so-called separate peace), but, second, they are imprudent in relations with authoritarian states. The validity of the democratic-peace thesis has been fiercely debated in the international relations literature.

other liberal or democratic states but they *will* go to war with nonliberal or undemocratic states. Historical evidence supports this point. Thus, Kant's idea that democratic states will not go to war cannot be supported.

An alternative explanation for the democratic peace thesis might be that liberal states tend to be wealthy and therefore have less to gain—and more to lose—by engaging in conflicts than poorer, authoritarian states. Perhaps the most convincing explanation of all is the simple fact that liberal states tend to be in relations of amity with other liberal states. War between Canada and the United States is unthinkable, perhaps not because of their liberal democratic constitutions but because they are friends with a high degree of convergence in economic and political matters (Wendt 1999, 298–99). Indeed, war between states with contrasting political and economic systems may also be unthinkable because they have a history of friendly relations. An example here is Mexico and Cuba, which maintain close bilateral relations despite their history of divergent economic ideologies.

Irrespective of the scholarly search for the reasons why liberal democratic states are more peaceful, it is important to note the political consequences of this hypothesis. In 1989 Francis Fukuyama wrote an article entitled "The End of History" that celebrated the triumph of liberalism over all other ideologies, contending that liberal states were more stable internally and more peaceful in their international relations (Fukuyama 1989, 3–18). Other defenders of the democratic peace thesis were more circumspect. As Doyle recognized, liberal democracies are as aggressive as any other type of state in their relations with authoritarian regimes and stateless peoples (Doyle 1995b, 100). The behavior of the United States after September 11, 2001, illustrates this possibility. How, then, should states inside the liberal zone of peace conduct their relations with nonliberal regimes? How can the Kantian legacy of restraint triumph over the historical record of international imprudence on the part of liberal states? These are fascinating and timely questions that will be taken up in the final section of the chapter.

Two centuries after Kant first called for a "pacific federation," the validity of the idea that democracies are more pacific continues to attract a great deal of scholarly interest. The claim has also found its way into the public discourse of Western states' foreign policy, appearing in speeches made by US presidents as diverse as Ronald Reagan, Bill Clinton, George W. Bush, and Barack Obama. Less crusading voices within the liberal tradition believe that a legal and institutional framework must be established that includes states with different cultures and traditions. At the end of the eighteenth century Jeremy Bentham advocated such a belief in the power of law to solve the problem of war. "Establish a common tribunal" and "the necessity for war no longer follows from a difference of opinion" (Luard 1992, 416). Like many liberal thinkers after him, Bentham showed that federal states such as the German Diet, the American Confederation, and the Swiss League were able to transform their identity from one based on conflicting interests to a more peaceful federation. As Bentham famously argued, "between the interests of nations there is nowhere any real conflict."

free trade An essential element of capitalism that argues for no barriers or minimal barriers to the exchange of goods, services, and investments between states.

Because liberal politics and capitalism are intimately linked, many writers believe, with Adam Smith, that the elimination of tariffs, duties, and other restrictions on imports would be a vital step in dissemination of liberalism's program. For example, Cobden's belief that **free trade** would create a more peaceful world order is a core idea of nineteenth-century liberalism. Trade brings mutual gains to all the players, irrespective of their size or the nature of their economies. It is perhaps not surprising that this argument found its most vocal supporters in Britain. The supposed universal value of free trade brought disproportionate gains to the hegemonic power. There was never an admission that free trade among countries at different stages of development would lead to relations of dominance and subservience. Indeed, since the Second World War this is one of the problems that both the General Agreement on Tariffs and Trade (GATT) and its successor, the World Trade Organization (WTO), have faced. (See Chapters 11 and 12 for more information on these international organizations.)

Like free trade, the idea of a "natural harmony of interests" in international political and economic relations came under challenge in the early part of the twentieth century. The fact that Britain and Germany had highly interdependent economies before World War I (1914–1918) seemed to confirm the fatal flaw in the association of economic interdependence with peace. From the turn of the century, the contradictions within European civilization, of progress and exemplarism on the one hand and the harnessing of industrial power for military purposes on the other, could no longer be contained. Europe stumbled into a horrific war killing 15 million people. The war not only brought an end to three **empires** but also was a contributing factor to the Russian Revolution of 1917.

The First World War shifted liberal thinking toward a recognition that peace is not a natural condition but one that must be constructed. In a powerful critique of the idea that peace and prosperity were part of a latent natural order, the publicist and author Leonard Woolf argued that peace and prosperity required "consciously devised machinery" (Luard 1992, 465). But perhaps the most famous advocate of an international authority for the management of international relations was Woodrow Wilson. According to this US president, peace could only be secured with the creation of an international organization to regulate the international anarchy. Security could not be left to secret bilateral diplomatic deals and a blind faith in the balance of power. Just as peace had to be enforced in domestic society, the international domain had to have a system of regulation for coping with disputes and an international force that could be mobilized if nonviolent conflict resolution failed. In

empire A distinct type of political entity, which may or may not be a state, possessing both a home territory and foreign territories. This may include conquered nations and colonies.

Liberal institutionalists believe that meetings such as the ASEAN-USA summit depicted here build international cooperation; realists warn against putting a country's trust in such arrangements. Which position makes most sense to you?

this sense, more than any other strand of liberalism, idealism rests on the idea that we can replicate the liberalism we know domestically at the international level (Suganami 1989, 94–113).

Along with calls for free trade and self-determination, in his famous "Fourteen Points" speech, addressed to Congress in January 1918, Wilson argued that "a general association of nations must be formed" to preserve the coming peace—the League of Nations was to be that general association. For the League to be effective, it had to have the military power to deter aggression and, when necessary, to use a preponderance of power to enforce its will. This was the idea behind the **collective security** system that was central to the League of Nations. Collective security refers to an arrangement where "each state in the system accepts that the security of one is the concern of all, and agrees to join in a collective response to aggression" (Roberts and Kingsbury 1993, 30). It can be contrasted with an alliance system of security, where a number of states join together, usually as a response to a specific external threat (sometimes known as "collective defense"). In the case of the League of Nations, Article 16 of the League's charter noted the obligation that, in the event of war, all member states must cease normal relations with the offending state, impose sanctions, and, if necessary, commit their armed forces to the disposal of the League Council should the use of force be required to restore the status quo.

The League's constitution also called for the self-determination of all nation-states, another founding characteristic of liberal-idealist thinking on international relations. Going back to the mid-nineteenth century, self-determination movements in Greece, Hungary, and Italy received support among liberal powers and public opinion. Yet the default support for self-determination masked a host of practical and moral problems that were laid bare after Woodrow Wilson issued his proclamation. What would happen to newly created minorities within a territory who felt no allegiance to the new state created by this emphasis on self-determination? How would minorities be protected if the majority population denied them rights? Could a democratic process adequately deal with questions of identity—who was to decide what constituency was to participate in a ballot? And what if a newly self-determined state rejected liberal-democratic norms?

Although the organization was able to be a mediator to relatively minor disputes—over the Åland Islands, for example—the overall experience of the League of Nations as a peacekeeper was a failure. While the moral rhetoric at the creation of the League was decidedly liberal and idealist, in practice states remained imprisoned by self-interest in the style of realism. There is no better example of this than the United States' decision not to join the institution it had created. With the Soviet Union initially outside the system for ideological reasons, the League of Nations quickly became a debating society for the member states. Hitler's decision in March 1936 to reoccupy the Rhineland, a designated demilitarized zone according to the terms of the Treaty of Versailles, effectively pulled the plug on the League's life-support system (it had been put on the critical list following the Manchurian crisis in 1931 and the Ethiopian crisis in 1935).

collective security Refers to an arrangement where "each state in the system accepts that the security of one is the concern of all, and agrees to join in a collective response to aggression" (Roberts and Kingsbury 1993, 30).

US president Woodrow Wilson thought that the key to international security was an international organization, the League of Nations. Why did the league fail?

According to the realist's version of the history of the discipline of international relations, the collapse of the League of Nations dealt a near-fatal blow to liberal idealism. There is no doubt that the language of liberalism after 1945 was more pragmatic; how could anyone living in the shadow of the Holocaust be optimistic? Yet familiar core ideas of liberalism—belief in the benefits of progress, free trade, and respect for human rights—remained. Even as the Second World War raged, key political leaders in Europe and North America recognized the need to replace the League with another international institution with responsibility for international peace and security. Only this time, in the case of the United Nations, there was an awareness of the need for a consensus between the great powers in order for enforcement action to be taken. The framers of the UN Charter therefore included a provision (Article 27) allowing any of the five permanent members of the Security Council the power of veto. This revision constituted an important modification to the classical model of collective security (A. Roberts 1996, 315). The framers of the UN Charter also acknowledged that security was more than guns and thus created the Economic and Social Council (see Chapter 6) to build what became known as "human security," which we will examine in Chapter 10. With the ideological polarity of the Cold War, the UN procedures for collective security were stillborn (as either of the superpowers and their allies would veto any action proposed by the other). It was not until the end of the Cold War that a collective security system was put into operation, following the invasion of Kuwait by Iraq on August 2, 1990.

An important argument advanced by liberals in the early postwar period concerned the state's inability to cope with modernization. David Mitrany (1943), a pioneer **integration theorist**, argued that transnational cooperation was required in order to resolve common problems. His core concept was **functionalism**, meaning the likelihood that cooperation in one sector would lead governments to extend the range of collaboration across other sectors. This process is known as "spillover." As states become more embedded in an integration process, the benefits of cooperation and the costs of withdrawing from cooperative ventures increase. The history of the European Union supports Mitrany's assertion.

Academic interest in the positive benefits from transnational cooperation is one that informed a new generation of scholars (particularly in the United States) in the 1960s and 1970s. Their argument was not simply about the mutual gains from trade, but that other **transnational nonstate actors** were beginning to challenge the dominance of sovereign states. World politics, according to pluralists (as they are often called, using a term from the study of domestic politics), was no longer an exclusive arena for states, as it had been for the first three hundred years of the Westphalian states system. The inability of the United States to win the Vietnam War—not simply an academic pursuit—provided the impetus to this research, for that conflict seemed to challenge realism's central claims about power determining outcomes in international politics. In one of the central texts of this genre, Robert Keohane and Joseph Nye (1972) argued that the centrality of other actors, such as interest groups, transnational corporations (e.g., Shell oil or AIG), and nongovernmental organizations (NGOs), like Oxfam or Human Rights Watch, had to be taken into consideration. They also asserted that military power had a declining utility in international politics. The overriding image of international relations is one of a cobweb of diverse actors linked through multiple channels of interaction.

Although the phenomenon of transnationalism was an important addition to the international relations theorists' vocabulary, it remained underdeveloped as a theoretical

integration A process of ever-closer union between states, in a regional or international context. The process often begins with cooperation to solve technical problems.

functionalism An idea formulated by early proponents of European integration that suggests that cooperation should begin with efforts aimed at resolving specific regional or transnational problems. It is assumed that resolution of these problems will lead to cooperation, or spillover, in other policy areas.

transnational nonstate actor Any nonstate or nongovernmental actor from one country that has relations with any actor from another country or with an international organization.

pluralism The political theory of pluralism holds that political power and influence in society does not belong just to the citizens, nor to elite groups in various sectors of society, but is distributed among a wide number of groups in the society. It can also mean a recognition of ethnic, racial, and cultural diversity.

interdependence A condition where states (or peoples) are affected by decisions taken by others. Interdependence can be symmetric, i.e., both sets of actors are affected equally, or it can be asymmetric, where the impact varies between actors. If political or economic costs of interdependence are high, a state is in a vulnerable position. If costs are low, it is a situation of sensitivity interdependence.

relative gains One of the factors that realists argue constrain the willingness of states to cooperate. States are less concerned about whether everyone benefits (absolute gains) and more concerned about whether someone may benefit more than someone else.

neoliberalism Shaped by the ideas of commercial, republican, sociological, and institutional liberalism. Neoliberals see the international system as anarchic but believe relations can be managed by the establishment of international regimes and institutions. Neoliberals think that actors with common interests will try to maximize absolute gains.

concept. Perhaps the most important contribution of **pluralism** was its elaboration of **interdependence**. Due to the expansion of capitalism and the emergence of a global culture, pluralists recognized a growing interconnectedness in which "changes in one part of the system have direct and indirect consequences for the rest of the system" (Little 1996, 77). Absolute state autonomy, so keenly entrenched in the minds of state leaders, was being circumscribed by interdependence. Such a development brought with it enhanced potential for cooperation as well as increased levels of vulnerability.

In his 1979 work *Theory of International Politics*, the neorealist Kenneth Waltz attacked the pluralist argument about the decline of the state. He argued that the degree of interdependence internationally was far lower than the constituent parts in a national political system. Moreover, the level of economic interdependence—especially between great powers—was less than that which existed in the early part of the twentieth century. Waltz concludes that "if one is thinking of the international-political world, it is odd in the extreme that 'interdependence' has become the word commonly used to describe it" (1979, 144).

In the course of their engagement with Waltz and other neorealists, early pluralists modified their position. Neoliberals, as they came to be known, conceded that the core assumptions of neorealism were indeed correct: the anarchic international structure, the centrality of states, and a rationalist approach to social scientific inquiry. Where they differed was apparent primarily in the argument that anarchy does not mean durable patterns of cooperation are impossible: the creation of international regimes matters here, as they facilitate cooperation by sharing information, reinforcing reciprocity, and making defection from norms easier to punish. Moreover, in what became the most important difference between neorealists and neoliberals, the latter argued that actors would enter into cooperative agreements if the gains were evenly shared. Neorealists dispute this hypothesis, saying that what matters is a question not so much of mutual gains as of **relative gains**: in other words, a neorealist (or structural-realist) state has to be sure that it has more to gain than its rivals from a particular bargain or regime.

Neoliberalism

There are two important arguments that set **neoliberalism** apart from democratic-peace liberalism and the liberal idealists of the interwar period. First, academic inquiry should be guided by a commitment to a scientific approach to theory building. Whatever deeply held personal values scholars maintain, their task must be to observe regularities, formulate hypotheses as to why that relationship holds, and subject these to critical scrutiny. This separation of fact and value puts neoliberals on the positivist or social scientific research side of the methodological divide. Second, writers such as Keohane are critical of the naive assumption of nineteenth-century liberals that commerce breeds peace. A free-trade system, according to Keohane, provides incentives for cooperation but does not guarantee it. Here he is making an important distinction between cooperation and harmony. "Co-operation is not automatic," Keohane argues, "but requires planning and negotiation" (1989b, 11).

Neoliberal institutionalism (or institutional theory) shares many of the assumptions of neorealism; however, its adherents claim that neorealists focus excessively on conflict and competition and minimize the chances for cooperation even in an anarchic international system. Neoliberal-institutional organizations such as the Bank for International Settlements, the IMF, and the World Bank are both the mediators and the means to achieve cooperation among actors in the system. Currently, neoliberal institutionalists are focusing their research on issues of global governance and the creation and maintenance of institutions associated with managing the processes of globalization.

For neoliberal institutionalists the focus on mutual interests extends beyond trade and development issues. With the end of the Cold War, states were forced to address new security concerns like the threat of terrorism, the proliferation of weapons of mass destruction, and an increasing number of internal conflicts that threatened regional and global security. Graham Allison (2000) states that one of the consequences of the globalization of security concerns like terrorism, drug trafficking, and pandemics like HIV/AIDS is the realization that threats to any country's security cannot be addressed unilaterally. Successful responses to security threats require the creation of regional and global regimes that promote cooperation among states and the coordination of policy responses to these new security threats.

Liberal theory holds that networks of cooperation involving average people exist in order to help strengthen state-to-state ties. What did you do to commemorate World AIDS Day?

Robert Keohane (2002) suggests that one result of the 9/11 terrorist attacks on the United States was the creation of a very broad coalition against terrorism involving a large number of states and key global and regional institutions. Neoliberals support cooperative multilateralism and are generally critical of the preemptive and unilateral use of force as is condoned in the 2002 Bush Doctrine. Most neoliberals would believe that the US-led war with Iraq undermined the legitimacy and influence of global and regional security institutions that operated so successfully in the first Gulf War (1990–1991) and continue to work effectively in Afghanistan.

The neoliberal-institutional perspective is more relevant in issue areas where states have mutual interests. For example, most world leaders believe that we will all benefit from an open trade system, and many support trade rules that protect the environment. Institutions have been created to manage international behavior in both areas. The neoliberal view may have less relevance in areas in which states have no mutual interests. Thus, cooperation in military or national-security areas, where someone's gain is perceived as someone else's loss (a zero-sum perspective), may be more difficult to achieve.

Liberalism in Practice: Globalization

When applying liberal ideas to international relations today, we find two clusters of responses to the problems and possibilities posed by globalization. Before outlining these responses, let's quickly recall the definition of liberalism set out at greater length earlier, the four components being *juridical equality*, *democracy*, *liberty*, and the *free market*. As we will see below, these same values can be pursued by very different political strategies.

The first response we'll address is that of the **liberalism of privilege** (Richardson 1997, 18). According to this perspective, the problems of globalization need to be addressed by a combination of strong democratic states in the core of the international system, robust regimes, and open markets and institutions. For an example of the working out of such a

liberalism of privilege
Developed democratic states have a responsibility to spread liberal values for the benefit of all peoples of the earth.

strategy in practice, we need to look no further than the success of the liberal hegemony of the post-1945 era. The US writer G. John Ikenberry is an articulate defender of this liberal order. In the aftermath of the Second World War, the United States took the opportunity to embed certain fundamental liberal principles into the rules and institutions of international society. Most importantly, and contrary to realist thinking, the leaders of the United States chose to forfeit short-run gains in return for a durable settlement that benefited all the world's states.

According to Ikenberry, the United States signaled the cooperative basis of its power in a number of ways. First, in common with liberal-democratic principles, the United States was an example to other members of international society insofar as its political system is open and allows different voices to be heard. Foreign policy, like domestic policy, is closely scrutinized by the media, public opinion, and political committees and opposition parties. Second, the United States advocated a global free-trade regime in accordance with the idea that free trade brings benefits to all participants (it also has the added advantage, from the hegemon's point of view, of being cheap to manage). Third, the United States appeared, to its allies at least, as a reluctant hegemon that would not seek to exploit its significant power-political advantage. Fourth, and most importantly, the United States created and participated in a range of important international institutions that constrained the country's actions. The Bretton Woods system of economic and financial accords and the NATO security alliance are the best examples of the highly institutionalized character of American power in the post-1945 period. Advocates of this liberal hegemonic order note that it was so successful that allies were more worried about abandonment than domination.

The post-1945 system of regulatory regimes and institutions has been successful in part due to the fact that they exist. In other words, once one set of institutional arrangements becomes embedded, it is very difficult for alternatives to make inroads. There are two implications that need to be teased out here. One is the narrow historical "window" that exists for new institutional design; the other is the durability of existing institutions. "In terms of American hegemony, this means that, short of a major war or a global economic collapse, it is very difficult to envisage the type of historical breakpoint needed to replace the existing order" (Ikenberry 1999, 137).

Let us accept for a moment that the neoliberal argument is basically correct: the post-1945 international order has been successful and durable because US hegemony has been of a liberal character. The logic of this position is one of institutional conservatism, meaning that in order to respond effectively to global economic and security problems, there is no alternative to working within the existing institutional structure. This is a manifesto for managing an international order in which the Western states that paid the start-up costs of the institutions are now experiencing significant returns on their institutional investment. At the other end of the spectrum, the current order is seen by many critics of the liberal international order as highly unresponsive to the needs of weaker states and peoples. According to the United Nations Development Programme, the resulting global inequality is "grotesque." One statistic is particularly graphic: the richest 20 percent of the world's population holds three-quarters of the income; the poorest 20 percent receive only 1.5 percent.

Given that liberalism has produced such unequal gains for the West and the rest, it is not surprising that the hegemonic power has become obsessed with the question of preserving and extending its control of

WHAT'S YOUR WORLDVIEW ❓

The new liberal order has left many countries and their people in poverty. Are there ways to create programs that give capitalism a human face? What do you think could be done to address global poverty?

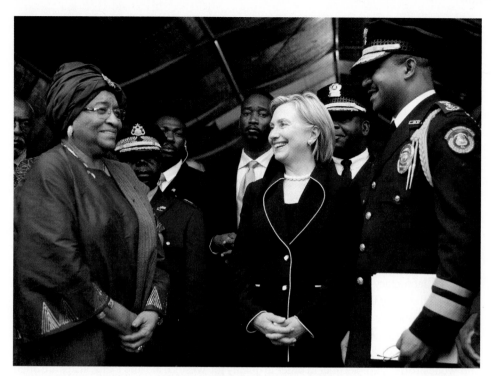

Visits by high-level diplomats, such as US secretary of state Hillary Rodham Clinton with Liberian president Ellen Johnson Sirleaf, send a signal of support for the leaders of a state. How do visits like these strengthen the image and influence of both states?

institutions, markets, and resources, just as realists predicted it would. When this hegemonic liberal order comes under challenge, as it did on 9/11, the response is uncompromising. It is notable in this respect that President George W. Bush mobilized the language of liberalism against Al Qaeda, the Taliban, and also Iraq. He referred to the 2003 war against Iraq as "freedom's war," and the term "liberation" is frequently used by defenders of "Operation Iraqi Freedom."

Given the primacy of the neoconservative ideology underpinning the most recent Bush presidency, one needs to proceed with caution when advancing the claim that many liberal principles underpin contemporary American foreign policy. Nevertheless, the official discourse of US foreign policy overlaps in interesting ways with a number of liberal values and ideas (Rhodes 2003), as can be seen in Bush's speech at the West Point graduation ceremony in June 2002. A key opening theme in the speech is how force can be used for freedom: "We fight, as we always fight, for a just peace." Bush then went on to locate this argument in historical context. Prior to the twenty-first century, great-power competition manifested itself in war. Today, "the Great Powers share common values" such as "a deep commitment to human freedom." In his State of the Union address of 2004, he even declared that "our aim is a democratic peace."

The tendency for liberalism to embrace imperialism has a long history (Doyle 1986, 1151–69). We find in Machiavelli a number of arguments for the necessity for republics to expand. Liberty increases wealth and the concomitant drive for new markets; soldiers who are at the same time citizens are better fighters than slaves or mercenaries; and expansion is often the best means to promote a state's security. In this sense, contemporary

US foreign policy is no different from the great expansionist republican states of the premodern period such as Athens and Rome. Few liberals today would openly advocate imperialism, although the line between interventionist strategies to defend liberal values and privileges and imperialism is very finely drawn. Michael Doyle advocates a policy mix of forcible and nonforcible instruments that ought to be deployed in seeking regime change in illiberal parts of the world.

This strategy of preserving and extending liberal institutions is open to a number of criticisms. For the sake of simplicity, these will be gathered up into an alternative to the liberalism that is seen to benefit only a few states and individuals that we will call **radical liberalism**. An objection made by proponents of radical liberalism concerns the understanding of liberalism embodied in the neoliberal defense of contemporary international institutions. The liberal character of those institutions is assumed rather than subjected to critical scrutiny. As a result, the incoherence of the purposes underpinning these institutions is often overlooked. The kind of economic liberalization advocated by Western financial institutions, particularly in economically impoverished countries, frequently comes into conflict with the norms of democracy and human rights. Three examples illustrate this dilemma.

First, the more the West becomes involved in the organization of developing states' political and economic infrastructure, the less those states are able to be accountable to their domestic constituencies, thereby cutting through the link between the government and the people which is so central to modern liberal forms of representative democracy (Hurrell and Woods 1995, 463). Second, in order to qualify for Western aid and loans, states are often required to meet harsh economic criteria requiring cuts in many welfare programs; the example of the poorest children in parts of Africa having to pay for primary school education (Booth and Dunne 1999, 310)—which is their right according to the Universal Declaration of Human Rights—is a stark reminder of the fact that economic liberty and political equality are frequently opposed. Third, the inflexible response of the IMF, World Bank, and other international financial institutions to various crises in the world economy has contributed to a backlash against liberalism. Richard Falk puts this dilemma starkly: there is, he argues, a tension between "the ethical imperatives of the global neighborhood and the dynamics of economic globalization" (1995a, 573). Radical liberals argue that the hegemonic institutional order has fallen prey to the neoliberal consensus, which minimizes the role of the public sector in providing for welfare and elevates the market as the appropriate mechanism for allocating resources, investment, and employment opportunities.

A second line of critique pursued by radical liberals concerns not so much the contradictory outcomes but the illiberal nature of the regimes and institutions. To put the point bluntly, there is a massive **democratic deficit** at the global level. Only fifteen members of international society can determine issues of international peace and security, and five of the fifteen can exercise a power of veto. In other words, it is hypothetically possible for up to two hundred states in the world to believe that military action ought to be taken—but such an action would contravene the UN Charter if one of the permanent members were to cast a veto. If we take the area of political economy, the power exerted by the West and its international financial institutions perpetuates structural inequality. A good example here is the issue of free trade, which the West has pushed in areas where it gains from an open policy (such as in manufactured goods and financial services) but resisted in areas that it stands to lose (agriculture and textiles). At a deeper level, radical liberals worry that *all* statist models of governance are undemocratic, as elites are notoriously self-serving.

radical liberalism This is the utopian side of liberalism best exemplified by the academic community called the World Order Models Project (WOMP). These scholars advocated a world in which states promote values like social justice, economic well being, peace, and ecological balance. These scholars see the liberal order as predatory and clearly in need of transformation.

democratic deficit Leaders have created many policy-making institutions at the global, regional, and national levels with policy-making power led by individuals who are appointed and not elected. Thus policy decisions are not subject to review by citizens.

These sentiments underpin the approach to globalization taken by writers such as Daniele Archibugi, David Held, Mary Kaldor, and Jan Aart Scholte, who believe that global politics must be democratized (Held and McGrew 2002). Held's argument is illustrative of the analytical and prescriptive character of radical liberalism in an era of globalization. His diagnosis begins by revealing the inadequacies of the "Westphalian order" (or the modern states-system that is conventionally dated from the middle of the seventeenth century). During the latter stages of this period, we have witnessed rapid democratization in a number of states, but this has not been accompanied by democratization of the **society of states** (Held 1993). This task is increasingly urgent given the current levels of interconnectedness, since "national" governments are no longer in control of the forces that shape their citizens' lives (for example, the decision by one state to permit deforestation has environmental consequences for all states). After 1945, the UN Charter set limits to the sovereignty of states by recognizing the rights of individuals in a whole series of human rights conventions. But even if the UN had lived up to its charter in the post-1945 period, it would still have left the building blocks of the Westphalian order largely intact: namely, the hierarchy between great powers and the rest (symbolized by the permanent membership of the Security Council); massive inequalities of wealth between states; and a minimal role for nonstate actors to influence decision making in international relations.

In place of the Westphalian and UN models, Held outlines a **cosmopolitan model of democracy**. This requires, in the first instance, the creation of regional parliaments and the extension of the authority of such regional bodies (like the European Union) that are already in existence. Second, human rights conventions must be entrenched in national parliaments and monitored by a new International Court of Human Rights. Third, reform of the UN, or the replacement of it, with a genuinely democratic and accountable global parliament "is necessary." Without appearing to be too sanguine about the prospects for the realization of the cosmopolitan model of democracy, Held is nevertheless adamant that if democracy is to thrive, it must penetrate the institutions and regimes that manage global politics.

Radical liberals place great importance on the civilizing capacity of global society. While the rule of law and the democratization of international institutions is a core component of the liberal project, it is also vital that citizens' networks are broadened and deepened to monitor and cajole these institutions. These groups form a linkage between individuals, states, and global institutions. It is easy to portray radical-liberal thinking as utopian, but we should not forget the many achievements of global civil society so far. The evolution of international humanitarian law, and the extent to which these laws are complied with, is largely due to the millions of individuals who are active supporters of human rights groups like Amnesty International and Human Rights Watch (Falk 1995b, 164). Similarly, global protest movements have been responsible for the heightened sensitivity to environmental degradation everywhere.

society of states An association of sovereign states based on their common interests, values, and norms.

cosmopolitan democracy A condition in which international organizations, transnational corporations, and global markets are accountable to the peoples of the world.

Conclusion

In this chapter we learned that realism provides what its advocates call a "parsimonious" model of global politics. It tells us that if we look for a few simple factors in any event, crisis, or pattern of interactions, we can understand why leaders picked a certain path of action. For realists, global politics is an endless struggle for dominance and power. Power can be control over something tangible, like resources and territory or power, or it can be a struggle for an intangible, like prestige. Realism is valuable because it helps us to understand some kinds of interactions. However, because of its often bleak opinion about human nature, realist theory tends to see enemies or competitors everywhere. The doctrine assumes that all leaders of all countries are constantly on the verge of war. While it shares some of realism's ideas about international systemic anarchy, liberalism offers a less violent explanation for global politics. Many proponents of the liberal perspective believe that long-term international cooperation is possible and will lead to human material and spiritual progress.

We turn now in the next chapter to several theories that are more recent intellectual inventions. These theories that we call "alternative" suggest other ways in which to interpret global events.

Contributors to Chapter 3: Tim Dunne, Brian C. Schmidt, and Steven L. Lamy.

REVIEW QUESTIONS

1. How does the Melian dialogue (see Case Study in this chapter) represent key concepts such as self-interest, the balance of power, alliances, capabilities, empires, and justice?

2. Do realists confuse a *description* of war and conflict for an *explanation* of why it occurs?

3. Is realism anything more than the ideology of powerful, satisfied states?

4. How would a realist explain the war on terrorism?

5. What is at stake in the debate between defensive and offensive realism?

6. Can realism help us to understand the globalization of world politics?

7. Should liberal states promote their values abroad? Is force a legitimate instrument in securing this goal?

8. Are democratic-peace theorists right, but for the wrong reasons?

9. Whose strategy of dealing with globalization do you find more convincing: those who believe that states and institutions should maintain the current order, or those who believe in reform driven by global civil society?

10. Are liberal values and institutions in the contemporary international system as deeply embedded as neoliberals claim?

FURTHER READING

For a general survey of the realist tradition:

Smith, M. J. (1986), *Realist Thought from Weber to Kissinger* (Baton Rouge: Louisiana State University Press). An excellent discussion of many of the leading realist thinkers.

Twentieth-century classical realism:

Carr, E. H. (2001), *The Twenty Years' Crisis 1919–1939: An Introduction to the Study of International Relations* (London: Palgrave). An important critique of liberal idealism.

Morgenthau, H. J. (1948), *Politics Among Nations: The Struggle for Power and Peace* (New York: Alfred A. Knopf). A foundational text for the discipline of international relations.

Structural realism:

Mearsheimer, J. (2001), *The Tragedy of Great Power Politics* (New York: W. W. Norton). This is the definitive account of offensive realism.

Waltz, K. (1979), *Theory of International Politics* (Reading, MA: Addison-Wesley). This is the exemplar for structural realism.

Neoclassical realism:

Rose, G. (1998), "Neoclassical Realism and Theories of Foreign Policy," *World Politics* 51: 144–72. An important review article that is credited with coining the term "neoclassical realism."

Liberalism in international relations:

Doyle, M. (1997), *Ways of War and Peace* (New York: W. W. Norton). The best textbook on the principal theories of international relations. There are over one hundred pages of analysis on liberalism in the book. See also, in a shorter and modified form, his article: Doyle, M. (1986), "Liberalism and World Politics," *American Political Science Review* 80(4): 1151–69.

Held, D., and McGrew, A. (eds.) (2002), *The Global Transformation Reader*, 2nd ed. (Cambridge: Polity Press). A useful collection of essays with many contributors who represent radical liberalism.

INTERNET RESOURCES

Internet Classics Archive
http://classics.mit.edu/index.html

Online Library of Liberty
http://oll.libertyfund.org/

Perseus Digital Library
http://www.perseus.tufts.edu/hopper/

For more information, quizzes, case studies, and other study tools, please visit us at **www.oup.com/us/lamy**

CHAPTER 4

Alternative Approaches

THE **LONDON**
SUMMIT **2009**
STABILITY | GROWTH | JOBS

Philosophers have only interpreted the world in various ways; the point, however, is to change it.

—*Karl Marx*

Theory is always *for* some one, and *for* some purpose.

—*Robert W. Cox*

Take a moment to consider this photograph of Gordon Brown, Barack Obama, and other world leaders at the 2009 G-20 meeting—and then let's start this chapter by asking some questions. For example, why might these world leaders be meeting? How might they plan to address whatever issues the world faces today? What kind of diplomatic, economic, or security means might they have at their disposal? Or, more fundamentally, we might ask—why are these specific people world leaders? Where are they meeting, and is that meeting open to the public? How did they become world leaders? What economic paths led them to this moment in time? And why are there so few women in this picture?

In this chapter we will learn to ask other kinds of questions: about the connections between social relations and political structures, about money—who controls it, for example—and about the critical concept that has guided our study so far, which is to say the state. The perspectives on international relations that we call "alternative approaches" ask us to reconsider our assumptions about politics.

In Chapter 3 we saw how realism and liberalism gained dominance in the study of international relations during the twentieth century. Both theories offer valuable insights into the interplay of states; however, as we saw, both realism and liberalism have certain shortcomings. With the exception of Marxism, the theories we will examine in this chapter have recently become part of the international relations discourse, in part as a response to these shortcomings but also in reaction to a different set of stimuli. Indeed, Marxism, constructivism, and feminist theory each

As the global economic recession deepened in 2009, leaders of some of the world's largest economies met to discuss methods to stop the slide. Were these policies effective?

can provide important tools to understand trends and events in global politics and globalization in ways that realism and liberalism cannot. Many might ask, why spend time on Marxism, when the Soviet Union collapsed? Most socialists or Marxists have two very convincing answers. First, the Soviet Union never provided a model of the ideal socialist or Marxist state. Michael Harrington (1989, 79), an American socialist, describes Soviet socialism as follows:

> [Soviet] Socialism was a bureaucratically controlled and planned economy that carried out the function of primitive accumulation and thus achieved rapid modernization. The state owned the means of production, which made some people think it must be socialist; but the party and the bureaucracy owned the state by virtue of a dictatorial monopoly of political power.

Harrington called the Soviet system a moral disaster for socialism. It was a totalitarian state and not an ideal Marxist state.

A second reason is globalization. Marx and Engels (1967) described how increasing interdependence will inevitably create a single global market and a global consumer culture:

> The need for a constantly expanding market for its products chases the bourgeoisie over the surface of the globe. In place of wants, satisfied by the production of country, we find new wants, requiring for their satisfaction the products of distant lands and climes.

A global economy shifts the key elements of Marxist thought from the domestic level to the global level.

Introduction

interparadigm debate This is the debate between the two main theoretical approaches in the field of global politics: realism versus liberalism. Some present this debate as one between neorealism and neoliberalism. Critics argue that this is no real debate because the two theoretical approaches share many assumptions.

normative theory Systematic analyses of the ethical, moral, and political principles that either govern or ought to govern the organization or conduct of global politics. The belief that theories should be concerned with what ought to be, rather than merely diagnosing what is.

Chapter 3 introduced us to the **interparadigm debate** between realism and liberalism. However, this mainstream debate by no means covers the complete range of issues linked to globalization that any contemporary theory of world politics needs to address. Instead, the debate tends to be a rather conservative and scholarly exercise, a study of the status quo, because it gives the impression of open-mindedness and intellectual pluralism, whereas, in fact, realism in its various forms often dominates university departments and academic journals. One factor that proponents of realism stress is its ability to describe everyday life as most people understand it. Thus alternative views can be dismissed as value laden, or **normative**, to be negatively compared with the allegedly scientific objectivity of realism. The theories discussed in this chapter challenge convincingly that assertion of objectivity.

In the past fifteen to twenty years the dominance of the mainstream theories has changed dramatically in two ways. First, there has been a lively academic debate between advocates of structural realism, or neorealism, and advocates of neoliberalism. This debate within the mainstream of scholarly thinking has exposed the shortcomings of both approaches. The second change has been the steadily growing intellectual appeal of a range of new approaches developed to understand world politics. These new perspectives complemented the long-standing Marxist criticism of a capitalist-dominated international system. In part, these changes reflect a transformed world. The end of the Cold War system in the early 1990s significantly reduced the credibility of realism, especially in its structural-realist guise where the stability of the bipolar system was seen as an enduring feature of world politics. The most obvious failure was the inability for either of the mainstream theories—realism or liberalism—to predict the end of the Cold War. To be fair to the scholars, however, we must remember that leaders of states around the world—and their intelligence agencies and military planners—did not expect the collapse of the Soviet Union that brought an end to the Cold War. As the bipolarity of the international system dramatically disappeared, so too did the explanatory power of the theory that most relied on it.

But this was not by any means the only reason for the rise of new approaches. There are three other obvious reasons. First, realism's dominance was called into question by a resurgence of its historical main competitor, liberalism, in the form of neoliberal institutionalism, as we discussed in Chapter 3. The debate between the two now comprised the mainstream of the discipline. Second, there were other changes under way in world politics that made the development of new approaches important, such as the kinds of factors discussed under the heading "globalization." Whatever the explanatory power of realism, it did not seem very good at dealing with economic, sociological, and cultural issues, such as the rise of **nonstate actors**, race and gender politics, transnational social movements, and information technology. In short, new approaches were needed to explain these features of world politics, even if proponents of realism still claimed that their theory was good at analyzing power politics between states. Third, there were major developments under way in other academic disciplines in the social sciences and philosophy that attacked the underlying methodological (i.e., how to undertake study) assumption of realism, a position known as **positivism** (see Chapter 5). This is the idea that political scientists can conduct research following the scientific method that guides the physical sciences like physics, chemistry, and biology. In its place, a host of alternative ways of thinking about the social sciences were being proposed, and the academic field of international relations simply caught up. Since then, scholars have proposed many alternative approaches as more relevant to world politics in the twenty-first century. In this chapter we will examine the three most influential alternatives to realism and liberalism.

We turn our attention first to Marxism, the oldest of the challengers to the teachings of realism and liberalism. Although the Communist Party state of the Soviet Union is gone and never reached the goal of a pure Marxist state, and the authoritarian Chinese Communist Party permits a form of capitalism in China, the central ideas of Marxism can still help us understand the inequality that characterizes the globalized economy.

WHAT'S YOUR WORLDVIEW

In Chapter 2, we learned about how the Cold War ended: specifically, what transpired and how the events unfolded. But how did ideas, as distinct from actions, also help to end the Cold War? More recently, how have ideas shaped global politics since September 11, 2001?

nonstate actor A term widely used to mean any actor that is not a government. Often it is not clear whether the term is being used to cover bodies such as the United Nations. Ambiguity is best avoided by referring separately to two categories, transnational actors and international organizations.

positivism and postpositivism Positivists (social scientists) and postpositivists (critical and constitutive theorists) form the basis for fierce debates among scholars. At the core lies a disagreement about whether or not social science theory can be value free. Positivists believe we can explain the social world as effectively as natural and physical scientists explain their phenomena. Postpositivists believe we cannot possibly be objective—value free—observers since we are actively or passively a part of the events and issues unfolding before us.

The Essential Marxism

A Marxist interpretation of world politics has been influential since the mid-1800s. In his inaugural address to the Working Men's International Association in London in 1864, Karl Marx told his audience that history had "taught the working classes the duty to master [for] themselves the mysteries of international politics." However, despite the fact that Marx himself wrote copiously about international affairs, most of this writing was journalistic in character. He did not incorporate the international dimension into his theoretical description of capitalism. This omission should perhaps not surprise us. The sheer scale of the theoretical enterprise in which he was engaged, as well as the nature of his own methodology, inevitably meant that Marx's work would remain contingent and unfinished.

Table 4.1

Alternative International Relations Theories at the Beginning of the Twenty-first Century

	Central Idea	View of International System	Key Authors
Marxist: Dependency School	Global capitalist system eliminates harmony of interests of workers.	Core-periphery relationship. Unfair terms of international trade. Underdevelopment in periphery.	Prebisch, Frank, Cardoso, O'Donnell
Marxism: World-System	Expansion of European capitalist system. Systems have life cycle, new ones develop.	Hegemonic powers. Core-periphery-semiperiphery relationship. Exploitation on a global scale, semiperiphery elites benefit.	Wallerstein, Chase-Dunn
Constructivism	Seeks to understand change. Ideas are social creations. Relationships result from historical processes. Ideas can evolve, replace older ways of thinking.	A process. Result of hegemonic ideas. Can change as result of evolving ideas.	Onuf, Walker, Wendt
Liberal Feminism	Change women's subordinate position in existing political systems.	Improve women's representation in INGOs. End gender bias in INGOs and NGOs.	Caprioli, Enloe, Elshtain, Tickner, Tobias
Socialist and Marxist Feminism	Ideas about gender relations impact economic relations.	States encourage gendered division of labor.	Chin, Hennessy, Ingraham, Whitworth
Standpoint Feminism	Ideas about gender are social constructs.	Ideas about gender shape international system.	Hartsock, Prügl, Zalewski
Postmodern Feminism	Perceptions of gender determine positions on gender. Dichotomized language.	Distinctions like order/anarchy, public/private, developed/underdeveloped linked to gender.	Fausto-Sterling, Hooper, Kinsella, Longino
Postcolonial Feminism	Effects of colonial experience on gender identity.	Challenges Western portrayals of third world women. Globalization perpetuates colonial-era gender-based exploitation.	Mohanty, Spivak

Marx was an enormously prolific writer whose ideas developed and changed over time. The *Collected Works* produced by Progress Publishers in Moscow, for instance, contains fifty volumes of very thick books. Hence, it is not surprising that his legacy has been open to numerous interpretations. In addition, real-world developments have led to the revision of his ideas in the light of experience. A variety of schools of thought have emerged that claim Marx as a direct inspiration or whose work can be linked to Marx's legacy.

Four strands of contemporary Marxist thought have made major contributions to thinking about world politics. Before we discuss what is distinctive about these approaches, it is important that we examine their essential commonalities.

First, all the theorists discussed in this section share with Marx the view that the social, political, and economic world should be analyzed as a totality. The academic division of the social world into different areas of inquiry—history, philosophy, economics, political science, sociology, international relations, and so on—is both arbitrary and unhelpful. None can be understood without knowledge of the others: the social world has to be studied as a whole. Given the scale and complexity of the social world, this requirement clearly makes great demands of the analyst. Nonetheless, for Marxist theorists, the disciplinary boundaries that characterize the contemporary social sciences need to be transcended if we are to generate a proper understanding of the dynamics of world politics.

Another key element of Marxist thought, which serves further to underline this concern with interconnection and context, is the materialist conception of history. The central contention here is that processes of historical change are ultimately a reflection of the economic development of society. That is, economic development is effectively the motor of history. The central dynamic that Marx identifies is tension between the means of production and relations of production that

The founders of "scientific socialism," Karl Marx and Friedrich Engels, sit together in a park that was once in communist-controlled East Berlin. Can you think of ways in which socialist ideas still influence politics in your country?

together form the **economic base** of a given society. As the means of production develop, for example through technological advancement, previous relations of production become outmoded, which restricts the most effective utilization of the new productive capacity. This in turn leads to a process of social change whereby relations of production are transformed in order to better accommodate the new configuration of means. For example, computer-driven machines for manufacturing might replace auto-factory workers, or because of the labor costs their jobs might be sent to a country where labor and production costs are lower. Workers are still needed, but fewer, and most of those must be retrained to repair computers or develop software and no longer make car doors. The current crisis in the US auto industry will have profound negative effects in industrial cities like Detroit, forever changing the political, economic, and social landscape. In other words, developments in the economic base act as a catalyst for the broader transformation of society as a whole. This is because, as Marx argues in the preface to his *Contribution to the Critique of Political Economy*, "the mode of production of material life conditions the social, political and intellectual life process in general." Thus the legal, political, and cultural institutions and practices of a given society reflect and reinforce—in a more or less mediated form—the pattern of power and control in the economy. It follows logically, therefore, that change in the economic base ultimately leads to change in the "legal and political **superstructure**."

And so, as you might have guessed by now, **class** plays a key role in Marxist analysis. Marx defines class as "social relations between the producers, and the conditions under which they exchange their activities and share in the total act of production" (Marx 1847). For most Americans, class is simply a way of designating an individual's position within the income distribution of a society. We talk about upper, middle, and lower income classes, and these represent income groups in our society. For Marxists, your income does not determine your class. Instead, your class is defined by your position within the hierarchy of production. In contrast to liberals, who believe that there is an essential harmony of interest between various social groups, Marxists hold that society is systemically prone to class conflict. Indeed, *The Communist Manifesto*, which Marx coauthored with Friedrich

economic base The substructure of the society is the relationship between owners and workers. Capitalists own the means of production and control technology and resources. The workers are employed by the capitalists, and they are alienated, exploited, and estranged from their work and their society.

superstructure This is the government or political structure that is controlled by those who own the means of production.

class A social group that in Marxism is identified by its relationship with the means of production and the distribution of societal resources. Thus, we have the bourgeoisie, or the owners or upper classes, and the proletariat, or workers.

Engels, argues that "the history of all hitherto existing societies is the history of class struggle" (Marx and Engels 1967). In capitalist society, says Marx, the main axis of conflict is between the bourgeoisie (the capitalists) and the proletariat (the workers).

The Marxist perspective on globalization seeks to describe the ways inequality affects the lives of millions of people. Marx and his co-author Friedrich Engels predicted that capitalism would spread around the world and then, and only then, would the proletariat become aware of their exploitation as workers, alienation from their government, and estrangement from society ruled by the bourgeoisie. In this situation, globalization might be the catalyst for awareness and eventual transformation. As we see in the data presented in Table 4.2, for example, despite the wealth generated in the global economy in the ten years prior to the economic depression of 2008–2009, that prosperity did not improve the living conditions of most of the world's population.

Despite his commitment to rigorous scholarship, Marx did not think it either possible or desirable for the analyst to remain a detached or neutral observer of this great clash between capital and labor. As he argued in a famous phrase that encouraged student radicals around the world in the 1960s, "philosophers have only interpreted the world in various ways; the point, however, is to change it" (Marx, *Theses on Feuerbach*, 1845). Marx was committed to the cause of emancipation. He was not interested in developing an understanding of the dynamics of capitalist society simply for the sake of it. Rather, he expected such an understanding to make it easier to overthrow the prevailing order and replace it with a communist society—a society in which wage labor and private property are abolished and social relations transformed.

Table 4.2

Indicators of World Inequality

- Worldwide, more than 1.2 billion people live on less than $1 per day.
- In 1990 the average American was 38 times richer than the average Tanzanian. By 2005 this had risen to 61 times richer.
- More than 1.1 billion people lack access to clean water.
- Average incomes in more than 50 developing countries are now at a lower level than they were in 1990. In 21 countries a larger proportion of the people are hungry. In 14 countries a higher proportion of children are dying before reaching the age of 5, and in 34 countries life expectancy has decreased.
- Tariffs on manufactured goods from the developing world are four times higher than those on manufactured goods from other OECD countries.
- One-sixth of the world's adults are illiterate (two-thirds of the world's illiterates are women).
- In the developed world, subsidies to agricultural producers are six times higher than overseas development aid.
- More than 10 million children die every year from easily preventable diseases.
- A child born in Zambia today is less likely to live past the age of 30 than a child born in 1840 in England.
- In Africa only one child in three completes primary education.
- In sub-Saharan Africa a woman is 100 times more likely to die in childbirth than women in high-income OECD countries.
- African countries pay out $40 million every day on debt repayment.

Sources: World Bank, United Nations Development Program, Jubilee Research

What Makes a Theory "Alternative"?

If you grew up in the United States you have probably internalized a combination of the liberal and realist perspectives. To keep with our metaphor that theories are like eyeglasses, you are in essence wearing bifocals, combining both liberal and realist visions of different worlds. You probably think that you live in a basically peaceful and law-abiding society with a free market economic system in which anyone can potentially become rich. This is the rough outline of the liberal model. And, while you have this view of the domestic situation, you most likely look at international events quite differently. Here, the realist model describes what you see: If countries are not at war, then they are constantly seeking some kind of an advantage—in trade negotiations, for example. Individuals and states are self-interest oriented, and international politics is a constant struggle for power and material resources, so even in trade negotiations self-help and self-interest rule.

But for someone who grew up in the former Eastern Bloc of communist countries, the view of your society could be quite different, especially if that person were a child of a member of the ruling Communist Party. For that person, Marxism, not capitalism, is the dominant political-economic model. In fact, in some ways, the theory of Marxism in the USSR was like a religion: it had an explanation for history, it described how to live properly, and it offered a utopian workers' paradise as a reward for living correctly.

A Marxist could look at life in the United States and see exploitation everywhere. Workers in factories are alienated from the products they make. Without an employee discount, for instance, an assembly line worker at a General Motors factory could never even think about owning the car that went by on the conveyor belt. Schools are designed to create good future workers by teaching the benefits of arriving on time, being polite to the teacher, and submitting perfect homework. The income gap between rich and poor is wide and getting wider.

For this imagined child of the Communist Party in the USSR, life is very good and not based on exploitation. There are special shops for party members, where shortages of meat are rare and you can purchase white bread, not the rough rye loaves found in other stores. You would probably also attend school with other children like yourself and have science labs with the latest equipment, while being taught by instructors who do not seem bored with their work. When you catch the flu in the winter, you do not have to wait in long lines for your turn to see the doctor in a clinic.

The Marxist perspective on international affairs would sound a bit like realism, but with a communist spin. For where realism sees constant struggles for power, the Marxist doctrine of the USSR saw capitalist encirclement of the Soviet Union and the exploitation of the developing world. The doctrine preached class warfare on a global scale, and the USSR extended foreign aid in "fraternal cooperation" with its socialist friends.

Imagining still that you were a student born into the USSR, in your classes on foreign relations you would learn that the "correlation of forces" was beginning to turn in the direction of the socialist world. You would also learn that your country was peace loving and had pledged that it would never use nuclear weapons first in a war with the capitalist NATO countries.

Of course, this is a stylized reality we've asked you to imagine, but one to prove a point: what is "alternative" depends on your perspective. In all likelihood, you, this hypothetical student in the USSR, would know that you had a privileged status in society. You might be uncomfortable with it, because you could see the exploitation of people in the "workers' paradise": tiny apartments with a shared bathroom down the hall; food shortages; drab clothing selections; a yearlong wait to purchase a car, and then no choice of color. In the workplace, people seem like the assembly line workers in the capitalist West: bored and underpaid. A popular joke in the 1970s Soviet Union was "we pretend to work, and the state pretends to pay us."

However, for all its shortcomings, it would be *your* Marxist perspective, and you might very well feel good about it; meanwhile, it would be the liberal capitalist model that you considered perilous until perhaps 1989, when you would learn what it meant to see things from the other perspective.

It is important to emphasize that the essential elements of Marxist thought, all too briefly discussed in this section, are also essentially contested. That is, they are subject to much discussion and disagreement even among those contemporary writers who have been influenced by Marxist writings. There is disagreement as to how these ideas and concepts should be interpreted and how they should be put into operation. Analysts also differ over which elements of Marxist thought are most relevant, which have been proven to be mistaken, and which should now be considered as outmoded or in need of radical overhaul. Moreover, there are substantial differences between them in terms of their attitudes toward the legacy of Marx's ideas. The work of the more contemporary Marxists, for example, draws far more directly on Marx's original ideas than does the work of the critical theorists. Indeed, the critical theorists would probably be more comfortable being viewed as post-Marxists than as straightforward Marxists. But even for them, as the very term post-Marxism suggests, the ideas of Marx remain a basic point of departure.

> ### WHAT'S YOUR WORLDVIEW ?
>
> *Marxists believe that globalization has created an uneven distribution of wealth, power, and influence. Do you think it is possible to manage and reform globalization to address the growing disparities? Are there examples of NGOs or governments addressing these concerns?*

World-System Theory

As we noted earlier, Marx did not devote much attention in his writing to the international aspects of capitalism, in particular leaving out the European colonial occupations of Asia and Africa. In fact, Marx seems to think that colonization might actually help to move the people of the non-European world out of their premodern modes of production into the capitalist mode. This in turn would create conditions of exploitation that would spark a proletarian revolution of the kind Marx and Engels predicted in *The Communist Manifesto*.

The origins of contemporary world-system theory can be traced back to the first systematic attempt to apply the ideas of Marx to the international sphere, that is, to the critique of **imperialism** advanced by a number of thinkers at the start of the twentieth century (see Brewer 1990). The most well-known and influential work to emerge from this debate is the pamphlet written by Lenin, published in 1917, called *Imperialism: The Highest Stage of Capitalism*. Lenin accepted much of Marx's basic thesis but argued that the character of capitalism had changed since Marx published the first volume of *Capital* in 1867 (Marx 1992). Capitalism had entered a new stage—its highest and final stage—with the development of **monopoly capitalism**. Under monopoly capitalism, a two-tier structure had developed within the world economy: a dominant core exploiting a less-developed periphery. With the development of a core and periphery, there was no longer an automatic harmony of interests between all workers. The bourgeoisie in the core states could use profits derived from exploiting the periphery to improve the lot of their own proletariat. In other words, the capitalists of the core could pacify their own working class through the further exploitation of the periphery.

The Latin American dependency school writers developed Lenin's views, especially the notion of core and periphery, in greater depth. In particular, Raul Prebisch, though not a Marxist scholar, argued that states in the periphery were suffering as a result of what he called "the declining terms of trade." He suggested that the price of manufactured goods increased more rapidly than that of raw materials. So, for example, year by year more tons of coffee are required to pay for a refrigerator. As a result of their reliance on primary goods, states of the periphery become poorer relative to the core. Writers such as Guillermo O'Donnell, Andre Gunder Frank, and Fernando Henrique Cardoso developed

imperialism The practice of foreign conquest and rule in the context of global relations of hierarchy and subordination. It can lead to the establishment of an empire.

monopoly capitalism A term introduced by Lenin that suggested that competitive capitalism had been replaced by large corporations that control the market in specific sectors.

these arguments further. It is from the framework developed by such writers that contemporary world-system theory emerged.

The Key Features of Wallerstein's World-System Theory

In order to outline the key features of world-system theory, we begin with the work of perhaps its most prominent protagonist, Immanuel Wallerstein. For Wallerstein, history has been marked by the rise and demise of a series of world systems. The modern world system emerged in Europe at around the turn of the sixteenth century. It subsequently expanded to encompass the entire globe. The driving force behind this seemingly relentless process of expansion and incorporation has been capitalism, defined by Wallerstein as "a system of production for sale in a market for profit and appropriation of this profit on the basis of individual or collective ownership" (1979, 66). Within the context of this system, all the institutions of the social world are continually being created and re-created. Furthermore, and crucially, it is not only the elements within the system that change. The system itself is historically bounded. It had a beginning, has a middle, and will have an end.

In terms of the geography of the modern world system, in addition to a core-periphery distinction, Wallerstein identified an intermediate "semiperiphery." According to Wallerstein, the semiperipheral zone displays certain features characteristic of the core and others characteristic of the periphery. Although dominated by core economic interests, the semiperiphery has its own relatively vibrant indigenously owned industrial base. Because of this hybrid nature, the semiperiphery plays important economic and political roles within the modern world system. In particular, it provides a source of labor that counteracts any upward pressure on wages in the core and also provides a new home for those industries that can no longer function profitably in the core (for example, car assembly and textiles). The semiperiphery also plays a vital role in stabilizing the world political structure.

Another theorist, Robert W. Cox, provides a transition from contemporary Marxism to more recent theoretical developments. In his 1981 article "Social Forces, States, and World Orders: Beyond International Relations Theory" Cox analyzes the state of international relations theory as a whole and one of its major subfields, international political economy. This article became an important wedge in the process of toppling realism's dominance in international relations. The sentence that has become one of the most often-quoted lines in all of contemporary international relations theory reads as follows: "Theory is always *for* some one, and *for* some purpose" (1981, 128). This echoes Marx's statement we cited above that philosophy must change the world. It

World-system theorists proposed that goods, such as these car parts made in China, are made in the periphery for sale in the core. Will globalization increase the division between rich and poor or reduce the gap between core and periphery?

expresses a worldview that follows logically from a broad Marxist position that has been explored in this section. If ideas and values are (ultimately) a reflection of a particular set of social relations, and are transformed as those relations are themselves transformed, then this suggests that all knowledge of political relations must reflect a certain context, a certain time, a certain space. Politics, in other words, cannot be objective and timeless in the way some traditional realists and contemporary structural realists, for example, would like to claim.

One key implication of this is that there can be no simple separation between facts and values. Whether consciously or not, all theorists inevitably bring their values to bear on their analysis. This leads Cox to suggest that we need to look closely at each theory, each idea, each analysis that claims to be objective or value-free, and ask who or what is it for, and what purpose does it serve? He subjects realism, and in particular its contemporary variant structural realism, to an extended criticism on these grounds.

According to Cox, these theories are for—or serve the interests of—those who prosper under the prevailing order, that is, the inhabitants of the developed states, and in particular the ruling elites. Their purpose, whether consciously or not, is to reinforce and legitimate the status quo. They do this by making the current configuration of international relations appear natural and immutable. When realists (falsely, according to Cox and many other analysts) claim to be describing the world as it is, as it has been, and as it always will be, what they are in fact doing is reinforcing the ruling hegemony in the current world order.

Washington Consensus The belief of key opinion-formers in Washington that global welfare would be maximized by the universal application of neoclassical economic policies that favor a minimalist state and an enhanced role for the market.

problem-solving theory Realism and liberalism are problem-solving theories that address issues and questions within the dominant paradigm or the present system. How can we fix capitalism? How can we make a society more democratic? These are problem-solving questions that assume nothing is wrong with the core elements of the system.

critical theory Theories that are critical of the status quo and reject the idea that things can be fixed under the present system. These theories challenge core assumptions of the dominant paradigm and argue for transformation and not just reform.

constructivism An approach to international politics that concerns itself with the centrality of ideas and human consciousness. As constructivists have examined world politics they have been broadly interested in how the structure constructs the actors' identities and interests, how their interactions are organized and constrained by that structure, and how their very interaction serves to either reproduce or transform that structure.

WHAT'S YOUR WORLDVIEW ?

Do you think critical theories like Marxism are no longer important for you, as a student of global politics, to explore? Why or why not?

In the same way, goes a contemporary neoliberal argument, blindly accepting globalization as a beneficial process reinforces the hegemony of the countries, corporations, and their stockholders.

Cox extends his argument by contrasting **problem-solving theory** with **critical theory**. Problem-solving theory accepts the parameters of the present order while attempting to fix its problems and thus helps legitimate an unjust and deeply iniquitous system, whereas critical theory attempts to challenge the prevailing order by seeking out, analyzing, and, where possible, assisting social processes that can potentially lead to transformation of the existing system.

Constructivism

Most writers who call themselves **constructivists** argue that our actions and words make society—and society, in turn, shapes our actions and words. As part of this process, we construct rules that first identify for us the key players (i.e., who has agency) in a given situation, recognizing that no one actor in the international system is an agent in all policy situations; then those rules instruct, direct, and commit actors to take certain actions. For example, realist rules during the Cold War dictated that all states were subservient to and would follow the lead of the US or the USSR. However, actual practice does not always comply with the rules: frequently states found areas where these superpowers had little interest—e.g., development or peacekeeping—and established a niche to serve their interests. The George W. Bush administration tried to assert a similar pattern of hegemonic rules after the attacks of September 11, 2001, with phrases like "coalition of the willing" and "you are either with us or you are with the terrorists."

The Power of Ideas: Politics and Neoliberalism

A very good example of the hegemonic power of the United States, many Marxists would argue, is the success that it has had in getting neoliberal policies accepted as the norm throughout the world. The set of policies most closely associated with the neoliberal project (in particular, reduction of state spending, currency devaluation, privatization, and the promotion of free markets) are, revealingly, known as the **Washington Consensus**. Many would argue that these are "commonsense" policies and that those third world countries that have adopted them have merely realized that such economic policies best reflect their interests. However, Marxists would argue that an analysis of the self-interest of the hegemon, and the use of coercive power, provide a more convincing explanation of why such policies have been adopted.

The adoption of neoliberal policies by third world countries has had a number of implications. Spending on health and education has been reduced, they have been forced to rely more on the export of raw materials, and their markets have been saturated with manufactured goods from the industrialized world. It does not take a conspiracy theorist to suggest that these neoliberal policies are in the interests of capitalists in the developed world. There are three main areas where the adoption of neoliberal policies in the third world is in the direct interest of the developed world. First there is the area of free trade. We need not enter into arguments about the benefits of free trade, but it is clear that it will always be in the interest of the hegemon to promote free trade—this is because, assuming it is the most efficient producer, its goods will be the cheapest anywhere in the world. It is only if countries put up barriers to trade, to protect their own production, that the hegemon's products will be more expensive than theirs. Second, there is the area of raw materials. If third world countries are going to compete in a free trade situation, the usual result is that they become more reliant on the export of raw materials (because their industrial products cannot compete in a free trade situation with those of the developed world). Again this is in the interest of the hegemon, as increases in the

supply of raw material exports mean that the price falls. Additionally, where third world countries have devalued their currency as part of a neoliberal package, the price of their exported raw materials goes down. Finally, when third world governments have privatized industries, investors from North America and Europe have frequently been able to snap up airlines, telecommunications companies, and oil industries at bargain prices. Duncan Green (1995) gives an eloquent description of the impacts of neoliberalism on Latin American countries.

If neoliberal policies appear to have such negative results for third world countries, why have they been so widely adopted? This is where the coercive element comes in. Through the 1970s and 1980s and continuing to today there has been a major debt crisis between the third world and the West. This debt crisis came about primarily as a result of excessive and unwise lending by Western banks. Third world countries were unable to pay off the interest on these debts, let alone the debt itself. They turned to the major global financial institutions, such as the International Monetary Fund, for assistance. Although the IMF is a part of the United Nations, it is heavily controlled by Western countries, in particular the United States. For example, the United States has 18 percent of the votes, while Mozambique has only 0.07 percent. In total, the ten most industrialized countries have over 50 percent of the votes. For third world countries, the price of getting assistance was that they would implement neoliberal policies. Only once these were implemented, and only on condition that the policies were maintained, would the IMF agree to provide aid to continue with debt repayment.

Hence Marxists would argue that a deeper analysis of the adoption of neoliberal policies is required. Such an analysis would suggest that the global acceptance of neoliberalism is very much in the interests of the developed world and has involved a large degree of coercion. That such policies seem "natural" and "commonsense" is an indication of the hegemonic power of the United States.

Over time, rules and practices can form a stable pattern that serves the interests of key agents. These patterns become "institutions." The Cold War, described above, was a twentieth-century institution, and the global economy is a good example of a twenty-first-century institution. Its rules and practices are based on neoliberal free market capitalism that best serves the interests of corporations, global economic institutions, and the wealthy states. The wealthy states' power in the system is based on both material factors (e.g., control of resources) and discursive power (power based on knowledge and the control of language and ideas within a society).

A leading constructivist, Alexander Wendt, seeks to understand "how world politics is socially constructed" (Wendt 1995, 71). Famous for his claim that "anarchy is what states make of it" (Wendt 1992, 391), Wendt argues that anarchy in the international system does not have to result in competition, security dilemmas, arms races, or conflict. States have plenty of options; they are only limited by rules, practices, and institutions that they themselves have created. How a country reacts to anarchy reflects its particular understanding of that condition.

Constructivists argue that the international system is defined by socially constructed realities, and therefore, to understand the system, one must focus on shared rules, practices, meanings, identities, and norms. These help define the system for each actor. These factors define the interests, identities, preferences, and actions of each state in the system. By emphasizing the social construction of reality we also are questioning what is frequently taken for granted. This raises several issues. One is a concern with the origins of those social constructs that now appear to us as natural and are now part of our social vocabulary. After all, the notion of sovereignty did not always exist, as we have learned in Chapter 2; it was a product of historical forces and human interactions that generated new distinctions regarding where political authority resided. Also, the category of "weapons of mass destruction" (WMD) is a modern invention. Although individuals have been forced to flee their homes throughout the course of human history, the political and legal category of "refugees" is only a century old. To understand the origins of these concepts requires attention to the interplay between existing ideas and institutions, the political calculations by leaders who had ulterior motives, and morally minded actors who were attempting to improve humanity.

Also of concern to constructivist thinkers are alternative "pathways." Although history appears path-dependent, which is to say that world history can be seen as patterned and somewhat predictable, there are contingencies—historical accidents and human intervention that can force history to change course. The events of 9/11 and the response by the Bush administration arguably transformed the direction of world politics. But how would the world be different today if Al Gore had taken the presidential oath of office in January 2001, before those attacks?

This interest in possible and counterfactual worlds works against historical determinism. Wendt's (1992) claim that "anarchy is what states make of it" calls attention to how different beliefs and practices will generate divergent patterns and organization of world politics. A world of Mahatma Gandhis would be very different from a world of Osama bin Ladens.

Constructivists also examine how actors make their activities meaningful. Following Max Weber's insight that "we are cultural beings with the capacity and the will to take a deliberate attitude toward the world and to lend it *significance*" (1949, 81), constructivists attempt to

Some political theorists believe that citizens are not powerless in the face of state power. But if the state seeks to fight back, how much can these Greek citizens accomplish with their protest?

recover the meanings that actors give to their practices and to the objects they create. Constructivists argue that culture, rather than private belief, informs the meanings people give to their action. Sometimes constructivists have presumed that such meanings derive from a hardened culture. But because culture is fractured and society comprises different interpretations of what is meaningful activity, scholars need to consider these cultural fault lines; to pinpoint or fix any precise meaning is largely a political and temporary accomplishment—it is not to discover some transcendent truth.

Some of the most important debates in world politics are about how to define particular activities. Development, human rights, security, humanitarian intervention, sovereignty—topics that we discuss in later chapters—are important, orienting concepts that can have any number of meanings. States and nonstate actors have rival interpretations of the meanings of these concepts and will fight to try to have collectively accepted their preferred meaning.

Indeed, the fact that these meanings are fixed through politics, and that once these meanings are fixed they have consequences for the ability of people to determine their fates, suggests an alternative way of thinking about power. Most international relations theorists treat power as the ability of one state to compel another state to do what it otherwise would not and tend to focus on the material technologies, such as military firepower

material This refers to things that we can see, measure, consume, and use, such as military forces, oil, and currency.

ideational This refers to ideas like democracy, capitalism, peace, and social justice.

legitimacy A legitimate authority is respected and recognized by those it rules and by other rulers or leaders of other states. The source of legitimacy can be laws or a constitution and the support of the society.

and economic statecraft, that have this persuasive effect. Constructivists have offered two important additions to this view of power. The forces of power go beyond **material**: they also can be **ideational** or discursive. Ideational power is more than control over meaning—it is also the acceptance of ideas or a way of life. The notion that *your* way of thinking is "the norm" is but one example of ideational power.

Consider the issue of **legitimacy**. States, including great powers, crave legitimacy—the belief that they are acting according to, and pursuing, the values of the broader international community. There is a direct relationship between state legitimacy and the costs associated with a course of action: the greater the legitimacy, the easier time state leaders will have convincing others to cooperate with their policies. The lesser the legitimacy, the more costly the action. This means, then, that even great powers will frequently feel the need to alter their policies in order to be viewed as legitimate—or bear the consequences. Further evidence of the constraining power of legitimacy is offered by the tactic of "naming and shaming" by human rights activists. For example, Iran's release of a US reporter in 2009, who was charged with spying, shows how the international media and NGOs dedicated to promoting and protecting press freedoms can be influential in changing government policy. Similarly, human rights advocates led by Mia Farrow used the threat of a boycott of the 2008 Olympics to persuade China to stop jailing dissidents and persecuting religious and ethnic minorities. China did allow for some changes, but because of its economic and political power, it was able to ignore calls for major reforms. If states did not care about their legitimacy—about their reputation, and the perception that they were acting in a manner consistent with prevailing international standards—then such a tactic would have little visible impact; it is only because law-breaking governments want to be perceived as acting in a manner that is consistent with international norms that they can be taunted into changing their conduct.

Other scholars look for points of connection and evaluate the relative strengths of each approach in order to see when they might be combined to enrich our understanding of the world. One possibility is strategic social construction (Finnemore and Sikkink 1998). Actors attempt to change the norms that subsequently guide and constitute state identities and interests. Human rights activists, for instance, try to encourage compliance with human rights norms not only by naming and shaming those who violate these norms but also by encouraging states to identify with these norms because it is the right thing to do. Another possibility is to consider the relationship between the normative structure and strategic behavior. Some use constructivism to elucidate how identity shapes the state's interests and then turn to rational choice for understanding strategic behavior. In this view, the American identity shapes national interests, and then the structure of the international system informs its strategies for pursuing those interests. Yet some scholars go further and argue that the cultural context shapes not only identities and interests of actors but also the very strategies they can use as they pursue their interests. In other words, while "game" metaphors are most closely associated with **game theory** and rational choice, some constructivists also argue that the normative structure shapes important features of the game, including the identity of the players and the strategies that are appropriate.

game theory A branch of mathematics that explores strategic interaction.

And, as it turns out, not all is fair in love and war—or any other social endeavor, for that matter. For decades Arab nationalism shaped the identities and interests of Arab states, contained norms that guided how Arab leaders could play the game of Arab politics, and encouraged Arab leaders to draw from the symbols of Arab politics to try to maneuver around their Arab rivals and further their own interests. They had very intense rivalries, and as they vied for prestige and status they frequently accused each other of being a traitor to the Arab nation or harming the cause of Arabism. But rarely did they use military force. Until the late 1970s, the idea of relations with Israel was a taboo, violated by Egyptian Anwar Sadat's trip to Jerusalem in 1977 and separate peace treaty in 1979. Arab states did not respond through military action but rather by evicting Egypt from the Arab League, and then Sadat paid the ultimate price for his heresy when he was assassinated in 1981 by supporters of the Muslim Brotherhood—who were reacting to Sadat's actions but also their own suppression within Egypt. But how does constructivism help us understand how and why things change? Proponents of constructivism scolded structural-realist and neoliberal-institutionalist scholars for their failure to explain contemporary global transformations. The Peace of Westphalia, for instance, helped to establish sovereignty and the norm of noninterference, but in recent decades various processes have worked against the principle of noninterference and suggested how state sovereignty is conditional on how states treat their populations. **World orders** are created and sustained not only by great-power preferences but also by changing understandings of what constitutes a legitimate **international order**. Until the Second World War, the idea of a world organized around **empires** was not illegitimate—but now it is.

In the next section we see how one socially constructed idea—gender—has become an important critical perspective in the study of international relations. Feminist theory is the last of the three most influential alternative theories that we will discuss in this chapter. We will see that a simple notion—that ideas of "correct" or "proper" gender roles vary from society to society—can offer a powerful lens through which we can analyze global politics.

Feminist Theory

Often misunderstood as an attack on males, feminist theory provides useful tools with which to analyze a range of political events and policy decisions. In this section we offer an overview of five main types of feminist theory, which have become common since the mid-1980s—liberal, socialist/Marxist, standpoint, postmodern, and postcolonial. Although this section is titled "feminist theory," it is a both deliberate and misleading heading. It is deliberate in that it focuses on the socially constructed roles that "women" occupy in world politics. It is misleading because this question has to be understood— as we noted in the previous section—in the context of the construction of differences between women and men, and contingent understandings of masculinity and femininity. In other words, the focus could more accurately be on gender rather than on women, because the very categories of women and men, and the concepts of masculinity and femininity, are highly contested in much feminist research. Similarly, distinctions such as liberal and socialist are slightly misleading, for, as we will discuss in more detail below, these categories do not exactly correspond to the diverse thinking of feminist scholars, especially in contemporary work, in which elements from each "type" are often integrated.

The term "gender" usually refers to the social construction of the difference between "men" and "women." Although it is a complex concept, here is one way to think of it: biology determines your sex; gender is determined by a mix of social and cultural norms,

WHAT'S YOUR WORLDVIEW

What is your image of the world? How do you construct the world in which we live? Is it a peaceful and hopeful place with a chance for reform, or is it a place of violence, despair, and misery? Whose ideas do you embrace in your construction of the world?

world order This is a wider category of order than the "international." It takes as its units of order not states, but individual human beings, and assesses the degree of order on the basis of the delivery of certain kinds of goods (be they security, human rights, basic needs, or justice) for humanity as a whole.

international order The normative and the institutional pattern in the relationship between states. The elements of this may be thought to include such things as sovereignty, the forms of diplomacy, international law, the role of the great powers, and the codes circumscribing the use of force. It is a shared value and condition of stability and predictability in the relations of states.

empire A distinct type of political entity, which may or may not be a state, possessing both a home territory and foreign territories. This may include conquered nations and colonies.

as well as your own sense of identity. Some of the theories covered in this section assume natural and biological (e.g., sex) differences between men and women. Some of the approaches do not. What all of the most interesting work in this field does, however, is analyze how gender both *affects* world politics and *is an effect of* world politics. In other words, feminist theorists examine how different concepts (such as "the state" or "sovereignty") are "gendered" and, in turn, how this gendering of concepts can have differential consequences for men and women (Steans 1998). It is important to note that feminists have always been interested in how understandings of gender affect the lives of men and women. (Brittan 1989; Seidler 1989; Connell 1995; Carver 1996; Zalewski and Parpart 1998). As with all theoretical traditions, there are different shades of feminism that combine with some of the more traditional theoretical ideas in global politics. We will discuss five forms, or varieties, of feminist thinking.

feminism A political project to understand so as to change women's inequality, liberation, or oppression. For some, the aim is to move beyond gender, so that it no longer matters; for others, to validate women's interests, experiences, and choices; for others, to work for more equal and inclusive social relations overall. Feminist theories tend to be critical of the biases of the discipline. Many focus their research on the areas where women are excluded from the analysis of major international issues and concerns.

liberal feminism A position that advocates equal rights for women but also supports a more progressive policy agenda that would include social justice, peace, economic well-being, and ecological balance.

    Feminist theory in international relations originally grew from work on the politics of development and peace research. But by the late 1980s a first wave of feminism, **liberal feminism**, was more forcefully posing the question of "where are the women in world politics?" The meaning of "liberal" in this context is decidedly *not* the same as the meaning we discussed in Chapter 3. This definition is more in line with traditional views of liberalism that put equal and nondiscriminatory liberty at the center of the international debate.

    In the context of feminism, the term *liberal* starts from the notion that the key units of society are individuals, that these individuals are biologically determined as either men or women, and that these individuals possess specific rights and are equal. Thus, one strong argument of liberal feminism is that all rights should be granted to women equally with men. Here we can see how the state is gendered insofar as rights, such as voting rights, right to possess property, and so on, have been predicated solely on the experiences and expectations of men—and, typically, a certain ethnic/racial class of men. Thus, taking women seriously made a difference to the standard view of world politics. Liberal feminists look at the ways in which women are excluded from power and prevented from playing a full part in political activity. They examine how women have been restricted to roles critically important for the functioning of things but not usually deemed important for theories of world politics.

    To ask "where are the women?" was at the time quite a radical political act, precisely because women were absent from the standard texts of international relations, and thus they appeared invisible. Take a moment to look back at the photograph of the G-20 leaders from 2009, found at the beginning of this chapter. How many world leaders pictured here are women? Writers such as Cynthia Enloe (1989, 1993, 2000) began from the premise that if we simply started to ask "where are the women?" we would be able to see their presence and importance to world politics, as well as the ways in which their exclusion from world politics was presumed a "natural" consequence of their biological or natural roles. After all, it was not that women were actually absent from world politics. Indeed, they played absolutely central roles, either as cheap factory labor, as prostitutes around military bases, or as tourist hotel maids.

WHAT'S YOUR WORLDVIEW?

How would your view of the wars in Iraq and Afghanistan change if you analyzed the wars based on the role of women and the impact of women in all the societies involved?

    The point is that traditional international theory either ignored these contributions or, if it recognized them at all, designated them as less important than the actions of states-*men*. Enloe demonstrated just how critically important were the activities of women—for example as wives of diplomats and soldiers or as models of correct European behavior—to the functioning of the inter-

Feminist thinkers ask "where are the women?" as a means to understand power relationships. If German chancellor Angela Merkel had more female counterparts at this summit meeting, would the world be different?

national economic and political systems, both during the era of European colonialism and afterward. She illustrated exactly how crucial women and the conventional arrangements of "women's and men's work" were to the continued functioning of international politics.

Most specifically, Enloe documented how the concept and practice of militarization influenced the lives and choices of men and women around the world. "Militarization," she writes, "is a step-by-step process by which a person or a thing gradually comes to be controlled by the military or comes to depend for its well-being on militaristic ideas" (2000, 3; also see Elshtain 1987; Elshtain and Tobias 1990). Enloe is an example of a scholar who begins from a liberal premise—that women and men should have equal rights and responsibilities in world politics—but draws on socialist feminism to analyze the role of economic structures and on standpoint feminism to highlight the unique and particular contributions of women.

A second strand of feminist theory is socialist/Marxist feminism, with its insistence on the role of material and primarily economic forces in determining the lives of women. This approach is also sometimes known as materialist feminism (Hennessy and Ingraham 1997). For Marxist feminism, the cause of women's inequality is to be found in the capitalist system; overthrowing capitalism is the necessary route for the achievement of

Percentage of Women Legislators Around the World. What does this graph suggest about the feminist movement worldwide? Do you find these percentages as expected or surprising? *Source: Inter-Parliamentary Union.*

the equal treatment of women (Sargent 1981). Socialist feminism, noting that the oppression of women occurred in precapitalist societies and continues in capitalist societies, differs from Marxist feminism in that it introduces a second central material cause in determining women's unequal treatment, namely, the patriarchal system of male dominance (Braun 1987; Gottlieb 1989). According to Marxist feminists, then, capitalism is the primary oppressor; for socialist feminists it is capitalism plus patriarchy. For socialist/Marxist feminists the focus of a theory of world politics would be on the patterns by which the world capitalist system and the patriarchal system of power lead to women being systematically disadvantaged compared to men. The approach, therefore, has much in common with postcolonial feminism, which is discussed later in this section. Both are especially insightful when it comes to looking at the nature of the world economy and its differential advantages and disadvantages that apply to women. But postcolonial feminism, as we will see, criticizes socialist/Marxist feminism for presuming the "sameness" of patriarchy throughout the world and across time.

The third version of feminist theory we'll discuss is standpoint feminism (Zalewski 1993 Hartsock 1998). This variant emerged out of socialist feminism and the idea of a particular class system. The goal was to try to think about how women as a class might be able to envision politics from a perspective denied to those who benefited from the subordination of women. Drawing on socialist-feminist interpretations of structure, standpoint feminism began to identify how the subordination of women, as a particular class, by virtue of their sex rather than economic standing (although the two are seen as related), possessed a unique perspective—or standpoint—on world politics as a result of their subordination. This first insight was later developed to consider also how the knowledge, concepts, and categories of world politics were predicated upon a norm of masculine behavior and masculine experiences and therefore represented not a universal standard—but a highly specific, particular standard.

Standpoint feminists argue that seeing the world from the standpoint of women radically alters our understanding of that world. We can appreciate this when we think about the gendered effects of free trade on the global economy: women work as underpaid employees in factories around the world; harried single-parent-family women shop for those products as bargains at the local Walmart; and female register workers scan those low-priced items but are blocked from promotion because of gender bias in the workplace. Standpoint feminism has undergone dramatic changes, since its first articulation, to incorporate the critiques of women of color, who argued that, as socialism had presumed class identity as a primary affiliation, standpoint feminism presumed sex identity as the primary affiliation of all women and, accordingly, the single source of their oppression. The standpoint position also runs the risk of "essentializing," or fixing the views and nature of women, by saying that *this one perspective* is how *all* women see the world (Gioseffi 2003). For example, it is unlikely that Hillary Rodham Clinton, Condoleezza Rice, Sarah Palin, and Queen Latifah all share the same beliefs about politics. Nonetheless, despite these dangers, standpoint feminism has been very influential in showing just how male-dominated the main theories of world politics are.

In an important book, J. Ann Tickner (1992) examines the ways in which gendered identities have shaped the international politics in security, economics, and the environment. Looking at war and peace, for example, Tickner demonstrates how the seemingly objective rules of Morgenthau's realism in fact reflect conventional ideas of masculine values and definitions of reality, rather than feminine ones. Tickner reformulates these same rules, taking women's (as opposed to men's) experiences as the starting point. Her point is to show that traditional Western European and North American notions of "proper" gender roles have underpinned decisions about security.

The fourth version is postmodern feminism, which develops the work of poststructuralism (especially that of Michel Foucault and Jacques Derrida) to analyze specifically the concept of gender. Essentially, postmodern feminism criticizes the basic distinction between **sex and gender** that earlier feminist theories found so useful in thinking about the roles of men and women in world politics and in analyzing the gendered concepts of world politics itself. This distinction between sex and gender was useful because it allowed feminists to argue that the position of women and men in the world was not natural but highly contingent and dependent on the meaning given to biological differences. Yet, while extremely useful, the acceptance of the sex-gender distinction retained the binary opposition of male-female and presumed that, while gender was constructed, sex was wholly natural. However, as a number of scholars demonstrated, what we understood sex to be, what biological differences were, was heavily influenced by our understanding of gender—that is, that sex was as constructed as gender (Fausto-Sterling 1992, 2000; Haraway 1989, 1991; Fox-Keller 1985; Longino 1990). This does not mean that our biological bodies or "the determination of sex" is not important. Rather, it suggests that "understanding this process leads to questions concerning how sex and gender operate to create the reality through which bodies materialize as sexed, as sexualized . . . as objects of knowledge and subjects of power" (Kinsella 2003, 296; also see Kinsella 2005a, 2005b, 2006).

The final form of feminism to mention is postcolonial feminism. Postcolonial feminists work at the intersection of class, race, and gender on a global scale. They especially analyze the gendered effects of transnational culture and the unequal division of labor in the global political economy. From this perspective, it is not good enough to simply demand (as liberal feminists do) that men and women should have equal rights in a Western-style democracy. Such a move ignores the way in which poor women of color in the global South or developing world remain subordinated by the global economic sys-

sex and gender "Sex" is biological difference, born male or female; the sex act; sexual difference. "Gender" is what it means to be male or female in a particular place or time; the social construction of sexual difference.

Constructivists assert that ideas shape how we view the world. If your social, ethnic, or economic identity were different, how would you see the world?

Table 4.3
Some Models of the International System

	Realist	Liberal, Institutionalist	Marxist	Constructivist, Feminist
Primary Unit	State	States, NGOs, MNCs, TNCs	State	Various
International system is...	Anarchic	Self-interestedly cooperative	Based on capitalist exploitation	Various: sum of ideas, a fiction, gendered
Leaders are...	Rational	Rational	Capitalists	Biased

tem—a system that liberal feminists were slow to challenge. In other words, the concerns and interests of feminists in the West and those in the rest of the world may not, therefore, so easily fit together. Postcolonial feminists are also critical of Western, privileged academic intellectuals (men and women) who claim to be able to "speak for" the oppressed, a form of cultural imperialism with important material effects. Perhaps the most influential postcolonial feminist scholar in this vein is Gayatri Spivak, who combines Marxism and feminism to interpret imperialism, past and present, and ongoing struggles for decolonization. In an influential essay "Can the Subaltern Speak?," Spivak (1988) acknowledged the ambiguity of her own position in a privileged Western university and argued that elite scholars should be wary of homogenizing the "subaltern" and trying to speak *for* them in their "true" voice (what she calls a form of "epistemic violence"). The term "subaltern" refers to subordinated groups, and in this instance to underprivileged women in the global South. In not recognizing the heterogeneity of experience and opinion of these diverse women, goes the argument, seemingly benevolent and well-meaning academics are at once patronizing in their desire to redeem them and unwittingly complicit in new forms of colonialism. Some postmodernists have also been criticized along similar lines for being too Western-centric and gender-blind. Thus the combination of colonialism and **patriarchy** has made it doubly difficult for the resistance and agency of the subordinated groups to be heard and recognized.

patriarchy A persistent society-wide structure within which gender relations are defined by male dominance and female subordination.

Conclusion

Although the proponents of the alternative theories presented in this chapter seek to challenge the conventionally dominant theories of international relations, their work does more than that. In addition to offering new critical ways in which to view the field, the alternative theories, if combined with aspects of realism and liberalism, give us a richer understanding of international processes (as summarized in Table 4.3). We can see, for example, that war might not only result from countries' struggle for material power but also from the power of ideas or constructed notions of a proper masculine role in society.

In the final part of this book we will learn about contemporary issues of globalization. As you read, think of the various theories as glasses to help you to see the central problem of each issue. You should be open to multiple interpretations of events, while remembering that no one theory can explain everything, since by accepting a single theory as your basis for understanding and explaining world politics you are excluding other perspectives that might also be valid.

Contributors to Chapter 4: Stephen Hobden, Richard Wyn Jones, Patricia Owens, Steve Smith, and Steven L. Lamy.

REVIEW QUESTIONS

1. Why have alternative theoretical approaches to realism become more popular in recent years?
2. How would you explain the continuing vitality of Marxist thought in a post–Cold War world?
3. How did Lenin's approach to international relations differ from that of Marx?
4. What is Wallerstein's notion of a semiperiphery? Why might it be useful?
5. What is the core concept of constructivism?
6. What do you think are the core issues for the study of global change, and how does constructivism help you address those issues? Alternatively, how does a constructivist framework help you identify new issues that you had not previously considered?
7. Feminists define gender as a social construction. What does this mean? What kinds of questions does international relations feminism try to answer using gender as a category of analysis?
8. Women's participation at the highest levels of international and national policy making has been extremely limited. Do you think this is important for understanding global politics?
9. Do you think women's roles—as diplomats' and soldiers' wives, domestic servants, sex workers, homemakers, and home-based workers—are relevant to the business of international politics? If so, how?
10. Which variant of feminist theory, or any combination of them, seems to capture most accurately what Enloe calls "gender makes the world go around"?
11. Why has international relations ignored issues concerning race for so long? What does postcolonialism suggest on the subject?
12. What is it about Marxism, constructivism, and feminism that makes them a threat to realism and liberalism?
13. Which of the three alternative theories discussed in this chapter do you think offers the best account of world politics? Why?

FURTHER READING

Campbell, D. (1998), *Writing Security: United States Foreign Policy and the Politics of Identity,* rev. ed. (Manchester: Manchester University Press). This important book shows how the identity of the United States is constructed through perceptions of danger in foreign policy discourse.

Chowdhry, G., and Nair, S. (eds.) (2002), *Power, Postcolonialism, and International Relations: Reading Race, Gender, and Class* (London: Routledge). An edited volume looking at how the intersection of race, class, and gender structures much of world politics.

Enloe, C. (1989), *Bananas, Beaches and Bases: Making Feminist Sense of International Politics* (London: Pandora). This was the classic text charting the way forward for feminist IR.

Gilroy, P. (1993), *The Black Atlantic: Modernity and Double Consciousness* (Cambridge, MA: Harvard University Press). A look at the unique racial and cultural identity of those black people forced to move from their native countries to the West and how Europeans were also affected by this cultural exchange.

Said, E. (1979), *Orientalism* (New York: Vintage). A decisive postcolonial text showing how colonial literary and artistic texts create the "other" with devastating material consequences.

Walker, R. J. B. (1993), *Inside/Outside: International Relations as Political Theory* (Cambridge: Cambridge University Press). An important early contribution to postmodern IR theory, which challenged some of the central categories of the discipline.

INTERNET RESOURCES

Following are four sources of primary texts of philosophy that can be useful to students for outside reading assignments:

Internet Classics Archive

http://classics.mit.edu/index.html

Online Library of Liberty

http://oll.libertyfund.org/

Perseus Digital Library

http://www.perseus.tufts.edu/hopper/

Project Gutenberg

http://promo.net/pg/

Marxists Internet Encyclopedia

www.marxists.org

> The source for anything to do with the past, present, and future of Marx and his followers. Includes biographical sketches, texts, and letters. The latter includes letters from Jenny Marx to Engels and others.

United Nations WomenWatch: Women, Peace and Security

http://www.un.org/womenwatch/feature/wps/

> The UN site for information on all aspects of women in international politics.

For more information, quizzes, case studies, and other study tools, please visit us at **www.oup.com/us/lamy**

PART THREE

Global Actors

I n this part of the book we present an overview of the primary actors in the global system and the ways in which they interact. Our **first** goal is to give you information about the numerous kinds of actors. We begin with Chapter 5 on **states and foreign policy making**. We show the ways in which nationalism, resources, and size help to determine the foreign policy goals of a state. Building on this foundation of "the state," Chapter 6 looks at **international law and international organizations**. In this chapter you will see the limits and possibilities for collective action in global politics. Our **second** goal is to show you that global politics is more than simply the interactions of states in various policy areas. Therefore, the last chapter of this part, Chapter 7, looks at the important role that **nongovernmental organizations** play in global politics.

States and Foreign Policy

Statecraft is the strategy of power. Power is the capacity to direct the decisions and actions of others. Power derives from strength and will.

—*Charles Freeman*

It is possible to achieve goals only by persuasion, eloquence, threats and—if need be—intimidation.

—*Abba Eban*

I n late August 2009 voters in Japan overwhelmingly rejected the almost fifty-year rule of the Liberal Democratic Party (LDP) and gave a clear mandate for change to the Democratic Party of Japan (DPJ) and its leader Yukio Hatoyama. Asserting that voters were, in his words, "fed up" with the old patterns of LDP politics, Hatoyama promised change in all aspects of the country's political life. The DPJ also promised voters more independence for Japan in its foreign relations with the United States. Yet—after only eight months in office—Prime Minister Hatoyama resigned for failing to fulfill an election promise to move a US military base away from the Japanese island of Okinawa.

Like Yukio Hatoyama, Barack Obama entered office seeking change and engagement with other world leaders. However, as we will see in this chapter, there may be both tangible and intangible limits to what one person can accomplish in foreign policy, even if that person is elected with a strong majority of votes. We will learn about the methods that political leaders around the world use to try to attain their foreign policy goals, including promoting and securing what they see as the national interests of their countries. All countries in the post–Cold War world—rich and poor, large and small, democratic and authoritarian— operate within the same set of limits and possibilities in the domestic and international arenas. Understanding how citizens and their leaders manage to articulate, promote, and eventually secure their interests in this global setting is the focus of this chapter.

Prime Minister Elect Yukio Hatoyama celebrates his victory in 2009, ending the dominance of the Liberal Democratic Party in Japan. Why did he resign nine months later?

Introduction

Each of the theories that we examined in Chapters 3 and 4 described the behavior of an actor called the state. As you will recall from Chapter 1, there is a lot of disagreement in international relations theory about what we mean by "the state." But for this chapter we need to begin by accepting that the state *exists* and that it is the most important actor in the contemporary globalized international system, so that we can better understand the relationship among nations and states, nationalism and national interests, and globalization and global politics. Only then will we be able to discuss the process by which this system of states interacts: We call this process **foreign policy**.

We begin this chapter with a brief discussion of the state, nationalism, and national interests, and then we define foreign policy and explore the tools of **statecraft** used by governments to secure and promote their national interests. We also explore the growing importance of soft power in the post–Cold War era, which is defined more by globalization and global challenges. We will see how, in global politics, foreign policy actors will often pursue different goals simultaneously because foreign policy connects domestic politics and international relations. For example, a leader might advocate human rights policy to satisfy domestic interest groups but maintain trade relations with an authoritarian state because of its need for natural resources.

In the next section of the chapter we will offer an analytical framework of the foreign policy process, providing an overview of how foreign policy is made in most states. We then present a brief overview of levels of analysis and the study of foreign policy behavior. Here we will learn to explain *why* states make certain choices over others. In the final section of the chapter, we will review foreign policy styles and traditions across great, middle, and small states around the world, while placing some emphasis on foreign policy in the United States.

States and Nationalism

To understand the relationship between states, nationalism, and national interests, we must first remember these points:

1. From about the mid-seventeenth century, an order of sovereign, territorial states known as the Westphalian system (see Chapter 2) developed in Europe.
2. The rise of nationalism from the late eighteenth century nationalized this state order, later extending beyond Europe until the whole world was organized as a series of nation-states (see Table 5.1). International relations were relations between nation-states.
3. Globalization may undermine this political order by eroding sovereign territorial power and by creating competing identities and multiple loyalties. But before considering propositions 2 and 3, we will first outline key concepts and debates concerning nationalism and nation-states.

Nationalism is the idea that the world is divided into nations, and these nations provide the overriding focus of political identity and loyalty that in turn demands **national self-determination**. Nationalism can be considered as ideology, as politics, and as sentiments. Definitions of nationalism usually frame it as ideology, a political worldview. However, we might ignore this ideology unless it becomes significant. This can happen if nationalism shapes people's sense of identity: nationalism as sentiments. It can also

foreign policy The articulation of national interests and the means chosen to secure those interests, both material and ideational, in the international arena.

statecraft The methods and tools that national leaders use to achieve the national interests of a state.

nationalism The *idea* that the world is divided into nations that provide the overriding focus of political identity and loyalty, which in turn should be the basis for defining the population of states. Nationalism also can refer to this idea in the form of a strong sense of identity (*sentiment*) or organizations and movements seeking to realize this idea (*politics*).

national self-determination The right or desire of distinct national groups to become states and to rule themselves.

Table 5.1
The Development of a World of Nation-States

Date	Rough Number of Nation(al) States*
1500	4 (England, France, Spain, and Portugal)
1800	6 (Britain, France, Holland, US, Spain, and Portugal)
1900	30 (including Belgium, Germany, Italy, Serbia, Romania, Greece, Brazil, Argentina, Japan, and Canada)
1923	45 members of the League of Nations
1945	51 states established the United Nations (UN)
1950	60 members of UN
1960	99 members of UN
1970	127 members of UN
2009	192 members of UN (195 countries worldwide)

*Before 1923 this is an estimate based on historical judgment. Thereafter it is based on membership of the League of Nations and the United Nations.

happen if nationalism is taken up by movements able to form nation-states: nationalism as politics empowered via self-determination.

Nationalism is an important element of any country's foreign policy and the formation of national interests. In the case of the United States, many believe that it is a nation unlike all others, with values and traditions that other states should emulate; this is often called "American exceptionalism." Many of the original settlers to the United States, especially in the New England colonies, brought with them an idea that they had a covenant with God to create a new nation that would lead humanity to greatness. In his introduction to Reinhold Niebuhr's critically important book, *The Irony of American History*, an international relations scholar, Andrew Bacevich (2008, x–xi), describes the American view of exceptionalism:

> As a Chosen People with what Niebuhr refers to as a "Messianic consciousness," Americans came to see themselves as set apart, their motives irreproachable, their actions not to be judged by standards applied to others.

This notion of "exceptionalism" has often translated into a foreign policy that promotes US values and traditions across the world and frames all US actions as being blessed by a higher power. Presidents from Washington to George Bush sought to promote US democracy and free market values around the world, and with the end of the two world wars, Woodrow Wilson and Franklin Roosevelt sought to build a rule-based system that reflected US interests and ideals and was led by America. More recently, the idea of American exceptionalism was embraced by the Clinton administration and reflected in the foreign policy guiding principle of enlargement. Clinton, inspired by Wilsonian ideals, thought peace, prosperity, and stability for the world would result if the United States was able to use its power and resources to enlarge the number of capitalist and democratic states. Similarly, part of the neoconservatives' message that shaped the foreign

	Disagree	Agree
United States	32	64
Canada	43	56
Italy	29	68
France	46	53
Germany	48	51
Great Britan	46	51
Russia	19	78
Mexico	21	76
India	4	76
Pakistan	6	71
China	31	64
Japan	35	63

Nationalism Around the World. This graph depicts opinions from people around the world who were asked whether they agreed or disagreed with the statement "*Our way of life needs protecting from foreign influences.*" Would you agree or disagree with this statement? Which countries shown here have citizens who express strong nationalist sentiments? *Source: Pew Research Center, "Views of a Changing World" (2003).*

state-strengthening nationalism The use of nationalist ideology to bolster or reform a government or seek to regain territory at the expense of other states.

secessionist nationalism The use of nationalist ideology to create a new state, often by seceding from an existing multiethnic state.

mass nationalism The use of nationalist ideology to encourage separation from an existing state. This is a tactic often employed with secessionist nationalism.

policy of G. W. Bush was the aggressive promotion of US values and traditions around the world. President G. W. Bush described his administration's goals in his second inaugural address: "It is the policy of the United States to seek and support the growth of democratic movements and institutions in every nation and culture, with the ultimate goal of ending tyranny in our world."

Of course this idea of exceptionalism and national purpose is not unique to the United States. In Russia, after the fall of the Soviet Union, some argued for Russian exceptionalism based on a more humanitarian, postcapitalist, Russian spiritualism. Raymond Aron (1966) suggested that security, power, glory, and ideals are "heterogeneous objectives" that shape a country's national interests. Every state has a vision about how the world should be ordered, but only a few have the means to actually follow through with their beliefs about order, security, and justice. In short, this is how nationalism can shape foreign policy as a sentiment and political ideology.

Nationalist sentiments can be held by elites within a society or by the masses. Some nationalist ideas only appeal to a small portion of the population, whereas others have popular resonance. In terms of politics, nationalism can be state strengthening or state subverting. **State-strengthening nationalism** accepts an existing state as broadly legitimate but seeks to strengthen it, internally by "purifying" the nation and reforming government, externally by reclaiming "national" territory and extending power. **Secessionist nationalism** aims to create a new state, usually by separation from a larger state, sometimes by unifying smaller states. The relationship of nationalism to global politics varies with these types. **Mass nationalism**, using ethnic ideas to subvert an existing state, is very different from **elite nationalism**, using civic ideas to strengthen an existing state.

Robert Cooper (2000) provides an interesting view of the evolution of the nation-state and the role of nationalism in a global age. Cooper suggests that the world can be divided into three types of states: premodern states, modern states, and postmodern states. In premodern states, individuals are more loyal to subnational, religious, and ethnic communities. People do not always identify as citizens of these very weak states, which are essentially what we call **failed or failing states**. These states do not have a monopoly of force at home and lack complete control over their own territory. Similarly, these **premodern states** do not have the capacity to provide even the basic services for their citizens. These are states that have minimal or nonexistent foreign policies except for the relationships they have with states that provide them with aid and essential services. Often, these relationships are dependent ones and they are with a former colonial power. Afghanistan, Zimbabwe, Somalia, North Korea, and Burma are examples of premodern states.

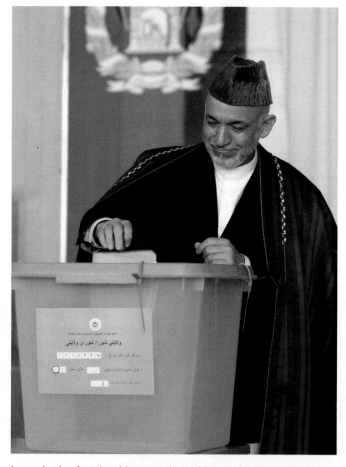

In an election fraught with accusations of fraud, Afghan president Hamid Karzai casts his ballot in his bid to retain the job in 2009. Should NATO countries have pledged to help the fledgling democracy, given the flawed election results?

Modern states are traditional nation-states with control over their territory and the ability to protect their citizens and provide services that allow for the accumulation of wealth. China, India, and Brazil are examples of modern states. Their foreign policies tend to be dominated by economic interests and a desire to become a major power in their region and gain a seat at the table with other global leaders or major powers. In these states, citizens identify with the state and nationalism tends to be very high. For example, the 2008 Olympics in China gave world viewers an indication of the strength of Chinese nationalism. Also, India's expressed desire to become a nuclear power, and the favorable nationalist reaction within India, is one more example of the relationship between nationalism and foreign policy.

Postmodern states are best represented by the states that make up the liberal western world. The United States and the European states provide the best examples. Postmodern states are linked with other states in both formal and informal arrangements at the regional and global levels. Citizens are less nationalistic and more cosmopolitan in their outlook on both domestic and foreign policy. Indeed, in most of the postmodern states, the distinction between domestic and foreign policies is virtually nonexistent. Policy-making authority is shared with a variety of actors at the local, national, regional, and international levels. For example, the European Union now develops common foreign policy positions, and most states depend on NATO for their external security. Sovereignty is shared, traded, and borrowed with other public and private actors. Not surprisingly, these are the states that tend to support calls for global governance and efforts aimed at resolving global problems, like the Kyoto Protocol and the International Criminal Court (ICC). These same

elite nationalism The use of nationalist ideology to encourage unity within an existing state. This is often a tactic that state-strengthening nationalists use.

failed (or failing) state A state that does not command the primary loyalty of its citizens or subjects. These states have no monopoly of force at home and lack complete control over their own territory.

premodern state A state within which the primary identity of citizens or subjects is to national, religious, or ethnic communities. People think of themselves as members of the subnational group first, rather than the state.

modern state Political unit within which citizens identify with the state and see the state as legitimate. This state has a monopoly over the use of force and is able to provide citizens with key services.

postmodern state A political unit within which citizens are less nationalistic and more cosmopolitan in their outlook on both domestic and foreign policy. Policy-making authority for this kind of state is shared with a variety of actors at the local, national, regional, and international levels.

Hosting the Olympics can enhance a state's international prestige. How do exhibitions such as this help build a country's reputation?

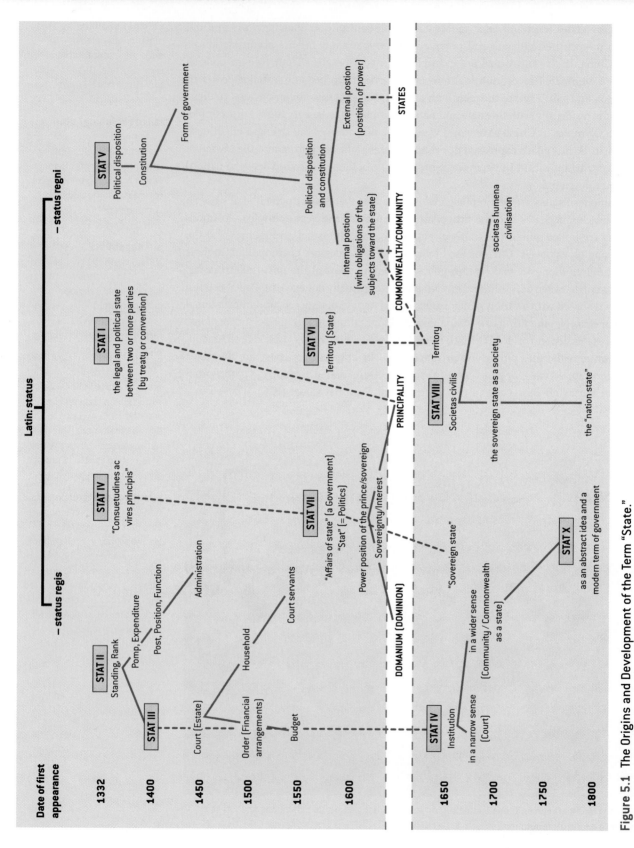

Figure 5.1 The Origins and Development of the Term "State."

The simple word "state" conjures several different meanings, depending on the context of the discussion. This chart traces the historical definitions of the term, and you may find it of assistance when, as in the following chapters (6 and particularly 7), we begin to analyze the term "state" more critically.

states took the lead to promote the 2005 UN resolution that established the new "responsibility to protect" initiative that fundamentally challenges the traditional Westphalian view of national sovereignty (for a visual representation of the historical development of the term "state," see Figure 5.1).

While modern states are all consumed with economic growth and building up their power and authority at home and abroad, postmodern states are multilateralists, who are busy building regional and global regimes to deal with the security challenges presented by the modern and premodern states. Premodern states present the biggest challenges to global security, since they can become incubators for terrorism and they provide profitable homes for drug sales, human trafficking, arms trading, and even piracy.

Such national interests—whether for good or ill—inevitably lead to discussions of foreign policy, which is the topic of our next section. Policy decisions result from these domestic political circumstances. It should be noted that even in undemocratic or authoritarian states, domestic interests such as those favored by military leaders, government bureaucrats, and business leaders shape both domestic and foreign policy. Citizens might not have as much to say about what their leaders decide to do in the international system, but bureaucratic agencies and elites do have a voice. Consider how the Chinese business community has worked to open up the communist regime in that country. The leaders of a state may often seem to be like Janus, the Roman god of doors and beginnings, who had two aspects—one facing inward and the other outward. But as we will see in the next section, the foreign policy process is essentially that—the act of balancing domestic and international factors.

What Is Foreign Policy?

Foreign policy is the articulation of national interests and the means chosen to secure those interests, both material and ideational, in the international arena. **Material interests** may be trade agreements, energy resources, and even control over strategic territory. **Ideational interests** include the promotion of values, norms, and policy ideas that enhance the security and prosperity of a nation-state. The national interests of any state are shaped by individuals, especially political leaders or elites, interest groups, geographic position, traditions, norms, and values that are part of a country's political culture. International events and the actions of both friends and enemies can also influence a country's national interests.

When discussing national interests, the most important questions are: *Which interests are national? Why these interests over others? Who determines these interests?* So far in this book, we have learned that different theoretical views provide different perspectives on both issues and policies. For realists, **national interests** are relatively unchangeable over time. Hans Morgenthau argues that a state's national interest is the pursuit of power, and that power, once acquired, is used to secure material aims, protect social and physical quality of life, and promote specific ideological or normative goals. However, neoclassical realists believe that domestic political interests also shape foreign policy, and thus a state's priorities may change. As we saw in Chapter 3, realists like Morgenthau believe in a state-centric international system in which states act as a single coherent actor that pursues national interests in a rational manner. Here, "rational" means selecting a policy path that maximizes benefits for the state and minimizes risks. Morgenthau and his disciples considered "national interest as the pursuit of power" the essence of politics.

material interest The tangible physical goals of state officials as they set foreign and domestic policy.

ideational/ideal interest The psychological, moral, ethical goals of a state as it sets foreign and domestic policy.

national interest The combination of material and ideal goals that comprise the goals of the government of a state.

Refugees

Who is a refugee? As refugees, can they be called citizens of any country? Why does this category matter, and how has it changed? How do refugee issues challenge those making foreign policy? There are many ways to categorize people who leave their homes, including migrants, temporary workers, displaced peoples, and refugees.

Prior to the twentieth century, "refugee" as a legal category did not exist, and it was not until the First World War that states recognized people as refugees and gave them rights. Who was a refugee? Although many were displaced by the First World War, Western states limited their compassion to Russians who were fleeing the Bolsheviks (it was easier to accuse a rival state of persecuting its people); only they were entitled to assistance from states and the new refugee agency, the High Commissioner for Refugees. However, the High Commissioner took his mandate and the category and began to apply it to others in Europe who also had fled their country and needed assistance. Although states frequently permitted him to expand into other regions and provide more assistance, states also pushed back and refused to give international recognition or assistance to many in need—most notably when Jews were fleeing Nazi Germany. After the Second World War, and as a consequence of mass displacement, states reexamined who could be called a refugee and what assistance they could receive. Because Western states were worried about having obligations to millions of people around the world, they defined a refugee as an individual "outside the country of his origin owing to a well-founded fear of persecution" as a consequence of events that occurred in Europe before 1951. In other words, their definition excluded those outside Europe who were displaced because of war or natural disasters because of events after 1951. Objecting to this arbitrary definition that excluded so many, the new refugee agency, the United Nations High Commissioner for Refugees, working with aid agencies and permissive states, seized on events outside Europe and argued that there was no principled reason to deny to them what was given to Europeans. Over time the political meaning of refugee came to include anyone who was forced to flee his or her home and crossed an international border, and eventually states changed the international legal meaning to reflect the new political realities.

In the contemporary era of Rwanda, Darfur, and Bosnia after the Cold War, we are likely to call someone a refugee if he or she is forced to flee home because of manmade circumstances, without having to cross an international border. To capture the idea of those who flee but are still in their homeland, we use the term "internally displaced peoples." Indeed, the concept of refugees has expanded impressively over the last one hundred years, and the result is that there are millions of people who are now entitled to forms of assistance that are a matter of life and death. Watching this world tragedy unfold has led many states to support the human-security move-

Refugees like the more than 300,000 Tamils displaced in the Sri Lankan civil war present a moral and practical dilemma for states. Do states have a responsibility to accept political refugees?

ment and the October 2005 UN resolution on the responsibility to protect (see Chapter 10).

One reason why states wanted to differentiate "statutory" refugees from internally displaced peoples is because they have little interest in extending their international legal obligations to millions of people and do not want to become too involved in the domestic affairs of states. For example, in the early 1990s refugees fleeing the civil war in Yugoslavia flooded into Germany. However, the German government was already paying for the reunification with East Germany and could not afford to support more refugees at the time. Therefore, because of domestic political reasons, the German government had to look to other states for a solution to a foreign policy problem. The German government chose to lobby for intervention by the European Union, NATO, and the UN.

For realists, the principal "national interest" is national security, or maintaining the integrity of a country's territory and its economic, political, and cultural institutions. Morgenthau argued that to understand foreign policy one has to understand the "political and cultural context within which foreign policy is formulated," and that interests and ideas shape foreign policy actions and priorities. He quotes the noted scholar Max Weber to make his point: "Interests (material and ideal), not ideas, dominate directly the actions of men. Yet the 'images of the world' created by these ideas have very often served as switches determining the tracks on which the dynamism of interests kept actions moving" (1960, 9).

The objectives of foreign policy, according to many realists, must be defined in terms of material national interests and must be supported by adequate power. Military power is the dominant coin of the realm, from a realist view; however, in this era of globalization the tools of statecraft have changed in both their utility and efficacy. All the major states today, for instance, have substantial armed forces, yet all states face the potential of attacks by terrorist groups, and a strong military is not always an effective deterrent.

Robert Pastor (1999) argues that a state's leaders rank their foreign policy goals from *vital* or *essential* to *desirable*. From his realist view, Pastor ranks national interests as follows:

1. National security that includes the defense of borders and the prevention of external influence over domestic affairs.
2. The pursuit of economic interests and securing vital resources.
3. The defense of a country's traditions and values, and the promotion of its ideals in the international system.
4. The implicit and explicit effort to make the world more like itself.

Moreover, as we learned in Chapter 3, proponents of the liberal perspective on international relations believe that a state's power is not measured by force alone. Liberals may define national interest in terms of maintaining rule of law in the international system and empowering international institutions and regimes that promote global governance in policy areas such as economic development and global finance. Liberal internationalists like the former Canadian foreign minister Lloyd Axworthy (2003, 5) have taken bold steps to reform the international system and shift foreign policy priorities from narrow national interests to a much more universal focus on human security and human interests. Axworthy described a goal that many liberal middle powers have embraced:

> We propose a way of seeing the world and tackling global issues that derived from serving individual human needs, not just those of the nation-state or powerful economic interests.

Liberal internationalism in this case has evolved to embrace a more Kantian or normative view of national priorities and interests.

Constructivists, meanwhile, believe that state interests and foreign policy goals are "defined in the context of internationally held norms and understandings about what is good and appropriate" (Finnemore 1996b, 2). This normative context changes over time, and this helps us understand shifts in foreign policy behavior and interests promoted by national leaders. For example, with the end of the Cold War, many states returned to their own traditions and values as guideposts for foreign policy; and the more internationalist context supported this shift away from ideological conflict to engagement and cooperation.

Marxists and many utopians, on the other hand, believe that foreign policy is generally controlled by economic and political elites who also control power at home. National interests are determined by the wealthy and powerful, not the average citizen. This leads to conclusions that wars are fought primarily for economic reasons and that the goal of a country's development-assistance programs is to make poor countries dependent on the donor state and to ensure that the developing regions of the world are kept in the position of providing cheap labor, cheap resources, and a welcome place for foreign investors. Utopians like the academics who comprised the World Order Models Project (WOMP) advocated a foreign policy that shifts national interests to more global interests such as peace, social justice, economic well-being, and ecological balance.

What Do We Expect from Foreign Policy?

National interests are usually related to what we, as citizens, expect from our governments. At the basic level we want the state to protect our borders, provide internal security, and support and maintain a means of exchange or a marketplace. This is the point at which domestic and international policy distinctions begin to blur. Foreign policy and domestic policies are clearly interdependent in this global age. Most foreign policy experts believe citizens expect their state's foreign policy to deliver in seven areas (Hill 2003, 44–45):

1. Protecting citizens living or traveling in a foreign country.
2. Projecting an image or identity in the international system that enhances a state's prestige and makes that state's values, beliefs, and traditions attractive to other states in the international system.
3. Maintaining the "status quo" in terms of providing stability and protecting citizens against external threats.
4. Advancing prosperity and providing the ways and means for accumulating wealth.
5. Assisting leaders in making decisions about whether to intervene in a global crisis or get involved in an alliance or international institution.
6. Providing support for international negotiations aimed at creating and maintaining a stable world order.
7. Working toward protecting the global commons (e.g., oceans) and for providing global public goods (e.g., clean air).

These foreign policy goals are influenced and shaped by a variety of internal and external actors and structures. Globalization has pushed domestic and foreign policy processes into a complex and interconnected relationship. Domestic societies are more exposed to external or international developments, and foreign policies both shape and are shaped by domestic developments. In capitols across the world, foreign policy leaders talk about policy issues that are transnational in nature, like migration, poverty, environmental challenges, and trade. In crafting government policies to slow global warming, for example, political leaders must contend with the demands of business and industry groups and those of concerned citizens at home—not to mention those demands that leaders, corporations, and citizens of other states bring to negotiations. These leaders also understand how domestic interests often prevent the realization of foreign policy goals. One of the most difficult issues for foreign policy leaders is how to make bold foreign policy decisions without alienating a powerful domestic group that might influence the next election. For example, the leaders of the world know that genocide is taking place in Darfur, and yet few states are willing to intervene in the area to stop the killing. Humanitarian intervention presents a difficult policy choice for most leaders. It is hard to convince domestic groups to sacrifice blood and treasure for people from distant lands.

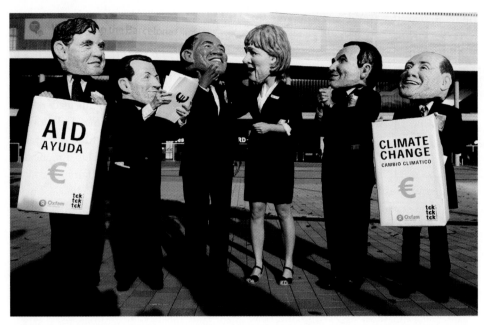

Moral suasion—naming and shaming—can influence world leaders. Do parodies like these of world leaders affect what you think?

Now that we've covered some foundational aspects of what foreign policy is, and what we expect from it, we turn to a discussion about how foreign policy is accomplished; and we will examine the strategies and tools that states might use to secure their goals and meet their priorities in the international system.

Foreign Policy Strategies and Tools

The organized statements of goals and beliefs that political leaders formulate, and the methods they intend to employ to achieve those goals, are called foreign policy strategies. For the political leaders of a state, a foreign policy doctrine provides a sextant, or, in current technology, a GPS system, that leaders use to chart policy strategies and determine national priorities. The doctrine guides decisions, such as where to invest critical resources to secure both long- and short-term goals. Like most countries, the United States has had one dominant strategy for protecting national interests—a combination of military, economic, and diplomatic resources aimed at protecting our homeland and maintaining an open global economy. During the Cold War the strategy developed a global reach and was identified with the presidents at the time. The Truman, Nixon, and Reagan doctrines were all aimed at either containing or confronting communist expansion. The Carter Doctrine was aimed at protecting US interests in the Middle East, and the recent Bush Doctrine included policies aimed at confronting extremist groups that use terrorism and the states that support them. Unilateralism and preemptive war were also core principles in the Bush Doctrine.

Most states have coherent foreign policy strategies to attain both material and ideal goals. For example, after emerging from apartheid and exclusive white rule in the late 1980s, the new South African state has developed a foreign policy that promotes human rights across the world and supports an African Renaissance. For China, the 2008 Summer Olympics was a symbolic announcement of its leadership status in world affairs. It is hoped that South Africa's sponsorship of the World Cup soccer/football matches in 2010 will signal to the world that South Africa is capable of leading an economic, political, and cultural resurgence of African states. Similarly, after years of rule by military dictators, Chilean democratic leaders have decided that an activist foreign policy based on the theme of "diplomacy for development" will help them overcome their structural constraints of size and geographic location and allow them to develop a niche as a regional leader and an honest broker in international affairs.

> ## WHAT'S YOUR WORLDVIEW ?
>
> *Do you think power gives rise to responsibility? Should powerful states be expected to right the world's wrongs and solve the world's problems?*

All countries have three kinds of foreign policy tools from which to choose: sticks, carrots, and sermons. "Sticks" refers to threats, "carrots" to inducements, and "sermons" to what diplomats might call "moral suasion." We could also add the power that comes with having a positive image or reputation in the international system. Being an "honest broker" or a moral leader seeking to help resolve regional conflicts can also become a source of power in the international world. Norway, for example, took the lead to resolve the Middle East conflict and the conflict in Sri Lanka. Norwegian leaders are supported in these endeavors because Norwegian citizens see it as their responsibility to the global community. Norwegian nationalism includes a strong sense of internationalism. It is important to remember that, because of differences in resources, population, and level of economic development, some countries might not be all able to use some or all of the options we discuss below.

Sticks, or Military Tools

In the international system of the realist perspective that influences many political leaders, states must secure their interests by military power. Since there is no common power or central government and no agreement on rules governing the system, some countries use force or the threat of force to secure their interest and gain more power and influence in the international system. Other military tools include military aid or assistance, sharing intelligence, alliances, military research, and technological innovations (see Table 5.2). Sometimes the decision to deploy a weapon system can be a stick for diplomats to use. The G.W. Bush administration supported the development and deployment of a ballistic missile defense system in Eastern Europe to defend Europe against missiles from Iran or terrorist groups in the Middle East. Perhaps fearing growing US power and influence in the region, the Russian government saw the installation of such a defense system as a menace to Russia's security needs. Most recently, the Obama administration offered the Russians a carrot by declining to build the missile defense system.

Countries will adopt some weapons system to deter their enemies, but many countries seek military power to protect their interests in what international relations specialists call a "self-help world." Unfortunately, spending scarce national resources on military equipment does not guarantee safety. For instance, the United States enjoys military hegemony in the world today. The US spends more on its military than any other nation-state. Yet the sale of weapons by private actors and even many states has created real security challenges for the entire world. New security challenges presented by global terrorism networks have resulted in a number of new security arrangements and the sharing of both technical resources and military personnel. NATO, for example, has expanded its mandate to address the wars in both Iraq and Afghanistan. The United States is funding

Table 5.2

2004–2008 5 Largest Suppliers and Recipients of Major Conventional Weapons

Recipient	Share of global arms imports (%)	Main supplier (share of recipient's transfers)	Supplier	Share of global arms exports (%)	Main recipients (share of supplier's transfers)
USA	31	South Korea (15%)	**China**	11	Russia (92%)
		Israel (13%)			
		UAE (11%)	**India**	7	Russia (71%)
Russia	25	China (42%)			
		India (21%)	**UAE**	6	USA (54%)
		Algeria (8%)			
Germany	10	Turkey (15%)	**South Korea**	6	USA (73%)
		Greece (13%)			
		South Africa (12%)	**Greece**	4	Germany (31%)
France	8	UAE (32%)			
		Singapore (13%)			
		Greece (12%)			
UK	4	USA (21%)			
		India (14%)			
		Chile (9%)			

These facts and data are taken from chapter 7, appendix 7A, 'The suppliers and recipients of major conventional weapons', by the SIPRI Arms Transfers Project, and appendix 7B, 'The financial value of the arms trade', by Mark Bromley, and are based in part on the SIPRI Arms Transfers Database, http://armstrade.sipri.org/.

SIPRI Yearbook 2009: Armaments, Disarmament and International Security. Published in June 2009 by Oxford University Press on behalf of Stockholm International Peace Research Institute

The data in the table above was located on pages 14 and 15 of the SIPRI Yearbook 2009 Summary Booklet found at http://www.sipri.org/yearbook/2009/

some of these efforts and providing new technology, equipment, and training for its partners in the current war in Afghanistan.

The use of foreign policy "sticks" is not limited to leaders who have adopted the realist perspective on global politics. Liberals also recognize the importance of military tools of statecraft. Woodrow Wilson did not shy away from using America's military resources to help end WWI. However, he called for a collective security arrangement with the League of Nations. Wilson also supported arms-control treaties and pushed for more rules of war. Even today, progressive-liberal states like Canada, the Netherlands, and Denmark are active members of NATO and have willingly deployed their armed forces in Iraq and Afghanistan. Many middle and small powers are active participants in peacekeeping forces in conflict regions around the world. Collective humanitarian interventions and peacekeeping are military tools that are becoming more important in areas where states have failed to provide basic security or are disintegrating. The UN has some seventeen current peacekeeping operations, eight in Africa alone.

A new form of warfare may present major challenges for both liberals and realists. Cyberwarfare, or an attack on a country's computer and information systems, could be aimed at causing an economic collapse. Russia used cyberattacks in Estonia and Georgia to weaken confidence in these governments and make their citizens and leaders feel vulnerable to outside forces. Military resources are not much help here. How do you prevent this kind of attack and protect vital information networks? Most states are not well prepared for such an attack, and the perpetrators could be states, terrorist networks, or a single computer expert.

In addition to military inducements, states can also employ economic sticks. This type of influence can include product or economic boycotts, trade embargoes, sanctions, and punitive tariffs. Sanctions are used to both alter domestic politics and influence the foreign policy behavior of a target state. In the war on terrorism, the United States froze bank and investment assets from Afghanistan and Iraq as well as several Islamic charity organizations. Blocking access to multilateral lending institutions such as the World Bank and investment restrictions have become major tools in attempts to influence state behavior at home and abroad. Monetary sanctions involving the buying and selling of large quantities of a target state's currency in order to manipulate its exchange rate and create an economic crisis are another economic tool. Additionally, restrictions on travel and business are often used to force change in a society.

The best example of an effective sanction effort was the global, cultural, political, and economic boycott of South Africa during its apartheid regime. Currently, the United States is working with other members of the UN Security Council to punish North Korea for its production and testing of nuclear weapons. Similarly, the UN has initiated sanctions against Iran for its refusal to submit to inspections by the International Atomic Energy Agency. Economic tools need not be all negative. States often use the promise of material assistance to reach a desired goal.

Carrots: Foreign Assistance

Most of the wealthy states in the international system are donor states, or those states that give a significant amount of development assistance or aid to less wealthy or poor states. For donor states, development assistance is a means of pursuing foreign policy objectives. There are at least five forms of foreign assistance:

1. *Project aid* provides a grant or loan to a country or an NGO for a specific project.
2. *Program aid* is given to a government to create certain policy conditions in the recipient country, such as opening a market or supporting balance of payments.
3. *Technical assistance* provides a country with equipment or technicians in a given policy area.
4. *Humanitarian* or *disaster assistance* provides states funds for food, materials, and medicine and other basic supplies.
5. *Military* or *security aid* is often given to allies or partners in programs like the war on terrorism or to those participating in UN peacekeeping activities.

As we will discuss more fully in Chapter 13, aid is given for a variety of purposes, but even when giving humanitarian aid most states will tie their aid to national interests such as security, economic growth, or prestige. Food aid helps the hungry, but it also helps farmers in the donor state who sell their crops and cattle to the government. Even the most

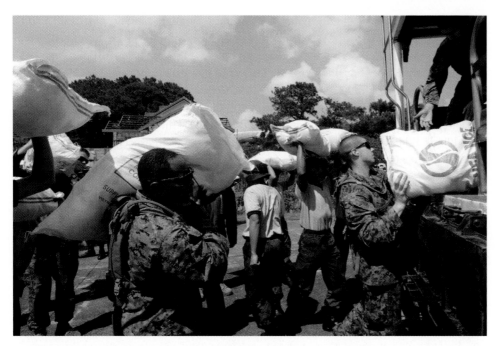

The United States no longer has bases in the Philippines, but marines provided humanitarian assistance after typhoons struck the country in October 2009. How is this an example of a "carrot"?

generous states use this economic tool to serve some of their own domestic interests. Assistance programs include the sharing of expertise and technology. Giving humanitarian assistance may also enhance a state's prestige and its image in the international system. Christine Ingebritsen (2006, 283) argues that the small countries of Scandinavia, consistently major donors, have played a pivotal role in promoting global social justice and strengthening norms of ethical behavior (see Chapter 10). These small and middle powers have used carrots such as development assistance, trade agreements, and other nonforce resources to encourage peaceful resolution of conflict, promote multilateralism, and work toward a more equitable distribution of global wealth. A typical Nordic aid program might include funding for public health and education, environmental protection, promotion of human rights and democracy, and family planning. The Nordic countries also give a high percentage of their aid to multilateral organizations and NGOs working in developing regions of the world (see Figure 5.2). About 40 percent of UNICEF's budget comes from Nordic countries, and organizations like Oxfam and Save the Children receive funds from Nordic governments.

Development assistance or aid programs in the United States are administered by the US Agency for International Development (USAID). Under the Clinton administration, USAID goals were trimmed from thirty to five. These reflected the neoliberal goals of the administration, for the enlargement of democratic and capitalist states:

1. Provision of human relief
2. Stabilization of population growth
3. Promotion of democracy
4. Environmental protection
5. Economic growth

These goals changed slightly with the Bush administration. Namely, a focus was placed on preventing HIV/AIDS, and family planning programs were no longer supported.

Other economic tools include trade agreements, the provision of loans, and the sharing of development or trade experts. Countries give economic resources in two main methods: directly to another country, in what are called "bilateral agreements"; or indirectly, through global institutions like the World Bank, the International Monetary Fund (IMF), and a variety of regional development banks like the Asian Development Bank. World Bank aid in the developing world can finance a range of projects, such as rural electrification or creating an export-driven agricultural market.

Sermons: Diplomatic Messaging and the Use of the Media

Military and economic sticks address material interests. "Sermons" address ideal interests. These might include *demarches,* or simple warnings, directives, or position statements sent to governments as a form of moral suasion. A charismatic leader giving a speech to the world can be a powerful diplomatic tool. President Obama's speech on June 4, 2009, given in Cairo, Egypt, addressed a global audience and was a clear attempt to convince the Muslim world that the US policy toward Islam was going to change. Minutes after its completion, the United States government had it on the Internet in several languages. Time will tell if this particular speech will succeed; as a kind of public diplomacy it is an effective use of modern media and global communications to serve political purposes.

Raymond Aron, a renowned international relations scholar, called diplomacy the art of convincing without the use of force. **Diplomacy** plays a critical role in the preservation of peace and world order. Many experts consider diplomacy as a lost art undermined by advanced communications, summit meetings, the increasing importance of international and regional organizations, and the demands of a global media industry that is persistently looking for information and often exposing secret agreements. Traditional diplomatic historians assert that diplomacy performs four important functions:

diplomacy The process by which international actors communicate as they seek to resolve conflicts without going to war and find solutions to complex global problems.

1. Communication between actors
2. Negotiation
3. Participation in regional and international organizations
4. Promotion of trade and other economic interests

Figure 5.2 Top Ten Foreign Aid Donors, 2007
Do you see a pattern among the countries that are on this list? What motivates these states to give such large amounts of aid?

Top Ten Aid Donors in 2007

Norway, Sweden, Luxembourg, Netherlands, Denmark, Ireland, Australia, Belgium, Finland, France

Percent of GNI

Diplomats today must deal with a host of new global challenges that require cooperation among state and nonstate actors. Diplomatic meetings aimed at addressing global challenges like climate change, terrorism, organized crime, human rights, and international investments are becoming major sources of power for countries with basic knowledge, scientific expertise, and the means to implement the policies. The role states play in the development of global regimes (see Chapter 8) is an important source of power in this era of globalization. Small and middle powers tend to value the role of diplomacy and use some of their most qualified foreign policy experts in diplomatic roles.

Public diplomacy is fast becoming an important foreign policy tool. In the past this form of diplomacy might have been called propaganda, but today it involves telling the world about the positive characteristics of your society. These educational, cultural, and informational programs are also an important source of power. Countries can provide funds for educational exchanges of students, faculty, and diplomats. The United States Fulbright Program, for example, sends students and scholars from the United States around the world and brings foreign scholars to the United States. Concerts, book tours, movies, and art exhibits are all part of a country's efforts to promote its values and cultural attributes. During the Cold War, the US Information Agency sponsored tours of jazz bands to the Soviet Union and other communist countries.

> **public diplomacy** The use of media, the Internet, and other social culture outlets to communicate the message of a state.

Media sources are also ways to promote a state's interests and make a state attractive to others. For example, the BBC and the Voice of America provide global radio programs that attract listeners and learners across the world, and during the Cold War, Radio Moscow provided a Soviet perspective on news events.

Finally, in a world of nuclear weapons and internal wars that kill both civilians and soldiers, **coercive diplomacy** has become a valuable foreign policy tool because "it seeks to persuade an opponent to cease his aggression" rather than going to war (George 1991, 5). In 1990, the first Bush administration used a strategy of coercive diplomacy in an attempt to get Saddam Hussein to leave Kuwait. The Bush administration made a clear demand, or *ultimatum,* that the Iraqi government ignored. The administration then took a variety of steps that involved the buildup of forces, economic sanctions, and diplomatic maneuvers in the United Nations. This strategy of gradually turning the screw was aimed at getting Iraq to see how costly a war with the United States and a coalition of forces representing some thirty-six countries would be. In this case, coercive diplomacy failed because Iraq did not back down, and the US-led coalition destroyed the Iraqi military with the blessings of the UN and most of the world community.

> **coercive diplomacy** The use of diplomatic and military methods that force a state to concede to another state. These methods may include the threat of force and the actual mobilization of military forces so as to gradually "turn the screw" but exclude the actual use of force. The implication is that war is the next step if diplomacy fails.

Soft and Hard Power in Foreign Policy

One way to understand the methods of foreign policy making is to think of both carrots and sticks as **hard power** tools. However, these inducements and threats are only part of the diplomatic process in the international system. Harvard professor and former Clinton administration official Joseph Nye introduced the concept of **soft power**, or the ability to "shape the preferences of others" (2004, 5–15). Soft power, as Nye presented the concept, tries to co-opt people and countries rather than to simply threaten or coerce them. Political leaders can use soft power to encourage cooperation and to shape what other states want in the international system. A country's culture and ideology are important sources of soft power.

> **hard power** The material threats and inducements leaders employ to achieve the goals of their state.
>
> **soft power** Influence and authority deriving from the attraction that a country's political, social, and economic ideas, beliefs, and practices have for people living in other countries.

Nye asserts that the soft power of any country is based on three sources: (1) its culture, (2) its political values, and (3) its foreign policy. If a country's culture is attractive to others, it can be a source of power. Similarly, if a country's political values—like democracy and

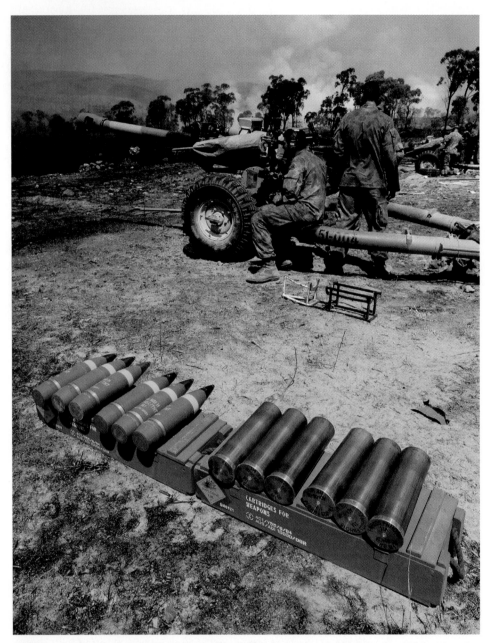

Middle powers like Australia can also face security threats and need "hard power" to attain their goals. How might diplomacy help the country achieve its security needs?

respect for human rights—are attractive to other citizens and other states, then that country can gain power and influence in the international system. Finally, a country with a moral foreign policy can also have power and influence in the international system. From this view, the United States may have lost its international standing because of its use of torture and prisoner abuse in Iraq and secret prisons around the world; when the United States lost moral credibility, its foreign policy activities were more likely to be seen as unethical by most of the global community. Nye suggests that if a country promotes values that other states want, leadership will cost less.

Soft power is not merely the same as influence. After all, influence can also rest on the hard power of threats or payments. Soft power is more than just persuasion, or the ability to move people by arguments, though that is an important part of it. It is also the ability to attract, and attraction often leads to acquiescence. Simply put, in behavioral terms soft power is *attractive power*.

Both hard- and soft-power tools will be an important part of any future leader's foreign policy doctrine and policy agenda. In this **nonpolar** world (Haass 2008), where no one state or group of states controls all power and authority, and where power and influence are distributed among a variety of state and nonstate actors, it will be harder to control these actors and even harder to build multilateral alliances to respond to global chal-

Salam Fayyad, prime minister of the Palestinian Authority, Jens Stoltenberg, center, prime minister of Norway, and Tony Blair, special envoy of the Middle East Quartet and former UK prime minister, represent small states and an informal international organization. How might their actions fit the model of "soft power"?

lenges. With no clear concentration of power in many policy areas, the number of threats and vulnerabilities is likely to increase, and states will need to work harder to maintain order and stability. Most experts predict that all states and transnational actors will need to combine resources to address the most significant global problems the world faces. The entire global effort aimed at addressing climate change, for example, will require major collective action. Globalization may not have changed enduring national interests such as the search for security and prosperity, but it has certainly changed how states pursue these interests.

nonpolar An international system in which power is not concentrated in a few states but is diffused among a variety of state and nonstate actors.

Explaining Foreign Policy

As a student of foreign policy, you might be interested in finding answers to puzzles or unexpected actions by a state. Why did North Korea's leaders decide to develop nuclear weapons? Why do Nordic governments give so much development assistance? Why does China's government continue to seek influence with the regime in Sudan that supports—or does little to stop—the killing in Darfur? These are complex issues, but there are some explanations that are better than others. Foreign policy analysis is the search for factors or variables that explain the most about a state's behavior. Scholars doing research in this area are interested in questions like the following: Why do states behave in a certain way? What factors explain a state's behavior? Why do leaders pick one option over another? If a state spends a significant amount of money on its military, what factors explain that choice? Although there are always questions about "agency," or which actors actually make foreign policy, foreign policy analysis offers plausible explanations for foreign policy behavior. We say "plausible explanations" because this is not an exact science: the social scientist trying to explain foreign policy puzzles can never replicate the certainty of the natural scientist working in the lab and controlling all the variables. Yet if the social scientist can identify factors that shape foreign policy, it might help us better understand the foreign policy process and even predict how states might behave in similar situations. In the next section, we will discuss one such approach to the agency question: levels of analysis.

Levels of Analysis in Foreign Policy. There are many factors that influence foreign policy. Based on what you've read here, which level of factors is more important in a crisis situation?

Levels of Analysis

In Chapter 1, we discussed how some research in international relations attempts to replicate the research methods and assumptions of the natural sciences. The idea here is that one can develop theories, test them by gathering evidence, and find useful explanations for the decisions made by leaders. Foreign policy analysis, a subfield of international relations, puts the individual at the center of decision making. Most studies of decision making begin with the assumption that all decision makers act rationally or always act to maximize benefits and minimize costs. In his classic study of decision making in a crisis situation, *Essence of Decision*, Graham Allison (1971) introduces three models, or analytical tools, for explaining decision making. The first, the rational-actor model, or RAM, provides a useful example of using rationality. The other two models, organizational behavior and bureaucratic politics, are second-level or domestic-level tools. Unfortunately, some foreign policy decision makers cannot meet the requirements of rationality. For example, it may not be possible for policy makers to know all of their options and assign values to those options. They may lack access to information that is essential to selecting policies that result in value maximization. Thus, other factors, like a decision maker's belief system, the political structure of a state, or the distribution of power in the international system, may influence the range of choices and the eventual policy choice.

Most texts suggest that there are three levels of analysis: *individual*, or the human dimension, *national* attributes, or domestic factors, and *systemic* conditions, or the nature of the international system. A number of scholars have added a fourth level that focuses on *global* conditions or factors. Discussions about the importance of globalization and technological innovations like the Internet suggest that these are potentially factors that influence decisions made by national leaders.

Individual, or the Human Dimension

We assume that all leaders are rational actors (i.e., always selecting a policy path that maximizes benefits and minimizes costs), but other factors like beliefs, personality factors, images, and perceptions also shape decision making. Foreign policy research suggests that these other factors or filters are most important in a crisis situation, a decision requiring secrecy and thus involving few actors, or a decision demanding a quick response. This level is also important when a leader is given a great deal of latitude to make a decision and when the decision maker has an interest or expertise in foreign policy. To act rationally, leaders must be able to know all of their options, be capable of assigning values to these options, and have enough information to select the higher valued options. Those who use these other idiosyncratic factors like *belief systems* or *personality types* to explain behavior do not believe any decision maker can be rational all of the time. Most decision makers operate in an environment of uncertainty with imperfect information. Many leaders talk about "going with their gut" when they are making decisions in crises, but they are usually relying on previous experience (e.g., analogical reasoning) or their worldview (e.g., realism or liberalism). Leaders filter information based on their worldviews and generally seek programs that fit with these beliefs. Former British prime minister Margaret Thatcher, with a strong realist belief system, convinced George H. W. Bush to take the 1990 Iraqi invasion of Kuwait seriously and respond militarily. She also decided to use force rather than diplomacy to take back the Falkland Islands after the Argentine invasion in 1982.

Domestic Sources, or National Attributes

At the domestic or national level, researchers look at a country's history, traditions, and its political, economic, cultural, and social structures. More permanent elements like geographic location and resource base also matter in this set of factors. Changing elements such as military power, economic wealth, and demographic factors also shape policy. A powerful variable in many democratic societies is domestic politics, or electoral calculations. Politicians often find that they are unable to achieve their desired goals because of demands of the election cycle. A further complication is the role of bureaucracies in the policy process. Unelected civil servants can influence outcomes that the politicians want. Examples of this are found in the range of academic work, beginning with Graham Allison's study of the Cuban missile crisis, *The Essence of Decision*. In his exploration of crisis decision making within the Kennedy administration, Allison found that **standard operating procedures (SOPs)**, or the way things are usually done in an organization, employed by governmental agencies, as well as the inherent goal of all bureaucrats to gain more power and influence in the decision-making process, are major determinants of foreign policy behavior. Large organizations employ SOPs to respond to a range of events. For instance, when a natural disaster like a hurricane or earthquake happens, agencies have plans ready to provide the correct kind of assistance. Normally, a state's agencies of all kinds—military, intelligence, foreign affairs—all have SOPs ready for every foreseeable eventuality. Bureaucratic politics, Allison's third model, suggests that within every government, bureaucratic agencies compete with each other for control over resources and policy. The result of this competition is eventually the policy.

standard operating procedures (SOPs) The prepared-response patterns that organizations create to react to general categories of events, crises, and actions.

Systemic Factors

The anarchic nature of the international system may be the most important factor at this level. However, as we have seen in this book, countries take individual and collective actions to cope with the lack of global central authority. Thus treaties, alliances, and trade conventions, which states agree to abide by, are seen as systemic constraints. These are formal contracts created by states in an attempt to provide order in the system.

A country's behavior is also shaped by more informal constraints based on traditions, common goals, and shared norms. For example, most states respect the sovereignty of all states, and most follow the rule of international law. These laws cannot be enforced, but states abide by them because they expect others to do the same. This notion of **reciprocity** is the primary incentive for states to support a rule-based international system. The distribution of power in the system (e.g., bipolar, multipolar, or nonpolar) and the nature of order (e.g., balance of power, collective security) are also important system-level factors. Neorealists believe that the lack of a common power or a central government at the global level is the defining element of international relations, and a state's foreign policy is primarily aimed at survival in this anarchic system. This anarchic condition of the system is described by Kenneth Waltz (1959, 238).

reciprocity A form of statecraft that employs retaliatory strategy, only cooperating if others do likewise.

> Each state pursues its own interests, however defined, in ways it judges best. Force is a means of achieving the external ends of states because there exists no consistent, reliable process of reconciling the conflicts of interest that inevitably arise among similar units in a condition of anarchy.

Liberals, on the other hand, believe that anarchy forces states to create rules and develop regimes or governing arrangements aimed at encouraging cooperation and multilateralism.

The threat of terror attacks by people claiming to be Muslims have pushed Dmitry Medvedev, Russian Federation president, and Mukhu Aliev, leader of the primarily Muslim Dagestan region of the Federation, to present a front of cordial relations.

Today, many liberals are focused on more effective global governance across policy areas. As the world has learned with the recent global economic crisis, rules and regulations that govern all markets are indeed essential.

Global Factors

These variables are often confused with system-level factors. Global-level variables can be the outcome of decisions made by individuals, interest groups, states, or nonstate actors. They may also be the results of natural conditions. These factors cannot be traced to the actions of any one state or even group of states. In fact, they usually challenge the ideas of boundaries and sovereignty. A technological innovation that is diffused through the system by a variety of actors but does not belong to any single actor comes to mind. The Internet and the information revolution may be an appropriate example here. The movement of capital by multinational banks, the broadcasts of CNN, and the revolutionary ideas of religious fundamentalists all represent global factors that might shape policy behavior. These global factors are pushed and promoted by the process of globalization. On the natural side, pollution, pandemics like HIV/AIDS, SARS, the swine flu, and weather patterns may also have an impact on foreign policy. Environmental conditions such as global warming and drought may lead to new alliances or to conflicts over the control of critical resources. As writers such as Peter Gleik and Michael Klare have shown, there is a very real possibility of "water wars" in the Middle East and Africa. These conditions may be the result of actions taken by specific national or transnational actors, but the effects are felt globally.

For our last example of global factors, consider how the Internet and other forms of telecommunication technology have been used by both radical groups and humanitarian groups to rally support for their causes and to challenge the power of key states. No one state owns the Internet, or the various messaging services, and yet these can be valuable tools aimed at shaping foreign policy.

positivists Analysts who use the scientific method to structure their research.

Usually social scientists do not combine variables to reach an explanation of a particular foreign policy decision. They are guided by the goals of precision and parsimony. Advocates of the scientific approach, or **positivists**, want to be able to say that US policy toward Iraq can best be explained by looking at the personality of George W. Bush or the power of the Defense Department and the Office of the Vice President in shaping policy. Each of these bureaucratic organizations made the case for war. What is exciting about research in our field is that there is always disagreement about which variables explain the most. Thus, someone could say with equal certainty that US economic interests, namely our dependency on oil, offer a better explanation for the decisions to launch a "war of choice," something we will discuss more in Chapter 8. The strength of anyone's argument is based on the quality of the empirical evidence that one collects to support the hypothesis being tested. We use the work of historians, public policy records, government documents, interviews, budgets, and journalists' accounts to gather evidence to confirm or reject our hypotheses.

We should remember that by explaining foreign policy we might be able to predict what states would do in a given situation. Likewise, we can use previous decisions as analogues and make suggestions or prescriptions for future foreign policy.

The Foreign Policy Process

So far we have examined the explanations and influences of foreign policy, answering questions of "why" and "what for"; in this section, we'll get down to the nuts and bolts and look at the process of "how" foreign policy comes about. You may be surprised to learn that the foreign policy–making apparatus of most democratic countries is basically the same. Political systems tend to divide the responsibility for decision making between members of the executive branch, which carries out the policies, and the deliberative or legislative branch, which sets spending priorities and guidelines for the executive to follow. Deliberative bodies often have a responsibility to oversee the actions of the executive branch. Both branches of government might subdivide responsibility further into geographic regions, economic sectors, or military affairs. In addition to the formal governmental actors with legal authority, there are also any number of individuals and groups outside the formal government structure that might seek to influence the policy process. The actors that comprise this informal sector vary by issue area, but they can include business groups, religious groups, news media, and private citizens.

As we suggested earlier in the chapter, even authoritarian or totalitarian states have decision-making processes in which government ministries debate issues and work with private interests to promote specific policy positions. Leaders rarely act alone and create a foreign policy that adheres specifically to their own interests. For example, the intransigence of North Korea and Cuba in their defiance of the United States and the international community is supported by military leaders and various bureaucrats within each state. However, in both states there are also oppositional groups.

Four Phases of Foreign Policy Making

The study of foreign policy making assumes that governmental officials with the legal authority to act do so in a logical manner. Political scientists call this the "rational-actor model" of foreign policy making. Proponents of this model assert that a government's foreign policy officials are able to (1) define a problem, (2) develop responses to the problem, (3) act upon one or more of the responses, and then (4) evaluate the effectiveness of the policy. In the following sections, we'll discuss these four phases in more depth.

Phase One: Initiation or Articulation Phase

Issues are often first articulated or otherwise promoted by media and interest groups attempting to influence the policy-making process. Information about a foreign policy issue is disseminated, and as public awareness of an issue increases, this informed public may pressure elected officials to either act on the issue or, in some cases, stay clear of the problem.

Both internal (or formal) and external (or informal) actors may push a particular position and pressure political leaders to take action. For example, in the case of the ongoing conflict and genocide in Darfur, NGOs using the Internet have been providing the public with information about the atrocities. These same NGOs have initiated further global-awareness campaigns with celebrities and notable public leaders that have attracted the attention of major media outlets and many elected officials who recognize the importance of the issue for either moral reasons or more pragmatic electoral calculations.

Individuals and research institutes (often called "think tanks") can initiate a debate about a foreign policy issue. Once public awareness increases, attentive members of the public might pressure a government to act. A natural disaster or an unexpected tragedy or crisis might also inspire some official reaction from governments. For example, in general the US public is not very supportive of increasing foreign aid, but if a flood or earthquake devastates an area, US citizens generally want the government to supply emergency aid. New technologies like the Internet and cell phones may actually contribute to the democratization of foreign policy. Today, citizens in industrialized states have an opportunity to be better informed than ever before, and they are presented with a variety of options to become actively involved in a particular issue area. Citizen involvement also now transcends borders: global or transnational social movements have mobilized citizens to work to end hunger, forgive debt, and end the use of certain weapons. These campaigns have been successful in their efforts to persuade governments to use official foreign policy tools to address their concerns. For example, Bono, the lead singer from the musical group U2, spent time with the late Senator Jesse Helms and other members of Congress as a representative of the Jubilee movement that urged wealthy states to forgive the debts of poor states. Other celebrities have joined members of the domestic Christian Coalition to increase awareness of the issues surrounding poverty and third world debt and to lobby both the executive branch of government and members of Congress.

Global and domestic actors also have an impact on policy makers in authoritarian or nondemocratic states. China continues to be a favorite target for human rights groups,

Table 5.3
Some US Policy Think Tanks

> **Brookings Institution** is a highly authoritative nonprofit public-policy organization whose mission is to conduct high-quality independent research and provide innovative, practical recommendations that strengthen American democracy; foster the economic and social welfare, security, and opportunity of all Americans; and secure a more open, safe, prosperous, and cooperative international system.
>
> **Council on Foreign Relations** is an independent, nonpartisan membership organization, think tank, and publisher dedicated to being a resource for its members, government officials, business executives, journalists, educators and students, civic and religious leaders, and other interested citizens in order to help them better understand the world and the foreign policy choices facing the United States and other countries. The council publishes *Foreign Policy*, a leading journal of international affairs and US foreign policy.
>
> **Heritage Foundation** is a conservative-leaning think thank committed to building an America where freedom, opportunity, prosperity, and civil society flourish.
>
> **Carnegie Endowment for International Peace (CEIP)** is one of America's leading institutions for researching and analyzing international affairs and making recommendations for US foreign policy. The CEIP, with over 100 employees, is headquartered in Washington, DC, with offices in four other countries.
>
> **RAND Corporation** is a nonprofit think tank first formed to offer research and analysis to the United States armed forces. The organization has since expanded to work with other governments, private foundations, international organizations, and commercial organizations on a host of nondefense issues.
>
> **American Enterprise Institute (AEI)** is a conservative think thank, founded in 1943. Its mission is "to defend the principles and improve the institutions of American freedom and democratic capitalism—limited government, private enterprise, individual liberty and responsibility, vigilant and effective defense and foreign policies, political accountability, and open debate."
>
> **Center for American Progress** is a liberal political-policy research and advocacy organization. Its website describes it as "a nonpartisan research and educational institute dedicated to promoting a strong, just and free America that ensures opportunity for all."

and they have had some impact on Chinese domestic policies. Tragically, many of these NGOs have had no impact on policy makers in failed states like Zimbabwe or extremist states like Sudan and Somalia.

Phase Two: The Formulation of Foreign Policy

The formulation phase involves the actual creation of an official government policy. Internal and external actors—individuals, interest groups, corporations, and foreign governments—initiate policy debates and put pressure on policy makers to act. The formulation phase is when parliaments, executive offices, ministries, and bureaucratic agencies work to develop an effective foreign policy. The idea to forgive the debt of third world countries is now discussed by relevant agencies within a government. Now the legislative branches debate the cost and benefits of forgiving debt, and specialists in various financial departments provide the essential information for the final policy position.

Specialists inside and outside of government provide the essential information for policy makers. Often, in the policy-making process, the original intention of the policy is loaded with other priorities that might help the politician get reelected or might help a bureaucracy gain more power and more resources. In noncrisis situations, foreign policy is formulated much like domestic policy. It is a complex process involving legislatures, executive agencies, ministries and departments, and a wide variety of interest communities.

In crisis situations, foreign policy is made by a smaller group of individuals and agencies. Since the end of the First World War, in the United States and many other Western democracies, the executive branch or cabinet has taken over the foreign policy process. Foreign ministries, defense departments, and special advisors to the prime minister or president are usually charged with responding to crisis. In the recent George W. Bush administration, decisions about the war in Iraq were made by a group of advisors scattered in the National Security Council, the vice president's office, and the Defense Department—while the State Department was often left out or its ideas dismissed by the president's inner circle.

Phase 1 - Initiate
Define the problem

Phase 2 - Formulate
Develop responses to the problem

Phase 3 - Implement
Act upon one or more of the responses

Phase 4 - Evaluate
Act upon one or more of the responses

A Typical Decision-Making Process. What do we mean by "rational actor"? What about this model suggests rationality? Of course this graphic is a simplification, for the sake of visualization. Can you draw a more complex process model, or flow-chart, based on what you have read so far? What other steps or loops would your model represent?

Although in most democracies elected members of legislatures serve on committees with foreign policy oversight, most of these committees react to policy plans formulated by the head of government and that person's advisors. Most legislative bodies do have budget responsibilities and can use this power to support or change foreign policy priorities. However, shrewd leaders who appeal to the public for support of their foreign policy actions can neutralize the legislature's power of the purse. Recently, for example, few members of the United States Congress challenged funding for military actions or aid programs for an important ally for fear of being called antimilitary or unpatriotic. Generally, when dealing in areas of foreign policy the old adage applies: "partisanship ends at the water's edge." After 9/11, it was very easy for the Bush administration to get congressional support for any program that could be framed as part of the global war on terror. Prime Minister Blair had the same advantages after the July attacks in Britain.

The British and Soviet war experiences in Afghanistan provided the background for the Dec. 8, 2009, House Armed Services Committee session with Stanley McChrystal, then-commander of US forces in Afghanistan, and Karl Eikenberry, US ambassador to Afghanistan, who were called to testify. How does the US war in Afghanistan illustrate the limits and possibilities of power in global politics?

US presidents since the end of WWII used the Cold War and the containment of communism around the world as justifications for financing an expansionary foreign policy. Hundreds of anticommunist organizations, the defense industries, and many ethnic communities, such as Polish and Hungarian Americans, kept pressure on US leaders to never ease up on the Soviet Union.

Phase Three: Foreign Policy Implementation

Once a policy is decided in a legislature or in a department or ministry, it is usually assigned to policy actors in a ministry or department and other affiliated actors in the field. These actors are expected to implement the policy. For example, if Congress passes a bill allocating funds for development assistance or foreign aid, the money is sent to the most appropriate agency: in this case, the US Agency for International Development (USAID), which receives the funds and distributes them to its various field offices. The money is then given to development projects that may have been organized by local governments, NGOs, and development agencies from other countries. It is not unusual for countries to form coalitions with local communities, NGOs, and other aid agencies. Funds are not always spent on intended projects, and they are often not spent at all. Corruption, project delays, new priorities, and leadership changes often get in the way of intended consequences. US agencies intending to reduce poverty in developing countries must deal with a variety of factors that might delay a program or prevent it from reaching its goals.

Phase Four: Foreign Policy Evaluation

Policy evaluation is the final step in the process, and it is rare that this step occurs. Although the review provision might be built into the program, the administrators of the policy might have a personal interest in keeping the program active. The media may focus their attention on the policy outcomes if the policy program was a success or a failure. All interested parties will have a position and will try to influence future decisions in this policy area. Often, the very public and private actors involved in the previous phases of the policy process will be involved in the evaluation of policy outcomes.

Most legislatures conduct public hearings related to major foreign policy expenditures. These hearings can become particularly important if a policy program has failed or had a major impact on a society. Consider, for instance, the Iraq Study Group's hearings on the Iraq War, or congressional committee hearings on the future of NATO or US trade policy toward China. Congress tends to use every opportunity to evaluate the foreign policy activities of a particular administration. In some political systems, like the UK and Canada, the prime minister must face the parliamentary opposition during a legislative session called "question time." This is a form of evaluation that generally attracts a great deal of public attention and comments from opposition politicians.

Another form of evaluation that usually triggers policy actions are comprehensive studies done by universities, think tanks, research institutions, and NGOs. Human Rights Watch, Greenpeace, the International Crisis Group, the International Committee of the Red Cross, and hundreds of other interest groups provide policy makers with comprehensive studies on just about every foreign policy issue area (see Chapter 7 for more on NGOs). To illustrate, in 2007 the Red Cross (ICRC) released a report on the "treatment of high value detainees" being held by the CIA. This report may have a major impact on future decisions about how to treat individuals taken prisoner in the war on terrorism.

Central America: A Perpetual Pursuit of Union?

The foreign policies of Central American states can seem to present a paradox. The observer sees a number of small countries, with a common history, a relatively high degree of common identity, and apparently everything to gain from integration, but which have consistently failed, so far, to achieve the ambitious regional goals they proclaim. This is a case of particularistic domestic goals undermining what seems to some outside observers to be a logical regional option.

Following independence, the Captaincy-General of Guatemala became the Federal Republic of Central America (1823–1839), before splitting into Guatemala, El Salvador, Honduras, Nicaragua, and Costa Rica. Restoration of this union has been a constant theme in integrationist discourse. Yet Central America was more a collection of communities than a clearly defined overarching entity, local elites elsewhere resisted leadership by Guatemala, and Costa Rica early on showed a tendency toward isolationism. Nationalism grew, unionism was undermined by conflict, and outside involvement was often unhelpful. A powerful mythology of union thus coexisted with various sources of division.

A first Central American Peace Conference in Washington, convened in 1907 to help end local conflicts, led to a short-lived Central American Court of Justice (1908–1918). The Organization of Central American States (ODECA) was created in 1951. The first organizations of functional cooperation emerged around this time. Some twenty-five such bodies now exist, covering everything from water to electrical energy, creating a complex web of regional interactions. Formal economic integration began in 1960, with the Central American Common Market (CACM). Intraregional trade grew, but the system entered crisis at the end of the 1960s. Efforts at reform in the 1970s were overtaken by political crisis and conflicts. In the 1980s, integration became associated with the Central American peace process. In this context of confidence building, a Central American Parliament was created as a forum for regional dialogue. In

1991, with conflicts in El Salvador and Nicaragua ended, the Cold War over, and a new wave of regional integration across the world, a new period began with the Central American Integration System (SICA). This aimed to provide a global approach to integration, with four subsystems—political, economic, social, and cultural.

The institutional system is concentrated around the presidential summits. The Central American Parliament is directly elected but has no powers. It does not include Costa Rica. As of 2006, only El Salvador, Honduras, and Nicaragua participated in the Central American Court of Justice. There have been repeated discussions of institutional reform. By 2005, intraregional trade represented around 27 percent of exports and 12 percent of imports. Most goods originating in Central American countries enjoy free circulation. The same levels of external tariff were being applied for 95 percent of goods. General negotiations for a Central American customs union began in 2004. The future is being shaped also by international agreements. The Central American countries signed a free trade agreement with the US in 2004, modeled on NAFTA, and in 2006 also began to negotiate an association agreement with the European Union including a free trade agreement. The pursuit of union continues at the international level, hindered by goals and motivations found at the individual and domestic levels of analysis.

Effective regional cooperation has eluded the countries of Central America. Can prestige and power help us to understand why?

Foreign Policy Styles and Traditions

Now that we have considered the many moving parts of foreign policy, let's take a step back and consider the bigger picture, how it all works together—i.e., the various styles and traditions of foreign policy, as well as the various ways in which great powers, middle powers, and weak states may differ in their approaches.

Analysts of foreign policy behavior often assert that factors such as the geographic size of a country, its resource base, and its population can determine the kind of foreign policy—or style—that a country will undertake. A **foreign policy style** is often the result of the ways in which the country deals with other members of the international community. When this style continues over a long period of time, we call it a **foreign policy tradition**. Both the foreign policy style and tradition include a common set of public assumptions about the role of the state in the international system. A tradition includes national beliefs about how the world works and what leaders must do to secure their national interests. Styles and traditions promote different foreign policy strategies, and each suggests different sets of policy priorities. In this section we discuss some aspects of foreign policy style and foreign policy tradition.

Great Powers, Middle Powers, and Small States

The foreign policy of all states is aimed at securing national interests and responding to the needs, values, and interests of their citizens. All states seek a role, or *niche*, in the international system. James Rosenau (1981) suggested that all states develop a strategy for adapting to the conditions created by the international system. Smaller states with limited resources and little capacity to influence other powers by unilateral actions are likely to select an acquiescent strategy. This strategy suggests they will adapt their interests to fit with the interests of larger and more powerful regional or global leaders. Consider for example the role of "client states" and alliances during the Cold War. These states followed the lead of the US or the USSR and were rewarded with the promise of security and prosperity in the form of aid, military assistance, and trade agreements.

Those states that were once global leaders and even hegemonic powers at times seek policies aimed at preserving their power and status in the international system. This preservative strategy is employed by countries like the United Kingdom and France. Preservative policies include taking a leadership role in international and regional organizations, identifying issues that need attention, and taking the lead in responding to these challenges. The UK's efforts to lead the debt-relief campaign and France's role in the Middle East peace talks are examples of this behavior.

The most powerful states seek to retain and possibly increase their power and authority by adapting a **promotive foreign policy**. The United States and the Soviet Union promoted their views, values, and interests after WWII as they competed for the hearts and minds of all citizens around the globe. Each superpower created an alliance structure that divided the world into two armed camps with the capacity to destroy the world as we know it. After the Cold War, the US leaders talked about establishing a new world order that served the interests of the United States and its allies. Some experts talked about the unipolar moment, a time when the United States could promote its values, traditions, and interests to create a peaceful and prosperous world.

There are always states that believe that the existing international system is unfair, oppressive, violent, and alienating. These states seek to transform the international system

foreign policy style Often shaped by a state's political culture, history, and traditions, this describes how a country deals with other states and how it approaches any decision-making situation. For example, does it act unilaterally or multilaterally; does it seek consensus on an agreement or does it go with majority rule?

foreign policy tradition A tradition includes national beliefs about how the world works and a list of national interests and priorities based on these beliefs. It also refers to past actions or significant historical events that act as analogs and give guidance to leaders about what strategy would best secure their national interests.

promotive foreign policy A foreign policy that promotes the values and interests of a state and seeks to create an international system based on these values.

by promoting an **intransigent foreign policy**. These states do not accept the "rules of the game" and mobilize their resources to challenge the great powers in the international system. During the 1960s and 1970s, leaders of the Nonaligned Movement (NAM)—namely, Cuba, Pakistan, India, and Indonesia—pushed intransigent policy programs challenging the dominant rules of the game. Today, North Korea and Iran are challenging great-power rules, namely, the rules that restrict the number of states with nuclear weapons.

To a certain extent, these four **adaptation strategies** describe the foreign policies of states today. Some international relations theorists propose that the choice from among these strategies is linked to a given country's size or influence in the international system. This assertion has been, at times, the center of a significant debate among academics. While it is clear that countries choose a foreign policy strategy because of their resources and needs, it is not always the case that size determines a particular policy option. A brief overview of what we might expect from great, middle, and small powers follows. States are constantly adapting to changes in the international system and to the domestic factors that might limit a state's ability to act in the system or, conversely, provide opportunities for more active participation.

Great-Power Foreign Policy

Most of the research about **great power** politics and foreign policy is shaped by traditional realist assumptions about world politics and as a result tends to ignore cases that contradict the academic goal of a parsimonious theory. It is also, as we learned in Chapter 3, an arguably bleak perspective, because it sees enemies everywhere. For example, John Mearsheimer (2001, 29–32), an influential realist scholar, contends that great powers always seek to maximize their share of world power and all great powers seek hegemony in the international system.

For all great powers, survival is the primary goal. These states all think strategically about how to survive in a system in which all states are potential threats. More specifically, the goals of great powers include advancing the economic and political interests of their people and maintaining the rules and institutions in the international system that serve their interests. The United States and its allies created the primary institutions of global governance after WWII. The only significant challenge to that system was advanced by the Soviet Union. Some have called the Cold War a war about whose rule book would be followed. With the end of the Cold War, there is now only one rule book, and the current battle is over which rules to apply and how to apply them. Those countries invited to the G-8 and G-20 meetings are all great global powers and great regional powers. They are meeting to debate about the best way to respond to the current economic crisis, and what they decide will affect the entire world.

Mistrust and uncertainty force states to act always in accordance with their own self-interest. Mearsheimer (2001, 33) suggests that great powers act "selfishly in a self-help world." This means the foreign policies of great powers are focused on gaining power and authority in the military world and beyond. Great powers seek to lead in all policy sectors. The dominant currency is military power, and all great powers must respond to the **security dilemma**. Without any form of central authority in the international system, states must seek security through military power and security alliances. Since all states are potential threats, foreign policy for great powers might be described as a "ceaseless competition" for security, power, and authority in all policy sectors.

intransigent foreign policy
A foreign policy that challenges the rules established by the great powers or rule-making states.

adaptation strategies
A foreign policy based on reacting to international events and adjusting national goals to conform to the effects of events external to that state.

great power State that has the political, economic, and military resources to shape the world beyond its borders. In most cases such a state has the will and capacity to define the rules of the international system.

security dilemma In an anarchic international system, one with no common central power, when one state seeks to improve its security it creates insecurity in other states.

middle powers These states, because of their position and past roles in international affairs, have very distinctive interests in the future order. Middle powers are activists in international and regional forums, and they are confirmed multilateralists in most issue areas. They support an equitable and pluralistic rule-based system. They are, for the most part, trading states and thus favor a relatively open and stable world market. Since stability is so important to them, most middle powers see themselves as global problem solvers, mediators, and moderators in international disputes [Wood 1998 and Holbraad 1984].

niche diplomacy Every state has its national interests and its areas of comparative advantage over others international actors. This is their area of expertise and where they have the greatest interests. Hence, this is where the state concentrates its foreign policy resources.

Middle-Power Foreign Policy

Relying again on realist assumptions and definitions, a scholar might focus on national attributes such as land area, resource base, population, and military capabilities to distinguish **middle powers** from small or weak states and great powers. However, in a world where power and influence are no longer solely defined in terms of physical attributes and military strength, a state's behavior or experience in various policy situations may provide better insights into how that state sees itself and how others see its role in the international system. Most middle powers are liberal states with social democratic political systems and economies based on trade. This means their survival and prosperity depend on global stability and order. These states seek incremental reform by extending a liberal world order, which they see as the most effective way to achieve both human and national security. Canada, Australia, and the Nordic countries are great examples of active middle powers.

In describing the importance of a "behavioral" measure of middle powers, Cooper, Higgot, and Nossal (1993) describe their attributes as follows:

A. *Catalysts*: States that provide resources and expertise to take leadership roles in global initiatives.
B. *Facilitators*: States that play active roles in setting agendas in global policy discussions and building coalitions for collaborative responses.
C. *Managers*: Middle powers that support institution building at the international level and encourage support for existing international organizations and multinational activities.

The same authors quote Gareth Evans, a former Australian minister for foreign affairs and trade, in describing a concept called **niche diplomacy**. This form of middle-

Mahmoud Ahmadinejad is the controversial leader of Iran, whose military has limited power-projection capability and whose territory possesses few resources beyond oil. How has Ahmadinejad attempted to change the role and power of Iran in the international system?

power activism "involves concentrating resources in specific areas best able to generate returns worth having, rather than trying to cover the field" (Cooper et al. 1993, 25–26).

The middle powers, because of their position and past roles in international affairs, have very distinctive interests in the future order. Middle powers are activists in international and regional forums, and they are confirmed multilateralists in most issue areas. They actively support an equitable and pluralistic rule-based system. They are, for the most part, trading states and thus favor a relatively open and stable world market. Since stability is so important to them, most middle powers see themselves as global problem solvers, mediators, and moderators in international disputes (Wood 1998 and Holbraad 1984). Middle powers usually play a leadership role in regional organizations (e.g., the European Union) and in functionally specific institutions such as the World Health Organization (WHO) and the Development Assistance Committee (DAC) of the Organization of Economic Cooperation and Development (OECD).

A third view of middle powers places an emphasis on the **normative orientation** of this group of states. Although subject to much criticism, the image of middle powers as potentially more wise and virtuous than other states is usually promoted by national leaders and progressive interest groups in order to gain domestic support for international activism and to enhance the reputation of their states in the international community. This image of global moral leaders, bridging the gap between rich and poor communities, fits well with the egalitarian social democratic values of most Western middle powers. Robert Cox (1989, 834–35) argues that the traditional normative aims of middle powers, namely, greater social equity and a call for more diffusion of power in the system, might give them more leverage as principled problem solvers in continuing economic and political challenges faced by all states in the system today.

normative orientation in foreign policy this means promoting certain norms and values and being prescriptive in one's foreign policy goals .

The middle powers may play a critical role as the catalysts of problem-solving initiatives or the managers of regimes initiated by greater powers with less interest for internationalism and little domestic support for egalitarian goals and values.

Small-State Foreign Policy

Researchers agree that small states are defined by a small land mass, GNP, and population. In addition, they usually do not have large military forces or the resources to have a significant impact on global politics. However, if they act in concert with other states, it is possible for small states to have an impact on the system. For example, the like-minded states that played a pivotal role in the formation of the International Criminal Court (ICC) included a coalition of small and middle powers.

Small states can also identify a niche and develop expertise in a given policy area. Most wealthy small states, like Belgium or New Zealand, often focus their foreign policy on trade and economic issues. They will also participate in regional organizations and at times take leadership roles in crisis situations. New Zealand, along with Australia and the island state of Vanuatu, took the lead to create a nuclear-free zone in the Pacific in 1985. The Reagan administration's response to this

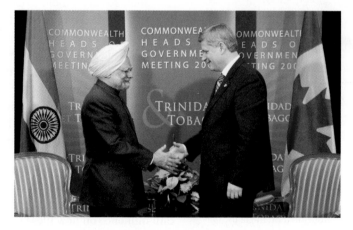

Organizations like the Commonwealth Heads of Government provide a forum for like-minded states to work together to solve regional and global problems. Given what you have learned about the concept of power in global politics, why should large and powerful states listen to less powerful states?

action demonstrates the limits to small-state actions: when the New Zealand Labour government banned nuclear-capable US Navy ships from its harbors, the United States terminated security cooperation with the country. Belgium is one of the most active members of the European Union, NATO, and every other regional and international organization. Because of its colonial past, it has worked with many African states in development and peacekeeping activities.

It should be stated that with the end of the Cold War and the intensity of forces of globalization there has been a change in the valuation of states' capacities and their potential influence in the international system. After all, military power may not be as important as policy expertise or technology in this new world where new security challenges include climate change, pandemics, poverty, and cyberwarfare. Foreign policy in a **nonpolar world** (i.e., power is diffused and held by a variety of state and nonstate actors) is less constrained by the structure of the system and allows for more flexibility and independence. Globalization has also increased the number of opportunities for citizen participation, and technology like the Internet makes it much easier to organize for a specific cause or policy position and to promote a small state's national interest in the global community.

Some small states have taken on the role of norm entrepreneurs in the international system. Christine Ingebritsen (2006, 275) describes this role:

> Thus, Scandinavia, a group of militarily weak, economically dependent small states, pursues "social power" by acting as a norm entrepreneur in the international community. In three policy areas (the environment, international security, and global welfare), Scandinavia has acted to promote a particular view of the good society.

Other attributes of small-state foreign policy include the following (Henderson et al. 1980, 3–5):

- Most small states have limited financial and human resources and thus have to decide carefully when and where to participate. Generally, this means a limited global role and a focus on their geographic region and the interests of their own citizens.
- With limited resources (their citizens), most small states focus on economic and trade issues.
- Small states generally take an active role in regional and international organizations. Multilateralism is a preferred strategy, and small states consider it the best way to secure their interests.
- Small states can play critical roles in alliances and in global policy regimes. Many of these states have resources and expertise, and they seek roles as global problem solvers in policy areas of importance to their domestic population.

As the space between domestic and foreign policy sectors blurs or even disappears, domestic politics and the interests of citizens play a greater role in shaping foreign policy. In both small and middle powers, what citizens expect from states at home has a significant influence on how these states behave internationally.

The Evolution of US Foreign Policy

As we noted earlier, the foreign policy traditions of all countries include sets of assumptions about the role of a country in the international system. A tradition includes beliefs about how the world works and what leaders must do to secure their national interests.

nonpolar world a world in which there are many power centers and many of them are not nation-states. Power is diffused and is in many hands in many policy areas.

Satisfied   Dissatisfied

Power and Political Satisfaction. Citizens who live in "great powers" report higher satisfaction with the status quo than those in middle powers. Based on what you have read in this chapter, why do you think that is so? *Source: Adapted from Kugler, Tammen, and Elfired (2004, 165).*

Theory in Practice

The Impact of Globalization on Different Kinds of States

The Asian economic crisis highlights the different capacities that states have to respond to globalization. Even though all states in the region were affected by the crisis, their responses suggested that some enjoyed more choice or "sovereignty" than others. Indonesia, Thailand, and Korea turned to the International Monetary Fund for assistance conditional on several policies mostly defined by the IMF, itself in Washington, DC. Meanwhile, Malaysia formulated its own strategy for adjustment and imposed policies such as capital controls, which were greatly disapproved of in Washington, DC. Although globalists and skeptics treat all states as equal in their arguments about globalization, it is worth questioning this.

One way to think about the impact of globalization is to distinguish between strong states and weak states. At the extreme end, strong states are those that shape the rules and institutions which have made a global economy possible: we have already seen the way US policies shaped the creation, implementation, and breakdown of the Bretton Woods system. A more general description of strong states is that they can control—to some degree—the nature and speed of their integration into the world economy. Into this category we might place not only relatively strong industrialized countries but also developing countries such as Brazil, Malaysia, China, Iraq, and Iran. In all of these cases, globalization is having a powerful effect, as evidenced by the restructuring of national and private industries in industrialized countries, the past decade of economic liberalization in Brazil, and, in a radically different way, through international

coercive interventions in Iraq. Yet at the same time, in each of these countries there are high protective barriers in important sectors of the economy and serious debates about capital controls and the regulation of international capital. The capacity of these countries to control their integration into the world economy is doubtless related to their size, resources, geostrategic advantages, and economic strength. However, interestingly, it seems also to be related to their national ideology and the domestic power of the state. One thing that all strong states have in common is that they guard with equal ferocity their independence in economic policy, foreign policy, human rights, and security issues.

Weak states, by contrast, suffer from a lack of choice in their international economic relations. They have little or no influence in the creation and enforcement of rules in the system, and they have exercised little control over their own integration into the world economy. For example, in

the aftermath of the debt crisis of the 1980s, many weak states opened up their economies, liberalized, and deregulated, more as a result of coercive liberalization than of a democratic policy choice. In the 1990s, this continued with what an international economist called "forced harmonization," whereby, for instance, in the case of trade negotiations on intellectual property, developing countries were coerced into an agreement that transferred "billions of dollars' worth of monopoly profits from poor countries to rich countries under the guise of protecting the property rights of inventors" (Rodrik 1999).

Distinguishing among states according to their capacity to shape and respond to globalization is vital in analyzing the impact on the global economy. The example of the collapse of the international financial system in late 2008 demonstrates that some states, in particular the United States, are rule makers in the world economy, while less powerful states are rule *takers*.

The pressure to develop resources to stay competitive in the global economy can lead to tensions within a state. For example, in August 2009 Brazil's president Luiz Inacio Lula da Silva addressed protesters from Greenpeace who opposed the government's plan to develop offshore oil fields.

Traditions promote different foreign policy strategies, and each tradition suggests differ-ent sets of policy priorities.

Many scholars believe that a country's foreign policy remains constant. Thus we can think of a distinctively "French," "Russian," or "Chinese" foreign policy. Many policy makers seem to agree with US secretary of state (and at the time future president) John Quincy Adams, who said, "I know of no change in [foreign] policy, only change of circum-stances." Scholars of US foreign relations often assert that the direction of the country's foreign policy has been relatively stable over the years. John Lewis Gaddis, for example, finds that the effects of surprise have led to a foreign policy for the United States that seeks hegemony and is willing to act unilaterally when necessary (Gaddis 2004). Another analyst finds that there are four basic traditions in US foreign policy (Mead 2001). We will examine these traditions in the next section.

Hamiltonian

Proponents of this tradition believe that US foreign policy is all about trade and economic prosperity. They support a strong alliance between US government and big business. For Hamiltonians, free trade is an essential element of US power and critical to maintaining US political and economic hegemony. US foreign policy is all about business, and for Hamiltonians "the dollar and the flag" work closely together to secure national interests.

Hamiltonians are liberal internationalists who support creating and maintaining global institutions to manage the international economic system. The recent global eco-nomic crisis and the G-20 summits aimed at finding a global economic framework for reform at a national level are exactly the priorities of Hamiltonians.

Jeffersonian

Jeffersonians believe that our foreign policy should focus on policies that strengthen our society and safeguard the values and institutions of American democracy. They do not believe in grandiose global campaigns to spread American values around the world, as Wilsonians and some Hamiltonians would have us do. They are generally very concerned about costly global entanglements such as memberships in alliances or global institutions that might commit US troops or US funds to risky and uncertain endeavors. The greatest threat for Jeffersonians is international overreach.

Jeffersonians believe we should be spending our resources on making America strong at home—a more perfect union and a shining "city on the hill." They want those in power to achieve our strategic goals and secure our national interests at the lowest possible costs. Most Jeffersonians thought that, with the end of the Cold War, the United States would cash in on the **peace dividend**: reduce NATO forces and programs and bring US military forces home from around the world.

peace dividend The misplaced belief that the end of the Cold War would bring about a fundamental change in international relations and provide funds for domestic programs or even result in a reduction in taxes.

Wilsonian

The Wilsonian tradition in US foreign policy focuses on the idea that power comes with obligations and responsibilities. The United States has a moral obligation to spread Amer-ican values and to build an international community based on the rule of law.

Wilsonians focus on legal and moral aspects of world order, and they believe in creating international or global institutions (e.g., the United Nations, the International Criminal Court) that encourage global cooperation and seek multilateral responses to the transnational challenges that threaten peace and stability in the international system. For example, Wilsonians would have few problems with a global treaty to manage climate change, and they would be open to participating in a multilateral force aimed at stopping the genocide in Sudan.

The Wilsonians are "political missionaries" with the goal of creating and maintaining a universal moral order based on what is good for the United States and what has worked in the United States. As foreign policy activists, Wilsonians would support a major expansion of the US role in world affairs. The neoconservatives (discussed later in this chapter) were Wilsonians of a kind. They supported US hegemony and the spreading of American values, ideals, and practices, but they dismissed multilateralism, international treaties, and international institutions. Instead of combining Wilsonian ideas with Hamiltonian notions of global economic cooperation, the Bush neoconservatives embraced the more militaristic views of the Jacksonians.

Jacksonian

Jacksonians believe that the United States must be stronger than all other countries, and its leaders must use their power to protect the citizens of the United States and promote its national interests. Jacksonians do not believe that the United States should travel around the world starting wars or facing down evil, but when wars start and our interests, values, and citizens are at risk, we fight to win! "Don't tread on me" and "No substitute for victory" are slogans Jacksonians would use on their T-shirts. The Jacksonian tradition is seen in some Americans' emphasis on patriotism and in the "popular culture of honor" that encourages self-reliance, courage, and military pride, and it has significant influence on both domestic and foreign policy. The credit we give military leaders in the political process supports this point. Jacksonians are comfortable with a greater role for the military in the US society.

These four traditions are represented in most US foreign policy debates. Most US administrations, perhaps unintentionally, have individuals representing each of these views. Some of these traditions combine to create new traditions, like the neoconservative doctrine that shaped the foreign policy of the Bush administration after the 9/11 terrorist attacks in New York, Washington, and Pennsylvania.

Now that we have discussed the various foundations, processes, and traditions of foreign policy, we'll turn to some extended examples, including a close look at the ideas and actions of the neoconservatives in the United States in the 1990s, as well as an early examination of President Obama's foreign policy.

Rise of the Neoconservatives

In 1996, William Kristol and Robert Kagan, two prominent voices in the neoconservative camp, laid out a foreign policy plan for the republican presidential candidate Robert Dole. Their foreign policy doctrine was based on the ideas of both Theodore Roosevelt and Ronald Reagan. Simply stated, these two neoconservatives and the others who would play prominent roles as both informal advisors and key policy makers in the George W. Bush administration believed that America is an *exceptional nation* and we should be willing and able to play the role of a benevolent hegemon.

This notion of **exceptionalism** was not new, as we have learned earlier in this chapter. Indeed, syllabi of many United States foreign policy classes include Puritan pastor John Winthrop's early seventeenth-century "City on a Hill" sermon that first presented the notion. Exceptionalism has served to justify American expansionism and the view held by

exceptionalism The belief that a country has a unique set of domestic and foreign policy traditions. An implication is that other countries should embrace the same set of policies.

many that the United States has a duty to spread its ideas, values, and traditions around the world. These views and rationales for global activism are well described by Andrew Bacevich in his book *The Limits to Power* (2008, 20): "We touted our status as God's New Chosen People, erecting a 'city upon a hill' destined to illuminate the world." Notions of "manifest destiny," "God's will" and "leading the nations of the world to democracy" recall the words and deeds of Teddy Roosevelt, Woodrow Wilson, and Ronald Reagan.

Many policy makers who became powerful decision makers in the first Bush administration embraced the neoconservatives' ideas. These advisors believed that the United States should secure and maintain its hegemony with military superiority and moral confidence. US foreign policy was to be based on more defense spending, a building-up of nationalism and patriotism, and an awareness of America's special role as a global leader. American foreign policy became a global policy strategy to promote the neoconservatives' ideas of what were the core American principles of democracy: free markets and individual freedom and liberty. The issue of moral clarity might be the most controversial, because it suggests that US leaders should not accept moral relativism, and they should not wait for threats to arrive. Instead, the neoconservatives contended, the United States needed to act preemptively to secure its interests. None of this was as new as the neoconservatives believed, however: unilateralism and preemption have been central components of US foreign policy since the early 1800s (Gaddis 2004).

The basic assumptions of this neoconservative group that controlled foreign policy in the Bush years represented a combination of Jacksonian and Wilsonian ideas. The first assumption is that the world is divided between "good and evil." This Manichean view of the world makes it clear that the United States represents the good and our enemies are all evil. More importantly, the United States is an exceptional nation with the special role as the slayer of evil states and networks.

A second assumption is that the United States must maintain its military superiority and use it for moral purposes: regime change and the creation of democratic and capitalist states. This emphasis on military power to change the world comes with a disdain for multilateralism, binding international treaties, and global institutions. The neoconservatives are skeptical about the rule of law and any collective security arrangements.

preventive war Launching a war to eliminate a perceived threat from another country, often started prior to the escalation of a crisis or before the enemy is itself prepared to attack.

The most controversial neoconservative assumption was the idea of **preventive war**. The Bush administration made it clear that it was willing to go to war with another state if it might be a threat in the future. Further, the Bush administration and the neoconservatives did not believe that they needed permission from other nation-states or international institutions to initiate their foreign policy. The 1991 Gulf War was a "good war" from a traditional realist or even a Wilsonian view. The first Bush administration moved carefully and gained support of the international community through UN resolutions condemning the unilateral invasion of Kuwait by Iraq forces. The Iraqi invasion was a clear violation of the sovereignty of Kuwait and therefore violated international law.

Not only did the United States obtain the support of the UN but most of the international community sent troops or provided financial support for the war. The second Bush administration, however, chose to go it alone in the second war against Iraq. Using fabricated information from Iraqi exiles and other enemies of Saddam Hussein's regime, and from questionable intelligence extracted from members of the Al Qaeda organization under torture in the so-called CIA secret prisons, the Bush administration was convinced that Iraq was developing nuclear weapons and supporting terrorist groups that were planning more attacks. At special sessions of the UN Security Council, Colin Powell, the sec-

In 1991, during the first Gulf War, then secretary of defense Dick Cheney and chairman of the US Joint Chiefs of Staff Colin Powell had a strong working relationship. That changed when the two were vice president and secretary of state, respectively. What helps to explain that shift?

retary of state, and other US officials presented intelligence information aimed at proving their view of Saddam Hussein's regime and convincing the world to support another multilateral war against Iraq.

This time the world was not convinced. The UN did not support the United States, and subsequently, the entire world learned that the information about weapons of mass destruction and links to the 9/11 attacks was fabricated by neoconservative members of the Bush administration who sought to start a war with Iraq. As early as 1992, in the first Bush administration, key decision makers like Paul Wolfowitz made a case for ridding the world of authoritarian leaders who sought to extend their power and influence in areas of strategic importance to the United States and the West. More traditional realists with an understanding of the importance of strategic regions opposed the war with Iraq as an unnecessary war of choice. They disagreed with the neoconservatives' desire to promote regime change and democratic peace.

Pragmatic Internationalism: Obama's Foreign Policy

In its global outlook, the Obama administration is more Wilsonian than the previous G. W. Bush administration. The new president has surrounded himself with liberal internationalists who believe in engaging with the world and using diplomacy and nonforce options to secure US national interests. Yet many of his advisors are also "liberal interventionists" who believe that US military power is essential for the future of global security. They also believe that the United States must use both hard and soft power to secure US interests in the world. Moreover, the Obama administration wishes to make certain that the United States will be the country to lead the world. Clearly, the era of unilateralism and chasing monsters across the world is over. In the coming months and years, the Obama administration will likely increase its efforts at building connections with global institutions and other democracies interested in global security, prosperity, and problem solving. Certainly, the global economic crisis has made it clear to all world leaders that working together is critical.

The Obama foreign policy strategy could be described as "pragmatic meliorism," which is simply the idea that humankind has the capacity to solve the problems that we face and that incrementally we can work cooperatively to find the answers. Remember that a doctrine is a road map both for the policy makers and for building domestic support for policy positions. The following describe Obama's foreign policy:

- Obama is making certain that the entire world knows that Bush unilateralism is over and that the United States seeks common or cooperative responses to global problems.
- Obama has adopted a more traditional realist position, in which the United States uses both national and international resources to secure national interests.
- The Obama administration is willing to "speak truth to power." The administration is willing to admit that the wars in Iraq and Afghanistan are not going well and that the United States may need international assistance to win these wars.
- Early on, the administration seems to be more interested in imaginative and creative diplomacy. The Obama administration has sent special envoys to lead discussions aimed at managing if not resolving conflicts in the Middle East and the troubled areas of Pakistan and Afghanistan. The Obama administration has also indicated that it is willing to begin talks with leaders from Syria, North Korea, and Iran—states that the Bush administration had isolated as enemies and members of the axis of evil.

The rhetoric previously used by the Bush administration has now been set aside to facilitate serious and "tough-minded diplomacy." The Obama administration is not afraid to talk with "enemies" or adversaries, and some of the preliminary discussions have already led to productive outcomes. Rather than fight with the Russians over the planned US missile defense system, the Obama administration has agreed to discuss its implementation with Russian leaders. Further, it has suggested that if Russia were willing to help the United States with Iran's nuclear weapons program, this might lead to the cancellation of the missile defense program. The United States has cancelled the missile system in Europe, and now the Obama administration will see if the Russians reciprocate. This kind of "diplomatic horse trading" can only work if one is willing to talk with both friends and adversaries.

The Obama administration is taking a very hard-line realist position on Iraq, Afghanistan, and Pakistan. This is because these are the countries where Al Qaeda is operating and where fundamentalists are continuing to plan and carry out attacks. What is missing from the Bush years is the unilateralism and the disdain for multilateralism. The Obama administration has made it clear that the world must act in concert to end terrorist activities and to address the deplorable human conditions that often cause someone to join extremist groups.

Conclusion

In this chapter we provided an overview of the primary issues and actors in the foreign policy process. We saw that many variables shape the world of diplomacy in the contemporary international system: material needs, ideas, and people themselves. The rational-actor model offers one way to understand the policy-making process. We also learned about different styles and traditions in foreign policy. In the following chapters we will turn to specific topics that comprise the critical challenges in the international system;

When President Barack Obama addressed the United Nations General Assembly in 2009 he spoke of a world in which states had eliminated the threat nuclear weapons pose to world peace. Has what you learned in this chapter convinced you that this is likely or unlikely? Why?

for example, we will see how globalization is undermining the autonomy of the nation-state. International and regional organizations like the United Nations and the European Union, nongovernmental organizations (NGOs), and multinational corporations are each eroding the power and influence some of the core policy areas that were once the sole responsibility of nation-states. This trend is an important factor shaping relations in the contemporary world that we will examine in depth in the next chapters.

Chapter 5 authored by Steven L. Lamy.

REVIEW QUESTIONS

1. Why has nationalism spread across the world in the last two centuries?
2. How has the rise of the modern state shaped the development of nationalism?
3. What are the ways in which personal characteristics can affect outcomes in the rational-actor model?
4. What are the four levels of analysis? How are they used to explain the behavior of states?
5. How do bureaucracies influence the foreign policy process?
6. Do "small states" have any power and influence in the international system?
7. "Contemporary globalization erodes nation-state sovereignty but does *not* undermine nationalism." Discuss.
8. Who are the actors in creating foreign policy? What are the phases?
9. What is a foreign policy doctrine?
10. Do you think the foreign policy process is shifting away from the state?

FURTHER READING
Foreign Policy in International Relations

Henderson, J., Jackson, K., and Kennaway, R. (1980), *Beyond New Zealand: The Foreign Policy of a Small State* (Auckland, NZ: Methuen). A case study of the foreign policy of a small state that provides useful ideas that apply to other small states.

Hill, C. (2003), *The Changing Politics of Foreign Policy* (Houndmills, Basingstoke, UK: Palgrave MacMillan). Excellent review of the analytical and theoretical issues in the field of foreign policy analysis.

Ingebritsen, C., Neumann, I., Gstöhl, S., and Beyer, J. (2006), *Small States in International Relations* (Seattle, WA: University of Washington Press). A recent study of small states, primarily the Nordic states, that focuses on their role as norm entrepreneurs in the post–Cold War world.

Johansen, R. C. (1980), *The National Interest and the Human Interest* (Princeton, NJ: Princeton University). An analysis of US foreign policy decision-making in four cases from the mainstream realist view that are compared with a more utopian World Order Models Project view of the same issues. It is Machiavelli versus Kant.

Mead, W. R. (2001), *Special Providence: American Foreign Policy and How It Changed the World* (NY: Alfred A. Knopf). Excellent study of the history of US foreign policy traditions and the four traditions that shape debates and policies.

Mearsheimer, J. J. (2001), *The Tragedy of Great Power Politics* (New York: W. W. Norton). A study of great powers in the post Cold War world written by one of the leading realist thinkers.

Morgenthau, H. J. (1962), *Politics Among Nations* (NY: Knopf). The most important modern realist text that shaped. US foreign policy after WWII and maybe the most influential text in shaping world politics.

Rosenau, J. N. (1980), *The Scientific Study of Foreign Policy* (London: Nichols Pub Co). An early study that helped to shape the study of foreign policy analysis.

Slaughter, A.-M., Jentleson, B., Daalder, I., et al. (July 2008), *Strategic Leadership: Framework for a Twenty-First-Century National Security Strategy* (Center for a New American Security). The game plan for the Obama Administration's foreign policy that was written by some of the most prominent liberal internationalist thinkers in the US.

INTERNET RESOURCES

Most state-members of the international community have official web sites. Here is a sample:

Australian Ministry of Foreign Affairs
http://www.dfat.gov.au/

Chinese Ministry of Foreign Affairs
http://www.fmprc.gov.cn/eng/default.htm

French Ministry of Foreign Affairs
http://www.diplomatie.gouv.fr/en/

Indian Ministry of External Affairs
http://meaindia.nic.in/

Japanese Ministry of Foreign Affairs
http://www.mofa.go.jp/

New Zealand Ministry of Foreign Affairs and Trade
http://www.mfat.govt.nz/

Nigerian Ministry of Foreign Affairs
www.mfa.gov.ng

Norwegian Ministry of Foreign Affairs
http://www.regjeringen.no/en/dep/

Saudi Arabian Ministry of Foreign Affairs
http://www.mofa.gov.sa/

Brookings Institution
http://www.brookings.edu

The Brookings Institution is a nonprofit public policy organization based in Washington, DC. Their mission is to conduct high-quality, independent research and, based on that research, to provide innovative, practical recommendations that strengthen American democracy, foster the economic and social welfare, security and opportunity of all Americans, and secure a more open, safe, prosperous, and cooperative international system.

Council on Foreign Relations (CFR)
www.cfr.org

The website of the Council on Foreign Relations (CFR) is designed to be an online resource for everyone in these turbulent times who wants to learn more about the complex international issues challenging policy makers and citizens alike.

Fund for Peace

http://www.fundforpeace.org

The Fund for Peace is an independent, nonpartisan research and educational organization that works to prevent war and alleviate the conditions that cause conflict. The organization promotes sustainable security through research, training and education, engagement of civil society, bridging bridges across diverse sectors, and developing innovative technologies and tools for policy makers. This site has a failed-state index and other pertinent info.

International Coalition for the Responsibility to Protect

www.responsibilitytoprotect.org/

The RESPONSIBILITY TO PROTECT ("RtoP" or "R2P") is a new international security and human rights norm to address the international community's failure to prevent and stop genocides, war crimes, ethnic cleansing, and crimes against humanity.

For more information, quizzes, case studies, and other study tools, please visit us at **www.oup.com/us/lamy**

Global and Regional Governance

Only in a universal union of states can the property and rights of states become settled and a true state of peace come into being.

—*Immanuel Kant*

This is an ungoverned world. The UN has no autonomous power; it is what its members want it to be, and usually its members don't want it to be anything much... When it is said that it is better if things are done multilaterally, too often this means accepting the lowest common denominator.

—*Stanley Hoffmann*

Those who used to chastise America for acting alone in the world cannot now stand by and wait for America to solve the world's problems alone. We have sought in word and deed a new era of engagement with the world, and now is the time for all of us to take our share of responsibility for a global response to global challenges.

—*Barack Obama*

In his first address to the leaders of all the member states of the United Nations, President Barack Obama called for a real change in global politics and a renewal of commitment to multilateralism, international organizations, and the rule of law. President Obama also promised that the United States would lead a new era of global engagement and collective action. He referred to the founders of the United Nations, who in 1945 believed that the world could only solve the most pressing problems by working together. Dedicated to preventing another world war, the United Nations was built on the principle that peace could only be achieved with the cooperative efforts of the entire world. It is the only international organization with a global mandate.

President Obama outlined a policy agenda for global action that would be led by the UN and all of its members. This agenda focused on the most critical issues that threaten peace and stability in the world today. His first pillar called for the end of nuclear proliferation and the prevention of

In December 2009 President Barack Obama received the Nobel Peace Prize.

a nuclear arms race. He mentioned the importance of the Nuclear Nonproliferation Treaty and the important role of the UN and the International Atomic Energy Agency (IAEA). The second pillar focused on the pursuit of peace and the end of violence and terrorism in the world. Here the president talked about the importance of UN peacekeeping and peace enforcement. The third pillar emphasized the importance of global cooperation to clean up the environment and preserve the planet. International and regional organizations will play a critical role in formulating treaties and rules that protect the environment. Finally, President Obama's fourth pillar addressed the economic crisis that has hurt people in rich and poor states. The World Health Organization and the UN Development Programme, as well as the World Trade Organization, the International Monetary Fund, and the World Bank, will need to work with regional organizations like the European Union, the Asian Development Bank, and the African Union to increase economic growth and find ways to address global poverty.

President Obama, like other world leaders, is calling for global engagement and acknowledging the necessity of working together through international organizations in this age of globalized challenges. Most world leaders embrace the idea that by following the concept of rule of law and by working through international organizations it is possible to create a safer world order.

Introduction

Leaders in all countries are faced with the challenge of managing the processes of globalization. States seek to create international institutions and laws that enable them to secure their national interests in a more globalized society. **Global governance** describes the formal

global governance
Involves the regulation and coordination of transnational issue areas by nation-states, international and regional organizations, and private agencies through the establishment of international regimes. These regimes may focus on problem-solving or the simple enforcement of rules and regulations.

The United Nations General Assembly has seen memorable speeches from world leaders. How well has the international organization translated rhetorical flourishes into concrete programs?

and informal processes and institutions that guide and control the activities of both state and nonstate actors in the international system; global governance does not mean the creation of a world government. After all, this governance is not always led by states, nor is it always led by international organizations that are created by states. Indeed, multinational corporations and even NGOs create rules and regulations to govern behavior in some policy areas. For example, banks will set up informal rules for exchanging currencies, and NGOs have set up ethical rules for fund-raising and intervention in crisis regions. As the work of Elinor Ostrom, 2009 Nobel Prize winner in economics, demonstrates, sometimes private, nongovernmental groups can do a better job of creating rules for governing a shared resource. In this case the state is the primary actor but not the only one in global governance (in Chapter 7 we will talk more about transnational and nongovernmental actors).

In this complex and increasingly global system, states are working with international and regional organizations like the UN and the European Union and nonstate actors like Oxfam, Save the Children, and Amnesty International through diplomacy, international law, and regimes or international governing arrangements to solve common regional and global problems. Coglianese (2000, 299–301) suggests that international organizations and international law are critical in responding to three types of problems:

1. Coordinating global linkages: In this area, rules and laws are critical for managing the exchanges of information, products, services, money, and finance, and even for managing collective responses to criminal activity.
2. Responding to common problems: The global community faces common problems like global warming, poverty, human rights abuses, refugees, and pandemics, all of which require some form of coordination and collective policy response.
3. Protecting core values: Institutions and laws are essential for protecting and promoting core values like equality, liberty, democracy, and justice across the world.

The problems listed above and others increase with globalization. States will undoubtedly become more dependent on international and regional institutions like the United Nations or the African Union to promote international and regional cooperation in these critical areas. The global system is a legal order with strong enforcement mechanisms and institutions capable of coordinating responses to global crises. The legal effectiveness and problem-solving success depend on voluntary compliance by both state and nonstate actors. If the laws, regimes, and institutions are considered fair and legitimate by global actors, compliance will be high and the processes of globalization will be more effectively managed. Here we mean international laws, or the body of legal standards, procedures, and institutions that govern the interactions of sovereign states. **Regimes** are governing arrangements that guide states as well as transnational actors and institutions (described in detail in the next section); they are sets of rules, norms, and practices that shape behavior of all actors in a given issue area. **International law** is an international institution.

Regionalism has become a pervasive feature of international affairs. According to the World Trade Organization (WTO), by July 2005 only one WTO member—Mongolia—was not party to any regional trade agreement, and a total of 330 such agreements had been notified. Regional peacekeeping forces have become active in some parts of the world. Regionalism has in the last decades become one of the forces challenging the traditional centrality of states in international relations.

That challenge comes from two directions. The word "region" and its derivatives denote one distinguishable part of some larger geographical area. Yet they are used in different

regimes Sets of implicit or explicit principles, norms, rules, and decision-making procedures around which actors' expectations converge in a given area of international relations. Often simply defined as governing arrangements in a regional or global policy area.

international law The formal rules of conduct that states acknowledge or contract between themselves.

ways. On the one hand, regions are territories within a state, occasionally crossing state borders. On the other, regions are particular areas of the world, covering a number of different sovereign states. We will focus on this latter description of regionalism in our discussion.

In this chapter we discuss three linked topics. First we introduce the basics of international law that provide a framework for the interactions of states in global politics. Next we turn to the United Nations, the largest international organization with a mandate to prevent future world wars and protect human rights. In the final section we discuss the concept of regional integration with a focus on the European Union, the most successful and comprehensive regional organization.

Introduction to International Law

In this section we will consider the practice of modern international law and the debates surrounding its nature and efficacy. For our purposes, there is one central question: What is the relationship between international law and international politics? If the power and interests of states are what matters, as we discussed in Chapter 5, then international law is either a servant of the powerful or an irrelevant curiosity. And yet—if international law does *not* matter, then why do states and other actors devote so much effort to negotiating new legal regimes and augmenting existing ones? Why does so much international debate revolve around the legality of state behavior, around the applicability of legal rules, and around the legal obligations incumbent on states? And why is compliance with international law so high, even by domestic standards? In other words, there seems to be a paradox at work.

Our starting point, therefore, should be made clear: international law is best understood as a core international institution—a set of norms, rules, and practices created by states and other actors to facilitate diverse social goals, from order and coexistence to justice and human development. It is, however, an institution with distinctive historical roots, and understanding these roots is essential to grasping its unique institutional features.

International Order and Institutions

Realists portray international relations as a struggle for power, a realm in which states are "continuously preparing for, actively involved in, or recovering from organized violence in the form of war" (Morgenthau 1985, 52). While war has certainly been a recurrent feature of international life, it is a crude and deeply dysfunctional way for states to ensure their security or realize their interests. Because of this, states have devoted as much, if not more, effort to liberating themselves from the condition of war than to embroiling themselves in violent conflict. Creating some modicum of international order has been an abiding common interest of most states most of the time (Bull 1977, 8).

international organization
Any institution with formal procedures and formal membership from three or more countries. The minimum number of countries is set at three, rather than two, because multilateral relationships have significantly greater complexity than bilateral relationships.

To achieve international order, states have created international institutions. People often confuse institutions and organizations, incorrectly using the two terms interchangeably. International institutions are commonly defined as complexes of norms, rules, and practices that "prescribe behavioral roles, constrain activity, and shape expectations" (Keohane 1989a: 3). **International organizations**, like the United Nations, are physical entities that have staffs, head offices, and letterheads. International institutions can exist without any organizational structure—the 1997 Ottawa Convention banning land mines is an institution, but there is no land mines head office. Many institutions have organizational dimensions, though. The World Trade Organization (formerly the General

Agreement on Tariffs and Trade) is an institution with a very strong organizational structure. While institutions can exist without an organizational dimension, international organizations cannot exist without an institutional framework, as their very existence presupposes a prior set of norms, rules, and principles that empower them to act and which they are charged to uphold. If states had never negotiated the Charter of the United Nations, the organization simply could not exist, let alone function.

In modern international society, states have created three levels of institutions. There are deep constitutional institutions, such as the principle of sovereignty, which define the terms of legitimate statehood. Without the institution of sovereignty, the world of independent states, and the international politics it engenders, would simply not exist. States have also created fundamental institutions, like international law and **multilateralism**,

For many years GATT, the predecessor to the World Trade Organization (WTO), was considered a club for rich exporting states. How has the growth of importance of countries like India, Argentina, and Brazil altered that perception?

which provide the basic rules and practices that shape how states solve cooperation and coordination problems. These are the institutional norms, techniques, and structures that states and other actors invoke and employ when they have common ends they want to achieve or clashing interests they want to contain. Lastly, states have developed issue-specific institutions or regimes, such as the Nuclear Nonproliferation Treaty (NPT), which enact fundamental institutional practices in particular realms of interstate relations. The NPT is a concrete expression of the practices of international law and multilateralism in the field of arms control.

multilateralism The process by which states work together to solve a common problem.

We are concerned here with the middle strata of fundamental institutions. "Fundamental institutions are the elementary rules of practice that states formulate to solve the coordination and collaboration problems associated with coexistence under anarchy" (Reus-Smit 1999, 14). In modern international society, a range of such institutions exists, including international law, multilateralism, bilateralism, diplomacy, and management by the great powers. Since the middle of the nineteenth century, however, the first two (international law and multilateralism) of these have provided the basic framework for international cooperation and the pursuit of order.

How do states develop international law? Why do states follow international law if there is no international government to enforce these laws? Why is international law not given a higher priority in the study of international relations? These are important questions that might help us understand the development of international law as an international institution.

The principal mechanism modern states employ to legislate international law is multilateral diplomacy, which is commonly defined as cooperation between three or more states based on, or with a view to formulating, reciprocally binding rules of conduct. It is a norm of the modern international legal system that states are obliged to observe legal rules because they have consented to those rules. A state that has not consented to the rules of a particular legal treaty is not bound by those rules. The only exception to this concerns rules of customary international law, and even then implied or tacit consent plays an important role in the determination of which rules have customary status.

Table 6.1

Levels of International Institutions

Constitutional institutions

Constitutional institutions comprise the primary rules and norms of international society, without which society among sovereign states could not exist. The most commonly recognized of these is the norm of sovereignty, which holds that within the state, power and authority are centralized and hierarchical, and outside the state no higher authority exists. The norm of sovereignty is supported by a range of auxiliary norms, such as the right to self-determination and the norm of nonintervention.

Fundamental institutions

Fundamental institutions rest on the foundation provided by constitutional institutions. They represent the basic norms and practices that sovereign states employ to facilitate coexistence and cooperation under conditions of international anarchy. They are the rudimentary practices states reach for when seeking to collaborate or coordinate their behavior. Fundamental institutions have varied from one historical system of states to another, but in the modern international system, contractual international law and multilateralism have been the most important.

Issue-specific institutions, or "regimes"

Issue-specific institutions, or "regimes," are the most visible or palpable of all international institutions. They are the sets of rules, norms, and decision-making procedures that states formulate to define legitimate actors and legitimate action in a given domain of international life. Examples of regimes are the Nuclear Nonproliferation Treaty, the Framework Convention on Climate Change, the Ottawa Convention on antipersonnel land mines, and the International Covenant on Civil and Political Rights. Importantly, issue-specific institutions or regimes are concrete enactments of fundamental institutional practices such as international law and multilateralism.

In many historical periods, and in many social and cultural settings, the political and legal realms have been entwined. For instance, the absolutist conception of sovereignty bound the two realms together in the figure of the sovereign. In the modern era, by contrast, the political and legal realms are thought to be radically different, with their own logics and institutional settings. Domestically, this informs ideas about the constitutional separation of powers; internationally, it has encouraged the view that international politics and law are separate spheres of social action. This has not only affected how the academic disciplines of international relations and law have evolved, but also how state practice has evolved.

Realists generally believe that international law should serve the interests of the powerful states. This has led to criticisms of international law and of international organizations like the UN, which protects the interests of major powers by focusing decision-making power in the Security Council. Other criticisms are raised by non-Western states who claim that many of these laws do not account for their interests, traditions, and values.

Criticisms of International Law

From one perspective, international law is easily cast as a Western, even imperial institution. As we have seen, its roots lie in the European intellectual movements of the sixteenth and seventeenth centuries. Ideas propagated at that time not only drew on ideas of natural law, which could be traced back to ancient Greek and Roman thought; they also drew a clear distinction between international laws that were appropriate among Christian peoples and those that should govern how Christians related to peoples in the Muslim world, the Americas, and later Asia. The former were based on assumptions of the inherent equality of Christian peoples, the latter on the inherent superiority of Christians over non-Christians.

Further evidence of this Western bias can be found in the "standard of civilization" that European powers codified in international law during the nineteenth century (Gong 1984). According to this standard, non-Western polities were granted sovereign recognition only if they exhibited certain domestic political characteristics and only if they were willing and able to participate in the prevailing diplomatic practices. The standard was heavily biased toward Western political and legal institutions as the accepted model. On the basis of the standard, European power divided the world's peoples into "civilized," "barbarian," and "savage" societies, a division they used to justify various degrees of Western tutelage.

Many claim that Western bias still characterizes the international legal order. Cited here is the Anglo-European dominance of peak legal institutions, most notably the United Nations Security Council, and international human rights law, which is said to impose a set of Western values about the rights of the individual on non-Western societies where such ideas are alien. These biases are seen as coming together around the issue of humanitarian intervention. Western powers are accused of using their privileged position on the Security Council, and of brandishing human rights norms, to intervene in the domestic politics of weak, developing countries.

All of these criticisms have veracity. However, the nature and role of international law in contemporary world politics is more complex than it first appears. To begin with, at the heart of the modern international legal system lies a set of customary norms that uphold the legal equality of all sovereign states, as well as their rights to self-determination and nonintervention. Non-Western states have been the most vigorous proponents and defenders of these cardinal legal norms, and their survival as independent political entities depends on the continued salience of such principles. Second, non-Western peoples were more centrally involved in the development of the international human rights regime than is commonly acknowledged. The Universal Declaration of Human Rights was the product of a deliberate and systematic process of intercultural dialogue, a dialogue involving representatives of all of the world's major cultures (Glendon 2002). The International Covenant on Civil and Political Rights, which is often portrayed as a reflection of Western values, was shaped in critical ways by newly independent postcolonial states (Reus-Smit 2001a). What is more, international human rights law has been an important resource in the struggles of many subject peoples against repressive governments and against institutions such as colonialism.

From International to Supranational Law?

So long as international law was designed primarily to facilitate international order—to protect the negative liberties (i.e., freedom from outside interference) of sovereign states—it remained a relatively circumscribed, if essential, institution. This was apparent in four characteristics of international law, at least until developments of the last three decades. First, states were the primary *subjects* of international law, the principal bearers of rights and obligations. "The classic view has been that international law applies only to states" (Higgins 1994, 40). The 1933 Montevideo Convention on the Rights and Duties of States establishes the "state as a person of international law," defines what constitutes a state,

The genocide of World War II brought about a global understanding that states should respect human rights, but it was not clear which rights states must protect. For example, must North Korea respect the rights of North Korean defector Kim Hae-young, shown here with her son?

and lays down the principal rights and obligations enjoyed by states (Weston et al. 1990, 12). Second, and related to the above, states were the primary *agents* of international law, the only actors empowered to formulate, enact, and enforce international law. International law was thus viewed as an artifact of state practice, not the legislation of a community of humankind. Third, international law was concerned with the regulation of interstate relations. How states interacted with one another fell within the purview of international law; how they operated within their territorial boundaries did not. This distinction was enshrined in the twin international norms of self-determination and nonintervention. Finally, the scope of international law was confined—or attempted to be confined—to questions of order, not justice. The principal objective of international law was the maintenance of peace and stability based on mutual respect for each state's territorial integrity and domestic jurisdiction; issues of distributive justice and the protection of basic human rights lay outside its brief.

In recent decades states have sought to move beyond the simple pursuit of international order toward the ambitious yet amorphous objective of global governance, and international law has begun to change in fascinating ways. First, although states are "still at the heart of the international legal system" (Higgins 1994, 39), individuals, groups, and organizations are increasingly recognized as subjects of international law. The development of an expansive body of international human rights law, supported by evolving mechanisms of enforcement, has given individuals, as well as some collectivities, such as minority groups or indigenous peoples, clear rights under international law. And recent moves to hold individuals criminally responsible for violations of those rights—evident in the war crimes tribunals that we discuss later in this chapter for Rwanda and the former Yugoslavia, the creation of a new International Criminal Court, and the arrest in London of Augusto Pinochet, the former Chilean dictator, for crimes against humanity—indicate the clear obligations individuals bear to observe basic human rights. Second, nonstate actors are becoming important agents in the international legal process. While such actors cannot formally enact international law, and their practices do not contribute to the development of customary international law, they often play a crucial role in shaping the normative environment in which states are moved to codify specific legal rules, in providing information to national governments that encourages the redefinition of state interests and the convergence of policies across different states, and, finally, in actually drafting international treaties and conventions. This last role was first seen when the International Committee of the Red Cross drafted the 1864 Geneva Convention (Finnemore 1996b, 69–88) and more recently when nonstate actors aided in the development of the Ottawa Convention on antipersonnel land mines (Price 1998) and in the creation of the International Criminal Court.

Third, international law is increasingly concerned with global, not merely international, regulation. Where the principles of self-determination and nonintervention once erected a fundamental boundary between the international and domestic legal realms, this boundary is now being breached by the development of international rules that regulate how states should behave within their territories. International law is a crucial element of global governance. Notable here is international trade law, the growing corpus of international environmental law, as well as the previously mentioned body of international human rights law. The penetration of these laws through the boundaries of the sovereign state is facilitated by the growing tendency of national courts to draw on precepts of international law in their rulings. Finally, the rules, norms, and principles of international law are no longer confined to maintaining international order, narrowly defined. Not only does the development of international humanitarian law indicate a broadening of international law to address questions of global justice, but recent decisions by the United Nations Security Council have treated gross violations of human rights by sovereign states as threats to international peace and security, thus legitimating action under Chapter 7 of the UN Charter. (An example is the international intervention in East Timor.) In doing so, the Security Council implies that international order is dependent on the maintenance of at least minimum standards of global justice.

Because of these changes, it has been suggested that international law may be gradually transforming into a system of supranational law. Once states are no longer the only subjects and agents of international law, once international law is involved in global regulation, and once its scope has been extended to encompass issues of justice as well as order, it has broken the bounds of both its initial intent and original practice. While these changes have not yet prompted the rewriting of international legal texts, and both international lawyers and international relations scholars are responding cautiously, current developments have injected new excitement and energy into the field of international law, which many previously regarded as moribund, and have caused international relations scholars to look afresh at the role of legal norms in shaping world politics, something often dismissed as idealism.

This desire to promote a rule-based global society that would protect the rights of humankind and prevent the scourge of war led world leaders to create the United Nations in 1945. We now take a step back in time and turn to a discussion of this important international institution.

UN Membership. Over the years, what factors have lead to the increase of UN membership? Which countries have yet to join? *Source: www.un.org.*

The United Nations

The **United Nations (UN)** has the unique status of being the largest **supranational global organization** and the only one that has a universal focus. Other supranational organizations with more specific responsibilities include the World Bank, the International Monetary Fund, and the World Trade Organization. The states that comprise the UN created a group of international institutions, which include the central system located in New York: the Specialized Agencies, such as the World Health Organization (WHO) and the International Labor Organization (ILO), and the Programmes and Funds, such as the United Nations Children's Fund (UNICEF) and the United Nations Development Programme (UNDP). When created more than half a century ago in the aftermath of the Second World War, the United Nations reflected the hope for a just and peaceful global community.

Unlike the other multinational organizations that we will discuss in the next chapter, the UN is the only global institution with legitimacy that derives from universal membership and a mandate that encompasses security, economic and social development, and, more specifically, the protection of human rights and the environment. Yet the UN was created by states for states, and the relationship between **state sovereignty** and the protection of the

supranational global organization An authoritative international organization that operates above the national state.

state sovereignty The concept that all countries are equal under international law and that they are protected from outside interference; this is the basis on which the UN and other international and regional organizations operate.

needs and interests of people has not been fully resolved. This debate was complicated by the 2005 decision by the UN to support the Responsibility to Protect resolution (R2P). This resolution was meant to resolve the impasse between those people who believe the outside world has the power to intervene in countries where human security is threatened and those who believe sovereignty precludes any outside intervention. Questions about the meaning of sovereignty and the limits of UN action have remained key issues. Since the founding of the UN, there has been an expansion of UN activities to address conditions within states, an improvement in UN capacity in its economic and social work, and an increased tendency to accord the UN a moral status. Threats to global security addressed by the UN now include interstate conflict and threats by **nonstate actors**, as well as political, economic, and social conditions within states. Despite the growth in UN activities, however, there are some questions about the relevance and effectiveness of the UN. Most recently, the failure by the United States and the United Kingdom to get clear UN Security Council authorization for the war in Iraq in 2003 led to well-publicized criticism of the UN and a crisis in international relations. Yet the troubled aftermath of the invasion and persistent questions about the legitimacy of a war that was not sanctioned by the UN show that the UN has acquired important moral status in international society.

After describing the main organs of the UN, this section will look at the changing role of the UN in addressing matters of peace and security and then matters of economic and social development. We will also focus our attention on how the UN's role has evolved in response to changes in the global political context and on some of the problems that it still faces.

A Brief History of the United Nations and Its Principal Organs

The United Nations was established on October 24, 1945, by fifty-one countries as a result of initiatives taken by the governments of the states that had led the war against Italy, Germany, and Japan. As early as 1939, American and British diplomats were discussing the need for a more effective international organization like the UN. It was intended to be a **collective security** organization. Often illustrated with the example of the stag hunt found in an essay by Jean-Jacques Rousseau (described in Chapter 3), this concept of collective security is simple: members of an organization agree that if one of them commits an offense to peace, all members of the organization will fight the aggressor. Unfortunately, as we will see later in this chapter, the Cold War bipolar international system undermined the effectiveness of the UN in security affairs.

By 2006, 192 states were members of the United Nations—nearly every state in the world. Notable exceptions include Western Sahara and Kosovo (neither of which are recognized as self-governing territories), Taiwan (which is not recognized as a separate territory from China), and Palestine and Vatican City (both of which enjoy nonmember observer status). When joining, member states agreed to accept the obligations of the **United Nations Charter**, an international treaty that set out basic principles of international relations. According to the Charter, the UN had four purposes: to maintain international peace and security; to develop friendly relations among nations; to cooperate in solving international problems and in promoting respect for human rights; and to be a center for harmonizing the actions of nations. At the UN, all the member states—large and small, rich and poor, with differing political views and social systems—had a voice and a vote in this process. Interestingly, while the United Nations was clearly created as a grouping of

nonstate actor Any participant in global politics that is neither acting in the name of government nor created and served by government. NGOs, terrorist networks, global crime syndicates, and multinational corporations are examples.

collective security Refers to an arrangement where "each state in the system accepts that the security of one is the concern of all, and agrees to join in a collective response to aggression" (Roberts and Kingsbury 1993, 30).

United Nations Charter (1945) The charter of the United Nations is the legal regime that created the United Nations as the world's only "supranational" organization. The charter defines the structure of the United Nations, the powers of its constitutive agencies, and the rights and obligations of sovereign states party to the charter. Among other things, the charter is the key legal document limiting the use of force to instances of self-defense and collective peace enforcement endorsed by the United Nations Security Council.

states, the Charter referred to the needs and interests of peoples as well as those of states (see Table 6.2).

In many ways, the United Nations was set up to correct the problems of its predecessor, the **League of Nations**. The League of Nations had been established after the First World War and was intended to make future wars impossible, but it lacked effective power. There was no clear division of responsibility between the main executive committee (the League Council) and the League Assembly, which included all member states. Both the League Assembly and the League Council could only make recommendations, not binding resolutions, and these recommendations had to be unanimous. Any government was free to reject any recommendation. Furthermore, there was no mechanism for coordinating military or economic actions against miscreant states. Key states, such as the United States, were not members of the League. By the Second World War, the League had already failed to address a number of acts of aggression.

San Francisco was the scene of the signing of the Charter of the United Nations in 1945. Has the time come to revise the document and reform the UN?

The structure of the United Nations was intended to avoid some of the problems faced by the League of Nations. The United Nations has six main organs: the Security

League of Nations The first permanent collective international security organization aimed at preventing future wars and resolving global problems. The League failed due to the failure of the US to join and the inability of its members to commit to a real international community.

Table 6.2
The UN Charter Contains References to Both the Rights of States and the Rights of People

> **The Preamble** of the UN Charter asserts that "We the peoples of the United Nations [are] determined [...] to reaffirm faith in fundamental human rights, in the dignity and worth of the human person, in the equal rights of men and women and of nations large and small."
>
> **Article 1(2)** states that the purpose of the UN is to develop "friendly relations among nations based on respect for the principle of equal rights and self-determination of peoples and to take other appropriate measures to strengthen universal peace."
>
> **Article 2(7)** states that "Nothing contained in the present Charter shall authorize the United Nations to intervene in matters which are essentially within the domestic jurisdiction of any state."
>
> **Chapter VI** deals with the "Pacific Settlement of Disputes."
>
> **Article 33** states that "The parties to any dispute, the continuance of which is likely to endanger the maintenance of international peace and security, shall, first of all, seek a solution by negotiation, enquiry, mediation, conciliation, arbitration, judicial settlement, resort to regional agencies or arrangements, or other peaceful means of their own choice."
>
> **Chapter VII** deals with "Action with Respect to Threats to the Peace, Breaches of the Peace, and Acts of Aggression."
>
> **Article 42** states that the Security Council "may take such action by air, sea, or land forces as may be necessary to maintain or restore international peace and security." The Security Council has sometimes authorized member states to use "all necessary means," and this has been accepted as a legitimate application of Chapter VII powers.
>
> **Article 99** authorizes the secretary-general to "bring to the attention of the Security Council any matter which in his opinion may threaten the maintenance of international peace and security."

Council, the General Assembly, the Secretariat, the Economic and Social Council, the Trusteeship Council, and the International Court of Justice (see Figure 6.1).

The Security Council

The UN Security Council was given the main responsibility for maintaining international peace and security. It was made up initially of eleven states and then, after 1965, of fifteen states. It includes five permanent members (sometimes called "the P-5"), namely, the United States, Britain, France, Russia (previously the Soviet Union)—the victors in the Second World War—and China, as well as ten nonpermanent members. (China was first represented by Nationalist China and not the People's Republic of China.) In contrast to the League of Nations, the United Nations recognized great power prerogatives in the Security Council, offering each of the P-5 a **veto power** over all Security Council decisions. The convention emerged that abstention by a permanent member is not regarded as a veto. Unlike with the League, the decisions of the Security Council are binding and must only be passed by a majority of nine out of the fifteen members. However, if one permanent member dissents, the resolution does not pass.

The five permanent members of the Security Council were seen as the major powers when the UN was founded, and they were granted a veto on the view that if the great powers were not given a privileged position, the UN would not work. This recognition of a state's influence being proportional to its size and political and military power stems from the realist notion that power determines who rules in the international system. Indeed, this tension between the recognition of power politics through the Security Council veto and the universal ideals underlying the United Nations is a defining feature of the organization. There have been widespread and frequent calls for the reform of the Security Council, but this is very difficult. In both theoretical and policy terms the inability to reform the Security Council also shows the limits of a collective security system and liberal thinking that suggests all states are equal.

When the Security Council considers a threat to international peace, it first explores ways to settle the dispute peacefully under the terms of Chapter VI of the UN Charter. It may suggest principles for a settlement or may suggest mediation. In the event of fighting, the Security Council tries to secure a cease-fire. It may send a peacekeeping mission to help the parties maintain the truce and to keep opposing forces apart (see the discussion of peacekeeping below). The Council can also take measures to enforce its decisions under Chapter VII of the Charter. It can, for instance, impose **economic sanctions** or order an **arms embargo**. (See Chapter 5 for a discussion of these foreign policy tools.) On rare occasions, the Security Council has authorized member states to use all necessary means, including collective military action, to see that its decisions are carried out. The Council also makes recommendations to the General Assembly on the appointment of a new secretary-general and on the admission of new members to the UN.

The General Assembly

The recognition of power politics through veto power in the Security Council can be contrasted with the universal principles underlying the other organs of the United Nations. All UN member states are represented in the General Assembly—a "parliament of nations"—which meets to consider the world's most pressing problems. Each member

veto power The right of the five permanent members of the Security Council (United States, Russia, China, France, and Great Britain) to forbid any action by the United Nations.

economic sanctions A tool of statecraft that seeks to get a state to behave by coercion of a monetary kind: for example, freezing banking assets, cutting aid programs, or banning trade.

arms embargo Similar to economic sanctions, an arms embargo stops the flow of arms from one country to another.

The United Nations System

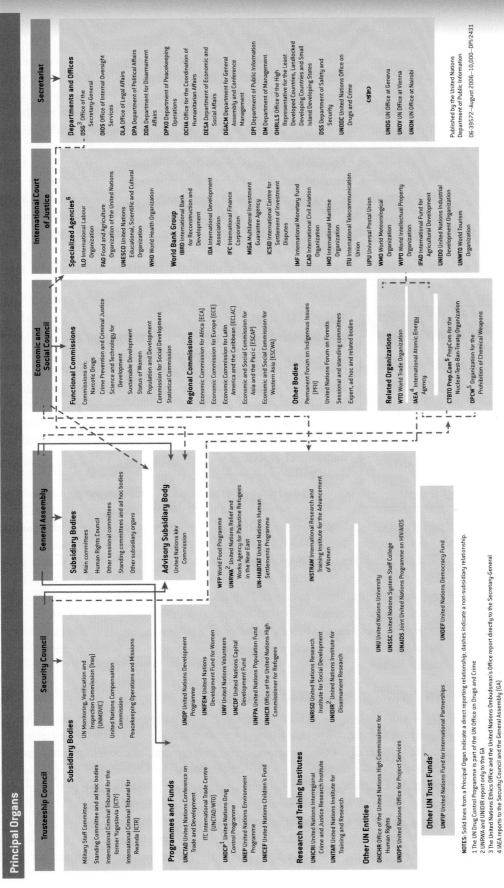

Principal Organs

Trusteeship Council

Security Council

Subsidiary Bodies

Military Staff Committee

Standing Committee and ad hoc bodies

International Criminal Tribunal for the former Yugoslavia (ICTY)

International Criminal Tribunal for Rwanda (ICTR)

UN Monitoring, Verification and Inspection Commission (Iraq) (UNMOVIC)

United Nations Compensation Commission

Peacekeeping Operations and Missions

General Assembly

Subsidiary Bodies

Main committees

Human Rights Council

Other sessional committees

Standing committees and ad hoc bodies

Other subsidiary organs

Advisory Subsidiary Body

United Nations kkv Commission

Programmes and Funds

UNCTAD United Nations Conference on Trade and Development

  ITC International Trade Centre (UNCTAD/WTO)

UNDCP[1] United Nations Drug Control Programme

UNEP United Nations Environment Programme

UNICEF United Nations Children's Fund

UNDP United Nations Development Programme

  UNIFEM United Nations Development Fund for Women

  UNV United Nations Volunteers

  UNCDF United Nations Capital Development Fund

UNFPA United Nations Population Fund

UNHCR Office of the United Nations High Commissioner for Refugees

WFP World Food Programme

UNRWA[2] United Nations Relief and Works Agency for Palestine Refugees in the Near East

UN-HABITAT United Nations Human Settlements Programme

Research and Training Institutes

UNICRI United Nations Interregional Crime and Justice Research Institute

UNITAR United Nations Institute for Training and Research

UNRISD United Nations Research Institute for Social Development

UNIDIR[2] United Nations Institute for Disarmament Research

INSTRAW International Research and Training Institute for the Advancement of Women

Other UN Entities

OHCHR Office of the United Nations High Commissioner for Human Rights

UNOPS United Nations Office for Project Services

UNU United Nations University

UNSSC United Nations System Staff College

UNAIDS Joint United Nations Programme on HIV/AIDS

Other UN Trust Funds[7]

UNFIP United Nations Fund for International Partnerships

UNDEF United Nations Democracy Fund

Economic and Social Council

Functional Commissions

Commissions on:

Narcotic Drugs

Crime Prevention and Criminal Justice

Science and Technology for Development

Sustainable Development

Status of Women

Population and Development

Commission for Social Development

Statistical Commission

Regional Commissions

Economic Commission for Africa (ECA)

Economic Commission for Europe (ECE)

Economic Commission for Latin America and the Caribbean (ECLAC)

Economic and Social Commission for Asia and the Paci c (ESCAP)

Economic and Social Commission for Western Asia (ESCWA)

Other Bodies

Permanent Forum on Indigenous Issues (PFII)

United Nations Forum on Forests

Sessional and standing committees

Expert, ad hoc and related bodies

Related Organizations

WTO World Trade Organization

IAEA[4] International Atomic Energy Agency

CTBTO Prep.Com[5] PrepCom for the Nuclear-Test-Ban-Treaty Organization

OPCW[5] Organization for the Prohibition of Chemical Weapons

International Court of Justice

Specialized Agencies[6]

ILO International Labour Organization

FAO Food and Agriculture Organization of the United Nations

UNESCO United Nations Educational, Scientific and Cultural Organization

WHO World Health Organization

World Bank Group

IBRD International Bank for Reconstruction and Development

IDA International Development Association

IFC International Finance Corporation

MIGA Multilateral Investment Guarantee Agency

ICSID International Centre for Settlement of Investment Disputes

IMF International Monetary Fund

ICAO International Civil Aviation Organization

IMO International Maritime Organization

ITU International Telecommunication Union

UPU Universal Postal Union

WMO World Meteorological Organization

WIPO World Intellectual Property Organization

IFAD International Fund for Agricultural Development

UNIDO United Nations Industrial Development Organization

UNWTO World Tourism Organization

Secretariat

Departments and Offices

OSG[3] Office of the Secretary-General

OIOS Office of Internal Oversight Services

OLA Office of Legal Affairs

DPA Department of Political Affairs

DDA Department for Disarmament Affairs

DPKO Department of Peacekeeping Operations

OCHA Office for the Coordination of Humanitarian Affairs

DESA Department of Economic and Social Affairs

DGACM Department for General Assembly and Conference Management

DPI Department of Public Information

DM Department of Management

OHRLLS Office of the High Representative for the Least Developed Countries, Landlocked Developing Countries and Small Island Developing States

DSS Department of Safety and Security

UNODC United Nations Office on Drugs and Crime

      ∾∾∾

UNOG UN Office at Geneva

UNOV UN Office at Vienna

UNON UN Office at Nairobi

Published by the United Nations
Department of Public Information
06-39572—August 2006—10,000—DPI/2431

NOTES: Solid lines from a Principal Organ indicate a direct reporting relationship; dashes indicate a non-subsidiary relationship.

1 The UN Drug Control Programme is part of the UN Office on Drugs and Crime

2 UNRWA and UNIDIR report only to the GA

3 The United Nations Ethics Office and the United Nations Ombudsman's Office report directly to the Secretary-General

4 IAEA reports to the Security Council and the General Assembly (GA)

5 The CTBTO Prep.Com and OPCW report to the GA

6 Specialized agencies are autonomous organizations working with the UN and each other through the coordinating machinery of the ECOSOC at the intergovernmental level, and through the Chief Executives Board for coordination (CEB) at the inter-secretariat level

7 UNFIP is an autonomous trust fund operating under the leadership of the United Nations Deputy Secretary-General. UNDEF's advisory board recommends funding proposals for approval by the Secretary-General.

Figure 6.1 The Structure of the United Nations

Source: Reproduced by permission of the United Nations Department of Public Information.

171

state has one vote. A two-thirds majority in the General Assembly is required for decisions on key issues such as international peace and security, the admission of new members, and the UN budget. A simple majority is required for other matters. However, the decisions reached by the General Assembly only have the status of recommendations, rather than binding decisions. One of the few exceptions is the General Assembly's Fifth Committee, which makes decisions on the budget that are binding on members.

The General Assembly can consider any matter within the scope of the UN Charter. There were 156 items on the agenda of the sixty-first session of the General Assembly (2006–2007), including topics such as globalization, the role of diamonds in fueling conflict, international cooperation in the peaceful uses of outer space, peacekeeping operations, sustainable development, and international migration. Since General Assembly resolutions are nonbinding, they cannot force action by any state, but the Assembly's recommendations are important indications of world opinion and represent the moral authority of the community of nation-states.

WHAT'S YOUR WORLDVIEW ?

In his 2008 global agenda address, Secretary-General Ban Ki-moon called for a strategy of "principled pragmatism" with a focus on three critical issues: humanitarian intervention, especially in the case of Darfur; aiding the world's poor by meeting the Millennium Development Goals (MDG); and global climate change. Can the UN do much about these issues without the support of the major powers? Why or why not?

nongovernmental organization (NGO) An organization, usually a grassroots one, with policy goals, but not governmental in makeup. An NGO is any group of people relating to each other regularly in some formal manner and engaging in collective action, provided the activities are noncommercial and nonviolent and are not on behalf of a government.

civil society (1) The totality of all individuals and groups in a society who are not acting as participants in any government institutions, or (2) all individuals and groups who are neither participants in government nor acting in the interests of commercial companies.

The Secretariat

The Secretariat carries out the substantive and administrative work of the United Nations as directed by the General Assembly, the Security Council, and the other organs. It is led by the secretary-general, who provides overall administrative guidance. In December 2006, Ban Ki-moon from South Korea was sworn in as the eighth secretary-general. The Secretariat consists of departments and offices with a total staff of 8,900 under the regular budget and a nearly equal number under special funding.

On the recommendation of the other bodies, the Secretariat also carries out a number of research functions and some quasi-management functions. Yet the role of the Secretariat remains primarily bureaucratic, and it lacks the political power and the right of initiative of, for instance, the Commission of the European Union. The one exception to this is the power of the secretary-general, under Article 99 of the Charter, to bring situations that are likely to lead to a breakdown of international peace and security to the attention of the Security Council. This article, which may appear innocuous at first, was the legal basis for the remarkable expansion of the diplomatic role of the secretary-general, compared with its League predecessor. The secretary-general is empowered to become involved in a large range of areas that can be loosely interpreted as threats to peace, including economic and social problems and humanitarian crises.

The Economic and Social Council

The Economic and Social Council (ECOSOC), under the overall authority of the General Assembly, is intended to coordinate the economic and social work of the United Nations and the UN family of organizations. It also consults with **nongovernmental organizations (NGOs)**, thereby maintaining a vital link between the United Nations and **civil society**. ECOSOC's subsidiary bodies include functional commissions, such as the Commission on the Status of Women; regional commissions, such as the Economic Commission for Africa; and other bodies (see Figure 6.1).

Along with the Secretariat and the General Assembly, ECOSOC is responsible for overseeing the activities of a large number of other institutions known as the United

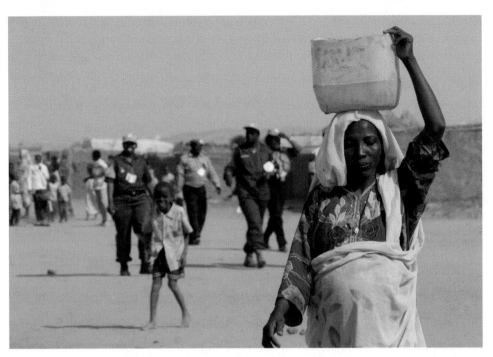

United Nations peacekeeping forces—called "the Blue Helmets"—can provide protection for refugees at camps like this one in the Darfur region of Sudan. With UN members supporting the Responsibility to Protect document, will peacekeeping become more aggressive and comprehensive?

Nations system. This includes the Specialized Agencies and the Programmes and Funds. The Specialized Agencies, such as the World Health Organization (WHO) and the International Labor Organization (ILO), have their own constitutions, regularly assessed budgets, executive heads, and assemblies of state representatives. They are self-contained constitutionally, financially, and politically and not subject to the management of the central system.

The Programmes and Funds are much closer to the central system in the sense that their management arrangements are subject to direct General Assembly supervision, can be modified by Assembly resolution, and are largely funded on a voluntary basis. Since the establishment of the United Nations in 1945, a number of new issues have come onto the international agenda, such as the rights and interests of women, climate change, resource depletion, population growth, terrorism, and the spread of HIV/AIDS. Frequently, those issues led to a new organization in the Programmes and Funds. Examples of Programmes and Funds include the United Nations Development Programme (UNDP) and the United Nations Children's Fund (UNICEF).

Whereas the League of Nations attributed responsibility for economic and social questions to the League Assembly, the Charter of the United Nations established ECOSOC to oversee economic and social institutions. This change was a consequence of thinking in more functionalist terms. Functionalism is a liberal idea that suggests that states will cooperate in functionally specific areas like a health pandemic, and, if successful, that cooperative activity will "spill over" into other policy areas (see Chapter 4). Organizations were set up to deal with specific economic and social problems. However, ECOSOC was not given necessary management powers. It can only issue recommendations and receive reports from the Specialized Agencies. In consequence, the UN's economic and social organizations have continually searched for better ways of achieving effective management.

The Trusteeship Council

When the United Nations was created, the Trusteeship Council was established to provide international supervision for eleven Trust Territories administered by seven member states and to ensure that adequate steps were taken to prepare the territories for self-government or independence. By 1994, all Trust Territories had attained self-government or independence, either as separate states or by joining neighboring independent countries. The last to do so was the Trust Territory of the Pacific Islands, Palau, which had been previously administered by the United States under special rules with the UN called a Strategic Trust. Its work completed, the Trusteeship Council now consists of the five permanent members of the Security Council. It has amended its rules of procedure to allow it to meet when necessary.

> ### WHAT'S YOUR WORLDVIEW?
>
> *Given the global economic troubles we now face, should the UN create an Economic Security Council? What could it do, and could it be effective?*

The International Court of Justice

The International Court of Justice (ICJ) is the main judicial organ of the UN. Consisting of fifteen judges elected jointly by the General Assembly and the Security Council, the Court decides disputes between countries. Participation by states in a proceeding is voluntary, but if a state agrees to participate, it is obligated to comply with the Court's decision. The Court also provides advisory opinions to other UN organs and Specialized Agencies on request. Only states may bring cases before the ICJ. If people who live in one state want to bring a suit against another state, they must get their home state to file the suit.

Three factors reduce the effectiveness of the ICJ. First, the competence, or jurisdiction, of the Court is limited, as noted above, to cases that states bring against states. The Court's statutory jurisdiction extends to anything related to a state's undertakings by signing the UN Charter and any matter related to a ratified treaty. If a state is not a signatory, there can be no recourse to the good offices of the ICJ. In addition, if the UN itself is a party to the case, at least one state party of the ICJ must be an applicant as well. This happened with the South-West Africa cases of the 1970s. A second factor that reduces the ICJ's effectiveness is the question of compulsory jurisdiction. States that are party to the ICJ statute are bound by compulsory jurisdiction unless they agree to it; this is the "option clause" problem. For example, in the *Aerial Incident of July 27, 1955 (Israel v. Bulgaria)* the court found that Bulgaria was not liable for damages because its compulsory jurisdiction option had expired. A third factor—the state reservations—limits the effectiveness of the ICJ and follows from the option-clause problems. For not only may a state let its compulsory jurisdiction lapse, it can also refuse to accept the ICJ jurisdiction if the state claims that its own existing national law covers the issue before the courts. This occurred, for example, in a 1957 case in which Norway sued France over a debt owed to Norwegian investors. France claimed that its domestic legal system had jurisdiction in the matter, and Norway lost.

Maintenance of International Peace and Security

The performance of the United Nations in questions of peace and security has been shaped by the global political context. Clearly, there have been changes in international society since the UN was founded in 1945 that have had an impact on the UN system.

The Cold War between the United States and the Soviet Union hampered the functioning of the UN Security Council, since the veto could be used whenever the major interests of the United States or Soviet Union were threatened. From 1945 to 1990, 193 substantive vetoes were invoked in the Security Council, compared to only 19 substantive vetoes from 1990 to 2007. Furthermore, while the UN Charter provided for a standing army to be set up by agreement between the Security Council and consenting states, the East-West Cold War rivalry made this impossible to implement. The end result was that the UN Security Council could not function in the way in which the UN founders had expected.

Since member states could not agree on the arrangements laid out in Chapter VII of the Charter, especially with regard to setting up a UN army, there followed a series of improvisations to address matters of peace and security. First, a procedure was established under which the Security Council agreed to a mandate for an agent to act on its behalf. This occurred in the Korean conflict in 1950 and the Gulf War in 1990, when action was undertaken principally by the United States and its allies.

Second, there have been many instances of what analysts call "classical peacekeeping." Classical peacekeeping involves the establishment of a UN force under UN command to be placed between the parties to a dispute after a cease-fire. Such a force only uses its weapons in self-defense, is established with the consent of the host state, and does not include forces from the major powers. No reference to peacekeeping exists in the UN Charter, but classical peacekeeping mandates and mechanisms are based on Chapter VI of the UN Charter. This mechanism was first used in 1956, when a UN force was sent to Egypt to facilitate the exodus of the British and French forces from the Suez Canal area and then to stand between Egyptian and Israeli forces. Since the Suez crisis, there have been a number of classical peacekeeping missions: for instance, monitoring the Green Line in Cyprus, in the Golan Heights, and after the decade-long Iraq-Iran War. The primary drawback to this kind of peacekeeping operation is that it is not effective if the war parties do not want to have peace. Second, once these peacekeeping missions are initiated, they are very difficult to conclude.

Third, there has been a new kind of peacekeeping, sometimes called multidimensional peacekeeping or **peace enforcement**, which emerged after the end of the Cold War. These missions are more likely to use force to achieve humanitarian ends. The new peacekeeping mandates are sometimes based on Chapter VII of the UN Charter. Such forces have been used when order has collapsed within states and therefore address civil wars as well as international conflict. A key problem has been that the peacekeepers have found it increasingly difficult to maintain a neutral position and have been targeted by belligerents. Examples include the intervention in Somalia in the early 1990s and intervention in the former Yugoslavia in the mid-1990s. In both cases, until the EU, NATO, or the United States was directly involved in the operations, peace was elusive. Certainly even after the US intervention in 1993 in Somalia, sadly best known for the "Black Hawk Down" incident, the country remains a failed state, characterized by clan-based violence.

In the early 1990s, after the end of the Cold War, the UN agenda for peace and security expanded quickly. The secretary-general at the time, Boutros Boutros-Ghali, outlined a more ambitious role for the UN in his seminal report, *An Agenda for Peace* (1992). The report described interconnected roles for the UN to maintain peace and security in the post–Cold War context. These included four main kinds of activities: **preventive diplomacy** that involves confidence-building measures, fact-finding, and preventive deployment of UN authorized forces; **peacemaking**, designed to bring hostile parties to agreement,

peace enforcement Designed to bring hostile parties to agreement and may occur without the consent of the parties.

preventive diplomacy Measures that states take to keep a disagreement from escalating.

peacemaking Active diplomatic efforts to seek a resolution to an international dispute that has already escalated.

peacekeeping The interposition of third-party military personnel to keep warring parties apart.

post-conflict peace building Activities launched after a conflict has ended that seek to end the condition that caused the conflict.

essentially through peaceful means; **peacekeeping**, which is the deployment of a UN presence in the field with the consent of all parties (this refers to classical peacekeeping); and **post-conflict peace building**, which, it is hoped, will develop the social, political, and economic infrastructure to prevent further violence and to consolidate peace. However, when all peaceful means have failed, peace enforcement authorized under Chapter VII of the Charter may be necessary. Peace enforcement may occur without the consent of the parties in conflict.

UN peacekeeping went through a rapid expansion in the early 1990s. In 1994, UN peacekeeping operations involved nearly 80,000 military personnel around the world, seven times the figure for 1990 (Pugh 2001, 115). In early 2007, the total number of peacekeeping personnel (military and police) in the UN's fifteen ongoing peacekeeping operations was just over 82,000.

Increased Attention to Conditions Within States

The new peacekeeping was the product of a greater preparedness to intervene within states. This challenged the traditional belief that diplomats should ignore the internal affairs of states in order to preserve international stability. An increasing number of people believed that the international community, working through the UN, should address individual political and civil rights, as well as the right to basic provisions like food, water, health care, and accommodation. Under this view, violations of individuals' rights were a major cause of disturbances in relations between states: a lack of internal justice risked international disorder. The UN reinforced this new perception that pursuing justice for individuals, or ensuring **human security**, was an aspect of national interest. (See Chapter 10 for more information on the topic of human security.)

human security The security of people, including their physical safety, their economic and social well-being, respect for their dignity, and the protection of their human rights. Simply put, it is freedom from fear and freedom from want.

In some states, contributions to activities such as peacekeeping were defended in terms of national interest. Indeed, states like Canada and Norway could justify their contributions to peacekeeping as a "moral" course of action, but it was also in their national interest since both countries gained status in the international community through such contributions. The Japanese also responded to moral pressure founded in national interest when they contributed substantially to defraying the cost of British involvement in the 1990–1991 Gulf War. This act can be explained in terms of the synthesis of morality and interest. For some states, reputation in the United Nations had become an important national good.

> **WHAT'S YOUR WORLDVIEW ?**
>
> *Why would a country decide to participate in a UN peacekeeping operation? What factors would motivate them to participate in such a collective action?*

These actions reflected an increasing concern with questions of justice for individuals and conditions within states. Yet in the past, the United Nations had helped to promote the traditional view of the primacy of international order between states over justice for individuals, so the new focus on individual rights was a significant change. What accounts for this change?

First, the international environment had changed. The Cold War standoff between the East and the West had meant that member states did not want to question the conditions of the sovereignty of states. Jeanne Kirkpatrick's (1979) influential essay, which recommended tolerating abhorrent dictatorships in Latin America in order to fight communism, was a reasonable report of the situation at that time. Unsavory right-wing regimes in Latin America were tolerated because they were anti-Soviet, and interfering in the other's sphere risked escalation of conflict (Forsythe 1988, 259–60).

Second, the process of decolonization had privileged statehood over justice. The UN respected the claims of colonies to become states and had elevated the right to statehood

Why Some Realists Have Concerns About the UN

For analysts of the realist school of thought, states exist in an anarchic, self-help world. As we saw in Chapter 3, the condition of anarchy means that states must look to their own power resources for national security. It would be wrong to assume that all realist thinkers and policy makers are opposed to international organizations. However, most are wary of those organizations that prevent them from securing their national interests. Alliances should only be short-term events, because allies might desert you in a crisis. For some realists, committing security to a collective security organization is even worse than an alliance, because in a worst-case situation, the alliance might gang up on your country. Even in the best-case situation, it would be a bad idea to submit your military forces to foreign leadership.

In its early years, prior to the wave of decolonization in Africa and Asia, the UN's US-based realist critics did not have the ear of the country's political leadership. Presidents Truman and Eisenhower both found a way around the USSR's Security Council veto by working through the General Assembly, a body that at that time was very friendly to the United States and its goals. However, with the end of European control of Africa and Asia, the General Assembly changed. The body frequently passed resolutions condemning the United States and its allies. One result was a growing movement to end US involvement in the UN, especially among the key foreign policy advisors to President Reagan.

US president George W. Bush, himself a critic of multilateralism, chose, in a controversial recess appointment, John Bolton to be the US ambassador to the UN. Bolton had worked in the administrations of presidents Reagan and the elder Bush, but his appointment as a UN envoy was a surprise to many in the international diplomatic community, primarily because he was such a staunch opponent of multilateral organizations in general, with the UN drawing his most specific vituperation.

In the 1980s the intellectual explanation for this antipathy toward the UN had a logic based on problems

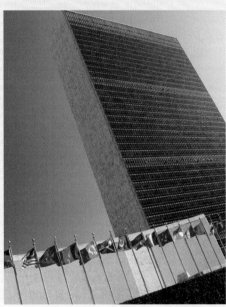

The UN headquarters in New York City. Do the five permanent members of the Security Council have too much power over the operations of the organization?

that the organization itself would later recognize to a certain extent. Reagan administration critics did not like what they said was the socialist ideological bias found in UNESCO programs and the fact that the head of UNESCO was a critic of US foreign policy in Central America. US critics also did not like the pro-abortion policy of some UN-sponsored development programs. In 1985, the US delegate to the UN's Nairobi Conference on the status of women was President Reagan's daughter, Maureen, who often cast the sole dissenting vote on measures designed to improve women's lives. Political realists saw no tangible benefit for the United States to remain active in the UN once the leaders in Washington could no longer count on a UN rubber stamp for US policies. For a number of years the United States did not pay its dues to the UN. Only after Richard Holbrooke, the US ambassador to the UN in the Clinton administration, negotiated a reduction in the American contribution to the UN in 2000 did the US repay its arrears, with the help of prominent media businessman Ted Turner.

The rejection of UN-style multilateralism revived with the Bush presidency in 2001. The Bush foreign policy advisors did not like the peacekeeping operation in the former Yugoslavia. In her criticism of the Clinton foreign policy, National Security Advisor Rice said the United States would not send its troops to countries for nation building. More importantly, the Bush administration did not want to have its hands tied when dealing with Iraq and its alleged store of nuclear, chemical, and biological weapons. President Bush and his top advisors believed that sanctions—an important weapon in the UN's moral-suasion arsenal—would never force Iraq to disarm and that only force could do so. The irony is that after the 2003 invasion the US's own weapons inspectors could find no evidence that Iraq had any of the banned weapons.

above any tests of viability, such as the existence of a nation, adequate economic performance, defensibility, or a prospect for achieving justice for citizens. This unconditional right to independence was enunciated in the General Assembly Declaration on the Granting of Independence to Colonial Countries and Peoples in 1960. There emerged a convention that the claims of elites in the putative states could be a sufficient indication of popular enthusiasm, even when the elites were crooks and the claims misleading.

Charles Beitz was one of the first to question this when he concluded that statehood should not be unconditional and that attention had to be given to the situation of individuals after independence (Beitz 1979). Michael Walzer and Terry Nardin produced arguments leading to similar conclusions: states were conditional entities in that their right to exist should be dependent on a criterion of performance with regard to the interests of their citizens (Walzer 1977; Nardin 1983). Such writings helped alter the moral content of diplomacy.

The new relationship between order and justice was, therefore, a product of particular circumstances. After the Cold War, it was felt that threats to international peace and security did not only emanate from aggression between states. Rather, global peace was also threatened by civil conflict (including refugee flows and regional instability), humanitarian emergencies, violations of global standards of human rights, and other conditions such as poverty and inequality.

More recently, other types of non-state-based threats, such as terrorism and the proliferation of small arms and weapons of mass destruction, have an increasingly prominent place on the UN security agenda. Partly due to the terrorist attacks in the United States in 2001, as well as the impasse reached in the UN Security Council over Iraq in 2003, then secretary-general Kofi Annan named a high-level panel to examine the major threats and challenges to global peace. The 2004 final report, *A More Secure World: Our Shared Responsibility*, emphasized the interconnected nature of security threats and presented development, security, and human rights as mutually reinforcing. Many of the report's recommendations were not implemented, but some were, notably the establishment of a new UN Peacebuilding Commission.

The UN Peacebuilding Commission was established in December 2005 as an advisory subsidiary body of the General Assembly and the Security Council. It was proposed first by the secretary-general's High-level Panel on Threats, Challenges, and Change in December 2004 and again in the secretary-general's report *In Larger Freedom* in March 2005 (UN 2005). Existing mechanisms at the UN were thought to be insufficient in responding to the particular needs of states emerging from conflict. Many countries, such as Liberia, Haiti, and Somalia in the 1990s, had signed peace agreements and hosted UN peacekeeping missions but reverted to violent conflict. The Peacebuilding Commission aims to provide targeted support to countries in the volatile postconflict phase to prevent the recurrence of conflict. It will propose integrated strategies and priorities for postconflict recovery, in order to improve coordination among the myriad of actors involved in postconflict activities. The establishment of the Peacebuilding Commission is indicative of a growing trend at the UN to coordinate security and development programming.

The organizational committee of the Peacebuilding Commission is made up of thirty-one member states, and the first session was held in June 2006. The Peacebuilding Support Fund, with a target of $250 million, is designed to support the activities of the commission. There are also country-specific meetings to look at the postconflict strategies, priorities, and programming for specific countries. The first two states considered by the Peacebuilding Commission were Sierra Leone and Burundi.

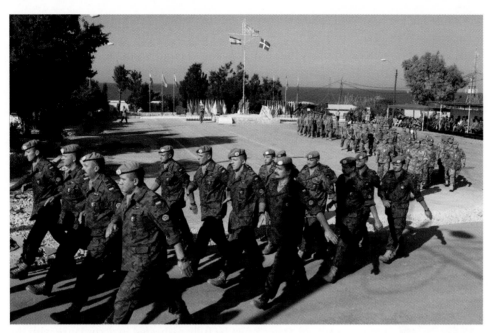

The UN has deployed peacekeepers to the Israel-Lebanon border for more than forty years. Why have transboundary raids by forces on both sides continued?

Intervention Within States

As issues of peace and security were increasingly understood to include human security and justice, the UN was expected to take on a stronger role in maintaining standards for individuals within states. A difficulty with carrying out the new tasks was that it seemed to run against the doctrine of nonintervention. **Intervention** was traditionally defined as a deliberate incursion into a state, without its consent, by some outside agency, in order to change the functioning, policies, and goals of its government and achieve effects that favor the intervening agency (Vincent 1974).

At the founding of the UN, sovereignty was regarded as central to the system of states. States were equal members of international society and were equal with regard to international law. Sovereignty also implied that states recognized no higher authority than themselves and that there was no superior jurisdiction. The governments of states had exclusive jurisdiction within their own frontiers, a principle that was enshrined in Article 2(7) of the United Nations Charter. Intervention in the traditional sense was in opposition to the principles of international society, and it could only be tolerated as an exception to the rule.

In earlier periods, however, states had intervened in each other's business and thought that they had a right to do so. The United States refused to accept any curtailment of its right to intervene in the internal affairs of other states in its hemisphere until 1933, when it conceded the point at the Seventh International Conference of American States. The US position was very similar to the Brezhnev doctrine of the 1970s, which held that the Soviet Union had the right to intervene in the member states of the socialist commonwealth to protect the principles of socialism.

Much earlier, the British had insisted on the abolition of slavery, in their relations with other states. They stopped ships on the high seas and imposed the abolition of slavery as

intervention Direct involvement within a state by an outside actor to achieve an outcome preferred by the intervening agency without the consent of the host state.

a condition in treaties (Bethell 1970). There were also occasions when states tried to bind other states to respect certain principles in their internal affairs. A number of states in Eastern Europe, such as Hungary and Bulgaria, were bound to respect the rights of minorities within their frontiers based on agreements made at the 1878 Congress of Berlin by the great powers. In practice, then, intervention was a common feature of international politics.

By the 1990s, some believed that there should be a return to this earlier period, when intervention was justified, but it was felt that a wider range of instruments should be used to protect generally accepted standards. Supporters of this idea insisted on a key role for the United Nations in granting a license to intervene. It was pointed out that the UN Charter did not assert merely the rights of states but also the rights of peoples: statehood could be interpreted as being conditional on respect for such rights. There was ample evidence in the UN Charter to justify the view that extreme transgressions of human rights could be a justification for intervention by the international community.

The major pronouncements of the UN General Assembly on humanitarian assistance referred to the primary responsibility of states for dealing with complex crises within their frontiers. A 1991 General Assembly resolution implied some relaxation of this principle when it held that "the sovereignty, territorial integrity, and national unity of States must be fully respected in accordance with the Charter of the United Nations. In this context, humanitarian assistance should be provided with the consent of the affected country and in principle on the basis of an appeal by the affected country" (A/RES/46/182). The use of the phrase "in principle," and the term "should," imply that there could be occasions where intervention was necessary even when consent in the target state was not possible. In the Outcome Document of the 2005 World Summit, the General Assembly said that if national authorities are "manifestly failing to protect their populations from genocide, war crimes, ethnic cleansing and crimes against humanity" and if peaceful means are inadequate, the international community could take collective action through the UN Security Council according to Chapter VII of the Charter (A/RES/60/1, para. 138 and 139). This document echoes recommendations from the **Responsibility to Protect**, the 2001 final report of the International Commission on Intervention and State Sovereignty.

Yet the number of occasions where a UN resolution justified intervention due to gross infringements of the rights of individuals has remained limited. The justification of intervention in Kosovo represented a break from the past in that it included a clear humanitarian element. Kosovo was arguably the first occasion in which international forces were used in defiance of a sovereign state in order to protect humanitarian standards. NATO launched the air campaign in March 1999 in Kosovo against the Republic of Yugoslavia without a mandate from the Security Council, since Russia had declared that it would veto such action. Nonetheless, NATO states noted that by intervening to stop ethnic cleansing and crimes against humanity in Kosovo they were acting in accordance with the principles of the UN Charter.

The Iraq War in 2003 was another case, although the legality of intervention under existing Security Council resolutions is contested, especially in view of the failure to obtain a second UN Security Council resolution to give an explicit mandate for the action (see the Case Study in this chapter). The US action against Afghanistan in 2001 is an exceptional case in which the UN Security Council acknowledged the right of a state that had

---

WHAT'S YOUR WORLDVIEW

Is the idea of national sovereignty now obsolete? With globalization becoming a more important factor in shaping our quality of life, should we be more open to collective multilateralism and global governance?

Responsibility to Protect
The 2001 final report of the International Commission on Intervention and State Sovereignty; a UN publication that asserted the moral obligation for states to intervene in a state when that state violates the human rights of people living there.

been attacked—referring to the events of 9/11 in the United States—to respond in its own defense.

Arguably, earlier instances of intervention did not explicitly breach sovereignty. The 1991 Security Council resolution sanctioning intervention in Iraq (S/Res/688) at the end of the Gulf War did not breach Iraqi sovereignty insofar as its implementation depended on Saddam Hussein's consent. The 1992 Security Council resolution (S/Res/733) that first sanctioned UN involvement in Somalia was based on a request by Somalia. A later resolution (S/Res/794) authorizing the United States to intervene in Somalia did not mention the consent of Somali authorities, but by that time a central Somali government did not exist.

The difficulty in relaxing the principle of nonintervention should not be underestimated. For instance, the UN has been reluctant to send peacekeepers to Darfur without the consent of the Sudanese government. Some fear a slippery slope whereby a relaxation of the nonintervention principle by the UN will lead to military action by individual states without UN approval. It could be argued that the action against Iraq in 2003 illustrates this danger (see the Case Study in this chapter). There are significant numbers of non-UN actors, including regional organizations, involved in peace operations, and several states are suspicious of what appears to be the granting of a license to intervene in their affairs.

An increasing readiness by the UN to intervene within states in order to promote internal justice for individuals would indicate a movement toward global governance and away from unconditional sovereignty. There have been some signs of movement in this direction, but principles of state sovereignty and nonintervention remain important. There is no clear consensus on these points. There is still some support for the view that Article 2(7) of the UN Charter should be interpreted strictly: that there can be no intervention within a state without the express consent of the government of that state. Others believe that intervention within a country to promote human rights is only justifiable on the basis of a threat to international peace and security. Evidence of a threat to international peace and security could be the appearance of significant numbers of refugees or the judgment that other states might intervene militarily. Some liberal internationalists argue that this condition is flexible enough to justify intervention to defend human rights whenever possible.

Overall, then, the UN's record on the maintenance of international peace and security has been mixed. On the one hand, there has been a stronger assertion of the responsibility of international society, represented by the United Nations, for gross offenses against populations. Nonetheless, the practice has been patchy. Intimations of a **new world order** in the aftermath of the Gulf War in 1991 quickly gave way to despondency with what were seen as failures in Somalia, Rwanda, other parts of Africa, and the former Yugoslavia, and increasing disagreement about the proper role of the UN in Kosovo and Iraq. Compared to the enthusiasm about the potential for the UN in the early 1990s, the debates and disagreements at the time of the war in Iraq in 2003 were striking.

Economic and Social Questions

As described above, there has been an increased tendency to view threats to peace and security not only in terms of traditional threats such as aggression between states but also in terms of civil conflict within states, threats emanating from nonstate actors, and threats relating to economic and social conditions within states. This view includes the belief that conditions within states, including human rights, justice, development, and equality, have

new world order This refers to the post–Cold War rhetoric of President George Herbert Walker Bush, who called for a new world order based on neoliberal values of democracy, capitalism, and the rule of law. After periods of turmoil or war, the victors often call for a new world order based on their values, beliefs, and interests.

The 2003 Intervention in Iraq

In March 2003, a US-led coalition launched a highly controversial war in Iraq, which removed Saddam Hussein from power. The justification for war stressed Iraq's possession of weapons of mass destruction, in defiance of earlier UN resolutions. Unlike in Kosovo, gross violations of human rights were not given as a main justification for the invasion until later. Yet the failure to find weapons of mass destruction in Iraq, as well as the ongoing civil war, have fueled the claims of critics that the war was unjustified.

There was no agreement over whether the UN Security Council authorized military action in Iraq. American and British diplomats pointed to UN Security Council Resolution 687 of 1991, which required the destruction of Iraqi weapons of mass destruction under UN supervision, and UN Security Council Resolution 1441 of 2002, which threatened "serious consequences" if this were not done. Yet efforts to reach a Security Council resolution in the winter of 2003 that would clearly authorize the use of force against Iraq were unsuccessful. France and Russia threatened to veto a second Security Council resolution authorizing force.

The decision of the US and British administrations, along with a small number of allies, to use force against Iraq without clear UN authorization undermined the credibility of the UN. This action renewed the fears that great powers like the United States and the United Kingdom would be willing at any time to act without UN authorization. The Bush administration's National Security Strategy of September 2002 states that "[W]e will be prepared to act apart when our interests and unique responsibilities require" (NSS 2002, 31).

Nonetheless, the aftermath of the invasion and the continued difficulties in establishing security in Iraq highlight the need for international cooperation. The UN enhances the legitimacy of military action and can also help share in global risks, burdens, and strategies for rebuilding.

Prior to the invasion of Iraq in 2003, the International Atomic Energy Agency (IAEA) took a lead role in the nuclear weapons inspections regime. What might the IAEA report have said that would have convinced German foreign minister Joschka Fischer (shown here outside a Security Council meeting) to keep his country out of the war?

---

a bearing on global peace. The more integrated global context has meant that economic and social problems in one part of the world may impact other areas. Furthermore, promoting social and economic development is an important UN goal in itself. The preamble of the UN Charter talks of promoting "social progress and better standards of life in larger freedom," and the need to "employ international machinery for the promotion of the economic and social advancement of all peoples."

The number of institutions within the UN system that address economic and social issues has significantly increased since the founding of the UN. Nonetheless, the main contributor states have been giving less and less to economic and social institutions. By the mid-1990s, there was a crippling financial crisis in the regular Assessed Budget for the UN and in the budget for peacekeeping operations. This was only mitigated when the United States agreed, under certain conditions, to repay what it owed the UN and when it returned to full funding in December 2002.

Global Perspective

The UN and Environmental Protection

The UN is an organization of states that claim the right of sovereign equality. In practical terms this means that if the leaders of a country do not want to act on a UN resolution, declaration, or action plan, the leaders can assert the right to make a national-level decision. On matters of peace and war this can, perhaps, be excused as protecting the national interest in an uncertain self-help world.

However, should national interest *not* apply to the topic of environmental protection? Many problems of pollution are becoming globalized as industrial production moves around the world. What has the UN done to stop pollution?

The UN Conference on Environment and Development (Earth Summit) held in 1992 in Rio de Janeiro was unprecedented for a UN conference in both its size and its scope of concerns. Representatives from 172 countries and over 2,400 NGOs discussed ways to help reach the goal of sustainable development in the global community. The Rio Earth Summit was held twenty years after the first UN Conference on the Human Environment in Stockholm. That 1972 conference had stimulated the creation of national environmental ministries around the world and established the United Nations Environment Program (UNEP).

The central concern of the Rio Earth Summit was the need for broad-based, environmentally sustainable development. As a result of the summit, 108 governments adopted three major agreements concerned with changing the traditional approach to development. These agreements included the Rio Declaration on Environment and Development (a series of principles defining the rights and responsibilities of states), the Statement of Forest Principles, and Agenda 21 (a comprehensive program of action to attain sustain-

able development on a global scale). In addition, the UN Framework Convention on Climate Change and the Convention on Biological Diversity were signed by many governments.

The UN Commission on Sustainable Development was formed after the 1992 Earth Summit to ensure follow-up and to report on the implementation of Earth Summit agreements at the local, national, regional, and international levels. A five-year review of Earth Summit progress took place in New York in 1997, and a ten-year review took place at the World Summit on Sustainable Development held in Johannesburg in 2002. There were significant divisions at the Johannesburg Summit. The conference was thought to be too large and the outcome was generally seen as disappointing. Nonetheless, by 2002 it was clear that environmental questions were prominent issues on the UN agenda.

Were these UN-level actions successful in fighting environmental problems? If you believe that the UN's greatest tool is that of moral suasion, then yes, the UN has taken a leading role in seeking to apply pressure to national governments to get them to regulate polluters in their countries. However, as you will see in Chapter 14, actions, not only moral suasion, are needed to solve the menace of the world's environmental problems.

Climate change will impact all countries of the world. What role can the UN take in facilitating cooperation?

In 2000, the UN convened a Millennium Summit, where heads of state committed themselves to a series of measurable goals and targets, known as the Millennium Development Goals (MDGs). These goals, to be achieved by 2015, include reducing by half the number of people living on less than a dollar a day, achieving universal primary education, and reversing the spread of HIV/AIDS and malaria (A/55/L.2). Since 2000, the UN has been integrating the MDGs into all aspects of its work at the country level, but progress on reaching the MDGs has been very uneven.

The Reform Process of the United Nations

In his important book *The Parliament of Man* (2006), Paul Kennedy suggests that any reform of the UN will need to be partial, gradual, and carefully executed. He argues that the need to make the UN more effective, representative, and accountable to its members is greater today than it was in the past because of a number of global developments, including the following:

1. The emergence of new great powers like India and Brazil and older powers like Japan and Germany who have been left out of the Security Council. Are the current members of the Security Council willing to add new members or even change the decision-making structure?
2. The presence of truly global issues that threaten the world as we know it. This includes environmental degradation, terrorism, the proliferation of weapons of all kinds, and the persistence of global poverty. Is the UN interested in or capable of responding to these issues?

In the mid- to late 1990s, alongside growing UN involvement in development issues, the UN economic and social arrangements underwent reform at two levels: first, reforms concerned with operations in the country (field) level; and second, reforms at the general or headquarters level.

Country Level

The continuing complaints of NGOs about poor UN performance in the field served as a powerful stimulus for reform. A key feature of the reforms at the country (field) level was the adoption of Country Strategy Notes. These were statements about the overall development process tailored to the specific needs of individual countries. They were written on the basis of discussions between the Specialized Agencies, Programmes and Funds, donors, and the host country, and described the plans of the various institutions and donors in a particular country. The merit of the Country Strategy Notes is that they clearly set out targets, roles, and priorities.

Another reform at the country level was the strengthening of the resident coordinator, usually an employee of the United Nations Development Program (UNDP). He or she became the responsible officer at the country level and was provided with more training to fulfill this role. Field-level officers were also given enhanced authority so that they could make decisions about the redeployment of funds within a program without referring to headquarters. There was also an effort to introduce improved communication facilities and information sharing. The activities of the various UN organizations were brought together in single locations, or "UN houses," which facilitated interagency communication and collegiality. The new country-level approach was called an "integrated programs" approach. The adoption of the Millennium Development Goals framework has also helped country field staff achieve a more coherent approach to development. This can be contrasted to earlier arrangements whereby the various agencies would work separately on distinct projects, often in ignorance of each other's presence in the same country.

Headquarters Level

Since the Security Council is the main executive body within the United Nations, with primary responsibility for maintaining international peace and security, it is not surprising that many discussions of UN reform have focused on the Security Council.

The founders of the UN deliberately established a universal General Assembly and a restricted Security Council that required unanimity among the great powers. Granting permanent seats and the right to a veto to the great powers of the time—the United States, the Soviet Union (now Russia), France, the United Kingdom, and China—was an essential feature of the deal.

The composition and decision-making procedures of the Security Council were increasingly challenged as membership of the United Nations grew, particularly after decolonization. Yet the only significant reform of the Security Council occurred in 1965, when the Council was enlarged from eleven to fifteen members and the required majority from seven to nine votes. Nonetheless, the veto power of the permanent five (P-5) members was left intact.

The Security Council does not reflect today's distribution of military or economic power, and it does not reflect a geographic balance. Germany and Japan have made strong cases for permanent membership. Developing countries have demanded more representation on the Security Council, particularly South Africa, India, Egypt, Brazil, and Nigeria. However, it has proved impossible to reach agreement on new permanent members. Should the European Union be represented instead of Great Britain, France, and Germany individually? How would Pakistan feel about India's candidacy? How would South Africa feel about a Nigerian seat? What about representation by an Islamic country? These issues are not easy to resolve. Likewise, it is very unlikely that the P-5 states will relinquish their veto. Nonetheless, while large-scale reform has proved impossible, there have been changes in Security Council working procedures that have made it more transparent and accountable to the member states.

If the UN role in economic and social affairs at the country level was to be effective, reform was also required at the headquarters level. The United Nations family of economic and social organizations has always been a polycentric system. Historically, there was no organization or agent within the system that was capable of managing the wide range of economic and social activities under the UN umbrella. Reform efforts in the 1990s focused on the reorganization and rationalization of the Economic and Social Council (ECOSOC).

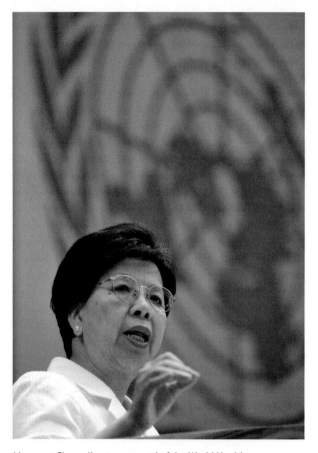

Margaret Chan, director-general of the World Health Organization, has stated that WHO can do more to eradicate infectious diseases. Should the organization be more than an information clearinghouse, if this means that states must share their sovereignty over the health of citizens?

In the UN Charter, the powers given to the General Assembly and ECOSOC were modest. ECOSOC could only issue recommendations and receive reports. By contrast, UN reform in the mid- to late 1990s allowed ECOSOC to become more assertive and to take a leading role in the coordination of the UN system. ECOSOC was to ensure that General Assembly policies were appropriately implemented on a systemwide basis. ECOSOC was given the power to make final decisions on the activities of its subsidiary bodies and on other matters relating to systemwide coordination in economic, social, and related fields (A/50/227, para. 37).

One of ECOSOC's responsibilities was to review common themes in the work of the nine functional commissions, such as the Commission on Narcotic Drugs, the Commission on Sustainable Development, and the Commission on the Status of Women. The reform effort aimed to eliminate duplication and overlap in the work of the functional commissions. ECOSOC would integrate their work and provide input to the General Assembly, which was responsible for establishing the broader economic and social policy framework. The boards of the Programmes and Funds were also reformed to enhance their day-to-day management.

Overall, economic and social reorganization meant that the two poles of the system were better coordinated: the pole where intentions are defined through global conferences and agendas and the pole where programs are implemented. Programs at the field level were better integrated and field officers were given enhanced discretion. The reform of ECOSOC sharpened its capacity to shape broad agreements into cross-sectoral programs with well-defined objectives. At the same time, ECOSOC acquired greater capacity to act as a conduit through which the results of field-level monitoring could be conveyed upward to the functional commissions. These new processes had the effect of strengthening the norms, values, and goals of a multilateral system.

Other Intergovernmental Organizations

The International Criminal Court

Established with the Rome Statute of July 1998, the International Criminal Court (ICC) is the first international court with the potential of a truly global jurisdiction. As we will see in Chapter 10, the ICC conducts trials of individuals accused of war crimes, genocide, and crimes against humanity. As of February 2009, 108 states had ratified the statute and were parties to the ICC. The court was needed because national political leaders could otherwise claim immunity from prosecutions because of their protected diplomatic status.

Regional Organizations

The "New Regionalism" taking place since the late 1980s has been more a response to new forms of globalization, as well as to the new multipolar environment after the end of the Cold War. Various common features could be seen in the 1990s. Regional arrangements tended to be more open than before in terms of economic integration, as well as more comprehensive in scope. The new open regionalism indeed seemed to lose some of the very defining characteristics of regionalism, forming part of "a global structural transformation in which non-state actors are active and manifest themselves at several levels of the global system [and] can therefore not be understood only from the point of view of the single region" (Hettne 1999, 7–8).

Yet regionalism may also be seen as one of the few instruments available to states to try to manage the effects of globalization. If individual states no longer have the effective capacity to regulate in the face of uncontrolled movements of capital, then regionalism may be seen as a means to regain some control over global market forces—and to counter the more negative social consequences of globalization. The debate is far from over.

The Process of European Integration

In Europe, regionalism after 1945 has taken the form of a gradual process of integration leading to the emergence of the European Union. It was initially a purely West European creation between the "original six" member states, born out of the desire for reconciliation between France and Germany in a context of ambitious federalist plans for a united Europe. Yet the process has taken the form of a progressive construction of an institutional architecture, a legal framework, and a wide range of policies, which in 2007 encompassed twenty-seven European states.

The European Coal and Steel Community was created in 1951 (in force in 1952), followed by the European Economic Community and the European Atomic Energy Community in 1957 (in force in 1958). These treaties involved a conferral of Community competence, or standards, in various areas—the supranational management of coal and steel, the creation and regulation of an internal market, and common policies in trade, competition, agriculture, and transport. Since then, powers have been extended to include new legislative competences in some fields such as the environment. Since the 1992 Treaty on European Union (the Maastricht Treaty, in force in 1993) the integration process has also involved the adoption of stronger forms of unification, notably monetary union, as well as cooperation in economic and employment policy, and more intergovernmental cooperation in foreign and security policy.

From very limited beginnings, in terms of both membership and scope, the EU has therefore gradually developed to become an important political and economic actor whose presence has a significant impact internationally and domestically (see Table 6.3). This gradual process of European integration has taken place at various levels. The first is the signature and reform of the basic treaties. These are the result of Intergovernmental Conferences (IGCs), where representatives of national governments negotiate the legal framework within which the EU institutions operate. Such treaty changes require ratification in each country and are the "grand bargains" in the evolution of the EU.

Within this framework, the institutions have been given considerable powers to adopt decisions and manage policies, although the dynamics of decision making differ significantly across arenas. There are important differences between the more integrated areas of economic regulation on the one hand and the more intergovernmental pillars of foreign policy and police or judicial cooperation in criminal matters on the other. In some areas, a country may have to accept decisions imposed on it by the (qualified) majority of member states. In other areas, it may be able to block decisions.

To understand the integration process, one needs to take account of the role played by both member states *and* supranational institutions. Moreover, member states are not just represented by national governments, since a host of state, nonstate, and transnational actors participate in the processes of domestic preference formation and direct representation of interests in Brussels. The relative openness of the European policy process means that political groups and economic interests will try to influence EU decision making if

Table 6.3

Important Agreements in the History of the European Union

Year	Treaty	Main Subjects
1951	Paris Treaty	Regulation of coal and steel production in the member states; creation of supranational institutions
1957	Rome Treaties	European Economic Community—creation of a customs union (removal of all intraunion duties and creation of a common customs tariff); plans for a common market and common policies; Euratom—cooperation in atomic energy
1986	Single European Act	Removal of all nontariff barriers to the movement of persons, goods, services, and capital (the 1992 program); foreign policy cooperation included in the treaty provisions
1992	Maastricht Treaty	Creation of the European Union, encompassing the European Community and two parallel pillars for Common Foreign and Security Policy (CFSP) and justice and home affairs; economic and monetary union (the euro)
1997	Amsterdam Treaty	Various institutional reforms; creation of the post of high representative for CFSP; provisions for enhanced cooperation
2001	Nice Treaty	Reform of commission and council (voting weights); expansion of majority voting
2004	Constitutional Treaty (signed but not ratified)	Simplification of the treaties; incorporation of the European Charter of Fundamental Rights; creation of the post of president of the council and EU foreign minister

they feel that their position is not sufficiently represented by national governments. That is one reason the EU is increasingly seen as a system of multilevel governance, involving a plurality of actors on different territorial levels: supranational, national, and substate.

The complexity of the EU institutional machinery, together with continuous change over time, has spawned a lively debate among integration theorists (Rosamond 2000; Wiener and Diez 2004). Some approaches are applications of more general theories of

If the EU takes a larger role in global politics, European states will lose some of their responsibilities and autonomy. Is that transfer of state power necessarily bad?

Table 6.4
Institutions of the European Union

EU Institution	Responsibilities	Location
European Commission	Initiating, administering, and overseeing the implementation of EU policies and legislation	Brussels and Luxembourg
European Parliament (EP)	Acting as directly elected representatives of EU citizens, scrutinizing the operation of the other institutions, and, in certain areas, sharing with the council the power to determine EU legislation	Strasbourg (plenary sessions); Brussels (MEP offices, committee meetings, and some plenary sessions); Luxembourg (administration)
Council of Ministers	Representing the views of national governments and determining, in many areas jointly with the EP, the ultimate shape of EU legislation	Brussels (some meetings in Luxembourg)
European Council	Holding regular summits of the heads of state or government and the president of the commission, setting the EU's broad agenda, and acting as a forum of last resort to find agreement on divisive issues (note: different from the Council of Europe)	Brussels
European Court of Justice	Acting as the EU's highest court (supported by a Court of First Instance): annulment of Community acts, infringement procedures against member states for failing to comply with obligations, and preliminary rulings on the validity or interpretation of EC law on request from national courts	Luxembourg
European Central Bank	Setting the interest rates and controlling the money supply of the single European currency, the euro	Frankfurt am Main
Court of Auditors	Auditing the revenues and the expenditure under the EU budget	Luxembourg

international relations. For example, the literature on both realism and liberalism has contributed to theorizing integration. Other scholars have regarded the European Union as sui generis—in a category of its own—and therefore in need of the development of dedicated theories of integration. The most prominent among these has been neofunctionalism, which sought to explain the evolution of integration in terms of "spillover" from one policy sector to another as resources and loyalties of elites were transferred to the European level. More recently, as aspects of EU politics have come to resemble the domestic politics of states, scholars have turned to approaches drawn from comparative politics or the study of governance in different states.

However, the exchange between "supranational" and "intergovernmental" approaches has had the greatest impact on the study of European integration. Supranational approaches regard the emergence of supranational institutions in Europe as a distinct feature and turn these into the main object of analysis. Here, the politics above the level of states is regarded as the most significant, and consequently the political actors and institutions at the European level receive most attention.

Intergovernmental approaches, on the other hand, continue to regard states as the most important aspect of the integration process and consequently concentrate on the study of

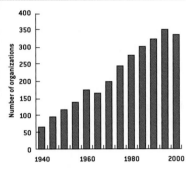

Intergovernmental Organizations. What factors are driving the increasing number of intergovernmental organizations? Why has there been a small decline in the early twenty-first century? *Source: Jon C. Pevehouse, Timothy Nordstrom, and Kevin Warnke, "The COW-2 International Organizations Dataset Version 2.0," Conflict Management and Peace Science 21, no. 2 (2004); 101–19.*

politics *between* and *within* states. But whatever one's theoretical preferences, most scholars would agree that no analysis of the EU is complete without studying both the operation and evolution of the central institutions and the input from political actors in the member states. More recently, debate in EU studies has also centered on a wider fault line in the social sciences: the difference between rationalist and constructivist approaches. Constructivists have challenged the implicit rationalism of much integration research until the 1990s (see Chapter 3). Their critique focused on the tendency of rationalist studies to privilege rational decision making over agenda setting and outcomes over process. The social-constructivist research agenda instead concentrates on the framing of issues *before* decisions about them are made, and therefore emphasizes the role of ideas, discourses, and social interaction in shaping interests (Christiansen, Jørgensen, and Wiener 2001).

The prospect of an ever *wider* European Union has raised serious questions about the nature and direction of the integration process. The 2004 enlargement has generally been seen as a qualitative leap for the EU. Concerns that the enlarged Union, if not reformed substantially, would find it difficult to make decisions and maintain a reliable legal framework led to several attempts to reform the treaties. The most wide-ranging proposals, and the most significant change in the language of integration, came with the treaty establishing a constitution for Europe that EU governments signed in 2004. The very fact that the EU should discuss something referred to in the media as a "European Constitution" is a sign of how far it has developed from its modest beginnings. However, the time may still not be right for such a project. The Constitutional Treaty was rejected in referendums in France and the Netherlands, raising serious doubts not only about this attempt at institutional reform but also about ambitions for a formal constitutional process more generally. In 2007, with intergovernmental negotiations about a revised "reform treaty," the EU seemed likely to continue along the established path of a succession of gradual developments rather than big leaps.

After eight years of debate and several disappointing negative national votes, the European Union's reform treaty came into force on December 1, 2009. EU leaders believe the now ratified Lisbon Treaty will rejuvenate the decision-making apparatus of all of the EU institutions, making the functioning of the twenty-seven-member Union more efficient and democratic.

Conclusion

International and regional organizations and international law play an important role in the governance of our global society. These institutions provide the infrastructure of a truly global system in which it is possible to think about a global common good and a world where human interests trump national interests. There are three pillars of global governance (Muldoon 2004pa):

1. A political pillar that includes diplomacy, international law, and global and regional organizations like the UN, the WTO, and the European Union.
2. An economic pillar that includes multinational corporations, international banking and industry associations, global labor movements, and global economic movements.
3. A social pillar that includes actors within the global civil society, such as NGOs, and global social movements, like the Jubilee movement led by U2 and Radiohead that sought to get states to forgive developing countries' debt.

Clearly, international and regional organizations play a critical role in governing the policy areas that transcend the nation-state. The effectiveness and perhaps the fairness of global policy will often depend on the efficacy of international law. Thus, all these institutions play a role in the governance of this global society.

As we have seen in this chapter, the capacity of the UN in its economic and social work, its development work, and its management of peacekeeping and postconflict reconstruction has expanded since the 1990s. Nonetheless, the predominance of US military power, the possibility that the United States will act again without clear UN authorization, the heightened concern over terrorism and weapons of mass destruction, the inability to respond effectively to the crisis in Darfur, and the pervasiveness of inequality and injustice across the world signal that further changes and adaptations within the UN system will be necessary.

With regard to regional organizations, the European Union is the best example of how far the integration process can go and how much sovereignty states are willing to share or surrender. The prospect of an ever-wider European Union has raised serious questions about the nature and direction of the integration process. The most wide-ranging proposals, and the most significant change in the language of integration, came with the treaty establishing a constitution for Europe that EU heads of state or government signed in 2004. The very fact that the EU should discuss something referred to in the media as a "European Constitution" is a sign of how far it has developed from its modest beginnings. However, the time may still not be right for such a project.

For all of these reasons, international law and international organizations remain works in progress.

Contributors to Chapter 6: Devon Curtis, Christian Reus-Smit, Paul Taylor, and Steven L. Lamy.

REVIEW QUESTIONS

1. Can you think of other factors, in addition to the ones listed in the chapter, that contributed to the rise of modern international law in the last two centuries?
2. Do you find the argument that states create institutions to sustain international order persuasive?
3. What do you think are the strengths and weaknesses of the international legal system?
4. What have been the driving forces behind processes of regional integration and cooperation?
5. What impact have processes of regional integration had on the state?
6. Compare and contrast European integration with regional cooperation in other areas of the world.
7. How does the UN try to maintain world order?
8. How has UN peacekeeping evolved?
9. Has reform of the economic and social arrangements of the UN been effective?
10. Does increased UN activity undermine the sovereignty of states?

FURTHER READING

Archer, C. (2001), *International Organisations,* 3rd ed. (London: Routledge). A succinct survey of the range of international institutions and their main purposes.

Barker, J. C. (2000), *International Law and International Relations* (London: Continuum). A good survey on the relationship between international law and international relations.

Berdal, M., and Economides, S. (eds.) (2007), *United Nations Interventionism, 1991–2004* (Cambridge: Cambridge University Press). Includes case studies of eight UN operations and discusses the impact of the "new interventionism" on international order.

Byers, M. (2000), *The Role of Law in International Politics* (Oxford: Oxford University Press). An excellent collection of advanced essays on the politics of international law.

Cassese, A. (2001), *International Law* (Oxford: Oxford University Press). An excellent international legal text by a leading scholar and jurist.

Claude, I. L. Jr. (1971, 1984), *Swords into Plowshares: The Progress and Problems of International Organization,* 4th ed. (New York: Random House). A classic text on the history of international institutions, particularly concerned with their role in war and peace. Useful for the history of the UN.

Dodds, F. (ed.) (1997), *The Way Forward: Beyond Agenda 21* (London: Earthscan). An account of the involvement of the UN system in the issues raised in the functional commissions, such as social development, the status of women, and environmental protection.

Goldsmith, J. L., and Posner, E. A. (2006), *The Limits of International Law* (New York: Oxford University Press). A vigorous critique of the institution of international law and its capacity to produce substantial goods for international society.

Higgins, R. (1994), *Problems and Process: International Law and How We Use It* (Oxford: Oxford University Press). A very good introduction to international law by a justice of the International Court of Justice.

Karns, M., and Mingst, K. (2004), *International Organizations: The Politics and Processes of Global Governance* (Boulder, CO: Lynne Rienner). A comprehensive overview of the main actors and processes of global governance.

Kennedy, P. (2006), *The Parliament of Man: The Past, Present, and Future of the United Nations* (New York: Random House). A review of the origins and evolution of the UN and a discussion of its future challenges.

Kratochwil, F. (1989), *Rules, Norms, and Decisions* (Cambridge: Cambridge University Press). The most sustained and advanced constructivist work on international legal reasoning.

Lynch, C., and Loriaux, M. (eds.) (2000), *Law and Moral Action in World Politics* (Minneapolis: University of Minnesota Press). A good collection of essays on the relationship between international law and ethics.

Malone, D. (ed.) (2004), *The UN Security Council: From the Cold War to the Twenty-first Century* (Boulder, CO: Lynne Rienner). Discusses the history of the UN Security Council and major UN operations.

Reus-Smit, C. (ed.) (2004), *The Politics of International Law* (Cambridge: Cambridge University Press). An edited collection that presents a constructivist perspective on international law, illustrated by a range of contemporary case studies.

Roberts, A., and Kingsbury, B. (eds.) (1993), *United Nations, Divided World: The UN's Roles in International Relations,* 2nd ed. (Oxford: Clarendon Press). An important collection of readings by practitioners and academics.

Taylor, P., and Groom, A. J. R. (eds.) (2000), *The United Nations at the Millennium* (London: Continuum). A detailed account of the institutions of the central UN system.

Thakur, R. (2006), *The United Nations, Peace and Security* (Cambridge: Cambridge University Press). Discusses the changing role of the UN peace operations.

Von Glahn, G. (1995), *Law Among Nations: An Introduction to Public International Law,* 7th ed. (New York: Addison-Wesley). A traditional yet comprehensive introduction to international law by a political scientist.

SELECTED DOCUMENTS RELATED TO THE CHANGING ROLE OF THE UNITED NATIONS SYSTEM

Development of the economic and social organizations:

A/32/197, Dec. 1977. The first major General Assembly resolution on reform of the economic and social organizations.

A/48/162, Dec. 1993. A major step toward reform of the economic and social organization of the United Nations, especially ECOSOC.

Development of the UN's role in maintaining international peace and security:

SC Res. 678, Nov. 1990. Sanctioned the use of force against Saddam Hussein.

SC Res. 816, Apr. 1993. Enforced the no-fly zone over Bosnia in that it permitted NATO war planes to intercept Bosnian Serb planes in the zones.

SC Res. 1160, 1199, and 1203. Contained arguments relevant to the action on Kosovo. SC Res. 1244 contained the agreement at the end of the bombing.

Development of humanitarian action through the UN:

SC Res. 688, Apr. 1991. Sanctioned intervention at the end of the Gulf War to protect the Kurds in northern Iraq.

SC Res. 733, Jan. 1992. Sanctioned UN involvement in Somalia. A/46/182, Apr. 1992, is the major document on the development of the machinery for humanitarian assistance.

SC Res. 794, Dec. 1992, sanctioned American intervention in Somalia under Chapter VII of the UN Charter. The government of Somalia had ceased to exist in the eyes of the member states of the Security Council.

SC Res. 1441, Nov. 2002, resolution on Iraq that threatened serious consequences if Saddam Hussein failed to reveal his weapons of mass destruction to the team of UN inspectors.

INTERNET RESOURCES

The network of websites regarding international law and international organizations provides reliable information for students to use in their work. Here is a sample of these websites:

European Union
http://europa.eu/

International Court of Justice
http://www.icj-cij.org/

International Criminal Court
http://www.icc-cpi.int/

UN High Commissioner for Refugees
http://www.unhcr.org/cgi-bin/texis/vtx/home

UN High Commissioner of Human Rights
http://www.ohchr.org/EN/Pages/WelcomePage.aspx

UN Office of Peacekeeping Operations
http://www.un.org/Depts/dpko/dpko/dpko.shtml

United Nations internet portal
www.un.org

For more information, quizzes, case studies, and other study tools, please visit us at **www.oup.com/us/lamy**

Transnational Actors

The rhetoric about the growing strength of international institutions notwithstanding, there is little evidence that they can get great powers to act contrary to the dictates of realism.

—*John Mearsheimer*

NGOs and other civil society actors are now perceived not only as disseminators of information or providers of services but also as shapers of policy, be it in peace and security matters, in development or in humanitarian affairs. The involvement of NGOs and other actors, such as parliamentarians, local authorities and business leaders, in the United Nations global conferences demonstrates this. It would now be difficult to imagine organizing a global event and formulating multilateral agreements and declarations without the active participation of NGOs.

—*Kofi Annan, UN Secretary-General*

In the previous chapter, we learned about the United Nations—an institution whose members are governments—and about several regional organizations also with governments as their members. In this chapter we will see that there are many more international or transnational organizations, some composed of governments, some composed of nongovernmental organizations and private citizens—and some with a mixture of both.

Amnesty International, the International Campaign to Ban Landmines (ICBL), and Doctors Without Borders all have been awarded the Nobel Peace Prize for their contributions to humanity. These nongovernmental organizations (NGOs) have stepped in to protect human rights where governments have failed, to limit the impact of war on civilians, or to respond to medical emergencies and address the causes of pandemics. NGOs and other transnational actors provide information, expertise, and services that many governments cannot offer. The list of

Amnesty International is a leading advocate for the rights of what it calls prisoners of conscience, successfully gaining the release of people worldwide. Are you a member of the AI chapter on your campus?

195

global civil-society actors that occupy the space between government and the corporate world is growing as governments fail to provide basics like education for all, clean water, or even minimal health care. Global networks of NGOs are playing a greater role in maintaining human security in many failed or failing states.

Even terrorist organizations and criminal networks challenge governments, and in some cases control territory and act as if they have legitimate governmental authority. The recent occupation of the Swat Valley in Pakistan by the Taliban and elements of Al Qaeda illustrates this point. As a noted scholar has remarked, "National governments are not simply losing autonomy in a globalizing economy. They are sharing powers with businesses, with international organizations, and with a multitude of citizens groups, known as non-governmental organizations (NGOs)" (Mathews 1997). As the issues we face become more transnational and more complex, there is a need for building global networks that include both governments and transnational actors. For example, the Bill and Melinda Gates Foundation, the Howard G. Buffett Foundation, and the Belgian government are working with the World Food Program (WFP) to transform how the WFP buys food. The new program buys from small local farmers. This initiative, Purchase for Progress (P4P), is focusing on farmers in Central America and sub-Saharan Africa and is providing services that we expect governments to offer.

In this chapter we will take a closer look at some of the more important transnational actors—their various approaches, activities, and structures—to see how they are transforming our world.

Introduction

In diplomacy, international law, journalism, and academic analysis, it is widely assumed that international relations consist of the relations between coherent units called states. This chapter will argue that better understanding of political change is obtained by analyzing the relations between governments and many other actors from each country. Global politics also includes companies or corporations and **nongovernmental organizations (NGOs)**. Thus the five main categories of political actors in the global system are these:

- Nearly 200 governments, including 192 members of the UN
- 77,200 transnational companies (TNCs), such as Ford, Shell, Microsoft, De Beers, and Nestlé, plus just over 800,000 foreign affiliates of these parent companies
- More than 10,000 single-country nongovernmental organizations that have significant transnational activities, such as the Sierra Club (US) and Population Concern (UK)
- 246 **intergovernmental organizations (IGOs)**, such as the UN, NATO, the European Union, and the International Coffee Organization
- Approximately 7,300 **international nongovernmental organizations (INGOs)**, such as Amnesty International, the Baptist World Alliance, and the International Chamber of Shipping, plus a similar number of less well-established international caucuses and networks of NGOs

nongovernmental organization (NGO) An organization, usually a grassroots one, with policy goals, but not governmental in makeup. An NGO is any group of people relating to each other regularly in some formal manner and engaging in collective action, provided the activities are noncommercial and nonviolent and are not on behalf of a government.

intergovernmental organization (IGO) A formal, legally constituted organization established by states to handle common problems or issues; membership and decision-making authority is limited to governments.

international nongovernmental organization (INGO) A formal international organization, with transnational members from at least three countries. There are many different types, with membership from national NGOs, local NGOs, companies, political parties, or individual people. A few have other INGOs as members, and some have mixed membership structures.

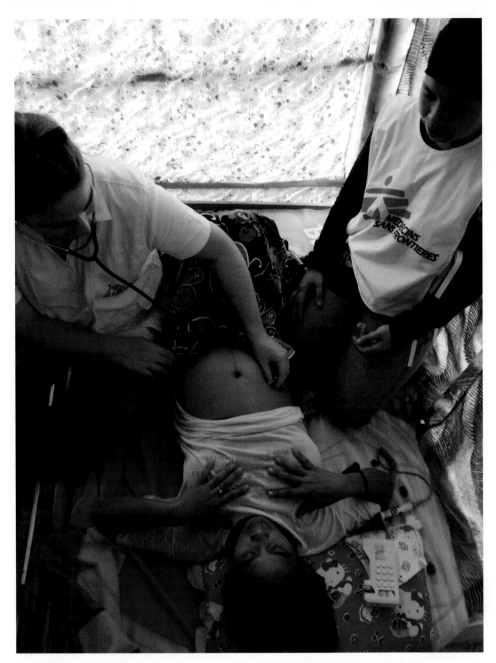

Doctors Without Borders provides free medical treatment to refugees, victims of war, and others whom states ignore. Will activities like these increase if the world leaders fail to address the challenge presented by failed states?

We have discussed governments and foreign policy in Chapter 5 and international and regional organizations with governments as members in Chapter 6. In this chapter we will discuss those actors that are critical players in global civil society, or what has been described as the public space where citizens and groups can engage in political activities independent of the state. For example, you might be a member of the ONE Movement to end global poverty and address the scourge of HIV/AIDS. As a member of that organization you work to shape policy of many governments and intergovernmental organizations, like the UN or the World Health Organization (WHO), by providing information and educating others to put pressure on their own governments to act. You might also partner with another category of nonstate actors that we call multinational or transnational corporations or companies. Nike, the Gap, or Starbucks might provide funding and platforms to promote your ideas. All these actors play a regular part in global politics, and each government interacts with a diverse range of **nonstate actors**. Sometimes guerrilla groups challenge the authority of particular governments. In addition, even though they are not considered legitimate participants in the system, terrorists and other criminal gangs have an impact—often minor, but sometimes major. Very many more companies and NGOs only operate in a single country but have the potential to expand into other countries, and they influence both domestic and foreign policy.[1]

> **nonstate actor** Any participant in global politics that is neither acting in the name of government nor created and served by government. NGOs, terrorist networks, global crime syndicates, and multinational corporations are examples.

As we learned in Chapter 3, one goal of realism is to provide parsimonious explanations for international events. A more open-ended approach, known as pluralism, drawing on the study of domestic politics, is based on the assumption that all types of actors can affect political outcomes. Nobody can deny the number of nonstate organizations and the range of their activities. The controversial question is whether to accept the pluralist assertions that the nonstate world has significance in its own right and that it affects the analysis of interstate relations. It is possible, as realists do, to adopt a state-centric approach and to *define* international relations as covering only the relations between states. Then it is only a tautology (true by definition) to say that nonstate actors are of secondary importance.

> **transnational actor** Any nongovernmental actor, such as a multinational corporation or one country's religious humanitarian organization, that has relations with any actor from another country or with an international organization.

The very words "nonstate actors" imply that states are dominant and other actors are secondary. An alternative phrase, **transnational actors**, has been coined by academics in order to assert forcefully that international relations are not limited to governments and that other actors operate across country boundaries. This term was developed in the 1970s and revived in the 1990s, when first détente and then the end of the Cold War persuaded liberal institutionalists and pluralists that traditional academic theories could not explain world events and global conditions.

For pluralist scholars it is an unacceptable analytical bias to decide, before research starts, that only states have any influence. Proponents of the transnational-actors approach believe that until the evidence indicates otherwise, we must assume that governments also interact with NGOs, companies, and international organizations. This chapter will first consider how assumptions made about "states" inhibit analysis of transnational actors and international organizations. Then we will describe the different types of transnational actors, after which we will consider the argument for always considering the activities of a diverse range of political actors.

Problems with the State-centric Approach

The great advantage of the state-centric approach is that the bewildering complexity of world politics is reduced to the relative simplicity of the interactions of less than two hundred units we call countries. However, there are at least four problems that suggest that the benefits of simplification and parsimony have been gained at the expense of a clear picture.

Ambiguity Between Different Meanings of a "State"

Writers who refer to the state often fail to use the term consistently. The standard approach in the analysis of international politics is to consider the state to be composed of territorial exclusivity, people, and a government that has sovereign power and authority. There is a very dissimilar concept among sociologists and democratic theorists of the state as the apparatus of **government**. As we mentioned before, in Chapter 1, an additional usage confusion is closer to home for North American students: the fifty states that comprise the United States. Unfortunately, no standard method exists to handle the ambiguity of the term "state," and most people blur these three distinctions:

- *In international law, the state is a legal person.* This is a highly abstract legal fiction. The law of each country treats corporations, universities, and other organizations as legal persons, so that they can be taken to court. Similarly, a state has to be imagined as a single coherent immortal "person," so that treaties can be agreed and honored for decades or even centuries.
- *In international politics, the state is a country, forming a political community.* This is recognizable in a practical, true-to-life manner when we read the newspapers. The United States, Germany, India, and Brazil are examples of distinct political systems made up of people sharing some common values, residing in a specific geographic space, and focusing on elections, lawmaking, taxation, and public expenditure, within the country's boundaries.
- *In sociology and political philosophy, the state is the government system.* These two fields explore questions about the relations between society and the state. We can recognize this definition in various bureaucratic structures. Here we have the concept of a state as the whole apparatus of government, including the executive, the legislature, the judiciary, the armed forces, and the police.

Logically, the first two meanings are compatible with each other, but the third is very different from the first two. Those working within international law and the traditional study of international politics assume **civil society** *is part of the state* and so it need not be analyzed. In contrast to this, for those focusing on the state as government, *civil society is separate from the state* and hence it can be analyzed independently. Thus, in international law or when the state means the whole country, there is very little room to acknowledge the existence of distinct transnational actors. Alternatively, when the state means the government and does not encompass civil society, we can investigate both intergovernmental relations and the intersociety relations of transnational actors. To keep things simple, in this textbook we are using the word "state" to indicate the abstract legal concept, while "country" and "government" will be used to analyze political behavior.

The Lack of Similarity Between Countries

The second problem is that giving all "states" the same legal status implies they are all essentially the same type of unit, when in fact they are not remotely similar in terms of the power resources that realists consider. Traditional studies of foreign policy acknowledge differences in size between the great powers and middle and small powers (see Chapter 5).

government The people and agencies that have the power and legitimate authority to determine who gets what, when, where, and how within a given territory.

civil society (1) The totality of all individuals and groups in a society who are not acting as participants in any government institutions, or (2) all individuals and groups who are neither participants in government nor acting in the interests of commercial companies.

WHAT'S YOUR WORLDVIEW

Many corporations have hired their own security forces, and in some cases states hire private security forces. Even the United States government hired the Blackwater security company to escort diplomats and private contractors in Iraq. Do you think this is a good idea? Does this undermine the power and influence of states? Will leaders find it easier to go to war with these new mercenary armies?

Nevertheless, the emphasis on legal equality does not take into account that at the end of the Cold War the United States economy was twice the size of the Soviet Union's economy, nor that at the start of this century the US economy was eight times China's, sixty-four times Saudi Arabia's, more than fourteen hundred times Ethiopia's, and over one hundred thousand times greater than Kiribati's. In terms of population, the divergences are even greater. The small island countries of the Caribbean and the Pacific with populations measured in tens of thousands are not comparable entities to ordinary small countries, let alone to China or India: they are truly "microstates." Alternatively, comparing the governments of the world reveals a diverse range of democracies, feudal regimes, ethnic oligarchies, economic oligarchies, populist regimes, theocracies, military dictatorships, and idiosyncratic combinations. The only thing that the countries have in common is the general recognition of their right to have their own government. They are legally equal and politically very different.

The consequence of admitting the differences in size is to make it obvious that the largest transnational actors are considerably larger than many of the countries. The 50 largest transnational industrial companies, by sales in 2007 (such as ExxonMobil, Shell, BP, and Wal-Mart), each had annual revenues greater than the GNP of 133 members of the United Nations. Using people as the measure, many NGOs, particularly trade unions, churches, and campaigning groups in the fields of human rights, women's rights, and the environment, have their membership measured in millions, whereas 42 of the 192 countries in the UN have populations of less than 1 million—of which 12 are less than one hundred thousand.[2] There is also great variation in the complexity and diversity of the economies and the societies of different countries and hence the extent to which they are each involved in transnational relations.

State Systems and International Systems

A third problem is found in the underlying analytical inconsistency in supposing states are located in an anarchic international system, a supposition that we learned in Chapter 3 when we discussed Hobbes. Whether it means a legal entity, a country, or a government, the state is seen as a coherent unit, acting with common purpose and existing as something more than the sum of its parts (the individual people). At the same time, most advocates of the state-centric approach deny the possibility of such collective entities existing at the global level. The phrase "the international system" is denied its full technical meaning of a collectivity in which the component elements (the individual states) lose some of their independence. No philosophical argument has been put forward to explain this inconsistency in the assumptions made about the different levels of analysis. By exaggerating the coherence of states and downplaying the coherence of global politics, both transnational relations and intergovernmental relations are underestimated.

The Difference Between State and Nation

A final intellectual problem with the state-centric approach is the behavioral assumption that politics within states is significantly different from politics between states. This is based on the idea, central to all realists since Morgenthau, that people's loyalty to their **nation** is more intense than other loyalties. Clearly, it cannot be denied that **nationalism**

nation A community of people who share a common sense of identity, which may be derived from language, culture, or ethnicity; this community may be a minority within a single country or live in more than one country.

nationalism The *idea* that the world is divided into nations that provide the overriding focus of political identity and loyalty, which in turn should be the basis for defining the population of states. Nationalism also can refer to this idea in the form of a strong sense of identity (*sentiment*) or organizations and movements seeking to realize this idea (*politics*).

and national **identity** invoke powerful emotions for most people, but various caveats must be made about their political relevance. First, communal identities form a hierarchy from the local through the national to wider groupings. Thus, both local communities and much broader groups than the nation can also make claims on a person's loyalty. "Americans" can simultaneously identify with their hometown, their state, the United States, North America, and America as a continent. Second, many individuals have dual national identities, whether through mixed parentage or through family ancestry, as with "African Americans" or "Irish Americans."

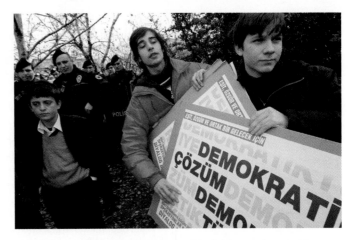

Kurds have protested for social and political rights and recognition within Turkey. Occasionally, people acting in the name of the Kurdish nation have bombed public facilities in Turkish cities. The Turkish government sees Kurds as terrorists while Kurds see themselves as national liberation fighters. What do you think?

Third, there has been a long-standing linguistic trick whereby national loyalty is made to appear as if it is focused on the nation-state. Both inter*national* relations and trans*national* relations cover relations across state boundaries, although logically the words refer to relations between national groups, such as the Scots or the Kurds. In the real world, only a few countries, such as Iceland, Poland, and Japan, can make a reasonable claim that their people are from a single nation, and in all such cases, significant numbers of the national group reside in other countries, often the United States. Most countries are multinational, and many national groups are present in several countries. Thus national loyalty is actually quite different from loyalty to a country.

identity The understanding of the self in relationship to an "other." Identities are social and thus always formed in relationship to others. Constructivists generally hold that identities shape interests; we cannot know what we want unless we know who we are. But because identities are social and produced through interactions, identities can change.

Transnational Companies as Political Actors

All companies that import or export are engaging in transnational economic activities. If they lobby foreign governments about trade, they become transnational political actors. However, they are not known as transnational companies (TNCs) until they have branches or subsidiaries outside their home country. The first companies to expand in this way were in agriculture, mining, or oil, operating in the European empires. Now they occur in all economic sectors, while industrialized countries that never had empires and most developing countries have seen some of their companies expand transnationally. In 2004, among the one hundred TNCs with the highest levels of assets outside their home country, fifty-three were from eleven Western European countries, twenty-five from the United States, four had dual headquarters in Western countries, nine from Japan, three from Canada, one from Australia, and one each from China, Malaya, Singapore, Hong Kong, and South Korea. Only developed countries, East and Southeast Asia, a few Latin American countries, India, and South Africa host large TNCs. Nevertheless, there are now transnational companies based in as many as 138 countries—35 from developed countries and 103 from transition and developing countries, including 31 African countries.[3]

WHAT'S YOUR WORLDVIEW

The United States can be seen as a country made up of many nations, with many Native American nations and many different ethnic nations. Or is the United States the world's only "nation-state"? Do you see yourself as a member of a nation? How do you identify yourself?

Financial Flows and Loss of Sovereignty

The consequences of the extensive transnationalization of major companies are profound. It is no longer possible to regard each country as having its own separate economy. Two

Table 7.1

Transnational Corporations from Developing Countries

The classical image of a TNC is a large company from the United States that has expanded production and sales overseas, dominating a global market and exploiting cheap labor in developing countries. In contrast to this, in the twenty-first century, TNCs from developing countries have become increasingly important.

- More than one-quarter of all TNCs now have their headquarters in developing countries.
- The top one hundred developing-country TNCs are from fourteen countries: China, Hong Kong, Taiwan, India, Malaysia, Singapore, Korea, the Philippines, Thailand, Brazil, Mexico, Venezuela, South Africa, and Egypt. However, the total foreign assets of all these companies in 2004 were less than those of one US company, General Electric, the world's biggest TNC.
- Most developing-country TNCs are small, but some are becoming major players in particular industries, such as cars, electronics, steel, and container shipping. The Chinese TNC Lenovo now owns the IBM PC brand, and the Indian TNC Tata has taken over Corus, the major European steel manufacturer, and its auto and truck division now owns Land Rover and Jaguar.
- Developing-country TNCs are more likely to invest in neighboring countries, but they are increasingly investing in the developed world as well. They own more than 500 affiliates in the US and a similar number in Britain.
- In the United States, opposition in Congress to developing-country TNCs has been strong enough to block a Chinese takeover of the US oil company UNOCAL and to force Dubai Ports World to divest itself of six US ports.

Two examples illustrate this new world of successful developing-country TNCs: Marcopolo, a Brazilian company, manufactures buses in several South American countries and sells them in more than eighty countries; and Hikma Pharmaceuticals, a Jordanian company, manufactures in two other Arab countries and in Portugal, having strong sales in West Asia and North Africa, along with recent expansion in Europe and the United States.

Source: *World Investment Report 2006* (UNCTAD 2006b)

sovereignty The condition of a state having control and authority over its own territory and being free from any higher legal authority. It is related to, but distinct from, the condition of a government being free from any external political constraints.

of the most fundamental attributes of **sovereignty**—control over the currency and control over foreign trade—have been substantially diminished. The two factors combined mean governments have lost control of financial flows. In the case of the currency, the successive crises in the 1980s and the 1990s for the dollar, the British pound, the French franc, and the Japanese yen established that even the governments with the greatest financial resources were helpless against the transnational banks and other speculators. In the twenty-first century, the global financial system became even more integrated, as all the major banks expanded their transnational activities more than their activities at home and the financial instruments became ever more complex (see Chapter 12).

The effects of trade on finance are less obvious. When goods move physically across frontiers, it is usually seen as being trade between the relevant countries, but it may also be intrafirm trade. As the logic of intrafirm trade is quite different from intercountry trade, governments cannot have clear expectations of the effects of their financial and fiscal policies on TNCs. A company may respond to higher tax rates by changing its transfer prices to reduce its tax bill. Several other motives might induce a company to distort transfer prices, including evasion of controls on the crossborder movements of profits or capital.

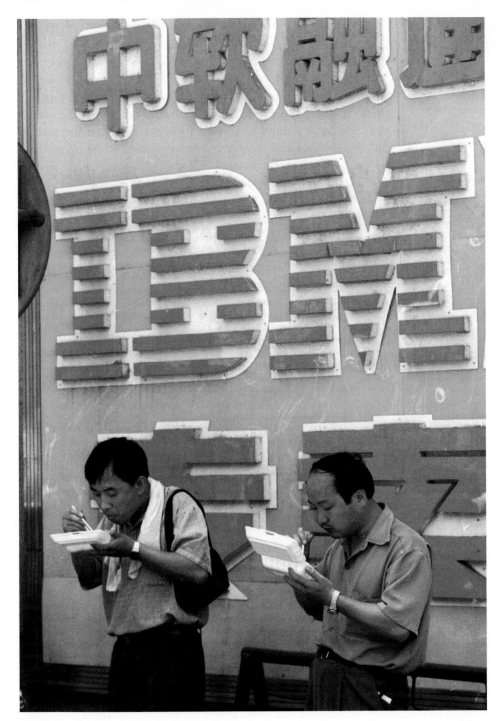

Transnational corporations like IBM have offices and production facilities around the world. What kind of power does this give them in global politics?

WHAT'S YOUR WORLDVIEW ?

To what extent did the global financial crisis of 2007–2009 demonstrate the limits of sovereignty of states and the ability of governments to control transactions within their borders?

triangulation This occurs when trade or communication between two countries is routed indirectly via a third country. For example, in the early 1980s, neither the Argentine government nor the British government permitted trade between the two countries, but some companies simply sent their exports via Brazil or Western Europe.

regulatory arbitrage In the world of banking, the process of moving funds or business activity from one country to another in order to increase profits by escaping the constraints imposed by government regulations. By analogy, the term can be applied to any transfer of economic activity by any company in response to government policy.

Triangulation of Trade and Loss of Sovereignty

Governments have great difficulty regulating international transactions. Even the US administration was unable to prevent some of its citizens from visiting communist Cuba or the Soviet Union during the Cold War. It may be possible to prevent the *direct* import or export of goods. However, there is no guaranteed method of preventing *indirect* trade from one country to another. This is known as **triangulation**. Only if a UN Security Council resolution obliges all the countries of the world to impose sanctions is there a reasonable prospect of a determined government preventing TNCs from evading sanctions. However, in such a situation, sovereignty over the relevant trade then lies with the Security Council and not with the individual governments.

Regulatory Arbitrage and Loss of Sovereignty

It is difficult for governments to regulate the commercial activities of companies within their country, because companies may choose to engage in **regulatory arbitrage**. If a company objects to one government's policy, it may threaten to limit or close down its local production and increase production in another country. The government that imposes the least demanding health, safety, welfare, or environmental standards will offer competitive advantages to less socially responsible companies. As a result, there can be a race to the bottom, unless governments unite to agree on minimum standards. There is also a strong global trend toward the reduction of corporation taxes. It thus becomes difficult for any government to set high standards and maintain taxes. In the case of banking, the political dangers inherent in the risks of a bank collapsing through imprudent or criminal behavior are so great that the major governments have set common capital standards, under the Basel Committee rules. Evasion of these rules, by the creation of new financial instruments, contributed to the 2007–2009 financial crisis, so the major countries in the G-20 have responded by agreeing to tighten the rules. Whatever control is achieved does not represent the successful exercise of sovereignty over companies: it is the partial surrender of sovereignty by states to an intergovernmental body or an international regime.

Extraterritoriality and Sovereignty

In addition, transnational companies generate clashes of sovereignty between different governments. Let us consider the example of a company that has its headquarters in the United States and a subsidiary company in the United Kingdom. Three lines of authority exist. The United States government can control the main company and the United Kingdom government can control the subsidiary. Each process would be the standard exercise of a government's sovereignty over its internal affairs. In addition, both governments would accept that the TNC can, within certain limits, control its own policies on purchasing, production, and sales. Under normal circumstances these three lines of authority can be exercised simultaneously and in harmony. However, when the US-government decisions cover the global operations of the TNC, there is a clash of sovereignty. Does the subsidiary obey the UK government or the orders of the US government issued via its headquarters? This problem of **extraterritoriality** is inherent in the structure of all TNCs.

A Transnational Challenge: The War on Drugs

While for many people in the United States the trade in illegal recreational drugs like marijuana is a joke, in Mexico it is not at all funny. Beginning in the 1960s, Mexico became a source of the weed in addition to being a transit country for other illegal drugs destined for the US markets. The actions of the drug gangs were often simply another part of life along the border. However, something changed dramatically during 2008, and by early 2009 open warfare began between Mexican drug kingpins and the Mexican federal government. In a change from the past, the federal police often found themselves outgunned by the drug gangs, which were armed with machine guns and rocket-propelled grenades. In the terms you learned in this chapter, the transnational criminal gangs represent a direct challenge to the authority of the governments of Mexico and the United States. It has become a significant transnational problem.

The central propositions of the Westphalian system are that each country is sovereign and has a legitimate monopoly on the use of force within its own specific territory. The transnational character of the drug trade has undermined the ability of governments to control the use of force within their borders. In the case of Mexico and the United States, the televised images of shoot-outs provide vivid examples of this phenomenon. The interdependent nature of this relationship goes beyond the fact that the drugs are on their way

to users in the United States. Mexican officials complained that lax gun-purchasing laws in the United States are part of the problem, because so-called straw purchasers buy firearms in the United States and then ship them south of the border.

Modern globalized mass culture also has a role in this drug-war drama. Movies, music, and video games that seem to glorify the violent drug culture play an important, if unwitting,

The Taliban in Afghanistan places a tax on opium poppy production to fund its war against NATO and Afghan government forces. Would you expect this from a group that professes to have strong religious values?

part in the erosion of governmental authority. It becomes "cool" to swagger like a gangster or to run up a high score on Grand Theft Auto. At parties on Thursday night at the dormitory or during a free period from high school, some think it is cool to have drugs.

In these overt and subtle ways, the norms on which the government's authority is based are diluted. In some regions of the world—the Golden Triangle of northern Burma and Thailand, Medellín in Colombia, Afghanistan—the drug kingpins have their private armies and administer their own form of jus-

tice in the territories they control. The drug traffickers provide a stable, if illegal, income for many people. Ironically, the drug lords also provide an alternative form of government, with their own quasi-legal code that features swift retribution for transgressions.

Paradoxically, the legitimacy of governments can be further undermined when their drug interdiction agencies cooperate to stem the international drug trade. We can see this at work in the relations of the United States with Mexico, Colombia, Bolivia, and Peru. For more than thirty years the US government has tried a number of means to control the supply of illegal drugs from these countries. These have included economic incentives to farmers to switch to legal crops, military assistance to the governments, and application of herbicides to kill the illegal plants. All of these methods have failed to end the drug-based agribusiness and have aggravated the perception that the gringo from *el norte* is continuing its meddling in the internal affairs of the Latin American countries.

Although some scholars who subscribe to the realist tradition might discount the significance of transnational actors as participants in international relations, it is clear that many of these actors do indeed have a substantial impact on a globalized society. They provide food aid, medical care, and development assistance. Unfortunately, some transnational agents also bring dangerous illegal drugs and narco-terrorism that present very real challenges to the legitimacy of the states.

As a matter of routine policy implementation, clashes now have to be resolved between different decisions in different jurisdictions on competition policy, mergers and acquisitions, accounting procedures, and anticorruption measures. Will US accounting standards apply to European companies because some of their operations are in the US? Can the directors of parent TNCs be prosecuted for the payment of bribes by their overseas branches? The long-term trend is for such questions to be resolved by global standardization of domestic policy. For example, the Organization for Economic Cooperation and Development (OECD) has developed a Convention on Combating Bribery of Foreign Public Officials in International Business Transactions.

From Domestic Deregulation to Global Re-regulation

For most companies most of the time, their interests will be in accord with the government's policy of increasing employment and promoting economic growth. Conflicts will arise over the regulation of markets to avoid the risks of market failures or externalization of social and environmental costs of production. Domestic deregulation and globalization of economic activity mean regulation is now occurring at the global level rather than within individual countries. Three factors involving TNCs push toward the globalization of politics. First, governments can only reassert control by acting collectively. Second, consumer pressures are leading to acceptance and implementation of global codes of conduct by companies in collaboration with NGOs. A third push is for global companies to submit to social and environmental auditing. These factors are coming together in the collaboration between governments, NGOs, and the UN Secretariat to recruit the major TNCs as voluntary partners in what is known as the Global Compact, to implement ten principles of corporate social responsibility on human rights, labor standards, the environment, and anticorruption.

Nonlegitimate Groups and Liberation Movements as Political Actors

A variety of groups engage in violent or criminal behavior on a transnational basis. A distinction can be made between activity that is considered criminal around the world, such as theft, fraud, personal violence, piracy, or drug trafficking, and activity that is claimed by those undertaking it to have legitimate political motives. In reality, the distinction becomes blurred when criminals claim political motives or political groups are responsible for acts such as terrorism, torture, or involving children in violence. For all governments, neither criminal activity nor political violence can be legitimate within their own jurisdiction and generally not in other countries.

Transnational Criminals and Their Political Impact

Politically, the most important criminal industries are illicit trading in arms and in drugs. For example, in early 2009, a war broke out in Mexico between police and drug smugglers moving their products into the United States. As travel has increased, trafficking in people has become easier and increased significantly in recent years. One result of this trend is the growth of new slave trade that has evolved mainly for sexual exploitation of young women and children. As you will have seen, TNCs are most concerned to prevent trade in counterfeit goods and theft of intellectual property, particularly of music, films, and computer software. The same four sovereignty problems arise with tackling criminals as with regulating TNCs. First, criminal financial flows can be massive, and money

laundering threatens the integrity of banking and other financial institutions. Second, criminal trade has been so extensively diversified
through triangulation that no government can confidently claim that its
country is not a transit route for drugs or arms. Third, as with regulatory arbitrage by TNCs, police action may displace well-organized gangs
to another country rather than stop their activities. Fourth, illicit drugs
and money laundering involve questions of extraterritorial jurisdiction.
However, in contrast to the regulation of TNCs, transnational police activities involve high levels of cooperation.

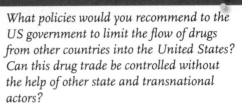

Terrorists, Guerrillas, and National Liberation Movements

Political violence is most common when broadly based nationalist movements, ethnic
minorities, or fundamentalist religious groups reject the legitimacy of a government.
As we will see in Chapter 9, these groups are often called "terrorists" to express disap-
proval, "guerrillas" by those who are more neutral, or "national liberation movements"
by their supporters. In the past, nationalists were usually able to obtain some external
support. Now, because of widespread revulsion against political violence, national groups
and ethnic minorities are subject to pressure to negotiate instead of fighting. Political
violence is more likely to be considered legitimate when a group has widespread support;
when political channels have been closed to them; when the target government is excep-
tionally oppressive; and when the violence is limited to "military targets." Groups that
fail to match these four characteristics only obtain very limited transnational support.
When Palestinian groups first used terrorist methods, the Palestine Liberation Organization (PLO) gained attention, but not support. When they limited these violent attacks in
the mid-1970s, the PLO achieved membership in the Arab League, along with observer
status at the UN. However, suicide bombing targeted at civilians by some Palestinians

Long labeled a terrorist organization, the Palestine Liberation Organization (PLO) gained observer
status at the UN, and the Palestinian Authority sits at the diplomatic table as an equal with states,
including Israel and the United States.

during and since the second intifada of the late 1980s greatly reduced the PLO's international legitimacy.

Since September 11, 2001, the political balance has changed substantially. The scale of the destruction wrought by Al Qaeda organizing nineteen hijackers simultaneously taking control of four passenger aircraft and using these as weapons against New York and Washington did much to delegitimize *all* groups who use violence for political purposes. Historically, terrorism has mainly been an instrument of internal conflict within a single society, but Al Qaeda suddenly presented the world with a new threat of a transnational global network. Within a few years they staged attacks in Kenya, Tanzania, Yemen, Saudi Arabia, the United States, Tunisia, Indonesia, Turkey, and Spain. And yet contemporary terrorism is not a single phenomenon. The Basque, Palestinian, Kashmiri, Tamil, and Chechnya disputes clearly have roots that are totally independent of each other and have little or no connection to Al Qaeda. There are different transnational processes for different conflicts generating terrorism. Even Al Qaeda itself is a disparate coalition of anti-American fundamentalist groups rather than a coherent disciplined organization.

Extensive political violence used by governments against their citizens was commonplace and immune from diplomatic criticism as recently as the 1970s. Because of a widespread desire to end the impunity of individual government leaders, soldiers, and officials responsible for the horrors of large-scale political violence at the end of the twentieth century, a revolution has occurred in international law. Initially, temporary tribunals were established to cover atrocities in Yugoslavia and Rwanda. Then, a new permanent International Criminal Court (ICC) was created in July 2002 to prosecute those who commit genocide, war crimes, or crimes against humanity. The ICC is a modification of the traditional interstate system, because it was created by political campaigning of human rights NGOs, because bitter opposition from the sole "superpower" was defeated, and because the sovereign responsibility to prosecute criminals has been assumed by a global court. In September 2005, the United Nations went further, replacing state sovereignty with a collective global responsibility to protect (R2P) when national authorities are manifestly failing (General Assembly Resolution 60/1).

The Significance of Criminals, Terrorists, and Guerrillas

Before September 11, 2001, analysis of transnational criminals and guerrillas did not present a challenge to orthodox state-centric theory. Criminals seemed to be marginal because they were not legitimate and were excluded from normal international transactions. Pirates operating in the Strait of Malacca or off the coast of Somalia rarely became international news. The violent groups that gained military, political, and diplomatic status on a transnational basis could be presented as nationalist groups aspiring to gain their place in the interstate system. Such arguments ignore the way globalization has changed the nature of sovereignty and the processes of government. The operations of criminals and other nonlegitimate groups have become more complex, spread over a wider geographical area, and larger in scale because the improvements in communications have made it so much easier to transfer people, money, weapons, and ideas on a transnational basis. Government attempts to control such activities have become correspondingly more difficult, as the case of the Somali pirates demonstrates. The legal concept of sovereignty may nominally still exist, but political practice has become significantly different. Now virtually every government feels it has to mobilize external support in order to exercise "domestic jurisdiction" over criminals. Defeat of Al Qaeda will not be achieved by military counterterrorism but by global political change that delegitimizes fundamentalism and violence. Oppressive action by governments is subject to extensive review under global human rights mechanisms and, in some situations, may be subject to prosecution at the ICC.

Nongovernmental Organizations as Political Actors

The politics of an individual country cannot be understood without knowing what groups lobby the government and what debate there has been in the media. Similarly, international diplomacy does not operate on some separate planet, cut off from global civil society. Because diplomats like to claim that they are pursuing the national interest of a united society, they will not admit to relations with interest groups or pressure groups, and they use the bland title "nongovernmental organizations," or simply "NGOs."

WHAT'S YOUR WORLDVIEW

In its campaign against terrorism, the Bush administration in the United States violated many critical tenets of international law and basic principles of human rights. Are these practices acceptable in the global war on terrorism, or do they serve the purposes of the terrorists to undermine the moral authority of the US government?

Consultative Status at the UN for NGOs

As a result of pressure, primarily from American groups, the United Nations Charter contains Article 71, providing for the Economic and Social Council (ECOSOC) to consult

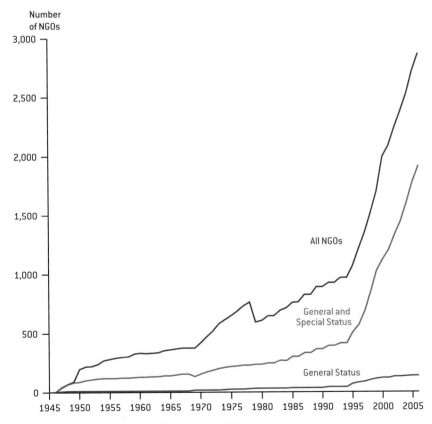

Figure 7.1 The Growth of NGOs at the UN.
What is behind the increase of NGOs at the UN in the last twenty years? Do you think this trend will continue?

with NGOs. In 1950, the council formally codified its practice in a statute for NGOs. It recognized *three categories* of groups:

1. A small number of high-status NGOs, concerned with most of the council's work;
2. Specialist NGOs, concerned with a few fields of activity and having a high reputation in those fields;
3. A roster of other NGOs that are expected to make occasional contributions to the council.[4]

Since then the term "NGO" has, for diplomats, been synonymous with a group that is eligible for ECOSOC consultative status. As of September 2009, there are 3,287 NGOs in consultative status, with 138 of these in the high-status category.

The UN Definition of an Acceptable NGO

Many NGO activists believe the UN should be more restrictive and only accept groups that are "true" NGOs, contributing to "progressive" social movements. For example, environmentalists are often upset that business federations are accepted, and the whole NGO community at the UN agonized over the National Rifle Association being admitted to the roster in November 1996.

The ECOSOC statute and the way it has been applied embodies six principles:

1. An NGO should support the aims and the work of the UN. However, it is very rare that objections are made to the political purposes of NGOs.
2. Officially, an NGO should be a representative body, with identifiable headquarters, and officers who are responsible to a democratic policy-making conference. In practice, many highly prestigious NGOs, particularly development and environment NGOs, are not membership organizations.
3. An NGO cannot be a profit-making body. Individual companies cannot gain consultative status, but trade federations of commercial interests are recognized as NGOs.
4. An NGO cannot use or advocate violence.
5. An NGO must respect the norm of "noninterference in the internal affairs of states." This means an NGO cannot be a political party, but parties can, like companies, form international federations. Also, NGOs concerned with human rights should not restrict their activities to a particular group, nationality, or country.
6. An international NGO is one that is not established by intergovernmental agreement.

Globalization and the Expansion of NGOs

The creation of a complex global economy has had effects way beyond the international trade in goods and services. Most companies, in each distinct area of activity, have formed organizations to facilitate communication, to harmonize standards, and to manage adaptation to complex change. Equally, the employees have found they face common problems in different countries, and so trade unions and professional bodies have developed their own transnational links. Any form of international regime to formulate policy for an industry, whether it is nongovernmental or intergovernmental, will encourage the strengthening of the global links among the NGOs concerned with its activities.

For most of the twentieth century, any individual could travel in person or communicate in writing to most parts of the world. The technical revolution in recent years lies in the increased density, increased speed, and reduced cost of communication and travel.

The Baby Milk Advocacy Network

The prototype for global campaigning by NGOs has been the International Baby Food Action Network (IBFAN), which challenges the marketing of dried milk powder by the major food and pharmaceutical TNCs. In the early 1970s, medical staff in developing countries gradually became aware that the death rate for babies was rising because of decreased breast feeding. If the family was poor and used insufficient milk powder, the baby was undernourished. If the water or the bottle was not sterile, the baby developed gastric diseases. Bottle feeding today causes around one and a half million deaths a year.

The question was first taken up by the *New Internationalist* magazine and War on Want (WoW) in Britain in 1973–1974. A Swiss NGO, the Third World Action Group (AgDW), then published a revised translation of WoW's report, under the title "Nestlé Kills Babies." When Nestlé sued for libel, AgDW mobilized groups from around the world to supply evidence for their defense. The Swiss Court found AgDW guilty in December 1976 on one of Nestlé's four original counts, on the technical basis that Nestlé was only indirectly responsible for the deaths.

The question moved to the United States when religious groups involved in Latin America fought another court case against Bristol-Myers. Increased awareness led to organization by a new group, the Infant Formula Action Coalition, of a boycott of Nestlé's products that spread to many countries. In the hope of diffusing the increasing pressure, the International Council of Infant Food Industries accepted a proposal by Senator Edward Kennedy for the World Health Organization (WHO) and UNICEF to hold a meeting on infant feeding in October 1979. Rather than seeing the issue depoliticized, the companies found they were facing demands to limit their marketing. The meeting also taught a group of NGOs how much they could benefit from working together with a common political strategy. They decided to continue to cooperate by forming IBFAN, as a global advocacy network.

The new network was able to mobilize a diverse coalition of medical professionals, religious groups, development activists, women's groups, community organizations, consumer lobbies, and the boycott campaigners.

Against intense opposition from the TNCs and the US administration, IBFAN succeeded in achieving the adoption of an International Code of Marketing of Breast-milk Substitutes, by WHO's assembly, in May 1981. The key provisions of the code were that "there should be no advertising or other form of promotion to the general public" nor any provision of free samples to mothers.

As of 2006, thirty-two countries had implemented the code by means of a comprehensive law, another forty-four countries had implemented many, but not all, provisions as law, and a further sixty-four countries had weak legal provisions or voluntary policies. IBFAN's work continues along two tracks: it monitors and reports violations of the code by companies, including in countries where marketing is now illegal; and it also seeks to upgrade the law in countries that are only partially implementing the code.

This account is based on A. Chetley (1986), The Politics of Baby Foods (London: Pinter) and information at www.ibfan.org, the IBFAN website.

The political revolution lies in these changes bringing rapid global communication within the capabilities of most people. This includes even the poor, if they band together to fund a representative to articulate their case or gain access to the news media. Changes in communications constitute a fundamental change in the structure of world politics. Governments have lost control over the transnational relations of their citizens. They may attempt to monitor or limit transboundary communications, but closing the border is no longer technologically possible.

The Shift of NGOs from the Local to the Global

One effect of the globalization of communication is to make it physically and financially feasible for small groups of people to establish and maintain cooperation, even though they may be based thousands of miles apart from each other. Thus it is very easy for NGOs to operate transnationally, but not all NGOs make this choice. They vary from local organizations solely operating in one small town to large global bureaucracies with a presence in most countries.

When NGOs cooperate transnationally, they may use one of four different types of structure. In the past, a formal joint organization known as an "INGO" (an international NGO) was usually established, with a permanent headquarters, a secretariat, and a regular program of meetings. With the creation and expansion of the Internet, it is now just as likely that a looser network will be formed, often with a single NGO providing the technical support for e-mail communications and a joint website. The most famous networks, such as Jubilee 2000, the Coalition for an International Criminal Court, and the International Campaign to Ban Landmines, have united around a single policy domain, brought together hundreds of NGOs from all around the world, and achieved major policy changes against the opposition of leading governments. These are known as **advocacy networks**. At the meetings of intergovernmental organizations, NGOs may combine in a caucus. This is a temporary network formed solely for the purpose of lobbying on the agenda items at the particular meeting. Finally, there are governance networks, formed by NGOs to maintain and enhance the participation rights of NGOs in intergovernmental meetings. They differ from advocacy networks and caucuses in not having common political goals, other than their common interest in being allowed access to the policy-making process. An example of the variety of actors involved in different policy areas is presented in Table 7.2.

advocacy networks Groups of regional, national, and international NGOs bound together by shared values. They coordinate activity to frame political debate and to influence policy outcomes.

International Organizations as Structures of Global Politics

International organizations—in the form of intergovernmental organizations, international NGOs, and hybrids (explained below)—provide the focus for global politics. The new physical infrastructure of global communications makes it easier for them to operate. In addition, when the sessions of the organizations take place, they become distinct structures for political communication. Face-to-face meetings produce different outcomes from telephone or written communications, and multilateral discussions produce different outcomes from interactions in networks of bilateral communications.

It was argued earlier that it is inconsistent to see states as coherent entities while asserting that anarchy exists at the global level. We can be consistent by accepting the existence of systems at all levels of world politics. In the modern world, human groups are never so coherent that they are independent, closed systems (perhaps excepting monastic orders). Equally, once distinct organizational processes are established, they are never so

Table 7.2

The Variety of Political Actors Involved in Different Policy Domains

	Apartheid in South Africa	Human Rights	Population Planning	Environment
Main Governments Involved	South Africa, UK, US versus African governments	Democratic versus authoritarian governments	All types of governments	Those who feel threatened by problems versus those who do not
Transnational Companies	Wide range, but especially mining and oil	Any working with oppressive governments	Medical, pharmaceutical, and food	Mainly industrial, energy, and transport
Guerrillas	ANC, PAC, and SWAPO	Any taking hostages	Any in control of territory	Generally not concerned
Grassroots NGOs	Anti-Apartheid Movement	Human rights groups and the oppressed	Religious, women's, and health groups	Friends of the Earth, WWF, Greenpeace, etc.
UN Intergovernmental Policy Forum	Committee Against Apartheid and Security Council	Human Rights Council	Commission on Population and Development	Commission on Sustainable Development
UN Secretariat	Centre Against Apartheid	Office . . . for Human Rights	UNICEF, UN Population Fund	UNDP, UNEP
Other IGOs	Organization of African Unity	Council of Europe, OAS, and AU	WHO, World Bank	World Bank
International NGOs	Many involved, with a secondary concern	Amnesty International and others	International Planned Parenthood Federation	Environment Liaison Centre International and other networks
Hybrid IOs	Those concerned with trade	ILO	None	World Conservation Union (IUCN)

open that the boundaries become insignificant. Thus international organizations of all types transcend country boundaries and have a major impact on the governmental actors and transnational actors composing them.

For a system to exist, there must be a sufficient density of interactions, involving each of its elements, at a sufficient intensity to result both in the emergence of properties for the system as a whole and in some consistent effect on the behavior of the elements. Generally, international organizations will have founding documents defining their goals, rules of procedure constraining the modes of behavior, secretariats committed to the status and identity of the organization (or at least committed to their own careers), past decisions that provide norms for future policy, and interaction processes that socialize new participants. All these features at the systemic level will be part of the explanation of the behavior of the members, and thus the political outcomes will not be determined solely by the members' initial goals. The statement that international organizations form systems is a statement that they are politically significant and that global politics cannot be reduced to "interstate" relations.

Normally a sharp distinction is made between intergovernmental organizations and international nongovernmental organizations. This conveys the impression that interstate

hybrid international organizations Organizations that provide full membership and equality of status both to governmental actors and to transnational actors. They create policy to govern specific areas of international relations.

diplomacy and transnational relations are separate from each other. In practice, governments do not rigidly maintain the separation. There is an overlapping pattern of relations in another category of international organizations, **hybrid international organizations**, in which governments work with NGOs. Among the most important hybrids are the International Red Cross, the World Conservation Union (IUCN), the International Council of Scientific Unions, the International Air Transport Association, and other economic bodies combining companies and governments.

In order to be regarded as a hybrid INGO, the organization must admit as full members *both* NGOs, parties, or companies *and* governments or governmental agencies. Both types of members must have full rights of participation in policy making, including the right to vote on the final decisions. When the principle of formal equality of NGOs and governments is acknowledged by both sides in such a manner, the assumption that governments can dominate must be totally abandoned.

The Power of NGOs

A critical question is, how much power do NGOs and other transnational actors have to implement their own strategic plans and affect the policy of governments and intergovernmental organizations? We know that transnational corporations have money and the promise of jobs, investment, and access to new technologies to use to influence governments, but what about religious organizations like World Vision or think tanks like the Brookings Institute? Let's just look at NGOs to assess their sources of influence.

In many societies, especially the pluralist social-democratic states (e.g., Sweden, Denmark, the Netherlands), NGOs may play an important role as partners in the policy process. Some NGOs are not as independent from public agencies as they claim to be. NGOs are often supported by governments to carry out policy programs that governments cannot or will not complete.

To illustrate, NGOs have played a critical role in implementing development-assistance programs throughout the world. The International Red Cross claims the NGOs working in the development and human-security areas give out more money than the World Bank. Most of this money comes from governments and public agencies. From 1990 to 1994, the percentage of European Union aid that was distributed by NGOs rose from 47 percent to 67 percent. Organizations like Oxfam in the United Kingdom, World Vision (the largest privately funded Christian relief-and-development NGO), and Médecins Sans Frontières (MSF)—Doctors Without Borders—receive anywhere from 25 percent to 50 percent of their funding from various government sources.

Obviously, government funding increases the ability of NGOs to assist people in need and to help governments carry out some of their foreign policy goals. As governments are forced to cut back their workforce, many duties are being transferred to NGOs. Not only do NGO employees deliver services to the poor and protect citizens in conflict areas, but NGOs like Amnesty International and Human Rights Watch provide policy makers and interested citizens with valuable information and research reports that can be used to develop new laws and policy programs. Their research expertise gives them access to policy makers, and often their ideas and interests become part of public policy.

Other forms of power discussed by Keck and Sikkink (1998, 18–24) include information politics, symbolic politics, leverage politics, accountability politics, and global campaign politics. Now we will provide a brief discussion of each of these forms of power, after which we will conclude the chapter by closely examining the role of NGOs in a "Global Perspective" feature highlighting NGOs that advocate children's rights around the world.

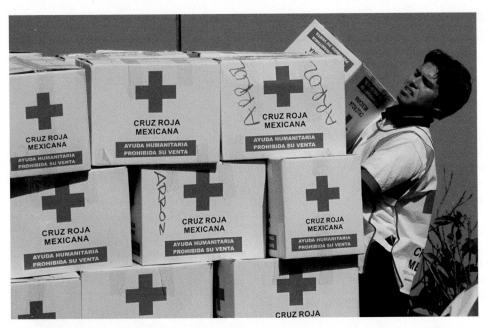

The International Committee of the Red Cross, often in association with its national counterparts, offers disaster-relief services in what is meant to be a nonpolitical manner. Here we see a member of the Red Cross stacking crates of food for victims of the devastating earthquake in Haiti in January 2010. How do states benefit by permitting NGOs to provide these essential services?

Information Politics

NGOs and other civil-society actors use e-mail, fax machines, newsletters, and web pages to keep their followers informed, solicit donations, and mobilize citizens to take positions supporting their causes. During antiglobalization demonstrations at WTO or G-8 talks, many activists use digital cameras and audio streams to share the day-to-day events with other activists in distant lands. This builds support and a stronger sense of community among NGOs and other activist groups.

Another part of information politics is the research and studies that many NGOs provide media reporters and government officials. Because of their expertise and their access to critical players in crisis situations, NGOs can also provide important technical and strategic information.

Symbolic Politics

Activist leaders of NGOs identify a critical issue or event and provide explanations that frame the issue so it becomes a catalyst for growth of the movement. The shelling of a café in Sarajevo by Bosnian Serb forces during the civil war in Yugoslavia was used as a symbolic event by human rights NGOs who were demanding US intervention to stop the ethnic cleansing in Bosnia.

NGOs use their position in society and their role in crises that occur as a way of increasing awareness and expanding support for their cause. When the Red Cross, Médecins Sans Frontières, and the International Campaign to Ban Landmines were awarded the Nobel Peace Prize, it called attention to their cause and gave the groups more legitimacy throughout the world. NGOs and the transnational social movements that they participate in often use big stories to gain public attention, more members, financial contributions, and the attention of those with political power. In the 1980s, Irish rock star Bob Geldof

Global Perspective

NGOs and Protecting the Rights of Children

Do nongovernmental organizations matter? That is the central question of the academic disputes that you read about at the start of this chapter. As you saw, people on one side in this discourse believe that NGOs are important actors that influence a range of behaviors in international relations. On the other side are many realists who believe that governments are the most important—and some believe the only—actor that matters in the study of the discipline. Somewhere in the middle are analysts who think that by combining the study of states and NGOs we can begin to understand the complexities of international relations. This dispute is primarily a disagreement of the kind you learned about in Chapters 3 and 4: What is the proper unit of analysis in the study of globalization and international relations?

For children around the world, these academic exercises miss the point: NGOs matter. Without the work of NGOs to supply food, provide education, and promote awareness, the lives of children would be much worse. In countries around the world each day children are forced to be soldiers in civil wars; children starve; children lack basic health services; children are forced to work in factories for less pay than adults; children are physically abused and forced into sex slavery.

Each day, workers for local and transnational NGOs strive to improve living conditions for millions of people under the age of eighteen. Hundreds of organizations attempt to implement the United Nations Millennium Development Goals that you read about already in this book. NGOs also do the important task of holding each country accountable for its ratification of the 1989 Convention on the Rights of the Child. Because the United Nations is an organization of sovereign and nominally equal countries, as you saw in Chapter 6, sometimes it is unable to do as much as some governments would like. NGOs, because they are not responsible to national governments, can apply moral suasion through public-awareness campaigns to help those people in need.

There are hundreds of NGOs working around the world to help children. Two of the more famous are Oxfam and Human Rights Watch, which focus on three main areas of children's rights: basic needs such as food, clothing, shelter, and health care; education; and security, including juvenile justice and ending war. Al-

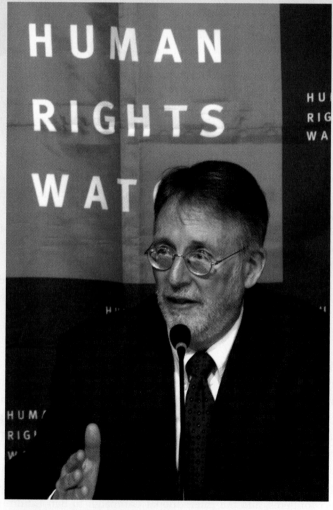

NGOs like Human Rights Watch shine a moral spotlight on human rights abuses in the Middle East and around the world. What kind of power do NGOs have and how do they influence states?

Global Perspective

though these are also problems in industrialized countries, they represent greater challenges in the developing world where governments lack the resources to provide for these needs. For example, according to the website of Oxfam International (http://www.oxfam.org/), its thirteen member groups work in more than one hundred countries helping people to help themselves by providing the tools and seeds for them to grow their own food. Oxfam also works in the area of arms control, seeking to encourage governments to stop expensive weapons sales and to redirect the money to basic human needs in developing countries.

Human Rights Watch has programs aimed at ending abuses of people regardless of age; however, the organization believes that children are at risk because of their vulnerable status in many societies. The group's website (http://www.hrw.org/en/category/topic/ children's-rights) has grim stories about the horrible conditions that children face around the world: detention in "social protection centers" in Vietnam where they are forced to work long hours for much less than the prevailing local wage scale; being forced to fight in civil wars in Africa and Asia; or use as sex workers in some countries, where they are then denied access to medical care, including HIV/AIDS medicines. The Children's Rights Division of Human Rights Watch has worked with the International Criminal Court to try to end the use of child soldiers and sexual trafficking in children.

Academic analysts of international politics might disagree about the worth of NGOs in the study of international society, but NGOs clearly have a positive effect daily on the lives of millions of people who are most at risk. NGOs are able to assume tasks that governments are unable or unwilling to do themselves.

(who played Wall in the Pink Floyd–inspired movie) turned the world's attention to famine in Western Africa. His activism led musicians in the United Kingdom, the United States, and Canada to each produce their own "We Are the World" records and sponsor a series of globally televised concerts to raise public awareness and collect funds for famine relief.

Some of these big stories that are picked up by the media are based on false or incomplete information. A good example is the Brent Spar incident. Greenpeace launched an attack on an obsolete oil rig, called the Brent Spar, in the North Sea to protest the decision by Shell to sink it. Greenpeace claimed that the environmental damage would be worse by sinking the rig than by towing it to shore and dismantling it there. Yet independent environmental studies did not support this position. These studies clearly showed that the environmental damage would be greater if the rig was towed to shore and dismantled. Still, Greenpeace continued with its campaign and forced the government of Germany and Shell Oil to dismantle the rig on land.

Leverage Politics

NGOs often use material leverage (e.g., money or goods) or moral leverage to persuade governments to act in certain ways or to encourage other NGOs to support their position on an issue. NGOs often shame governments into acting in a certain way. NGOs are adept at using the media to expose hypocritical behaviors and to make certain the public is aware of unpopular practices by governments, transnational corporations, and other actors. With greater access to media and information technology, NGOs have greater access to larger audiences. These NGOs demand more accountability and have increasing power and influence.

Accountability Politics

NGOs are able to use a number of information and media sources to force governments and political leaders to follow up on their public promises. These groups act as watch dogs, making certain that political leaders follow through with commitments that they make when running for office or addressing a current public concern. Unfortunately, this pressure does not always work. Both George H. W. Bush and Bill Clinton promised to push China to improve its human rights record before they would support new trade relations. Once elected, both presidents caved in to trade interests and failed to address human rights concerns. Although NGOs are not always successful, they continue to use all of their resources to pressure governments to close the gap between promises and performances.

The Global Campaign

A relatively new tool for NGOs and other civil-society actors and like-minded governments is a global campaign that uses the media, local activist networks, and if necessary product boycotts like the one described in the Nestlé case study. The use of the social networking sites on the Internet and the proliferation of NGOs across the world have made it easier to establish and maintain such campaigns. The One Campaign aimed at addressing global poverty and recent campaigns seeking to provide assistance to victims of natural disasters in New Orleans and Haiti have also benefitted from what we know as celebrity diplomacy. We are all familiar with the role played by Bono, Radiohead and Wyclef Jean in mobilizing public support for their humanitarian cause.

Conclusion

In this chapter we learned that the process of globalization is more than the interactions of governments and international organizations comprising governments. Since the mid-nineteenth century, nongovernmental organizations and other transnational actors like corporations have played an increasingly important role in global affairs. Global corporations, banks, and investment firms make choices that challenge the sovereignty and power of states. The recent global economic meltdown gave the world clear insights into how difficult it is for governments to control investment flows.

NGOs as members of global civil society occupy the "space between" the corporate world and the governmental or public world. Among their activities, NGOs provide vital health services, education, and legal services to people around the world. The organizations have gained official recognition within the United Nations system as partners in issue areas like environmental protection and peace building. As Rischard (2002) argues in his book on global problems, NGOs tend to work in three broad areas:

- *Sharing-our-planet* issues, or global common concerns such as climate change, ocean pollution, or biodiversity loss.
- *Sharing-our-humanity* issues, or human-security issues that focus on global health, education, human rights, and issues of war, violence, and repression.
- *Sharing-our-rule-book* issues, or governance issues that involve international laws and institutions.

In the next part of the book, we will examine the ways in which governments, intergovernmental organizations, and transnational actors such as NGOs and global corporations interact in the areas of war, security, and human rights.

Contributors to Chapter 7: Peter Willetts and Steven L. Lamy.

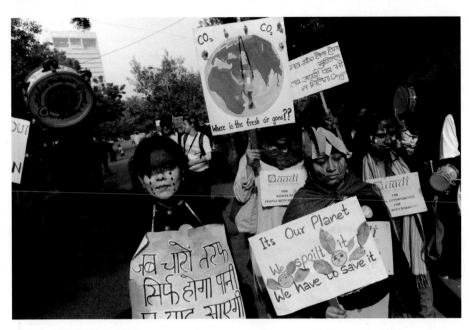

The government of India faces the conflicting pressures of economic growth and environmental protection.

REVIEW QUESTIONS

1. What are three meanings of "state"? Explain the implications of each for the study of transnational actors.
2. What are the different types of transnational actor? Give examples of each type.
3. What is a nation? How does the concept differ from that of a state?
4. How do transnational companies affect the sovereignty of governments?
5. What measures could you use to compare the size of countries, TNCs, NGOs, and international organizations? Are countries always larger than transnational actors?
6. What types of NGOs are, and what types are not, eligible to obtain consultative status with the Economic and Social Council of the United Nations? Why?
7. Explain the expansion in the number of NGOs engaging in transnational activities.
8. What are hybrid international organizations, and why are they significant?
9. How is it possible for NGOs to exercise influence in global politics? (Note: This question can be answered both in theoretical terms and in practical empirical terms.)
10. Explain the difference between analyzing international relations as a single international system (the realist model) and as the global politics of many different policy domains (the pluralist model).

FURTHER READING

Case study materials

Edwards, M., and Gaventa, J. (2001), *Global Citizen Action: Lessons and Challenges* (Boulder, CO: Lynne Rienner). Focuses on broadly based campaigning networks, with six case studies on civil-society interaction with the international financial institutions and seven case studies on environment, human rights, and development campaigns.

Keck, M. E., and Sikkink, K. (1998), *Activists Beyond Borders: Advocacy Networks in International Politics* (Ithaca, NY: Cornell University Press). A major contribution to the literature on the nature of modern transnational advocacy networks, with case studies on Latin America, the environment, and violence against women.

Risse-Kappen, T. (ed.) (1995), *Bringing Transnational Relations Back In* (Cambridge: Cambridge University Press). Provides a set of six case studies around the theme that transnational influence depends on the structures of governance for an issue area at both the domestic level and in international institutions.

Weiss, T. G., and Gordenker, L. (eds.) (1996), *NGOs, the UN and Global Governance* (Boulder, CO: Lynne Rienner). Six studies of NGO activity and three chapters addressing cross-cutting themes, set within a pluralist approach.

Willetts, P. (ed.) (1982), *Pressure Groups in the Global System: The Transnational Relations of Issue-Orientated Non-Governmental Organizations* (London: Pinter). In reaction against the omission of noneconomic groups by Keohane and Nye, examines how pressure groups move from single-country to global activity.

——(ed.) (1996), *"The Conscience of the World": The Influence of Non-Governmental Organizations in the UN System* (London: Hurst and Co.). Defines an NGO, gives the history of the League and the UN consultative arrangements, and offers seven case studies of the influence of NGOs in the UN system.

Theoretical debate

Rosenau, J. N. (1980), *The Study of Global Interdependence: Essays on the Transnationalisation of World Affairs* (London: Pinter). A fruitful source of theoretical ideas for a pluralist approach.

Viotti, P. R., and Kauppi, M. V. (1998), *International Relations Theory: Realism, Pluralism, Globalism*, 3rd ed. (New York: Macmillan). Gives excellent focus on the fundamentals of the theoretical debate.

Willetts, P. (1990), "Transactions, Networks and Systems," in A. J. R. Groom and P. Taylor (eds.), *Frameworks for International Co-operation* (London: Pinter), ch. 17. More detailed coverage of the development of international relations theory on transnational and intergovernmental relations. See also the editors' chapters in the case study books.

UN materials

Kaul, I., et al. (1993), *Human Development Report* (New York: Oxford University Press). An official UN annual report, which in this edition concentrates on the contribution made by NGOs to development.

UNCTAD, Division on Transnational Corporations and Investments (1991–), *World Investment Report* (New York: UN). An official UN annual report, which assesses the scale of TNC participation in global production, investment, and trade.

NOTES

1. Data on transnational corporations is given in annual reports from the United Nations. The figures quoted come from *World Investment Report 2006* (UNCTAD 2006b: 270–273 and 280–284). The numbers of different types of transnational and international organizations are from the *Yearbook of International Organizations 2005–2006*, vol. 5, p. 7 (Munich: K. G. Saur, 2006).

2. The *World Investment Report 2008* lists the 100 largest nonfinancial TNCs, ranked by foreign assets: of these, 50 had global sales of $60 billion or more in 2007. Data for each country on GNP and population are given each year in the *World Development Indicators, 2006* (Washington, DC: World Bank).

3. *World Investment Report 2006*, Annex tables A.I.6 and A.I.11.

4. ECOSOC Resolution 288(X)B, Arrangements for Consultation with Nongovernmental Organizations, was passed in February 1950. It was amended and replaced by Resolution 1296(XLIV) in May 1968 and again by Resolution 1996/31 in July 1996.

INTERNET RESOURCES

Amnesty International
www.amnesty.org
A leading NGO working to protect human rights around the world.

Foundation for Sustainable Development
http://www.fsdinternational.org/
An NGO that works to promote economic development in an environmentally sound manner.

International Committee of the Red Cross
www.icrc.org
A politically neutral NGO whose mission is to provide humanitarian assistance.

Multinational Monitor
http://multinationalmonitor.org/monitor.html
A nongovernmental organization that provides news and information about MNCs and TNCs.

United Nations Department of Public Information NGO Section
http://www.un.org/dpi/ngosection/index.asp
The UN resource page for NGO information.

World Federalist Society
http://www.wfm-igp.org/site/
An NGO that promotes world government as a solution to war and strife.

For more information, quizzes, case studies, and other study tools, please visit us at **www.oup.com/us/lamy**

PART FOUR

Global Issues: Security

In the final two parts of the book we want to give you a wide-ranging overview of the main issues in contemporary world politics. The previous three parts have been designed to give you a comprehensive foundation for the study of contemporary international issues. As with the other sections, this one also has two aims: **first**, we want to give you an understanding of some of the more important pressing problems of war and peace that appear every day in the media headlines and that, directly and indirectly, affect our lives. These issues are the stuff of globalization, and they take a number of different forms. Some, like **war and nuclear proliferation**, pose dangers of global catastrophe, which we will discuss in Chapter

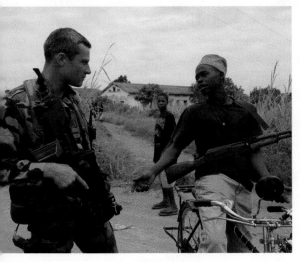

8. Yet other issues, such as **terrorism** (Chapter 9), **human rights**, and **human security** (Chapter 10), are fundamentally intertwined with globalization. Our **second** aim, of course, is that by providing overviews of these issues we are posing questions about the nature of globalization. By the end of Parts Four and Five you should be able to answer critical questions about how globalization shapes global issues. Does it make it easier or harder to deal with the problems covered in these chapters? The picture that emerges is that the process of globalization is a highly complex one, with major disagreements existing about its significance and its impact.

CHAPTER 8

International Security and Military Power

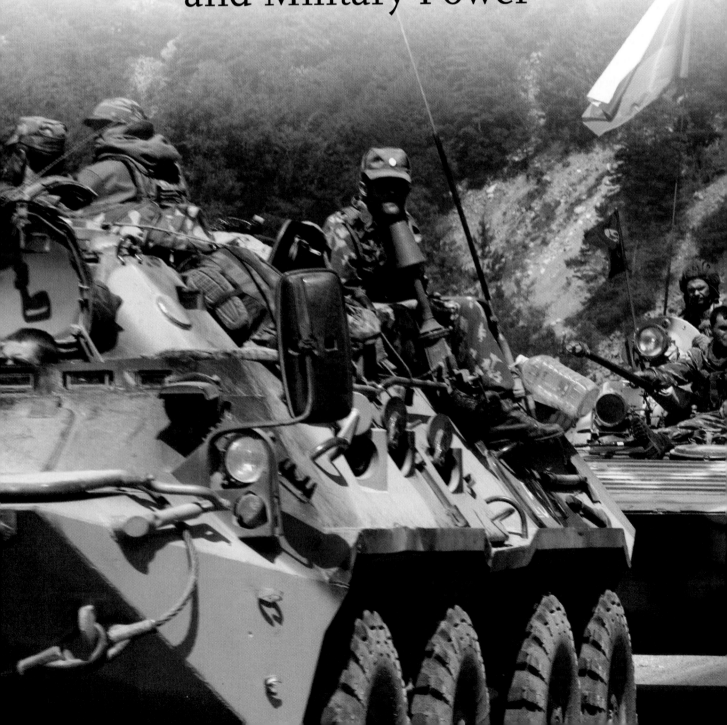

Only the dead have seen the end of war.

—*Plato*

I learned early on that war forms its own culture. The rush of battle is a potent and often lethal addiction, for war is a drug, one I ingested for many years. It is peddled by mythmakers—historians, war correspondents, filmmakers, novelists, and the state—all of whom endow it with qualities it often does possess: excitement, exoticism, power, chances to rise above our small stations in life, and a bizarre and fantastic universe that has a grotesque and dark beauty.

—*Chris Hedges*

The city-states of ancient Greece stopped all wars during the Olympic Games. With the best athletes also the best warriors, this temporary truce was a practical solution in an age when the javelin was also a weapon. Today the javelin, although still dangerous, is not the weapon of choice in armed conflict. For some countries, contemporary warfare is conducted with precision-guided munitions, night-vision goggles, and stealth bombers. Remotely piloted aircraft can fire highly accurate missiles on their targets while the controller of the aircraft sits in an air-conditioned office halfway around the world.

Despite these advances in military technology, however, most people killed in armed conflicts die from bullets and stab wounds. And today, unlike in Athens, Sparta, and the other ancient Greek city-states, we do not call a truce during the Olympics. In fact, during the 2008 Olympics a brief war broke out between Russia and Georgia, both former members of the Soviet Union and both newly democratized countries. For whatever reason, war has been a feature of life for most of recorded history. In this chapter we will examine national security, international or global security, and conflict from a number of academic perspectives. We will try to determine if the shape of war has changed in an age of globalization.

As the Beijing Olympic Games went on, Russia and Georgia fought a brief war over a territory both claimed. Why did the two countries not ask for outside assistance to mediate in the dispute?

Introduction

Is international security possible to achieve, given the kind of world in which we live? For much of the intellectual history of the world, a debate has raged about the causes of war. For some writers, especially historians, the causes of war are unique to each case. Other writers believe that it is possible to provide a wider, more generalized explanation. Some analysts, for example, see the causes lying in human nature, others in the outcome of the internal organization of states, and yet others in international anarchy. As we saw in Chapter 3, Kenneth Waltz and other structural realists put particular emphasis on the nature of international anarchy, but they also recognize that a comprehensive explanation requires an understanding of individual and societal causes. Here we return to our discussion of levels of analysis and contending explanations for why states go to war. War is rarely explained by a single variable. Factors often combine and then lead to wars. In *Man, the State and War* (1959), Waltz suggests we look at the nature of men, the political and economic structure of states, and the nature of order in the international system, as we look for the causes of war. In other words, the international system is a permissive setting in which aggressive leaders of antagonistic countries believe that war is a proper solution to disputes.

With the end of the Cold War, however, the debate began again. Some liberal and many alternative theorists like constructivists and radical liberals (discussed in Chapter 4) claimed to see the dawn of a new world order in the end of the ideological confrontation between East and West. For other analysts, however, realism or neorealism remained the best approaches to thinking about international security. In their view, very little of substance had changed as a result of the events of 1989. The end of the Cold War initially brought into existence a new, more cooperative era between the superpowers. But this more harmonious phase in international relations was only temporary, because countries still interacted in an anarchic system. For the thousands of people who have died, events seemed to support the realist and neorealist worldviews. With the first Gulf War (1990–1991), the ongoing civil wars in Africa and Asia, and then the 9/11 attacks, it became increasingly clear that states and nonstate actors (including international terrorist groups) continued to view force as an effective way to achieve their objectives.

We begin with a look at the basic definitions and disagreements central to the field, including what is meant by "security," and we probe the relationship between national security and international security. Then we examine the traditional ways of thinking about national security, and the influence these ideas about national security have had on contemporary thinking. This is followed by a survey of alternative ideas and approaches that have emerged in the literature in recent years. Next we turn to the pressing question of nuclear weapons proliferation, including a brief overview of these weapons and a discussion of attempts to prevent their spread in the years after the Cold War ended. Finally, we will provide an assessment of these ideas about national security before returning to the central question of whether greater global security is more, or less, likely in the new century.

What Is "Security"?

Most writers agree that **security** is a contested concept. There is a consensus that it implies freedom from threats to core values (for both individuals and groups), but there is a major disagreement about whether the main focus of inquiry should be on *individual, national,* or *international* security. For much of the Cold War period, most writing on the subject was

security Measures taken by states to ensure the safety of their citizens, the protection of their way of life, and the survival of their nation-state. Security can also mean the ownership of property that gives an individual the ability to secure the enjoyment or enforcement of a right or a basic human need.

dominated by the idea of **national security**, which was largely defined in militarized terms. The main area of interest for both academics and political leaders tended to be, as the realist model asserts, the military capabilities that their own states should develop to deal with the threats that faced them. More recently, however, this idea of security has been criticized for being ethnocentric (culturally biased), gendered, and too narrowly defined. Instead, a number of contemporary writers have argued for an expanded conception of security outward from the limits of parochial national security to include a range of other considerations. It is known as the **widening school of international security** because of proponents' desire to widen the definition to include economic, political, social, and even environmental issues as part of a global security agenda.

This focus on the tension between national and international security is not accepted by all who study security issues. There are those who argue that the emphasis on state and interstate relations ignores the fundamental changes that have been taking place in world politics especially in the aftermath of the Cold War. For some, the dual processes of integration and fragmentation that characterize the contemporary world mean that much more attention should be given to "societal security." According to this view, growing regional integration is undermining the classical political order based on nation-states, leaving states exposed within larger political frameworks. We see this development in the European Union. Plans for an expanded North American Free Trade Agreement (NAFTA) might indicate a similar trend in the Western Hemisphere. At the same time, the fragmentation of various states, like the Soviet Union and Yugoslavia, has created new problems of boundaries, minorities, and organizing ideologies that are causing increasing regional instability (Weaver et al. 1993, 196). This has led to the argument that ethnonational groups, rather than states, should become the center of attention for security analysts.

Disagreements about definitions matter, because these academic arguments often influence the policy decisions that political leaders make. If the political leaders believe their primary responsibility is national security, then building a safe international system for all countries is of secondary importance. Consider the following definitions of security:

- "In the case of security, the discussion is about the pursuit of freedom from threat. When this discussion is in the context of the international system, security is about the ability of states and societies to maintain their independent identity and their functional integrity." (Barry Buzan)
- "Acceptance of **common security** as the organizing principle for efforts to reduce the risk of war, limit arms, and move towards disarmament, means, in principle, that cooperation will replace confrontation in resolving conflicts of interest. This is not to say that differences among nations should be expected to disappear . . . The task is only to ensure that these conflicts do not come to be expressed in acts of war, or in preparations for war. It means that nations must come to understand that the maintenance of world peace must be given a higher priority than the assertion of their own ideological or political positions." (Palme Report 1992)

At the same time, there are other commentators who argue that the stress on national and international security is less appropriate because of the emergence of an embryonic global society in the post–Cold War era. Academics called "societal-security theorists" point to the fragmentation of some nation-states, and they argue that more attention should be given, not to society at the ethnonational level, but to global society or, as the Islamic

national security A fundamental value in the foreign policy of states secured by a variety of tools of statecraft including military actions, diplomacy, economic resources, and international agreements and alliances. It also depends on a stable and productive domestic society.

widening school of international security Sometimes called the Copenhagen School, this refers to authors who extend the definition of security to include economic, political, societal, and environmental policy areas.

common security At times called "cooperative security," it stresses noncompetitive approaches and cooperative approaches through which states—both friends and foes—can achieve security. Sometimes expressed as until all people are secure from threats of war, no one is secure.

globalization A historical process involving a fundamental shift or transformation in the spatial scale of human social organization that links distant communities and expands the reach of power relations across regions and continents.

terrorism The use of violence by nonstate groups or, in some cases, states to inspire fear, by attacking civilians and/or symbolic targets, and eliminating opposition groups. This is done for purposes such as drawing widespread attention to a grievance, provoking a severe response, or wearing down an opponent's moral resolve, to effect political change.

community A human association in which members share common symbols and wish to cooperate to realize common objectives.

Peace of Westphalia, 1648 The treaties of Osnabrück and Münster, which together form the Peace of Westphalia, ended the Thirty Years' War and were crucial in delimiting the political rights and authority of European monarchs.

movements after 2001 suggest, to religious affiliation. These writers argue that one of the most important contemporary trends is the broad process of **globalization** that is taking place. They accept that this process brings new risks and dangers. These include international **terrorism**, a breakdown of the global monetary system, global climate change and the dangers of nuclear accidents. These threats to security, on a planetary level, are viewed as being largely outside the control of nation-states. Only the development of a global **community**, societal-security theorists believe, can deal with this adequately.

At the same time, there are other writers on globalization who stress the transformation of the state (rather than its demise) and the new security agenda in the early years of the new century. In the aftermath of 9/11, and the new era of violence that followed it, Jonathan Friedman argued that we are living in a world "where polarization, both vertical and horizontal, both class and ethnic, has become rampant, and where violence has become more globalized and fragmented at the same time, and is no longer a question of wars between states but of sub-state conflicts, globally networked and financed, in which states have become one actor, increasingly privatized, amongst others" (Friedman 2003, ix). For many who feel like this, the post–September 11 era is a new and extremely dangerous period in world history. Whether the world is so different today from in the past is a matter of much contemporary discussion. In order to consider this issue we need to begin by looking at the way security has been traditionally conceived.

The Mainstream Approaches to National Security

As Chapter 2 has shown, from the **Peace of Westphalia** in 1648 onward, states have been regarded as the only legitimate, and by far the most powerful, actors in the international

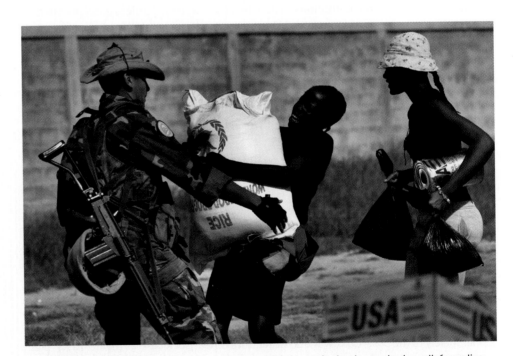

Peacekeeping troops have multiple roles, including making certain that humanitarian relief supplies arrive safely. To what extent are the concepts of national sovereignty and failed states to blame for refugee crises?

system. They have been the universal standard of political legitimacy, with no higher authority to regulate their relations with each other. This has meant that security has been seen as the priority obligation of state governments. They have taken the view that there is no alternative but to seek their own protection, in what has been described as a **self-help** world. For most modern political leaders and academics, realism has been the analytical lens best suited to understanding war and security. As a result, the assumptions of realism, in all their permutations, have dominated discussions. The other lenses that we discuss below all must respond to realism.

Realist Views on Security

In the historical debate about how best to achieve national security, writers like Thucydides, Hobbes, Machiavelli, and Rousseau tended to paint a rather pessimistic picture of the implications of state sovereignty. The international system was viewed as a rather brutal arena in which states would seek to achieve their own security at the expense of their neighbors. Interstate relations were seen as a struggle for power as states constantly attempted to take advantage of each other. According to this view, permanent peace was unlikely to be achieved. All that states could do was to try to balance the power of other states to prevent any one from achieving overall hegemony. This was a view shared by writers like E. H. Carr and Hans Morgenthau, who developed what became known as the realist (or "classical" realist) school of thought in the aftermath of both world wars.

Other contemporary writers, like Kenneth Waltz and John Mearsheimer, share the realist's pessimistic view of international relations. The pessimism of these structural realists rests on a number of key assumptions they make about the way the international system works (see Chapter 3).

Key Structural-Realist Assumptions

The following assumptions, structural realists argue, produce a tendency for states to act aggressively toward each other:

- The international system is anarchic. They do not mean by this that it is necessarily chaotic. Rather, anarchy implies that there is no central authority capable of controlling state behavior.
- States claiming sovereignty will inevitably develop offensive military capabilities to defend themselves and extend their power. As such they are potentially dangerous to each other.
- Uncertainty, leading to a lack of trust, is inherent in the international system. States can never be sure of the intentions of their neighbors, and, therefore, they must always be on their guard.
- States will want to maintain their independence and sovereignty, and, as a result, survival will be the most basic driving force influencing their behavior.
- Although states are rational, they will often make miscalculations. In a world of imperfect information, potential antagonists will always have an incentive to misrepresent their own capabilities to keep their opponents guessing. This may lead to mistakes about real state interests.

According to this view, national security, or insecurity, is largely the result of the structure of the international system. The condition of anarchy is seen as highly durable. The

self-help In realist theory, in an anarchical environment, states cannot assume other states will come to their defense even if they are allies. *Each state must take care of itself.*

balance of power In realist theory, this refers to an equilibrium between states; historical realists regard it as the product of diplomacy (contrived balance), whereas structural realists regard the system as having a tendency toward a natural equilibrium (fortuitous balance). It is a doctrine and an arrangement whereby the power of one state (or group of states) is checked by the countervailing power of other states.

implication is that international politics in the future is likely to be as violent as international politics in the past. In an important article entitled "Back to the Future," written in 1990, John Mearsheimer argued that the end of the Cold War was likely to usher in a return to the traditional multilateral **balance of power** politics of the past in which extreme nationalism and ethnic rivalries would lead to widespread instability and conflict. Mearsheimer viewed the Cold War as a period of peace and stability brought about by the bipolar structure of power that prevailed. With the collapse of this system, he argued that there would be a return to the kind of great-power rivalries that had blighted international relations since the seventeenth century.

For most contemporary structural-realist writers there is little prospect of a significant change in the nature of security in the post–Cold War world. Pointing to the Gulf War in 1991, the violent disintegration of the former Yugoslavia and parts of the former Soviet Union, continuing violence in the Middle East, the Iraq War after the 2003 invasion, and the war in Afghanistan that drags on into 2010, they argue that we continue to live in a world of mistrust and constant security competition. They tend to downplay the effect of politicians' choices to make war and to undervalue cooperation between states that occurs, saying it is difficult to achieve and even more difficult to sustain. There are two main factors, structural realists suggest, that continue to make cooperation difficult, even after the changes of 1989. The first is the prospect of cheating; the second is the concern that states have about what are called "relative gains."

WHAT'S YOUR WORLDVIEW ?

Do regions of the world have their own unique set of security challenges, or are the structural realists correct when they argue that all states respond to anarchy and the security dilemma in the same fashion?

The Problem of Cheating

Structural-realist writers do not deny that states often cooperate or that in the post–Cold War era there are even greater opportunities than in the past for states to work together. They argue, however, that there are distinct limits to this cooperation because the people that lead states have always been, and remain, fearful that others will cheat on any agreements reached and attempt to gain advantages. This risk is regarded as particularly important given the nature of modern military technology, which can bring about very rapid shifts in the balance of power between states. "Such a development," Mearsheimer has argued, "could create a window of opportunity for the cheating side to inflict a decisive defeat on the victim state" (1994/5, 20). States realize that this is the case, and although they join alliances and sign arms-control agreements, they remain cautious and aware of the need to provide for their own national security in the last resort. For example, believing the country needed a missile-defense system, the Bush administration eliminated a key piece of the Cold War international security system, the ABM Treaty of 1972, thus provoking a reaction from the Putin administration in Russia.

The United States equips its armed forces with the most advanced weapons the world has seen. How has the Taliban in Afghanistan managed to confound the US and its NATO allies?

The Problem of Relative Gains

Cooperation is also inhibited, according to many neorealist writers, because states tend to be concerned with **relative gains** rather than **absolute gains**. Instead of being interested in cooperation because it will benefit both partners, states always have to be aware of how much they are gaining compared with the state they are cooperating with. Because all states will attempt to maximize their gains in a competitive, mistrustful, and uncertain international environment, cooperation will always be very difficult to achieve and hard to maintain. We can see this thinking at work when we examine the acts that countries took in response to the global economic collapse of 2008–2009. Although the situation needed coordinated actions, leaders seemed reluctant to take the first step for fear of harming their domestic economies and preferred to wait to see what other key players did first.

Liberal Institutionalists on Global Security

One of the main characteristics of the structural-realist approach to international security is the belief that international institutions do not have a very important part to play in the prevention of war. Institutions are seen as the product of state interests and the constraints imposed by the international system itself. It is these interests and constraints that shape the decisions on whether to cooperate or compete, rather than the institutions to which states belong.

Such views have been challenged by both political leaders and a number of international relations specialists, particularly following the end of the Cold War. The British foreign secretary Douglas Hurd, for example, made the case in June 1992 that institutions themselves had played, and continued to play, a crucial role in enhancing security, particularly in Europe. He argued that the West had developed "a set of international institutions which have proved their worth for one set of problems." He went on to argue that the great challenge of the post–Cold War era was to adapt these institutions to deal with the new circumstances that prevailed (Hurd, quoted in Mearsheimer 1994/5).

This view reflected a belief, widely shared among Western leaders, that a framework of complementary, mutually reinforcing institutions—the EU, **NATO**, WEU (Western European Union), and the Organization for Security and Cooperation in Europe (OSCE)—could be developed to promote a more durable and stable European security system for the post–Cold War era. It is a view shared by a distinctive group of academic writers active since the 1980s and early 1990s. These writers hold the conviction that the developing pattern of institutionalized cooperation between states opens up unprecedented opportunities to achieve greater international security in the years ahead. Although the past may have been characterized by frequent wars and conflict, important changes are taking place in international relations at the beginning of the

relative gains One of the factors that realists argue constrain the willingness of states to cooperate. States are less concerned about whether everyone benefits (absolute gains) and more concerned about whether someone may benefit more than someone else.

absolute gains All states seek to gain more power and influence in the system to secure their national interests. This is absolute gain. Offensive neorealists are also concerned with increasing power relative to other states. One must have enough power to secure interests and more power than any other state in the system—friend or foe.

North Atlantic Treaty Organization (NATO) Organization established by treaty in April 1949 comprising twelve (later sixteen) countries from Western Europe and North America. The most important aspect of the NATO alliance was the American commitment to the defense of Western Europe. Today NATO has twenty-eight member states.

Collective defense organizations like NATO promise a united front against aggression. How might this lead to trouble if Ukraine and Russia have a dispute over former Soviet boundaries, like Russia and Georgia had in 2009?

twenty-first century that create the opportunity to dampen down the traditional security competition between states. Certainly the fact that there has not been a war in Western Europe in over sixty years supports this perspective.

This approach, known as liberal institutionalism, argues that international institutions are much more important in helping to achieve cooperation and stability than structural realists realize (see Chapter 3). Supporters of these ideas point to the importance of European economic and political institutions in overcoming the traditional hostility of European states. They also point to the developments within the European Union and NATO in the post–Cold War era and claim that, by investing major resources, states themselves clearly demonstrate their belief in the importance of institutions. The creation of the euro zone of shared currency and NATO's deployment of troops outside Europe provide evidence of this trend.

As such, it is suggested that in a world constrained by state power and divergent interests, international institutions operating on the basis of reciprocity at least will be a component of any lasting peace. In other words, international institutions themselves are unlikely to eradicate war from the international system, but they can play a part in helping to achieve greater cooperation between states.

A striking feature of war in some parts of the contemporary world is its absence. The North Atlantic region has been described as a **security community**, a group of states for whom war has disappeared as a means of resolving disputes with each other, though they may continue to use war against opponents outside the security community. One common characteristic of these states is that they are all democracies, and it has been suggested that while democracies will go to war, they are not prepared to fight against a fellow democracy. The assumption of this **democratic peace** argument is that where groups of democracies inhabit a region, war will become extinct in that region, and that as democracy spreads throughout the world, war will decline. Neoconservative advisors in the Bush administration pushed the country into war, believing that democratic Iraq would become the seed from which democracy would grow in the Middle East. However, there is a danger that some wars will occur as democracies attempt to overthrow nondemocratic regimes to spread the "democratic zone of peace," so that wars will be fought in the name of peace. This was clearly the result of the 2003 invasion of Iraq.

Alternative Views on Global Security

We saw in Chapter 4 that many academics have developed theories attempting to explain international politics as something other than a struggle between power-seeking countries. These alternatives to both realism and some strains of liberalism became vibrant intellectual challenges to those mainstream ideas about the causes of war and peace.

Constructivist Theory and War

Writers who describe themselves as "constructivist" theorists often assert that international relations are not only affected by power politics but also by ideas. This assertion clearly places most constructivist thinkers in the liberal tradition. According to this view, the fundamental structures of international politics are **social** rather than strictly **material**. This leads constructivists to argue that changes in the nature of social interaction between states can bring a fundamental shift toward greater international security (see Chapter 4).

Constructivists think about international politics in a very different way from structural realists. The latter tend to view structure as made up only of a distribution of mate-

security community A regional group of countries that have the same guiding philosophic ideals—usually liberal-democratic principles, norms, and ethics—and tend to have the same style of political systems.

democratic peace A central plank of liberal-internationalist thought, the democratic-peace thesis makes two claims: first, liberal polities exhibit restraint in their relations with other liberal polities (the so-called separate peace), but, second, they are imprudent in relations with authoritarian states. The validity of the democratic-peace thesis has been fiercely debated in the international relations literature.

social structure An arrangement based on ideas, norms, values, and shared beliefs. According to constructivists, the social domain does not exist in nature but is constructed through processes of interaction and the sharing of meaning.

material structure An arrangement based on economic, political, and military resources.

rial capabilities. On the other hand, constructivists view structure as the product of social relationships. Social structures are made possible by shared knowledge, material resources, and practices. This means that social structures are defined, in part, by shared understandings, expectations, or knowledge. According to this perspective, the security dilemma is a social structure composed of intersubjective understandings in which leaders of states are so distrustful that they make worst-case assumptions about each other's intentions and, as a result, define their interests in "self-help" terms. In contrast, a security community is a social structure composed of shared knowledge, in which states trust one another to resolve disputes without war.

The emphasis on the structure of shared knowledge is important in constructivist thinking. Social structures include material things, like tanks and economic resources, but these only acquire meaning through the shared knowledge in which they are embedded. The idea of power politics, or **realpolitik**, has meaning to the extent that states accept the idea as a basic rule of international politics. According to social-constructivist writers, power politics is an idea that does affect the way states behave, but it does not describe all interstate behavior. States are also influenced by other ideas and **norms**, such as the rule of law and the importance of institutional cooperation and restraint. In his study "Anarchy Is What States Make of It" (1992), Wendt argues that security dilemmas and wars can be seen, in part, as the outcome of self-fulfilling prophecies. The "logic of reciprocity" means that states acquire a shared knowledge about the meaning of power and act accordingly. Equally, he argues, policies of reassurance can also help to bring about a structure of shared knowledge that can help to move states toward a more peaceful security community.

Although constructivists argue that security dilemmas are not ruled by fate—or any higher, autonomous power—they differ over whether they can be escaped. For some, the fact that structures are socially constructed does not necessarily mean that they can be changed. Many constructivist writers, however, are more optimistic. They point to the changes in ideas represented by perestroika and glasnost, concepts that Soviet Communist Party General Secretary Mikhail Gorbachev introduced in the USSR during the second half of the 1980s, which led to a shared knowledge about the end of the Cold War. Once both sides accepted that the Cold War was over, it really was over. According to this view, understanding the crucial role of social structure is important in developing policies and processes of interaction that will lead toward cooperation rather than conflict. If there are opportunities for promoting social change, most constructivists believe it would be irresponsible not to pursue such policies.

Critical Security Studies: Feminism

Despite the differences between constructivists and realists about the relationship between ideas and material factors, they tend to agree on the central role of the state in debates about international security. There are other theorists, however, who believe that the state has been given too much prominence. Keith Krause and Michael C. Williams have defined critical security studies in the following terms: "Contemporary debates over the nature of security often float on a sea of unvoiced assumptions and deeper theoretical issues concerning to what and to whom the term *security* refers... What most contributions to the debate thus share are two inter-related concerns: what security is and how we study it" (1997, 34). What they also share is a wish to deemphasize the role of the state and a belief in the need to reconceptualize security. For critical security theorists, states should

realpolitik First used to describe the foreign policy of Bismarck in Prussia, it describes the practice of diplomacy based on the assessment of power, territory, and material interests, with little concern for ethical realities.

norms These specify general standards of behavior and identify the rights and obligations of states. Together, norms and principles define the essential character of a regime, and these cannot be changed without transforming the nature of the regime.

not be the center of analysis, because they are not only extremely diverse in character but also often part of the problem of insecurity in the international system. They can be providers of security, but they can also be a source of threat to their own people. According to this view, therefore, attention should be focused on the individual rather than the state. A number of different approaches make up critical security studies, however. These include feminist approaches, which we will discuss in the rest of this section.

Feminist writers challenge the traditional emphasis on the central role of the state in studies of international security. While there are significant differences between feminist theorists, all share the view that books and articles on international politics in general,

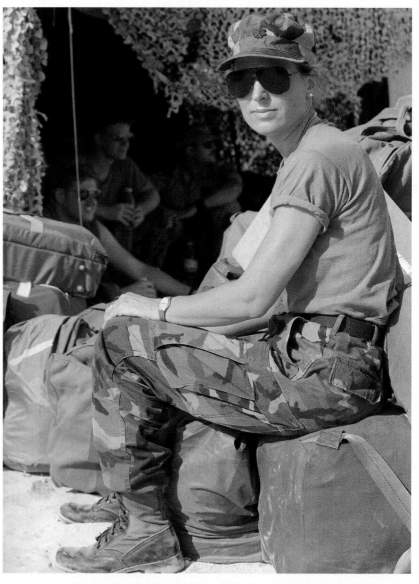

As US military commitments expand, the country must rely increasingly on women. Have US government restrictions on formally deploying women to ground combat units become obsolete?

and international security in particular, have been written from a "masculine" point of view. In her work, Ann Tickner (1992, 191) argues that women have "seldom been recognized by the security literature" despite the fact that conflicts affect women as much as, if not more than, men. The vast majority of casualties and refugees in war are women and children, and, as the recent war in Bosnia confirms, the rape of women is often used as a tool of war.

Feminist writers argue that if gender is brought more explicitly into the study of security, not only will new issues and alternative perspectives be added to the security agenda, but the result will be a fundamentally different view of the nature of international security. According to Jill Steans, "Rethinking security involves thinking about militarism and patriarchy, maldevelopment and environmental degradation. It involves thinking about the relationship between poverty, debt and population growth. It involves thinking about resources and how they are distributed" (Steans 1998; see also Smith 1999, 72–101). If we look at the language used to describe war, we can see one way in which security is gendered. As Carol Cohn wrote in her important essay "Sex and Death in the Rational World of Defense Intellectuals" (1987), the defense-policy-making world tends to be dominated by men who employ sexual and other euphemisms to describe their work: "servicing the target" instead of "bombing it"; "collateral damage" instead of "dead civilians"; "patting the missile" instead of "getting a tour of a Trident missile–carrying submarine." Cohn and others write that this is the result of war being "man's work."

Conflicts like those in Bosnia and Sudan pose a critical problem for the international community of whether to intervene in the domestic affairs of sovereign states to safeguard minority rights and individual human rights (see Chapter 10). This dilemma reflects the historic transformation of human society that is taking place at the beginning of the twenty-first century. Although states continue to limp along, many global theorists argue that it is now increasingly necessary to think of the security of individuals and of groups within the emergent global society. Other writers on globalization, however, argue that states are not withering away but are being transformed as they struggle to deal with the range of new challenges—including those of security—that face them.

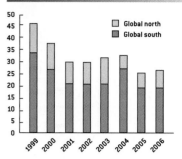

Arms Delivery (in Billions of Dollars). Which region accounts for the most arms delivery—the North or the South? Based on what you have studied so far in this course, how would you explain the trends you see in this graph? *Source: Congressional Research Service (2007): 38.*

Changing Character of War

In the contemporary world there are powerful pressures producing changes to national economies and societies. Some of these pressures reflect the impact of globalization, others are the result of the broader effects of **postmodernity**, but their cumulative effect has been to bring about significant political and social changes, which have resulted in changed perceptions of the threats coming from the external environment. These changed perceptions have in turn influenced beliefs regarding the utility of force as an instrument of policy and regarding the forms and functions of war. In the past two centuries, the modern era of history, war has traditionally been seen as a brutal form of politics: a way in which some states sought to resolve certain issues in international relations and an outcome of their willingness to amass military power for defense and deterrence and to project it in support of their foreign and defense policies. The two world wars of the twentieth century typified this approach to the instrumentality of war. In the post–Cold War period, the kinds of threats that have driven the accumulation of military power in the developed world have not taken the form of traditional state-to-state military rivalry but have been a response to rather more amorphous and less predictable threats such as terrorism, insurgencies, and internal crises in other countries.

postmodernity The postmodern international system is one where domestic and international affairs are intertwined, national borders are permeable, and states have rejected the use of force for resolving conflict. The European Union is seen as an example of the evolution of the state-centric system (Cooper 2003).

Global Perspective

The Democratic Republic of the Congo

Events in the Democratic Republic of the Congo (DRC) since the end of the Cold War provide a good illustration of the complexities of contemporary conflict and the dangers of providing simple explanations of why wars occur. Between 1996 and 2006, in this "forgotten war" (sometimes called "Africa's World War"), nearly 4 million people lost their lives as a result of ethnic strife, civil war, and foreign intervention, as well as starvation and disease. The key events are as follows:

In 1996 the conflict and genocide in neighboring Rwanda (in which 800,000 people died) spilled over into the Congo (named Zaire at the time). Rwandan Hutu forces, who fled after a Tutsi-led government came to power, set up bases in the eastern part of the country to launch attacks on Rwanda. This resulted in Rwandan forces invading the Congo with the aim of ousting the existing government of Mobutu Sese Seko and putting its own government under Laurent Désiré Kabila in power. This was achieved in May 1997. Kabila soon fell out with his backers in August 1998, however, and Rwanda and Uganda inspired a rebellion designed to overthrow him. This led to further intervention, this time by Zimbabwe, Angola, Namibia, Chad, and Sudan, in support of the Kabila government. Although a cease-fire was signed in 1999, fighting continued in the eastern part of the country. In January 2001 Kabila was assassinated and replaced by his son, Joseph Kabila. Fighting continued until 2003, partly due to ethnic divisions (the DRC is a country of 250 ethnic groups and 242 different languages), but also because of the continuing occupation of foreign troops (often engaged in illegal mining of minerals and diamonds). These foreign troops frequently formed alliances with local militias to fight their enemies on DRC soil. Negotiations designed to broker a peace agreement eventually led to the Pretoria Accord in April 2003. As a result, some

of the foreign troops left, but hostilities and massacres continued, especially in the east of the country, as rival militias backed by Rwanda and Uganda continued to fight and to plunder the resources of the DRC.

On July 18, 2003, a transitional government was set up as a result of what was known as the Global and All-inclusive Agreement. The agreement required parties to help reunify the country, disarm and integrate the warring factions, and hold elections. Continued instability, however, meant that the elections did not take place un-

The complex political situation in the Democratic Republic of the Congo has led foreign peacekeeping troops to form alliances with one of the warring militias.

til July 2006, and even after these elections, the peace remained very fragile.

This conflict in the DRC highlights the utility of a broader definition of "security" and the importance of new ideas relating to "human" and "societal" security. It also illustrates the relative shift from interstate wars to intrastate conflicts, involving ethnic militias, in what are sometimes called "failed states." Nevertheless, the war also highlights the continuing importance of conflict across state boundaries and traditional, regional balance-of-power rivalries.

War has been a brutal experience for humanity. The cost in terms of lives lost defies understanding. For example, around 14,400 wars have occurred throughout recorded history, claiming the lives of some 3.5 billion people. From 1815 to the present there have been between 224 and 559 wars, depending on the definition of war that is used (Mingst 2004, 198). The Uppsala University Conflict Data Program and the International Peace Research Institute in Norway define wars as having at least one thousand battle-related deaths per year, while conflicts have at least twenty-five battle-related deaths per year. Since the end of the Cold War, the annual number of wars, battle deaths, and war-related massacres have all declined sharply compared with the Cold War period. And finally, between 1989 and 1992 nearly one hundred wars came to an end, and in terms of battle deaths, the 1990s were the least violent decade since the end of the Second World War. In 1992, more than fifty armed conflicts involving states were being waged globally, and by 2003 the number of conflicts had dropped to twenty-nine. Conflicts within states, not between states, now make up 95 percent of all conflicts in the world. The Human Security Report of 2005 states that during the 1990s the number of wars actually declined and these wars were less deadly. Today's wars are more low-intensity asymmetric wars in which major powers with the best equipment and technologically sophisticated weapons are fighting battles with poorly armed gangs and extremist networks in urban settings or in isolated rural regions.

For some observers, the current era has seen a major evolution in the structure of international relations, with the dramatic political changes that followed the end of the Cold War and the dissolution of the Soviet Union. Changes in the international system on this scale are not common in history and, when they occur, can be expected to have a major impact on the mechanisms by which the international system is governed. At the same time, and partly as a result of the evolution of the international environment, changes are

The US Air Force B-2 strategic bomber is designed to make it difficult for radar to see the aircraft.

Americanization The spread of American values, practices, popular culture, and way of life.

also occurring in the domestic attributes of many of the states that make up the international system. There has, for example, been a notable increase in the number of democratic political systems, but in the same period many other states have disintegrated into civil wars and insurgency. The identity of the key players in international relations has also changed since the end of the Cold War. Some analysts contend the world has become temporarily subject to the hegemonic control of a single state, the United States, so that, for many, the processes of globalization and **Americanization** have become synonymous—and the response has been fierce cultural and political resistance.

The influential nineteenth-century strategist Carl von Clausewitz argued that the fundamental nature of war is immutable. The characteristics or form of war typical in any particular age might change, but the essential nature of war could not. For Clausewitz, the novel characteristics of war were not the result of new inventions but of new ideas and social conditions. In his view, wars are a socially constructed form of large-scale human group behavior and must be understood within the wider contexts of their political and cultural environments. If, indeed, wars are taking distinctive and perhaps novel forms in the post–Cold War world, this is a reflection of broader changes in the international system—including changing perceptions of threat—rather than war being the primary agent of those changes.

In an era of unprecedented communications technologies, new fields of warfare have emerged. Nonstate actors in the post–Cold War period have moved to transform both cyberspace and the global media into crucial battlegrounds, alongside terrestrial military and terrorist operations, so that war is now fought on a number of different planes of reality simultaneously, and reality itself is subverted in the cause of war through sophisticated strategies of informational and electronic deception. The battlefield of the past has now become the "battlespace": three-dimensional in the sense of including airpower and the use of space satellites, nondimensional in that it also embraces cyberspace and communications wavebands.

At the same time, the tangible capacity for war making has also been developing. Military technology with enormous destructive capacity is becoming available to more and more states. This is important, not just because the technology to produce and deliver **weapons of mass destruction** is spreading, but because highly advanced conventional military technology is becoming more widely available. One of the effects of the end of the Cold War was that there was a massive process of disarmament by the former Cold War enemies. This surplus weaponry flooded the global arms market, much of it highly advanced equipment being sold off comparatively cheaply.

weapons of mass destruction A category defined by the United Nations in 1948 to include "atomic explosive weapons, radioactive material weapons, lethal chemical and biological weapons, and any weapons developed in the future which have characteristics comparable in destructive effects to those of the atomic bomb or other weapons mentioned above."

The Nature of War

Wars are fought for reasons. The Western understanding of war, following Clausewitz, is that it is instrumental, a means to an end. Wars in this perspective are not random violence; they reflect a conscious decision to engage in them for a rational political purpose. Clausewitz defined war as an act of violence intended to compel one's opponent to fulfill one's will. Oftentimes, people who initiate wars rationalize them by appealing to common belief and value systems.

War is a form of social and political behavior. This was one of the central arguments of Clausewitz. It remains true at the start of the twenty-first century, but only if we operate with a broad and flexible understanding of what constitutes politics. As our understanding of politics, and the forms it can take, has evolved in the postmodern era, we should expect the same to be true of the character of war, since that is itself a form of politics.

Re-imaging War

Realism is often called the dominant, traditional, or mainstream theory of international relations. As we have seen in this book, this means that the central assumptions of realism—anarchy, a self-help world, an enduring struggle for power—provide the framework for academic discussions of all aspects of the discipline. Foreign policy makers in all countries use the vocabulary of realism. However, unlike in the academic world, where an essay on political theory only receives a grade, in the world of political leaders a political theory can impact the lives of millions of people. What if politicians used one of the other theoretical perspectives, like constructivism or feminism?

Let's begin with what the former Bush administration in the United States called the "global war on terror." We see territory-based political units—countries in the customary Westphalian style of sovereign states—trying to defeat attacks from nonstate actors: terrorist organizations claiming their legitimacy from religious texts. This is not only an armed struggle; in terms of political theories it is a confrontation between two kinds of theories, explanatory and constitutive. Leaders in Western Europe and the United States use the former when they look at the world; the followers of Islamic fundamentalist leaders employ the latter as they seek to create a new world with their ideas. This dichotomy in perspectives has practical policy implications. The United States leaders of the Bush administration, in line with the teaching of realism, believed that if they attacked terrorist strongholds and leaders around the world, they could

defeat the terrorists. Islamists who employ terror as a means of conflict are equally convinced that the deaths of individual people will not kill the idea of re-creating the caliphate and, with it, the rule of Islamic law.

The alternative theories we have studied offer another take on events and ideas surrounding this global war on terror. They would begin by pointing to the overall lack of success in the attempt to eliminate terrorists. Indiscriminate attacks by remotely piloted aircraft have killed people who were Muslims but not necessarily members of terrorist organizations. However, as

Families of US military personnel have suffered from the repeated deployments of troops to Iraq and Afghanistan.

continued

Theory in Practice *continued*

news reports tell us, attacks on wedding ceremonies mistakenly believed by US mission planners to be Islamist cell meetings have created more anger directed against the United States and its interests around the world. A gendered perspective on the global war on terror would contend that the methods the Bush administration adopted are stereotypically masculinist: instead of seeking to open a dialogue with the Islamists, the United States followed a realist path, focusing on its own view of national security, and launched a military attack. The same set of alternative-theory lenses can help us to understand events leading up to the 2003 US-led invasion of Iraq and the occupation of the country. Rejecting the consensus-building approach that his father (the former president) adopted prior to the 1991

Iraq War, George W. Bush made it clear early on that the invasion would happen whether or not United Nations arms-control inspectors (permitted by Saddam Hussein's government) found the banned nuclear, biological, and chemical (NBC) weapons. Adopting the realist perspective, the Bush administration seemed convinced that Al Qaeda planned the September 2001 attacks with active material assistance from the Iraq government. The Americans were apparently convinced that such a coordinated event was beyond the capabilities of a non-state actor operating out of Afghanistan. The Bush foreign policy team labeled critics of their strategy as "not tough enough," or "soft on terrorism," or "weak on security," all terms that attract the attention of advocates of the gendered perspective.

Perspective matters in the arena of public policy. Many pessimists tend to gravitate to the realist lens. They see a dangerous world in which war is always about to happen and their allies of today might desert them tomorrow. This is not to say that the alternative theories of international relations are not pessimistic; for instance, some advocates of the gendered perspective see disheartening patterns of sexualized language to describe wars. And yet, if we do not try to use a range of theories to understand events, we might miss opportunities to learn or to make better policy choices. Certainly both the global war on terror and the belief that Iraq had nuclear/biological/chemical weapons demonstrate what can happen if leaders act on faulty assumptions.

Table 8.1
Chronology of Nuclear Development

1945	United States detonates the world's first nuclear weapon.
1946/7	United States and Soviet Union submit plans for the international control of atomic energy to the newly formed United Nations Atomic Energy Commission (UNAEC).
1949	Soviet Union tests its first nuclear weapon.
1952	United Kingdom tests its first nuclear weapon.
1953	President Eisenhower of the United States introduces his "Atoms for Peace" proposal to the United Nations General Assembly.
1957	International Atomic Energy Agency (IAEA) inaugurated.
1958	European Atomic Energy Community (Euratom) begins its operation within the European Community.
1960	France becomes the fourth state to test a nuclear weapon.
1961	United Nations General Assembly adopts the "Irish Resolution" calling for measures to limit the spread of nuclear weapons to additional states.
1963	Partial Test Ban Treaty (PTBT) enters into force.
1964	China becomes the fifth state to test a nuclear weapon.
1967	Treaty for the Prohibition of Nuclear Weapons in Latin America (the Tlatelolco Treaty) is opened for signature.
1968	Treaty on the Nonproliferation of Nuclear Weapons (the NPT) is opened for signature.

1969	Tlatelolco Treaty enters into force.
1970	NPT enters into force.
1971	IAEA concludes the INFCIRC (Information Circular)/153 Safeguards Agreement; Zangger Committee also adopts a set of nuclear-export guidelines pursuant to the NPT.
1972	Anti–Ballistic Missile (ABM) Treaty is signed between United States and Soviet Union.
1974	India detonates a nuclear explosive device declared to be for peaceful purposes; Nuclear Suppliers Group (NSG) is formed.
1975	First Review Conference of the NPT is held in Geneva; by the end of the year, 97 states are party to the treaty.
1978	First United Nations Special Session on Disarmament (UNSSOD-1) provides the forum for the five nuclear weapon states to issue unilateral statements on negative security assurances.
1980	Second NPT Review Conference is held in Geneva.
1983	United States announces its Strategic Defense Initiative (SDI).
1985	Third NPT Review Conference is held in Geneva. Treaty of Rarotonga creates South Pacific Nuclear-Free Zone.
1987	Missile Technology Control Regime (MTCR) is established.
1990	Fourth NPT Review Conference is held in Geneva.
1991	A United Nations Special Committee (UNSCOM) is established to oversee the dismantling of Iraq's undeclared nuclear weapons program. United States announces its Safety, Security, Dismantlement (SSD) Program following the dissolution of the Soviet Union.
1993	South Africa announces that it had produced six nuclear devices up until 1989 and then dismantled them prior to signing the NPT. Democratic People's Republic of Korea (DPRK) announces its intention to withdraw from the NPT following allegations concerning its nuclear program.
1995	Review and Extension Conference of the NPT is held in New York; the 179 parties decide to extend the NPT indefinitely and also establish a new treaty review process and a set of principles and objectives for nonproliferation and disarmament.
1996	The Comprehensive Test Ban Treaty (CTBT) is opened for signature.
1997	First Preparatory Committee (PrepCom) for the new NPT treaty review process convenes in Geneva.
1998	India and Pakistan conduct a series of nuclear and missile tests.
1999	United States announces its National Missile Defense (NMD) Act.
2000	Sixth NPT Review Conference is held in New York for the now 188 parties to the treaty. The five nuclear weapon states reiterate the undertaking "to accomplish the total elimination of their nuclear arsenals."
2002	Cuba becomes the 189th party to the NPT; The Hague Code of Conduct for missile-technology transfers is initiated.
2003	The issue of noncompliance and responses to it becomes the focus of attention as the DPRK announces its "withdrawal" from the NPT and intervention occurs in Iraq.
2004	A transnational nonstate nuclear supply network is discovered; Libya agrees unconditionally to dismantle its weapons-of-mass-destruction infrastructure in compliance with international agreements; United Nations Security Council passes Resolution 1540.
2005	Seventh NPT Review Conference is held in New York.
2006	DPRK announces that it has tested a nuclear weapon.
2008	Iran announces progress on its uranium-enrichment program. DPRK has successful test of Taep'o-dong-2C/3 ballistic missile.
2009	Iran successfully launches a satellite into Earth orbit using booster based on DPRK Taep'o-dong-2C/3 ballistic missile.

All Others, 18.6%
United States, 38.9%
Major West European, 22.4%
China, 2.3%
Russia, 17.6%
2001-2004

All Others, 15.4%
United States, 42.6%
Major West European, 22.8%
China, 2.9%
Russia, 16.3%
2005-2008

Arms Transfer Agreements Worldwide. The conventional arms suppliers here are shown as percentages. Do you notice a shift between the two date-ranges compared here? Is it significant? How would you explain the relative stability of conventional arms suppliers worldwide? *Source: U.S. Government.*

The political nature of war has been evolving in recent decades under the impact of globalization, which has increasingly eroded the economic, political, and cultural autonomy of the state. Contemporary warfare takes place in a local context, but it is also played out in wider fields and influenced by nongovernmental organizations, intergovernmental organizations, regional and global media, and users of the Internet. In many ways, contemporary wars are partly fought on television, and the media therefore have a powerful role in providing a framework of understanding for the viewers of the conflict. Reaching beyond even the effect of twenty-four-hour-a-day television news channels desperate for items to broadcast, Al Qaeda, for instance, uses the Internet to disseminate its propaganda. The award-winning documentary *Control Room* showed how the 2003 invasion of Iraq became an exercise in the United States government trying to restrict the images a globalized audience saw on its televisions. One effect of the constant coverage of international violence by the global media may be to gradually weaken the legal, moral, and political constraints against the use of force by making it appear routine, thereby reversing the moral questioning of war that was a feature of the second half of the twentieth century. The advent of such "war fatigue" might make recourse to war appear a normal feature of international relations.

Nevertheless, war, both in terms of preparation for it and its actual conduct, may be a powerful catalyst for change, but technological or even political modernization does not necessarily imply moral progress. Evolution in war, including its contemporary forms, may involve change that is morally problematic, as indeed is the case with the forces of globalization more generally. War is a profound agent of historical change, but it is not the fundamental driving force of history. There are a wide variety of factors that can contribute to the outbreak of war, such as nationalism, class conflict, human nature, and so on. These are the main drivers of change rather than war itself. War is not something imposed by an outside force. The willingness to go to war comes from within states and societies.

For many analysts of war, war's nature, as the use of organized violence in pursuit of political goals, always remains the same and is unaltered even by radical changes in political forms, in the motives leading to conflict, or by technological advances (Gray 1999b, 169). For Colin Gray, if war's nature were to change, it would become something else, so he, like Clausewitz, insists that all wars have the same political nature, one fundamentally based on the idea that war is a political act: the use of force for conscious political ends.

For Clausewitz and Gray, there is an important distinction between the *nature* and the *character* of war. The former refers to the constant, universal, and inherent qualities that ultimately define war throughout the ages, such as violence, chance, and uncertainty. The latter relates to the impermanent, circumstantial, and adaptive features that war develops and that account for the different periods of warfare throughout history, each displaying attributes determined by sociopolitical and historical preconditions while also influencing those conditions. Clausewitz also distinguished between the *objective* and *subjective* nature of war, the former comprising the elements common to all wars and the latter consisting of those features that make each war unique.

A number of questions follow from this survey of war in relation to its contemporary and future forms. Does the current era have a dominant form of war, and if so, what is it? In what ways are the processes associated with globalization changing contemporary warfare? In what ways are the characteristics of postmodernity being reflected in contemporary modes of warfare?

The Revolution in Military Affairs

Although many observers have suggested that the character of war is changing significantly, their reasons for coming to this conclusion are often quite different. One school of thought focuses on the so-called **revolution in military affairs (RMA)**. The concept of the revolution in military affairs became popular after the dramatic American victory in the 1991 Gulf War. The manner in which superior technology and doctrine appeared to give the United States an almost effortless victory, if the Iraqi war deaths are ignored, suggested that future conflicts would be decided by the possession of technological advantages such as advanced guided weapons and space satellites. However, the subsequent popularity of the RMA concept has not produced a clear consensus on what exactly the RMA is or what its implications might be. Although analysts agree that RMAs involve a radical change or some form of discontinuity in the history of warfare, there is disagreement regarding how and when these changes or discontinuities take place, or what causes them.

RMA proponents argue that recent breakthroughs and likely future advances in military technology mean that military operations will be conducted with such speed, precision, and selective destruction that the whole character of war will change and this will profoundly affect the way military and political affairs are conducted in the next few decades. Most of the RMA literature focuses on the implications of developments in technology. In the conflicts in Kuwait (1991), Serbia (1999), and Iraq (2003), American technology proved vastly superior to that of the opponent. In particular, computing and space technology allowed the US forces to acquire information about the enemy to a degree never before seen in warfare and allowed precision targeting of weapon systems. Advanced communications allowed generals to exercise detailed and instant control over the developing battle and to respond quickly to developments. The speed, power, and accuracy of the weapons allowed them to be carefully targeted so as to destroy vital objectives without inflicting unnecessary casualties on civilian populations, though absolute precision and reliability proved impossible to achieve. Opponents lacking counters to these technologies found themselves helpless in the face of overwhelming American superiority. However, the RMA emphasis on military technology and **tactics**, while understandable, risks producing an oversimplified picture of what is an extremely complex phenomenon, in which nontechnological factors can play a crucial part in the outcome.

In addition, most of the literature and debate on the RMA has been American and has tended to take for granted the dominance conferred by technological superiority. The current RMA is based on a particularly Western concept of war fighting and may well only be useful in certain well-defined situations. For example, there is little discussion of what might happen if the United States were to fight a country that has a similar capability or is able to deploy countermeasures. There has been far less discussion of how a state might use unconventional or asymmetric responses to fight

revolution in military affairs (RMA) This is the effect generated by the marriage of advanced communications and information processing with state-of-the-art weapons and delivery systems. It is a means of overcoming the uncertainty and confusion that are part of any battle in war.

tactics The conduct and management of military capabilities in or near the battle area.

Remote-controlled aircraft like this US Predator can locate and destroy targets while the operator sits miles away in relative safety. How have Predator attacks on the tribal areas of Pakistan near the Afghan border harmed US-Pakistani relations?

asymmetric conflicts In symmetrical warfare, armies with comparable weapons, tactics, and organizational structures do battle. Wars are fought on near-equal terms. When stakes are high and those actors in conflict are not equal in terms of weapons and technology, the weaker side adopts asymmetrical tactics. These include guerrilla warfare, roadside bombs, attacks on civilians, and other terrorist tactics.

effectively against a more technologically sophisticated opponent. Asymmetry works both ways. **Asymmetric conflicts** since 1990 have been fought by US-led "coalitions of the willing" against Iraq (1991 and again in 2003), Yugoslavia, and Afghanistan. Because of the extreme superiority in combat power of the coalition, the battle phases of these asymmetric conflicts have been fairly brief and have produced relatively few combat deaths compared to the Cold War period. However, in the postconventional insurgency phases in Iraq and Afghanistan, the asymmetry has produced guerrilla-style conflict against the technological superiority of the coalition forces. As we noted at the start of this chapter, most battle deaths since 1945 have been caused by bullets and knives, not high-tech military equipment.

The conflicts in Iraq and Afghanistan (see Case Study in this chapter) raised major questions about the pattern of warfare likely after the RMA. Who are the most likely future opponents of states capable of adopting the RMA technologies? Does the RMA influence all forms of war or simply large-scale, conventional interstate war? What about urban warfare or nuclear weapons? What about the use of unmanned drones and the targeting of civilian areas? What is the likely response of opponents such as terrorists, insurgents, and armed forces unable to acquire RMA technology themselves?

Postmodern War

Global society is moving from the modern to the postmodern age. This is a process that has been under way for several decades and is the result of a wide range of economic, cultural, social, and political changes that are altering the meaning of the "state" and the "nation." It has been marked by a shift from production to information as a core output of advanced economies. As this happens, it will affect the character of war. In some parts of the world, the state is deliberately transferring functions, including military functions, to private authorities and businesses, such as Blackwater and other contractors in Iraq and Afghanistan. In other areas, these functions are being seized from the state by other political actors. Many of the world's armies are relying more on child soldiers, paramilitary forces, and private armies. At the same time, globalization has weakened the national forms of identity that have dominated international relations in the past two centuries and reinvigorated earlier forms of political identity and organization, such as religious, ethnic, and clan loyalties.

The greatly increased role of the media is one feature of this evolution. Portable satellite dishes enabling live broadcasts make media far more important in terms of shaping or even constructing understandings of particular wars. Media warfare has made war more transparent. Each side now goes to great lengths to manipulate media images of the conflict, and journalists have effectively been transformed from observers into active participants, facing most of the same dangers as the soldiers and helping to shape the course of the war through their reporting. This reflects a broader change. Just as modernity and its wars were based on the mode of production, so postmodernity and its wars reflect the mode of information.

Another postmodern development has been the increasing "outsourcing" of war to modern-day mercenaries and private contractors. Over the past decade more and more states have contracted out key military services to private corporations. Privatized military firms (PMFs) like Blackwater (now known as Xe Services LLC) sell a wide range of war-related services to states, overwhelmingly in the logistical and security roles rather than direct combat. Hundreds of PMFs have operated in more than fifty countries since the

The Iraq War, 2003–2009

On March 20, 2003, US-led coalition forces invaded Iraq with the objective of locating and disarming suspected Iraqi weapons of mass destruction. The coalition forces conducted a swift and overwhelmingly successful campaign, leading to the capture of Baghdad and the collapse and surrender of the Iraqi armed forces. President George W. Bush declared the official end of major combat operations on May 2, 2003. While casualties during this conventional phase of fighting were historically low for a major modern war, the fighting quickly evolved into an insurgency in which guerrilla and terrorist attacks on the coalition forces and Iraqi civilian population were the norm. By the spring of 2007 the coalition had suffered around 3,500 deaths and 24,000 wounded. Estimates of total Iraqi war-related deaths ranged from a conservative 60,000 to a maximum figure of 650,000.

The Iraq War illustrates a number of the themes that have been prominent in discussions of the possible future development of war. The rapid coalition victory saw the Iraqi armed forces shattered by the technological superiority of the advanced weapons and information systems of the United States forces, suggesting that a revolution in military affairs was under way.

The doctrine employed by the American forces was also vital. The allied success was the result not just of technological superiority but also of a superior maneuver-oriented operational doctrine. The swift and comparatively bloodless victory for the American-led forces reinforced the view that in the post–Cold War strategic environment, there were few inhibitions on the use of force by the United States. With the trauma of Vietnam laid to rest, war had become swift, decisive, and affordable for the United States, and the end of the Cold War removed the threat of regional conflict escalating into a nuclear conflict with another superpower.

A central feature of the conflict was the American dominance of information warfare, both in the military sense, meaning the ability to use satellite systems for reconnaissance, communications, and weapons targeting, and in the postmodern sense, meaning the manipulation of the civilian communications and global media images of the war to produce an international understanding of the fighting that reflected what the US administration wished the watching world to perceive.

However, the conflict did not end with the surrender of the regular Iraqi forces, confirming, in turn, some of the arguments made by proponents of the "postmodern" and "new wars" (see the next section of this chapter). The ability to operate using complex informal military networks allowed the insurgency to conduct effective asymmetric warfare, despite the overwhelming superiority of the US military technology. In addition, the insurgents were able to use the global media to manipulate perceptions of the strategy of terrorism and destabilization. The techniques used by the insurgents were brutal, ruthless, and targeted against the civilian population, in a campaign supported by outside forces and finance, and sustained by an overtly identity-based campaign, again reflecting features of the postmodern and "new wars" conceptions.

Pre-Inspection Materiel Removal, Ibn al Haytham

Having the ability to collect information about an enemy's capability does not mean that you have information about the enemy's intent. Was it moral for the US to base its invasion of Iraq in 2003 on inaccurate or false intelligence reports?

end of the Cold War. The growth of PMFs reflects a broader global trend toward the privatization of public assets. Through the provision of training and equipment, PMFs have influenced the outcomes of several recent wars, including those in Angola, Croatia, Ethiopia, and Sierra Leone. PMFs played a significant role in the 2003 US-led invasion of Iraq. They also have become the targets of criticism and lawsuits for wrongful death, as with the case of the Blackwater guards who in 2007 killed several unarmed Iraqi civilians.

Globalization and New Wars

new wars Wars of identity between different ethnic communities or nations, and wars that are caused by the collapse of states or the fragmentation of multiethnic states. Most of these new wars are internal or civil wars.

Mary Kaldor has suggested that a category of **new wars** has emerged since the mid-1980s. Just as earlier wars were linked to the emergence and creation of states, the new wars are related to the disintegration and collapse of states, and much of the pressure on such states has come from the effects of globalization on the international system. In the past decade, 95 percent of armed conflicts have taken place within states rather than between them. The new wars occur in situations where the economy of the state is performing extremely poorly, or even collapsing, so that the tax revenues and power of the state decline dramatically, producing an increase in corruption and criminality. As the state loses control, access to weapons and the ability to resort to violence are increasingly privatized and paramilitary groups proliferate, organized crime grows, and political legitimacy collapses. One of the effects of these developments is that the traditional distinction between the soldier and the civilian becomes blurred or disappears altogether.

For Kaldor, a significant feature of these conflicts is the combatants' focus on questions of identity, which she sees as a result of the pressures produced by globalization. In the postmodern world there has been a breakdown of traditional cleavages based on class and ideology and a greater emphasis on identity and culture. To the extent that war is a continuation of politics, therefore, war has become increasingly driven by questions of culture and identity. A major cause of the wars since 1990 has been the demands of various groups for national self-determination. Questions of identity in a broader sense have also underpinned recent wars. It can be argued that Islamic fundamentalists are not fighting for control of territory or political power in the traditional Westphalian sense but in order to defend or expand a particular cultural autonomy against the globalizing pressures of Westernization and secularism. They are, ironically perhaps, rejecting in a postmodernist way the seventeenth-century European concept of the state and replacing it with a tenth-century Middle Eastern concept of the state.

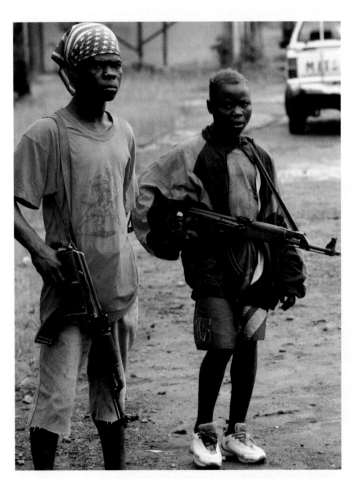

In civil conflicts around the world, children have been forced to fight. What role should international governments play in preventing the conscription of children into such violent lives? What role should NGOs play? Should states work with NGOs to resolve the problem of child soldiers?

The relationship between identity and war is also shifting in terms of the gender and age of the combatants. The "feminization" of war has grown as women have come to play increasingly visible and important roles, from auxiliaries in the late modern period to direct front-line roles in the postmodern period, from uniformed military personnel to female suicide bombers in Iraq and Israel. Children have also become more visible as participants rather than noncombatants in war. Helen Brocklehurst has drawn attention to the meaning and implications of the increasing visibility of children as victims of war at many different levels. Child soldiers can be found on every continent but have been particularly prevalent in recent African conflicts. In the civil war in Sierra Leone, nearly 70 percent of the combatants were under the age of eighteen. Children fight in around three-quarters of today's armed conflicts and may make up 10 percent of current armed combatants (Brocklehurst 2007, 373). Nearly one-third of the militaries that use child soldiers include girls in their ranks.

Many of the features of the new wars are not new, in that they have been common in earlier periods of history—ethnic and religious wars, for example, or conflicts conducted with great brutality. Looting and plunder have been a feature of most wars in history. Low-intensity conflicts have in fact been the most common form of armed conflict since the late 1950s. However, it can be argued that the initiators of the new wars have been empowered by the new conditions produced by globalization, which have weakened states and created parallel economies and privatized protection. These new wars are made possible by the inability of many governments to successfully exercise many of the functions associated with the traditional Westphalian state. Such conflicts will typically occur in **failed states**, countries like Somalia where the government has lost control of significant parts of the national territory and lacks the resources to reimpose control. Steven Metz (2004) has termed the countries falling into this category as the **third-tier states** of the global political system.

For some observers, the economic rationale, rather than politics, is what drives the new wars, so that war has become a continuation of economics by other means. It is the pursuit of personal wealth, rather than political power, that is the motivation of the combatants. In some conflicts, therefore, war has become the end rather than the means.

third-tier states Sometimes called the "less-developed states" or the "premodern states." These countries fail to provide the basics, such as border protection, law and order, and maintenance of a functioning economy.

Nuclear Proliferation and Nonproliferation

Although all wars since 1945 have been fought *without* the actual use of nuclear weapons, the issue of nuclear proliferation represents one of the more marked illustrations of the globalization of world politics. Although only five states (China, France, Russia [Soviet Union], United Kingdom, and United States) are acknowledged by the Treaty on the Non-proliferation of Nuclear Weapons (NPT) as possessing nuclear weapons, others have the capability to construct nuclear devices. This was emphasized in May 1998 when India and Pakistan, previously regarded as "threshold" or near-nuclear states, demonstrated their respective capabilities by conducting a series of nuclear tests followed by ballistic missile launches. These events highlighted another aspect of nuclear globalization: the potential emergence of a regionally differentiated world. While in some regions nuclear weapons have assumed a lower significance in strategic thinking than they once held, other regions may be moving in the opposite direction. In Latin America, the South Pacific, Southeast Asia, Africa, and Central Asia the trend has been toward developing the region as a Nuclear Weapon Free Zone (NWFZ). In other regions, such as South Asia, the trend appears to be toward a higher profile for nuclear capabilities. What is unclear is the impact that nuclearization (meaning nuclear weapons acquisition) in some regions will have on those moving toward denuclearization (meaning a process of removing nuclear weapons).

WHAT'S YOUR WORLDVIEW?

The new wars tend to be internal wars between cultural or ethnic groups. Adversaries in these wars seek to eliminate those from different culture communities. Ethnic cleansing and genocide are the results. Does the international community have a responsibility to prevent these types of war?

Developments stemming from the dissolution of the Soviet Union have also raised novel problems. This is the only case where a previously acknowledged **nuclear weapon state (NWS)** has been subjected to political disintegration. At the time, there was little understanding of what the nuclear consequences would be from such a tumultuous state implosion, and only in hindsight can we judge its full significance. It was unquestionably a period of unprecedented nuclear transformation requiring long-term cooperation between previously hostile states. Less obvious is that this period of transition was facilitated by the foresight of policy makers from both sides of the former Cold War divide who had created a framework of arms-control and disarmament agreements. Ensuring nuclear stability during this period might have been more difficult had it not been for policies such as the Cooperative Threat Reduction Program and agreements like the multilateral NPT and bilateral Strategic Arms Reduction Treaties (START), signed initially between the United States and the Soviet Union (and later between the United States and Russia).

Proliferation Optimism and Pessimism

One thesis that has sparked diverging responses asserts that the gradual spread of nuclear weapons to additional states should be welcomed rather than feared. The thesis is based on the proposition that, just as nuclear **deterrence** maintained stability during the Cold War, so can it induce stabilizing effects on other conflict situations. This argument is challenged by those who hold that more will be worse, not better, and that measures to stem nuclear proliferation represent the best way forward (Sagan and Waltz 1995 and 2003). In a series of articles, two leading thinkers on nuclear matters, Kenneth Waltz and Scott Sagan, present the arguments. Waltz writes that a controlled spread of nuclear weapons in countries like Pakistan and India is better than a rapid arms race. He contends that leaders of the new nuclear weapons countries would show the same restraint that the US and the USSR demonstrated when they developed their nuclear arsenals.

Sagan disagrees strongly with Waltz's argument. His argument is based on the internal political dynamics of the second generation of nuclear weapons states. According to Sagan, developing countries lack the stable political institutions that the United States and the Soviet Union had during the late 1940s and early 1950s. Instead, they have military-run or weak civilian governments, without the positive constraining mechanisms of civilian control, while military biases may serve to encourage nuclear weapons use—especially during a crisis.

The responses to nuclear proliferation encompass unilateral, bilateral, regional, and global measures that collectively have been termed the nuclear nonproliferation regime. Advocates of this regime argue it is these measures (including treaties like the NPT, export controls, international safeguards, nuclear-supplier agreements, and other standard-setting arrangements) that have constrained nuclear acquisition. Conversely, there have been several criticisms of this regime, and even some long-term supporters acknowledge it is in "need of intensive care" (Ogilvie-White and Simpson 2003). Among the criticisms are that it is a product of a bygone first nuclear age (1945–1990) and is not suited to the demands of the potentially more dangerous second nuclear age (1990–present); it is unable to alleviate the security dilemma that many states confront and, hence, does not address the security motivation driving nuclear weapons acquisition; and it is a discriminatory arrangement because the NPT only requires that the five NWSs pursue nuclear disarmament in good faith (under its Article VI), while all other parties—designated as **non–nuclear weapon states (NNWS)**—must forgo the acquisition of nuclear weapons. Thus, there has

Modifying an existing North Korean missile, rocket scientists in Iran have developed guided missiles that can reach Saudi Arabia, Central Asia, and Israel. How do these ballistic missiles influence global politics?

always been a tension between two notions of the NPT: as primarily a nonproliferation measure (for preventing the emergence of additional nuclear-armed states) or as a means for achieving nuclear disarmament. This tension was in evidence during discussion at the NPT Conference in 1995, when the treaty was extended indefinitely after an initial twenty-five years in operation (under Article X). It also featured at the NPT Review Conference in 2000, when the five NWSs reiterated their commitment to the goal of nuclear weapons elimination. India was a leading critic of this position, asserting that states have an inherent right to provide for their defense. During these dialogues, emphasis was placed on the need for all parties to improve transparency in their nuclear operations and for additional measures to enhance verification and compliance.

Nature of Nuclear Weapons

Unless a nuclear weapon or the materials required for its manufacture can be obtained "off the shelf" as a result of purchase or theft, the usual route for any state or nonstate actor seeking nuclear weapons would be to acquire the necessary technological infrastructure. This includes a range of nuclear, conventional, computational, and electronic technologies. It also requires individuals with key scientific skills.

Nuclear reactors and nuclear weapons differ in their management of the nuclear chain reaction and the energy produced. Whereas in a reactor, energy output is achieved through a sustained and regulated process, in a nuclear weapon the objective is a large explosive yield from a critical mass of nuclear material created by an uncontrolled and rapid chain reaction (Gardner 1994, 6–7). Nuclear weapons consequently derive their explosive energy either from techniques designed to split the atoms rapidly, thus creating a chain reaction (in "fission" weapons), or by using fission weapons as a primary initiator to compress and heat hydrogen atoms so they combine, or fuse (in "thermonuclear," or "fusion," weapons). Energy production in a nuclear reactor involves a means for regulating the chain reaction, a moderator that surrounds the fissile core for maintaining the chain reaction, and a means for removing the heat produced from the reactor core by the chain reaction, which can also provide the steam to drive turbines and generate electricity.

Nuclear Weapons Effects

The effects of nuclear weapons are considerable. Because of this, the United Nations Commission for Conventional Armaments in 1948 introduced a new category, **weapons of mass destruction (WMD)**, to distinguish nuclear weapons from conventional forms. More recently, another concept, known as CBRN (referring to chemical, biological, radiological, and nuclear capabilities), has appeared in academic and policy papers. Some analysts have also argued that the term "WMD" should be unraveled because each of the weapons types has different effects, with nuclear weapons being the true WMD (Panofsky 1998).

A nuclear weapon produces its energy in three distinct forms: blast, heat or thermal radiation, and nuclear radiation. Experience of nuclear testing has also indicated another feature of a nuclear weapons explosion, the phenomenon known as electromagnetic pulse (EMP). This can cause acute disruption to electronic equipment (Grace 1994, 1).

Extensive damage to human populations may result from a nuclear weapons detonation. Awareness of the effects stems from the two weapons dropped on Hiroshima and Nagasaki at the end of the Second World War, which remains the only time nuclear weapons have been used. What is also known is that the weapons that destroyed these Japanese cities were relatively small in comparison to the destructive forces generated by later testing of thermonuclear weapons. The largest weapon of this kind known to have been tested was estimated to be a fifty-megaton device (i.e., the equivalent of 50 million tons of TNT) produced by the Soviet Union in 1961. In recent years there has been a trend away from nuclear weapons with large explosive potential toward designs with lower yields.

Nuclear Defense

The US Congress passed the National Missile Defense (NMD) Act in 1999. This act proposed that the United States develop the technical means to counter a possible small-scale ballistic missile attack on the US mainland. The announcement generated a range of reactions within the United States and elsewhere. The overall program cost and technical feasibility became central elements of the US domestic debate, for, unlike the 1983 Strategic Defense Initiative, which intended to use a range of technologies—including nuclear explosions—to intercept incoming missiles, the new Ballistic Missile Defense (BMD) system was developed primarily using kinetic energy. This means the intention is to hit an incoming missile with another defensive missile during its flight path. Such a system inevitably requires considerable early-warning and computational capabilities and a missile that is fast and maneuverable enough to hit a target potentially traveling at seven kilometers per second. International reaction to US missile-defense proposals met with concerns in Russia and China about the impact on stability if the Anti–Ballistic Missile (ABM) Treaty was eroded, while in Europe similar reservations were expressed.

weapons of mass destruction (WMD) A category defined by the United Nations in 1948 to include "atomic explosive weapons, radioactive material weapons, lethal chemical and biological weapons, and any weapons developed in the future which have characteristics comparable in destructive effects to those of the atomic bomb or other weapons mentioned above."

During the recent G. W. Bush administration the United States eventually moved forward with a testing program for missile interceptors, withdrew from the ABM Treaty, negotiated a new agreement with Russia known as the Strategic Offensive Reductions Treaty (SORT), and began initial BMD deployments. Japan and Israel also decided to deploy missile defenses, while a debate emerged in Europe over the proposed stationing of US BMD in Poland, the Czech Republic, and possibly elsewhere. Russia responded negatively to the latter proposal because of concerns about the effects on stability in the region and its implications for arms-control agreements. However, Vice President Biden signaled a change in US policy when he announced in Munich in February 2009 that the new Obama administration was reconsidering the BMD plans of the Bush administration. In an apparent effort to persuade Russia to play a more active role in halting the Iranian program to build nuclear weapons, the Obama administration announced in the late summer of 2009 that it would not build missile-defense installations in Poland and the Czech Republic. In March 2010, President Obama and Russian President Dmitry Medvedev reached agreement on a nuclear arms treaty that will cut nuclear weapons to the lowest levels since 1960s. This treaty replaces the Strategic Arms Reduction Treaty of 1991 and it is a positive step toward Obama's goal of reducing the global stockpile of nuclear weapons.

Theorizing Nuclear Proliferation

One question that has provoked interest is what constitutes nuclear proliferation: is it a single decision to acquire a nuclear weapon, or is it a process that may stretch over several years, and consequently no one identifiable decision can be located? Research on what has been referred to as "the proliferation puzzle" has embraced several conceptual issues (Meyer 1984; Davis and Frankel 1993; Lavoy 1995; Ogilvie-White 1996; Hymans 2006). While much literature endorses the propositions derived from political realism, which asserts that in an anarchic international environment states will seek nuclear weapons to enhance their security, insights from other theoretical positions have become more commonplace (see chapters in Part Two). This has generated questions concerning what the level of analysis should be in studying nuclear proliferation. Should the focus be on the individual, the organization, the cultural group, the state, the international system, or some combination of these?

> **WHAT'S YOUR WORLDVIEW**
>
> *What, in your opinion, is the cause of nuclear proliferation? What theory best describes the causes for nuclear proliferation? What theory poses the best solution(s)?*

The argument has also been advanced that norms, taboos, and **epistemic communities** have played an important role in the nuclear context (Adler 1992; Price and Tannenwald 1996). One viewpoint sees international norms as increasingly significant both as constraints on nuclear behavior and in setting appropriate standards among a range of actors. Similarly, some analysts stress the role played by culture and identity factors in fostering nonproliferation dialogues (Krause and Williams 1997). Scholars have also drawn attention to the important roles played by nongovernmental organizations (NGOs) and epistemic communities, referring to groups of individuals often from different disciplines and countries that operate as conduits for ideas on nonproliferation.

Another issue with enduring resonance concerns the question of what can explain nuclear "nonuse" since 1945. This debate started early in the nuclear calendar as authors like Bernard Brodie argued that nuclear weapons were useful only in their nonuse (Brodie 1946; C. S. Gray 1996). Over the years the main explanation of nonuse has centered on the notion of **nuclear deterrence**: states have been deterred from using nuclear weapons

epistemic community
A knowledge-based transnational community of experts and policy activists.

nuclear deterrence Defined by nuclear strategists as the possession of sufficient power to inflict unacceptable damage on a potential adversary. Nuclear deterrence must involve explicit threats in order to effectively prevent a state from using weapons. These threats must be seen as credible and must be clearly communicated.

because of concerns of retaliation in kind by adversaries. On the US side, this became known as Mutually Assured Destruction, or MAD. Defense intellectuals in the United States believed that if both the US and the USSR were able to absorb a surprise nuclear attack and still retaliate with what the analysts called "unacceptable damage," then neither side would risk a preemptive strike.

Nuclear Motivations

Traditional analysis of the motivations for nuclear proliferation has focused at the state and interstate levels. For much of the post–Second World War period the pattern of nuclear weapon acquisition established by the five NWSs was considered the one most likely to be followed by any future proliferating state. Analysis of the motivational aspect consequently addressed the strategic, political, and prestige rationales that led these states to seek nuclear weapons. The strategic motivation focused on the role nuclear weapons played in the Second World War and its immediate aftermath, when initially they were seen as war-fighting or war-winning weapons. Later, attention shifted to the role nuclear weapons played in deterrence, leading to the assumption that one of the principal motivations for acquisition was the deterrence of other nuclear weapons–capable states. Similarly, the political and prestige benefits that nuclear weapons conferred on those states with the wherewithal to manufacture them were also deemed significant. Nuclear weapons were seen as the most modern form of weaponry, and their custodians were automatically afforded a seat at the "best table of international affairs."

It is now more difficult to explain nuclear proliferation by focusing on a single variable. With reference to levels of analysis, specialists have argued that it is necessary to consider a range of factors that may influence nuclear weapons acquisition. These may include militarism and traditional technological factors, the availability of nuclear technology, and a cadre of trained nuclear scientists who encourage acquisition; domestic politics, imperatives within a political party, or the domestic political situation may propel a state towards nuclear weapons; diplomatic bargaining, that acquisition of a nuclear capability can be used to influence or bargain with both perceived allies and enemies; and nonintervention, that a nuclear capability can deter or prevent intervention by other states.

transnational actor Any nongovernmental actor, such as a multinational corporation or one country's religious humanitarian organization, that has relations with any actor from another country or with an international organization.

Further complexity is added when attention is focused at the substate or **transnational actor** level as the motivations of nonstate actors may be different from those associated with states. In much traditional thinking, only states were considered to have the wherewithal to acquire nuclear capabilities. Nuclear commerce was conducted on a state-to-state basis, and it was states that entered into international arms control and disarmament treaties. Today, states are no longer the sole focus of attention, as nonstate actors have also featured.

nuclear terrorism The use of or threat to use nuclear weapons or nuclear materials to achieve the goals of rogue states or revolutionary or radical organizations.

Studies conducted during the 1970s and 1980s on **nuclear terrorism** indicated that there were risks associated with particular groups acquiring a nuclear device or threatening to attack nuclear installations. One study by the International Task Force on Prevention of Nuclear Terrorism concluded that it was possible for a terrorist group to build a crude nuclear device provided it had sufficient quantities of chemical high explosives and weapons-usable fissile materials. More significantly, it was felt that such a group would be more interested in generating social disruption by making a credible nuclear threat rather than actually detonating a nuclear device and causing mass killing and destruction (Leventhal and Alexander 1987). More recent occurrences have served to alter this latter judgment.

Events in the mid-1990s, such as the first bombing of the World Trade Center in New York in 1993 and the attack against the US government building in Oklahoma in April 1995, revealed the extent of damage and loss of life that could be caused. While both instances involved traditional methods of inflicting damage, the use of nerve agents (chemical weapons) in an underground train network in central Tokyo in March 1995 to cause both death and widespread panic has been viewed as representing a quantum change in methods. These concerns have intensified since the tragic events of September 11, 2001, when the World Trade Center was destroyed by a coordinated attack using civilian aircraft loaded with aviation fuel as the method of destruction. The attack not only produced mass casualties, it also changed the assumption about terrorist use of CBRN capabilities (Wilkinson 2003).

Nuclear Capabilities and Intentions

The nuclear programs in Iraq, Iran, Pakistan, and North Korea have raised important issues concerning capabilities and intentions. These instances reveal the difficulties in obtaining consensus in international forums on how to respond to **noncompliance** and the problems associated with verifying treaty compliance in situations where special inspection or nuclear development arrangements are agreed. In the case of Iraq, a special inspection arrangement known as UNSCOM (United Nations Special Committee) was established following the 1991 Gulf War to oversee the dismantlement of the WMD program that had come to light as a result of the conflict. By the late 1990s, problems were encountered over access to particular sites, and UNSCOM inspectors were withdrawn. Disagreements also surfaced among the five permanent members of the United Nations Security Council concerning how to implement the UN resolutions that had been passed in connection with Iraq since 1991. These had not been resolved at the time of the

noncompliance The failure of states or other actors to abide by treaties or rules supported by international regimes.

The IAEA is intended to work with states to control the spread of nuclear technology. If states like Iran, Iraq, and North Korea refuse to cooperate, what should the agency do?

2003 intervention in Iraq, and subsequent inspections in that country were unable to find evidence of significant undeclared WMD.

The complexity associated with compliance is evident in the case of Iran. The country became the subject of attention from the International Atomic Energy Agency (IAEA) over delays in signing a protocol, added to Iran's safeguards agreement, requiring increased transparency by non–nuclear weapons states. Although Iran later did sign the protocol, the discovery by the IAEA of undeclared facilities capable of enriching uranium fueled speculation. In an effort to find a solution, a dialogue between Iran and the so-called EU-3 (France, Germany, and the United Kingdom) began in October 2003. While an agreement was reached in Paris in November 2004, the situation was not resolved, and by 2006 the UN Security Council passed resolutions, under Chapter VII of the UN Charter, requiring Iran to comply with its international obligations. The Iranian case is a destabilizing factor in regional—and international—politics. The Ahmadinejad government has denounced Israel, with the Iranian president himself calling for the destruction of

Figure 8.1 A Global View of Highly Enriched Uranium and Plutonium.
The essential ingredients of nuclear weapons exist in dozens of countries, with security that ranges from excellent to appalling. Programs sponsored by the US Energy and Defense departments help remove such materials to secure locations and assist other nation-states in improving security at facilities that hold nuclear material.

the country. Thus, the difficulty of getting Iran to agree to verification mechanisms has complicated an already dangerous Middle East security picture.

Post–Cold War Antiproliferation Efforts

In 1987, seven missile-technology exporters established identical export guidelines to cover the sale of nuclear-capable ballistic or cruise missiles. Known as the Missile Technology Control Regime (MTCR), this supply arrangement seeks "to limit the risks of nuclear proliferation by controlling transfers of technology which could make a contribution to nuclear weapons delivery systems other than manned aircraft" (Karp 1995). Membership of the MTCR has expanded to include many of the major missile producers, and the guidelines now embrace missile systems capable of carrying chemical and biological payloads. Over time, concerns have been expressed about the long-term viability of the MTCR. While observers acknowledge that the arrangement has fulfilled its initial purpose in slowing down missile proliferation, there are calls for new measures. Missile defenses are one means for dealing with the problem, but other suggestions include global or regional ballistic-test notification centers and multilateral arms-limitation measures for missiles with certain ranges. Also, in 2002, a new initiative, known as The Hague Code of Conduct, was launched (M. Smith 2002). As the name implies, the code seeks to develop standards of appropriate behavior in the transfer of missiles and missile parts.

Will the future see an end to conflict?

At the time of the 1995 NPT Extension Conference, expectations were high that the documents adopted by consensus then would provide the foundation for strengthening the treaty. Events afterward indicated that this assessment was premature, as differences surfaced between the parties over how these documents should be interpreted. Similarly, in 1995, expectations were high that a CTBT would soon be agreed and implemented, but again this proved premature. Although a CTBT was opened for signature in 1996, it has not entered into force. This will only occur once a group of forty-four states (including the five NWSs and states such as India, Pakistan, and North Korea) have signed and ratified the treaty. This has meant that the success or failure of the CTBT is dependent on developments in several states. Significantly, also, not everyone agrees that this treaty is a worthwhile measure. Proponents claim that the restriction on nuclear testing will limit both **vertical** and **horizontal proliferation**. Critics of a CTBT argue that any such testing prohibition is unverifiable and will therefore be unable to constrain proliferation.

Problems have similarly been encountered over attempts to negotiate a Fissile Material Cutoff Treaty (FMCT). One issue has been whether the FMCT should only prevent future production of fissile materials or include an agreement to remove existing stockpiles. The verification provisions of any such treaty have also been the subject of differing proposals. One feature of this debate that inevitably will demand innovative thinking is how any excess fissile material can be disposed of, as safely and cost effectively as possible, given the large quantities involved.

vertical proliferation An increase in the number of nuclear weapons a state possesses and in other technologies used for delivery of weapons. Recently, concerns were raised about the production of tactical nuclear weapons like bunker busters that could be used to destroy caves and underground facilities in Afghanistan.

horizontal proliferation An increase in the number of actors who possess nuclear weapons.

The document tabled at the 1995 conference by the Arab states party to the NPT, known as the Resolution on the Middle East, calls on all states in the region to accede to the NPT. The debate over this resolution has highlighted how difficult it is to ensure universal adherence to the treaty. For although signatories to the NPT have increased to the point where 188 states are now party, Israel, India, and Pakistan have remained nonsignatories, while North Korea withdrew in 2003. The question is therefore how, if at all, the treaty can be made universal.

Thus, as the new millennium dawned, the context of nuclear proliferation was undergoing change. It became urgent to be more responsive to the complexities of globalized proliferation. This urgency generated measures like the Proliferation Security Initiative (PSI), established originally by eleven states in June 2003 and now involving fifteen, with sixty others participating on an ad hoc basis. The PSI is designed as a means to interdict trafficking in WMD, delivery systems, and related materials. There have also been calls to reappraise the prospects for creating new multilateral nuclear fuel centers (an idea that has been around for several decades). Regional safeguards organizations, such as the one established in the European Union (known as Euratom), provide possible models for facilitating greater regional oversight of nuclear energy developments.

Conclusion

Questions of war and peace are central to the existence of every country. In this chapter we have examined the many ways academics analyze security affairs and how these ideas influence the decisions political leaders make on war and weapons procurement, especially nuclear weapons and nuclear proliferation. In the next chapter we turn to the globalizing of unconventional warfare through the use of terrorism.

Contributors to Chapter 8: John Baylis, Darryl Howlett, and Steven L. Lamy.

REVIEW QUESTIONS

1. Why is security a "contested concept"?
2. What do neorealist writers mean by "structure"?
3. According to realists, why do states find it difficult to cooperate? How do constructivists explain cooperation?
4. What is distinctive about constructivist views of international security?
5. Is the tension between national and global security resolvable?
6. Has international security changed since 9/11?
7. What are the main arguments for and against the proliferation of nuclear weapons?
8. What role do norms, taboos, and scientists play in the context of nuclear proliferation?
9. What nuclear-proliferation concerns have stemmed from the dissolution of the Soviet Union?
10. Does the nonstate actor represent a new nuclear-proliferation challenge?
11. To what extent is globalization a cause of war?
12. Why do some authors believe that war between the current great powers is highly unlikely?
13. What is "asymmetric warfare"?
14. How is gender important in understanding war?
15. What is the relationship between children and contemporary war?

FURTHER READING

International and global security

K. N. Waltz's study *Man, the State and War* (New York: Columbia University Press, 1954) is one of the best sources for the study of the causes of war, and see also J. C. Garnett, "The Causes of War and the Conditions of Peace," in J. Baylis, J. Wirtz, E. Cohen, and C. S. Gray (eds.), *Strategy in the Contemporary World*, 2nd ed. (Oxford: Oxford University Press, 2006).

B. Buzan's *People, States and Fear* (London: Harvester, 1983) provides an excellent starting point for the study of national and international security. The book is written largely from a neorealist perspective.

M. J. Smith, *Realist Thought from Weber to Kissinger* (Baton Rouge: Louisiana State University Press, 1986), covers the development of what has been described as classical realism and discusses some of the major thinkers in the field. For neoclassical approaches see T. Christensen, *Useful Adversaries: Grand Strategy, Domestic Mobilization and Sino-American Conflict, 1947–1958* (Princeton, NJ: Princeton University Press, 1996); R. Schweller, *Deadly Imbalances: Tripolarity and Hitler's Strategy of World Conquest* (New York: Columbia University Press, 1998); W. Wohlforth, *The Elusive Balance: Power and Perceptions During the Cold War* (Ithaca, NY: Cornell University Press, 1993); and F. Zakaria, *From Wealth to Power* (Princeton, NJ: Princeton University Press, 1998). For an interesting account of "ethical realism," see A. J. H. Murray, *Reconstructing Realism: Between Power Politics and Cosmopolitan Ethics* (Edinburgh: Keele University Press, 1997), and A. Lieven and J. Hulsman, *Ethical Realism: A View of America's Role in the World* (New York: Pantheon Books, 2006).

A. Wendt's article "Anarchy Is What States Make of It: The Social Construction of Power Politics," in *International Organization* 46(2) (1992), gives a very useful analysis of the constructivist perspective. See also A. Wendt, *Social Theory of International Politics* (Cambridge: Cambridge University Press, 1999).

O. Waever, B. Buzan, M. Kelstrup, and P. Lemaitre, *Identity, Migration and the New Security Agenda in Europe* (London: Pinter, 1993), provides an original perspective for studying the kind of nonstate aspects of security that have affected Europe in the post–Cold War period.

Very useful discussions about the changing nature of security can be found in C. Bretherton and G. Ponton (eds.), *Global Politics: An Introduction* (Oxford, Blackwell, 1996);

T. Terriff, S. Croft, L. James, and P. Morgan, *Security Studies Today* (Cambridge: Polity Press, 1999); K. Krause and M. C. Williams (eds.), *Critical Security Studies: Concepts and Cases* (London: UCL Press, 1997); S. Lawson (ed.), *The New Agenda for Global Security: Cooperating for Peace and Beyond* (St. Leonards: Allen and Unwin, 1995); R. D. Kaplan, *The Coming Anarchy: Shattering the Dreams of the Post–Cold War* (New York: Random House, 2000); K. Booth and T. Dunne, *Worlds in Collision: Terror and the Future of Global Order* (London: Palgrave, 2002); and I. Clark, *Globalization and International Relations Theory* (Oxford: Oxford University Press, 1999).

For a discussion of different theoretical approaches to security and some of the contemporary debates about security studies, see A. Collins (ed.), *Contemporary Security Studies* (Oxford: Oxford University Press, 2006), and S. Smith, "The Increasing Insecurity of Security Studies: Conceptualizing Security in the Last Twenty Years," in *Contemporary Security Policy* 20(3) (Dec. 1999). See also R. Stubbs, "The Many Faces of Asian Security," *Contemporary Southeast Asia* 24(1) (April 2002), and J. A. Tickner, *Gender in International Relations: Feminist Perspectives on Achieving Global Security* (New York: Columbia University Press, 1992).

The best guide to the use of the Internet on the subject of international security is W. M. Arkin, *The Internet and Strategic Studies* (Baltimore, MD: The Center for Strategic Education, the Paul Nitze School of Advanced International Studies, Johns Hopkins University, 1998).

Nuclear proliferation: theoretical aspects

Buzan, B., and Herring, E. (1998), *The Arms Dynamic in World Politics* (London: Lynne Rienner). This text covers theoretical and empirical aspects associated with the arms dynamic in the context of nuclear weapons.

Campbell, K. M., Einhorn, R. J., and Reiss, M. B. (2004), *The Nuclear Tipping Point: Why States Reconsider Their Nuclear Choices* (Washington, DC: Brookings Institute Press). This volume explores the factors that lead states to reconsider their nuclear options.

Hymans, J. E. (2006), *The Psychology of Nuclear Proliferation* (Cambridge: Cambridge University Press). Using four case studies, the author draws on materials from the humanities, social sciences, and natural sciences to analyze nuclear decision-making in the states chosen for study.

Sagan, S. D., and Waltz, K. N. (1995), *The Spread of Nuclear Weapons. A Debate* (New York and London: W. W. Norton, and 2nd ed. 2003). This book juxtaposes the contrasting arguments of the two authors concerning the spread of nuclear weapons.

On nuclear use and nonuse

Herring, E. (ed.) (2000), *Preventing the Use of Weapons of Mass Destruction* (special issue), *Journal of Strategic Studies*, 23(1) (March). The contributors to this volume concentrate on the issues associated with preventing the use of WMD.

Lavoy, P. R., Sagan, S., and Wirtz, J. J. (eds.) (2000), *Planning the Unthinkable: How New Powers Will Use Nuclear, Biological and Chemical Weapons* (Ithaca, NY: Cornell University Press). The authors compare how military threats, strategic cultures, and organizations shape the way leaders intend to employ WMD.

Historical context and background

Walker, W. (2004), *Weapons of Mass Destruction and International Order*, Adelphi Paper 370 (Oxford: Oxford University Press for the International Institute for Strategic Studies). This IISS paper addresses the "problem of order" associated with weapons of mass destruction by drawing on historical evidence and ideas.

Nonproliferation/antiproliferation measures

Bosch, O., and Van Ham, P. (eds.) (2007), *Global Non-Proliferation and Counter-Terrorism* (Washington, DC: Brookings Institute Press). This volume assesses the impact of UN Security Resolution 1540.

Dhanapala, J., with Rydell, R. (2005), *Multilateral Diplomacy and the NPT: An Insider's Account* (Geneva: United Nations Institute for Disarmament Research). This book provides an analysis of the multilateral diplomacy surrounding the 1995 NPT Review and Extension Conference and is written by two authors who were closely involved in the negotiating process (one of whom was the president of that conference).

Simpson, J., and Howlett, D. (eds.) (1995), *The Future of the Non-Proliferation Treaty* (New York: St Martin's Press). This explores the background issues associated with the NPT in the lead-up to the 1995 Review and Extension Conference.

Alternative nuclear futures

Baylis, J., and O'Neill, R. (eds.) (2000), *Alternative Nuclear Futures* (Oxford: Oxford University Press). This edited volume provides an overview of the different positions related to the nuclear future.

Changing character of war

Biddle, S. (2004), *Military Power: Explaining Victory and Defeat in Modern Battle* (Princeton, NJ: Princeton University Press). An interesting and stimulating study of warfare since 1900, analyzing the techniques and technologies that have aided the offense and defense to achieve victory in modern wars.

Blank, S. J. (1996), "Preparing for the Next War: Reflections on the Revolution in Military Affairs," *Strategic Review* 24: 17–25. An analysis of the post–1990 revolution in military affairs, which argues cogently that in order to benefit from the technological advantages in the RMA, states must embrace necessary organizational and doctrinal changes.

Brocklehurst, H. (2006), *Who's Afraid of Children? Children, Conflict and International Relations* (Aldershot: Ashgate). A groundbreaking study of the place of children in modern warfare, exploring their roles as warriors, as victims, and as witnesses. The book raises searching questions about the meaning of "childhood" and "child" in the light of contemporary conflict.

Clausewitz, C. V. (1989), *On War*, ed. and trans. by M. Howard and P. Paret (Princeton, NJ: Princeton University Press). Clausewitz remains essential reading for the serious student of war.

Cohen, E. A. (2004), "Change and Transformation in Military Affairs," *Journal of Strategic Studies* 27(3): 395–407. An engaging article in which the author argues that the changes in the structures of military forces and the nature of battle mean that there has been fundamental change in the character of war in the past two decades.

Coker, C. (2001), *Humane Warfare* (London: Routledge). A challenging book that argues that the horrors of mid-twentieth-century warfare have led Western democracies to seek to fight "humane wars" characterized by minimal civilian and military casualties on both sides.

Duyvesteyn, I., and Angstrom, J. (eds.) (2005), *Rethinking the Nature of War* (London: Frank Cass). A collection of excellent essays debating the changing nature of war in the post–Cold War era.

Gray, C. S. (2002), *Strategy for Chaos: Revolutions in Military Affairs and the Evidence of History* (London: Frank Cass). A very good introduction to the RMA debates with useful historical case studies of earlier RMAs.

Ignatieff, M. (1997), *The Warrior's Honor: Ethnic War and the Modern Conscience* (New York: Henry Holt). An examination of the motivations of "moral interventionists" such as aid workers, journalists, and peacekeepers, and those of the ethnic warriors with whom they engage in postmodern war zones.

Kaldor, M. (1999), *New and Old Wars: Organized Violence in a Global Era* (Cambridge: Polity, Press). Kaldor argues that key features of the conflicts waged since 1990 allow them to be termed "new wars." Sadly, the long history of warfare demonstrates that there is little genuinely novel about such conflicts.

Record, J. (2004), *Dark Victory: America's Second War Against Iraq* (Washington, DC: US Naval Institute Press). This study presents the 2003 war against Iraq as a long-delayed completion of business begun in 1990–1991. Although he does not deal with the insurgency phase of the war, Record strongly advocates a comprehensive program for postwar reconstruction as a key to long-term success.

Van Creveld, M. (1991), *The Transformation of War* (New York: Free Press). An analysis that is particularly strong in bringing out the socioeconomic demands of modern warfare.

INTERNET RESOURCES

Battle of Salamis, Aeschylus
http://www.poetry-archive.com/a/the_battle_of_salamis.html
Poetry provides a most unacademic insight into war.

First World War.com—Vintage Photographs—Home Front
http://www.firstworldwar.com/photos/homefront.htm
Part of a larger private First World War hobbyist site, the photos are useful for student activities.

Global Security: Reliable Security Information
http://www.globalsecurity.org/
This web site has an extensive selection of information about the armed forces of most countries. It also has current news from the world of international security.

Imperial War Museum
http://www.iwm.org.uk/
The definitive war museum has a large and growing online collection.

International Atomic Energy Agency
http://www.iaea.org
The international organization created to control the dissemination of nuclear technology. More recently at the center of debate regarding Iran's nuclear program.

International Institute for Strategic Studies
http://www.iiss.org/
An academic source for information about international policy.

International Physicians for the Prevention of Nuclear War
http://www.ippnw.org/
A leading NGO committed, as its name suggests, to ending the threat of nuclear war.

For more information, quizzes, case studies, and other study tools, please visit us at **www.oup.com/us/lamy**

Terrorism and Globalization

Asymmetry gives terrorists and cybercriminals their strength, since adversaries operate beyond accepted international norms and value systems on a plane where atrocity is a legitimate form of war.

—Robert D. Kaplan

With respect to terrorism, the locus of global concern is mainly restricted to Islamic countries with no willingness to address the terrorism of "covert operations" in the North, or to address the social causes of terrorism to the extent that recourse to such forms of political violence rests on injustices.

—Richard Falk

Malika El Aroud is a 48-year-old Belgian citizen and is one of the most prominent Internet jihadists in Europe. She is proud to be a female warrior for Al Qaeda, and she uses her time to recruit Muslim men and women to join the global jihad against the West. El Aroud does not conceal her identity, and she certainly takes advantage of living in a democratic society that has laws that protect the freedoms of its citizens. She has been detained for supposed plots within Belgium, but the system requires the release of suspects if no charges are brought within twenty-four hours. She continues to seek recruits out of her home although under constant police surveillance, while getting $1,100 each month in unemployment benefits. El Aroud seeks to inspire other people to wage jihad. The director of Belgium's federal police force says that El Aroud enjoys the protections offered by Belgium and at the same time she is a threat to her country and the rest of the world.

Terrorism is a tactic that is used by individuals and groups around the world who seek to change what they believe are unjust or immoral systems. The violence of terrorism presents serious problems for governments, whose primary mission is to provide security for their citizens. To achieve their goals, terrorists exploit globalization, which makes it easier for radicals to travel, communicate, finance, organize, and purchase the weapons. What should be done?

Jihadi online recruiter Malika El Aroud at home in her secular-government-subsidized apartment in Belgium.

Should we sacrifice our rights to control these potential terrorists? Can globalization bring a solution to these threats to safety and security?

Introduction

The relationship between terrorism and globalization is difficult to describe accurately. Each phenomenon is complicated in its own right and defies simple characterization. It is inaccurate to suggest that globalization is responsible for terrorism, but technologies associated with globalization have been exploited by terrorists. In particular, the Internet has improved the ability of terrorist groups to work together, share information, and reach out to previously unavailable audiences. Technology, however, cannot change the character of the terrorist message or the nature of the struggle. Terrorism, often called a weapon of the weak, is conducted by a minority of individuals who promote an extremist ideology. The global community is not powerless in the face of such violence. In order to succeed, the global community must utilize the resources at its disposal collaboratively to diminish support for terrorism and demonstrate the illegitimacy of terrorist messages and aspirations. But it must do this while still respecting the values and institutions that terrorists seek to destroy.

Defining Terrorism

Terrorism and globalization share at least one quality—both are complex phenomena open to subjective interpretation. Definitions of terrorism vary widely, but all depart from a common point. **Terrorism** is characterized, first and foremost, by the use of violence. This tactic of violence takes many forms and often indiscriminately targets noncombatants. The purpose for which violence is used, and its root causes, is where most of the disagreements about terrorism begin. Historically, the term "terrorism" described state violence against citizens, for example during the French Revolution or the Stalinist era of the Soviet Union. Over the past half-century, however, the definition of terrorism has evolved to mean the use of violence by small nonstate groups to achieve political change. Terrorism differs from criminal violence in its degree of political legitimacy. Those sympathetic to terrorist causes suggest that violence, including the death of innocent people, is the only remaining option that can draw attention to the plight of the aggrieved. Such causes have included ideological, ethnic, and religious exclusion or persecution.

Defining terrorism can be difficult, as groups often advocate multiple grievances and compete with one another for resources and support. In addition, the relative importance of these grievances within groups can change over time. Those targeted by terrorists are less inclined to see any justification, much less legitimacy, behind attacks that are designed to spread fear by killing and maiming civilians. As a result, the term "terrorist" has a pejorative value that is useful in delegitimizing those who commit such acts.

Audrey Kurth Cronin, an academic authority on terrorism, has outlined different types of terrorist groups and their historical importance in the following way:

> There are *four types* of terrorist organizations currently operating around the world, categorized mainly by their source of motivation: left-wing terrorists, right-wing terrorists, ethnonationalist/separatist terrorists, and religious or "sacred" terrorists. All four types have enjoyed periods of relative prominence in the modern era, with left-wing terrorism

terrorism The use of violence by nonstate groups or, in some cases, states to inspire fear, by attacking civilians and/or symbolic targets and eliminating opposition groups. This is done for purposes such as drawing widespread attention to a grievance, provoking a severe response, or wearing down an opponent's moral resolve to effect political change.

WHAT'S YOUR WORLDVIEW ?

Most people think that all groups that use terrorism are nonstate actors, but states can also use terrorist tactics. Do you think that terrorism is a legitimate use of force if used by a state?

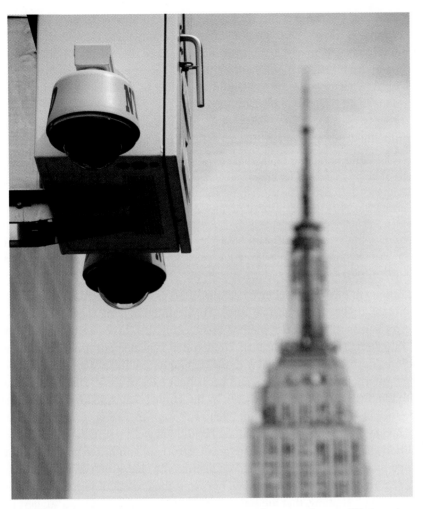

Once rare in the United States, security cameras have become a fixture of life in major cities. Does technology intrude on our right to privacy?

intertwined with the Communist movement and currently practiced by Maoists in Peru and Nepal, right-wing terrorism employed by skinheads in several European countries drawing its inspiration from Fascism, and the bulk of ethnonationalist/separatist terrorism accompanying the wave of decolonization especially in the immediate post–World War II years and in places like Northern Ireland and Spain. Currently, "sacred" terrorism is becoming more significant . . . Of course, these categories are not perfect, as many groups have a mix of motivating ideologies—some ethnonationalist groups, for example, have religious characteristics or agendas—but usually one ideology or motivation dominates. (Cronin 2002/3, 39)

Academics and political leaders have difficulty deciding what actions constitute terrorism, in part because the tactics of wars of **national liberation**, **guerrilla wars**, and **asymmetric conflict** can resemble those that terrorists use. The legitimacy of terrorist means and methods is the foremost reason for disagreement. Some people view terrorist acts as legitimate only if they meet the criteria associated with the "just war" tradition that developed in Europe (see Chapters 2 and 8). These criteria, which apply to all applications

national liberation This was a doctrine promoted by the Soviet Union that encouraged anticolonial or anti-Western insurgencies in the developing world.

guerrilla wars Conflicts or insurgencies that involve irregular forces. Fighters in these wars use unconventional methods of warfare, such as sabotage, ambushes, roadside bombs, and sniping.

asymmetric conflict In symmetrical warfare, armies with comparable weapons, tactics, and organizational structures do battle. Wars are fought on near-equal terms. When stakes are high and those actors in conflict are not equal in terms of weapons and technology, the weaker side adopts asymmetrical tactics. These include guerrilla warfare, roadside bombs, attacks on civilians, and other terrorist tactics.

of force, have been expanded to include a just cause, proportional use of violence, and the use of force as a last resort. For academics who study these issues, another problem is that the terrorists themselves, their justifications, and their methods do not fit conveniently into international relations theories. Realists, for example, suggest that the political violence used by terrorist groups is illegitimate on the basis that states alone have a monopoly on the legitimate use of physical force.

Terrorism expert Martha Crenshaw provides an analytic, though subjective, approach to determine the legitimacy of terrorist acts of violence:

> The value of the normative approach [to terrorism] is that it confronts squarely a critical problem in the analysis of terrorism, and indeed any form of political violence: the issue of legitimacy. Terrorists of the left deny the legitimacy of the state and claim that the use of violence against it is morally justified. Terrorists of the right deny the legitimacy of the opposition and hold that the violence in the service of order is sanctioned by the values of the status quo . . . the need for scholarly objectivity and abstraction does not excuse us from the obligation to judge the morality of the use of force, whether by the state or against. (Crenshaw 1983, 2–4)

Yet even with the use of violence by states, there is disagreement on what constitutes the legitimate application of armed force. For example, during the 1980s Libya sponsored terrorist acts as an indirect method of attacking the United States, France, and the United Kingdom. Those states, in turn, condemned Libyan sponsorship as contravening international norms and responded with the customary methods of international politics: sanctions, international court cases, and occasional uses of force. Disagreement associated with the invasion of Iraq in 2003, led by the United States, relates to interpretations over whether or not the conditions for "just war" were met prior to commencement of military operations. Some suggest that the conditions were not met and that actions by the coalition should be considered as an "act of terrorism" conducted by states. Leaders in the United States and the United Kingdom dismiss the charge on the basis that a greater evil was removed. Violating international norms in the pursuit of terrorists runs the risk of playing into perceptions that the state itself is a terrorist threat. Critics suggest that US policy toward terrorist detainees and "extraordinary renditions" damages America's credibility as a global champion for individual rights and freedoms.

As with other forms of irregular, or asymmetric, warfare, terrorism is designed to achieve political change for the purpose of obtaining power in order to right a perceived wrong. However, according to some analysts, terrorism is the weakest form of irregular warfare with which to alter the political landscape. The reason for this weakness is that terrorist groups rarely possess the broader support of the population that characterizes insurgency and revolution, and the methods of terrorists often alienate potential supporters of the cause. Terrorist groups often lack support for their objectives because the changes they seek are based on radical ideas that do not have widespread appeal. In order to effect change, terrorists must provoke drastic responses that act as a catalyst for change or weaken their opponent's moral resolve. In a few cases, terrorist acts have achieved relatively rapid change.

The bombings in Madrid in 2004, for example, seemed to influence the outcome of elections in Spain in a dramatic fashion, and news-media editorials suggested that the attack was designed with just such a purpose in mind. An alternative explanation says that many Spanish voters were already unhappy with their conservative government's support for the US invasion of Iraq; the train bombings, in this interpretation, had no direct effect on voting behavior. Many terrorist leaders hope that their actions will lead to disproportionate reactions by a state that in turn disaffects public or international opinion and increases support for their cause. Terrorist campaigns, however, often take years or decades to achieve meaningful results, and the amount and nature of force used can be problematic. Terrorist groups risk fading into obscurity if they do not alarm the public or conduct newsworthy attacks. However, attacks by terrorists that are too horrific, such as the publicized beheadings in Iraq after the US invasions, put support for terrorist causes at risk. Although states can also engage in terrorist activities, terrorism is defined here as the use of violence by substate groups to inspire fear, by attacking civilians and/or symbolic targets, for purposes such as drawing widespread attention to a grievance, provoking a severe response, or wearing down their opponent's moral resolve to effect political change. Many of these substate groups have used various technologies to extend their reach to distant communities. These groups have become part of **transnational terrorist networks**.

As with definitions of terrorism, there is general agreement on at least one aspect of globalization. Technologies allow the transfer of goods, services, and information almost anywhere quickly and efficiently. In the case of information, the transfer can be secure and is nearly instantaneous. The extent of social, cultural, and political change brought on by globalization, including increasing interconnectedness and homogeneity in the international system, remains the subject of much disagreement and debate, as other chapters in this volume have outlined. These disagreements, in turn, influence discussion of the extent to which globalization has contributed to the rise of modern terrorism. There is little doubt that the technologies associated with globalization have been used to improve the effectiveness and reach of terrorist groups. The relationship between globalization and terrorism is best understood as the next step in the evolution of political violence since terrorism became a transnational phenomenon in the 1960s. In order to understand the changes perceived in terrorism globally, it is useful to understand the evolution of terrorism from a primarily domestic political event to a global phenomenon.

transnational terrorist networks Terrorists use existing global or transnational economic, transportation, and communication systems to manage and maintain terrorist organizations around the world. These networks facilitate the movement of followers and material to locations around the world.

> ### WHAT'S YOUR WORLDVIEW
>
> *Why would an individual resort to terrorism? Why would people decide to join extremist groups and use terrorism to achieve their goals?*

Terrorism: From Domestic to Global Phenomena (1968–2001)

Historically, nonstate terrorist groups have used readily available means to permit small numbers of individuals to spread fear as widely as possible. In the late nineteenth and early twentieth centuries, anarchists relied on railroads for travel and killed with revolvers and dynamite. Yet terrorists and acts of terrorism rarely had an impact beyond national borders, in part because the activists often sought political change within a specific country. Three factors led to the birth of transnational terrorism in 1968: the expansion of commercial air travel, the availability of televised news coverage, and broad political and ideological interests among extremists that converged on a common cause. As a result, terrorism grew from a local to a transnational threat. Air travel gave terrorists unprecedented mobility. For example, the Japanese Red Army trained in one country and attacked in another, as with the 1972 Lod Airport massacre in Israel. In the United States, some radicals forced airplanes to go to Cuba. Air travel appealed to terrorists for other reasons. Airport security measures, including passport control, were almost nonexistent when terrorists began hijacking airlines. These **skyjackings** suited terrorist purposes well.

skyjacking The takeover of a commercial airplane for the purpose of taking hostages and using these hostages to bargain for a particular political or economic goal.

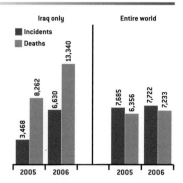

Terrorist Incidents and Fatalities. What conclusions can you draw from studying this data? What does this data say (if anything) about the "globalization of terrorism"? *Source: U.S. National Counter-Terrorism Center (NCTC 2007).*

Hijacked airlines offered a degree of mobility, and therefore security, for the terrorists involved. States also acquiesced to terrorist demands, frequently for money, which encouraged further incidents. The success of this tactic spurred other terrorist groups, as well as criminals and political refugees, to follow suit. As a result, incidents of hijacking skyrocketed from five in 1966 to ninety-four in 1969. Shared political ideologies stimulated cooperation and some exchanges between groups as diverse as the Irish Republican Army (IRA) and the Basque separatist organization Euzkadi Ta Askatasuna (ETA). Besides sharing techniques and technical experience, groups demanded the release of imprisoned "fellow revolutionaries" in different countries, giving the impression of a coordinated global terrorist network. The reality was that groups formed short-term relationships of convenience, based around weapons, capabilities, and money, to advance local political objectives. For example, members of the IRA did not launch attacks in Spain to help the ETA, but they did share resources.

Televised news coverage and the Internet also played a role in expanding the audience, who could witness the theater of terrorism in their own homes. People who had never heard of what was called "the plight of the Palestinians" became very aware of the issue after live coverage of incidents such as the hostage taking conducted by Black September during the 1972 Munich Olympics. Although some considered media coverage to be "the oxygen that sustains terrorism," terrorists discovered that reporters and audiences lost interest in repeat performances over time. In order to sustain viewer interest and compete for coverage, terrorist groups undertook increasingly spectacular attacks, such as the seizure of Organization of Petroleum Exporting Countries (OPEC) delegates

Members of the Basque national separatist group ETA have conducted a thirty-year-long campaign of sporadic bombings of Spanish government buildings, often killing civilians. Is this style of war for national independence legitimate?

by "Carlos the Jackal," whose real name was Ilich Ramírez Sánchez, in Austria in December 1975. Terrorism experts speculated that terrorist leaders understood that horrific, mass-casualty attacks might cross a threshold of violence. This may explain why few terrorist groups attempted to acquire or use **weapons of mass destruction**, including nuclear, chemical, and biological weapons.

The Iranian "Islamic Revolution" of 1979 was a watershed event in transnational terrorism. Although Israeli interests remained primary targets for attack, due to continued sympathy for the Palestinian cause, a number of groups began to target citizens and symbols of the United States. Certainly the kidnapping of fifty-three US workers in the Teheran embassy spurred this trend by demonstrating the inability of a global superpower to defend its embassy staff. The decade of terrorism (1980–1990) included incidents such as suicide bombings (the US Marine barracks in Beirut, Lebanon, 1983—an attack that killed more than two hundred service personnel) and hijackings (TWA Flight 847, 1985). During this decade three disturbing trends emerged: fewer, but more deadly and indiscriminate, attacks; increasing sophistication of attacks; and a greater willingness to perform suicide attacks.

Marxist-Leninist groups discovered that their sources of support in Western Europe disappeared at the end of the Cold War, in part because of the failure of the ideological preferences of the groups. In addition, national law enforcement and paramilitary forces were increasingly effective in combating terrorism. Other terrorist groups discovered that transnational attacks were counterproductive in achieving local aims. For example, ETA, the Basque ethnic separatist movement in Spain, and the IRA, the predominantly Catholic separatist group seeking independence from the UK, sought negotiations but still used terrorist attacks as a bargaining ploy and to remain visible domestically. Although Marxist-Leninist transnational terrorism was decreasing in scale and intensity, militant Islamic terrorism, symbolized by the group Al Qaeda and enabled by globalization, has become a global phenomenon.

Terrorism: The Impact of Globalization

Al Qaeda, "The Base" or "The Foundation," received global recognition as a result of its attacks conducted in New York and Washington on September 11, 2001. Over the past eight years, since the 2001 attacks, experts have continuously debated what Al Qaeda is, what it represents, and the actual threat that it poses. For example, in early 2006, the Office of the Chairman of the Joint Chiefs of Staff in the Pentagon released the *National Military Strategic Plan for the War on Terrorism*, which sought to characterize the fluid nature of the militant Islamic terrorism:

> There is no monolithic enemy network with a single set of goals and objectives. The nature of the threat is more complicated. In the GWOT [global war on terror], the primary enemy is a transnational movement of extremist organizations, networks, and individuals—and their state and non-state supporters—which have in common that they exploit Islam and use terrorism for ideological ends. The Al Qa'ida Associated Movement (AQAM), comprised of Al Qa'ida and affiliated extremists, is the most dangerous present manifestation of such extremism . . . The [Al Qaeda network's] adaptation or evolution resulted in the creation of an extremist "movement," referred to by intelligence analysts as AQAM, extending extremism and terrorist tactics well beyond the original organization. This adaptation has resulted in decentralizing control in the network and franchising its extremist efforts within the movement. (National Military Strategic Plan for the War on Terrorism [Unclassified], p. 13)

weapons of mass destruction A category defined by the United Nations in 1948 to include "atomic explosive weapons, radioactive material weapons, lethal chemical and biological weapons, and any weapons developed in the future which have characteristics comparable in destructive effects to those of the atomic bomb or other weapons mentioned above."

Al Qaeda Most commonly associated with Osama bin Laden, "The Base" (as it means in Arabic) is a religious-based group whose fighters swear an oath of fealty to bin Laden.

Global Perspective

The Shanghai Cooperation Organization: Fighting Terrorism in the Former Communist Bloc

Although this is often missing from the headlines of North American press reports, terrorism is a threat to countries not directly involved in the former president George Bush's global war on terror. Debates in the United States and Western Europe about the proper methods to stop attacks frequently center on matters of ethics and morality. To put it briefly, what *should* Western-style democracies do to confront terrorist groups, especially those with Islamist links that seek to destroy open societies based on tolerance? *Can* democracy and inclusive institutions survive if Western governments must occasionally bend their own laws to safeguard society?

Such questions of appropriate methods to combat terrorism tend not to restrain the governments of China and the former Soviet republics Russia, Kazakhstan, Kyrgyzstan, Tajikistan, and Uzbekistan, which together created the Shanghai Cooperation Organization (SCO) in June 2001. None of these countries are paragons of democratic virtue. Indeed, according to the annual survey of the human rights organization Freedom House, Kyrgyzstan ranks the highest of the six SCO countries, and it is only partly free.   (http://www.freedomhouse.org/template.cfm?page=363&year=2008)

Government officials in all of the countries regularly suppress and occasionally murder independent journalists who criticize those who hold political power. Opposition political parties find their offices closed, their assets seized, their telephones tapped, their members harassed and arrested. Religious minorities are often jailed if they practice their rituals in public. All of this sounds like the description of terror found at the beginning of this chapter: a state repressing its own subjects or citizens.

Yet from the time of its founding, the SCO called itself an antiterror institution and its greatest threat Islamist radical groups. Certainly, given the role that Taliban fighters played in defeating the Soviet invasion of Afghanistan in the 1980s and the Islamic aspect to the Russian war in Chechnya, it made sense

that Russia would see an Islamic threat. However, media organizations in the United States miss the effect that separatist groups have in Chinese politics: for example, the Muslim Uighurs who live in the Sinkiang region in the West of the country. In Kyrgyzstan, Tajikistan, and Uzbekistan, Islam is the primary religious identification for more than 80 percent of people. (https://www.cia.gov/library/publications/the-world-factbook/index.html) Each member state of the SCO must, therefore, take a different approach to its own Muslim problem. The leaders of the most Islamic states fear that a Taliban style of Sunni Islam might become popular and challenge the legitimacy of the secular governments. Both Russia and China fear that Islamic radicals might push for independence.

Thus, for SCO member states, the greatest threat is not external attack but internal collapse. As a result, terrorism and separatism are linked in the "Shanghai Convention on Combating Terrorism, Separatism, and Extremism," signed in June 2001. The SCO held its first

Leaders of the Shanghai Cooperation Council meet regularly to plan coordinated antiterrorist operations.

joint antiterror war games in August 2003 in Kazakhstan. There was perhaps a message in the choice of host country for the exercise. Kazakhstan's population

Continued

Global Perspective *continued*

is about 30 percent Russian and has, after China and Russia, the fewest number of people who self-identify as Muslims: about 47 percent. Therefore it is a country in which Russians have the most to fear from Islamic radicals, yet at the same time the exercises might offend the least number of Muslims.

Despite the antiterrorist stand of the SCO, the Bush administration was wary of the motives of the group. Some US officials feared that China and Russia might apply pressure to the Central Asian states to get them to force the United States to leave the bases it had in

Kyrgyzstan in support of its war against the Taliban in Afghanistan. Those neoconservatives in the United States who advocated the spread of democracy also expressed concerns that China and Russia might form an alliance similar to the Holy Alliance that Russia, Prussia, and Austria-Hungary created after the Napoleonic wars. That early-1800s alliance was strongly antidemocratic, repressing political and civil liberties. Some analysts believe that by seeking to slow an inevitable process of liberalism, the Holy Alliance brought about the destruction that it wanted to avoid.

Part of the reason for the disagreement of terms stems from the fact that Al Qaeda, as the standard-bearer for militant Islam, has evolved considerably since the US invasion of Afghanistan. Immediately after 9/11, Al Qaeda was depicted as the center of a global nexus of terrorism connected to almost all terrorist groups. More recently, however, Al Qaeda has appeared less as a group and more as a global movement that markets and exploits its own form of militant Islam in a loose network of "franchised" cells and groups. Regardless of how one views Al Qaeda, one cannot dispute the influence of its message across national boundaries. Efforts to explain the vitality of global terrorism in general—and Al Qaeda in particular—focus on three areas linked to aspects of globalization: culture, economics, and religion.

The attacks on September 11, 2001, have not led to improved living conditions for people in the Middle East.

Cultural Explanations

Culture is one way to explain why militant Islam's call for armed struggle has been successful in underdeveloped countries. Culture also explains many of the ethnic conflicts, violence between religious and language groups, across the world. The 1990s were a period of unprecedented ethnic violence and terrorism that included the genocide in Rwanda and the ethnic cleansing in the former Yugoslavia. Many fundamentalist groups believe that violence is the only method to preserve traditions and values against a cultural tsunami of Western products and **materialism**. Once sought after as an entry method to economic prosperity, Western secular, materialist values are increasingly rejected by those seeking to regain or preserve their own unique cultural identity. The phenomenon of rejecting the West is not new; one could argue that it began almost two hundred years ago as the strength of the Ottoman Empire waned. Since then, the social changes associated with globalization and the spread of free market capitalism appear to be overwhelming the identity or values of groups who perceive themselves as the losers in the new international system. In an attempt to

materialism In this context materialism means the spreading of a global consumer culture and popular-culture artifacts like music, books, and movies. Christopher Lasch called this the "ceaseless translation of luxuries into necessities." These elements are seen as undermining traditional cultural values and norms.

identity The understanding of the self in relationship to an "other." Identities are social and thus always formed in relationship to others. Constructivists generally hold that identities shape interests; we cannot know what we want unless we know who we are. But because identities are social and produced through interactions, identities can change.

preserve their threatened identity and values, groups actively distinguish themselves from despised "others." At the local level, this cultural friction may translate into conflicts divided along religious or ethnic lines to safeguard **identity**.

According to one explanation, however, the number of distinct civilizations is limited globally. They include Western, Confucian, Japanese, Islamic, Hindu, Slavic-Orthodox, and Latin American (Huntington 1993, 25). Geography and relative cultural stability limit abrasion between some of the civilizations. Where individuals perceive their own civilization to be weak, insecure, or stagnant, and interaction is high between weak and strong civilizations, conflict may be inevitable. Samuel Huntington suggests that a major fault line exists between the liberal Western civilization and an Islamic one "humiliated and resentful of the West's military presence in the Persian Gulf, the West's overwhelming military dominance, and . . . [unable] to shape their own destiny" (1993, 32).

Critics of Huntington suggest, among other things, that he ascribes a degree of homogeneity within the Islamic world that simply does not exist. Theologically and socially, the Islamic civilization contains a number of deep divisions that impede the cooperation required to challenge the West. The extremely bloody sectarian violence between Sunni and Shia in Iraq, after the US invasion in 2003, is only one example of these very real fissures. Militant Islamic calls to kill noncombatants and fellow Muslims represent another internal fault line. Nonbelievers fall into the categories of infidels (those of different religion) and apostates (those Muslims who do not share their interpretation of the Koran). As a result, Osama bin Laden's unequivocal sanction to now-deceased Abu Musab al-Zarqawi to kill Muslim Shia in Iraq in 2005 calls into question the morality of the means, and therefore the legitimacy of bin Laden and militant Islam as the champions of Muslim values among the wider and moderate Islamic community.

Economic Explanations

imperialism The practice of foreign conquest and rule in the context of global relations of hierarchy and subordination. It can lead to the establishment of an empire.

World Bank Group A collection of five agencies, the first established in 1945, with head offices in Washington, DC. The WBG promotes development in medium- and low-income countries with project loans, structural-adjustment programs, and various advisory services..

Not everyone agrees that defense of cultural identity is the primary motivation for globalized terrorist violence. Others see economic aspects as the crucial motivating factor in the use of violence to effect political change. Although globalization provides access to a world market for goods and services, the net result has also been perceived as a form of Western economic **imperialism**. The United States and the postindustrial states of Western Europe form the global North or economic core that dominates international economic institutions such as the **World Bank**, sets exchange rates, and determines fiscal policies. The actions and policies can be unfavorable to the underdeveloped countries, or global South, that comprise the periphery. Political decisions by the leaders of underdeveloped countries to deregulate or privatize industries to be competitive globally may lead to significant social and economic upheaval. The citizenry may shift loyalties to illegal activities such as terrorism if the state breaks its social contract (Junaid 2005, 143–4).

Wealth is also linked to personal security and violence. With little opportunity to obtain wealth locally, individuals will leave to pursue opportunities in other countries. The result is emigration and/or the rapid growth of burgeoning urban centers that act as regional hubs for the flow of global resources. Movement, however, is no guarantee that individual aspirations will be realized. In cases where they are not, individuals may turn to violence for criminal (i.e., personal gain) or political (i.e., to change the existing political system through insurgency or terrorism) reasons. Paradoxically, rising standards of living and greater access to educational opportuni-

WHAT'S YOUR WORLDVIEW

Poverty may not be a direct cause of terrorist activities, but do you think it contributes to attitudes that make people susceptible to recruitment by radical groups?

ties associated with globalization may lead to increased expectations. If those expectations are unmet, individuals can turn to extreme political views and action against "the system" that denies them the opportunity to realize their ambitions. A prominent study suggests that a sense of alienation and lack of opportunity among some Muslim males is a contributing factor for their decision to turn to violence globally (Sageman 2004, 95–96).

Other views offer a broader explanation. In particular, the writings of revolutionary Frantz Fanon provide insights into the use of political violence to right economic wrongs (Onwudiwe 2001, 52–56). In the 1960s, Fanon suggested that the end of colonialism would not end conflict between the West and the oppressed. This struggle would be replaced by another until the economic and power imbalances were removed (Fanon 1990, 74). Terrorist violence is motivated by inequalities of the global economy. Therefore terrorist attacks against the World Trade Center in 1993 and 2001 were not reactions against the policies of the United States per se, but rather a blow against an icon of global capitalism. Statements by fringe groups, including neo-Nazis, anarchists, and the "New, New Left," are additional evidence that globalization might be a stimulus for political violence (Rabasa, Chalk, et al. 2006, 86–93).

The explanation that recent terrorist violence is a reaction to economic globalization may be flawed for a number of reasons. These reasons include the personal wealth and social upbringing of a number of members of global terrorist groups, as well as trends in regional patterns of terrorist recruitment. Many former leaders and members of transnational terrorist groups, including the German Red Army Faction and the Italian Red Brigades, came from respectable middle- and upper-class families. The same holds true for a number of modern-day antiglobalization anarchists. Within militant Islamic groups, most of their leaders and senior operatives attended graduate schools around the globe in fields as diverse as engineering and theology and were neither poor nor downtrodden (Sageman 2004, 73–74). And, like the Bolshevik leaders, bin Laden and others have been able to convince less fortunate people to die for the cause.

The links between terrorism and poverty also vary considerably between regions. Many militant Islamic terrorists in Europe have employment rates and salaries that are close to EU averages for their age group (Bakker 2006, 41, 52). One might expect that the poorest region globally would account for a high percentage of terrorists, but this is not the case. Despite conditions that favor the outbreak of terrorist violence in sub-Saharan Africa against economic imperialism and global capitalism, the region has not proved a breeding ground for terrorism.

Religion and "New" Terrorism

In the decade prior to 9/11, a number of scholars and experts perceived that fundamental changes were taking place in the character of terrorism. The use of violence for political purposes, to change state ideology or the representation of ethnic minority groups, had failed in its purpose and a new trend was emerging. **Postmodern** or **"new" terrorism** was conducted for different reasons altogether and seemed to be driven by the power of ideas of the kind that constructivist international relations theory describes (see Chapter 4). Motivated by promises of rewards in the afterlife, some terrorists are driven by religious reasons to kill as many of the nonbelievers and unfaithful as possible (Laqueur 1996, 32–33). Although suicide tactics had been observed in Lebanon as early as 1983, militant Islam had previously been viewed as a state-sponsored, regional phenomenon (Wright 1986, 19–21).

Postmodern or **new terrorists**
Groups and individuals subscribing to millennial and apocalyptic ideologies and system-level goals. Most value destruction for its own sake, unlike most terrorists in the past, who had specific goals, usually tied to a territory.

People in the United States and Western Europe often do not understand the appeal of groups like Hamas and Hezbollah. Do you have a cause that you would be willing to die for?

jihad In Arabic, *jihad* simply means "struggle." Jihad can refer to a purely internal struggle to be a better Muslim or a struggle to make society more closely align with the teachings of the Koran.

New terrorism, which some authors use to explain the global jihad, is seen as a reaction to the perceived oppression of Muslims worldwide and the spiritual bankruptcy of the West. As globalization spreads and societies become increasingly interconnected, Muslims have a choice: accept Western beliefs to better integrate, or preserve their spiritual purity by rebelling. Believers in the global **jihad** view the rulers of countries such as Pakistan, Saudi Arabia, or Iraq as apostates who have compromised their values in the pursuit and maintenance of secular, state-based power. The only possible response is to fight against such influences through jihad. Jihad is understood by most Islamic scholars and imams to mean the internal struggle for purity spiritually, although it has also been interpreted historically as a method to establish the basis for just war. Extremists who espouse militant Islam, including Osama bin Laden and his intellectual associate, Ayman al-Zawahiri, understand jihad in a different way. For the jihadi terrorist, there can be no compromise with either infidels or apostates.

The difference in value structures between secular and religious terrorists makes the responses to the latter difficult. Religious terrorists will kill themselves and others because they believe that they will receive rewards in the afterlife. Differences in value structures make the deterrence of religious terrorism difficult, if not impossible, as secular states cannot credibly threaten materially the ideas that terrorists value spiritually. Secular terrorism has had as its goal the pursuit of power in order to correct flaws within society but retain the overarching system. Religious terrorism, by contrast, does not seek to modify but rather to replace the normative structure of society (Cronin 2002/3, 41).

The use of religion, as a reaction to and an explanation for the phenomenon of global terrorism, contains some of the same incongruities as those focused on cultural and economic aspects. For Western observers, religious reasons appear to explain how individual terrorists are convinced to take their own lives and kill others. Personal motivations can include promises of financial rewards for family members, gaining fame within a community, taking revenge for some grievance, or simply achieving a form of self-actualization. Yet few religious terrorist leaders, planners, and coordinators martyr themselves. Religion provides terrorist groups with a crucial advantage: the mandate and sanction of the divine to commit otherwise illegal or immoral acts. There is a substantial difference between religious motivation as the single driving factor for individuals to commit acts of terrorism and the ultimate purpose for which violence is being used. Scholars disagree on the ultimate political purpose of religiously inspired suicide violence. Such purposes can include competing with other terrorist groups for popular support, in a process of "outbidding" (Bloom 2005, 77–79), or convincing foreign occupiers to withdraw their forces, for the sake of self-determination (Pape 2005, 45–46). A common theme among jihadi statements is another political purpose: overthrowing apostate regimes and assuming political power. Political power is necessary to impose the militant Islamic form of **Sharia law** within a state and restore the just and pure society of the caliphate.

Sharia law Traditional Islamic law of the Koran ("al Qur'an") and the "Sunna," which are the interpretations of the life of the Prophet Muhammad.

Globalization, Technology, and Terrorism

Few challenge the point that terrorism has become much more pervasive worldwide due to the processes and technologies of globalization. The technological advances associated with globalization have improved the capabilities of terrorist groups to plan and conduct operations with far more devastation and coordination than their predecessors could have imagined. In particular, technologies have improved the capability of groups and cells in the following areas: proselytizing, coordination, security, mobility, and lethality.

Proselytizing

Terrorist groups have traditionally sought sympathy and support within national boundaries or in neighboring countries as a means to sustain their efforts. Sustaining terrorist causes has traditionally been more difficult, as terrorist messages, goals, and grievances tend to be extreme, and therefore less appealing, than those of insurgents. For example, land reform, government corruption, or foreign occupation motivates larger numbers of individuals to support or join insurgencies, whereas the radical political ideology espoused by groups, such as the Japanese Red Army, has less appeal in largely prosperous and stable democratic societies. States traditionally have had an advantage in their ability to control information flows and use their resources to win the battle of hearts and minds against terrorist groups. Terrorist leaders understand how the Internet has changed this dynamic: "We [know that we] are in a battle, and that more than half of this battle is taking place in the battlefield of the media. And that we are in a media battle in a race for the hearts and minds of our Umma" (Office of the Director of National Intelligence 2005, 10).

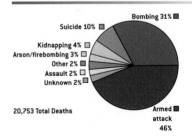

Terrorist Methods Used Worldwide. This data (from 2006) captures a snapshot of the major methods used by terrorists in fatal incidents. Based on what you have read in this chapter, is there anything in this graph that surprises you? Why or why not? *Source: U.S. National Counter-Terrorism Center (NCTC 2007).*

The continued expansion of the number of Internet service providers, especially in states with relaxed or ambivalent content policies or laws, combined with capable and cheap computers, software, peripherals, and wireless technologies, has empowered individuals and groups to post tracts on or send messages throughout the World Wide Web. One form of empowerment is the virtual presence that individuals have. Although prominent jihadi terrorists' physical presence can be removed through imprisonment or death, their virtual presence and influence is immortalized on the World Wide Web, as the case of Mustafa Setmariam Nasar suggests (see Case Study).

Another form of empowerment, brought on by globalization, for terrorist groups is the volume, range, and sophistication of propaganda materials. Terrorist groups were once limited to mimeographed manifestos and typed communiqués. Terrorist supporters and sympathizers now build their own websites. An early example was a website sympathetic to the Peruvian Tupac Amaru Revolutionary Movement. This website posted the group's communiqués and

Theory in Practice

The Realist-Theory Perspective and the War on Terror

Debates about political theories have had an important role in government debates about how secular Western democracies can best fight terrorism. The realist tradition asserts that countries are the most important, sometimes the only, actors that matter in international politics. Many political scientists in the realist tradition also maintain that questions of morality should not restrain the actions of a country that is under threat of an attack. These components of realism can explain why the Bush administration was seemingly surprised by the September 11, 2001, attacks and why the government reacted the way it did to those events. For example, on August 6, 2001, National Security Advisor Rice gave President Bush a briefing that included a memo titled "Bin Laden Determined to Strike in US" that documented plans of the Al Qaeda organization (*The 9/11 Commission Report*, NY: Norton; p. 261). This was the most recent of a series of warnings about possible terrorist attacks on the United States or on American interests around the world. Realist theory helps us to understand why the Bush administration did not act aggressively on these reports: the theory asserts that *states* are the primary threat to other *states*. Despite the previous successful Al Qaeda attacks on the US embassies in Kenya and Tanzania, and the near sinking of the destroyer USS *Cole*, members of the Bush administration might have believed that a small nonstate group was not able to

launch another attack. In addition, the Bush administration was preoccupied with North Korea's nuclear weapons program and an incident in which a Chinese fighter aircraft had damaged a US Navy maritime surveillance aircraft, forcing it to land in China. Logically for President Bush and his advisors, North Korea and China presented a more pressing threat to the United States.

Realist international relations theory also provides an explanation for the Bush administration's actions after September 11, 2001. If, as the memo said, bin Laden was determined to attack the United States, President Bush was equally determined that it would not happen again. Therefore, the United States soon attacked Afghanistan, seeking to depose the Taliban government that had offered sanctu-

ary to bin Laden and other members of the Al Qaeda leadership. More telling, however, was the Bush administration's decision to label as "unlawful combatants" anyone that US military personnel captured and detain them at the US Navy base at Guantanamo, Cuba, or in secret prisons around the world. The increasingly unpopular practice of "extraordinary rendition" was another component of the policy. Extraordinary rendition was the capture and transfer of suspected terrorists to unspecified foreign sites for purposes of detention and often torture. While some nongovernmental human rights organizations called the actions violations of international law, the Bush administration, echoing a key aspect of the realist perspective, called the decisions morally necessary to protect the United States.

The need to respond to the September 11, 2001, attacks caused a fundamental shift in power relationships within the US government and in US diplomatic relations. How should democracies combat terrorist threats?

videos during the seizure of the Japanese embassy in Lima in 1996. Webmasters sympathetic to terrorist groups also control the content and connotation of the material posted on their websites. The website of the Sri Lankan group Liberation Tigers of Tamil Eelam, for example, posts items that cast the group as an internationally accepted organization committed to conflict resolution. Messages, files, and polemics can be dispatched to almost anywhere on the globe via the Internet or text messaging, almost instantaneously.

For the purposes of spreading messages to the widest possible audience for those without Internet or text-messaging capabilities, and where speed of communication is not a requirement or a possibility for security reasons, terrorists need not rely exclusively on virtual methods. Any computer of modest capabilities can be used by members of terrorist groups and their sympathizers to create propaganda leaflets and posters at very low cost in large quantities. Whereas offset-printing machines and photocopiers are difficult to move, a laptop computer and printer can be packed in a suitcase, increasing the mobility of the terrorist cell generating the material and making the cell more difficult to locate.

Terrorist groups in Chechnya and the Middle East have also made increasing use of video cameras to record the preparations for attacks and their results, including successful roadside bombings and the downing of helicopters. With the right software and a little knowledge, individuals or small groups can download or obtain digital footage and music and produce videos that appeal to specific groups. Video footage is useful in inspiring potential recruits and seeking donations by support elements within the organization. For example, terrorist recruiters distributed videos of sniper and other attacks against coalition forces in Iraq, produced by the Al Qaeda media-production group As-Sahab. The competition between global news outlets like CNN, MSNBC, and Al Jazeera ensures that the images of successful and/or dramatic attacks reach the widest audience possible.

Coordination

During the era of transnational terrorism, groups planned and conducted individual attacks or mounted multiple attacks from a single staging base. The technologies associated with globalization have enabled terrorist cells and groups to mount coordinated attacks in different countries. Indeed, a hallmark of militant Islamic groups is their ability to conduct multiple attacks in different locations. The simultaneous bombings of the US embassies in Kenya and Tanzania in 1998 are one example. Other examples include the synchronized detonation of ten of thirteen bombs on packed commuter trains in Madrid in March 2004 and three of the four July 2005 London Underground bombings.

The technologies associated with globalization, including commercially available handheld radios and phones, have allowed terrorist cell members and groups to operate independently at substantial distances from one another and network together. The Global System for Mobile Communications (GSM) standard, for example, ensures that any compliant phone will work anywhere in the world where a GSM network has been established. E-mail and cell phone contact among geographically separated group members allows them to conduct their attacks in separate locations or converge on a specific target area. For example, the 9/11 hijackers utilized cheap and readily available prepaid phone cards to communicate between cell leaders and senior leadership and, according to at least one press account, to coordinate final attack authorization prior to the jets taking off from different locations.

Terrorist groups under pressure from aggressive countermeasures have utilized technologies and other innovations to maintain their activities tactically and strategically. On a tactical level, bomb manufacturers for the IRA and Al Qaeda have demonstrated the ability

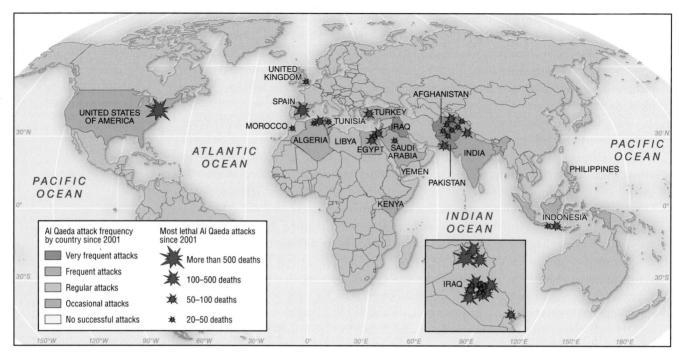

Map 9.1 Global Reach of Al Qaeda.
Can a nation-state respond to networks like this without global cooperation?

to respond rapidly to electronic countermeasures. At the strategic level, Al Qaeda has continued to evolve despite losing its sanctuary and training camps in Afghanistan since December 2001. Instead of a hierarchical organization with fixed training bases, what has developed is a virtual global militant Islamic "community of practice" characterized by individuals exchanging information and discussing the best ways to coordinate and conduct attacks. Some Western analysts have labeled the current decentralized version of global terrorism "Al Qaeda 2.0." Cells form around individuals sympathetic to militant Islamic goals accessible via webcast or online jihadi discussion forums. At present, law enforcement officials believe that there are more than five thousand active militant Islamic discussion sites along the lines of the now defunct Muntada al-Ansar al-Islami. Such diffuse violence can be thought of as a cruel variation on the environmentalist motto "Think globally, act locally," a motto that reinforces the perception of militant Islam's global depth, power, and reach.

Security

Terrorist cells without adequate security precautions are vulnerable to discovery and detection. Translations of captured Al Qaeda manuals, for example, demonstrate the high value their writers place on security, including surveillance and countersurveillance techniques. The technological enablers of globalization assist terrorist cells and leaders in preserving security in a number of ways, including distributing elements in a coordinated network, remaining mobile, and utilizing clandestine or encrypted communications.

The security of terrorist organizations has historically been preserved by limiting communication and information exchanges between cells. This ensures that if one cell is compromised, its members only know each other's identities and not those of other cells. Thus the damage done to the organization is minimized. Security is even more important to **clandestine** or **"sleeper" cells** operating on their own without central direction. The use of specific codes and ciphers, known only to a few individuals, is one way of preserving the security of an organization. Although code and ciphers inevitably have been broken and information obtained through interrogation, such activities take time. During that time, terrorist groups adjust their location and operating methods in an attempt to stay ahead of counterterrorist forces. Technological advancements, including faster processing speeds and software developments, now mean that those sympathetic to terrorist causes can contribute virtually through servers located hundreds or thousands of miles away.

> **clandestine** or **"sleeper" cell**
> Usually a group of people, sent by an intelligence organization or terrorist network, that remains dormant in a target country until activated by a message to carry out a mission, which could include prearranged attacks.

Terrorist groups have been able to leverage technological developments designed to shield a user's identity from unauthorized commercial or private exploitation (Gunaratna 2002, 35). Concerns about infringements on civil liberties and privacy during the early years of the Internet led to the development of 64- and 128-bit encryption freeware that is extremely costly and time-consuming to crack. In addition, access to hardware such as cell phones, personal data assistants, and computers can be restricted via the use of passwords. The use of Internet Protocol–address generators, anonymity-protection programs, and rerouted communications, as well as private chat rooms where password-protected or encrypted files can be shared, also provide a degree of security. In virtual jihadist discussion groups, youth sympathetic to the militant Islamic cause post information on circumventing electronic surveillance. They advise awareness of phishing and mobile-phone monitoring techniques and suggest using electronic "dead letters"—draft messages saved in shared third-party e-mail accounts, such as Hotmail—so that nothing is actually sent that could be intercepted.

Mobility

The reduced size and increased capabilities of personal electronics also give terrorists mobility advantages. Mobility has always been a crucial consideration for terrorists and insurgents alike, given the superior resources that states have been able to bring to bear against them. In open societies that have well-developed infrastructures, terrorists have been able to move rapidly within and between borders, and this complicates efforts to track them, as they exploit the very societal values they seek to destroy.

The globalization of commerce has also improved terrorist mobility. The volume of air travel and goods that pass through ports has increased exponentially through globalization. Between states, measures have been taken to ease the flow of goods, services, and ideas to improve efficiency and reduce costs. One example is the European Schengen Agreement, in which border security measures between EU member states have been relaxed to speed deliveries. Market demands for efficiencies of supply, manufacture, delivery, and cost have complicated states' efforts to prevent members of terrorist groups from exploiting gaps in security measures. Additional mobility also allows terrorist groups to transfer expertise, as demonstrated by the arrest of three members of the IRA suspected of training counterparts in the Fuerzas Armadas Revolucionarias de Colombia (FARC) in Bogota in August 2001.

The use of air travel by terrorists prior to 9/11 has been well documented. Mohamed Atta, for example, traveled extensively between Egypt, Germany, and the Middle East before the attacks. In this respect, the latest generation of terrorists resemble their transnational

What methods can democracies use to deter groups like Aum Shinrikyo ("Supreme Truth"), whose leader Shoko Asahara (shown here under arrest in Japan in 1995) believes that the end of the world is near and that death is preferable to life?

predecessors in exploiting travel methods for attacks. Terrorist use of transportation is not necessarily overt, as the volume of goods transported in support of a globalized economy is staggering and difficult to monitor effectively. For example, customs officials cannot inspect all of the vehicles or containers passing through border points or ports. To illustrate the scale of the problem, the United States receives 10 million containers per year, and one port, Los Angeles, processes the equivalent of twelve thousand twenty-foot containers daily. Western government officials fear that terrorist groups will use containers as a convenient and cheap means to ship weapons of mass destruction. Incidents in Italy in 2001 and Israel in 2004 confirm that terrorist groups are aware of the convenience and cheapness of globalized shipping to improve their mobility.

Lethality

Globalization has undoubtedly had a troubling influence on terrorism, but the one element that concerns counterterrorism experts and practitioners the most is future catastrophic attacks using weapons of mass destruction. Since the end of the Cold War, some terrorist leaders have expressed both the desire and the will to use weapons of mass destruction. In 1995 Aum Shinrikyo, a Japanese group, released the nerve agent sarin in the Tokyo subway system, killing six people and wounding more than three thousand. Evidence that US troops recovered in Afghanistan in 2001 outlined plans by Al Qaeda to produce and test biological and chemical weapons. In addition, a raid on a suspected Al Qaeda flat in London in 2004 revealed quantities of ricin, a toxin. Militant Islamic statements have mentioned, and one fatwa supports, the use of any means, including weapons of mass destruction, to kill as many infidels and apostates as possible. Globalized media, ironically, may have played a role in shaping terrorist plans. Al Qaeda leaders are alleged to have conjured up mass-casualty attacks as a result of spectacular special effects contained in Hollywood blockbuster movies.

In the absence of weapons of mass destruction, globalization has facilitated access to weapons, resources, and proficiency required to conduct smaller but more lethal attacks. Terrorist groups from Chechnya to Sri Lanka have shared their expertise in the manufacturing of lethal bombs triggered by increasingly sophisticated and globally available remote control devices. Within Iraq, since 2003, terrorist groups have been able to obtain the knowledge and resources required to build sophisticated **improvised explosive devices (IEDs)**. Such IEDs range in scale and complexity. The United States, for example, claims that Iran supports terrorist violence in Iraq through the supply of specific IED technology. State sponsorship, however, may no longer be necessary in a globalized world. Digital videos suggest that terrorists are already conducting distance learning through a **virtual jihad academy** in which prospective terrorists study everything from conducting ambush attacks to making and using IEDs in order to increase their effectiveness and lethality.

Combating Terrorism

States plagued by transnational terrorism responded individually and collectively to combat the phenomenon during the Cold War. These responses ranged in scope and

improvised explosive device (IED) This is usually a homemade device or a crude booby trap, designed to cause death or injury, that can be made of a variety of explosive materials.

virtual jihad academy The use of the Internet to plan, promote, and propagate physical and cyber attacks as well as train and educate future followers or jihadists.

effectiveness and included passing antiterrorism laws, taking preventative security measures at airports, and creating special-operations counterterrorism forces such as the West German Grenzschutzgruppe-9 (GSG-9). Successful rescues in Entebbe (1976), Mogadishu (1977), and Prince's Gate, London (1980), demonstrated that national counterterrorism forces could respond effectively both domestically and abroad. A normative approach to tackling the problem, founded on the principles of international law and collective action, was less successful. Attempts by the United Nations to define and proscribe transnational terrorism bogged down in the General Assembly over semantics (i.e., deciding on the definition of a terrorist), but other cooperative initiatives were successfully implemented. These included the conventions adopted through the International Civil Aviation Organization (ICAO) to improve information sharing, and legal cooperation, such as The Hague Convention for the Suppression of Unlawful Seizure of Aircraft (1970). Another collective response to improve information sharing and collaborative action was the creation of the Public Safety and Terrorism Sub-Directorate within Interpol in 1985. However, most initiatives and responses throughout this decade were unilateral, regional, or ad hoc in nature.

State leaders disagree on how best to deal with the current form of global terrorist violence. Much of the controversy relates to the nature of the threat and what approach should be taken to deal with it. Some national leaders view militant Islam as an intractable problem in which there can be no negotiation. After the 9/11 attacks, the leaders of the United States, Great Britain, and Australia suggested that all states should cooperate in a war on terror to deal with the threat. The stakes in what some have called "the Long War" consist of the preservation of basic freedoms and a way of life. In order to defeat terrorism, individual states have a responsibility to protect civilian populations while dealing with terrorist cells, supporters, and sympathizers within their own borders. Given the global, elusive, and adaptive character of the militant Islamic threat, the best approach for dealing with global terrorism is to pool resources in a coalition of the willing, in which forces from the global North are seeking to improve the capabilities of specific partner states in the global South. The end result will be the development of a global counterterrorism network (GCTN) of states able to detect, track, and eliminate terrorist threats while nonmilitary efforts address the root causes of terrorism.

> ### WHAT'S YOUR WORLDVIEW ❓
>
> *With the aspects of globalization—affordable travel, technology, and the free flow of capital—do you think it is possible to provide complete security and safety for all citizens in a society?*

Other national leaders are less comfortable with the concept of "war" against the tactics of terrorism. In their view, actions by the military can only lead to terrorist reprisals, or worse—the return of terrorism to its original connotation, the sanctioned use of terror by the state to repress its own citizenry. In their eyes, terrorism is a crime that is best dealt with through law enforcement methods. By dealing with terrorism as a police problem, states uphold the rule of law, maintain the high moral ground, preserve democratic principles, and prevent the establishment of martial law. Military force should only be used in extreme circumstances, and even then its use may have negative consequences. Terrorism is best dealt with inside state borders and through cooperative international law enforcement efforts to arrest suspects and provide them with due process. The law enforcement approach to terrorism must balance taking enough measures against terrorist groups without crossing over into the realm of "political justice, where the rules and rights enshrined in the principle of due process are either willfully misinterpreted or completely disregarded" (Chalk 1996, 98). To do little against domestic or global terrorism, in

Three Generations of Militant Islamic Terrorists   CASE STUDY

The first generation of militant Islamic terrorists closely affiliated with Al Qaeda shared a number of common traits. A significant number fought in Afghanistan against the Soviet Union and aligned with Osama bin Laden as a result of an intellectual split that occurred in 1994. Bin Laden believed it was necessary to fight next against the "far" enemy, the United States (and by extension, the West), which was responsible for a number of perceived injustices against Islam. Others continued to advocate the overthrow of "near" enemies who ruled over secular Islamic states. In preparation for the fight against the far enemy, bin Laden moved to Afghanistan in 1998 and established numerous training camps, research facilities, and a support bureaucracy. One of those who migrated to Afghanistan at this time was Mustafa Setmariam Nasar.

Nasar is better known as "Abu Musab al-Suri" or "the Syrian." Though a second-generation jihadist, he shares a number of traits with first-generation jihadists, including experience against the Soviets in Afghanistan and supporting local jihadist groups in Algeria and elsewhere. Prior to 9/11, Nasar was suspected of running training camps in Afghanistan and Pakistan for bin Laden. Like a number of members of this second-generation cohort, Nasar is well educated, and this is apparent in his writings. His works include the 1,600-page tract and

If Osama bin Laden is captured, should he be put on trial? Do you think his capture will end Al Qaeda attacks ?

detailed training manual entitled "Global Islamic Resistance Call." In addition, Nasar videotaped a number of his lectures based on it. US actions succeeded in removing or dispersing first-generation leaders, as well as Nasar himself, who was acting as a second-generation link to future jihadists by transferring his knowledge and skills to them. Both the manual and the videos continue to be circulated online despite Nasar's capture in Pakistan sometime in late 2005/early 2006. He is believed to be in custody in Syria.

Younis Tsouli represents another or third generation of militant Islamic terrorism, with different skills from his predecessors. His identity was unknown to authorities until just before his arrest. The same cannot be said for Tsouli's virtual persona, "*Irhabi 007*" ("Terrorist 007"). Irhabi 007 achieved notoriety in jihadist discussion forums for his technical acumen in hacking websites, circumventing online surveillance techniques, and posting militant Islamic training and propaganda videos. Law enforcement officials suspected that Irhabi 007 was in the United States when he hosted jihadi websites and hid other material on servers based there. Cooperation between British and American officials led to Tsouli's eventual discovery and arrest at a flat in West London in late 2005. His reputation in online jihadist circles was built in just over a year.

the name of upholding the rule of law, risks offering terrorist groups a sanctuary and the security of rights and laws.

The virtual opinion of a number of nongovernmental organizations (NGOs), members of blogs, and webmasters has also been critical of the "war" on terrorism. Those suspicious of the motives of the most recent Bush administration and the political elite of the United States range widely in their opinions. Conspiracy theorists online suggest that the war in Iraq, Afghanistan, and elsewhere is the first stage in the establishment of an Orwellian system that is constantly in conflict with the terrorist "other" to justify continued

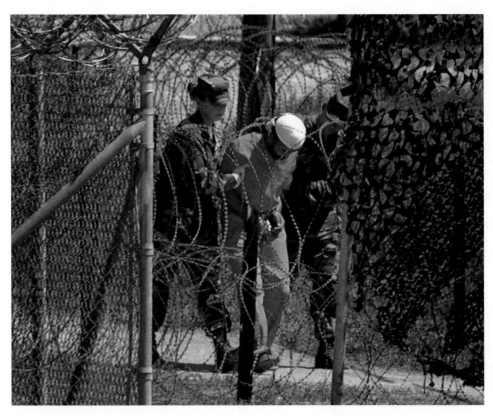

Are the prisoners (one shown here) held at the US Navy base at Guantanamo Bay civilians, unlawful combatants, or prisoners of war? Why is that designation so important? Are US civilian courts the place to conduct their trials?

violation of personal privacy. More objective communities of practice, and NGOs such as Human Rights Watch, routinely provide monitoring and online reporting of suspected government human rights and civil liberties abuses. One example is the persistent attention paid to the status of terrorist detainees held in US custody at Guantanamo Bay.

Although disagreements still exist over how best to deal with terrorism philosophically, pragmatically the largest problems reside in locating terrorists and isolating them from their means of support. Locating and identifying terrorists is a tedious and time-consuming process that requires collecting, assessing, and analyzing information from a range of sources. Information technologies associated with globalization have been useful in this process. Such technologies allow identification of terrorist patterns before and after attacks, with systems capable of performing calculations measured in the trillions per second (floating point operations, or flops). Terrorist finances and organizations are evaluated through link analysis to construct a more comprehensive picture of the way terrorist elements interact. In addition, huge volumes of information can be reduced and exchanged electronically between departments, agencies, and other governments or made available on secure servers whose capacities are measured in terabytes. For example, every day, the National Security Agency collects four times the amount of data in the Library of Congress. Discovering terrorist cells, however, has much to do with luck and pursuing nontechnical leads. State bureaucracies

WHAT'S YOUR WORLDVIEW ?

Providing security is the primary task of all nation-states. Do you think states will willingly share resources and intelligence with other states or international organizations to defeat terrorist networks? What factors work against multilateralism in this area?

Threats of terrorist attacks on airplanes have meant long lines and delays in airports. Are you willing to submit to full-body screening or personal interviews during your security screening if it means enhanced safety?

can impede or negate technical and resource advantages over terrorist groups.

In order to deal with global terrorism, the international community must address its most problematic modern aspects: the appeal of messages that inspire terrorists to commit horrific acts of violence. Killing or capturing individuals does little to halt the spread of extremist viewpoints that occur under the guise of discussion and education. In the case of Islam, for example, radical mullahs and imams twist the tenets of the religion into a doctrine of action and hatred, where spiritual achievement occurs through destruction rather than personal enlightenment. In other words, suicide attacks offer the promise of private goods (spiritual reward) rather than public good (positive contributions to the community over a lifetime). Precisely how the processes and technologies of globalization can assist in delegitimizing the pedagogy that incites terrorists will remain one of the most vexing challenges for the international community for years to come.

Conclusion

Terrorism remains a complex phenomenon in which violence is used to obtain political power to redress grievances that may have become more acute through the process of globalization. Globalization has improved the technical capabilities of terrorists and given them global reach, but it has not altered the fundamental fact that terrorism represents the extreme view of a minority of the global population. In other words, globalization has changed the scope of terrorism but not its nature. The benefits that globalization provides terrorists are neither one-sided nor absolute: the same technologies and processes also enable more effective means of states to combat terrorists. Global terrorists can only succeed through popular uprising or the psychological or physical collapse of their state-based adversary. Neither outcome is likely, given the limitations of terrorist messages and capabilities. Terrorist and counterterrorist campaigns are characterized by prolonged struggle to maintain advantages in legitimacy domestically and internationally. The challenge for the global community will be in utilizing its advantages to win the war of ideas that motivates and sustains those responsible for the current wave of terrorist violence.

Chapter 9 contributors: James D. Kiras and Steven L. Lamy.

REVIEW QUESTIONS

1. Why is linking terrorism with globalization so difficult to do theoretically? What does this difficulty suggest about the limits of political theory?

2. When did terrorism become a truly global phenomenon, and what enabled it to do so?

3. In what ways are the technologies and processes associated with globalization more beneficial to states? To terrorists?

4. Given that terrorism has been both a transnational and a global phenomenon, why has it not been more successful in effecting change?

5. Of all the factors that motivate terrorists, is any one more important than others, and if so, why?

6. What has changed in terrorism over the past half-century, and have any factors remained the same? If so, what are they, and why have they remained constant?

7. What is the role that technology plays in terrorism, and will it change how terrorists operate in the future? If so, how?

8. What are the dilemmas that terrorist groups face with respect to weapons of mass destruction?

9. What is the primary challenge that individual states and the international community as a whole face in confronting terrorism?

10. How can globalization be useful in diminishing the underlying causes of terrorism?

FURTHER READING

Ganor, B. (2005), *The Counter-Terrorism Puzzle: A Guide for Decision Makers* (New Brunswick, NJ: Transaction). Emphasizes the dilemmas and practical difficulties associated with various counterterrorism policy options.

Hoffman, B. (2006), *Inside Terrorism*, rev. and exp. ed. (New York: Columbia University Press). The best single-volume work on the development of terrorism, its evolution over time, and current and future prospects for defeating it.

Juergensmeyer, M. (2000), *Terror in the Mind of God: The Global Rise of Religious Violence* (Berkeley, CA: University of California Press). Highlights similarities between religious leaders across faiths and sects in how they justify killing noncombatants.

Office of the Chairman of the Joint Chiefs of Staff (2006), *National Military Strategic Plan for the War on Terrorism* (Washington, DC: The Pentagon). The unclassified version of this document is available for downloading at www.strategicstudiesinstitute.army.mil/pdffiles/gwot.pdf.

Rabasa, A., Chalk, P., et al. (2006), *Beyond al-Qaeda: Part 1, The Global Jihadist Movement, and Part 2, The Outer Rings of the Terrorist Universe* (Santa Monica, CA: RAND). This two-part report provides a comprehensive survey of current militant Islamic terrorist groups, the impact of Iraq on the global jihad, and the linkages between terrorism and organized crime. Available for downloading at www.rand.org/pubs/monographs/2006/RAND_MG429.pdf (Part 1) and www.rand.org/pubs/monographs/2006/RAND_MG430.pdf (Part 2).

Roy, O. (2004), *Globalized Islam: The Search for a New Ummah* (New York: Columbia University Press). A provocative work that challenges many of the assumptions about militant Islam, as well as explanations for its rise.

Sageman, M. (2004), *Understanding Terror Networks* (Philadelphia, PA: University of Pennsylvania Press). Analyzes Al Qaeda members based on information gathered from open sources and arrives at thought-provoking conclusions about the formation of the militant global jihad network.

Schmid, A. P., Jongman, A. J., et al. (1988), *Political Terrorism: A New Guide to Actors, Authors, Concepts, Data Bases, Theories, and Literature* (New Brunswick, NJ: Transaction Books). A still useful, if at times overwhelming, reference work that highlights the problems associated with defining and studying terrorism.

INTERNET RESOURCES

Special Operations Web site

www.specialoperations.com

Exhaustive collection devoted to all aspects of special operations, including national counter-terrorism units and historical operations.

Terrorism Files

www.terrorismfiles.org

A useful collection of news items, terrorist group overviews, individuals, and incidents.

Terrorism Research Center

www.Terrorism.com

This useful site has an excellent links section, including links to relevant reports and terrorism news.

This is Baader-Meinhof

www.baader-meinhof.com

This site contains information related to transnational terrorism, and in particular, the German Baader-Meinhof group.

US State Department – Patterns of Global Terrorism Annual Report

www.state.gov/s/ct/rls/pgtrpt/

Archived from 1995 onward, these reports contain valuable information and trends analysis on American perceptions of terrorism and the threat it poses.

For more information, quizzes, case studies, and other study tools, please visit us at **www.oup.com/us/lamy**

Human Rights and Human Security

The crime of genocide should be recognized therein as a conspiracy to exterminate national, racial or religious groups. . . The formulation of the crime may be as follows: Whoever, while participating in a conspiracy to destroy religious, national or racial groups undertakes—an attack against life, liberty or property of members of such groups is guilty of the crime of genocide.

—Raphael Lemkin

The punishment of the crime of genocide is a matter of international concern.

—United Nations General Assembly Resolution A/RES/96 (I) 11 December 1946

Human security naturally connects several kinds of freedom—such as freedom from want and freedom from fear, as well as freedom to take action on one's behalf.

—Commission on Human Security

The term **genocide** was created after World War II, as leaders of the antifascist coalition struggled to understand the magnitude of human tragedy before them. Immediately after the war, the victorious powers promised "never again" would countries stand by as tyrants massacred their own people or launched wars of aggression.

And yet, since then, Congo, Cambodia, East Timor, Rwanda, Kosovo, Chechnya, Somalia, and Darfur are but a few of the places where genocidal violence has occurred since 1945, and sadly there are many more. In this chapter we will examine the linked concepts of human rights and human security, both of which emerged from the effects of World War II. We will see that there are many reasons for hope that the world community will be able one day to stop human rights abuses and to provide security to people. Because the successful promotion of both human rights and human security depends on the international community, there may be as many reasons to be pessimistic about the prospects for a better world. After all, protecting the rights of individuals can infringe on the prerogatives of governments

genocide Deliberate and systematic extermination of an ethnic, national, tribal, or religious group.

CHAPTER OUTLINE

FEATURES

"Arbeit macht frei" literally means "work makes you free." This is a modern-day picture of the front gates leading into Auschwitz. In 1945, states pledged that genocide would never occur again. Have the states kept their promise?

and thus on the notion of sovereign equality of countries. However, as we have seen elsewhere in this book, globalization is changing many traditions in world affairs.

This tension between the rights of the *individual* and the rights of *society* is a significant barrier to the creation of human security. As we will see in the first section of this chapter, there were intellectual disagreements in the nineteenth and early twentieth centuries about answers to basic questions: What is a human right? What rights should be protected? And by whom? Must these rights be universal? We are still looking for answers to these questions. How can we discuss such a broad issue as global security on a smaller, human scale—what should it look like, and why is it important? What opportunities still exist for political and military leaders to circumvent, undermine, and exploit international laws?

Introduction

As in other issue areas of international relations, there are disagreements about human rights and human security. And, like the debates in other issue areas, the splits tend to be down the same lines as the international relations theory we discussed in Chapters 3 and 4. However, the fundamental question is a simple one: *Do countries have an obligation to improve the living conditions of people who live in other countries?*

Furthermore, if there is such an obligation, on what legal foundations does this obligation rest? And who would define the terms of human rights? Clearly such rights would rest within a legal system—but whose? And what kind? One source of contemporary disagreement about the obligation to promote human rights and human security is, quite simply, the result of geography. For example, the modern concept of individual human rights developed originally in Europe. Yet, as many European countries colonized other regions of the world (and other parts of Europe, even), these rights were often not extended to other peoples who were seen not as "human." Today, for many people who live in Africa and Asia these human rights may appear to derive from their problematic colonial heritage. Why should it necessarily mean something different to be human in Africa than in Europe?

What Are Human Rights?

The theory of rights developed in Europe during the Middle Ages, and it rested on the idea of **natural law**. Natural law theorists differed on many issues, but the central proposition is clear: There are, indeed, universal moral standards that support individual rights, and there is a general duty to adhere to these standards (Finnis 1980). Most importantly, this position is not limited in application to any particular legal system, community, state, race, religion, or **civilization**. This is the origin of our modern rhetoric concerning *universal* human rights.

Natural law provided the theory, but in the rougher world of medieval political practice, rights had rather different connotations. Here a "right" was a concession one extracted from a nominal superior, probably by force. The Magna Carta (1215) is a case in point. The barons of England obliged King John to grant to them and their heirs in perpetuity a series of liberties that are, for the most part, very specific and related to particular grievances. The Great Charter as a whole was based on the important principle that the subjects of the king owe him duty only if he meets their claims. This is clearly a political bargain or contract.

natural law The idea that humans have an essential nature, which dictates that certain kinds of human goods are always and everywhere desired; because of this, there are common moral standards that govern all human relations, and these common standards can be discerned by the application of reason to human affairs.

civilization The broadest construction of cultural identity to which individuals may subscribe. A number of broad cultures have emerged from world history, including the Western, Islamic, and Chinese civilizations.

There is no necessary incompatibility between the rights established by political bargaining between monarch and subjects and the rights entailed by natural law, but it should not be forgotten that these two sources of the notion of rights are actually based not on different but on *opposed* principles. Whereas rights based on natural law are derived from reason and the notion of human flourishing and are universal in time and space, **charter rights** simply describe in legal terms the result of a political bargain or contract and, by definition, are limited to the parties to the bargain, and thus restricted in time and space.

The complex language of medieval thinking on rights carried over into the modern period. Political philosophers such as Hugo Grotius, Thomas Hobbes, and John Locke continued to use notions of natural law, albeit in radically different ways from their predecessors. Political activists such as the Parliamentarians in the English Civil War drew on the rights and privileges they believed to have been granted to their forebears to sustain their notion of themselves as freeborn Englishmen. Gradually, a synthesis emerged that can be termed the **Liberal Account of Rights**. This position is made up of two basic components:

1. Human beings possess rights to life, liberty, the secure possession of property, the exercise of freedom of speech, and so on, which are inalienable—cannot be traded away—and unconditional. The only acceptable reason for constraining any one individual is to protect the rights of another.

2. The primary function of government is to protect these rights. Political institutions are to be judged on their performance of this function, and political obligation rests on their success in this. In short, political life is based on a kind of implicit or explicit contract between people and government.

From a philosophical and conceptual point of view, this position is easy to denigrate as a mishmash of half-digested medieval ideas. As G. W. F. Hegel and many subsequent communitarian thinkers have pointed out, it assumes that individual rights, indeed individuals, predate society—and yet it is difficult to see how one could exist as an individual without being part of a society. For Jeremy Bentham the function of government was to promote the general good (which he called utility), and the idea that individuals might have the right to undermine this seemed to him madness, especially since no one could tell him where these rights came from; the whole idea was "nonsense upon stilts." Karl Marx, on the other hand, and many subsequent radicals, pointed to the way in which the liberal position stresses property rights to the advantage of the rich and powerful. All these points raise compelling questions, but they underestimate the powerful rhetorical appeal of the liberal position. Most people are less likely to be worried about the conceptual inadequacies associated with the liberal position on human rights than they are to be attracted by the obvious benefits of living in a political system based on or influenced by it.

One of the uncertain features of the liberal position is the extent to which the rights it generates are considered to be universal. For example, the French Revolutionary Declaration of the Rights of Man and of the Citizen clearly, by its very title, is intended to be of universal scope, but even here the universalism of Article 1, "Men are born and remain free and equal in respect of rights," is soon followed by Article 3, "The nation is essentially the source of all sovereignty . . . " When Revolutionary and Napoleonic France moved to bring the Rights of Man to the rest of Europe, the end result looked to most contemporaries remarkably like a French empire. The liberal position, while universal in principle, is particular in application, and state boundaries are more or less taken for granted.

charter rights Civil liberties guaranteed in a written document such as a constitution.

Liberal Account of Rights The belief that humans have inherent rights that the state has a responsibility to protect.

People around the world live with poverty and insecurity. Is this our problem? Should the global community respond?

The humanitarianism and international standard-setting of the nineteenth and twentieth centuries brought these issues to the foreground. The Congress of Vienna of 1815 saw the great powers accept an obligation to end the slave trade, which was finally abolished by the Brussels Convention of 1890, while slavery itself was formally outlawed by the Slavery Convention of 1926. The Hague Conventions of 1907 and the Geneva Conventions of 1926 were designed to introduce humanitarian considerations into the conduct of war. The International Labor Office, formed in 1901, and its successor the International Labor Organization, attempted to set standards in the workplace via measures such as the Convention Concerning Forced or Compulsory Labor of 1930.

In short, for Western European proponents of the doctrine, human rights were initially intended to be protections for individuals against oppressive rulers, whether unelected monarchs or the will of democratic majorities. Eventually, the English and French colonizers of Asia and Africa took that notion of individual rights with them and believed that it could take root in other cultures. Thus our modern notion of human rights is clearly the result of the European historical experience—and over the centuries it has evolved, even as it has been the subject of many disagreements.

WHAT'S YOUR WORLDVIEW

Not all ideas regarding human rights come from Europe. Do some research and find out what ideas about human rights came from non-Western societies.

Human Rights and State Sovereignty

While humanitarian measures taken together do provide an elaborate framework for some kind of global governance, they nevertheless exist within a context in which notions of sovereignty and **nonintervention** are taken for granted and are only to be overridden with great reluctance. For example, abolishing the slave trade, which involves international transactions, was much easier than abolishing slavery, which concerns what states

nonintervention The principle that external powers should not intervene in the domestic affairs of sovereign states.

do to their own people—indeed, pockets of slavery survive to this day in parts of Africa, Asia, and the Middle East.

While sovereignty remains a norm of the system, humanitarian impulses often seem reduced to no more than laudable speech and standard–setting. For example, when nineteenth-century Europeans traveled to China, Japan, and other non-European countries in pursuit of trade, they were reluctant to put themselves (and their property) under the jurisdiction of local legal systems, which often violated what Europeans regarded as basic principles of justice—for example, by allowing the aristocracy and military elite to dispense summary justice. However, a basic principle of international society is the sovereignty of states, which requires respect toward, and noninterference with, the institutions of member states. Where they had the power to do so, Europeans solved this problem by requiring countries to respect European legal conventions (the "standards of civilization") before they were allowed full membership in international society. In the meantime, special courts would be established by and for Europeans and those who dealt with them. These restrictions were bitterly resented as implying inferior status, and removing the "regime of capitulations"—as they were called—was a key nationalist demand everywhere they were set in place.

In nineteenth-century England, Manchester School radical liberals such as John Bright and Richard Cobden were bitterly critical of traditional diplomacy but supported the norm of nonintervention on the grounds that their opponents used moral arguments in support of interventions that were really engaged in for reasons of power politics and general mischief making. This is, of course, a familiar line of argument most likely, in the twenty-first century, to be directed at the American heirs of Britain's position in the world.

Cobden was a consistent anti-interventionist and anti-imperialist—other liberals were more selective. Gladstone's 1870s campaign to throw the Ottoman Empire out of Europe was based on the more common view that different standards applied between "civilized" and "uncivilized" peoples. In Gladstone's view, the Ottoman Empire—although since 1856 a full member of international society—could not claim the rights of a sovereign state because its institutions did not come up to the requisite standards. Indeed, this latter position was briefly established in international law in the notion of **standards of civilization**. Now, in the early twenty-first century, this notion may disturb and unsettle us, yet current conventional wisdom on human rights is based on very similar ideas.

The willingness of liberals to extend their thinking on human rights toward direct intervention was characteristic of the second half of the twentieth century. The horrors of the 1914–1918 war stimulated attempts to create a peace system based on a form of international government, and although the League of Nations of 1919 had no explicit human rights provision, the underlying assumption was that its members would be states governed by the rule of law and respecting individual rights. The Charter of the United Nations of 1945, in the wake of the Second World War, does have some explicit reference to human rights—a tribute to the impact, on the general thought climate, of the horrors of that war and, in particular, of the murder of millions of Jews, Gypsies, and Slavs in the extermination camps of National Socialist Germany. In this context, the need to assert a universal position was deeply felt, and the scene was set for the burst of international human rights legislation of the postwar era.

In 1948, the United Nations General Assembly established a baseline of human rights for its member states to follow. The Universal Declaration of Human Rights set out

Life Expectancy. This chart shows combined data for both women and men. On average, women live longer than men, even in developing countries. Overall, life expectancy is steadily rising worldwide; but how do you explain the dramatic difference between rich and poor nations? Is there a link between guaranteeing human rights and increasing life expectancy? If so, what mitigating factors are there? *Source:* Oxford Essential World Atlas, *4th edition.*

standards of civilization A nineteenth-century, European discourse about which values and norms made a country "civilized," or "barbaric" and "uncivilized." The conclusion was that civilized countries should colonize barbaric regions for the latter's benefit.

thirty basic political, civil, economic, and social rights that sought to define which specific rights all people share as humans. In the words of the Preamble to the Declaration, "the peoples of the United Nations reaffirmed their faith in fundamental human rights, in the dignity and worth of the human person and of the equal rights of men and women. . . " The enumerated entitlements included freedom from torture; freedom of opinion; equal treatment before the law; freedom of movement with a country; right to own property; right to education; and right to work.

There were two shortcomings in the Universal Declaration. First, it was nonbinding on the member states of the United Nations. Countries' leaders could pledge to support the goals of the document but then point to a range of political or economic problems that

> ### WHAT'S YOUR WORLDVIEW ?
>
> *Do you think US constitutional rights should be extended to noncitizen residents? Why or why not?*

stopped them from full implementation. Article 29 suggested the rationale: "Everyone has duties to the community in which alone the free and full development of his personality is possible." A second difficulty was the European origins of these rights. As the wave of decolonization swept Asia and Africa, newly independent countries eagerly embraced the tenets of human rights law. Unfortunately, as civil strife threatened to split some of these countries, some leaders blamed the pattern of oppression that the colonizers created, and the provisions of Article 29 were seen as the political justification for postcolonial repression.

Building on the promise of the Universal Declaration, the UN took the lead in creating ten major legally binding international conventions that define rights of specific groups, including women, children, and migrant workers, and to eliminate torture and racial discrimination. These conventions provide the intellectual and legal basis for the concept of human security that we examine in the next section.

What Is Human Security?

human security The security of people, including their physical safety, their economic and social well-being, respect for their dignity, and the protection of their human rights.

Like the doctrines of human rights, the concept of **human security** represents a powerful but controversial attempt by sections of the academic and policy community to redefine and broaden the meaning of security. Traditionally, security meant protection of the sovereignty and territorial integrity of states from external military threats. This was the essence of the concept of national security, which dominated security analysis and policy making during the Cold War period. In the 1970s and 1980s, academic literature on security, responding to the Middle East oil crisis and the growing awareness of worldwide environmental degradation, began to think of security in broader, nonmilitary terms. Yet the state remained the object of security, or the entity to be protected.

The concept of human security challenges the state-centric notion of security by focusing on the individual. Human security is about security for the people, rather than for states or governments. As such, it has generated much debate. Critics wonder whether such an approach would widen the boundaries of security studies too much and whether "securitizing" the individual is the best way to address the challenges facing the international community from the forces of globalization. On the other side, advocates of human security find the concept effectively highlights the dangers to human safety and survival posed by poverty, disease, environmental stress, and human rights abuses, as well as armed conflict. These disagreements notwithstanding, the concept of human security captures a growing realization that, in an era of rapid globalization, security must encompass a broader range of concerns and challenges than simply defending the state from external military attack.

The origin of the concept of human security can be traced to the publication of the *Human Development Report* of 1994, issued by the United Nations Development Programme (UNDP 1994). The report defined the scope of human security to include seven areas:

- **Economic security**—an assured basic income for individuals, usually from productive and remunerative work or, in the last resort, from some publicly financed safety net.
- **Food security**—ensuring that all people at all times have both physical and economic access to basic food.
- **Health security**—guaranteeing a minimum protection from diseases and unhealthy lifestyles.
- **Environmental security**—protecting people from the short- and long-term ravages of nature, man-made threats in nature, and deterioration of the natural environment.
- **Personal security**—protecting people from physical violence, whether from the state or external states, from violent individuals and substate factors, from domestic abuse, or from predatory adults.
- **Community security**—protecting people from the loss of traditional relationships and values and from sectarian and ethnic violence.
- **Political security**—ensuring that people live in a society that honors their basic human rights, and ensuring the freedom of individuals and groups from government attempts to exercise control over ideas and information.

The seven areas appear to describe the basic purpose of every country; and yet, as with other United Nations programs, the *Human Development Report* has had numerous critics. The primary complaint was that the UNDP has issued an unfunded mandate: the report could be used to admonish countries that did not reach the standards, yet the UNDP provided little or no funding to reach them. As you will see in the next section, this tension between standard-setting in human rights and human security and assessing country performance has been a consistent strain since 1945. The leaders of many governments resent what they perceive as interference in the sovereign affairs of their countries.

> **WHAT'S YOUR WORLDVIEW**
>
> *Are the elements of human security rights or privileges? On what evidence and theoretical perspective do you base your argument?*

History of Humanitarian Challenges

The modern concepts of human rights and human security have developed over many years. All the while, there has been a growing awareness on the part of many opinion leaders and politicians in democratic societies that the state must take action in the face of challenges to human lives and dignity. In effect, many politicians have come to believe that the state should do more than defend borders and that cooperative and purposeful international action might be necessary to safeguard people. The post–Second World War humanitarian impulse led to the burst of lawmaking and standard-setting described in the previous section of this chapter. In this section we will examine the next steps in this process.

1948 and the Modern Agenda

Although the 1966 covenants now have the status of international law, and although the European Convention of 1950 has the most effective enforcement machinery, nonetheless, for all its declamatory status and lack of teeth, the Universal Declaration of Human

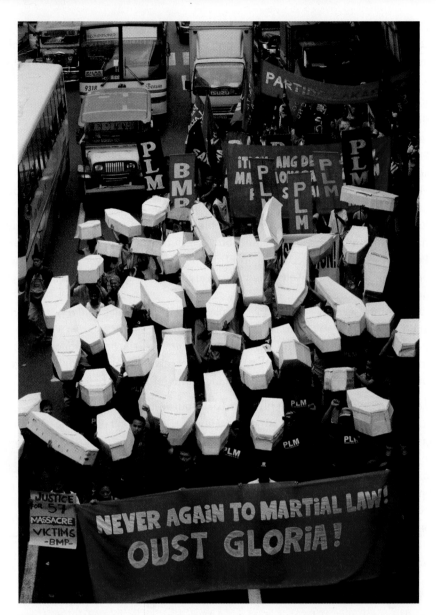

In December 2009, protesters marched demanding the prosecution of a government official implicated in the murders of fifty-seven people. What should states do when a member of the government is involved in human rights violations?

Rights by the UN General Assembly in 1948 is, symbolically, central. This was the first time in history that the international community had attempted to define a comprehensive code for the internal government of its members. During the late 1940s the United Nations was dominated by the West, and the contents of the Declaration represented this fact, with its emphasis on political freedom. The voting was forty-eight for and none against. Eight states abstained, for interestingly different reasons.

South Africa abstained. The white-dominated regime in South Africa denied political rights to the majority of its people and clearly could not accept that "all are born free and

Human Insecurity in Southeast Asia

Whether going by the narrow (freedom from fear) or broad (freedom from want) conception, Southeast Asia faces some of the most critical challenges to human insecurity in the world. The region, comprising Vietnam, Laos, Cambodia, Burma (Myanmar), Indonesia, Malaysia, Thailand, Philippines, Brunei, and Singapore, has witnessed some of the worst violence of the twentieth century. The Khmer Rouge regime in Cambodia killed about 1.7 million (a quarter of the Cambodian population) during its brutal rule between 1975 and 1979 (Yale University Cambodian Genocide Program). In Indonesia, anti-Communist riots in the mid-1960s, which accompanied the transition from President Sukarno to President Suharto, claimed about 400,000 lives (Schwarz 1999, 20). The US war in Vietnam produced 250,000 South Vietnamese, 1.1 million North Vietnamese, and 60,000 American casualties (J. S. Olson 1988). Ethnic and separatist movements in East Timor and Aceh have claimed 200,000 and more than 2,000 lives, respectively (Wessel and Wimhofer 2001). And while there are no proper collated figures for ethnic separatism in Myanmar—usually low-scale, random casualties and conflicts—600,000 internally displaced persons from these conflicts have been recorded (US Department of State 2003).

The region has been free of major conflict since the fighting in Cambodia (1979–1991) ended. But internal conflicts in southern Thailand, southern Philippines, and Myanmar pose a serious challenge to human security. Military rule, which accounted for some of the worst human rights violations in the region, continues in Myanmar, has returned in Thailand, and remains a possibility in Philippines.

Southeast Asia also faces other threats to human security. Absolute poverty levels have declined, but the prevalence of underweight children under five years of age in Southeast Asia is third highest in the world (28 percent), after sub-Saharan Africa (30 percent) and South Asia (47 percent). In Asia, national HIV-infection levels are highest in Southeast Asia. The outbreaks of highly patho-

genic H5N1 avian influenza, which began in Southeast Asia in mid-2003 and have now spread to parts of Europe, are the largest and most severe on record.

Southeast Asia has also experienced a range of transnational threats in recent years. These include the Asian economic crisis of 1997, described by the World Bank as "the biggest setback for poverty reduction in East Asia for several decades" (Ching 1999). Other challenges in-

An AIDS hospice in Thailand was the site of a test of anti-HIV drugs in 2009. Should states make such medicines available at reduced costs to all citizens in the world?

clude the recurring haze problem (1997, 2006) from forest fires in Indonesia, the severe acute respiratory syndrome (SARS) outbreak in 2003, and the Indian Ocean tsunami that devastated coastal areas in Indonesia, Thailand, and other Southeast Asian nations in December 2004 and killed at least 200,000 people in Asia, with Indonesia suffering 128,000 dead and 37,000 missing.

Conceptually, Southeast Asia shows a link between underdevelopment and conflict. Its poorest areas—Indonesia, Cambodia, Myanmar, and the southern regions of Thailand and Philippines—have been especially prone to conflict. Economic development has led to relative stability in Singapore and Malaysia.

Acharya 2007

equal in dignity and rights" (Article 1), claiming it violated the protection of the domestic jurisdiction of states guaranteed by Article 2(7) of the United Nations Charter. This is a clear and uncomplicated case of a first-generation (political) rights issue.

The Soviet Union and five Soviet-bloc countries abstained. Although Stalin's USSR was clearly a tyranny, the Soviet government did not officially object to the political freedoms set forth in the Declaration. Instead, the Soviet objection was to the absence of sufficient attention to social and economic rights by comparison to the detailed elaboration of "bourgeois" freedoms and property rights. The Soviets saw the Declaration as a Cold War document, designed to stigmatize socialist regimes—a not wholly inaccurate description of the motives of its promulgators.

Saudi Arabia abstained. Saudi Arabia was one of the few non-Western members of the United Nations in 1948 and just about the only one whose system of government was not, in principle, based on some Western model. Saudi Arabia objected to the Declaration on religious grounds, specifically objecting to Article 18, which specifies the freedom to change and practice the religion of one's choice. These provisions did not merely contravene specific Saudi laws, which, for example, forbade (and still forbid) the practice of the Christian religion in Saudi Arabia, they contravened the tenets of Islam, which does not recognize a right of apostasy. Here, to complete the picture, we have an assertion of third-generation rights and a denial of the universalism of the Declaration. Thus, the opening moment of the universal human rights regime sees the emergence of the themes that will make up the politics of human rights over the next sixty years.

Unlike many other efforts to redefine security, where political scientists played a major role, human security was the handiwork of a group of development economists, such as the late Pakistani economist Mahbub ul Haq, who conceptualized the UNDP's *Human Development Report*. They were increasingly dissatisfied with the orthodox notion of development, which viewed it as a function of economic growth. Instead, they proposed a concept of **human development** that focuses on building human capabilities to confront and overcome poverty, illiteracy, diseases, discrimination, restrictions on political freedom, and the threat of violent conflict: "Individual freedoms and rights matter a great deal, but people are restricted in what they can do with that freedom if they are poor, ill, illiterate, discriminated against, threatened by violent conflict or denied a political voice . . ." (UNDP 2005, 18–19).

Closely related to the attempt to create a broader paradigm for development was the growing concern about the negative impact of defense spending on development, or the "guns versus butter" dilemma. As a global study headed by Inga Thorsson of Sweden concluded, "the arms race and development are in a competitive relationship" (Roche 1986, 8). Drawing on this study, a UN-sponsored International Conference on the Relationship Between Disarmament and Development, in 1986 in Paris, sought "to enlarge world understanding that human security demands more resources for development and fewer for arms."

The move toward human security was also advanced by the work of several international commissions. They offered a broader view of security that looked beyond the Cold War emphasis on East-West military competition. Foremost among them was the Palme Commission of 1982, which proposed the doctrine of "common security." Its report stressed that "in the Third World countries, as in all our countries, security requires economic progress as well as freedom from military fear" (Palme Commission 1982, xii). In 1987, the report of the World Commission on Environment and Development (also known as the Brundtland Commission) highlighted the linkage between environmental

human development The notion that it is possible to improve the lives of people. Basically, it is about increasing the number of choices people have. These may include living a long and healthy life, access to education, and a better standard of living.

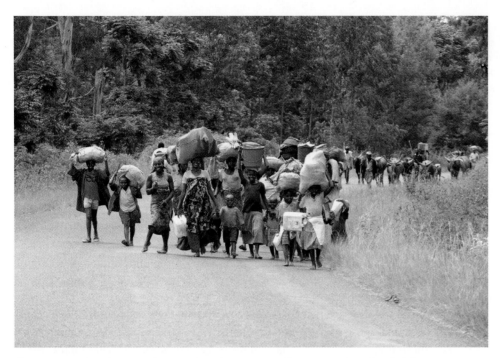

Civil wars, ethnic violence, and international intervention all cause people to flee their homes.

degradation and conflict: "The real sources of insecurity encompass unsustainable development, and its effects can become intertwined with traditional forms of conflict in a manner that can extend and deepen the latter" (Brundtland et al. 1987, 230)

Along with attempts to broaden the notion of security to include nonmilitary threats, there was also a growing emphasis on the individual as the central object of security. The Palme Commission's notion of **common security** became the conceptual basis of the Conference on Security and Cooperation in Europe (CSCE). The CSCE made East-West security cooperation conditional on the improvement of the human rights situation in the former Soviet bloc. The North-South Roundtable on the "Economics of Peace," held in Costa Rica in 1990, called for a shift from "an almost exclusive concern with military security . . . to a broader concern for overall security of individuals from social violence, economic distress and environmental degradation" (Jolly and Ray 2006, 3).

In the post–Cold War era, the importance given to people's security has grown in salience. One reason for this is the rising incidence of civil wars and intrastate conflicts involving huge loss of life, ethnic cleansing, displacement of people within and across borders, and disease outbreaks. Traditional national-security approaches have not been sufficiently sensitive toward conflicts that arise over cultural, ethnic, and religious differences, as happened in Eastern Europe, Africa, and Central Asia in the post–Cold War era (Tow and Trood 2000). Another reason is the spread of democratization and the post–Cold War emphasis on human rights and **humanitarian intervention**. The latter involves the principle that the international community is justified in intervening in the internal affairs of states accused of gross violation of human rights. This has led to the realization that while the concept of national security has not been rendered irrelevant, it no longer sufficiently accounts for the kinds of danger that threaten societies, states, and the international community. The

common security At times called "cooperative security," it stresses noncompetitive approaches and cooperative approaches through which states—both friends and foes—can achieve security. Sometimes expressed as until all people are secure from threats of war, no one is secure.

humanitarian intervention The use of military force by external actors to end a threat to people within a sovereign state.

notion of human security has also been brought front and center by the crises induced by accelerating globalization. For example, the widespread poverty, unemployment, and social dislocation caused by the Asian financial crisis 1997 underscored the vulnerability of people to the effects of economic globalization (Acharya 2004). More recently, during the 2008–2009 global economic recession, international aid agencies saw a sharp decline in donations for countries and individuals, thus undermining their ability to provide basic needs.

The 1990s: A Golden Era of Humanitarian Activism?

It has become common to describe the immediate post–Cold War period as something of a golden era for humanitarian activism. Thomas Weiss (2004, 136) argues that "the notion that human beings matter more than sovereignty radiated brightly, albeit briefly, across the international political horizon of the 1990s." There is no doubt that, during the 1990s, states began to contemplate intervention to protect imperiled strangers in distant lands. This was symbolized for many by NATO's intervention to halt Serb atrocities in Kosovo in March 1999 and the Australian-led intervention to end mass atrocities in East Timor. But the 1990s also saw the world stand aside during the genocides in Rwanda and Srebrenica. To make sense of these developments, let's focus on international interventions in northern Iraq, Somalia, Rwanda, and Kosovo and divide our discussion into three parts: the place of humanitarian impulses in decisions to intervene; the legality and legitimacy of the interventions; and the effectiveness of these military interventions.

In the case of northern Iraq in April 1991, but also Somalia in December 1992, domestic public opinion played an important role in pressuring policy makers into using force for humanitarian purposes. In the face of a massive refugee crisis caused by Saddam Hussein's oppression of the Kurds in the aftermath of the 1991 Gulf War, US, British, French, and Dutch military forces intervened to create protected "safe havens" for the Kurdish people. Similarly, the US military intervention in Somalia in December 1992 was a response to sentiments of compassion on the part of US citizens. However, this sense of solidarity disappeared once the United States began sustaining casualties. The fact that the White House pulled the plug on its Somali intervention after the loss of eighteen US Rangers in a firefight in October 1993 indicates how capricious public opinion is. Television pictures of starving and dying Somalis had persuaded the outgoing Bush administration to launch a humanitarian rescue mission, but once the US public saw dead Americans dragged through the streets of Mogadishu, the Clinton administration announced a timetable for withdrawal. What this case demonstrates is that the "CNN effect" is a double–edged sword: it can pressure governments into humanitarian intervention yet with equal speed produce public disillusionment and calls for withdrawal. However, these cases suggest that even if there are no vital national interests at stake, liberal states might launch humanitarian rescue missions if sufficient public pressure is mobilized. Certainly, there is no evidence in either of these cases to support the realist claim that states cloak power-political motives behind the guise of humanitarianism.

By contrast, the French intervention in Rwanda in July 1994 seems to be an example of abuse. The French government emphasized the strictly humanitarian character of the operation, but this interpretation lacks credibility given the evidence that it was covertly pursuing national self-interest. France had propped up the one-party Hutu state for twenty years, even providing troops when the Rwandan Patriotic Front (RPF), con-

Global Perspective

Asian Values

That Western states, intergovernmental organizations, and NGOs have sometimes taken it upon themselves to promote human rights has always been resented as hypocritical in the non-Western world, where the imperialist record of the West over the last four centuries has not been forgotten. In the 1990s, this resentment led a number of the leaders of the quasi-authoritarian newly industrializing nations of Southeast Asia to assert the existence of Asian values that could be counterposed to the (allegedly) Western values associated with the international human rights regime—in this they seemed to confirm the forthcoming "Clash of Civilizations" forecast by Huntington (1996). Such thinking was partially reflected in the Bangkok Declaration of 1993, made by Asian ministers in the run-up to the Vienna Conference of that year (for texts see Tang 1994). Western notions of human rights were seen as excessively individualistic, as opposed to Asian societies' stress on the family, and insufficiently supportive of (if not downright hostile to) religion. Further, some regarded the West as morally decadent because of the growth of gay rights and the relative success of the women's movement in combating gender discrimination. Some have argued that such positions are simply intended to legitimate authoritarian rule, although it should be noted that "Asian values" can only perform this task if the argument strikes a chord with ordinary people. More to the point, it may be doubted whether the conservative positions expressed

by proponents of Asian values are in any genuine sense "Asian"; many Western conservatives and fundamentalists share their critique of the West, while progressive Asian human rights activists are critical. Notions such as "the West" or "Asia" are unacceptably "essentialist"—all cultures and civilizations contain different and often conflicting tendencies; the world of Islam, or of "Confu-

Human rights activist Ka Hsaw Wa (left), an ethnic Karen from Burma, has led the struggle for minority national rights and environmentalism within that country.

cian capitalism," is no more monolithic than is Christianity or Western secularism. The Asian-values argument petered out at the end of the 1990s, but the problems it illustrated remain.

sisting largely of members of the rival Tutsi population and operating out of neighboring Uganda, threatened to overrun the country in 1990 and 1993. The French president, François Mitterrand, was reportedly anxious to restore waning French influence in Africa and was fearful that an RPF victory in French-speaking Rwanda would bring the country under the influence of Anglophones. France therefore did not intervene until the latter stages of the genocide against the Tutsis, which was ended primarily by the RPF's military victory. It seems, therefore, that French behavior accords with the realist premise that states will only risk their soldiers in defense of the national interest. French leaders may have been partly motivated by humanitarian sentiments, but this seems to be a case of a state abusing the concept of humanitarian intervention, since the primary purpose of the intervention was to protect French national interests.

The moral question raised by French intervention is why international society failed to intervene when the genocide began in early April 1994. French intervention may have saved some lives, but it came far too late to halt the genocide. Some 800,000 people were killed in a mere hundred days. The failure of international society to stop the genocide indicates that state leaders remain gripped by the mind-set of statism. There was no intervention for the simple reason that those with the military capability to stop the genocide were unwilling to sacrifice troops and treasure to protect Rwandans. International solidarity in the face of genocide was limited to moral outrage and the provision of humanitarian aid.

If the French intervention in Rwanda can be criticized for being too little, too late, NATO's intervention in Kosovo in 1999 was criticized for being too much, too soon. At the beginning of the war, NATO said it was intervening to prevent a humanitarian catastrophe. To do this, NATO aircraft were given two objectives: reduce Serbia's military capacity and coerce Milosevic into accepting the Rambouillet settlement, with the emphasis initially placed on the former. Three arguments were adduced to support NATO's claim that the resort to force was justifiable. First, it was argued that Serbian actions in Kosovo had created a humanitarian emergency and breached a whole range of international legal commitments. Second, NATO governments argued that the Serbs were committing crimes against humanity, possibly including genocide. Third, it was contended that the Milosevic regime's use of force against the Kosovar Albanians challenged global norms of common humanity.

Closer analysis of the justifications articulated by Western leaders suggests that while humanitarianism may have provided the primary impulse for action, it was by no means

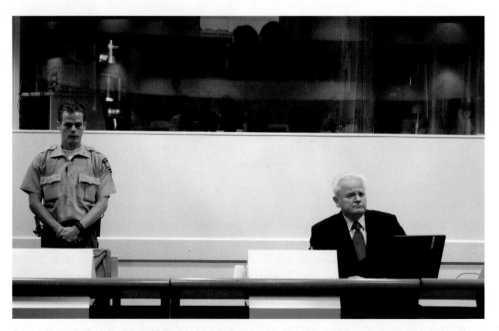

Former Yugoslavian president Slobodan Milosevic in the dock at his trial for crimes against humanity during the war against Bosnia. Prior to his 2006 death while in detention, Milosevic argued his innocence and that the international court had no jurisdiction over an internal matter. However, the International Criminal Court has jurisdiction over crimes against humanity and ethnic cleansing.

the exclusive impulse, and the complexity of the motives of the interveners colored the character of the intervention. Indeed, NATO was propelled into action by a mixture of humanitarian concern and self-interest gathered around three sets of issues. The first might be called the "Srebrenica syndrome"—a fear that, left unchecked, Milosevic's henchmen would replicate the carnage of Bosnia. The second is related directly to self-interest and was a concern that protracted conflict in the southern Balkans would create a massive refugee crisis in Europe. Finally, NATO governments were worried that if they failed to contain the crisis, it would spread and engulf several neighboring states, especially Macedonia, Albania, and Bulgaria (Bellamy 2002, 3). This suggests that humanitarian intervention might be prompted by mixed motives. This only becomes a problem if the nonhumanitarian motives undermine the chances of achieving the humanitarian purposes.

WHAT'S YOUR WORLDVIEW

Genocide continues and states have often not responded, despite the fact that many states have signed international agreements requiring it. Why do you think states have failed to act effectively?

Universalism Challenged

Paradoxically, the success of the global human rights regime caused a growing backlash to the development of international norms of behavior. If taken seriously and at face value, human rights laws after 1945 would create a situation where all states would be obliged to conform to a quite rigid template that dictated most aspects of their political, social, and economic structures and policies. And so, from 1945 opponents of both the human rights and the human-security regimes objected that the norms were an unwarranted intrusion in the affairs of sovereign states and that these norms also sought to overturn existing assumptions about the role of the state and its jurisdiction.

Conventional defenders of human rights argue that universalism would be a good thing—the spread of best practice in human rights matters is in the interest of all people. Others disagree. Does post-1945 law actually constitute best practice? The feminist critique of universal human rights is particularly appropriate here. The universal documents all, in varying degrees, privilege a patriarchal view of the family as the basic unit of society. Even such documents as the Convention on the Elimination of All Forms of Discrimination Against Women (CEDAW) of 1979 do no more than extend to women the standard liberal package of rights, and modern feminists debate whether this constitutes a genuine advance (Peters and Wolper 1995).

More fundamentally, is the very idea of "best practice" sound? We have already met one objection to the idea in the Saudi abstention of 1948. The argument is simple: universalism is destructive not just to undesirable differences between societies but to desirable and desired differences. The human rights movement stresses the *common* humanity of the peoples of the world, but for many, the things that distinguish us from one another are as important as the things that unify us. For example, the Declaration of Principles of Indigenous Rights adopted in Panama in 1984 by a nongovernmental group, the World Council of Indigenous Peoples, lays out positions that are designed to preserve the traditions, customs, institutions, and practices of indigenous peoples (many of which, it need hardly be said, contradict contemporary liberal norms). As with feminist critiques, the argument here is that the present international human rights regime rests too heavily on the experiences of one part of humanity, in this case Western Europe, Canada, and the United States—of course, in practice, the cultural critique and the feminist critique may lead in different directions.

This philosophical point took on a political form in the 1990s. In the immediate post–Cold War world, and especially after the election of US president Bill Clinton in

1992, there was some talk of the United States adopting active policies of democracy promotion, and a number of East Asian governments and intellectuals asserted in response the notion that there were specifically "Asian values" that required defending from this development. The argument was that human rights boil down to no more than a set of particular social choices that need not be considered binding by those whose values (and hence social choices) are differently formed—for example, by Islam or Confucianism rather than by an increasingly secularized Christianity. The wording of the Vienna Declaration on Human Rights of 1993, which refers to the need to bear in mind "the significance of national and regional particularities and various historical, cultural and religious backgrounds" when considering human rights, partially reflects this viewpoint—and has been criticized for this by some human rights activists.

Returning to the history of rights, it is here that the distinction between rights grounded in natural law and rights grounded in a contract becomes crucial. As noted above, it is only if rights are grounded in some account of human progress and reason that they may be regarded as genuinely universal in scope. But is this position, as its adherents insist, free of cultural bias, a set of ideas that all rational beings must accept? It seems not, at least insofar as many apparently rational Muslims, Hindus, Buddhists, atheists, utilitarians, and so on clearly do not accept its doctrines. It seems that either the standards derived from natural law (or a similar doctrine) are cast in such general terms that virtually any continuing social system will exemplify them, or, if the standards are cast more specifically, they are not in fact universally desired.

Of course, we are under no obligation to accept all critiques of universalism at face value. Human rights may have first emerged in the West, but this does not in itself make rights thinking "Western." It may be that an apparently principled rejection of universalism is, in fact, no more than a rationalization of tyranny. How do we know that the inhabitants of Saudi Arabia, say, actually prefer not to live in a democratic system with Western liberal rights, as their government asserts? There is an obvious dilemma here: if we insist that we will only accept democratically validated regimes, we will be imposing an alien test of legitimacy on these societies—yet what other form of validation is available?

In any event, does not the body of legal acts for the protection of universal human rights apply even if rights are, in effect, convenient fictions? Again, defenders of difference will argue that international law is itself a Western, universalist notion, and, in any event, they rightly note that the Western record of adherence to universal norms does not justify any claim to moral superiority. They point to the many crimes of the age of imperialism as well as to contemporary issues such as the treatment of asylum seekers and refugees, and, of course, the by-products of the global war on terror such as torture and imprisonment without trial.

The general point is that there is no neutral language with which to discuss human rights. Whatever way the question is posed reflects a particular viewpoint, and this is no accident. It is built into the nature of the discourse. Is there any way in which the notion of universal rights can be saved from its critics? Two modern approaches seem fruitful. Even if we find it difficult to specify human *rights*, it may still be possible to talk of human *wrongs*—similarly, some have argued that it is easier to specify what is *unjust* than what is *just* (see Booth 1999). To use Michael Walzer's terminology (1994), there may be no thick moral code that is universally acceptable, to which all local codes conform, but there may be a thin code that at least can be used to delegitimize some actions. Thus, for example, the Genocide Convention of 1948 seems a plausible example of a piece of international

see inset

1 THE SPREAD OF DEMOCRACY

Multiparty system:

- before 1939
- 1940–59
- 1960–79
- 1980–98
- Subsequent lapse from democracy
- Multiparty elections not held
- *LAOS* Country that had not ratified ICCPR by March 1999

Map 10.1 The Spread of Democracy to 2000.

During the second half of the twentieth century, democracy was introduced to most of the countries of Africa, Central America, and, following the collapse of their communist regimes in 1989–90, to the countries of Eastern Europe and Central Asia. Also, democratic processes were reinstated in many South American countries, which experienced periods of right-wing dictatorship during the 1970s and early 1980s. However, in many countries democracy is only tenuously established, and human rights abuses continue; some of the newly democratic countries in Africa have slipped back to being one-party states, and in other parts of the world there has been clear evidence of rigged elections, as in Afghanistan in 2009. The majority of the world's countries now support the International Covenant on Civil and Political Rights (ICCPR), adopted by the UN in 1966, which sets out a range of rights, including freedom of conscience, freedom from torture and slavery, and the right to demonstrate peaceably.

Human rights groups criticized the methods Russian troops used to combat separatist rebels in the Chechen Republic of the Russian Federation.

legislation that outlaws an obvious wrong, and, similarly, while some local variations in the rights associated with gender may be unavoidable, it is still possible to say that practices that severely restrict human capabilities, such as female genital mutilation, are simply wrong. Any code that did not condemn such suffering would be unworthy of respect.

This may not take us as far as some would wish—essential to this approach is the notion that there are going to be some practices that many would condemn but that will have to be tolerated—but it may be the most appropriate response to contemporary pluralism. An alternative approach involves recognizing that human rights are based on a particular culture—Richard Rorty (1993) calls this the "human rights culture"—and defending them in these terms rather than by reference to some cross-cultural code. This approach would involve abandoning the idea that human rights exist. Instead, it involves proselytizing on behalf of the sort of culture in which rights are deemed to exist. The basic point is that human life is safer, pleasanter, and more dignified when rights are acknowledged than when they are not.

Humanitarian Dimensions

Both human rights and human security have become part of an international discourse about proper norms of behavior and the best methods to promote these norms. The disagreements that exist today tend to be questions about the responsibilities of governments to live up to these standards. In this section we will discuss some dimensions of this discourse, with particular emphasis on political and economic rights; human rights during times of conflict; rights to natural resources; and women's rights.

Political and Economic Rights

"No one shall be subjected to torture or to cruel, inhuman or degrading treatment or punishment" (UN Declaration Article 5, Covenant on Civil and Political Rights Article 7, Convention on Torture, etc.). This is an immunity that is now well-established, but what in practice does this mean for someone faced with the prospect of such treatment? If the person is fortunate enough to live in a country governed by the rule of law, domestic courts may well uphold his or her immunity, and the international side of things will come into play only on the margins. Thus, a European who is dissatisfied with treatment at home may be able to take a legal dispute over a particular practice beyond his or her national courts to the European Commission on Human Rights and the European Court of Human Rights. In non-European countries governed by the rule of law, no such direct remedy is available, but the notion of universal rights at least reinforces the rhetorical case for rights that are established elsewhere.

The more interesting case emerges if potential victims do not live in such a law-governed society—if, that is, "their" government and courts are the problem and not the source of a possible solution. What assistance should they expect from the international community? What consequences will flow from their government's failure to live up to its obligations? The problem is that even in cases where violations are quite blatant, it may be difficult to see what other states are able to actually do, even supposing they are willing to act—which cannot be taken for granted, since states rarely if ever act simply in terms of human rights considerations.

Thus, during the Cold War, the West regularly issued verbal condemnations of human rights violations by the Soviet Union and its associates but rarely acted on these condemnations—the power of the Soviet Union made direct intervention imprudent, while even relatively minor sanctions would only be adopted if the general state of East-West relations suggested this would be appropriate (see Chapter 2). Similar considerations apply today to relations between Western countries and China. Conversely, violations by countries associated with the West were routinely overlooked or, in some cases, even justified—the global war on terror provides contemporary examples. With the ending of the Cold War it seemed possible that a more evenhanded approach to human rights violations might emerge, and, indeed, more active policies have been pursued in some cases, but expectations of major changes in attitude have not been met. In 1997, for example, the incoming Labour government in Britain declared its determination to place human rights at the heart of its foreign policy. Perhaps predictably, the actual policy of the government was frequently seen to be as determined by political and commercial considerations as in the past, and this was true even before the impact of 9/11 and the war on terror is taken into consideration (Smith and Light 2001).

All told, it seems unlikely that individuals ill-treated by nonconstitutional regimes will find any real support from the international community unless their persecutors are weak, of no strategic significance, and commercially unimportant—and even then it is unlikely that effective action will be taken unless one further factor is present, namely, the force of public opinion. This is the one positive factor that may goad states into action: the growth of humanitarian nongovernmental organizations (NGOs) has produced a context in which sometimes the force of public opinion can make itself felt, not necessarily in the oppressing regime, but in the policy-formation processes of the potential providers of aid.

The situation with respect to second-generation rights is more complicated. Consider, for example, "the right of everyone to an adequate standard of living for himself and his family, including adequate food, clothing and housing, and to the continuous improvement of living conditions" (Covenant on Economic, Social and Cultural Rights, Article 11.1), or the "right of everyone to be free from hunger" (Article 11.2). It has been argued by numerous cosmopolitan writers that such rights are, or should be, central. For example, Henry Shue (1996) argues that only if such basic rights are met can any other rights be claimed, and Thomas Pogge (2002) sees the relief of world poverty as a central task for the human rights regime.

The Covenant makes the realization of these rights an obligation on its signatories, but this is arguably a different kind of obligation from the obligation to refrain from, for example, "cruel or degrading" punishments. In the latter case, as with other basically political rights, the remedy is clearly in the hands of national governments. The way to end torture is, simply, for states to stop torturing. The right not to be tortured is associated with a duty not to torture. The right to be free from hunger, on the other hand, is not simply a matter of a duty on the part of one's own and other states not to pursue policies that lead to starvation. It also involves a duty to act to "ensure an equitable distribution of world food supplies in relation to need" (Covenant on Economic, Social and Cultural Rights, Article 11.2[b]). The distinction here is sometimes seen as that between "negative" and "positive" rights, although this is not entirely satisfactory, since negative (political) rights often require positive action if they are to be protected effectively. In any event, there are problems with the notion of economic rights.

First, it is by no means clear that, even assuming goodwill, these social and economic goals could always be met, and to think in terms of having a right to something that could not be achieved is to misuse language. In such circumstances, a right simply means "a generally desirable state of affairs," and this weakening of the concept may have the effect of undermining more precise claims to rights that actually can be achieved (such as the right not to be tortured). Second, some states may seek to use economic and social rights more directly to undermine political rights. Thus, dictatorial regimes in poor countries quite frequently justify the curtailment of political rights in the name of promoting economic growth or economic equality. In fact, there is no reason to accept the general validity of this argument—Amartya Sen argues cogently that development and freedom go together (Sen 1999)—but it will still be made, and not always in bad faith. Finally, if it is accepted that all states have a positive duty to promote economic well-being and freedom from hunger everywhere, then the consequences go beyond the requirement of the rich to share with the poor, revolutionary though such a requirement would be. Virtually all national social and economic policies become a matter for international regulation. Clearly, rich states would have a duty to make economic and social policy with a view to its consequences on the poor, but so would poor states. The poor's right to assistance creates a duty on the rich to assist, but this in turn creates a right of the rich to insist that the poor have a duty not to worsen their plight—for example, by failing to restrict population growth or by inappropriate economic policies. Aid programs promoted by the Commonwealth and World Bank, and the structural-adjustment programs of the International Monetary Fund, regularly include conditions of this kind. They are, however, widely resented because they contradict another widely supported economic and social right: "All peoples have the right of self-determination. By virtue of that right they freely determine their political status and freely pursue their economic, social and cultural development" (Covenant on Economic,

Social and Cultural Rights, Article 1.1). Even when applied in a well-meaning and consistent way, external pressures to change policy are rarely popular, even with those they are intended to benefit.

On the other hand, it is certainly true that people suffering from brutal poverty and severe malnourishment are unlikely to be able to exercise any rights at all unless their condition is attended to, and it may be true, as Pogge argues, that the transfers actually required to raise living standards to an acceptable level across the world are sufficiently modest that they would not actually raise the problems outlined above. Still, most economic and social "rights" are best seen as collectively agreed-on aspirations rather than as "rights" as the term has conventionally been used.

Conflict, Human Rights, and Human Security

Why the continued importance of national security over human security? For developing countries, state sovereignty and territorial integrity take precedence over security of the individual. Many countries in the developing world are artificial nation-states, whose boundaries were drawn arbitrarily by the colonial powers in the nineteenth century without regard for the actual ethnic composition or historical linkages between peoples. State responses to ethnic separatist movements (now conflated with terrorism), which are partly rooted in people's rejection of colonial-imposed boundaries, have been accompanied by the most egregious violations of human security by governments. Moreover, many third world states, as well as China, remain under authoritarian rule. Human security is stymied by the lack of political space for alternatives to state ideologies and by restrictions on civil liberties imposed by authoritarian regimes to ensure their own survival.

> **WHAT'S YOUR WORLDVIEW**
>
> *Economic, social, and cultural rights were very controversial during the Cold War and remain so today. Why do you think these proposed rights remain so controversial? Do they challenge the power and influence of certain economic and political interests?*

In the developed as well as the developing world, one of the most powerful challenges to human security has come from the war on terror led by the United States in response to the 9/11 attacks. These have revived the traditional emphasis of states on national security (Suhrke 2004, 365). Although terrorists target innocent civilians and thus threaten human security, governments have used the war on terror to restrict and violate civil liberties. The US decision to put Saddam Hussein on trial in an Iraqi court rather than the International Criminal Court (ICC) illustrates the continued US defiance of a key policy instrument of human security, even though it focuses on the more Western-oriented conception of "freedom from fear." The US questioning of the applicability of the Geneva Conventions, and the abandoning of its commitments on the issue of torture in the context of war in Iraq, have further undermined the agenda of human security. So have Russia's flouting of a wide range of its international commitments—including the laws of war, CSCE (Conference on Security and Co-operation in Europe) and OSCE (Organization for Security and Co-operation in Europe) commitments, as well as international and regional conventions on torture—in the context of its war in Chechnya.

A pioneering report released by the Human Security Center at the University of British Columbia (2005) points to several significant trends in armed conflicts around the world (see Table 10.1). What explains the downward trend? The report lists several factors: growing democratization (the underlying assumption here being that democracies tend to be better at peaceful resolution of conflicts); rising economic interdependence (which increases the costs of conflict); the declining economic utility of war, owing to the fact that resources can be more easily bought in the international marketplace than acquired through force; the growth in the number of international institutions that can mediate in conflicts; the impact of international norms against violence such as human sacrifice, witch burning, slavery, dueling, war crimes, and genocide; the end of colonialism; and the end of the Cold War. A specific reason identified by the report is the dramatic increase in the UN's role: its work in areas such as preventative diplomacy and peacemaking activities, its postconflict peacebuilding, the willingness of the UN Security Council to use military action to enforce peace agreements, the deterrent effects of war crime trials by the International Criminal Court (ICC) and other tribunals, and the greater resort to reconciliation and addressing the root causes of conflict (see Chapter 6 for more on the ICC and UN peacekeeping operations). The 80 percent decline in the most deadly civil conflicts since the early 1990s, argued the report, is due to the dramatic growth of international efforts at preventative diplomacy, peacemaking, and peacebuilding (University of British Columbia, *Human Security Report* 2005, Part V).

Yet the picture is not entirely positive. The decline in armed conflicts reported by the *Human Security Report* is from 1991 onward. The number of armed conflicts had actually increased between 1960 and 1990–1, especially intrastate conflicts (which jumped from 12 in 1960 to 49 in 1991). And there were still 121 active armed conflicts during the 1989–2005 period (some of them started before 1989). As Figure 10.1 shows, armed conflicts are now on the same level as during the 1970s and markedly higher than during the 1950s and early 1960s.

And there are some horrific costs associated with these conflicts. For example, deaths directly or indirectly attributed to the conflict in the Democratic Republic of the Congo since 1998 have surpassed casualties sustained by Britain in the First World War and Second World War combined. The conflict in Sudan's Darfur region displaced nearly 2 million people (UNDP 2005, 12). In Iraq, a team of American and Iraqi epidemiologists estimates that Iraq's mortality rate has more than doubled since the US invasion: from 5.5 deaths per 1,000 people in the year before the invasion to 13.3 deaths per 1,000 people per year in the postinvasion period. In all, some 655,000 more people have died in Iraq

Table 10.1

Trends in Conflict

- A 40 percent drop in armed conflicts in the world since 1991. (This counts only conflicts with at least twenty-five battle-related deaths where one of the parties was a state.)
- An 80 percent decline in the number of genocide and "politicides"* between the high point in 1988 and 2001.
- A 70 percent decline in the number of international crises between 1981 and 2001.
- A 45 percent decrease in the number of refugees between 1992 and 2003. The number of internally displaced persons has increased, although accurate information is hard to obtain.
- A 98 percent decline in the average number of battle deaths per conflict per year. In 1950, an average armed conflict killed 38,000 people. In 2002, the figure was 600.**

Source: Human Security Report, *University of British Columbia, Human Security Center (2005)*

* The term "politicide" describes policies that seek to destroy groups because of their political beliefs rather than religion or ethnicity (the latter being captured by the term "genocide").

** Most of the battle deaths in the Cold War period were accounted for by the Korean and Vietnam Wars. If these are excluded, the drop in battle deaths will be less dramatic.

Figure 10.1 Conflicts by Type, 1946–2009.
Source: @ Uppsala Conflict Data Project (UCDP), Uppsala University.

since the invasion in March 2003 than would have died if the invasion had not occurred (D. Brown 2006, A12).

The share of civilian casualties in armed conflict has increased since the Second World War. Civilians accounted for 10 percent of the victims during the First World War and 50 percent of the victims during the Second World War. They constitute between 80 and 85 percent of the victims of more recent wars. Many of these victims are children, women, the sick, and the elderly (*Gendering Human Security* 2001, 18). Although death tolls from organized campaigns against civilians have declined in recent years, the number of such campaigns increased by 55 percent between 1989 and 2005 (University of British Columbia, Human Security Center 2006, 3).

International terrorist incidents and related fatalities increased worldwide between 2002 and 2005. Most of the increases were associated with the war in Iraq, where the number of fatalities grew from about 1,700 in 2004 to approximately 3,400 in 2005 (National Counterterrorism Center 2005). Excluding Iraq, however, terrorist action killed fewer people worldwide in 2005—1,500 as opposed to 3,000 in 2004 (National Counterterrorism Center 2005).

Furthermore, some of the most serious issues of human security in armed conflicts still need to be overcome, such as child soldiers and land mines. According to one study, 75 percent of the armed conflicts today involve child soldiers (University of British Columbia, *Human Security Report* 2005, 35). Land mines and unexploded ordnance cause between 15,000 and 20,000 new casualties each year (United States Campaign to Ban Landmines, accessed February 3, 2007). Despite the justified optimism generated by the Ottawa Treaty (to be discussed later), there remain 80 million live mines undetected—someone steps on a land mine every 28 minutes—and 80 percent of those killed or injured by land mines are civilians (Koehler 2007).

Finally, the decline in armed conflicts around the world is not necessarily irreversible. Some of the factors contributing to the decline of conflicts, such as democratization

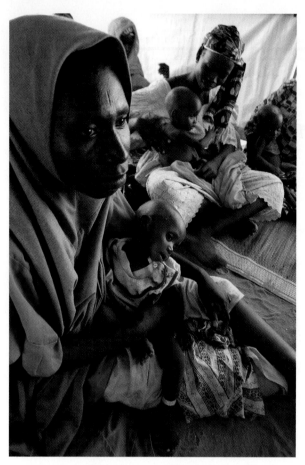

Too often it is women and children who suffer the most from war and human rights abuses.

and the peace-operations role of the UN, can suffer setbacks due to lack of support from major powers and the international community. And there remain serious possible threats to international peace and security that can cause widespread casualties, such as a conflict in the Korean Peninsula and war between China and Taiwan.

Battle deaths are not themselves an adequate indicator of threats to human security posed by armed conflict. Many armed conflicts have indirect consequences on human life and well-being. Wars are a major source of economic disruption, disease, and ecological destruction, which in turn undermine human development and thus create a vicious cycle of conflict and underdevelopment. As the *Human Development Report* (UNDP 2005, 12) puts it: "Conflict undermines nutrition and public health, destroys education systems, devastates livelihoods and retards prospects for economic growth." It found that out of the fifty-two countries that are reversing or stagnating in their attempts to reduce child mortality, thirty have experienced conflict since 1990. A British government white paper on international development notes:

Violent conflict reverses economic growth, causes hunger, destroys roads, schools and clinics, and forces people to flee across borders. . . Women and girls are particularly vulnerable because they suffer sexual violence and exploitation. And violent conflict and insecurity can spill over into neighboring countries and provide cover for terrorists or organized criminal groups. (Department for International Development 2006, 45)

Wars also damage the environment, as happened with the US use of Agent Orange defoliant during the Vietnam War and Saddam Hussein's burning of Kuwaiti oil wells in the 1990–1991 Gulf War, leading to massive air and land pollution. Similar links can be made between conflict and the outbreak of disease: "[W]ar-exacerbated disease and malnutrition kill far more people than missiles, bombs and bullets" (*Human Security Report* 2005, 7). Disease accounts for most of the 3.9 million people who have died in the conflict in the Democratic Republic of the Congo (UNDP 2005, 45).

Just as wars and violent conflict have indirect consequences such as economic disruption, ecological damage, and disease, levels of poverty and environmental degradation contribute to conflict and hence must be taken into consideration in human-security research (see Chapter 13). One study shows that a country at $250 GDP per capita has an average 15 percent risk of experiencing a civil war in the next five years, while at a GDP per capita of $5,000, the risk of civil war is less than 1 percent (Humphreys and Varshney 2004, 9; Department for International Development 2005, 8). While no direct link can be established between poverty and terrorism, terrorists often "exploit poverty and exclusion in order to tap into popular discontent—taking advantage of fragile states such as Somalia, or undemocratic regimes such as in Afghanistan in the 1990s, to plan violence" (UNDP 2005, 47).

WHAT'S YOUR WORLDVIEW

With the war on terrorism and the rise of new security challenges, one must ask if states are prepared to respond. In this era of globalization, can states deliver on their promise to provide security for their citizens and still maintain certain rights and freedoms?

Resources and Intervention

Environmental degradation, which is often linked to poverty, is another source of conflict (Homer-Dixon 1991, 1994). Analysts have identified competition for scarce resources such as water and arable land as a source of possible conflict between Israel and its Arab neighbors, between India and Pakistan, between Turkey and Syria, and even between countries that share use of an important waterway, like Egypt and Ethiopia (Rice 2006, 78). The world's poorer countries, where families often see the need for more children to compensate for a high infant mortality rate and to raise their income potential, account for a significant proportion of the growth in the world's population, which doubled between 1950 and 1998 (Rice 2006, 80). Population growth, in turn, contributes to resource scarcity and environmental stress, often resulting in conflict. For example, South Asia, one of the poorest and most heavily populated regions of the globe, faces intensified competition and the possibility of conflict over scarce water resources. Examples include the

Table 10.2
Key Facts About Disease

Those who take a broad definition of human security look at threats to the survival and safety of the individual, not only from violent conflict, but also from such nonviolent factors as disease, environmental degradation, and natural disasters. Below are some of the key trends in disease.

- The world has seen the appearance of at least thirty new infectious diseases, including avian flu, HIV/AIDS, severe acute respiratory syndrome, hepatitis C, and West Nile virus, in the past three decades. Twenty diseases previously detected have reemerged with new drug-resistant strains. (Rice 2006, 79)
- AIDS is the leading cause of death in Africa and the fourth leading cause of death worldwide. Around 40 million people worldwide are infected with HIV, 95 percent of whom live in developing countries. In 2004, approximately 5 million people were newly infected with the virus. HIV/AIDS killed more than 20 million people worldwide, and 3.1 million people died of AIDS-related causes in 2004. It is estimated that per capita growth in half of the countries in sub-Saharan Africa is falling by 0.5–1.2 percent each year as a direct result of AIDS. By 2010, per capita GDP in some of the hardest-hit countries may drop by 8 percent, and per capita consumption may fall even farther. (The Global Fund to Fight AIDS, Tuberculosis and Malaria, http://www.theglobalfund.org/en/hivaids/)
- Malaria causes about 350–500 million infections in humans and approximately 1–3 million deaths annually (Breman 2001, 1–11)—this would translate as about one death every thirty seconds (Greenwood et al. 2005, 1487–98). The majority, which amounts to 85–90 percent of malaria fatalities, occur in sub-Saharan Africa. The economic impact of malaria has been estimated to cost Africa $12 billion every year. (World Health Organization n.d.)
- Annually, 8 million people become ill with tuberculosis, and 2 million people die from the disease, worldwide (Centers for Disease Control 2005). Presently, tuberculosis is the world's greatest infectious killer of women of reproductive age and the leading cause of death among people with HIV/AIDS. (PR Newswire Europe 2002)
- The outbreaks of highly pathogenic H5N1 avian influenza that began in Southeast Asia in mid-2003 and have now spread to parts of Europe are the largest and most severe on record. To date, nine Asian countries have reported outbreaks (listed in order of reporting): the Republic of Korea, Vietnam, Japan, Thailand, Cambodia, the Lao People's Democratic Republic, Indonesia, China, and Malaysia. (World Health Organization 2006)

Indo-Pakistan dispute over the Wular Barrage, the Indo-Bangladesh water dispute over the Farakka Barrage, and the Indo-Nepal dispute over the Mahakali River Treaty (Power and Interest News Report 2006). The potential for political upheaval or war as a consequence of environmental problems is evident in a host of poor regions around the world, including North Africa, the sub-Saharan Sahel region of Africa (including Ethiopia, Sudan, Somalia, Mali, Niger, and Chad), the island nations of the western Pacific Ocean, the Ganges River basin (principally northeastern India and Bangladesh), and some parts of Central and South America (Petzold-Bradley, Carius, and Vincze 2001). Darfur illustrates the linkage between poverty, environmental degradation, and conflict. Traditional intercommunal conflict in Darfur over scarcity of resources and land deteriorated as a result of desertification and a shortage of rainfall. In the 1970s and 1980s, droughts in northern parts of Darfur sent its nomadic population southward in search of water and herding grounds, bringing it into conflict with the local tribes (Environmental Degradation and Conflict in Darfur 2004).

Natural disasters can also affect the course of conflicts by either exacerbating or mitigating them. The December 2004 Indian Ocean tsunami changed the course of two separatist conflicts: Aceh in Indonesia and Tamil separatism in Sri Lanka. In Aceh, where the government announced a cease-fire to permit relief work, prospects for reconciliation improved. In contrast, the conflict in Sri Lanka, where relief supplies did not reach rebel-held territory, saw an escalation of violence.

From the foregoing discussion, we can establish a conceptual link between the broader and narrower understandings of human security.

Women, Conflict, and Human Security

The relationship between gender and human security has multiple dimensions. The United Nations Inter-Agency Committee on Women and Gender Equality notes five aspects: (1) violence against women and girls; (2) gender inequalities in control over resources; (3) gender inequalities in power and decision making; (4) women's human rights; and (5) women (and men) as actors, not victims (United Nations Inter-Agency Committee on Women and Gender Equality 1999, 1). Recent conflicts have shown women as victims of rape, torture, and sexual slavery. For example, between 250,000 and 500,000 women were raped during the 1994 genocide in Rwanda. Such atrocities against women are now recognized as a crime against humanity (Rehn and Sirleaf 2002, 9).

War-affected areas often see a sharp increase in domestic violence directed at women and a growth in the number of women trafficked to become forced laborers or sex workers. Women and children comprise 73 percent of an average population but account for 80 percent of the refugees in the world today and perhaps a larger percentage as internally displaced persons. Another important aspect of the gender dimension of human security is the role of women as actors in conflicts. This involves considering the participation of women in combat. In the Eritrean war of independence, women made up 25–30 percent of combatants. A similar proportion of women are fighting with the Tamil Tigers. Women play an even larger role in support functions, such as logistics, staff, and intelligence services, in a conflict. It has been noted that women become targets of rape and sexual violence because they serve as a social and cultural symbol. Hence violence against them may be undertaken as a deliberate strategy to undermine the social fabric of an opponent. Similarly, securing women's participation in combat may be motivated by a desire, among the parties to a conflict, to increase the legitimacy of their cause. It signifies "a broad social

Gendered Perspective on Human Rights

Until recently, it has been conventional for human rights treaties to be cast in language that assumes that the rights bearer is a man and the head of a household. Many feminists argue that this reflects more than an old-fashioned linguistic convention. The classic political and civil rights (freedom of speech, association, from arbitrary arrest, and so on) assume that the rights bearer will be living, or would wish to live, a life of active citizenship, but, until very recently, such a life was denied to nearly all women in nearly all cultures. Instead of this public life, women were limited to the private sphere and subjected to the arbitrary and capricious power of the male head of the household. It is only very recently in the Western liberal democracies that women have been able to vote, to stand for office, or to own property in their own name, and such issues as the criminalization of rape in marriage and the effective prevention of domestic violence against women are still controversial. The situation is, if anything, rather worse in non-Western polities. It may be that a genuinely gender-neutral account of human rights is possible, but some radical feminists argue that an altogether different kind of thinking is required (see Mackinnon 1993).

Both cultural critics and feminists argue, convincingly, that the model of a rights bearer inherent in the contemporary international human rights regime is based on the experiences of Western men. Agreement collapses, however, when the implications of this common position are explored. Liberal feminists wish to see the rights of men extended to women, while radical feminists wish to promote a new model of what it is to be human that privileges neither men nor women. Most cultural critics, on the other hand, wish to preserve inherited status and power differences based on gender.

The contradictions here are sharpest when it comes to relations between the world of Islam and the human rights regime, largely because relations between Islam and the West

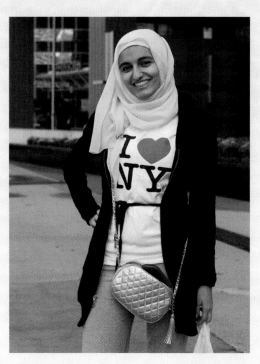

Increased international travel can put burdens on women who want to see the world while remaining true to the tenets of their religions.

are so fraught on other grounds that all differences are magnified. Radical or traditional Islamists argue for conventional gender roles, support quite severe restrictions on the freedom of women, and promote the compulsory wearing of restrictive clothing such as the *niqab* or the burqa. Many of these petty restrictions have no basis in the Koran or the sayings of the Prophet and can simply be understood as methods of preserving male dominance—although it should be said that they are often accepted by Muslim women as ways of asserting their identity. More serious for the human rights regime are those verses of the Koran that unambiguously deny gender equality. It is often, and truly, said that the Koran's attitude toward the status of women was in advance of much contemporary seventh-century thought—including Christian and Jewish thought of the age—but it remains the case that, for example, in a sharia court the evidence of a woman is worth less than that of a man, and sexual intercourse outside marriage is punishable for a woman even in the case of rape. The other Abrahamic religions continue to preserve misogynist vestiges, but mainstream Christian and Jewish theologians have reinterpreted those aspects of their traditions that radically disadvantage women. Given the importance attached to the literal text of the Koran, this will prove more difficult for Muslims. The role of women under Islam will be a continuing problem for the international human rights regime as it attempts to divest itself of its Western Judeo-Christian heritage and adopt a more inclusive framework. It will of course be an even bigger problem for those women who live in oppressive Muslim regimes.

consensus and solidarity, both to their own population and to the outside world" (*Gendering Human Security* 2001, 18).

In recent years, there has been a growing awareness of the need to secure the greater participation of women in international peace operations. The UN Department of Peacekeeping Operations noted in a 2000 report:

> Women's presence [in peacekeeping missions] improves access and support for local women; it makes male peacekeepers more reflective and responsible; and it broadens the repertoire of skills and styles available within the mission, often with the effect of reducing conflict and confrontation. Gender mainstreaming is not just fair, it is beneficial. (cited in Rehn and Sirleaf 2002, 63)

In 2000, the UN Security Council passed a resolution (Security Council Resolution 1325) mandating a review of the impact of armed conflict on women and the role of women in peace operations and conflict resolution. The review was released in 2002 and entitled *Women, Peace and Security* (UN 2002). In his introduction to the report, UN Secretary-General Kofi Annan noted that that "women still form a minority of those who participate in peace and security negotiations, and receive less attention than men in post-conflict agreements, disarmament and reconstruction" (UN 2002, ix). There is still a long way to go before the international community can fully realize the benefits of greater participation by women in UN peace operations and conflict-resolution activities.

Globalization has made it more difficult for leaders of countries to assert that national cultural norms are more important than global standards of behavior. Transnational corporations, the globalized entertainment industry, and the United Nations itself all penetrate national borders and erode traditional values. As we will see in the next section, the international community of countries is actively involved in this process.

The Role of the International Community

Because of the broad and contested nature of the idea of human security, it is difficult to evaluate policies undertaken by the international community that can be specifically regarded as human-security measures. But the most important multilateral actions include the International Criminal Court (ICC) and the Antipersonnel Landmines Treaty. The ICC was established on July 1, 2002, with its headquarters in The Hague, Netherlands, although its proceedings may take place anywhere. It is a permanent institution with "the power to exercise its jurisdiction over persons for the most serious crimes of international concern" (Rome Statute, Article 1). These crimes include genocide, crimes against humanity, war

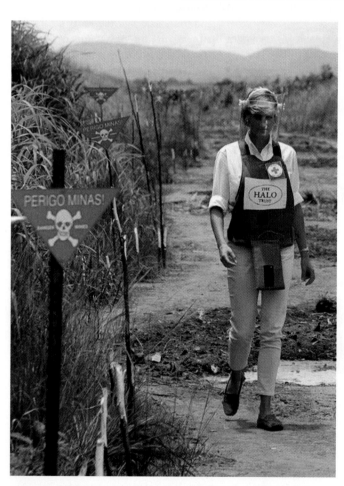

Prior to her death in an automobile accident, Princess Diana gave her name and face to the international campaign to ban the use of antipersonnel landmines. How do celebrities help or hinder such programs?

crimes, and the crime of aggression, although the court would not exercise its jurisdiction over the crime of aggression until such time as the state parties agree on a definition of the crime and set out the conditions under which it may be prosecuted. The ICC is a "court of last resort." It is "complementary to national criminal jurisdictions," meaning that it can only exercise its jurisdiction when national courts are unwilling or unable to investigate or prosecute such crimes (Rome Statute, Article 1). The court can only prosecute crimes that were committed on or after July 1, 2002, the date its founding treaty entered into force. Since its establishment, the ICC has been involved in the prosecution of some high-profile war criminals in the former Yugoslavia, Liberia, and Congo, including the former president of Yugoslavia, Slobodan Milosevic (whose trial ended without a verdict after he was found dead in his cell in March 2006) and former Liberian president Charles Taylor.

The Convention on the Prohibition of the Use, Stockpiling, Production, and Transfer of Anti-Personnel Mines and on Their Destruction, signed in Ottawa on December 3–4, 1997, bans the development, production, acquisition, stockpiling, transfer, and use of antipersonnel mines (Ottawa Treaty, Article 1, General Obligations, 1997). It also obliges signatories to destroy existing stockpiles. Among the countries that have yet to sign the treaty are the People's Republic of China, the Russian Federation, and the United States.

The surge in UN peacekeeping and peacebuilding operations has contributed to the decline in conflict and enhanced prospects for human security. The number of UN peacekeeping operations increased threefold between the first forty years of the UN's founding and the twenty years since—from thirteen to forty-seven missions (United Nations Peacekeeping website, n.d.). More recently, a UN Peacebuilding Commission was inaugurated in 2006. Its goal is to assist in postconflict recovery and reconstruction, including institution building and sustainable development, in countries emerging from conflict. The UN has also been center stage in promoting the idea of humanitarian intervention, a central policy element of human security. The concept of humanitarian intervention was endorsed by the report of the UN Secretary-General's High-Level Panel on Threats, Challenges and Change, *A More Secure World* (2004, 66, 106), the subsequent report by the secretary-general, entitled *In Larger Freedom* (UN 2005), and finally by the UN Summit in September 2005.

UN specialized agencies play a crucial role in promoting human security. For example, the UN Development Programme and the World Health Organization (WHO) have been at the forefront of fighting poverty and disease, respectively. Other UN agencies, such as the United Nations High Commissioner for Refugees (UNHCR), United Nations Children's Fund (UNICEF), and United Nations Development Fund for Women (UNIFEM), have played a central role in getting particular issues, such as refugees and the rights of children and women, onto the agenda for discussion and in providing a platform for advocacy and action (MacFarlane and Khong 2006).

Nongovernmental organizations (NGOs) contribute to human security in a number of ways: giving information and early warning about conflicts, providing a channel for relief operations (often being the first to do so in areas of conflict or natural disaster), and supporting government- or UN-sponsored peacebuilding and rehabilitation missions. NGOs also play a central role in promoting sustainable development. A leading NGO with a human-security mission is the International Committee of the Red Cross (ICRC). Established in Geneva, it has a unique authority based on the international humanitarian law of the Geneva Conventions to protect the lives and dignity of victims of war and internal violence, including the war wounded, prisoners, refugees, civilians, and other

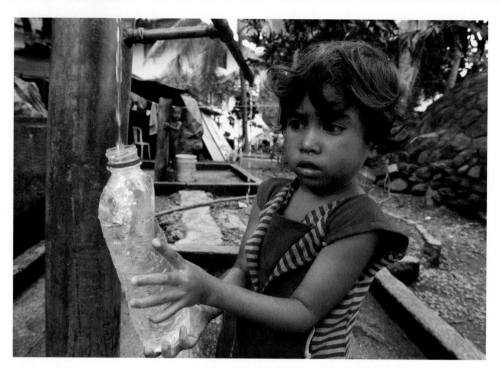

Should access to clean drinking water be a human right and a state responsibility?

noncombatants, and to provide them with assistance. Other NGOs include Médicins Sans Frontières (Doctors Without Borders; emergency medical assistance), Save the Children (protection of children), and Amnesty International (human rights).

At times these agencies overlap in the services they provide or the issue for which they advocate. As you will see, this tends to be the case in international relations. However, given the complex nature of international human rights law and the demands of providing for human security, each organization can play a part in helping to advance the international agenda.

Conclusion

For more than sixty years, leaders and citizens of countries have worked to develop the paired concepts of human rights and human security. Although governments around the world—including some in Europe and North America, the intellectual homelands of the concepts—from time to time violate the very freedoms they once endorsed, when they ratified the various human rights treaties, it is understood that these are transgressions of long-standing norms of behavior. Certainly, more can be done to promote freedom from fear and freedom from want. The *Human Development Report* of 2005 estimates that the rich nations of the world provide ten dollars to the military budget for every one dollar they spend on aid. For example, the current global spending on HIV/AIDS, "a disease that claims 3 million lives a year, represents three day's worth of military spending" (UNDP 2005, 8).

Perhaps the greatest challenge today in the issue area of human rights and human security is the need to change the ways in which gov-

> ### WHAT'S YOUR WORLDVIEW ?
>
> *Do you think the UN should have its own independent military force for humanitarian intervention, peacemaking, and even state building? Is this the only way to ensure that something is done about these crimes against humanity?*

ernment officials and citizens see the role of the state. Does it exist solely to defend the country, along the lines suggested in the Westphalian model of an independent and sovereign state? Or do we have an obligation as humans to help other humans in need? Until this is resolved, debates about human rights and human security will continue.

Contributors to Chapter 10: Amitav Acharya, Alex J. Bellamy, Chris Brown, Nicholas J. Wheeler, and Steven L. Lamy.

REVIEW QUESTIONS

1. What is the relationship between rights and duties?
2. Why is the promotion of human rights so rarely seen as an appropriate foreign policy goal of states?
3. What are the problems involved in assigning rights to peoples as opposed to individuals?
4. In what ways can gender bias be identified in the modern human rights regime?
5. What is the relationship between democracy and human rights? Is it always the case that democracies are more likely to respect human rights than authoritarian regimes?
6. Can the compromising of human rights in the face of the threat of terrorism ever be justified as the lesser of two evils?
7. What is human security? How is it different from the concept of national security?
8. Describe the main difference between the two conceptions of human security: "freedom from fear" and "freedom from want." Are the two understandings irreconcilable?
9. How do you link poverty and health with human security?
10. What are the main areas of progress in the promotion of human security by the international community?
11. What are the obstacles to human-security promotion by the international community?
12. Why do we need to give special consideration to the suffering of women in conflict zones?

FURTHER READING

Brownlie, I., and Goodwin-Gill, G. (eds.) (2006), *Basic Instruments on Human Rights,* 5th rev. ed. (Oxford: Clarendon Press). Contains the texts of all the most important treaties and declarations.

Finnis, J. (1980), *Natural Law and Natural Rights* (Oxford: Clarendon Press). The best introduction to modern natural law thinking.

Freeman, M. (2002), *Human Rights: A Multidisciplinary Approach* (Cambridge: Polity Press). Discusses the philosophical problems posed by the idea of rights.

Jones, P. (1994), *Rights* (Basingstoke: Macmillan). This book also discusses the philosophical problems posed by the idea of rights.

Steiner, H. J., and Alston, P. (2000), *International Human Rights in Context: Law, Politics, Morals: Texts and Materials,* 2nd ed. (Oxford: Clarendon Press). Contains abbreviated texts and a great deal of useful commentary in its 1,500 + pages! It is the single most useful book for the study of international human rights. A third edition was issued in 2007.

International human rights

Donnelly, J. (2002), *Universal Human Rights in Theory and Practice,* 2nd ed. (Ithaca, NY: Cornell University Press). Another valuable introduction to international human rights.

Smith, K. E., and Light, M. (eds.) (2001), *Ethics and Foreign Policy* (Cambridge: Cambridge University Press). Examines the problems involved in making human rights central to foreign policy.

Second-generation rights

Pogge, T. (2002), *World Poverty and Human Rights: Cosmopolitan Responsibilities and Reforms* (Cambridge: Polity Press). The most important and influential modern statement in this area.

Shue, H. (1996), *Basic Rights: Subsistence, Affluence and US Foreign Policy,* 2nd rev. ed. (Princeton, NJ: Princeton University Press). A very influential defense of second-generation rights as genuine rights.

Third-generation rights

Bauer, J., and Bell, D. A. (eds.) (1999), *The East Asian Challenge for Human Rights* (Cambridge: Cambridge University Press). The best collection of writings on the Asian value debate, covering a wide range of perspectives.

Sen, A. (1999), *Development as Freedom* (Oxford: Oxford University Press). Persuasively disposes of the argument that development requires the curtailment of human rights.

Academic disagreements about human rights

Huntington, S. (1996), *The Clash of Civilizations and the Remaking of World Order* (New York: Simon & Schuster). A key contribution, much criticized by academics, but which has entered the public consciousness, especially since 9/11.

Peters, J. S., and Wolper, A. (eds.) (1995), *Women's Rights, Human Rights: International Feminist Perspectives* (New York: Routledge). A good collection of feminist views.

Walzer, M. (1994), *Thick and Thin: Moral Argument at Home and Abroad* (Notre Dame, IN: University of Notre Dame Press). Argues for a "thin" cross-cultural moral code.

Human rights, the war on terror, and the "torture debate"

Greenberg, K. (ed.) (2006), *The Torture Debate in America* (New York: Cambridge University Press). A collection of essays, mostly by lawyers, focusing on Guantanamo and Abu Graib, as opposed to the more philosophically oriented papers collected in Levinson (ed.) (2004).

Ignatieff, M. (2005), *The Lesser Evil: Political Ethics in an Age of Terror* (Princeton, NJ: Princeton University Press) and

——— (2005), *American Exceptionalism and Human Rights* (Princeton, NJ: Princeton University Press). Both texts offer a more nuanced approach to the problem of the appropriate means to combat terrorism.

Levinson, A. (ed.) (2004), *Torture: A Collection* (New York: Oxford University Press). Contains essays by Michael Walzer, Jean Bethke Elshtain, and Alan Dershowitz.

The most useful journals in the field are *Human Rights Quarterly: A Comparative and International Journal of the Social Sciences, Philosophy and Law* (Baltimore, MD: Johns Hopkins University Press), *Ethics and International Affairs* (New York: Carnegie Institute), and *The International Journal of Human Rights* (London: Frank Cass).

Human security

Acharya, A. (2001), "Human Security: East Versus West," *International Journal*, 56(3): 442–60. Examines the debate between two conceptions of human security, "freedom from fear" and "freedom from want," with particular reference to Asia.

Commission on Human Security (2003), *Human Security Now: Protecting and Empowering People* (New York: United Nations).

Gough, I. (2004), *Insecurity and Welfare Regimes in Asia, Africa and Latin America: Social Policy in Development Contexts* (Cambridge: Cambridge University Press). A comparative study of social and economic welfare approaches to addressing human security challenges in the developing world.

Haq, M. (1995), *Reflections on Human Development* (Oxford: Oxford University Press). The book by the late Pakistani development economist, who played a pioneering role in the Human Development Report, outlines his thinking on human development and human security.

United Nations Development Programme (1995), *Human Development Report 1994* (Oxford: Oxford University Press). The original source of the idea of human security.

INTERNET RESOURCES

Amnesty International
www.amnesty.org
> A leading NGO working to protect human rights around the world.

Center for World Indigenous Rights
http://cwis.org/
> The political and economic rights of indigenous peoples have gained prominence recently. This is an excellent source of information on this topic.

European Human Rights Centre
http://www.ehrcweb.org/
> A clearinghouse for information on human rights.

Genocide Intervention Network
http://www.genocideintervention.net
> With student chapters in over 1,000 secondary schools and colleges, this organization seeks to educate citizens about genocide and mass atrocities and hold leaders accountable for their commitments to prevent further violence.

Global Centre for the Responsibility to Protect
http://globalr2p.org
> Created in 2007, this organization publishes materials and sponsors program to promote the R2P agreement that was approved at the World Summit in 2005.

Human Rights Watch
www.hrw.org
> A US-based NGO that exposes human rights abuses.

International Coalition for the Responsibility to Protect
http://www.responsibilitytoprotect.org/
> This is an organization of NGOs from around the world that seek to enhance our understanding of the normative dimensions of R2P and to strengthen the capacity of citizens and states to respond to genocide, ethnic cleansing, and other crimes against humanity.

United Nations Development Program
www.undp.org

United Nations Office of the High Commissioner of Human Rights
http://www.ohchr.org
> With offices in NY and Geneva and with over 200 human rights officers around the world, the Commissioner is the principal human rights official of the UN. This office works with the Human Rights Council and with other UN offices involved in human rights and human security issues.

For more information, quizzes, case studies, and other study tools, please visit us at **www.oup.com/us/lamy**

PART FIVE

Global Issues: Political Economy

While Part Four looked at questions of war, security, and violence, this final part looks at primarily economic issues with global impacts. Economic questions are at the core of the debates about globalization; how states and other actors address these questions will determine how millions of people around the world will live. This part looks at the crucial issues of trade, finance, poverty, hunger, and environment. First, in Chapter 11 we will discuss **international political economy** and examine the evolving relationship of states to corporations as the latter have internationalized their production sourcing and methods. In Chapter 12 we will see how new **trade tactics and financial instruments** have fueled this process of globalized production. The third chapter of this part, Chapter 13, looks at those people who have missed the benefits of economic globalization, as we investigate **poverty, hunger, and economic development**. That leaves Chapter 14 on **global environmental problems** to pull the other topics together. As you will see, every global issue you have studied has environmental impacts. Unless the world's leaders successfully address all the other issues, it could be that we will no longer have clean air to breathe and clean water to drink. Some contributors to this text see opportunities for greater cooperation because of globalization, while others see dangers of increased levels of conflict, at the beginning of the twenty-first century. But all of the contributors agree on one point: By the end of this book, you should have your own, well-informed position with regard to this debate.

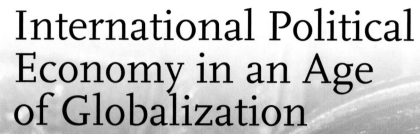

CHAPTER 11

International Political Economy in an Age of Globalization

The ideas of economists and political philosophers, both when they are right and when they are wrong, are more powerful than is commonly understood. Indeed, the world is ruled by little else.

—*John Maynard Keynes*

The market itself is a source of power that influences political outcomes. Economic dependence establishes a power relationship that is a fundamental feature of the contemporary world economy.

—*Robert Gilpin*

As the global economic crisis gained speed in October 2008, the government of Iceland shut down the stock market and seized control of the last major independent bank in the country. Long a member of the Western European financial system yet unable to find credit in the usual markets, the Icelandic government was forced to turn to Russia for a bridge loan to keep itself afloat. By early 2009, the country was bankrupt and the government leaders resigned in disgrace. Iceland was the most prominent example of the potential downside of globalization. The country supported the free flow of goods, services, and investments. Its lack of regulation led the country's banks to participate in a ten-year debt-fueled binge. Banks expanded aggressively and citizens borrowed and bought. When the value of their currency fell, they could not pay their debts. Iceland is a member of the Organization of Economic Cooperation and Development (OECD), the organization of the world's most advanced economies. Yet the government had to turn to the International Monetary Fund (IMF) for support to restore fiscal and monetary stability, a tactic that many developing countries resort to in time of emergency. Iceland was not alone.

By the end of 2008, Georgia, Ukraine, Hungary, the Seychelles, Pakistan, Latvia, and Belarus had all taken loans from the IMF. The financial crisis was the result of serious shortcomings in domestic financial regulation and the failure of global cooperation, especially with regard to

Iceland's currency took a pounding in the economic downturn of 2009–2010.

poverty In the orthodox view, a situation suffered by people who do not have the *money to buy food* and satisfy other basic *material needs*. In the alternative view, a situation suffered by people who are not able to meet their *material and nonmaterial needs* through their own effort.

World Bank Group A collection of five agencies, the first established in 1945, with head offices in Washington, DC. The WBG promotes development in medium- and low-income countries with project loans, structural-adjustment programs, and various advisory services.

World Trade Organization (WTO) Established in 1995 with headquarters in Geneva. Membership (2010) of 153 states. The WTO is a permanent institution to replace the provisional GATT. It has a wider agenda, covering services, intellectual property, and investment issues as well as merchandise trade. The WTO also has greater powers of enforcement through its dispute-settlement mechanism. The organization's Trade Policy Review Body conducts surveillance of members' commercial measures.

global financial institutions. Beginning in the late fall of 2008, many politicians and academic specialists argued that it was time for world leaders to reform the international economic institutions that were created after World War II. As you will see in this chapter, much has changed since 1945: there are now more state actors, more global financial actors, more transnational corporations. The world-wide economic collapse of 2008–2009 revealed that globalization has made all of this more difficult to manage, if not control. Open economies grew much faster than closed economies, but they also opened themselves to the spread of financial difficulties.

Introduction

International political economy (IPE) is about the interplay of economics and politics in world affairs. The core question of IPE is, what drives and explains events in the world economy? For some people, this comes down to a battle of "states versus markets." However, this is misleading. The "markets" of the world economy are not like local street bazaars, in which all items can be openly and competitively traded and exchanged. Equally, politicians cannot rule the global economy, much as they might like to. World markets—and countries, local firms, and multinational corporations that trade and invest within them—are all shaped by layers of rules, norms, laws, organizations, and even habits. Political scientists call all these features of the system "institutions." International political economy tries to explain what creates and perpetuates institutions and what impact institutions have on the world economy.

Since the 1970s, IPE has continued to advance as a core subject of international relations. As will be discussed below, globalization (with its causes and effects on states, processes of international cooperation, and institutions) has become a defining feature of international relations. Furthermore, the end of the Cold War curtailed many of the geostrategic aspirations and much of the influence the West had enjoyed. The challenge of integrating the former Eastern Bloc countries into the world system was soon defined primarily as one of economic transformation and integration. At the same time, an explosion of tribal, religious, and ethnic conflict on the edges of Europe (in the former Yugoslavia) as well as in Africa (such as in Rwanda), in Asia (such as in Indonesia), and in the Middle East forced analysts to examine more closely the links between **poverty**, economic stagnation, and the indebtedness of countries on the one hand and intrastate conflict on the other (see Chapters 10 and 13). Finally, the end of the Cold War thrust international institutions into the limelight. The United Nations, the International Monetary Fund (IMF), the **World Bank Group**, and the newly created **World Trade Organization (WTO)** all became an important focus of study and attention, providing further grist for the mill of IPE scholars concerned with examining the causes, determinants, and impact of international institutions and cooperation among states in economic affairs.

WHAT'S YOUR WORLDVIEW ?

How far should governments go to control or manage the world economy? Can the market self-regulate and create opportunities for all citizens across the world?

The Postwar World Economy

The institutions and framework of the world economy have their roots in the planning for a new economic order that took place during the last phase of the Second World War. In 1944, policy makers gathered in

After the stock market crash of 1929, governments opened relief stations that offered meals to families in need.

New Hampshire at the **Bretton Woods** resort to consider how to resolve two very serious problems. First, they needed to ensure that the **Great Depression** of the 1930s would not happen again. In other words, they had to find ways to ensure a stable global monetary system and an open world-trading system. Second, they needed to rebuild the war-torn economies of Europe.

At Bretton Woods, three institutions were planned in order to promote a new world economic order. The International Monetary Fund (IMF) was created to ensure a stable exchange rate regime and the provision of emergency assistance to countries facing a temporary crisis in their balance of payments regime. The International Bank for Reconstruction and Development (IBRD and later called the World Bank) was created to facilitate private investment and reconstruction in Europe. The bank was also charged with assisting **development** in other countries, a mandate that later became the main reason for its existence. Finally, the General Agreement on Tariffs and Trade (GATT) was signed in 1947 and became a forum for negotiations on **trade liberalization**.

The 1944 plans for the world economy, however, were soon postponed when in 1945 the United States made its first priority the containment of the Soviet Union. Fearing the rise of communism in war-ravaged Europe, the United States took a far more direct role than planned in reconstructing Europe and managing the world economy. The United States announced the **Marshall Plan** in 1947, which directed massive financial aid to Europe and permitted the United States to set conditions on it. The planned gold standard was replaced by the **dollar standard**, which the United States managed directly, backing the dollar with gold. Unsurprisingly, by the time the IMF, the World Bank, and the GATT began to function in the 1950s, they were distinctly Western-bloc organizations that depended heavily on the United States.

US support for the Bretton Woods system began to change when weaknesses emerged in the US economy. After 1965, the United States widened its costly military involvement in Vietnam and also started to spend more money on public education

Bretton Woods System The name given to the three institutions that comprise the post–Second World War international political economic system. It is called Bretton Woods after the hamlet in northern New Hampshire where the leaders from the United States, the United Kingdom, and forty-two other countries met in July 1944.

Great Depression A byword for the global economic collapse that ensued following the US Wall Street stock market crash in October 1929. Economic shockwaves soon rippled around a world already densely interconnected by webs of trade and foreign direct investment, with the result that the events of October 1929 were felt in countries as distant as Brazil and Japan.

development In the orthodox view, top-down; reliance on "expert knowledge," usually Western and definitely external; large capital investments in large projects; advanced technology; expansion of the private sphere. In the alternative view, bottom-up; participatory; reliance on appropriate (often local) knowledge and technology; small investments in small-scale projects; protection of the commons.

trade liberalization The removal or reduction of barriers to free trade such as tariffs or quotas on the trading of specific goods.

Marshall Plan Officially known as the European Recovery Program, it was a program of financial and other economic aid for Europe after WWII. Proposed by Secretary of State George Marshall in 1948, it was offered to all European states, including the Soviet Union, and these funds played a critical role in European recovery.

dollar standard By 1947, the British pound and gold could no longer serve as the world's money. The only currency strong enough to be used to meet the demands for international liquidity was the US dollar. For both political and economic reasons, the US government was willing to become the world's central bank and use dollars for the key currency in the international monetary system.

export-led growth An outward-oriented economy that is based on exploiting its own comparative advantages, such as cheap labor or resources, to capture a share of the world market in a given industry. Many of the countries in Asia took advantage of cheap labor to gain control of industries like electronics and textiles and thereby to control most of the exports to the world.

protectionism Not an economic policy but a variety of political actions taken to protect domestic industries from more-efficient foreign producers. Usually this means the use of tariffs, nontariff barriers, and subsidies to protect domestic interests.

and urban redevelopment programs at home (President Johnson's "Great Society" programs), and all this without raising taxes. The damage was dramatic. As prices rose within the US economy, the competitiveness of US goods and services in the world economy dropped. Likewise, confidence in the US dollar plummeted. Firms and countries turned away from the dollar, and the US capacity to back its currency with gold was brought into question. Meanwhile, other countries in the world economy were enhancing their position. European allies were benefiting from the growing and deepening economic integration in Europe. By the late 1960s, the development of the European Economic Community (EEC) provided a springboard for European policy makers to diverge from US positions on such subjects as NATO, military exercises, and support for the gold standard. In Asia, the phenomenal success of **export-led growth** in Japan and in newly industrializing countries such as South Korea and Taiwan created a new challenge to US trade competitiveness and a new agenda for trade negotiations.

Facing these pressures, the United States changed the rules of the international monetary system in 1971. The government announced that it would no longer convert dollars to gold at $35 per ounce and that it was imposing a 10 percent surcharge on import duties (to improve its trade balance by curtailing imports, which were flooding into the United States, and to try to stem the outflow of dollars to the rest of the world). These actions broke the Bretton Woods system. This was not the only change in the world economy in the 1970s.

In the 1970s, the period of high growth enjoyed after the Second World War came to an abrupt end, leaving very high inflation. Further compounding the problem, the first oil crisis in 1973 plunged the world economy into stagflation (a combination of economic stagnation, or low growth, and high inflation). In the monetary system, the role of the IMF collapsed when the Bretton Woods system broke down in 1971 and the major industrialized countries failed to find a way to coordinate their exchange rate policies within the IMF framework. Instead, the major currencies floated, and industrialized countries began to discuss monetary issues among themselves in groups such as the Group of Seven (comprising the United States, Japan, Germany, the United Kingdom, France, Italy, and Canada), which first met in 1975.

In the trading system, cooperation had steadily grown in negotiations under the auspices of the GATT. However, in the 1970s, the gains that had been made in reducing tariff barriers, especially among industrialized countries, were reversed by policies of new **protectionism**. As each country grappled with stagflation, many introduced new forms of barriers (or "nontariff barriers"), in particular to keep out the new competitive imports from successful developing countries like those experiencing export-driven growth. An egregious example of the new protectionism was the Multifiber Arrangement of 1973, which placed restrictions on all textile and apparel imports from developing countries, blatantly violating the GATT principle of nondiscrimination.

The General Agreement on Tariffs and Trade (GATT) was an interim agreement signed in 1947 in the expectation that it would be superseded by an international trade organization. A permanent trade organization was not created until 1994, and so for four decades the interim GATT continued to exist as an arrangement among "contracting parties," backed up by a very small secretariat based in Geneva and a minuscule budget. In essence, the GATT was a forum for trade negotiations. Numerous rounds of talks culminated in the very successful Kennedy Round of 1962–1967, where breakthroughs were made in the reduction of trade barriers among industrialized countries. However, when protectionism flourished in the 1970s, the GATT proved unable to restrain powerful members such as the United States and European countries from imposing trade barriers (e.g., the Multifiber Arrangement of 1973 restricting textile imports) and abusing the many exceptions and safeguards written into the agreement. The GATT also functioned as a forum for dispute settlement (i.e., upholding trade rules). However, it was both slow and impotent in this regard, constrained by the need for consensus on any decision regarding disputes. The GATT was replaced by the World Trade Organization (WTO) as a result of agreements forged in the last round of GATT talks, the Uruguay Round (1986–1994). Established on January 1, 1995, the WTO has the following functions: administering WTO trade agreements; providing a forum for trade negotiations; handling trade disputes; monitoring national trade policies; supplying technical assistance and training for developing countries; and cooperating with other international organizations. It is located in Geneva with a secretariat staff of five hundred.

The new protectionism in industrialized countries further fueled the anger of people in developing countries, who, in the 1970s, launched a concerted campaign in the United Nations General Assembly for a New International Economic Order (NIEO). Organized as the Group of 77 (G-77), the developing countries were determined to alter the rules of the game, and their strategy for change was bolstered by the success of OPEC oil-producing developing countries in raising oil prices in 1973. The agenda of the NIEO covered trade, aid, investment, the international monetary and financial system (including debt forgiveness), and institutional reform. Developing countries sought better representation in international economic institutions, a fairer trading system, more aid, the regulation of foreign investment, the protection of economic sovereignty, and reforms to ensure a more stable and equitable financial and monetary system.

A kind of **summit diplomacy** also took place in the 1970s between North (the industrialized countries) and South (developing countries). These negotiations were underpinned by a different kind of thinking and scholarship about IPE. The developing countries' push for reform of the international economic system reflected **dependency** and Marxist theories of international economic relations that highlighted negative aspects of **interdependence**, which we discussed in Chapter 4. In particular, as you remember, these theorists were concerned to identify aspects of the international economy and institutions that impeded the possibilities of development in the South. Their central concern was to answer why so many countries within the world economy remained underdeveloped, in spite of the promises of modernization and global growth. The most sympathetic official "Northern" answer to these concerns was voiced in

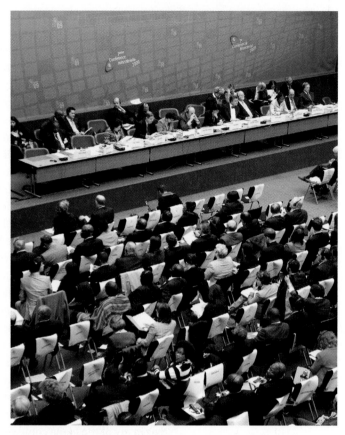

The framers of the Bretton Woods institutions wanted to create a system to manage the global economy in order to avoid another global collapse. How do we measure the success of the World Trade Organization (2009 meeting shown here)?

summit diplomacy A direct meeting between heads of government (of the superpowers in particular) to resolve major problems. The "summit" became a regular mode of contact during the Cold War.

WHAT'S YOUR WORLDVIEW

In the face of the 2008–2009 global economic collapse, how well did the leaders of countries coordinate their economic policies? Did these efforts include both rich and poor states?

dependency theory The world capitalist system divides the world into core, semiperiphery, and periphery states. The core states control both the economic and the political system and exploit the people and resources in the periphery and semiperiphery. The capitalist system is seen as impossible to reform, and only by withdrawing from the system can poor states break this dependency.

interdependence A condition where states (or peoples) are affected by decisions taken by others. Interdependence can be symmetric, i.e., both sets of actors are affected equally, or it can be asymmetric, where the impact varies between actors. If political or economic costs of interdependence are high, a state is in a vulnerable position. If costs are low, it is a situation of sensitivity interdependence.

free market A market ruled by the forces of supply and demand, where all buying and selling is not constrained by government regulations or interventions.

global capital markets These are banks, investment companies, insurance companies, trusts, hedge funds, and stock exchanges that transfer funds to industries and other commercial enterprises globally.

deregulation The removal of all regulation so that market forces, not government policy, control economic developments.

the Brandt Report in 1980, the findings of a group of high-level policy makers from rich and poor states who had been asked to examine how and why the international community should respond to the challenges of interdependence and development. The Brandt Report urged the wealthy states in the North to increase development assistance and to reduce trade and investment restrictions for poor countries in the South. Closing the gap between rich and poor states was presented as the biggest security challenge facing world leaders.

The NIEO campaign was unsuccessful for several reasons. The United Nations General Assembly (UNGA) was an obvious institution for developing countries to choose in making their case since, unlike the IMF or World Bank, it offers every country one vote. However, the UNGA had no power to implement the agenda of the developing countries. Furthermore, although many industrialized countries were sympathetic to the developing countries' case in the 1970s, these governments did not act, and by the 1980s a new set of governments with a distinctly less sympathetic **free market** ideology had come to power in the United States, the United Kingdom, and West Germany.

The 1980s opened with a shift in US economic policy. In 1979, the US Federal Reserve dramatically raised interest rates. This action was taken to stem inflation by contracting economic activity in the United States. However, the reverberations in the rest of the world economy were immediate and extensive. During the 1960s and 1970s, US and European policies had facilitated the rapid growth of **global capital markets** and financial flows. In the 1970s these flows were further buoyed by the investments of oil producers who needed to find outlets for the vast profits made from the oil-price rise of 1973. The money found its way to governments in developing countries, which were offered loans at knock-down prices. The rise in interest rates in 1979 was an abrupt wake-up call to both borrowers and creditors (many of whom were US-based banks), who suddenly realized that many of the loans could not be repaid. The IMF was immediately called in to prevent any developing country defaulting on these loans, since it was feared that such a default would cause a global financial crisis.

The debt crisis meant that the IMF's role in the world economy became largely one of ensuring that indebted countries undertook "structural adjustment" in their economies. Structural adjustment meant immediate measures to reduce inflation, government expenditure, and the role of the government in the economy, including trade liberalization, privatization, and **deregulation**. These "neoliberal" policies were in marked contrast to the Keynesian analysis that had prevailed until the 1980s, during the decades of growth in the world economy. Keynesians (named after economist John Maynard Keynes) believe that governments should play an active and interventionist role in the economy in order to ensure both growth and equity. By contrast, neoliberalism sought to roll back the state and the role of government, leaving decisions about allocation, production, and distribution in the economy to the market. By the late 1980s, the term **Washington Consensus** was being used, sometimes pejoratively, to imply that these policies were mainly a reflection of US interests.

The 1990s brought the end of the Cold War and the challenge of how to integrate Central and Eastern European countries and the former Soviet Union into the global economy. The IMF and World Bank became deeply involved, but the Washington Consensus was not broad enough for the purpose. Both institutions began to embrace a broader and deeper view of **conditionality** aimed at promoting "good governance" in member countries. But many thought conditionality had gone too far when, in the wake of the East Asian financial crisis in 1997, the IMF imposed far-reaching and overly draconian conditions on countries such as Korea. The impact would be felt in subsequent years as the IMF's lending role waned in most emerging market economies. Over this period, the World Bank sought to broaden its appeal through enhanced relations with governments as well as with nongovernmental organizations (NGOs). Its legitimacy seemed less tarnished. At the same time, the newly established World Trade Organization began operations in 1995, opening up a new forum within which a broad range of international issues would be negotiated, including not just traditional trade but such issues as **intellectual property rights**, trade-related investment measures, and food-safety standards.

> **WHAT'S YOUR WORLDVIEW**
>
> *In a global economy run by transnational corporations seeking cheap labor, cheap resources, and minimal rules concerning safety, health, and the environment, should governments seek to protect their citizens and protect their jobs?*

In the first decade of the twenty-first century, a shift in global economic power was occurring. In September 2003, during global trade negotiations in Mexico, a group of twenty countries, including Brazil, South Africa, India, and China, resisted the powerful United States and European Union and refused to engage unless some of their terms were heeded. In the IMF in 2006 a shift in voting power was conceded in favor of China, Mexico, Turkey, and Korea, and further shifts were conceded in the wake of the financial crisis. Yet few believed this would be enough to fully engage these countries in the institutions. Several emerging countries—with China in the lead—became more powerful donors in their own right. As world energy consumption grew, so too did the power of countries supplying energy resources. In Venezuela, President Hugo Chavez painted the world in the style made popular in the 1970s, blaming the US and other countries of the global North for the economic conditions in the global South. Meanwhile, across most industrialized countries, calls for greater efforts to reduce climate-changing emissions became ever stronger. For scholars of international relations, the twenty-first century brought serious questions about how international institutions might assist, not only in managing new challenges in the global economy, but equally in managing a shift in power among the states that make up—and make work—the existing institutions.

Washington Consensus The belief of key opinion formers in Washington that global welfare would be maximized by the universal application of neoliberal economic policies, which favor a minimalist state and an enhanced role for the market.

conditionality When regional or international lending agencies require that recipient national governments accept certain policy conditions in order to receive a loan or some form of economic assistance.

intellectual property rights Rules that protect the owners of content through copyright, patents, trademarks, and trade secrets. The World Intellectual Property Organization (WIPO) is the forum where states (184 members in 2010) discuss this issue.

Traditional Approaches to IPE: Liberal, Mercantilist, and Marxist

We have learned that in international relations there are contending theories or traditions that offer competing descriptions and explanations of conditions and events. As we try to understand the complexities of the global economy—past, present, and future—we should consider three competing traditions or economic belief systems. The liberal tradition dominated most discussion of the international economic system that was created after WWII and is still much used to explain the present global economy. The mercantilist tradition focuses on competition among states, stressing that states must protect their own interests and power in order to protect their citizens in the competitive international economy. The Marxist or socialist tradition favors a more equitable political economy that ends the exploitation of workers around the world and closes the gap between rich and poor states. These three traditions have a particular moral and analytical slant on global economic relations.

The Liberal Tradition

The liberal tradition is the free market one, in which the role of voluntary exchange and markets is emphasized as both efficient and morally desirable. The assumption is that free trade and the free movement of capital will ensure that investment flows to where it is most profitable to invest (for example, into less developed areas where maximal gains

Global Perspective

The Bretton Woods Institutions and the Global South

For many people in the developing world, the international finance institutions of the Bretton Woods system are yet another form of neocolonial exploitation. Politicians, news media, and ordinary people condemn the oppression of the globalized system based in the capital of the hegemon, the United States. Although the Bretton Woods system has not been the only cause of underdevelopment in the global South, there is some basis for these criticisms.

Both the International Monetary Fund and the International Bank for Reconstruction and Development (World Bank) were established in 1946, after wartime negotiations held at the Bretton Woods resort in New Hampshire, with headquarters (opposite one another) in Washington, DC. The IMF was created to promote international monetary cooperation and resolve the interwar economic problems, although several of these functions ended when the Bretton Woods system broke down in 1971. The IMF now has a membership of 186 countries, each of whom contributes a quota of resources to the organization (proportionate to the size of their economy), which also determines their percentage of voting rights and the amount of resources to which they can have automatic access. Since the 1980s, the IMF has become an institution offering financial and technical assistance to developing and transitional economies. The terms on which countries receive assistance include the government having to commit to specific "conditions" or policy reforms, called conditionality (see www.imf.org).

The World Bank started out as an agency to finance reconstruction in war-torn Europe as well as development in the rest of the world. It has since become the world's largest source of development assistance, providing nearly $16 billion in loans annually to eligible member countries, through the IBRD, the International Development Association (IDA), the International Finance Corporation (IFC), and the Multilateral Investment Guarántee Agency (MIGA). As with the IMF, the World Bank requires members to whom it lends to undertake specific reforms within their economy. Most recently, this has included requiring borrowing governments to demonstrate their commitment to reducing poverty within their countries. With the exception of IDA (which is funded by donations), the World Bank's resources come from its issue of bonds in the capital markets. These bonds are backed up by guarantees provided by the governments that belong to the institution (see www.worldbank.org).

At the time of their creation, the IMF and the World Bank were not intended to help what we now call the "developing world." In 1944 most of Africa and significant parts of Asia were colonies of European countries. The colonies of Africa and Asia might benefit indirectly from the IMF's exchange rate mechanism, but it was by design a procedure to bring stability to the international economic transactions of the Europeans' homelands. The weighted-voting procedure of the IMF was another indication of the lack of status of certain countries in the system. While weighted voting acknowledged the size of the United States' contribution to the IMF, and it gave leadership status as well, it also locked in place the subordinate status for the colonies as they won their independence from Europe. In the 1980s and early 1990s the IMF's Structural Adjustment Programs (SAP)—which demanded an end to price subsidies for basics like food and cooking oil—were, from the perspective of the Global South, an even greater intrusion in the affairs of the nominally sovereign developing countries.

Economic prosperity is not spread evenly around the world.

Global Perspective

The formal name of the World Bank, the International Bank for Reconstruction and Development, provides a clue to the inherent difficulties that the newly independent former European colonies had with the organization. "Reconstruction" came before "Development" in the name because the bank was originally founded primarily to deal with the needs of Europeans and reconstruction. With the increasing power of developing countries in the 1960s and 1970s, most visibly in the United Nations with the creation of the United Nations Conference on Trade and Development (UNCTAD, see Chapter 13) and later the Group of 77, the World Bank created special lending facilities such as IDA, mentioned above, to help the global South. However, like the IMF, the World Bank's facilities were still controlled from Washington, DC, with the decision-making bodies seemingly under the control of the United States. This impression is reinforced by the fact that the head of the World Bank has always been a citizen of the United States.

might be made). Free trade is crucial, for it permits countries to benefit from their comparative advantages. In other words, each country can exploit its own natural advantages, resources, and endowments and gain from specialization. The economy is oiled by freely exchangeable currencies and open markets that create a global system of prices, which, like an **invisible hand**, ensures an efficient and equitable distribution of goods and services across the world economy. This view was promoted by the Scottish economist Adam Smith and his influential book, *The Wealth of Nations* (1776), which promoted free trade over mercantilism. Order in the global economy is fairly minimal. The optimal role of governments and institutions is to ensure the smooth and relatively unfettered operation of markets. It is assumed that governments face a wide range of choices in the world system and likewise vis-à-vis their own societies and populations. This means that governments that fail to pursue "good" economic policies do so because decision makers are either too corrupt or too ignorant of the correct economic choices they might make.

invisible hand The concept found in the eighteenth-century writing of Adam Smith that proposed governments leave trade and financial sectors alone.

The Mercantilist Tradition

The mercantilist tradition stands in stark contrast to the liberal one. Whereas liberals have a view that all states can benefit from a free market (positive sum), mercantilists share the presumptions of realists in international relations that states exist in a **zero-sum world**. They do not focus on individual policy makers and their policy choices but rather assume that the world economy is an arena of competition among states seeking to maximize relative strength and power. Simply put, the international system is like a jungle in which each state has to do what it can to survive. For this reason, the aim of every state must be to maximize its wealth and independence. States will seek to do this by ensuring their self-sufficiency (sometimes called **autarchy**) in key strategic industries and commodities and by using trade protectionism (tariffs and other limits on exports and imports), subsidies, and selective investments in the domestic economy. Obviously, within this system some states have more power and capability than others. As we saw in Chapter 3, the most powerful states define the rules and limits of the system: through hegemony, alliances, and balances of power. Indeed, stability and order will only be achieved where one state can play the role of hegemon, or, in other words, is willing and able to create, maintain, and enforce basic rules. Amid this, the economic policies of any one government will always be subservient to its quest to secure the external and internal sovereignty of the state.

zero-sum world A pessimistic view of any interaction that suggests that another's gains are your losses.

autarchy The mercantilist recommendation that states strive for economic self-sufficiency by using trade protectionism or policies of complete isolation.

The Marxist Tradition

The Marxist tradition also sees the world economy as an arena of competition, but not among states. Capitalism is the driving force in the world economy. Using Marx's language, this means that world economic relations are best conceived as a class struggle between the oppressor and the oppressed. The oppressors, or capitalists, are those who own the means of production (trade and industry). The oppressed are the working class. The struggle between the two arises because capitalists seek to increase their profits and this requires them to exploit ever more harshly the working class. This description of class relations within a capitalist system has been applied to international relations in various ways. Lenin, founder of the USSR, believed that imperialism was the highest stage of capitalism. Theorists like Immanuel Wallerstein contend that between the core (industrialized countries) and periphery (developing countries) an unequal exchange occurs. Dependency theorists (who have focused mainly on Latin America) describe the ways classes and groups in the core link to the periphery. Underdevelopment and poverty in so many countries is explained as the result of economic, social, and political structures that have been deeply influenced by international economic relations. The global capitalist order within which these societies have emerged is, after all, a global capitalist order that reflects the interests of those who own the means of production.

It becomes clear in contrasting these traditions of thinking about international economic relations that each focuses on different actors and driving forces in the world economy and that each has a different conception of what "order" means and what is necessary to achieve it.

Comparing the different traditions also highlights two different levels of analysis (system and national levels): the structure of the international system (be that international capitalism or the configuration of power among states in the system), the nature of a particular government or competition within its institutions, and the role of interest groups and societal forces within a country (see levels of analysis discussions in Chapters 1 and 5). At each of these levels of analysis we need to ask what drives the actors concerned and how we might therefore explain their preferences, actions, and the outcomes that result. In answering this question we enter into more methodological preoccupations that today divide the study of IPE.

WHAT'S YOUR WORLDVIEW ?

If the present neoliberal system cannot address the inequalities in the system, will states become more mercantilist? Will a new Marxist movement emerge?

Table 11.1
Dominant Perspectives on IPE

Liberal	Mercantilist	Marxist
The world economy has the potential to be a seamless global marketplace in which free trade and the free movement of capital shape the policies of governments and economic actors. Order would be achieved by the "invisible hand" of competition in the global marketplace.	As an arena of interstate competition, the world economy is one in which states seek to maximize their wealth and independence vis-à-vis other states. Order is achieved only where there is a balance of power or hegemony.	The world economy is best described as an arena of capitalist competition in which classes (capitalists and workers) and social groups are in constant conflict. Capitalists (and the states they are based in) are driven by the search for profits, and order is achieved only where they succeed in exacting the submission of all others.

New Approaches to IPE

International political economy is divided by the different normative concerns and analytical questions that are highlighted by the traditions outlined above. The discipline is now subject to a lively methodological debate about how scholars might best explain policies and outcomes (see Table 11.2). In essence, this debate is about whether you can assume what states' (and other actors') preferences and interests are. If you can, then rational-choice (or "neoutilitarian") approaches to IPE make sense. However, if you open up the question as to why and how states and other actors come to have particular preferences, then you are pushed towards approaches now often labeled "constructivism" (see Chapter 4).

Political Economy: The Application of Rational Choice to Groups Within the State

In the United States, the study of IPE has become dominated by a "rational choice" or neoutilitarian approach. This borrows economic concepts to explain politics. Instead of exploring the ideas, personalities, ideologies, or historical traditions that lie behind policies and institutions, rational choice focuses on the incentive structure faced by those making decisions. It is assumed that actors' interests and preferences are known or fixed and that actors can make strategic choices as to how best to promote their interests. The term "rational choice" is a useful one to describe this approach since it proposes that, even though a particular policy may seem stupid or wrong, it may well have been rational. "Rational" in this sense means that for the actor or group concerned, this was the optimal choice given the specific incentives and institutional constraints and opportunities that existed at the time.

Rational choice has been applied to interest groups and their influence on IPE in what has been called a **political-economy approach**. This approach has its roots in explanations of trade policy that focus on interest groups. More recent applications have attempted to explain why countries adapt in particular ways to changes in the world economy (see Table 11.2). The analysis proceeds on the assumption that governments and their policies are important but that the policies and preferences of governments reflect the actions of specific interest groups within the economy. These groups may emerge along class or sectoral lines. Indeed, the assumptions of rational choice are applied to explain how particular groups within the economy emerge and what their goals and policy preferences are. Furthermore, rational choice provides a framework for understanding the coalitions into which these groups enter and their interactions with other institutions. For example, in explaining developing-country responses to the debt crisis of the 1980s, a political-economy approach starts out by examining the effect of **economic shocks**, such as high interest rates and structural adjustment, on interest groups. By demonstrating that the power of some interests (such as those working in the export sector) has increased and the power of others (such as those working in industries relying on diminishing state subsidies) has diminished, the approach proffers an explanation for radical shifts in government policies.

Institutionalism: The Application of Rational Choice to States

A different application of rational choice lies in the institutionalist approach to IPE. This approach applies the assumptions of rational choice to states in their interaction with other states. Drawing on theories of delegation and agency, it offers an explanation as to why institutions exist and for what purposes. The core assumption is that states create international institutions and delegate power to them in order to maximize utility within the

political-economy approach The study of the interactions between states or public actors and the market at domestic and international levels.

economic shock An event that produces a significant change within an economy, despite occurring outside of it. Economic shocks are unpredictable and typically impact supply or demand throughout the markets. A sudden rise in commodity process and a devaluation of a currency are two examples of shocks that would hurt economic actors.

Table 11.2
Examples of New Approaches to IPE

Institutionalist	Political Economy	Constructivist
Institutionalists regard the world economy as an arena of interstate cooperation. They see the core actors as governments and the institutions to whom they delegate power, and the key driving forces as rational choice at the level of the state motivated by the potential gains from cooperation. For institutionalists, the key condition for order is the existence of international institutions that permit cooperation to continue.	For political economists, the world economy is characterized by competition among vested interests within different kinds of states, and the core actors are interest groups formed within domestic economies. The key driving force is rational choice at the level of groups within the domestic economy, responding to changes in the international economy. Political economists are not concerned with theorizing about the conditions necessary for international order.	Constructivists see the world economy as an overarching structure of knowledge, ideas, and institutions that reflects the interests of dominant actors and within which competition takes place. They regard the structure of the system itself as vital in understanding the identities and preferences of the actors. The key driving force of the system is capitalist competition, which is constrained by the need of the powerful to gain the consent of the less powerful. Dominance by one state is an insufficient condition for international order. Hegemony requires control over the structures of knowledge and ideas as well.

constraints of world markets and world politics. Frequently, this comes down to the need to resolve collective-action problems. For example, states realize that they cannot achieve their goals in areas such as trade or environment unless all other states also embark on a particular course of action. Hence, institutions are created to ensure that there is no defection or free riding, and the collective goal is achieved.

Constructivism

In contrast to rational-choice analysis, other approaches to international political economy assume that policies within the world economy are affected by historical and sociological factors. Much more attention is paid to the ways in which actors formulate preferences, as well as to the processes by which decisions are made and implemented. In other words, rather than assuming that a state or decision maker's preferences reflect rational choices within given constraints and opportunities, analysts in a broader tradition of IPE examine the beliefs, roles, traditions, ideologies, and patterns of influence that shape preferences, behavior, and outcomes.

Interests, actions, and behavior in the world economy are conceived as taking place within a structure of ideas, culture, and knowledge. We cannot simply assume that the preferences of actors within the system reflect objectively definable competing "interests." Rather, the way actors understand their own preferences will depend heavily on prevailing beliefs and patterns of thinking in the world economy, many of which are embodied in institutions. The question this poses is, whose interests and ideas are embodied in the rules and norms of the system?

hegemony A system regulated by a dominant leader, or political (and/or economic) domination of a region. It is also means power and control exercised by a leading state over other states.

For some, the answer to the question *in whose interest* lies in **hegemony**. The dominant power within the system will achieve goals not just through coercion but equally by ensuring the consent of other actors. This means that dominant powers will promulgate institutions, ideologies, and ideas, all of which help to persuade other actors that their best interests converge with those of the dominant power. For example, constructivists interpret the dominance of neoliberalism since the 1980s as a reflection of US interests in the global economy, successfully projected through structures of knowledge (it became the dominant paradigm in top research universities), through institutions (such as the IMF, which became a forceful proponent of neoliberal policy prescriptions), and through broader cultural beliefs and understandings (the very language of "free" market contrasting with restricted or repressive regimes).

New approaches to IPE highlight a powerful debate about whether we should treat states' interests and preferences as given or fixed. We return to this question in the final section of this chapter. There we will examine why states form institutions and what role such institutions might play in managing globalization. First, though, we need to establish what globalization in the world economy is and what its implications are.

Meetings of the WTO attract a range of protesters opposed to what they see as the predatory nature of globalization.

The Globalization Debate in IPE

The nature and impact of globalization is the subject of profound debate within IPE (as within other areas of international relations discussed in this book). The term "globalization" is used to refer to at least four different sets of forces or processes in the world economy (see Table 11.3). Internationalization describes the increase in economic transactions across borders, which has been taking place since the turn of the century but which some argue has undergone a quantitative leap in recent decades. The technological revolution is a second aspect of globalization, identifying the effect of new electronic communication that permits firms and other actors to operate globally with much less regard for location, distance, and borders. One effect of the technological revolution is to speed up deterritorialization, or the lessening influence territorial distances, borders, and places have on the way people collectively identify themselves, act, and seek political voice or recognition. Finally, liberalization describes the policies, undertaken by states, that have made a new global economy possible. These include both the rules and the institutions created by powerful states to facilitate a new scale of transnational economic activity in certain sectors of the world economy. It also includes the policies of smaller and less powerful states (e.g., Iceland) in the system, which, by liberalizing trade, investment, and production, have integrated into the world economy.

In IPE, several competing claims are made about globalization. For example, while some scholars argue that globalization is nothing new, others posit that globalization is dramatically diminishing the role of the state (see Chapter 1). Still others claim that globalization is exacerbating inequalities and giving rise to a more unjust world. To make sense of these different arguments, and the evidence adduced to support them, it is worth thinking about the approaches to IPE covered in previous sections, for they help to identify key differences in emphasis that give rise to conflicting interpretations of globalization. For example, skeptics who deny that globalization is transforming world politics tend to focus on the "internationalization" element of globalization (see Table 11.3). They can

Table 11.3
Four Aspects of Globalization

1. **Internationalization** describes the increase in transactions among states, reflected in flows of trade, investment, and capital (see the argument that these flows have not increased as much as is claimed: UNDP 1997). The processes of internationalization have been facilitated and are shaped by international agreements on trade, investment, and capital, as well as by domestic policies permitting the private sector to transact abroad.

2. The **technological revolution** refers to the way modern communications (Internet, satellite communications, high-tech computers), made possible by technological advances, have made distance and location less important factors not just for government (including at local and regional levels) but equally in the calculations of other actors, such as firms' investment decisions or in the activities of social movements.

3. **Deterritorialization** is accelerated by the technological revolution and refers to the declining influence of territorial places, distances, and boundaries over the way people collectively identify themselves or seek political recognition. This permits an expansion of global civil society but equally an expansion of global criminal or terrorist networks.

4. **Liberalization** describes government policies that reduce the role of the state in the economy, such as through the dismantling of trade tariffs and barriers, the deregulation and opening of the financial sector to foreign investors, and the privatization of state enterprises.

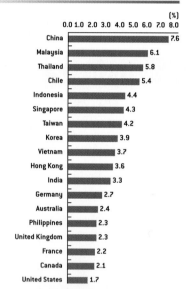

Real GDP Growth. This is a chart showing the per capita real GDP growth of selected countries (2009-2010). Does anything about this data surprise you? Based on what you have read in this book, and studied in your course, how would you explain the data presented here? *Source: "Report of the Globalization Working Group in the Economic Outlook Committee," by the Economic Council of Japan.*

then draw on evidence that throws into doubt whether the number of transactions taking place among states has indeed risen (UNDP 1997) and make the argument that there is "nothing new" in the growing interdependence of states. By contrast, liberal enthusiasts of globalization focus on technological innovation and the nonpolitical "objective" forces that are shrinking the world economy. They argue that this is creating a less political, more efficient, more unified world order. Those who focus on deterritorialization highlight that there is also a negative side to globalization. Just as technological innovation permits a more active global civil society, so too it permits the growth of an uncivil one.

Terrorist networks and transnational crime grow easily and are harder to combat in an era of globalization. This puts an important caveat on a final argument about globalization—one that prioritizes the role powerful states play in shaping the process. Focusing on liberalization, several analysts highlight the role of powerful states in setting the rules of the new globalized international economy and their increasing influence over less powerful states. Yet this has two faces. On the one hand, powerful states find it relatively easy to set down rules with little or no consultation with less powerful states. This is as true in the global economy as it has been in recent years in the United States' (and selected allies') war against terrorism and invasions of Afghanistan and Iraq. Yet in the latter case, the subsequent challenge of pacifying weakened states through military occupation reveals how difficult it is even for the most powerful states to control other countries.

Is Globalization Diminishing the Role of the State in the World Economy?

"A global economy is emerging," claim those who depict a world in which multinational trade, production, investment, and financing move in and out of countries ever more easily. The globalists tell us that, as a result, governments and states are losing their capacity to control economic interactions. This is partly because the quantity and rapidity

Microcredit: Empowering Women Through Investment

CASE STUDY

In 1976, a Bangladeshi economist, Muhammad Yunus, founded the Grameen Bank. The bank is a lending program that provides its largely female clientele with small loans for business investment. These small loans, which are called "microcredit," are directed toward women because women have a better record for investment and repayment than men. Women are more likely to invest the loans rather than spend them on themselves, and they are more likely to repay. Loan-repayment rates fluctuate between 96 percent and 100 percent. Loans directed toward women are also seen as a method of empowerment that gives women access to resources, economic security, and higher status in the household. Up to 5 percent of borrowers per year rise out of poverty. Borrowers also increase the educational and nutritional standards within their families.

In Bangladesh in 2006, Grameen Bank reported 6.83 million borrowers in 73,609 villages, 97 percent of whom were women. In addition to financing small enterprises, homebuilding, and education, the bank empowers women by fostering entrepreneurialism and encouraging family planning. Borrowers now own 94 percent of the bank, with the other 6 percent owned by the government. The bank earns a profit and, since 1995, has been self-sufficient. The Grameen Bank and its founder were jointly awarded the 2006 Nobel Peace Prize.

Microcredit is widely publicized as a successful model for development *and* the empowerment of women. However, many organizations, including commercial banks, who have tried to replicate the Grameen Bank have failed. This has led to a fierce debate about what makes microcredit effective. The Grameen Bank succeeded, not just by carefully managing its loans to ensure that individual women could repay, but because its programs actively addressed reasons for default. Only a few organizations have replicated this.

of flows make it more difficult for governments to regulate trade, investment, or capital. Equally important is the fact that firms and investors can more easily take their business elsewhere. This puts new constraints on governments trying to retain and encourage investment. The argument here is that footloose modern businesses will simply exit from a country if a government does not pursue liberalizing policies that foster corporate profitability and flexibility. For this reason, governments are under pressure to reduce taxes and to cut back state expenditure on health, education, pensions, and so forth. When it comes to regulating international business, governments are permitting investors themselves to set the rules, and these private actors are doing so though new private international networks and self-regulatory agencies. In sum, states are losing power in a global economic order in which state borders and governments are less influential. This eventuality is, of course, embraced by those interpreting it from a "liberal" starting point.

The Global Skeptics

A variety of skeptics counter the "global economy" view, pointing out flaws in the argument and the evidence that the state is losing power. The proposition that states are under pressure to cut taxes and reduce expenditure is attacked by scholars who examine data of industrialized countries and demonstrate that the evidence does not back up this claim. Nor does the evidence suggest that transnational corporations (TNCs) relocate investment to areas where there are lower wages and lower taxes. Rather, contemporary research into actual patterns of TNC investment discloses that in the new knowledge-intensive economy, factors such as the availability of skilled and semiskilled labor, good infrastructure, and proximity to market are crucial ingredients to choices of location. The conclusion drawn from this evidence is that the role of states is not eroding. To the

Volume of World Merchandise Exports. This graph represents the annual percentage change in the volume of world merchandise exports. What does this data tell you about world trade over the last twenty years? What patterns do you notice here? What factors may have influenced each of the significant fluctuations? *Source: WTO Secretariat.*

China, with its Communist Party government, has become a central player in the globalized capitalist economy. How do you explain this apparent paradox?

contrary, states and government still have a very important and substantial role to play in a successful economy.

New Constraints on States

While skeptics knock holes in some of the arguments about the erosion of state power in the face of global multinational enterprises, other aspects of globalization do constrain all states. In particular, the fact that billions of dollars can flood in—or out—of a country overnight sets a new constraint on monetary policy and opens up new vulnerabilities in the financial sectors of all countries. In other words, governments have to be very careful in managing interest rates and managing or floating exchange rates. In the same way, they need robust domestic banking and financial systems to weather the onslaught or recession of a tidal wave of capital. The punishment for poor policy is instantaneous and devastating. Furthermore, as the Asian financial crisis of 1997 (see Case Study) showed, it is not only the culprit country that bears the punishment. The financial crisis in Asia brought to light the potential vulnerability of all countries to massive inflows and outflows of capital. It also underlined that some states suffer the impact of globalization more than others.

> **WHAT'S YOUR WORLDVIEW**
>
> *Is globalization eroding the sovereignty of states? How has it influenced your own way of living?*

International Institutions in the Globalizing World Economy

We have seen that globalization is increasing interdependence among states. It is also increasing global interconnectedness and the capacity of some states to influence others. The Asian financial crisis exhibited all three of these changes. The countries of Asia had

Theory in Practice

The Prisoner's Dilemma

Game theorists are mathematicians interested in non-zero-sum games that focus on the strategic interaction between rational actors who can pursue either competitive or collaborative strategies. Their interaction produces a much more complex situation than is found in the purely competitive market setting; yet, by distilling the detail and working with a theoretical model, we can better understand the underlying dynamics of a complex situation, such as market failures, arms races, or any agreement that requires some form of collective agreement.

"The prisoner's dilemma" is a popular interpretation of this non-zero-sum game. It's a game in which two people each have two options whose outcome depends on the simultaneous choice made by the other, for example, whether to confess to a crime. A typical scenario would unfold something like this: A prison warden once had two prisoners. The warden required a voluntary confession of at least one of the prisoners before he could hang either one. So, he summoned the first prisoner (A) and offered him his freedom *and* a big cash reward if he would confess at least one day before the second prisoner (B), so that an indictment could be prepared and so that the second prisoner could be hanged. If prisoner B should confess at least a day before him, however, the first prisoner was told, then prisoner B would be freed and given the cash reward—and that he (prisoner A) would be hanged instead.

"And what if we both should confess on the same day?" asked prisoner A. "Then you each will keep your life but will get ten years in prison," the warden responded.

"And if neither of us should confess?" "Then both of you will be set free—without any reward, of course. But, are you willing to bet your life that your fellow prisoner—that crook—will not confess and pocket the reward? Now go back to your solitary cell and think about your answer until tomorrow." The second prisoner in his interview was told the same, and each man spent the night alone considering his dilemma (Deutsch 1968: 120).

Here the two actors are confronted with two possible strategies, generating a situation with four possible outcomes. Being rational, the prisoners can place these outcomes on a preference ranking. The matrix here reveals the preference rankings for the two prisoners. Both prisoners will pursue the strategy which will optimize their position in light of the strategies available to the other prisoner. To avoid being hanged, both prisoners will confess and end up in prison for ten years, thereby demonstrating how

		A	
		Silent	**Confess***
B	**Silent**	3, 3‡	4, 1
	Confess*	1, 4	2, 2†

Key

* Dominant strategy: both players have dominant rather than contingent strategies. A strategy becomes dominant if it is preferable to the alternative strategy no matter which strategy the other player adopts.

† Denotes an equilibrium outcome.

‡ A Pareto optimal outcome: Vilfredo Pareto (1848–1923) was an Italian sociologist and economist who developed a criterion for identifying when an exchange between two parties has reached its most efficient or optimum point. He argued, in essence, that the point is reached when one party is better off and the other party is no worse off than before the exchange took place.

In this figure, cell numerals refer to ranked preferences: 4 = best, 1 = worst. The first number in each cell refers to A's preference and the second number refers to B's preference.

Continued

Theory in Practice *continued*

individual rationality leads to collective irrationality. The sub-optimal outcome could only be avoided if the two prisoners possessed a mechanism which allowed them to collaborate.

We know that in the U.S. the study of international political economy is dominated by rational choice approaches. Rational means that for a group or individual this was the optimal choice. The prisoner's dilemma payoff structure may apply to any agreement or global issue that requires a global or collective response such as new regulations governing banking practices. To some actors in the banking industry, the optimal choice may be to defect rather than cooperate because of the short-term advantages of unilateral action over cooperation. This raises another problem addressed by the prisoner's dilemma: Without a collective will to enforce rules and the means to punish those who defect, states will not see cooperation as the optimal choice. Of course, what may seem irrational to the outside observer may seem perfectly rational to the people in power who are making the decision.

"liberalized" into global capital markets (with much encouragement from the United States and other industrialized countries) and soon became recipients of large inflows of short-term capital. As soon as confidence in Thailand faltered, reactions were instantaneously transmitted to investors (through the new communications networks). The subsequent debacle of 1997 demonstrated how quickly, easily, and devastatingly a financial crisis in one country can spill over into others.

The management of the Asian financial crisis led some policy makers to call for stronger, more effective international institutions, including a capacity to ensure better information and monitoring, deeper cooperation, and regulation in the world economy. At the same time, however, others argued that the crisis revealed the problems and flaws of existing international institutions and the bias or interests they reflect. These positions echo a larger debate in IPE about the nature and impact of institutions in the world economy. This debate is important in helping us to determine what role international institutions might play in managing the new problems and challenges arising from globalization (see Table 11.4).

Competing accounts of institutions echo the differences in approaches to IPE already discussed. Institutionalists (or neoliberal institutionalists; see Chapter 3) tell us that states will create institutions in order to better achieve gains through policy **coordination** and cooperation. However, several preconditions are necessary for this to occur. Under certain conditions, institutionalists argue, states will agree to be bound by certain rules, norms, or decisions of **international organizations**. This does not mean that the most powerful states in the system will always obey the rules. Rather, institutions affect international politics because they open up new reasons to cooperate, they permit states to define their interests in a more cooperative way, and they foster negotiations among states as well as compliance with mutually agreed rules and standards.

The institutionalist account offers reasons for a certain kind of optimism about the role international institutions will play in managing globalization. Institutions will smooth over many gaps and failures in the operation of markets and serve to ensure that states make genuinely rational and optimizing decisions to cooperate. Globalization

coordination A form of cooperation requiring parties to pursue a common strategy in order to avoid the mutually undesirable outcome arising from the pursuit of divergent strategies.

international organization Any institution with formal procedures and formal membership from three or more countries. The minimum number of countries is set at three, rather than two, because multilateral relationships have significantly greater complexity than bilateral relationships.

will be managed by existing institutions and organizations, and, indeed, new institutions will probably also emerge. Globalization managed in this way will ensure that the world economy moves more toward the liberal model and that both strong and weak states benefit. Although there have been many protests about international organizations, these are the result of people misunderstanding the advantages of free trade and free movements of capital in the world economy.

Realists (and structural realists in particular) disagree with institutionalists. Realists reject the idea that institutions emerge primarily as a solution to universal problems or market failures. They argue that international institutions and organizations will always reflect the interests of dominant states within the system. When these dominant states wish to coordinate policies with others, they will create institutions. Once created, however, these institutions will not (as the institutionalists argue) transform the way states define and pursue their interests. Institutions will be effective only for as long as they do not diminish the power of dominant states vis-à-vis other states.

Let us consider what this means in practice. Take a state deciding whether to sign up to a new trade agreement or support the decision of an international organization. The institutionalists argue that policy makers will consider the absolute gains to be made from the agreement, including the potential longer-term gains, such as advancing a more stable and credible system of rules. The structural realists, by contrast, argue that policy makers will primarily be concerned with relative gains. In other words, rather than asking, "Do we gain from this?", they will ask, "Do we gain more from this than other states?" If other states stand to gain more, then the advantages of signing up are outweighed by the fact that the power of the state will be diminished in relation to other states.

For realists, cooperation and institutions are heavily constrained by underlying calculations about power. Having signed an agreement or created an international organization, a powerful state will not necessarily be bound by it. Indeed, if it gets in the way

Table 11.4
Debates About Institutions

	Institutionalist (or "Neoliberal Institutionalist")	Realist (or "Neorealist")	Constructivist
Under what conditions will states create international institutions?	For mutual gains (rationally calculated by states).	Only where relative position vis-à-vis other states is not adversely affected.	Institutions arise as a reflection of the identities and interests of states and groups, which are themselves forged through interaction.
What impact do institutions have on international relations?	Expand the possible gains to be made from cooperation.	Facilitate the coordination of policies and actions but only insofar as this does not alter the balance of power among states.	Reinforce particular patterns of interaction, and reflect new ones.
What are the implications for globalization?	Institutions can manage globalization to ensure a transition to a more "liberal" economy.	Institutions will "manage" globalization in the interests of dominant and powerful states.	Changing patterns of interaction and discourse will be reflected in institutional responses to globalization.

of the state's interests (defined in realist terms), a powerful state will simply sweep the institution aside. The implications for globalization and its impact on weak states are rather grim. International institutions, including the IMF, the World Bank, the WTO, the G-20, and the EU, will manage globalization but in the interests of their most powerful members. Institutions will only accommodate the needs and interests of weaker states where in so doing they do not diminish the dominant position of powerful states. From a realist perspective, it follows that antiglobalization protesters are right to argue that the international institutions do not work for the interests of poor and developing countries. However, the realists are equally certain that such protests will have little impact.

Constructivists reject the idea that institutions reflect the "rational" calculations of states, either within interstate competition (realists) or as part of a calculation of longer-term economic advantage and benefits from cooperation (institutionalists). In fact, what constructivists reject is the idea that states' interests are objectively definable and fixed. Instead, they argue that any one state's interests are affected by its identity as a state and that both its interests and identity are influenced by a social structure of interactions, normative ideas, and beliefs. If we cannot assume that states have a particular identity or interest prior to their interactions, then the institutionalists are wrong to assume that institutions emerge as rational responses to the needs of markets, trade, finance, and the like. Equally, the realists are wrong to assume that institutions can only be reflections of power politics. To quote constructivist Alexander Wendt, "Anarchy is what states make of it" (1992). In other words, identities and interests are more fluid and changing than realists permit. Through their interactions and discourse, states change, and these changes can reflect in institutions.

The constructivist approach examines actors and processes involved in globalization that are neglected in realist and institutionalist accounts and have important ramifications for institutions. For example, the protesters against the WTO, the IMF, and the World Bank can be construed as part of an ongoing dialogue that affects states in several ways. The international attention to these issues places them on the agenda of international meetings and organizations. It also puts pressure on political leaders and encourages interest groups to form within the state. As a result, the beliefs, ideas, and conceptions of interest in international relations change, and this can shift the attention, nature, and functions of international institutions. On this view, globalization is not just a process affecting and managed by states. Several other actors are involved, both within and across societies, including international institutions, which play a dynamic role. The governance or management of globalization is shaped by a mixture of interests, beliefs, and values about how the world works and how it ought to be. The existing institutions doubtless reflect the interests of powerful states. However, these interests are the products of the way states interact and are subject to reinterpretation and change.

Conclusion

In this chapter we have seen the basics of the major post–Second World War international financial institutions and how they work. The global economic events of 2008–2009 put a major strain on the ability of these institutions to cope with the collapse. Some analysts of international political economy believe that the very institutions that were intended to bring stability to the system helped to cause the recent global recession. Institutions like

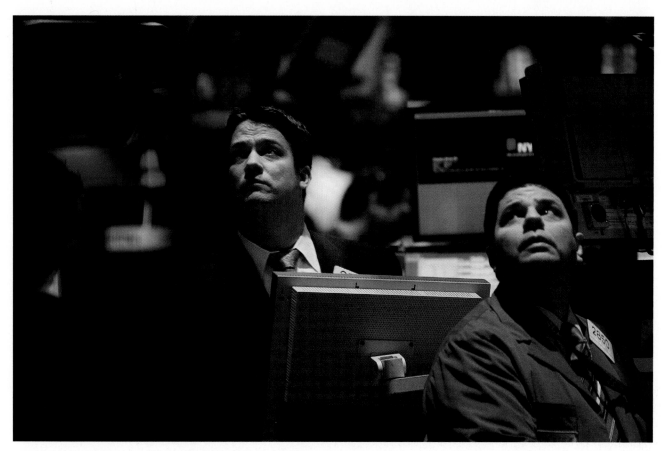

By mid-2010, key global economic indicators remained mixed.

the IMF and World Bank looked to adapt to a more pluralistic economic system in which economic power is diffused among a number of states and nonstate actors. The present economic system is no longer controlled by the United States. The 2008–2009 crisis has forced the rich and poor states to come together, reform the present global economic institutions, and create new ones—like the G-20 group of leaders, which first met in November 2008 in Washington DC, bringing together the Group of Seven and major emerging economies. When the subprime mortgage crisis struck the US markets in the summer of 2008, the effects were felt worldwide. World leaders must react and reform the present system or risk further turbulence as new crises emerge. We are facing several potential problems. First, we will need to address the growing inequality within and between states; second, we will need to address new vulnerabilities and risks unleashed by globalized financial markets; and third, the world must deal with the growing scarcity of critical resources like oil and water. Otherwise, we face a future of resource wars and collapsing economies.

Contributors to Chapter 11: Ngaire Woods and Steven L. Lamy.

REVIEW QUESTIONS

1. In what ways did the Bretton Woods framework for the postwar economy try to avoid the economic problems of the interwar years?
2. What was the "breakdown in the Bretton Woods system"?
3. Did a loss of US hegemony cause the breakdown of the Bretton Woods system?
4. Are there any issues on which mercantilists agree with liberals?
5. What is different about the Marxist and mercantilist depictions of power in the international economy?
6. Does rational-choice theory explain more about outcomes than actors' preferences?
7. In what way do constructivists invoke structure in their explanation of IPE?
8. Why do skeptics doubt that globalization is transforming IPE?
9. What vulnerabilities faced by states in the globalizing economy did the Asian financial crisis demonstrate?
10. How can we explain the different impact globalization has on different states?
11. How and why do institutionalists argue that institutions change the behavior of states?
12. For whom might the realist account of institutions and globalization be cheerful reading?

FURTHER READING

Frieden, J., and Lake, D. A., (eds.) (2000), *International Political Economy: Perspectives on Global Power and Wealth* (New York: St. Martin's Press). Offers very useful editors' introductions to core texts from each approach to international political economy.

Grieco, J. M., and Ikenberry, G. J. (2003), *State Power and World Markets: The International Political Economy* (New York: W. W. Norton & Company). An overarching text with an underlying realist view of the world economy.

Held, D., McGrew, A., Goldblatt, D., and Perrator, J. (1999), *Global Transformations: Politics, Economics and Culture* (Cambridge: Polity Press). A useful resource book on the empirical evidence of globalization in all aspects of international relations.

Helleiner, E. (1994), *States and the Reemergence of Global Finance: From Bretton Woods to the 1990s* (Ithaca, NY: Cornell University Press). Explains how the policies of states have shaped the emergence of the international financial system.

Katzenstein, P., Keohane, R., and Krasner, S. (1998), "International Organization and the State of World Politics," *International Organization* 52(4): 645–85. Reviews key developments in the study of international relations and international political economy.

Oatley, T., and Silver, M. (2003), *International Political Economy: Interests and Institutions in the Global Economy* (Harlow: Pearson). An example of the public or rational-choice approach to international political economy.

Palan, R. (ed.) (2000), *Global Political Economy: Contemporary Theories* (London: Routledge). A sampling of European approaches and theories of international political economy.

Rodrik, D. (1999), *The New Global Economy and Developing Countries: Making Openness Work* (Washington, DC: Overseas Development Council). A critical analysis of the advantages and disadvantages of globalization for developing countries.

Woods, N. (2006), *The Globalizers: The IMF, the World Bank, and Their Borrowers* (Ithaca, NY: Cornell University Press). An overview on the roles, evolution, and politics of the IMF and World Bank and their relations with developing countries.

INTERNET RESOURCES

Gapminder
www.gapminder.org
   An NGO that tracks the gap between rich and poor countries and people around the world.

International Monetary Fund
www.imf.org
   Part of the Bretton Woods system, this multilateral organization helps to manage the global economy.

The Group of Twenty

http://www.g20.org/

> The economic forum of the 20 leading national economies. The group gained prominence during the 2008-2010 global recession.

World Bank

www.worldbank.org

> The International Bank for Recovery and Development, or World Bank, is the most important multilateral international lending organization. It provides funding for both large-scale infrastructure and smaller-scale human development programs.

World Trade Organization

http://www.wto.org

> The prime multilateral organization that sets the "rules of the game" in international trade.

For more information, quizzes, case studies, and other study tools, please visit us at **www.oup.com/us/lamy**

Global Trade and Finance

Trade is the oldest and most important economic nexus among nations. Indeed, trade along with war has been central to the evolution of international relations.

—*Robert Gilpin*

There can be different brands of free-market vanilla and you can adjust your society to it by going faster or slower. But, in the end, if you want higher standards of living in a world without walls, the free market is the only ideological alternative left. One road. Different speeds. But one road.

—*Thomas L. Friedman*

How did it happen? One day the global economy was cruising along in the economic version of the fast lane. Stock prices seemed to have no ceiling, with each day bringing a new all-time high. The annual bonuses that CEOs of multinational corporations and bond traders of Wall Street gave themselves were more than the GDPs of most developing countries. Then, although the danger was there to see for some time, subprime mortgages in the United States managed to spark a worldwide economic collapse in 2008. Some economists had warned that the "Ownership Society" of the Bush administration could cause an economic catastrophe. We soon saw that the policy of encouraging people who barely met the income guidelines for mortgages to purchase houses with flexible-rate loans would lead to foreclosure and bankruptcy. These bad mortgages had become part of the new pattern of global investments for the most part unfettered by government regulation.

But the crisis of 2008–2009 was more than bad personal finances and massive government bailouts for banks and corporations. Indeed, in early 2009, Dennis Blair, the new director of national intelligence for the United States, warned members of the Senate that the global economic crisis was the most serious security challenge facing the United States and the world. Blair stated that 25 percent of the countries in the world have experienced low-level instability that is attributed to unemployment and poor economic conditions. Economic refugees might topple weak

Is the global economy recovering, or is progress limited to certain countries?

governments, and failed states might never get off the bottom. Even wealthy states have been adversely affected by the global economic crisis; after all, a working and effective global trade and financial system are also critical elements of global security.

Introduction

The globalization of world politics involves, among other things, a globalization of economics. As we discussed in previous chapters, politics and economics are inseparable within social relations. Economics does not explain everything, but no account of world politics (and hence no analysis of globalization as a key issue of contemporary world history) is adequate if it does not explore the economic dimension.

Like the Bretton Woods system that we learned about in the previous chapter, the global trade and finance systems developed in reaction to the events that followed World War I. The freewheeling capitalism of the Roaring Twenties, many people believed, helped to cause the Great Depression. In the United States, for example, overproduction and underconsumption, buying stocks on margin, the corrupt investment strategies known as Ponzi schemes (made famous again by the recent actions of Bernie Madoff), and land speculation were all parts of the problems inherent when governments did not regulate business activity. Once the Great Depression struck in 1929, international trade measures such as increased tariffs exacerbated the preexisting domestic market distortions.

International trade, however, did not lend itself to solutions like the IMF and World Bank of the Bretton Woods system. John Maynard Keynes, Harry Dexter White, and the other economists and political leaders who met in New Hampshire in July 1944 planned a third part of the system, the International Trade Organization. Unfortunately, largely because of opposition in the US Senate, the Havana Charter of the ITO never entered into force. In its place, the GATT secretariat—which was intended to oversee trade on a temporary basis—took on the task of organizing global trade negotiations.

Global Trade and Finance Actors

Countless discussions of globalization have brought its economic aspects front and center. For example, the late Milton Friedman, a Nobel Prize–winning economist, remarked that it has become possible "to produce a product anywhere, using resources from anywhere, by a company located anywhere, to be sold anywhere" (cited in Naisbitt 1994, 19). A senior researcher with American Express has described the global financial integration of recent decades as marking "the end of geography" (O'Brien 1992). Global governance bodies like the Bank for International Settlements (BIS), the Group of Eight (G-8), the International Monetary Fund (IMF), the Organization for Economic Cooperation and Development (OECD), the United Nations Conference on Trade and Development (UNCTAD), the World Bank Group (WBG), and the World Trade Organization (WTO) have all put economic globalization high on their agendas (see Table 12.1). Usually these official circles have endorsed and encouraged the trend, as have most national governments. Meanwhile, many social movements have focused their critiques of globalization on economic aspects of the process. Their analyses have depicted contemporary globalization of trade and finance as a major cause of higher unemployment, a general decline in working standards, increased inequality, greater poverty for some (see Chapter 13), recurrent financial crises, and large-scale environmental degradation (see Chapter 14).

The Main Trading Nations.
The white bars show the imports and exports of the top ten trading nations as a percentage of world trade. The blue bars show each country's trade manufactured, also as a percentage of world trade. What patterns do you see in this graph? What do these patterns suggest about global trade? *Source:* Oxford Essential World Atlas, *4th edition.*

Table 12.1

Major Public Global Governance Agencies for Trade and Finance

BIS Bank for International Settlements. Established in 1930 with headquarters in Basel. Membership (2010) of fifty-six shareholding central banks, although many other public financial institutions also use BIS facilities. Promotes cooperation among central banks and provides various services for global financial operations. For example, the Basel Committee on Banking Supervision, formed through the BIS in 1974, has spearheaded efforts at multilateral regulation of global banking. (www.bis.org)

G-8 Group of Eight. Established in 1975 as the G-5 (France, Germany, Japan, the UK, and the US); subsequently expanded as the G-7 to include Canada and Italy and since 1998 as the G-8 to include the Russian Federation. The G-8 conducts semiformal collaboration on world economic problems. Government leaders meet in annual G-8 summits, while finance ministers and/or their leading officials periodically hold other consultations.

G-20 Established in 1999, this group is made up of finance ministers and central bank governors of nineteen countries and the European Union. Members include Argentina, Australia, Brazil, Canada, China, France, Germany, India, Indonesia, Italy, Japan, Mexico, Russia, Saudi Arabia, South Africa, South Korea, Turkey, the United Kingdom, and the United States. This is an informal forum that was created after the financial crisis in the mid-1990s. The members discuss national policies, plans for international cooperation, and ideas for reforming institutions that manage the global economy. (http://www.g20.org)

GATT General Agreement on Tariffs and Trade. Established in 1947 with offices in Geneva. Membership had reached 122 states when it was absorbed into the WTO in 1995. The GATT coordinated eight rounds of multilateral negotiations to reduce state restrictions on cross-border merchandise trade. (www.wto.org)

IMF International Monetary Fund. Established in 1945 with headquarters in Washington, DC. Membership (2009) of 185 states. The IMF monitors short-term cross-border payments and foreign exchange positions. When a country develops chronic imbalances in its external accounts, the IMF supports corrective policy reforms, often called "structural-adjustment programs." Since 1978 the IMF has undertaken comprehensive surveillance both of the economic performance of individual member states and of the world economy as a whole. The IMF also provides extensive technical assistance. In recent years the fund has pursued various initiatives to promote efficiency and stability in global financial markets. (www.imf.org)

IOSCO International Organization of Securities Commissions. Established in 1983 with headquarters in Montreal; secretariat now in Madrid. Membership (2010) of 193 official securities regulators, as well as (nonvoting) trade associations and other agencies. IOSCO aims to promote high standards of regulation in stock and bond markets, to establish effective surveillance of transborder securities transactions, and to foster collaboration between securities markets in the detection and punishment of offenses. (www.iosco.org)

OECD Organization for Economic Cooperation and Development. Founded in 1962 with headquarters in Paris. Membership (2010) of thirty-one states with advanced industrial economies and further relationships with some seventy other states. Provides a forum for multilateral intergovernmental consultations on pretty well all policy issues except military affairs. OECD measures have especially addressed environmental questions, taxation, and transborder corporations. At regular intervals the OECD Secretariat produces an assessment of the macroeconomic performance of each member, including suggestions for policy changes. (www.oecd.org)

UNCTAD United Nations Conference on Trade and Development. Established in 1964 with offices in Geneva. Membership (2010) of 193 states. UNCTAD monitors the effects of world trade and investment on economic development, especially in the South. It provided a key forum in the 1970s for discussions of a New International Economic Order. (www.unctad.org)

WBG World Bank Group. A collection of five agencies, the first established in 1945, with head offices in Washington, DC. The WBG promotes development in medium- and low-income countries with project loans, structural-adjustment programs, and various advisory services. (www.worldbank.org)

WTO World Trade Organization. Established in 1995 with headquarters in Geneva. Membership (2010) of 153 states. The WTO is a permanent institution to replace the provisional GATT. It has a wider agenda, covering services, intellectual property, and investment issues as well as merchandise trade. The WTO also has greater powers of enforcement through its Dispute Settlement Mechanism. The organization's Trade Policy Review Body conducts surveillance of members' commercial measures. (www.wto.org)

In their different ways, all of these assessments agree that economic globalization is a key development of contemporary history. True, the scale and impact of the trend are often exaggerated. However, it is just as wrong to argue, as some skeptics have done, that claims about a new globalizing economy rest on nothing but hype and myth. Instead, as in the case of most historical developments, economic globalization involves an intricate interplay of changes and continuities. Certainly the economic crisis of 2008–2009 shows how interconnected and globalized the world's economy has become.

A Globalizing Economy

One key reason for disagreements over the extent and significance of economic globalization relates to the contrasting definitions that different analysts have applied to notions of what it means to be global. What, more precisely, is "global" about the global economy? The following paragraphs distinguish three contrasting ways the globalization of trade and finance has been broadly conceived, namely, in terms of (1) the crossing of borders, (2) the opening of borders, and (3) the transcendence of borders. Although the three conceptions overlap to some extent, they involve important differences of emphasis. Most arguments concerning economic globalization have pitted skeptics, who adopt the first perspective, against enthusiasts, who apply the second. However, the third conception of globality offers a more distinctive and revealing approach. Later sections of the present chapter therefore develop that alternative notion in relation to trade and finance.

Cross-Border Transactions

Skepticism about the significance of contemporary economic globalization has often arisen when analysts have conceived the process in terms of increased cross-border movements of people, goods, money, investments, messages, and ideas. From this perspective, globalization is seen as equivalent to internationalization. No significant distinction is drawn between global companies and international companies, between global trade and international trade, between global money and international money, between global finance and international finance.

When conceived in this way, economic globalization is nothing particularly new. Commerce between different territorial-political units has transpired for centuries and in some cases even millennia. Ancient Babylon and the Roman Empire knew forms of long-distance lending and trade, for example. Shipments between Arabia and China via South and Southeast Asia occurred with fair regularity more than a thousand years ago. Certain coins circulated widely around maritime Southeast Asia in a prototypical "international monetary regime" of the tenth century. Long-distance monies of the premodern Mediterranean world included the Byzantine solidus from the fifth century onward and the Muslim dinar from the eighth to the thirteenth centuries. Banks based in Italian city-states main-

All kinds of products have become globalized, including Coke products. If this trend continues, how will traditional taste preferences survive?

tained (temporary) offices along long-distance trade routes as early as the twelfth century. The Hanseatic League in the fourteenth century and companies based in Amsterdam, Copenhagen, London, and Paris in the seventeenth century operated overseas trading posts. The first brokerage houses with cross-border operations appeared in the eighteenth century with Amsterdam-based Hope & Co. and London-based Barings.

Indeed, on certain (though far from all) measures, cross-border economic activity reached similar levels in the late nineteenth century as it did a hundred years later. Relative to world population of the time, the magnitude of permanent migration was in fact considerably greater than today. When measured in relation to world output, cross-border investment in production facilities stood at roughly the same level on the eve of the First World War as it did in the early 1990s. International markets in loans and securities also flourished during the heyday of the gold–sterling standard between 1870 and 1914. Under this regime, the British pound, fixed to a certain value in gold, served as a global currency and thereby greatly facilitated cross-border payments. Again citing proportional (rather than aggregate) statistics, several researchers (for example, Zevin 1992) have argued that these years witnessed larger capital flows between countries than in the late twentieth century. Meanwhile, the volume of international trade grew at some 3.4 percent per annum in the period 1870–1913, until its value was equivalent to 33 percent of world output (Barraclough 1984, 256; Hirst and Thompson 1999, 21). By this particular calculation, cross-border trade was greater at the beginning than at the end of the twentieth century.

For the skeptics, then, the contemporary globalizing economy is nothing new. In their eyes, recent decades have merely experienced a phase of increased cross-border trade and finance, much as occurred a hundred years before. Moreover, they note, just as growth of international interdependence in the late nineteenth century was substantially reversed with a forty-year wave of protectionism after 1914, so economic globalization of the present day may prove to be temporary. Governments can block cross-border flows if they wish, say the skeptics of globalization, and national interest may well dictate that states once more tighten restrictions on international trade, travel, foreign exchange, and capital movements. Contemporary economic globalization gives little evidence, say these doubters, of an impending demise of the state, a weakening of national loyalties, and an end of war. Thus, for example, skeptics regularly point out that most so-called global companies (1) still conduct the majority of their business in their country of origin, (2) retain strong national character and allegiances, and (3) remain heavily dependent on states for the success of their enterprises.

Open-Border Transactions

In contrast to the skeptics, enthusiasts for contemporary globalization of trade and finance generally define these developments as part of the long-term evolution toward a global society. In this second conception, globalization entails not an extension of internationalization but the progressive removal of official restrictions on transfers of resources between countries. In the resultant world of open borders, global companies replace international companies, global trade replaces international trade, global money replaces international money, and global finance replaces international finance. This process results in markets that are much larger than regional arrangements like the European Union (EU) and the North American Free Trade Association (NAFTA). From this perspective, globalization is a function of liberalization: that is, the degree to which products, communications, financial instruments, fixed assets, and people can circulate throughout the world economy free from state-imposed controls. Whereas skeptics generally back up their arguments of historical repetition with proportional data, globalists usually substantiate their claims of historical change with aggregate statistics, many of which do indeed appear quite staggering (see Table 12.2).

Globalists regard the forty-year interlude of protectionism (ca. 1910–1950) as a temporary detour from a longer historical trend toward the construction of a single integrated world economy. In their eyes, the tightening of border controls in the first half of the twentieth century was a major cause of economic depressions, authoritarian regimes, and international conflicts such as the world wars. In contrast, the emergent open world economy (so runs the globalist promise) will yield prosperity, liberty, democracy, and peace for all humanity. From this perspective—which is often termed neoliberalism—contemporary economic globalization continues the universalizing project of modernity launched several centuries ago.

Recent history has indeed witnessed considerable opening of borders in the world economy. For one thing, a succession of interstate accords through the General Agreement on Tariffs and Trade (GATT) has, since 1948, in a series of negotiations called "rounds," brought major reductions in customs duties, quotas, and other measures that previously inhibited cross-border movements of merchandise. Average tariffs on manufactures in countries of the North fell from over 40 percent in the 1930s to less than 4 percent by 1999. Following the Uruguay Round of multilateral trade negotiations (1986–1994), the GATT was subsumed within the new World Trade Organization. This successor agency has greater competences both to enforce existing trade agreements and to pursue new avenues of liberalization: for example, with respect to shipping, telecommunications,

Table 12.2
Some Indicators of Contemporary Economic Globalization ($ Billion)

Measure (Worldwide Figures)	Earlier Level	Recent Level
Foreign direct investment	$68 (1960)	$10,672 (2005)
Exports	$629 (1960)	$10,159 (2005)
Official foreign exchange reserves	$100 (1970)	$5,028 (2006)
Daily turnover on foreign exchange markets	$100 (1979)	$1,880 (2004)
Bank deposits by nonresidents	$20 (1964)	$7,876 (1995)
Cross-border loan announcements	$9 (1972)	$1,465 (2000)
Cross-border bond issues	$1 (1960)	$1,157 (1999)
Euroequity* issues	Initiated 1984	$50 (1995)
Cross-border share dealing	$10 (1980)	$120 (1994)
Daily turnover of financial derivatives contracts	Small before 1980	$1,162 (1995)

Sources: BIS, IMF, OECD, UNCTAD, WTO.

* When a company's shares are made available internationally rather than just where the company has its home base (*Financial Times*).

and investment flows. Meanwhile, regional frameworks like the EU and NAFTA have (to varying degrees) removed official restrictions on trade between participating countries. Encouraged by such liberalization, cross-border trade expanded between 1950 and 1994 at an annual rate of just over 6 percent, thus almost twice as fast as in the late nineteenth century. Total international trade multiplied fourteenfold in real terms over this period, while expansion of trade in manufactures was even greater, with a twenty-six-fold increase (World Trade Organization 1995).

Borders have also opened considerably to money flows since 1950. As discussed in the previous chapter, the gold–dollar standard became fully operational through the IMF in 1959. Under this regime, major currencies—and especially the United States dollar—could circulate worldwide (though not in communist-ruled countries) and be converted to local monies at an official **fixed exchange rate**. The gold–dollar standard thereby broadly re-created the situation that prevailed under the gold–sterling standard in the late nineteenth century. Contrary to many expectations, the US government's termination of dollar–gold convertibility on demand in 1971 did not trigger new restrictions on cross-border payments. Instead, a regime of **floating exchange rates** developed: de facto from 1973 and formalized through the IMF in 1976. Moreover, from the mid-1970s onward most states with developed economies reduced or eliminated restrictions on the import and export of national currencies. In these circumstances the average volume of daily transactions on the world's wholesale foreign exchange markets burgeoned from $15 billion in 1973 to $1,900 billion in 2004.

Alongside the liberalization of trade and money movements between countries, recent decades have also witnessed the widespread opening of borders to investment flows. These movements involve both direct investments (i.e., fixed assets like research facilities and factories) and portfolio investments (i.e., liquid assets like loans, bonds, and stocks). One result of this is that the 2008 global economic implosion began with the sale of securities of unwise mortgages made in the United States.

Apart from a spate of expropriations in the South during the 1970s (many of them subsequently reversed), states have generally welcomed **foreign direct investment (FDI)** into their jurisdictions, in contemporary history. Indeed, many governments have actively lured externally based business by lowering corporate tax rates, reducing restrictions on the repatriation of profits, relaxing labor and environmental standards, and so on. Since 1960 there has been a proliferation of what are variously called "international," "multinational," "transnational," or "global" corporations (hence the frequently encountered abbreviations MNC and TNC). The number of such companies grew from 3,500 in 1960 to 64,000 in 2005. The aggregate stock of FDI worldwide increased in tandem from $68 billion in 1960 to $10,672 billion in 2005, as compared with only $14 billion in 1914 (UNCTAD 1996, ix, 4; UNCTAD 2006b). In this world of more open borders, various globalists have described MNCs as "footloose" and "stateless." This is a process that Cynthia Enloe calls "the globetrotting sneaker."

Substantial liberalization has also occurred since the 1970s with respect to cross-border portfolio investments, which provided another cause of the 2008 economic recession. For example, many a state now permits nonresidents to hold bank accounts within its jurisdiction. Other **deregulation** has removed legal restrictions on ownership and trading of stocks and bonds by nonresident investors. Further legislation has reduced controls on participation in a country's financial markets by externally based banks, brokers, and fund managers. As a result of such deregulation (e.g., the repeal of the Glass-Steagall Act

fixed exchange rate The price a currency will earn in a hard currency. Here a government is committed to keep it at a specific value.

floating exchange rate The market decides what the actual value of a currency is compared to other currencies.

foreign direct investment (FDI) Capital speculation by citizens or organizations of one country into markets or industries in another country.

deregulation The removal of all regulation so that market forces, not government policy, control economic developments.

in 1999), financial institutions from all over the world have converged on global cities like Hong Kong, New York, Paris, and Tokyo. Levels of cross-border banking and securities business have risen markedly since the 1960s in tandem with such liberalization, as several statistics in Table 12.2 indicate. It is important to note that corresponding indicators for the period between 1870 and 1914 come nowhere close to these current aggregate figures.

In sum, legal obstructions to economic transactions between countries have greatly diminished worldwide in contemporary history. At the same time, cross-border flows of merchandise, services, money, and investments have reached unprecedented levels, at least in aggregate terms. To this extent, enthusiasts for globalization as liberalization can argue against the skeptics that borders have opened more than ever. That said, significant official restrictions on cross-border economic activity persist. They include countless trade restrictions and continuing **capital controls** in many countries. While states have on the whole welcomed FDI, there is as yet no multilateral regime to liberalize investment flows, comparable to the GATT/WTO with respect to trade or the IMF with respect to money. (Negotiations for a Multilateral Agreement on Investment were abandoned at the end of 1998, although states have concluded hundreds of liberalizing bilateral investment treaties.) In addition, while many governments have loosened visa and travel restrictions in recent times, **immigration controls** are on the whole as tight as ever. Indeed, many have recently been reinforced. To this extent skeptics have grounds to affirm that international borders remain very much in place and can be opened or closed as states choose to do.

Transborder Transactions

As mentioned earlier, most debates concerning economic globalization have unfolded between skeptics, who regard the current situation as a limited and reversible expansion of cross-border transactions, and globalists, who see an inexorable trend toward an open world economy. However, these two most common positions do not exhaust the possible interpretations. Indeed, neither of these conventional perspectives requires a distinct concept of globalization. Both views resurrect arguments that were elaborated using other vocabulary long before the word "globalization" entered widespread circulation in the 1990s.

In a third conception, globalization refers to processes whereby social relations linked to certain economic sectors acquire relatively distanceless and borderless qualities, so that human lives are increasingly played out in the world as a single place. In this usage, "globalization" refers to a transformation of geography that occurs when a host of social conditions become less tied to territorial spaces.

Along these lines, a globalizing economy is one in which patterns of production, exchange, and consumption become increasingly de-linked from a geography of territorial distances and territorial borders. *Global* economic activity—for those industries and people linked to it—extends across widely dispersed terrestrial locations at the same time and moves between locations scattered across the planet, often in effectively no time. While the patterns of *international* economic interdependence are strongly influenced by territorial distances and national divisions, patterns of *global* trade and finance often have little correspondence to distance and state boundaries. With air travel, satellite links, the Internet, telecommunications, transnational organizations, global consciousness (i.e., a mind-set that conceives of the planet as a single place), and more, much contemporary economic activity

capital controls This is the monetary policy device that a government uses to regulate the flows into and out of a country's capital account, i.e., the flows of investment-oriented money into and out of a country or currency.

immigration controls When a government controls the number of people who may work, study, or relocate to its country. It may also include quotas for certain national groups for immigration.

Global Perspective

NAFTA and Mexico

Most people in the United States had not heard of the North American Free Trade Agreement (NAFTA) prior to the 1992 presidential election campaign. In the first televised presidential debate, independent candidate H. Ross Perot skewered then president George H. W. Bush, asserting that the NAFTA—the terms of which were largely unknown in the United States—would result in what Perot called "a giant sucking sound" as American jobs went south to Mexico. As expected, the three candidates said little about what the deal would mean for Mexico. With the agreement more than fifteen years old, what has the NAFTA done for Mexico?

According to statistics found on the website of the Office of the United States Trade Representative (USTR), by 2003 all sectors of the Mexican economy had benefited from the country's membership in the NAFTA. For example, exports of Mexican-grown agricultural products to the United States increased 103 percent from 1993 to 2000. Overall farm production increased by over 50 percent during the same period, with changes of 25 percent in pork production, 27 percent in fruit production, and a stunning 80 percent increase in poultry production.

In higher-wage industrial manufacture jobs, similar changes swept most sectors by 2003. In export-oriented industries, according to the USTR, the NAFTA is responsible for more than three and a half million new jobs, and these jobs on average pay 37 percent more than non-export-linked manufacturing employment. (http://www.ustr.gov/Document_Library/Fact_Sheets/2003/NAFTA_at_10_Myth_-_NAFTA_Was_a_Failure_for_Mexico.html)

Statistics, as Mark Twain famously said, can lie. Put somewhat more diplomatically, statistics are but one perspective on a complex economic situation. As noted in Chapters 11, 12, and 13 of this book, government-compiled economic figures tell only part of the story. Ignored in government data are those sectors of an economy in which payment for a job completed might be in the form of a basket of fruit or a chicken. Or, if people are paid in cash and do not report this payment on their income tax forms, the transaction escapes the notice of the government. This is often the case in developing countries with what is called "women's work."

There are several signs that the NAFTA is not working for most Mexicans, if people in the United States are willing to look beyond official data. When US college students on spring break trips descend on Cancun and Puerto Vallarta, they could, if they stopped to think, recognize the limited extent of the NAFTA's success. Jobs in support of the tourist industry are low paid, low status, and high stress. Cleaning up after tourists from *El Norte*, as the United States is called, is unrewarding at best.

Another sign of the very focused character of NAFTA's success for Mexico can be seen in the thousands of young Mexicans, primarily males but not entirely, who risk arrest and death by trekking across the Sonoran desert to gain illegal entry into the United States. Once here, these "illegal immigrants," as US opponents of the current immigration policies call them, compete for low-wage jobs. They can be seen in neighborhoods throughout Southern California, waiting to be hired as day laborers. The irony of the economic recession of 2008–2009 is seen in a surprising statistic: the United States Border Patrol is intercepting fewer people trying to gain illegal entry into the country. With few jobs in *El Norte*, why risk death in the desert, abuse at the hands of human traffickers, or arrest in the United States? Better, perhaps, to stay in Mexico and hope that the North American Free Trade Agreement will bring you a job.

NAFTA's terms have helped some economic sectors and harmed others.

transborder Economic, political, social, or cultural activities crossing or extending across a border.

supraterratoriality Social, economic, cultural, and political connections that transcend territorial geography.

transcends borders. In this third sense, globalization involves the growth of a **transborder** (as opposed to cross-border or open-border) economy.

This rise of **supraterritoriality** is evidenced by, among other things, increased transactions between countries. However, the geographical character of these transplanetary (as opposed to long-distance) movements is different from the territorial framework that has traditionally defined international interdependence. This qualitative shift means that contemporary statistics on international trade, money, and investment can only be crudely compared with figures relating to earlier times. Moreover, economic statistics ignore or simply do not count those activities that are not "modern" but are nonetheless vital in some societies. These can include such items as a woman gathering firewood to cook the evening meal in a traditional society or a grandparent providing unpaid childcare in present-day New York City. Hence the issue is not so much the amount of trade between countries but the way much of this commerce forms part of transborder production processes and global marketing networks. The problem is not only the quantity of money that moves between countries but also the instantaneity with which most funds are transferred. The question is not simply the number of international securities deals so much as the emergence of stock and bond issues that involve participants from multiple countries at the same time. In short, if one accepts this third conception of globalization, then both the skeptics and the enthusiasts are largely missing the crucial point of historical change.

WHAT'S YOUR WORLDVIEW ?

Why do these disputes about the character of globalization matter? In your own life, is globalization a positive or negative process?

Global Trade

The distinctiveness of transborder, supraterritorial economic relations will become clearer with illustrations. Examples concerning global trade are given in the present section. Others regarding global finance are discussed in the next section. In each case, it is seen that their significance relates mainly to contemporary history (although the phenomena in question made some earlier appearances).

The rules of the global trading system are to a great extent only those the countries themselves put on the firms that operate within their borders. Most of the world's trade takes place within the framework of the World Trade Organization; however, as the organization's press office indicates, it is a multilateral discussion forum, not a global trade system. Member states of the WTO agree, among other things, to lower tariffs and to eliminate nontariff barriers to trade, but it is left to the member states to enforce the agreements. Following the concept of international regime that you read about in Chapter 3, the principle that guides the WTO is that multilateral free trade pacts are better than bilateral deals. Another key principle is **most favored nation status**, whereby member states pledge not to discriminate against their trading partners.

most favored nation status This is the status granted to most trading partners that says trade rules with that country will be the same as those given to their most favored trading partner.

Of course, disputes occur in the world's trading system, often to serve a domestic political purpose. For example, the United States and the EU from time to time have disagreements about bovine growth hormone in beef products grown in the United States, and the United States has had a long-running dispute with China over intellectual property rights (TRIPS). To address such disagreements, the WTO has a dispute-resolution panel that keeps the process at the multilateral level, so that members will not take unilateral action that could undermine the WTO's goals. Frequently, however, once a country begins the Dispute Settlement Body process, both parties settle the dispute before it reaches the full

Figure 12.1 The Organizational Table of the World Trade Organization.

panel. From the creation of the WTO in 1995 to July 2005, members filed 332 unfair-trade complaints, but less than a third reached the DSB panel stage. Because of the risk of retaliation, members prefer to utilize the good offices, reconciliation, and mediation services of the secretary-general, as provided for in Article 5 of the WTO covenant.

Transborder Production

Transborder production arises when a single process is spread across widely dispersed locations both within and between countries. Global coordination links research centers, design units, procurement offices, material-processing installations, fabrication plants, finishing points, assembly lines, quality-control operations, advertising and marketing divisions, data-processing offices, after-sales services, and so on.

Transborder production can be contrasted with territorially centered production. In the latter instance, all stages of a given production process—from initial research to after-sales service—occur within the same local or national unit. In global production, however, the stages are dispersed across different and often widely scattered countries. Each of the various links in the transborder chain specializes in one or several functions, thereby creating economies of scale and/or exploiting cost differentials between locations. Through **global sourcing**, the company draws materials, components, machinery, finance, and services from anywhere in the world. Territorial distance and borders figure only secondarily, if at all, in determining the sites. Indeed, a firm may relocate certain stages of production several times in short succession in search of profit maximization.

What have been described as global factories were unknown before the 1940s. They did not gain major prominence until the 1960s and have mainly spread since the 1970s. Transborder production has developed mainly in the manufacture of textiles, garments, motor vehicles, leather goods, sports articles, toys, optical products, consumer electronics, semiconductors, airplanes, and construction equipment. As you can see, there is little that is not produced transnationally (see Chapter 1).

With the growth of global production, a large proportion of purportedly international transfers of goods and services have entailed **intrafirm trade** within transborder companies. When the intermediate inputs and finished goods pass from one country to another they are officially counted as "international" commerce; yet they primarily involve movements within a global company rather than between national economies. Conventional statistics do not measure intrafirm transfers, but estimates of the share of such exchanges in total cross-border trade have ranged from 25 to over 40 percent.

Much (though far from all) transborder production has taken advantage of what are variously called special economic zones (SEZs), export processing zones (EPZs), or free production zones (FPZs). Within these enclaves, the ruling national or provincial government exempts assembly plants, and other facilities for transborder production, from the usual import and export duties. The authorities may also grant other tax reductions, subsidies, and waivers of certain labor and environmental regulations. The first such zone was established in 1954 in Ireland, but most were created after 1970, mainly in Asia, the Caribbean, and the maquiladora areas along the Mexican frontier with the United States. Several thousand EPZs are now in place across more than one hundred countries. One distinguishing trait of these manufacturing centers is their frequent heavy reliance on female labor.

global sourcing Obtaining goods and services across geopolitical boundaries. Usually the goal is to find the least expensive labor and raw material costs and the lowest taxes and tariffs.

intrafirm trade International trade from one branch of a TNC to an affiliate of the same company in a different country.

global goods Products that are made for a global market and are available across the world.

Transborder Products

Much of the output of both transborder and country-based production has acquired a planet-spanning market in the contemporary globalizing economy. Hence a considerable proportion of "international" trade now involves the distribution and sale of **global goods**, often under a transworld brand name. Consumers dispersed across many corners of the planet purchase the same articles at the same time. The country location of a potential customer for, say, a Xerox photocopier, a Britney Spears CD, or Kellogg's corn flakes is of secondary importance. Design, packaging, and advertising determine the market far more than territorial distances and borders.

Like other aspects of globalization, supraterritorial markets have a longer history than many contemporary observers appreciate. For example, Campbell Soup and Heinz began to become household names at widely dispersed locations across the world in the mid-1880s, following the introduction of automatic canning. From the outset, Henry Ford regarded his first automobile, the Model T, as a world car. Coca-Cola was bottled in twenty-seven countries and sold in seventy-eight by 1929 (Pendergrast 1993, 174). On the whole, however, the numbers of goods, customers, and countries involved in these earlier global markets were relatively small.

In contrast, global goods pervade the contemporary world economy. They encompass a host of packaged foods, bottled beverages, tobacco products, designer clothes, household articles, music recordings, audio-visual productions, printed publications, interactive communications, office and hospital equipment, armaments, transport vehicles, and travel services. In all of these sectors and more, global products inject a touch of the familiar almost wherever on earth a person might visit. The countless examples include Nescafé

Where are your sneakers manufactured?

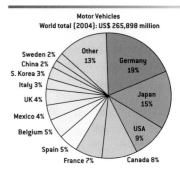

Motor Vehicles
World total (2004): US$ 265,898 million

Germany 19%, Japan 15%, USA 9%, Canada 8%, France 7%, Spain 5%, Belgium 5%, Mexico 4%, UK 4%, Italy 3%, S. Korea 3%, China 2%, Sweden 2%, Other 13%

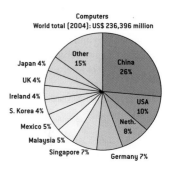

Computers
World total (2004): US$ 236,396 million

China 26%, USA 10%, Neth. 8%, Germany 7%, Singapore 7%, Malaysia 5%, Mexico 5%, S. Korea 4%, Ireland 4%, UK 4%, Japan 4%, Other 15%

Telecommunications Gear
World total (2004): US$ 405,989 million

China 26%, S. Korea 9%, Japan 9%, USA 7%, Germany 7%, Mexico 5%, UK 3%, Malaysia 3%, France 3%, Singapore 3%, Sweden 3%, Hungary 3%, Other 17%

Petrol Products
World total (2004): US$ 496,092 million

Russia 15%, Norway 8%, Venezuela 6%, UK 6%, Canada 5%, Mexico 5%, Algeria 4%, Netherlands 4%, USA 3%, Singapore 3%, Other 41%

Major Exports. These charts show a snapshot of the leading manufactured items and their exporters in 2004. What do these charts reveal about the nature of distribution and sale of global goods? *Source:* Oxford Essential World Atlas, *4th edition.*

WHAT'S YOUR WORLDVIEW

It may be comforting to travel around the world and find Nike shops, Xerox machines, and Starbucks—but what are the costs to local businesses? What is lost economically and culturally? Do you think this form of global homogenization is a good or bad thing?

electronic commerce
The buying and selling of products and services over the telephone or Internet. E-Bay and Amazon are examples of leaders in this area of commerce.

(sold in 200 varieties worldwide), Heineken beer (quaffed in over 170 countries), Kiwi shoe polish (applied in almost 200 countries), Nokia mobile phones (used in more than 130 countries), Thomas Cook tourist offices (available in 140 countries), American International Group insurance policies (offered in more than 130 countries), television programs by Globo of Brazil (distributed in 128 countries), and the *Financial Times* newspaper (printed in 19 cities across the globe). Covering smokers in 170 lands, "Marlboro Country" is a distinctly global place.

Today many shops are mainly stocked with transborder articles. Moreover, since the 1970s a number of retail chains have gone global. Examples include Italy-based Benetton, Japan-based 7-Eleven, Sweden-based IKEA, UK-based Body Shop, and US-based Toys "R" Us. Owing largely to the various megabrands and transborder stores, shopping centers of the twenty-first century are in good part global emporia. Unfortunately for many of these globalized corner stores, the economic recession of 2008–2009 has caused a global fire sale of products.

Other supraterritorial markets have developed since the 1990s through **electronic commerce**. Today's global consumer can—equipped with a credit card and telephone,

Table 12.3
Your Global Morning as a College Student

With an 8 a.m. class, you rely on a good working alarm clock this semester. You also rely on a global production and distribution system.
Your alarm clock is a product of the Sony Corporation, a Japanese-based multinational corporation. The clock was assembled in a Sony plant in Brazil from components produced in Japan, Mexico, and Germany. It was shipped to the United States in a Greek-owned ship manufactured in Sweden, licensed in Liberia, and staffed by a Portuguese crew.
Not much to wear to class because you have not had time to wash anything for a few weeks.
Now you are wearing the international. Your shorts were made in Japan from cotton exported to Japan from the United States. Your socks were made in Vietnam using wool grown in Australia.
Just enough time to stop at the dining hall for some breakfast.
Your stomach is full of the international. The bacon was brought to you by the UPS Corporation, a multinational shipping company. The pig your bacon came from consumed more grain than the majority of humans eat each year. The bread you ate was Wonder Bread, a product of International Telephone and Telegraph, another multinational company. The technology that heated your bread to make toast is a product from another multinational, General Electric. The butter that you put on your toast contains dried milk imported from Germany. Finally, the coffee is a product of the Nestlé Corporation, a Swiss multinational.
Wondering how the Red Sox did last night and whether the US team won its qualifying round for the World Cup, you take a look at the local newspaper.
Now you are reading the international. Much of the news on the front page that you skimmed is about events outside the United States and the role the US plays as a global leader. The newspaper received much of its news from the BBC, Agence France-Presse, the Associated Press, and Reuters, all transnational information agencies. The major sports story today is about the World Cup and the various international athletes.

Table 12.4

An Example of a Global Product: Your IBM ThinkPad X31

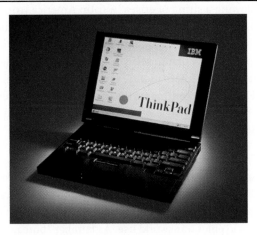

Was US national security harmed when American firm IBM sold its personal computer business to the Chinese corporation Lenovo?

Memory: Ten manufacturers worldwide, the largest in Korea

Case and keyboard: Made in Thailand

Wireless card: Intel, made in Malaysia

Battery: Made in Asia (various locations in the region possible)

Display screen: Two major screen makers are Samsung and LG Philips in South Korea

Graphics controller chip: ATI, made in Canada, or TMSC, made in Taiwan

Microprocessor: Intel, made in USA

Hard drive: Made in Thailand

Assembly: Mexico

television, or Internet link shop across the planet from home. Mail-order outlets and tele-sales units have undergone exponential growth, while e-commerce on the World Wide Web has expanded hugely.

Through transborder production and transworld products, global trade has become an integral part of everyday life for a notable proportion of the world's firms and consumers (see Tables 12.3, 12.4, and the Case Study on the iPod from Chapter 1). Indeed, these developments could help to explain why the recessions of contemporary history have not, in spite of frequently expressed fears of "trade wars," provoked a wave of protectionism. In previous prolonged periods of commercial instability and economic hardship (e.g., during the 1870s–1890s and 1920s–1930s), most states responded by imposing major protectionist restrictions on cross-border trade. Reactions to the 2008–2009 recession have been more complicated (see Milner 1988). While many territorial interests have pressed for protectionism, global commercial interests have generally resisted it. Thus, many transborder companies actively promoted the Uruguay Round and have, on the whole, vigorously supported the WTO.

Global Finance

Finance has attracted some of the greatest attention in contemporary debates on globalization, especially following a string of crises in Latin America (1994–1995), Asia (1997–1998), Russia (1998), Brazil (1999), Argentina (2001–2002), and the globalized collapse of 2008–2009. The rise of supraterritoriality has affected both the forms money takes and the ways it is deployed in banking, securities, derivatives, and (although not detailed below) insurance markets. As international, cross-border activities, such dealings have quite a long history. However, as commerce that unfolds through telephone and computer networks that make the world a single place, global finance has experienced its greatest growth since the 1980s.

Transplanetary Money

The development of global production and the growth of global markets have each encouraged—and been facilitated by—the spread of global monies. It was noted earlier that the fixed and later floating exchange regimes operated through the IMF have allowed a number of "national" currencies to enter transworld use. As familiar "bureau de change" signs indicate, today retail outlets in scores of countries deal in multiple currencies on demand.

No national denomination has been more global in this context than the US dollar. About as many dollars circulate outside as inside the United States. Indeed, in certain financial crises, this global money has displaced the locally issued currency in the everyday life of a national economy. Such "dollarization" has occurred in parts of Latin America and Eastern Europe. Since the 1970s, the German mark (now superseded by the euro), Japanese yen, Swiss franc, and other major currencies have also acquired a substantial global character. Hence huge stocks of notionally "national" money are now used in countless transactions that never touch the "home" soil.

Foreign exchange dealing has become a thoroughly supraterritorial business. This round-the-clock, round-the-world market has no central meeting place. Many of the deals have nothing directly to do with the countries where the currencies involved are initially issued or eventually spent. The trading itself has also taken place without distance. Transactions are generally concluded over the telephone and confirmed by telex or e-mail between buyers and sellers across whatever distance. Meanwhile, shifts in exchange rates are flashed instantaneously and simultaneously on video monitors across the main dealing rooms worldwide.

Transborder money also takes other forms besides certain national currencies. Gold has already circulated across the planet for several centuries, although it moves cumbersomely through territorial space rather than instantly through telecommunication lines. A newer and more fully supraterritorial denomination is the **Special Drawing Right (SDR)**, issued through the IMF since 1969. SDRs reside only in computer memories and not in wallets for everyday transactions.

Meanwhile, other supraterritorial money has entered daily use in plastic form. For example, many bank cards can extract local currency from automated teller machines (ATMs) worldwide. In addition, several types of smart card (e.g., Mondex, a part of the MasterCard network) can simultaneously hold multiple currencies as digital cash on a microchip. Certain credit cards like Visa and MasterCard are accepted at millions of venues the world over to make purchases in whatever local denomination.

In sum, contemporary globalization has—through the spread of transborder currencies, distinctly supraterritorial denominations, digital purses, and global credit and

Special Drawing Right (SDR) IMF members have the right to borrow this asset from the organization up to the amount that the country has invested in the IMF. The SDR is based on the value of a "basket" of the world's leading currencies: British pound, euro, Japanese yen, and US dollar.

debit cards—significantly altered the shape of money. No longer is money restricted to the national/state/ territorial form that prevailed from the nineteenth to the middle of the twentieth century.

Transplanetary Banking

Globalization has touched banking mainly in terms of (1) the growth of transborder deposits, (2) the advent of transborder bank lending, (3) the expansion of transborder branch networks, and (4) the emergence of instantaneous transworld interbank fund transfers.

Globalized banking lets you conduct your business nearly anywhere.

So-called eurocurrency deposits are bank assets denominated in a national money different from the official currency in the country where the funds are held. For instance, euroyen are Japanese yen deposited in, say, Canada. Eurocurrency accounts first appeared in the 1950s but mainly expanded after 1970, especially with the flood of "petrodollars" that followed major rises of oil prices in 1973–1974 and 1979–1980. Eurocurrencies are supraterritorial: they do not attach neatly to any country's money supply, nor are they systematically regulated by the national central bank that issued them.

Globalization has also entered the lending side of banking. Credit creation from eurocurrency deposits first occurred in 1957, when American dollars were borrowed through the British office of a Soviet bank. However, euroloans mainly proliferated after 1973 following the petrodollar deluge. Today it is common for a loan to be issued in one country, denominated in the currency of a second country (or perhaps a basket of currencies of several countries), for a borrower in a third country, by a bank or syndicate of banks in a fourth country or additional countries.

Global banking takes place not only at age-old sites of world finance like London, New York, Tokyo, and Zurich but also through multiple **offshore finance centers**. Much like EPZs in relation to manufacturing, offshore financial arrangements offer investors low levels of taxation and regulation. Although a few offshore finance centers, including Luxembourg and Jersey (a dependency of the UK that is part of the Channel Islands), predate the Second World War, most have emerged since 1960 and are now found in over forty jurisdictions. For example, less than thirty years after passing relevant legislation in 1967, the Cayman Islands hosted over five hundred offshore banks, with total deposits of $442 billion (S. Roberts 1994; BIS 1996, 7).

> **offshore finance centers**
> Extraterritorial banks that investors use for a range of reasons, including the desire to avoid domestic taxes, regulations, and law enforcement agencies.

The supraterritorial character of much contemporary banking also lies in the instantaneity of interbank fund transfers. Electronic messages have largely replaced territorial transfers by check or draft—and cost far less. The largest conduit for such movements is the Society for Worldwide Interbank Financial Telecommunications (SWIFT). Launched in 1977, SWIFT interconnected more than 8,300 financial institutions in 208 countries by 2009, carrying an average of 12.3 million payments per day.

Transplanetary Securities

Globalization has altered not only banking but also the shape of securities markets. First, some of the bonds and stocks themselves have become relatively detached from territorial space. Second, many investor portfolios have acquired a transborder character. Third, electronic interlinkage of trading sites has created conditions of anywhere/

Southern Debt in Global Finance

The global character of much contemporary finance is well illustrated by the struggles that many middle- and low-income countries have had with large transborder debts. The problems developed in the 1970s, when the surge in oil prices generated huge export earnings of so-called petrodollars, which were largely placed in bank deposits. The banks in turn needed to lend the money, but demand for loans in the OECD countries was low at the time owing to recession. So, instead, large bank loans went to countries of the South (in some cases partly to help pay for the increased cost of oil imports). Often the lenders were insufficiently careful in extending these credits, and often the borrowers were reckless in spending the money. Starting with Mexico in August 1982, a string of borrowing governments in the South defaulted on their transborder loans.

The initial response to this situation of unsustainable debts was to implement short-term emergency rescue packages for each country as it ran into crisis. Payments were rescheduled, and additional loans were provided to cover unpaid interest charges. This piecemeal approach only tended to make things worse. From 1987 onward, a series of comprehensive plans for third world debt relief were promoted. During the following decade, unsustain-able commercial bank loans were gradually written off or converted into long-term bonds. Many bilateral loans from Northern governments to Southern borrowers were also canceled. However, in the mid-1990s, major problems persisted in regard to debts owed by low-income countries to multilateral lenders such as the IMF and the World Bank. A much-touted Highly Indebted Poor Countries (HIPC) initiative, launched in 1996 and recast in 1999, has brought slow and limited returns. In 2005, the G-8 Summit in Gleneagles agreed to write off the debts of eighteen HIPCs to the multilateral agencies.

Throughout these twenty years, programs of debt relief for low-income countries have received major support from global citizen campaigns. Activists formed a first Debt Crisis Network in the mid-1980s. Regional coalitions such as the European Network on Debt and Development emerged in the early 1990s. These efforts coalesced and broadened in the global Jubilee 2000 campaign of the late 1990s, which, among other things, assembled seventy thousand people in a "human chain" around the G-8 Summit in Birmingham, UK, in 1998. Most commentators agree that these global citizen mobilizations significantly increased, improved, and accelerated programs of debt relief.

anytime securities dealing. Each of these factors contributed to the 2008 economic collapse: subprime US home mortgages were sold in European markets and traded twenty-four hours a day, seven days a week.

In regard to the first point, contemporary globalization has seen the emergence of several major securities instruments with a transborder character. These bonds and equities can involve issuers, currencies, brokers, and exchanges across multiple countries at the same time. For example, a so-called eurobond is denominated in a currency that is alien to a substantial proportion of the parties involved: the borrower who issues it; the underwriters who distribute it; the investors who hold it; or the exchange(s) that list it. This transborder financial instrument is thereby different from a foreign bond, which is handled in one country for an external borrower. Cross-border bonds of the latter type have existed for several hundred years, but eurobonds first appeared in 1963. In that year, the state highway authority in Italy issued bonds denominated in US dollars through managers in Belgium, Britain, Germany, and the Netherlands, with subsequent quotation on the London Stock Exchange.

On a similar pattern, a euroequity issue involves a transborder syndicate of brokers selling a new share release for simultaneous listing on stock exchanges in several countries. This supraterritorial process contrasts with an international offer, where a company based in one country issues **equity** in a second country. Like foreign bonds, international share quotations have existed almost as long as stock markets themselves. However, the first transborder equity issue occurred in 1984, when 15 percent of a privatization of British Telecommunications was offered on exchanges in Japan, North America, and Switzerland concurrently with the majority share release in the UK. Transworld placements of new shares have occurred less frequently than eurobond issues. However, it has become quite common for major transborder firms to list their equity on different stock exchanges across several time zones, particularly in Asia, Europe, and North America.

Not only various securities instruments but also many investor portfolios have acquired a transborder character in the context of contemporary financial globalization. Thus, for example, an investor in one country may leave assets with a fund manager in a second country who in turn places those sums on markets in a collection of third countries. In other words, even when individual securities have a territorial character, they can be combined in a supraterritorial investment package. Indeed, a number of pension funds, insurance companies, and unit trusts have created explicitly designated "global funds" whose component securities are drawn from multiple corners of the world. Many transborder institutional investors have furthermore registered offshore for tax and other cost advantages. For example, the Africa Emerging Markets Fund has its investments in Africa, its listing in Ireland, and its management office in the United States. As of 1995, Luxembourg hosted some $350 billion in offshore investment funds, largely outside the regulatory reach of the managers' home governments.

Finally, securities markets have gone global through the growing supraterritorial character of many exchanges since the 1970s. The open-outcry trading floors of old have largely given way to electronic transactions by telephone and computer networks. These telecommunications provide the infrastructure for distanceless deals (called "remote trading"), in which the brokers can, in principle, be located anywhere on earth. Most major investment banks (Daiwa Securities, Dresdner Kleinwort, Fidelity, etc.) now coordinate offices across several time zones in round-the-clock, round-the-world trading of bonds and shares. The first computerized order-routing system became operational in 1976, connecting brokers across the United States instantly to the trading floor of the New York Stock Exchange. Similar developments have, since 1996, begun to link brokers anywhere in the European Union directly to its main exchanges. For its part, the wholly computer-based National Association of Securities Dealers Automated Quotation system (Nasdaq) has, since its launch in 1971, had no central meeting place at all. This transborder cyberspatial network has become the world's largest stock market, listing around 3,200 companies with a combined market capitalization of over $4.1 trillion and annual trading of 580 billion shares as of 2006. Meanwhile, beginning with the Toronto and American stock exchanges in 1985, a number of securities markets have established electronic links to enable transborder dealing between them. This extensive growth of supraterritoriality in the securities markets helps to explain why, for example, the Wall Street crash of October 1987 triggered transworld reverberations within hours.

Much like global banking, transborder securities trading is mainly conducted through computerized clearing systems. The equivalents of SWIFT are the Euroclear network, established in 1968, and Cedel (now renamed Clearstream), launched in 1971. Euroclear alone handled a turnover of over €350 trillion (euros) in 2005.

equity Also called "stock" or "share"; a number of equal portions in the nominal capital of a company; the shareholder thereby owns part of the enterprise.

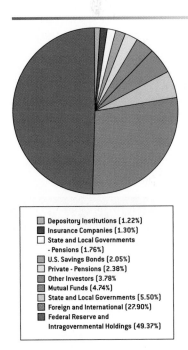

Depository Institutions (1.22%)
Insurance Companies (1.30%)
State and Local Governments - Pensions (1.76%)
U.S. Savings Bonds (2.05%)
Private - Pensions (2.38%)
Other Investors (3.78%)
Mutual Funds (4.74%)
State and Local Governments (5.50%)
Foreign and International (27.90%)
Federal Reserve and Intragovernmental Holdings (49.37%)

Estimated Ownership of all U.S. Treasury Securities (June 2008). What two groups own the most U.S. Treasury Securities? *Source: U.S. Treasury.*

Transplanetary Derivatives

A fourth area of finance suffused with globalization—and a major villain in the drama of the 2008–2009 economic crisis—is the derivatives industry. A derivative product is a contract, the value of which depends on (hence is "derived" from) the price of some underlying asset (e.g., a raw material or an equity) or a particular reference rate (e.g., an interest level or stock market index). Derivatives connected to tangible assets like raw minerals and land date from the middle of the nineteenth century, while derivatives based on financial indicators have proliferated since their introduction in 1972.

Derivatives contracts take two principal forms. The first type, called **futures** or "forwards," oblige a buyer and seller to complete a transaction at a predetermined time in the future at a price agreed on today. The second main type, called **options**, give parties a right (without obligation) to buy or sell at a specified price for a stipulated period of time up to the contract's expiry date. Other kinds of derivatives include "swaps," "warrants," and further—seemingly ever more obscure—financial instruments.

Additional technical details and the various rationales relating to derivatives need not detain us here. It suffices for present purposes to emphasize the magnitude of this financial industry and its near total lack of government regulation prior to 2009. Public derivatives exchanges have proliferated worldwide since 1982 along with even larger over-the-counter (OTC) markets. By 1995 the volume of trading on world derivatives markets totaled some $1.2 trillion per day. The notional value of outstanding OTC financial derivatives contracts alone reached $370 trillion in mid-2006 (BIS 1996, 27; BIS 2006).

Like banking and securities, much derivatives business has become relatively distanceless and borderless. For example, a number of the contracts relate to supraterritorial indicators, such as the world price of copper, the interest rate on euro–Swiss franc deposits, and so on. In addition, much derivatives trading is undertaken through global securities houses and transworld telecommunications links. A number of derivatives instruments are traded simultaneously on several exchanges in a round-the-world, round-the-clock market. For example, contracts related to three-month eurodollar interest rates have been traded concurrently on Euronext.liffe (a pan-European derivatives exchange), the New York Futures Exchange (NYFE), the Sydney Futures Exchange (SFE), and the Singapore Exchange (SGX).

Owing to these tight global interconnections, major losses in the derivatives markets can have immediate worldwide repercussions. For example, deficits of $1.3 billion accumulated by the Singapore-based futures trader Nick Leeson triggered a transborder collapse of the venerable Barings investment bank in 1995. A succession of similarly huge losses in other quarters caused some analysts to worry that global derivatives trading could undermine the world financial system as a whole, although the sector remained largely unregulated in Europe and the United States.

futures Derivatives that oblige a buyer and seller to complete a transaction at a predetermined time in the future at a price agreed on today. Futures are also known as "forwards."

options Derivatives that give parties a right (without obligation) to buy or sell at a specific price for a stipulated period of time up to the contract's expiry date.

WHAT'S YOUR WORLDVIEW

With all these transnational institutions and policies, is it possible for any state or even a group of states to manage the global economy? Who should be charged with protecting average people and their savings accounts?

Continuity and Change in Economic Globalization

Having now reviewed the development of a supraterritorial dimension in the contemporary world economy (summarized chronologically in Table 12.3), and emphasized its significance, we need to recognize continuities alongside these changes. One can appreciate the importance of globalization without slipping into globalism. In the following sections we will discuss four factors of continuity: the unevenness of globalization, which we call irregular incidence; the enduring importance of territoriality; the role of the state in an era of globalization; and the persistence of nationalism and cultural diversity.

Irregular Incidence

Globalization has not been experienced everywhere and by everyone to the same extent. In general, transborder trade and finance have developed furthest (1) in East Asia, North America, and Western Europe, (2) in urban areas relative to rural districts, and (3) in wealthier and professional circles. On the other hand, few people and places are today completely untouched by economic globalization.

Supraterritorial trade and finance have transpired disproportionately in what we are calling the North, and then most especially in its cities. For instance, although McDonald's fast food is dished up in 30,000 establishments across 119 countries, the vast majority of these meals are consumed in a handful of those lands. In contrast to currencies issued in the North, the national denominations of countries in Africa have had scarcely any mutual convertibility. Thus far, three-quarters and more of foreign direct investment, credit card transactions, stock market capitalization, derivatives trade, and transborder loans flowed within the North.

This marginalization of the South is far from complete, however. For instance, certain products originating in the South have figured significantly in global markets (e.g., wines from Chile and South Africa and package holidays in the Caribbean). Electronic banking has even reached parts of rural China. A number of offshore finance centers and large sums of transborder bank debt are found in the South. Global portfolios have figured strongly in the development of new securities markets in major cities of Africa, Asia, Eastern Europe, and Latin America since the mid-1980s. SGX and the São Paulo–based Bolsa de Mercadorias & Futuros (BM&F) have played a part in the burgeoning derivatives markets of recent decades.

Indeed, involvement in global trade and finance is often as much a function of class as of the North-South divide. The vast majority of the world's population—including many in the North—have lacked the means to purchase most global products. Likewise, placing investments in global financial markets depends on wealth, the distribution of which does not always follow a North-South pattern. For example, substantial petrodollars have been owned by elites in the oil-exporting countries of Africa, Latin America, and the Middle East.

Space limitations do not permit full elaboration of the point here, but transborder markets and investments can be shown to have contributed significantly to growing wealth gaps within countries as well as between North and South (Scholte 2005, Chapter 10). For example, the global mobility of capital, in particular to low-wage production sites and off-shore finance centers, has encouraged many countries, including the United States, to reduce upper tax brackets and to downgrade some social welfare provisions. Such steps have contributed to growing inequality across much of the contemporary world. Increasingly, poverty has become connected as much to supraterritorial class, gender, and race structures as to country of domicile (see Chapter 4).

> ### WHAT'S YOUR WORLDVIEW
>
> *Who has been left out of this global or transnational economy? Can these states and their citizens be brought into the system?*

The Persistence of Territory

Yet the transcendence of territorial space in the contemporary world economy must not be overestimated. True, evidence presented earlier in this chapter suggests that distance

Table 12.5

Some Key Events in Global Trade and Finance

1929	Institution of the first offshore finance arrangements (in Luxembourg)	1974	Formation of Basel Committee on Banking Supervision following the collapse of two banks heavily involved in foreign exchange dealing
1944	Bretton Woods Conference drafts constitutions of the IMF and the World Bank	1974	US government relaxes foreign exchange controls (other states follow in later years)
1954	Establishment of the first export processing zone (in Ireland)	1976	IMF meeting in Jamaica formalizes the regime of floating exchange rates
1954	Launch of the "Marlboro cowboy" as a global commercial icon	1977	Inauguration of the SWIFT system of electronic interbank fund transfers worldwide
1955	First McDonald's restaurant opens (operating in 119 countries 50 years later)	1982	Mexico's threatened default on global loans triggers third world debt crisis
1957	Issuance of the first eurocurrency loan	1983	Formation of the International Organization of Securities Commissions
1959	Gold–dollar standard enters into full operation	1984	First transborder equity issue (by British Telecommunications)
1963	Issuance of the first eurobond	1985	First transborder electronic link between stock exchanges
1965	Start of the maquiladora program in Mexico	1987	Stock market crash on Wall Street reverberates worldwide within hours
1968	Launch of Euroclear computerizes transworld settlement of securities deals	1994	Conclusion of the Uruguay Round of the GATT
1969	Introduction of the Special Drawing Right	1995	Inauguration of the World Trade Organization
1971	Establishment of the first wholly electronic stock exchange (Nasdaq)	1995	Leeson affair highlights the volatility of global derivatives markets
1972	Launch of markets in financial derivatives, starting with currency futures	1997–2002	Crises in Asia, Russia, Brazil, and Argentina raise concerns about underregulated global finance; in 1999, US Glass-Steagall Act repealed
1973	Quadrupling of oil prices floods euromarkets with petrodollars	2003	Doha Development Round of multilateral trade talks stalls, and bilateral trade agreements increase
		2007–2009	Growing concerns over subprime mortgages in US. US government nationalizes insurance giant AIG, General Motors, and several key banks; Italian carmaker Fiat buys controlling share of US firm Chrysler

and borders have often lost the determining influence on economic geography that they once had. However, this is not to say that the nation-state has lost all significance in the contemporary organization of production, exchange, and consumption.

On the contrary, after several decades of accelerated globalization, a great deal of commercial activity is still linked to a specific country and has only a secondary supraterritorial dimension. For example, although transborder manufacturing through global factories has affected a significant proportion of certain industries, most processes have remained contained within one country. Even many globally distributed products (Boeing jets, Ceylon teas) are prepared within a single country.

Many types of money, too, have remained restricted to a national or local domain. Likewise, the great bulk of retail banking has stayed territorial, as clients deal with their local branch offices. In spite of substantial growth since the 1980s, transborder share dealing remains a small fraction of total equity trading. Moreover, a large majority of turnover on most stock exchanges continues to involve shares of firms headquartered in the same country.

Nor has most global commercial activity been wholly detached from territorial geography. For example, local circumstances have strongly influenced corporate decisions regarding the location of transborder production facilities. In the foreign exchange markets, dealers have mainly been clustered in half a dozen cities, even if their transactions are largely cyberspatial and can have immediate consequences anywhere in the world. It remains rare for a transborder company to issue a large proportion of its stock outside its country of origin.

Hence the importance of globalization is that it has ended the monopoly of territoriality in defining the spatial character of the world economy. The trend has by no means eliminated territoriality. The global dimension of contemporary world commerce has grown alongside, and in complex relations with, its territorial aspects. Globalization has been reconfiguring economic, social, and political geography (alongside concurrent processes of regionalization and localization) rather than obliterating territory.

The Survival of the State

Similarly, globalization has repositioned the (territorial) state rather than signaled its demise. The expansion of transborder trade and finance has made claims of Westphalian sovereign statehood obsolete, but the significance of states themselves remains. Through both unilateral decisions and multilaterally coordinated policies, states have done much to facilitate economic globalization and influence its course.

As already mentioned, states have encouraged the globalization of commerce through various policies of liberalization and the creation of special economic zones and offshore finance centers. At the same time, some governments in the developing world have also slowed globalization within their jurisdiction by retaining certain restrictions on transborder activity. However, most states have sooner or later responded to strong pressures to liberalize. In any case, governments have often lacked effective means to fully enforce their territorially bound controls on globally mobile capital. Only with respect to immigration restrictions have states largely sustained their borders against economic globalization, and even then substantial traffic in unregistered migrants occurs.

Yet states are by no means powerless in the face of economic globalization. Even the common claim that global finance lies beyond the state requires qualification. After all, governments and central banks continue to exert major influence on money supplies and interest rates, even if they no longer monopolize money creation and they lack tight control over the euromarkets. Likewise, particularly through cooperative action, states can significantly shift exchange rates, even if they have lost the capacity to fix the conversion ratios and are sometimes overridden by currency dealers. We see examples of both kinds of behavior in 2008–2009 as political leaders tried to halt the economic collapse. Governments have also pursued collective regulation of transborder banking to some effect via the Basel Committee on Banking Supervision, set up through the BIS in 1974. The survival of offshore finance centers, too, depends to a considerable extent on the goodwill of governments, both the host regime and external authorities. Recent years have seen increased intergovernmental consultations, particularly through the OECD, to obtain tighter official oversight of offshore finance. Similarly, national regulators of securities markets have collaborated since 1984 through the International Organization of Securities Commissions (IOSCO).

In short, there is little sign that global commerce and the state are antithetical. On the contrary, the two have shown considerable mutual dependence. States have provided much of the regulatory framework for global trade and finance, albeit sharing these competences with other regulatory agencies. Sadly, despite the potential for collective action, none of the measures countries undertook could stop the pace of the economic collapse in late 2008.

The Continuance of Nationalism and Cultural Diversity

Much evidence also confounds the common presumption that economic globalization is effecting cultural homogenization and a rise of cosmopolitan orientations over national **identities**. The growth of transborder production, the proliferation of global products, the multiplication of supraterritorial monies, and the expansion of transworld financial flows have shown little sign of heralding an end of cultural difference in the world economy.

True, global trade and finance are moved by much more than national loyalty. Consumers have repeatedly ignored exhortations to buy American and the like in favor of global products. This is one reason US automakers Chrysler, Ford, and General Motors had to beg for cash bailouts from the federal government in 2008–2009. Shareholders and managers have rarely put national sentiments ahead of the profit margin. For example, the global media magnate Rupert Murdoch happily traded Australian for US citizenship in 1985 when it suited his commercial purposes. Foreign exchange dealers readily desert their national currency in order to reap financial gain.

However, in other respects national identities and solidarities have survived—and sometimes thrived—in the contemporary globalizing economy. Most transborder companies have retained a readily recognized national affiliation. Most firms involved in global trade and finance have kept a mononational board of directors, and the operations of many of these enterprises continue to reflect a national style of business practice connected with the country of origin. Different national conventions have persisted in global finance as well. For instance, since equities have traditionally held a smaller place in German finance, globalization in that country has mainly involved banks and the bond markets. Cultural diversity has also persisted in transborder marketing. Local peculiarities have often affected the way a global product is sold and used in different places. Advertising has often been adjusted to local tastes to be more effective.

In sum, then, like globalization in general, its economic dimension has not had universal scope. Nor has the rise of global trade and finance marked the end of territorial space, the demise of the state, or full-scale cultural homogenization. However, recognition of these qualifications does not entail a rejection of notions of globalization, on the lines of the skeptics noted earlier. After discounting for exaggeration and non sequiturs, the growth of global interactions remains a highly significant development in the contemporary world economy.

identity The understanding of the self in relationship to an "other." Identities are social and thus always formed in relationship to others. Constructivists generally hold that identities shape interests; we cannot know what we want unless we know who we are. But because identities are social and produced through interactions, identities can change.

Theory in Practice

What Course to Follow Out of the 2008 Global Recession?

The debates about international relations theories that you studied in Chapters 3 and 4 may have struck you as somewhat sterile. But if you were a political leader seeking a way to bring your country out of the economic recession of 2008–2009, you would probably have a clear idea of what the theories mean for the policies you were considering. Although in 2010 there is one socialist in the Senate, in the United States political leaders tend to follow one of two dominant models: realism or liberalism.

The realist perspective on international relations stresses the need to defend the state and its interests. In the past, the recommendations of realism tended to sound like mercantilism, popular in the seventeenth and eighteenth centuries. Countries should seek to be self-sufficient, a condition called autarchy, and keep as much gold and silver within national control as possible. In modern times, realists might not call it mercantilism, but their protectionist recommendations can sound like that doctrine: for example, increase tariff barriers to protect domestic industries, buy products made domestically, and stop outsourcing jobs to other countries.

Liberal international relations theories make a very different set of recommendations, many of which are embodied in the World Trade Organization. For adherents of this perspective, the way out of an economic recession is by increasing foreign trade, by making trade as free as possible. This means reducing or eliminating tariffs and nontariff barriers and encouraging the process of global sourcing of goods and services. The result of such outward-looking policies would hopefully be what economists call "comparative advantage." This is a complex idea that in simplest terms asserts that if a country produces and sells what it can make most efficiently, it will be able to buy the other products that it needs with the profits from its own production.

For our hypothetical political leader the choice is not as simple as it seems. In democratic political systems, politicians must stand for reelection, and they must account for their decisions. In some ways, the realist perspective is the easiest to defend. The politician has promised to defend American jobs and pursued policies that could do that. If the recession is made worse by these protectionist ideas, at least the politician can claim to have tried.

Working against the protectionist counsels of realism is the more than sixty years of effective trade practices, first in GATT and then after 1995 in the WTO. Therefore, a politician seeking reelection has the historical record to fall back on when debating with a realism-inspired opponent. Beginning in 1947 with twenty-three countries, the eight rounds of trade talks worked to reduced global restrictions on trade in goods and services. Of course, no politician would want to tell a worker that it is a good thing that the factory closed its doors and the jobs went to another country where production costs are lower. In good economic times, this is perhaps not necessary; during an economic recession, there is often no choice.

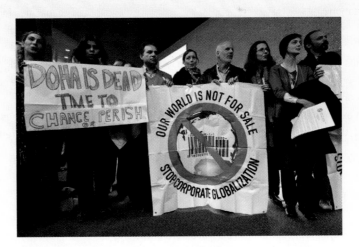

Do corporations have a social responsibility?

What is in store for the world's economy?

Conclusion

We began this chapter by asking, "How did it happen?" Prior to the summer of 2008, the world's economy seemed to be gaining wealth. Aside from the historic high price for petroleum products, most economic sectors showed no sign of distress. Yet the seeds of the economic recession that began in 2008 were already planted. As you read in this chapter, the complex relationship of trade in goods and financial instruments was seemingly doomed to fail. Too much of the money was invested in arcane instruments like derivatives and mortgages served up as secure investments. The globalized trade and finance sectors were largely unregulated by host countries. Even as this text goes to press, it is not clear what the ultimate fallout will be from this global crisis. Governments have tried the methods that have worked during past recessions, but as of late 2009, none have worked. Banks continue to fail, corporations continue to file for bankruptcy, and workers have lost their retirement savings and, far too often, their jobs.

Chapter 12 authored by Steven L. Lamy.

REVIEW QUESTIONS

1. What are the three main conceptions of economic globalization?
2. To what extent is economic globalization new to contemporary history?
3. How does transborder production differ from territorial production?
4. What is an offshore financial center?
5. To what extent has contemporary economic globalization marked "the end of geography"?
6. How has globalization of trade and finance affected state capacities for economic regulation?
7. How have global products altered ideas of cultural diversity?
8. To what extent can it be said that global capital carries no national flag?
9. Assess the relationship between globalization and income inequality.
10. In what ways might global commerce be reshaped to promote greater distributive justice?

FURTHER READING

Dunning, J. H. (ed.) (2004), *Making Globalization Good: Moral Challenges of Global Capitalism* (Oxford: Oxford University Press). Essays exploring ways to make global markets environmentally sustainable and socially equitable.

Held, D. et al. (1999), *Global Transformations: Politics, Economics and Culture* (Cambridge: Polity Press). Excellent text on indicators and repercussions of economic globalization.

Hirst, P., and Thompson, G. (1999), *Globalization in Question: The International Economy and the Possibilities of*

Governance, 2nd ed. (Cambridge: Polity Press). A critique of "globalist" presumptions that economic globalization is new, irreversible, and wholly beyond state control.

Hocking, B., and McGuire, S. (eds.) (2004), *Trade Politics*, 2nd ed. (London: Routledge). Covers the main issues of, and perspectives on, global trade.

O'Brien, R., and Williams, M. (2004), *Global Political Economy: Evolution and Dynamics* (Basingstoke: Palgrave

Macmillan). A thorough overview of the history and current challenges of global production and exchange.

Peterson, V. S., and Runyan, A. S. (1999), *Global Gender Issues*, 2nd ed. (Boulder, CO: Westview Press). A critical examination of the impacts of globalization on, inter alia, women's employment and the feminization of poverty.

Porter, T. (2005), *Globalization and Finance* (Cambridge: Polity Press). A thorough analysis of global finance and its governance.

Scholte, J. A. (2005), *Globalization: A Critical Introduction*, 2nd ed. (Basingstoke: Palgrave Macmillan). Elaborates the arguments presented in this chapter, including the implications of economic globalization for human security, social justice, and democracy.

Stubbs, R., and Underhill, G. R. D. (eds.) (2006), *Political Economy and the Changing Global Order*, 3rd ed. (Basingstoke: Palgrave). A textbook in international political economy with much concerning global trade and finance.

UNDP (1990–   ), *Human Development Report* (New York: Oxford University Press). This annual publication of the United Nations Development Program includes much on the welfare consequences of economic globalization. See especially the 1999 edition.

INTERNET RESOURCES

Bank for International Settlements
www.bis.org

The organization that encourages cooperation between national central banks.

European Union
http://europa.eu/

Website of the EU provides a treasure chest of information about the organization.

Gapminder
www.gapminder.org

An NGO that tracks the gap between rich and poor countries and people around the world.

Organization of Economic Co-operation and Development
www.oecd.org

The organization of the world's leading national economies.

Public Citizen NAFTA page
http://www.citizen.org/trade/nafta/

The website of a USA NGO that provides information about a range of topics.

United Nations Conference on Trade and Development
www.unctad.org

The forum for developing countries within the UN structure.

For more information, quizzes, case studies, and other study tools, please visit us at **www.oup.com/us/lamy**

CHAPTER 13

Poverty, Development, and Hunger

Wherever there is great property there is great inequality. For one very rich man there must be at least five hundred poor, and the affluence of the few supposes the indigence of the many.

—*Adam Smith*

All societies used to be poor. Most are now lifting out of it; why are others stuck? The answer is traps. Poverty is not intrinsically a trap, otherwise we would all still be poor. Think, for a moment, of development as chutes and ladders. In the modern world of globalization there are some fabulous ladders; most societies are using them. But there are also some chutes, and some societies hit them. The countries at the bottom are an unlucky minority, but they are stuck.

—*Paul Collier*

Can music solve the problems of global poverty and hunger? Bob Geldof thought so, and in 1985 he organized the first of the series of Live Aid concerts. Over the years, Bono and many other rappers, rockers, and Afro-pop musicians became active in seeking an end to starvation in developing countries. The most recent event was Live 8, held in cities around the world in 2005. The concerts were intended to raise money for the cause and, perhaps more importantly, to apply pressure on the political leaders of the Group of 8 countries, the richest countries in the global economic system, prior to their meeting in Scotland. As we will see in this chapter, advocacy campaigns linked to celebrities like Kanye West, Radiohead, U2, Angelina Jolie, Panjabi MC, 50 Cent, and Madonna have come to play an important part in shaping the range of choices that politicians make about eliminating poverty, building economic development, and ending hunger worldwide.

George Michael, Bob Geldof, and Paul McCartney, along with an African choir, sing their message at the London Live 8 concert.

human security The security of people, including their physical safety, their economic and social well-being, respect for their dignity, and the protection of their human rights. Simply put, it is freedom from fear and freedom from want.

Washington Consensus The belief of key opinion-formers in Washington that global welfare would be maximized by the universal application of neoliberal economic policies that favor a minimalist state and an enhanced role for the market.

global governance Involves the regulation and coordination of transnational issue areas by nation-states, international and regional organizations, and private agencies through the establishment of international regimes. These regimes may focus on problem-solving or the simple enforcement of rules and regulations.

Introduction

Since 1945 we have witnessed over sixty years of unprecedented official development policies and impressive global economic growth. Yet global polarization is increasing, with the economic gap between rich and poor states and people growing (see Figure 13.1). As we have seen in other issue areas in this book, people who work in the academic discipline of international relations have different ways of thinking about this gap:

- Traditionally, because of its focus on states in the international system, the dominant realist perspective concentrated on issues relating to war, and regarded security and development economics as separate issue areas.
- Mainstream realist and liberal scholars neglected the challenges presented to human well-being by the existence of global underdevelopment.
- Dependency theorists were interested in persistent and deepening inequality and relations between North and South, but they received little attention in the discipline.
- During the 1990s, debate flourished, and several subfields developed that touched on matters of poverty, development, and hunger, albeit tangentially (e.g., global environmental politics, gender, international political economy).
- Also in the 1990s, and more significant in raising within the discipline the concerns of the majority of humanity and states, were the contributions from postcolonial theorists, Marxist theorists (Hardt and Negri), scholars adopting a **human security** approach (Nef, Thomas), and the few concerned directly with development (Saurin, Weber).

Now, in the twenty-first century, the discipline is better placed to engage with the interrelated issues of poverty, development, and hunger by influencing the diplomatic world, where interest in these issues is increasing, spurred on by fears of terrorist threats and recognition of the uneven impact of globalization (Thomas and Wilkin 2004).

Poverty, hunger, and disease remain widespread, and women and girls continue to comprise the majority of the world's poorest people. Since the 1980s and 1990s, the worldwide promotion of neoliberal economic policies (the so-called **Washington Consensus**) by **global governance** institutions has been accompanied by increasing inequalities within and between states. During this period, the second world countries of the former Eastern Bloc have been incorporated into the third world grouping of states, and millions of people previously cushioned by their governments have been thrown into poverty with the transition to market economies. As a result, the developing world is characterized by rising social inequalities and, within the third world countries, the adverse impact of globalization has been felt acutely, as countries have been forced to adopt free market policies as a condition of debt rescheduling and in the hope of attracting new investment to spur development. The global picture is very mixed, with other factors such as gender, class, race, and ethnicity contributing to local outcomes (Buvinic 1997, 39).

More recently, the enormity of the current challenges was recognized by the UN in 2000 with the acceptance of the Millennium Development Goals (www .undp.org). These set time-limited, quantifiable targets

Rebels frequently target food-relief convoys, often to sell the food to purchase weapons.

across eight areas, including poverty, health, gender, education, environment, and development. The first goal was the eradication of extreme poverty and hunger, with the target of halving the proportion of people living on less than a dollar a day by 2015.

The attempts of the majority of governments, **international nongovernmental organizations (INGOs)**, and nongovernmental organizations (NGOs) since 1945 to address global hunger and poverty can be categorized into two very broad types, depending on the explanations they provide for the existence of these problems and the respective solutions they prescribe. These can be identified as the dominant mainstream, or orthodox, approach, which provides and values a particular body of developmental knowledge, and a critical alternative approach, which incorporates other, more marginalized understandings of the development challenge and process (see Table 13.1). Most of this chapter will be devoted to an examination of the differences between the mainstream/orthodox approach and the critical alternative approach in view of the three related topics of poverty, development, and hunger, with particular emphasis placed on the topic of development. The chapter concludes with an assessment of whether the desperate conditions in which so many of the world's citizens find themselves today are likely to improve. Again, two contrasting approaches are outlined.

Poverty

Different conceptions of poverty underpin the mainstream and alternative views of development. There is basic agreement on the material aspects of poverty, such as lack of food, clean water, and sanitation, but disagreement on the importance of nonmaterial aspects. Also, key differences emerge in regard to how material needs should be met, and hence about the goal of development.

Most governments, international organizations (like the IMF and World Bank), and citizens in the West, and many elsewhere, adhere to the orthodox conception of **poverty**, which refers to a situation where people do not have the money to buy adequate food or satisfy other basic needs and are often classified as un- or underemployed.

Since 1945, this mainstream understanding of poverty based on money has arisen as a result of the globalization of Western culture and the attendant expansion of the market. Thus a community that provides for itself outside monetized cash transactions and wage labor, such as a hunter-gatherer group, is regarded as poor. This meaning of poverty has been almost universalized. Poverty is seen as an economic condition dependent on cash

> **WHAT'S YOUR WORLDVIEW** ❓
>
> *How do intellectual models of poverty help us to understand it?*

international nongovernmental organization (INGO) A formal international organization, with transnational members from at least three countries. There are many different types, with membership from national NGOs, local NGOs, companies, political parties, or individual people. A few have other INGOs as members, and some have mixed membership structures.

poverty In the orthodox view, a situation suffered by people who do not have the *money to buy food* and satisfy other basic *material needs*. In the alternative view, a situation suffered by people who are not able to meet their *material and nonmaterial needs* through their own effort.

Table 13.1
Mainstream and Alternative Conceptions of Poverty, Development, and Hunger

	Poverty	Development	Hunger
Mainstream approach	Unfulfilled material needs	Linear path—traditional to modern	Not enough food to go around
Critical alternative approach	Unfulfilled material and nonmaterial needs	Diverse paths, locally driven	There is enough food, the problem is distribution and entitlement

transactions in the marketplace for its eradication. These transactions in turn are dependent on development defined as economic growth. The same economic yardstick is used to measure all societies and to judge if they merit development assistance.

Poverty has widely been regarded as characterizing the third world, and it has a gendered face that realist and liberal perspectives often ignore. By the mid 1990s an approach had developed whereby it was seen as incumbent on the developed countries to help the third world eradicate poverty. As studies show that women and children are most severely impacted by the consequences of poverty, development economists are increasingly addressing female poverty and women's roles in economic development. The solution advocated to overcome global poverty is the further integration of the global economy (C. Thomas 2000) and of women into this process (Pearson 2000; H. Weber 2002). Increasingly, however, as globalization has intensified, poverty defined in such economic terms has come to characterize significant sectors of the population in advanced developed countries such as the United States (see Bello 1994).

But for some, poverty cannot be measured merely in terms of cash. Critical, alternative views of poverty place the emphasis not simply on money but on spiritual values, community ties, and availability of common resources. In traditional subsistence methods, a common strategy for **survival** is provision for oneself and one's family via **community**-regulated access to common water, land, and fodder. The work of the United Nations Development Programme (UNDP) since the early 1990s is significant here for distinguishing between income poverty (a material condition) and human poverty (encompassing human dignity, opportunity, and choices).

The issue of poverty and the challenge of poverty alleviation moved up the global political agenda at the close of the twentieth century, as evidenced in the UN's first Millennium Development Goals, cited earlier in this chapter. While World Bank figures for the 1990s showed a global improvement in reducing the number of people living on less than a dollar a day (its orthodox measurement of extreme poverty), the picture was uneven: in sub-Saharan Africa the situation deteriorated, and elsewhere, such as the Russian Federation, the Commonwealth of Independent States, Latin America and the Caribbean, and some non-oil-producing Middle Eastern states, the picture remains bleak. In 2005, almost half the world—over three billion people—lived below the new poverty line, $2.50 a day, and at least 80 percent of the world's population lived on less than $10 a day. Most of the global improvement resulted from trends in China and India, and even there, extensive pockets of poverty remain.

Development

Having considered the orthodox and critical alternative views of poverty, we will now turn to an examination of the important topic of development. This examination will be conducted in three main parts. The first part will start by examining the orthodox view of development and then proceed to an assessment of its effect on postwar development in the third world. The second part will examine the critical alternative view of development and its application to subjects such as empowerment and democracy. In the third part, we will consider the ways the orthodox approach to development has responded to some of the criticisms made of it by the critical alternative approach.

When we consider the topic of **development**, it is important to realize that all conceptions of development necessarily reflect a particular set of social and political values. Since the Second World War, the dominant understanding—favored by the majority of

survival In this context it is the survival of the person by the provision of adequate food, clean water, clothing, shelter, medical care, and protection from violence and crime.

community A human association in which members share common symbols and wish to cooperate to realize common objectives.

development In the orthodox view, top-down; reliance on "expert knowledge," usually Western and definitely external; large capital investments in large projects; advanced technology; expansion of the private sphere. In the alternative view, bottom-up; participatory; reliance on appropriate (often local) knowledge and technology; small investments in small-scale projects; protection of the commons.

The Terms of Development

Can any theory of international relations explain the problems of economic underdevelopment? International relations specialists even have trouble deciding what to call the countries of the world once held in European colonial bondage. "Third world" made sense at one time. The term originated with Alfred Sauvy, a French demographer, who in 1952 compared the economic and political conditions of European colonies with those endured by the Third Estate in France prior to the Revolution. The typology was a simple one: first world countries had capitalist free market economies, second world countries in the Soviet bloc and China had centrally planned economies, and third world countries lacked industrial bases and provided raw materials for export. With the end of the Cold War, this tripartite typology made less sense.

Until 1989, "third world" provided a less demeaning alternative to terms often found in the political science literature on Africa, Asia, Oceania, and Latin America: "underdeveloped," or "less developed country" (LDC), sometimes called "least developed country" (also LDC). A brief look at a map reveals another problem. The "global South" is another term often used to indicate the former European colonies in Africa, Asia, and Latin America; the other side of this dyad is the "global North," meant to describe the former colonial occupiers. But not all countries in the global South are "poor," and not all countries that were once colonial occupiers—Portugal and Spain, for instance—are "rich." Instead, there are pockets of wealth and poverty in both the South and the North.

Beyond debates about terminology, there is another problem for theorists. What do we mean by the term "development" itself? The term might mean industrial output and its related exchange of goods and services. If that is the case, then the term implies that industrialization itself is a proper goal. The problem of global climate change suggests that industrialization, as it has been practiced, is not a good thing. (See Chapter 14.) Moreover, the term, according to some gender theorists, only considers transactions that can be counted, or that rely on an amount calculated in a currency. This method of accounting can overlook transactions that take place in a barter market, or economic activities traditionally done by women: raising crops for household consumption, cutting firewood, caring for children. In a capitalist economy, in Western Europe or the United States, such activities could have a dollar amount attached. For example, the US tax code gives a deduction for the cost of child care.

The realist perspective looks at the problems of economic and political underdevelopment, using the standard definitions found in scholarly books, with an almost Calvinist sensibility: countries are poor because they are poor. Since international politics is a constant struggle for power in conditions of anarchy, then some countries must lose in that struggle. This perspective can help to explain the series of internal and transborder

Slums, like this favela in Rio de Janeiro, Brazil, are home to poor people around the world who live mixed into pockets of wealth.

continued

Theory in Practice   *continued*

wars in central Africa since the late 1980s. Short on their own resources, the neighbors of the Congo tried to destabilize that country to gain access to mineral wealth.

Radical perspectives like Marxism once offered hope for a restructured global system. However, whatever comfort the doctrine once promised, the demise of the Soviet Union ended it. What was left was a theory that

outlined the causes and results of political and economic exploitation but proposed an apparently bankrupt solution.

For analysts in the liberal tradition, the policy prescription does not offer much hope either. This tradition tends to recommend that the former colonies integrate themselves into the global economy, perhaps by planting a cash crop for export, or to utilize

untapped resources. As we have seen in this chapter, however, countries that borrow money from international financial institutions can get caught in a debt trap if the price for the export commodity declines. This can leave the country economically worse off.

Unfortunately, no matter what they are called—the third world, the global South, the LDCs—for many countries, poverty and hunger prevail.

WHAT'S YOUR WORLDVIEW ?

In 2005, the World Bank stated that 2.5 billion people made less than two dollars a day. The poorest 1.1 billion were making less than one dollar a day. What would your life be like if you were in one of these categories? How do your choices keep the people in these categories? Could you make choices that might help the bottom billion?

governments and multilateral lending agencies—has been modernization theory, a theory that considers development synonymous with economic growth, within the context of a free market international economy. Economic growth is identified as necessary for combating poverty, defined as the inability of people to meet their basic material needs through cash transactions. This is seen in the influential reports of the World Bank, where countries are categorized according to their income. Those countries that have the lower national incomes per capita are regarded as being less developed than those with higher incomes, and they are perceived as being in need of increased integration into the global marketplace.

As the wave of decolonizations swept the world in the 1960s and early 1970s, an alternative view of development has, however, emerged from a few governments, UN agencies, grassroots movements, NGOs, and some academics. Their concerns have centered broadly on entitlement and distribution. Poverty is identified as the inability to provide for the material needs of oneself and one's family by subsistence or cash transactions and by the absence of an environment conducive to human well-being broadly conceived in spiritual and community terms. These voices of opposition are growing significantly louder, as ideas polarize following the apparent universal triumph of economic liberalism at the end of the Cold War. The language of opposition is changing to incorporate matters of democracy such as political empowerment, participation, meaningful self-determination for the majority, protection of the commons, and an emphasis on growth that benefits the poor. The fundamental differences between the orthodox and the alternative views of development can be seen in Table 13.2, supplemented by Case Study 13.1, which illustrates the impact of ideas about development from the contemporary coffee-producing sector. In the following two sections, we will examine how the orthodox view of development has been applied at a global level and assess what measure of success it has achieved.

Post-1945 International Economic Liberalism and the Orthodox Development Model

During the Second World War there was a strong belief among the Allied powers that the protectionist trade policies of the 1930s had contributed significantly to the outbreak

Ideas and Development in the Contemporary Coffee-Producing Sector

Contemporary debate on the coffee sector provides a graphic example of competing ideas and values concerning development and has relevance far beyond coffee. The impact of commodity price volatility and a long-term decline in terms of trade of primary products has profound effects on livelihoods of millions of rural householders in the poorest countries. In the case of coffee, about 25 million small farmers in over fifty countries depend directly on coffee production. During the 1980s, export production increased in poor countries, fueled significantly by policy advice from the World Bank and International Monetary Fund (IMF) that hard-currency earnings had to be boosted through increased commodity exports to pay off spiraling third world debt. Oversupply since the early 1980s has resulted in a decline of about 70 percent in nominal coffee prices, with prices reaching a thirty-year low in 2001. The impact on livelihoods of smallholder peasant farmers and plantation workers has been devastating. At the eleventh World Coffee Conference in Salvador da Bahia in September 2005, twelve groups representing peasant farmers and workers launched an alternative approach to coffee production, in the Salvador Declaration:

> For a truly sustainable coffee sector, all who take part in coffee production must share its wealth: small-scale producers, permanent and seasonal rural workers, industry and retail workers. Many say that the solutions to the crisis are only associated with methods of production, including increased investment in substitutes for local coffee varieties, use of toxic fertilisers and pesticides, and mechanization—all aimed at greater productivity. This vision . . . allows for the consolidation of production and marketing by a small group of companies that do not practise social responsibility but make decisions that impact millions of people while they reap the lion's share of the benefits of the trade. This vision is not sustainable. . .
>
> Real sustainability of the coffee sector should not be viewed through an economic lens alone but must include ethical and political perspectives.
>
> From an ethical perspective, the citizenship rights of people who participate in wealth generation must be guaranteed. Those rights are: stability of prices; recognition of efforts to protect the rural landscape and biological diversity by improving cultivation, harvest, and post harvesting practices; and recognition of the basic rights of rural workers, including the fundamental rights of association and collective bargaining, particularly for seasonal rural workers . . .
>
> From a political perspective, . . . governments (must) agree to and implement public policies that guarantee the rights of coffee producers and rural workers. It should be possible to develop a sustainable model based on food security and sovereignty.
>
> In conclusion, we expect the World Coffee Conference to acknowledge . . . the issue of sustainability from the perspective of all actors involved in the coffee chain and sanction space for direct representation by small-scale farmers and rural workers organisations . . . (and) seek to establish the basis for fair trade between nations.

(Oxfam 2006, 11–12)

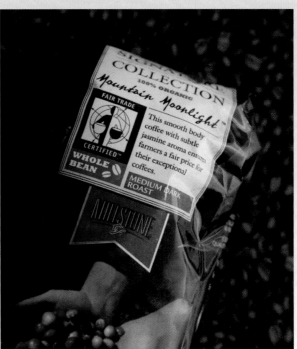

Fair trade NGOs seek to get a fair price for producers of tea, coffee, cocoa, and other food products grown in the developing world.

Fixed Phone Lines

Cell Phone Subscribers

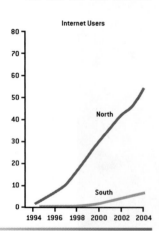

Internet Users

Digital Divide—North and South. The South is significantly behind the North in terms of connectivity and cell phone communications. Is this just a by-product of poverty or are there other factors involved? *Source: International Telecommunications Union.*

Table 13.2
Development: A Contested Concept

The orthodox view

Poverty: A situation suffered by people who do not have the *money to buy food* and satisfy other *basic material needs.*

Purpose: Transformation of traditional subsistence economies defined as "backward" into industrial, commodified economies defined as "modern." Production of surplus. Individuals sell their labor for money, rather than producing to meet their family's needs.

Core ideas and assumptions: The possibility of unlimited economic growth in a free market system. Economies would reach a "takeoff" point, and thereafter, wealth would trickle down to those at the bottom. Superiority of the Western model and knowledge. Belief that the process would ultimately benefit everyone. Domination, exploitation of nature.

Measurement: Economic growth; Gross Domestic Product (GDP) per capita; industrialization, including of agriculture.

Process: Top-down; reliance on "expert knowledge," usually Western and definitely external; large capital investments in large projects; advanced technology; expansion of the private sphere.

The alternative view

Poverty: A situation suffered by people who are not able to meet their *material and nonmaterial needs* through their own effort.

Purpose: Creation of human well-being through sustainable societies in social, cultural, political, and economic terms.

Core ideas and assumptions: Sufficiency. The inherent value of nature, cultural diversity, and the community-controlled commons (water, land, air, forest). Human activity in balance with nature. Self-reliance. Democratic inclusion, participation: for example, a voice for marginalized groups such as women and indigenous groups. Local control.

Measurement: Fulfilment of basic material and nonmaterial human needs of everyone; condition of the natural environment. Political empowerment of marginalized.

Process: Bottom-up; participatory; reliance on appropriate (often local) knowledge and technology; small investments in small-scale projects; protection of the commons.

of the war. As we learned in Chapters 11 and 12, even before the Second World War had ended, the United States and the United Kingdom drew the plans for the creation of a stable postwar international order, with the United Nations (UN), its affiliates the International Monetary Fund (IMF) and the World Bank Group, plus the General Agreement on Tariffs and Trade (GATT) providing the institutional bases. The latter three provided the foundations of a liberal international economic order, based on the pursuit of free trade but allowing an appropriate role for state intervention in the market in support of national security and national and global stability (Rapley 1996). This has been called "embedded liberalism." Because the decision-making procedures of these international economic institutions favored a small group of developed Western states, their relationship with the UN, which in the General Assembly has more democratic procedures, has not always been an easy one.

In the early postwar years, reconstruction of previously developed states took priority over assisting developing states. This reconstruction process really took off in the context of the Cold War, with the transfer of huge sums of money from the United States to Europe in the form of bilateral aid from the Marshall Plan of 1947. In the 1950s and 1960s, as decolonization progressed and developing countries gained power in the UN

General Assembly, the focus of the World Bank and the UN system generally shifted to the perceived needs of developing countries. The United States was heavily involved as the most important funder of the World Bank and the UN and also in a bilateral capacity.

There was a widespread belief in the developed Western countries, among the managers of the major multilateral institutions, and throughout the UN system that third world states were economically backward and needed to be "developed." Western-educated elites in those countries believed this process would require intervention in their economies. In the context of independence movements, the development imperative came to be shared by many citizens in the third world. The underlying assumption was that the Western lifestyle and mode of economic organization were superior and should be universally aspired to.

The Cold War provided a context in which there was a competition between the West and the Eastern Bloc to win markets in the third world. The United States believed that the path of liberal economic growth would result in development and that development would result in a global capitalist system, which favors the US. The USSR, by contrast, attempted to sell its centralized economic system as the most rapid means for the newly independent states to achieve industrialization and development. Unfortunately for the Soviet government, because of its own food-supply and consumer-goods production problems, the country's material foreign assistance was usually limited to military equipment.

The majority of third world states were born into and accepted a place within the Western, capitalist orbit, primarily because of preexisting economic ties with their former colonial occupiers, while a few, either by choice or lack of options, ended up in the socialist camp. Yet in the early postwar and postcolonial decades, all newly independent states favored an important role for the state in development.

With the ending of the Cold War and the collapse of the Eastern Bloc after 1989, this neoliberal economic and political philosophy came to dominate development thinking across the globe. The championing of unadulterated liberal economic values played an important role in accelerating the globalization process, representing an important ideological shift. The "embedded liberalism" of the early postwar decades gave way to the neoclassical economic policies that favored a minimalist state and an enhanced role for the market: the Washington Consensus. The belief was that global welfare would be maximized by the **liberalization** of trade, finance, and investment and by the restructuring of national economies to provide an enabling environment for capital. Such policies would also hopefully ensure the repayment of debt. The former Eastern Bloc countries were now seen to be in transition from centrally planned to market economies, and throughout the third world the role of government was reduced and the market given the role of major engine of growth and associated development. This approach was presented as common sense, with the attendant idea that "There Is No Alternative," or TINA (C. Thomas 2000). It informed the strategies of the IMF and World Bank, and, importantly, through the Uruguay Round of trade discussions carried out under the auspices of GATT, it shaped the **World Trade Organization (WTO)**.

By the end of the 1990s, the G-7 (later the **G-8**, when Russia joined in 1996) and associated international financial institutions were championing a slightly modified version of the neoliberal economic orthodoxy, labeled the **post–Washington Consensus**, which stressed growth benefiting the poor and poverty reduction based on institutional strength, continued domestic policy reform, and growth through trade liberalization. Henceforth,

liberalization Describes government policies that reduce the role of the state in the economy, such as the dismantling of trade tariffs and barriers, the deregulation and opening of the financial sector to foreign investors, and the privatization of state enterprises.

World Trade Organization (WTO) Established in 1995 with headquarters in Geneva. Membership (2010) of 153 states. The WTO is a permanent institution to replace the provisional GATT. It has a wider agenda, covering services, intellectual property, and investment issues as well as merchandise trade. The WTO also has greater powers of enforcement through its dispute-settlement mechanism. The organization's Trade Policy Review Body conducts surveillance of members' commercial measures.

G-8 (Group of Eight) Established in 1975 as the G-5 (France, Germany, Japan, the UK, and the US); subsequently expanded as the G-7 to include Canada and Italy; and since 1998 the G-8, to include the Russian Federation. The G-8 conducts semiformal collaboration on world economic problems. Government leaders meet in annual G-8 summits, while finance ministers or their leading officials periodically hold other consultations. See further www.g8online.org.

Post–Washington Consensus A slightly modified version of the Washington Consensus, promoting economic growth through trade liberalization coupled with pro-poor growth and poverty-reduction policies.

regional diversity Each region of the world has experienced economic development differently based on traditions, culture, historical development, and even geographic location.

locally owned national poverty-reduction strategy (PRS) papers would be the focus for funding (Cammack 2002). These papers quickly became the litmus test for funding from an increasingly integrated lineup of global financial institutions and donors.

The Post-1945 International Economic Order: Results

There has been an explosive widening of the gap between the rich and the poor since 1945 compared with previous history. Nevertheless, there have been major gains for developing countries since 1945 as measured by the orthodox criteria of economic growth, GDP per capita, and industrialization. The rates of total and per capita growth for developing countries in the period 1960–2004 are shown in Tables 13.3 and 13.4. A striking feature of both is the marked **regional diversity**. The East Asian experience has been generally positive throughout this period, the African experience not so. China has been strong since the early 1980s, and India has fared better since the late 1980s.

In the 1990s, the picture was far from positive. The UNDP reports "no fewer than 100 countries—all developing or in transition—have experienced serious economic decline over the past three decades. As a result, per capita income in these 100 countries is lower than it was 10, 20, even 30 years ago" (UNDP 1998, 37). Moreover, the 1990s saw twenty-one countries experience decadelong declines in social and economic indicators, compared with only four in the 1980s (UNDP 2003). Financial crises spread across the globe and indicated marked reversals in Mexico, the East Asian states, Brazil, and Russia.

Table 13.3
GDP Growth in Selected Developing Countries and Regions, 1960–2004 (average annual percentage change)

Region/country	1960–1965	1965–1970	1970–1975	1975–1980	1980–1985	1985–1990	1990–1995	1995–2000	2000–2004
Africa	5.4	4.9	4.4	3.8	2.2	2.6	1.1	3.4	3.9
Sub-Saharan Africa, excl. South Africa	3.9	3.9	3.9	1.9	1.7	3.2	1.5	3.7	4.2
Latin America	4.6	5.8	6.6	5.1	0.5	1.8	3.6	2.8	1.5
East Asia	5.0	7.5	6.8	7.6	7.1	8.2	8.8	4.9	6.2
China	2.1	5.3	5.1	6.1	11.0	7.8	12.9	8.5	9.4
First-tier NIEs	8.0	9.8	8.3	9.0	7.1	9.1	7.3	4.2	3.8
South Asia	4.5	4.9	2.3	3.6	5.3	5.9	5.0	5.3	5.7
India	4.2	4.9	2.4	3.0	5.3	6.6	5.3	5.8	6.1
Developing countries	4.8	6.0	6.4	5.1	2.9	5.4	5.4	4.1	4.4

Source: UNCTAD secretarial in org calculations, based on World Bank, *World Development Indicators*, various issues United Nations Statistics Division (UNSD), *National Accounts Main Aggregates* Database; and Taiwan Province of China, *MacroEconomics* Database

Note: Calculations are based on GDP in constant 1995 dollars. *Source:* UNCTAD (2006a, 46).

Table 13.4

Per Capita GDP Growth in Selected Developing Countries and Regions, 1960–2004
(average annual percentage change)

Region/country	1960–1965	1965–1970	1970–1975	1975–1980	1980–1985	1985–1990	1990–1995	1995–2000	2000–2004
Africa	2.8	2.2	1.6	0.9	0.7	−0.2	−1.5	1.0	1.6
Sub-Saharan Africa, excl. South Africa	1.3	1.2	1.1	−1.0	−1.2	0.2	−1.3	1.1	1.8
Latin America	1.7	3.1	4.0	2.7	−1.6	−0.2	1.9	1.2	0.1
East Asia	3.0	4.7	4.4	5.9	5.4	6.4	7.5	3.8	5.3
China	0.3	2.6	2.8	4.6	9.5	6.1	11.7	7.5	8.7
First-tier NIEs	5.0	7.2	6.1	7.1	5.5	8.0	6.1	3.2	3.2
South Asia	2.2	2.5	0.0	1.4	2.9	3.6	2.8	3.3	4.0
India	1.9	2.5	0.1	0.9	3.1	4.4	3.3	4.0	4.5
Developing countries	2.5	3.4	3.9	2.9	0.7	2.2	3.5	2.4	2.9

Source: UNCTAD secretariat calculations, based on World Bank, *World Development Indicators*, various issues UNSD, *Population* Database and *National Accounts Main Aggregates* Database; and Taiwan Province of China, *MacroEconomics* Database

Source: UNCTAD (2006a, 47).

The African continent looked increasingly excluded from any economic benefits of glo-balization, and thirty-three countries there ended the 1990s more heavily indebted than they had been two decades earlier (Easterly 2002). By the end of the century, not a single former second or third world country had joined the ranks of the first world in a solid sense. Significant growth occurred in a handful of countries, such as China, India, and Mexico—the "new globalizers"—but the benefits were not well distributed within those countries. Despite significant improvements in global social indicators like adult literacy, access to safe water, and infant mortality rates, global deprivation continues. This is illus-trated vividly in Figure 13.1.

Having outlined the broad development achievements and failures of the postwar international economic order, we will now evaluate these from two different development perspectives: a mainstream orthodox view and a critical alternative view.

Economic Development: Orthodox and Alternative Evaluations

The orthodox liberal assessment of the past sixty years of development suggests that states that have integrated most deeply into the global economy through trade liberalization have grown the fastest, and it praises these "new globalizers." It acknowledges that neo-liberal economic policy has resulted in greater inequalities within and between states but regards inequality positively as a spur to competition and the entrepreneurial spirit.

It was clear at least from the late 1970s that "trickle-down" (the idea that overall eco-nomic growth as measured by increases in the GDP would automatically bring benefits

Goals and Targets

Goals and Targets	Africa		Asia				Oceania	Latin America & Caribbean	Commonwealth of Independent States	
	Northern	Sub-Saharan	Eastern	South-Eastern	Southern	Western			Europe	Asia

GOAL 1 | Eradicate extreme poverty and hunger

	Northern	Sub-Saharan	Eastern	South-Eastern	Southern	Western	Oceania	Latin America & Caribbean	Europe	Asia
Reduce extreme poverty by half	low poverty	very high poverty	high poverty	high poverty	very high poverty	low poverty	...	moderate poverty	low poverty	high poverty
Productive and decent employment	very large deficit in decent work	very large deficit in decent work	large deficit in decent work	very large deficit in decent work	very large deficit in decent work	very large deficit in decent work	very large deficit in decent work	moderate deficit in decent work	small deficit in decent work	moderate deficit in decent work
Reduce hunger by half	low hunger	very high hunger	moderate hunger	high hunger	high hunger	moderate hunger	moderate hunger	moderate hunger	low hunger	moderate hunger

GOAL 2 | Achieve universal primary education

	Northern	Sub-Saharan	Eastern	South-Eastern	Southern	Western	Oceania	Latin America & Caribbean	Europe	Asia
Universal primary schooling	high enrolment	low enrolment	high enrolment	high enrolment	moderate enrolment	moderate enrolment	...	high enrolment	high enrolment	high enrolment

GOAL 3 | Promote gender equality and empower women

	Northern	Sub-Saharan	Eastern	South-Eastern	Southern	Western	Oceania	Latin America & Caribbean	Europe	Asia
Equal girls' enrolment in primary school	close to parity	close to parity	parity	parity	parity	close to parity	almost close to parity	parity	parity	parity
Women's share of paid employment	low share	low share	high share	medium share	low share	low share	medium share	high share	high share	high share
Women's equal representation in national parliaments	very low representation	low representation	moderate representation	low representation	low representation	very low representation	very low representation	moderate representation	low representation	low representation

GOAL 4 | Reduce child mortality

	Northern	Sub-Saharan	Eastern	South-Eastern	Southern	Western	Oceania	Latin America & Caribbean	Europe	Asia
Reduce mortality of under-five-year-olds by two thirds	low mortality	very high mortality	low mortality	low mortality	high mortality	low mortality	moderate mortality	low mortality	low mortality	moderate mortality
Measles immunization	high coverage	moderate coverage	high coverage	moderate coverage	moderate coverage	moderate coverage	low coverage	high coverage	high coverage	high coverage

GOAL 5 | Improve maternal health

	Northern	Sub-Saharan	Eastern	South-Eastern	Southern	Western	Oceania	Latin America & Caribbean	Europe	Asia
Reduce maternal mortality by three quarters *	moderate mortality	very high mortality	low mortality	high mortality	high mortality	moderate mortality	high mortality	moderate mortality	low mortality	low mortality
Access to reproductive health	moderate access	low access	high access	moderate access	moderate access	moderate access	low access	high access	high access	moderate access

GOAL 6 | Combat HIV/AIDS, malaria and other diseases

	Northern	Sub-Saharan	Eastern	South-Eastern	Southern	Western	Oceania	Latin America & Caribbean	Europe	Asia
Halt and reverse spread of HIV/AIDS	low prevalence	high prevalence	low prevalence	low prevalence	low prevalence	low prevalence	moderate prevalence	moderate prevalence	moderate prevalence	low prevalence
Halt and reverse spread of tuberculosis	low mortality	high mortality	moderate mortality	high mortality	moderate mortality	low mortality	high mortality	low mortality	moderate mortality	moderate mortality

GOAL 7 | Ensure environmental sustainability

	Northern	Sub-Saharan	Eastern	South-Eastern	Southern	Western	Oceania	Latin America & Caribbean	Europe	Asia
Reverse loss of forests	low forest cover	medium forest cover	medium forest cover	high forest cover	medium forest cover	low forest cover	high forest cover	high forest cover	high forest cover	low forest cover
Halve proportion without improved drinking water	high coverage	low coverage	moderate coverage	moderate coverage	moderate coverage	high coverage	low coverage	high coverage	high coverage	moderate coverage
Halve proportion without sanitation	moderate coverage	very low coverage	low coverage	low coverage	very low coverage	moderate coverage	low coverage	moderate coverage	moderate coverage	high coverage
Improve the lives of slum-dwellers	moderate proportion of slum-dwellers	very high proportion of slum-dwellers	high proportion of slum-dwellers	high proportion of slum-dwellers	high proportion of slum-dwellers	moderate proportion of slum-dwellers	moderate proportion of slum-dwellers	moderate proportion of slum-dwellers	...	...

GOAL 8 | Develop a global partnership for development

	Northern	Sub-Saharan	Eastern	South-Eastern	Southern	Western	Oceania	Latin America & Caribbean	Europe	Asia
Internet users	moderate usage	very low usage	high usage	moderate usage	low usage	moderate usage	low usage	high usage	high usage	low usage

---

The progress chart operates on two levels. The words in each box indicate the present degree of compliance with the target. The colors show progress towards the target according to the legend below:

- ■ Already met the target or very close to meeting the target.
- ■ Progress sufficient to reach the target if prevailing trends persist.
- ■ Progress insufficient to reach the target if prevailing trends persist.
- ■ No progress or deterioration.
- ☐ Missing or insufficient data.

* The available data for maternal mortality do not allow a trend analysis. Progress in the chart has been assessed by the responsible agencies on the basis of proxy indicators.

For the regional groupings and country data, see mdgs.un.org. Country experiences in each region may differ significantly from the regional average. Due to new data and revised methodologies, this Progress Chart is not comparable with previous versions.

Sources: United Nations, based on data and estimates provided by: Food and Agriculture Organization; Inter-Parliamentary Union; International Labour Organization; International Telecommunication Union; UNAIDS; UNESCO; UN-Habitat; UNICEF; UN Population Division; World Bank; World Health Organization - based on statistics available as of June 2009.

Compiled by Statistics Division, Department of Economic and Social Affairs, United Nations.

Figure 13.1 2008 Progress Chart for UN Millennium Development Goals.

Global Perspective

Life in Zimbabwe: Poverty, Hunger, Development, and Politics

It is possible the average person in Zimbabwe was not aware of the global economic downturn of 2009. If people in the southern African country did know about the collapse of banks and, according to the IMF, the loss of perhaps 51 million jobs worldwide, this knowledge would not have changed their lives very much. With a 2008 per capita gross domestic product (GDP) of $200 already, things could not have gotten much worse.

The previous year had seen an array of problems that few developing countries had seen recently. First, a series of bad harvests had pushed more people than usual to rely on food aid provided mainly by foreign aid agencies, such as the UN's World Food Program, and some European Union countries. In power since 1980, President Robert Mugabe's government had banned aid from Britain because the former colonial power had sought to have Zimbabwe suspended from the Commonwealth, an organization of now-independent former British colonies. Critics of Mugabe's government blame the famine not just on low rainfall but, even more, on the badly planned land reform effort that took land away from the most prosperous farmers and gave it to landless Zimbabweans. Although the Mugabe government called the reform program "Zimbabwe for Zimbabweans," it was not only people of European descent who lost land but also people who were not members of President Mugabe's ethnic group. Resistance to land reform led to riots, as government paramilitary units forced people from their farms and into illegal squatter camps.

The famine exacerbated preexisting economic problems. Zimbabwe had little to offer for export earnings beyond the agricultural sector, which provided more than 400,000 jobs. When the land reform began, unemployment increased, as did the inflation rate, because the government printed more money to cover its operating expenses. The US CIA World Factbook estimates that prior to the currency reform of January 2009, Zimbabwe's annual inflation rate was 11.2 million percent (https://www.cia.gov/library/publications/the-world-factbook/geos/zi.html#Econ). This internal economic debacle coincided with the rapid price rise for a barrel of oil. Like many other developing countries, Zimbabwe does not have domestic sources of petroleum products and must import what it needs.

Bad harvests, bad weather, and oil prices are not the source of Zimbabwe's troubles, say many analysts of African affairs. Rather, they assert, President Mugabe

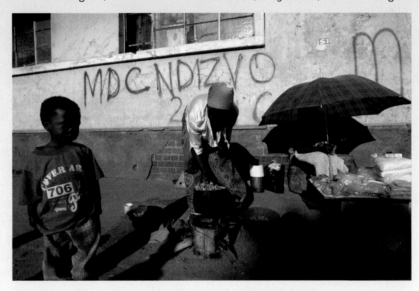

In Zimbabwe, ethnic-linked political unrest and violence have increased poverty rates and suffering.

himself is to blame for the current situation. Left alone by the British and other countries, the president established his personalist regime that favored his family and other members of his ethnic group and intimidated other ethnic groups in Zimbabwean society. If a person wanted to advance in the country, the person had to be a member of Mugabe's political party, Zimbabwe African National Union–Popular Front (Zanu-PF). Like other parties in the country but unlike political parties in most liberal democracies, it is linked to an ethnic group, but

continued

Global Perspective *continued*

membership in the party was not guaranteed. Parliamentary elections in March 2008 sparked another crisis. When the Movement for Democratic Change (MDC) won more seats than Zanu-PF, and Mugabe came in second to MDC's leader Morgan Tsvangirai in the presidential election, people knew that trouble was ahead. Mugabe's supporters began to violently harass MDC members, an action that caused Tsvangirai to withdraw from the race. (The current government of national unity is a coalition of ZANU-PF and the MDC and it was formed in February 2009.)

Given this string of unfortunate internal events, an average Zimbabwean can be forgiven if the failure of banks in Iceland, New York, and London is not a cause for great alarm. If workers at Macy's, Home Depot, or Merrill Lynch lose their jobs, this is not news for a resident of Harare. The subprime mortgage crisis in the United States must sound otherworldly to a person who lives in a galvanized metal shack in a shantytown on the outskirts of Bulawayo.

for the poorer classes) had not worked. Despite impressive rates of growth in GDP per capita enjoyed by some developing countries, this success was not reflected in their societies at large, and while a minority became substantially wealthier, the mass of the population saw no significant change. For some bankers in multilateral organizations, and conservative politicians in rich countries, the even greater polarization in wealth evident in recent decades is not regarded as a problem, so long as the social and political discontent the inequality creates is not so extensive as to potentially derail implementation of the liberalization project itself. This discontent will be alleviated by the development of national poverty-reduction strategies (PRS), which it is claimed put countries and their peoples in the driving seat of development policy, thus empowering the local community and ensuring a better distribution of benefits.

Advocates of a critical alternative approach emphasize the pattern of distribution of gains within global society and within individual states, rather than growth. They believe that the economic liberalism that underpins the process of globalization has resulted, and continues to result, in increasing economic differentiation between and within countries and that this is problematic. Moreover, they note that this trend has been evident over the very period when key global actors have been committed to promoting development worldwide and, indeed, when there were fairly continuous world economic growth rates and positive rates of GDP growth per capita (Brown and Kane 1995).

The increasing gap between rich and poor was regarded as inevitable, and undesirable, by dependency theorists such as Andre Gunder Frank (1967). Writing in the 1960s and 1970s, these theorists stressed how the periphery, or third world, was actively underdeveloped by activities that promoted the growth in wealth of the core Western countries and of elites in the periphery (see Case Study 13.2).

At the beginning of the twenty-first century, however, exponents of a critical alternative—in contrast to their orthodox colleagues—question the value of national PRSs, arguing that while a new focus on issues such as health and education is important, the more fundamental issue of possible links between Washington Consensus policies and poverty creation is ignored.

The orthodox and alternative evaluations are based on different values and they are measuring different things. Glyn Roberts's words are pertinent: "GNP growth statistics might mean a good deal to an economist or to a maharajah, but they do not tell us a thing about the quality of life in a Third World fishing village" (G. Roberts 1984, 6).

A Critical Alternative View of Development

Since the early 1970s, there have been numerous efforts to stimulate debate about development and to highlight its contested nature. Critical alternative ideas have been put forward that we can synthesize into an alternative approach. These have originated with various NGOs, grassroots development organizations, individuals, UN organizations, and private foundations. The Nobel Prize committee recognized the alternative approach when in 2006 it gave the Peace Prize to Muhammad Yunus and the microcredit loan institution, Grameen Bank, which he founded. Disparate **social movements** not directly related to the development agenda have contributed to the flourishing of the alternative viewpoints: for example, the women's movement, the peace movement, movements for democracy, and green movements (Thomas 2000). Noteworthy was the publication in 1975 by the Dag Hammarskjöld Foundation of *What Now? Another Development?* This alternative conception of development (see Ekins 1992, 99) argued that the process of development should be

- need-oriented (material and nonmaterial);
- endogenous (coming from within a society);
- self-reliant (in terms of human, natural, and cultural resources);
- ecologically sound; and
- based on structural transformations (of economy, society, gender, power relations).

Since then, various NGOs, such as the World Development Movement, have campaigned for a form of development that takes aspects of this alternative approach on board. Grassroots movements have often grown up around specific issues, such as dams (Narmada in India) or access to common resources (the rubber tappers of the Brazilian Amazon; the Chipko movement, which began as a women's movement to secure trees in the Himalayas). Such campaigns received a great impetus in the 1980s with the growth of the green movement worldwide. The two-year preparatory process before the UN Conference on Environment and Development (UNCED) in Rio, in June 1992, gave indigenous groups, women, children, and other previously voiceless groups a chance to express their views. This momentum has continued, and it has become the norm to hold alternative NGO forums, parallel to all major UN conferences. Also, the World Social Forum meets annually.

Democracy, Empowerment, and Development

Democracy is at the heart of the alternative conception of development. Grassroots movements are playing an important role in challenging entrenched structures of power in formal democratic societies. In the face of increasing globalization, with the further erosion of local community control over daily life and the further extension of the power of the market and **transnational corporations**, people are standing up for their rights as they define them. They are making a case for local control and local empowerment as the heart of development. They are protecting what they identify as the immediate source of their survival—water, forest, and land. They are rejecting the dominant agenda of private and public (government-controlled) spheres and setting an alternative one. Examples include the Chiapas uprising in Mexico, and Indian peasant protests against foreign-owned seed

social movement People with a diffuse sense of collective identity, solidarity, and common purpose that usually leads to collective political behavior. The concept covers all the different NGOs and networks, plus all their members and all the other individuals who share the common value(s). Thus, the women's movement and the environmental movement are much more than the specific NGOs that provide leadership and focus the desire for social change.

transnational company/ corporation (TNC) A company that has affiliates in a foreign country. The affiliates may be branches of the parent company, separately incorporated subsidiaries, or associates with large minority shareholdings.

factories. Protests at the annual meetings of the WTO, and protests of the IMF and World Bank, have become routine since the late 1990s and are indicative of an increasingly widespread discontent with the process of globalization and the distribution of its benefits. Such protests symbolize the struggle for substantive democracy that communities across the world are working for. In this context, development is about facilitating a community's participation and lead role in deciding what sort of development is appropriate for it; it is not about assuming the desirability of the Western model and its associated values. This alternative conception of development therefore values diversity above universality and is based on a different conception of rights.

For some commentators, national PRSs offer the opportunity—albeit as yet unrealized—for greater community participation in development policy making in the South. If all parties operate in the spirit that was intended, the PRS process could enhance representation and voice for states and peoples in the South, and it offers the best hope available for expanding national ownership of economic policy.

Now that we have looked at the critical alternative view of development, we will look at the way the orthodox view has attempted to respond to the criticisms of the alternative view.

The Orthodoxy Incorporates Criticisms

sustainable development
This has been defined as development that meets the needs of the present without compromising the ability of future generations to meet their own needs.

In the mainstream debate, the focus has shifted from growth to sustainable development. The concept was championed in the late 1980s by the influential Brundtland Commission (officially entitled the World Commission on Environment and Development—see Brundtland et al. 1987) and supported in the 1990s by a series of UN global conferences. Central to the concept of **sustainable development** is the idea that the pursuit of development by the present generation should not be at the expense of future generations. Similarly, when faced

The WTO is frequently the target of protests because of what demonstrators believe is a bias in favor of export-market-driven food production.

with critical NGO voices, the World Bank eventually in 1994 came up with its "Operational Policy 4.20" on gender. The latter aimed to "reduce gender disparities and enhance women particularly in the economic development of their countries by integrating gender considerations in its country assistance programs" (www.worldbank.org).

Most recently, the language of poverty reduction being incorporated into World Bank and IMF policies includes words like "growth with equity" and "pro-poor growth," which some would argue are nothing more than buzzwords, since they underlie macroeconomic policy that remains unchanged. An examination of the contribution of the development orthodoxy to increasing global inequality is not on the agenda. The gendered outcomes of macroeconomic policies are largely ignored.

Despite promises of new funding at the UN Monterrey Conference on Financing for Development in 2002, new transfers of finance from developed to developing countries have been slow in coming; meanwhile, most expected new promises to be made by the G-8 during their summit in 2009. In addition to new finance, that summit saw commitments to write off $40 billion of debt owed by the heavily indebted poor countries (HIPCs). However, the commitment was not implemented with immediate effect and didn't cover all needy countries. The North-South agenda has changed little in the years since the Rio Summit, when sustainable development hit the headlines.

It is important to note that some parts of the UN family have been genuinely responsive to criticisms of mainstream development. The UNDP is noteworthy for its advocacy of the measurement of development based on life expectancy, adult literacy, and average local purchasing power—the Human Development Index (HDI). The HDI results in a very different assessment of countries' achievements than does the traditional measurement of development based on per capita GDP (Thomas et al. 1994, 22). For example, China, Sri Lanka, Poland, and Cuba fare much better under HDI assessments than they do under more orthodox assessments, while Saudi Arabia and Kuwait fare much worse.

An Appraisal of the Responses of the Orthodox Approach to Its Critics

During 2000, a series of official "+ 5" miniconferences were held, such as Rio + 5, Copenhagen + 5, and Beijing + 5, to assess progress in specific areas since the major UN conferences five years earlier. The assessments suggested that the international community had fallen short in its efforts to operationalize conference action plans and to mainstream these concerns in global politics.

Voices of criticism are growing in number and range. Even among supporters of the mainstream approach, voices of disquiet are heard, as increasingly the maldistribution of the benefits of economic liberalism are seen to have been a threat to local, national, regional, and even global order. Moreover, the social protest that accompanies economic globalization is regarded by some as a potential obstacle to the neoliberal project. Thus supporters of globalization are keen to temper its most unpopular effects by modification of neoliberal policies. Small but nevertheless important changes are taking place. For example, the World Bank has guidelines on the treatment of indigenous peoples, resettlement, the environmental impact of its projects, gender, and disclosure of information. It is implementing social safety nets when pursuing structural-adjustment policies, and it is promoting microcredit as a way to empower women. With the IMF, it developed an HIPC initiative to reduce the debt burden of the poorest states. What is important, however, is whether these guidelines and concerns really inform policy and whether these new

Bono (right) and Damien Rice are activists for social justice and economic aid for less developed countries.

policies and facilities result in practical outcomes that impact the fundamental causes of poverty.

The bank has admitted that such changes have been incorporated largely due to the efforts of NGOs, which have monitored its work closely and undertaken vigorous international campaigns to change its general operational processes and the way it funds projects. These campaigns continue. The Bretton Woods Campaign, Fifty Years Is Enough, Jubilee 2000, and, most recently, the Make Poverty History campaign have been particularly significant in calling for open, transparent, and accountable decision making by global economic institutions, for local involvement in project planning and implementation, and for debt write-off. As noted at the start of this chapter, for many years Bob Geldof and Bono have been very active in advocating change. In addition to the NGO pressure for change, pressure is building within the institutional champions of the neoliberal development orthodoxy.

There is a tremendously long way to go in terms of gaining credence for the core values of the alternative model of development in the corridors of power, nationally and internationally. Nevertheless, the alternative view, marginal though it is, has had some noteworthy successes in modifying orthodox development. These may be significant for those whose destinies have up till now been largely determined by the attempted universal application of a selective set of local, essentially Western, values.

Hunger

In addressing the topic of global hunger, it is necessary to face the paradox that while "the production of food to meet the needs of a burgeoning population has been one of the outstanding global achievements of the post-war period" (ICPF 1994, 104, 106), there were nevertheless in 2006 around 852 million malnourished people in around eighty countries, and at least 40,000 die every day from hunger-related causes. The current depth of hunger across different world regions is shown in Map 13.1. While famines may be exceptional phenomena, hunger is ongoing. Why is this so?

The Orthodox, Nature-Focused Explanation of Hunger

The orthodox explanation of hunger, first mapped out in its essentials by Thomas Robert Malthus in his *Essay on the Principle of Population* in 1798, focuses on the relationship between human population growth and the food supply. It asserts that population growth naturally outstrips the growth in food production, so that a decrease in the per capita availability of food is inevitable, until eventually a point is reached at which starvation, or some other disaster, drastically reduces the human population to a level that can be sustained by the available food supply. This approach therefore places great stress on human overpopulation as being the cause of the problem and seeks ways to reduce the fertility of the human race, or, rather, that part of the human race which seems to reproduce faster than the rest—the poor of the third world. Recent supporters of this approach, such as Paul

Map 13.1 World Hunger Map, 2008, by Severity.
What patterns of world hunger do you see around the world? What responsibilities might industrial nation-states have toward helping less developed nation-states?

387

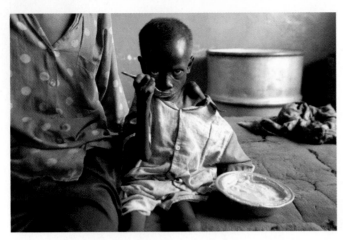

In parts of the developing world, more than 50 percent of the population is malnourished.

Ehrlich and Dennis and Donella Meadows (1972), argue that there are natural limits to population growth—principally that of the carrying capacity of the land—and that when these limits are exceeded, disaster is inevitable.

The available data on the growth of the global human population indicate that it has quintupled since the early 1800s and is expected to grow from six billion in 1999 to ten billion in 2050. Over 50 percent of this increase is expected to occur in seven countries: Bangladesh, Brazil, China, India, Indonesia, Nigeria, and Pakistan. Figure 13.2 provides data on world population growth from 1800, with projections through to 2050, and shows that the rate of world population growth is set to increase over the coming decades. Table 13.5 focuses on the most populous countries—almost all of which are located in the third world—and only eleven of them account for over half of the world's population. Figures like these have convinced many adherents of the orthodox approach to hunger that it is essential for third world countries to adhere to strict family-planning policies that one way or another limit their population growth rates. Indeed, in the case of the World Bank, most women-related efforts until very recently were in the area of family planning.

The Entitlement, Society-Focused Explanation of Hunger

Critics of the orthodox approach to hunger and its associated implications argue that it is too simplistic in its analysis and ignores the vital factor of food distribution. They point out that it fails to account for the paradox we observed at the beginning of this discussion

Table 13.5

Most populous countries, 2003			Most populous countries, 2050		
Rank	**Country**	**Population (millions)**	**Rank**	**Country**	**Population (millions)**
1	China	1,289	1	India	1,628
2	India	1,069	2	China	1,394
3	United States	292	3	United States	422
4	Indonesia	220	4	Pakistan	349
5	Brazil	176	5	Indonesia	316
6	Pakistan	149	6	Nigeria	307
7	Bangladesh	147	7	Bangladesh	255
8	Russia	146	8	Brazil	221
9	Nigeria	134	9	Congo, Dem. Rep. of	181
10	Japan	128	10	Ethiopia	173

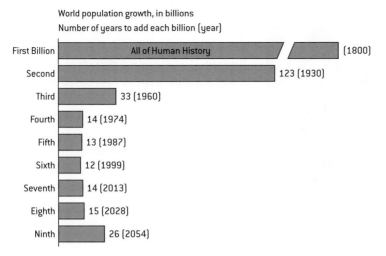

World population growth, in billions
Number of years to add each billion (year)

Figure 13.2 World Population Growth from 1800 with Projections to 2050.
Sources: First and second billion: Population Reference Bureau. Third through ninth billion: United Nations, World Population Prospects: The 1998 Revision (medium scenario). See www.prb.org.

on hunger: that despite the enormous increase in food production per capita that has occurred over the postwar period (largely due to the development of high-yielding seeds and industrial agricultural techniques), little impact has been made on the huge numbers of people in the world who experience chronic hunger. For example, the UN Food and Agriculture Organization (FAO) estimates that although there is enough grain alone to provide everyone in the world with 3,600 calories a day (i.e., 1,200 more than the UN's recommended minimum daily intake), there are still over 800 million hungry people.

Furthermore, critics note that the third world, where the majority of malnourished people are found, produces much of the world's food, while those who consume most of it are located in the Western world. Meat consumption tends to rise with household wealth, and a third of the world's grain is used to fatten animals. A worrying recent trend is the use of corn grown in the United States to produce green fuel, thus reducing what is available to feed the hungry overseas. Such evidence leads opponents of the orthodox approach to argue that we need to look much more closely at the social, political, and economic factors that determine how food is distributed and why access to food is achieved by some and denied to others.

A convincing alternative to the orthodox explanation of hunger was set forward in Amartya Sen's pioneering book, *Poverty and Famines: An Essay on Entitlement and Deprivation*, which was first published in 1981. From the results of his empirical research work on the causes of famines, Sen concluded that hunger is due to people not having enough to eat, rather than there not being enough to eat. He discovered that famines have frequently occurred when there has been no significant reduction in the level of per capita food availability and, furthermore, that some famines have occurred during years of peak food availability. For example, the Bangladesh famine of 1974 occurred in a year of peak food availability, yet because floods wiped out the normal employment opportunities of rural laborers, the latter were left with no money to purchase the food that was readily available, and many of them starved.

WHAT'S YOUR WORLDVIEW

The One Campaign and NGOs like Oxfam have worked hard to end global poverty and hunger, so why do poverty and hunger persist? What appear to be the root causes? Best solutions?

In parts of the developing world, enough food is available. However, the increased global demand for biofuels has started to push farmers to grow crops they can sell in that emerging market for a higher price.

security Measures taken by states to ensure the safety of their citizens, the protection of their way of life, and the survival of their nation-state. Security can also mean the ownership of property that gives an individual the ability to secure the enjoyment or enforcement of a right or a basic human need.

Therefore, what determines whether people starve or eat is not so much the amount of food available to them but whether or not they can establish an entitlement to that food. For example, if there is plenty of food available in the stores, but a family does not have the money to purchase that food and does not have the means of growing their own food, then they are likely to starve. With the globalization of the market, and the associated curtailing of subsistence agriculture, the predominant method of establishing an entitlement to food has become that of the exercise of purchasing power, and consequently it is those without purchasing power who will go hungry amid a world of plenty (Sen 1981, 1983).

Sen's focus on entitlement enables him to identify two groups who are particularly at risk of losing their access to food: landless rural laborers, such as in South Asia and Latin America, and pastoralists, such as in sub-Saharan Africa. The landless rural laborers are especially at risk because no arrangements are in place to protect their access to food. In the traditional peasant economy there is some **security** of land ownership, and therefore rural laborers have the possibility of growing their own food. However, this possibility is lost in the early stages of the transition to capitalist agriculture, when the laborers are obliged to sell their land and join the wage-based economy. Unlike in the developed countries of the West, no social security arrangements are in place to ensure that their access to food is maintained. In this context, it is important to note that the IMF/World Bank austerity policies of the 1980s ensured that any little welfare arrangements that were previously enjoyed by vulnerable groups in developing countries were largely removed, and therefore these policies directly contributed to a higher risk of hunger in the third world.

Building on the work of Sen, the researcher Susan George in *The Hunger Machine* (Bennett and George 1987, 1–10) details how different groups of people experience unequal levels of access to food. She identifies six factors that are important in determining who goes hungry:

1. The North-South divide between developed and developing countries
2. National policies on how wealth is shared
3. The rural-urban bias
4. Social class
5. Gender
6. Age

One could add to the list two other very important, and often neglected, factors determining hunger: race and disability. Consequently, a person is more likely to experience hunger if he or she is disabled rather than able-bodied, black rather than white, a child rather than an adult, poor rather than wealthy, a rural dweller rather than a town dweller, and an inhabitant of a developing country rather than an inhabitant of a developed country.

Globalization and Hunger

It is possible to explain the contemporary occurrence of hunger by reference to the process of globalization. Globalization means that events occurring in one part of the globe can

Haiti: Poverty and Hunger

With its per capita income of $556, Haiti is the poorest country in the Western hemisphere. Two-thirds of people live in rural areas; 80 percent are poor. Nearly half the population consumes less than 75 percent of the recommended intake of food energy. Rice is a major staple of the diet and mainly produced by small farmers. Twenty percent of people depend on rice cultivation for their livelihoods, and the sector has a major economic spin-off, with thousands of agricultural laborers, traders, and millers earning their living from it.

In recent years Haiti has undergone rapid trade liberalization, and it is now one of the most open economies in the world. Liberalization of the rice market started in the 1980s, but the final stroke came in 1994–1995, when, under pressure from the international community (notably the IMF and the United States), the tariff on rice was cut from 35 percent to 3 percent.

Rice producers reported that prices fell by 50 percent during 1986–1987, after the first wave of liberalization.

In 1995, local production fell by 27 percent. Rice imports increased by 30 times between 1985 and 1999 as a result of the market slump. Food aid in rice surged from zero in 1994 to 16,000 metric tons in 1999. Most rice imports are of subsidized US rice.

These trends have severely undermined the livelihoods of more than 50,000 rice-farming families and led to a rural exodus. While cheap imports initially benefited poor consumers, in recent years these benefits have vanished. The FAO says that overall malnutrition has increased since the start of the trade liberalization, affecting 48 percent of the population in 1979–1981 and 62 percent in 1996–1998. Even before the recent devastating earthquake, almost half of Haiti's food needs were met by imports.

Oxfam 2003, 10

affect, and be affected by, events occurring in other, distant parts of the globe. Often, as individuals, we remain unaware of our role in this process and its ramifications. When we drink a cup of tea or coffee, or eat imported fruit and vegetables, in the developed countries, we tend not to reflect on the changes experienced at the site of production of these cash crops in the developing world. However, it is possible to look at the effect of the establishment of a global system of food production, as opposed to a local, national, or regional one. This has been done by David Goodman and Michael Redclift in their book *Refashioning Nature: Food, Ecology and Culture* (1991), and the closing part of this discussion on hunger is largely based on their findings.

Since 1945, a global food regime has been established, and as we enter the twenty-first century we are witnessing an increasingly global organization of food provision and of access to food, with transnational corporations playing the major role. In other words, local subsistence producers, who traditionally have produced to meet the needs of their family and community, may now be involved in cash-crop production for a distant market. Alternatively, they may have left the land and become involved in the process of industrialization. The most important actor in the development and expansion of this global food regime has been the United States, which, at the end of the Second World War, was producing large food surpluses. These surpluses became cheap food exports and initially were welcomed by the war-ravaged countries of Europe. They were also welcomed by many developing countries, for the model of development prevalent then depended on the creation of a pool of cheap wage labor to serve the industrialization process. Hence, in order to encourage people off the land and away from subsistence production, the incentive to produce for oneself and one's family had to be removed. Cheap imported food provided this incentive, while the resulting low prices paid for domestic subsistence crops made them unattractive to grow; indeed, for those who continued to produce for the local market, such as in Sudan, the consequence has been the production of food at a loss (Bennett and George 1987, 78). Not surprisingly, therefore, in the developing world, the production of subsistence crops for local consumption drastically declined in the postwar period.

The postwar, US-dominated, global food regime has therefore had a number of unforeseen consequences. First, the domestic production of food staples in developing countries was disrupted. Second, consumer preferences in the importing countries changed in line with the cheap imports, and export markets for American-produced food were created. Effectively, a dependence on food aid was created (Goodman and Redclift 1991, 123). Third, there has been a stress on cash-crop production. The result has been the drive toward export-oriented, large-scale, intensively mechanized agriculture in the South. Technical progress resulted in the "Green Revolution," with massively increased yields produced from high-yield seeds and industrialized agricultural practices. This has in some respects been an important achievement. However, the cost has been millions of peasants thrown off the land because their labor was no longer required; the greater concentration of land in a smaller number of hands; and environmental damage from pesticides, fertilizers, and inappropriate irrigation techniques.

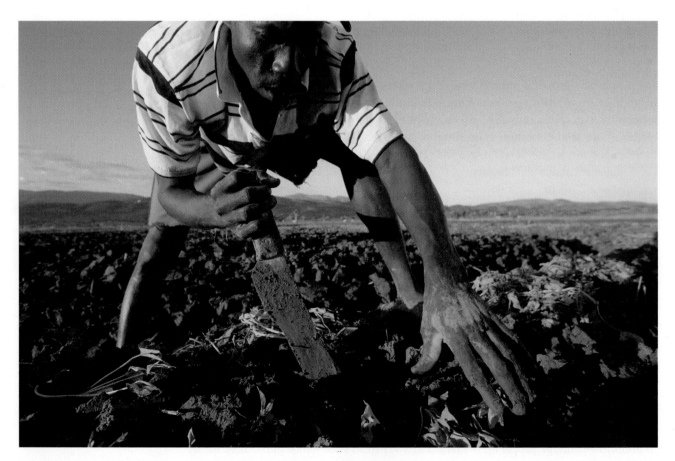

In many parts of the world, farmers use hand tools, not tractors, to cultivate their crops.

Since the early 1980s, the reform of national economies via structural-adjustment policies has given a further boost to the undermining of the national organization of agriculture and a further boost to the activities of agribusiness. Also, the aggressive pursuit of unilateralist trade policies by the United States, such as the invocation of free trade to legitimize opening the Korean agricultural market, has added to this. Global trade liberalization since the early 1980s, and especially the Uruguay Round's Agreement on Agriculture (the original text of which was drafted by the multinational Cargill's vice president Dan Amstutz; Oxfam 2003, 23), are further eroding local food security and throwing peasant producers and their families off the land. The Haitian example portrayed in Case Study 13.2 is repeated across the developing world; for example, the crisis facing Niger in 2005–2006 has been called a "free market famine" (Mousseau and Mittal 2006, 1). This has fueled resentment in the South about the global rules governing agriculture. For example, in India, disputes over intellectual property rights in regard to high-yielding crop seeds have resulted in violent protest by peasant farmers at foreign-owned seed factories. In the North, NGOs have campaigned against the double standards operated by their governments in expecting Southern countries to liberalize their food markets while the Northern countries continue to heavily subsidize and protect their own.

Conclusion

In this chapter we have seen the ways in which poverty, development, and hunger are more than merely domestic political issues. Academic theories of international relations tended to ignore these problems until the mid-1980s, when the third world debt crisis threatened to undermine key parts of the global financial system. Political leaders in the rich countries of the North—and in many cases the South—acted the way realism predicted: to protect the interests of their own states. For the areas of human rights and human security, a very different situation exists. In the next chapter, we will see that, without a clearly defined challenge to their interests, countries are less likely to act to promote human rights.

Contributors to Chapter 13: Caroline Thomas and Steven L. Lamy.

The global recession has caused a reduction in the flow of both bilateral and multilateral development assistance and donations from private individuals.

REVIEW QUESTIONS

1. What does poverty mean?
2. Explain the orthodox approach to development and outline the criteria by which it measures development.
3. Assess the critical alternative model of development.
4. How effectively has the orthodox model of development neutralized the critical alternative view?
5. Compare and contrast the orthodox and alternative explanations of hunger.
6. What are the pros and cons of the global food regime established since the Second World War?
7. Account for the increasing gap between rich and poor states and people after fifty years of official development policies.
8. Use a gendered lens to explore the nature of poverty.
9. Is the recent World Bank focus on poverty reduction evidence of a change of direction by the bank?
10. Which development pathway—the reformist or the alternative—do you regard as the more likely to contribute to global peace in the twenty-first century?
11. Are national poverty-reduction strategies contributing to national ownership of development policies in the Third World?

FURTHER READING

General

Adams, N. B. (1993), *Worlds Apart: The North-South Divide and the International System* (London: Zed). Presents a broad economic and political history of the North-South divide and focuses on the role of the international economic system. This book provides an effective introduction to the politics of North-South economic relations over the past half-century.

Kiely, R. (2006), *The New Political Economy of Development: Globalization, Imperialism and Hegemony* (Basingstoke: Palgrave Macmillan). An important text that examines development in a historic and political-economic context. This is a book for ambitious students who want to take their understanding of development to a deeper level.

Rapley, J. (1996), *Understanding Development* (Boulder, CO: Lynne Rienner). Analyzes the theory and practice of development in the third world since the Second World War in a straightforward, succinct manner. It provides the reader with a firm grasp of changing development policies at the international level and their take-up over time in different states.

Thomas, C. (2000), *Global Governance, Development and Human Security* (London: Pluto). Examines the global development policies pursued by global governance institutions, especially the IMF and the World Bank, in the 1980s and 1990s. It assesses the impact of these policies on human security and analyzes different paths toward the achievement of human security for the twenty-first century.

Development

Rahnema, M., with Bawtree, V. (eds.) (1997), *The Post-Development Reader* (Dhaka: University Press, and London: Zed). Challenges the reader to think critically about the nature of development and assumptions about meanings. This is an extremely stimulating interdisciplinary reader.

Hunger

Dreze, J., Sen, A., and Hussain, A. (eds.) (1995), *The Political Economy of Hunger* (Oxford: Clarendon Press). An excellent collection on the political economy of hunger.

Sen, A. (1981), *Poverty and Famines* (Oxford: Clarendon Press). Provides a groundbreaking analysis of the causes of hunger that incorporates detailed studies of a number of famines and convincingly challenges the orthodox view.

Wiesmann, D. (2006), *Global Hunger Index 2006: A Basis for Cross-Country Comparisons*, Issue Brief 47 (Washington, DC: International Food Policy Research Institute). The Global Hunger Index (GHI), published by the International Food Policy Research Institute, was developed in 2006 to increase attention on the hunger problem and to mobilize the political will to address it.

INTERNET RESOURCES

Commission for Global Governance
www.cgg.ch
An NGO that advocates expanded non-state authority in world affairs.

Foundation for Sustainable Development
www.fsdinternational.org
An NGO that promotes community development projects.

Oxfam International

www.oxfam.org

Perhaps the most famous anti-poverty NGO, with projects and programs globally.

UN Conference on Trade and Development

www.unctad.org

Created in 1964 as a caucus within the UN structure to provide a voice for the newly independent countries in UN deliberations about economic development. It offers a means to build consensus regarding the often contentious debates about development. UNCTAD also provides technical assistance and is a clearinghouse for data collection and analysis.

World Food Program

www.wfp.org

The UN agency that coordinates international famine relief and hunger efforts around the world. In an average year the organization provides 3.7 tons of food.

For more information, quizzes, case studies, and other study tools, please visit us at **www.oup.com/us/lamy**

CHAPTER 14

Environmental Issues

In the middle of the 20th century, we saw our planet from space for the first time. Historians may eventually find that this vision had a greater impact on thought than did the Copernican revolution of the 16th century, which upset the human self-image by revealing that the Earth is not the centre of the universe. From space, we see a small and fragile ball dominated not by human activity and edifice but by a pattern of clouds, oceans, greenery, and soils. Humanity's inability to fit its activities into that pattern is changing planetary systems, fundamentally. Many such changes are accompanied by life-threatening hazards. This new reality, from which there is no escape, must be recognized—and managed.

—From the United Nations' Call to Action, "Our Common Future, From One Earth to One World," A/42/427, 1987

So today, we dumped another 70 million tons of global-warming pollution into the thin shell of atmosphere surrounding our planet, as if it were an open sewer. And tomorrow, we will dump a slightly larger amount, with the cumulative concentrations now trapping more and more heat from the sun. As a result, the earth has a fever. And the fever is rising. The experts have told us it is not a passing affliction that will heal by itself. We asked for a second opinion. And a third. And a fourth. And the consistent conclusion, restated with increasing alarm, is that something basic is wrong. We are what is wrong, and we must make it right.

—Al Gore, from his Nobel Peace Prize acceptance speech, Oslo, Norway, 2007

I n 2006, Al Gore's documentary *An Inconvenient Truth* was released, a film in which Gore declares, "I've been trying to tell this story [about the climate crisis] for a long time and I feel as if I've failed to get the message across." Nearly twenty years before, in 1987, the Brundtland Commission released its UN-sponsored report on the global environment: "Our Common Future." At the time, the

A small blue-green planet, our home, as seen from the Apollo spacecraft.

commission introduced the global community to the goal of sustainable development, designed to meet the needs of present generations without abusing the environment and compromising the ability to meet the needs of future generations. To achieve this, the report said, we need to develop foresight capacity and become global stewards, protecting the environment and finding solutions to environmental problems like climate change, pollution, and the depletion of critical resources. Without a doubt, the world's environmental problems have only gotten worse since the UN report was agreed to and published in 1987. Despite recent leadership from past politicians such as Nobel Prize winner Al Gore, and despite strong grassroots efforts by citizens in some industrial countries to "Reduce, Reuse, and Recycle"—to "Think Globally, Act Locally"—why are other international leaders and many other citizens unwilling to change their lifestyles to respond to urgent challenges like climate change, air and water pollution, and resource scarcity? Why is it so hard to reach agreement when the scientific reports clearly confirm the severity of environmental degradation across the globe? While there are no easy answers to these global problems, such questions can at least be understood more clearly with a careful examination of the facts, along with some perspective afforded us by considering the history and theory of international cooperation involving environmental issues.

Introduction

Although humankind as a whole now appears to be living well above Earth's carrying capacity, the **ecological footprints** of individual states vary to an extraordinary extent. See, for example, the unusual map of the world (Map 14.1), where the size of countries is proportionate to their carbon emissions. Indeed, if everyone were to enjoy the current lifestyle of the developed countries, more than three additional planets would be required.

This situation is rendered all the more unsustainable by the process of **globalization**, even though the precise relationship between environmental degradation and the overuse of resources, on the one hand, and globalization, on the other, is complex and sometimes contradictory. Globalization has stimulated the relocation of industry to the global South, caused urbanization as people move away from rural areas, and contributed to ever-rising levels of consumption, along with associated emissions of effluents and waste gases. While often generating greater income for poorer countries exporting basic goods to developed-country markets, ever-freer trade can also have adverse environmental consequences by disrupting local **ecologies**, cultural habits, and livelihoods.

On the other hand, some analysts believe there is little evidence that globalization has stimulated a "race to the bottom" in environmental standards, and some even argue that increasing levels of affluence have brought about local environmental improvements, just as birth rates tend to fall as populations become wealthier. Economists claim that globalization's opening up of markets can increase efficiency and reduce pollution, provided that the environmental and social damage associated with production of a good is properly factored into its market price. Similarly, as we will see in this chapter, globalization has promoted the sharing of knowledge and the influential presence of **nongovernmental organizations (NGOs)** in global environmental politics. Whatever the ecological balance sheet of globalization, the resources on which human beings depend

ecological footprint Used to demonstrate the load placed on the Earth's carrying capacity by individuals or nations. It does this by estimating the area of productive land and water system required to sustain a population at its specified standard of living.

globalization A historical process involving a fundamental shift or transformation in the spatial scale of human social organization that links distant communities and expands the reach of power relations across regions and continents.

ecologies Communities of plants and animals in an environment that supplies raw materials for all living things.

nongovernmental organization (NGO) An organization, usually a grassroots one, with policy goals, but not governmental in makeup. An NGO is any group of people relating to each other regularly in some formal manner and engaging in collective action, provided the activities are noncommercial and nonviolent and are not on behalf of a government.

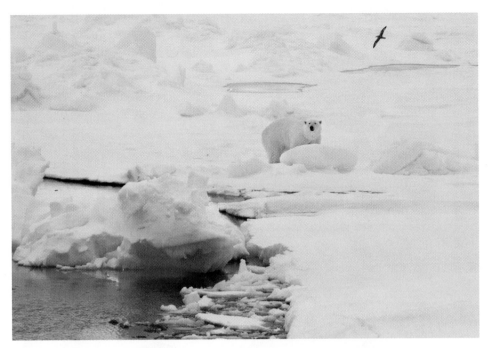

Debates about the causes of global warming do not matter to the polar bears that are dying as a result of the melting of the polar ice caps.

for survival, such as fresh water, a clean atmosphere, and a stable climate, are now under serious threat.

Global problems may need global solutions and pose a fundamental requirement for **global environmental governance**. Yet the history of environmental cooperation demonstrates that local or regional action remains a vital aspect of responses to many problems. One of the defining characteristics of environmental politics is the awareness of such interconnections and of the need to "think globally—act locally." NGOs have been very active in this respect, as we saw in Chapter 8.

Despite the global dimensions of environmental change, an effective response still has to depend on a fragmented international political system of over 190 sovereign states. Global environmental governance consequently involves bringing to bear interstate relations, international law, and transnational organizations in addressing shared environmental problems. Using the term "governance"—as distinct from *government*—implies that regulation and control have to be exercised in the absence of a central government, delivering the kinds of service that a world government would provide if it were to exist. In this chapter we will briefly explore essential concepts employed in regime analysis, which is commonly applied in the study of international governance.

global environmental governance Governance is the performance of regulative functions, often in the absence of a central government authority. Global environmental governance usually refers to the structure of international agreements and organizations but can also involve governance by the private sector or NGOs.

At the 1992 Earth Summit in Brazil, the world's leaders pledged to protect the environment, yet they could not agree on the methods to do this.

Total CO$_2$ emissions

from fossil-fuel burning, cement production and gas flaring

Japan

South Korea

Taiwan

Hong Kong

China

Singapore

India

Country size is proportionate to national carbon dioxide emissions in 2004.

Germany

United Kingdom

France

Italy

Spain

South Africa

United States

The United Nations Framework Convention on Climate Change (UNFCCC), adopted in 1992, divides countries into Annex I (industrialized countries and countries with economies in transition) and Non-Annex parties (mostly developing countries).

Some of them committed to reduce their greenhouse gas emissions by adopting the Kyoto Protocol (1997).

Annex I countries

Non-Annex countries

Non-parties to the UNFCCC

Cartography: SASI Group, University of Sheffield; Mark Newman, University of Michigan, 2006 (updated in 2008), www.worldmapper.org.
Data source: Gregg Marland, Tom Boden, Bob Andres, Oak Ridge National Laboratory. Please note that data for Norway is inaccurate.

Map 14.1 World Carbon Emissions.

What patterns of CO$_2$ emission do you see around the world? Does a nation's responsibility toward ending global climate change increase if its CO$_2$ emission is higher? Which laws govern the global emissions of CO$_2$? How can they be enforced?

Environmental Issues on the International Agenda: A Brief History

Before the era of globalization there were two traditional environmental concerns: conservation of natural resources and damage caused by pollution. Pollution, like wildlife, does not respect international boundaries, and action to mitigate or avert environmental harm sometimes had to involve more than one state. Early international agreements were designed to conserve specific resources, such as fisheries (1867 convention between France and Great Britain) or fur seals (1891, 1892, 1911 conventions between Great Britain, the United States, and Russia). In 1935, with the Trail Smelter case, leaders of countries recognized that reducing transboundary pollution required joint effort and could be accomplished peacefully. In this landmark case, pollutants from a mineral smelter in Canada drifted south to contaminate portions of the US state of Washington. The resulting treaty between the two countries asserted the legal principle that countries are liable for damage that their citizens cause in another country. There were also numerous, mostly unsuccessful, attempts to regulate exploitation of maritime resources lying beyond national jurisdiction, including several multilateral fisheries commissions. The 1946 International Convention for the Regulation of Whaling (and its International Whaling Commission [IWC]) offers an interesting move away from the goal of the late nineteenth-century fur seal conventions, which entailed conserving an industry by regulating catches, toward the preservation of the great whales per se by declaring an international moratorium on whaling. This shift still generates bitter confrontation between NGOs, most IWC members, and the small number of nations—Japan, Norway, and Iceland—that wish to resume commercial whaling and still kill what they call "research whales."

After the Second World War, global economic recovery brought with it evidence of damaging pollution of the atmosphere, of watercourses, and of the sea, notably the Mediterranean, leading to international agreements in the 1950s and 1960s covering such matters as discharges from oil tankers. This worthy activity was, though, hardly the stuff of great power politics. Such "apolitical" matters were the domain of new United Nations **specialized agencies**, like the Food and Agriculture Organization (FAO), but were hardly central to diplomacy at the UN General Assembly (UNGA) in New York.

However, the salience of environmental issues grew in the 1960s, and in 1968 the UNGA accepted a Swedish proposal for what became the 1972 UN Conference on the Human Environment (UNCHE) "to focus governments' attention and public opinion on the importance and urgency of the question." The Stockholm Conference led to the creation of the United Nations Environment Programme (UNEP) and the establishment of environment departments by many governments. Yet it was already clear that for the countries of the South, constituting the majority in the UNGA, environmental questions could not be separated from their demands for development, aid, and the restructuring of international economic relations. This was the political context surrounding the emergence of the concept of **sustainable development** (also see Chapter 13), but before this was formulated by the Brundtland Commission in 1987, the environment had been pushed to the periphery of the international agenda by the global economic downturn of the 1970s and then the onset of the second Cold War (see Chapter 2).

Environmental degradation continued nonetheless. Awareness of new forms of transnational pollution, such as sulfur dioxide, or "acid," rain, joined existing concerns over point-source pollution (when the pollutant comes from a definite source), followed

WHAT'S YOUR WORLDVIEW

Do you think that citizens should pressure governments to take action to protect the environment? At what level of government do citizens have the greatest influence on environmental issues—local, state, or national? Why do you think this is so?

specialized agencies
International institutions that have a special relationship with the central system of the United Nations but are constitutionally independent, having their own assessed budgets, executive heads and committees, and assemblies of the representatives of all state members.

sustainable development
This has been defined as development that meets the needs of the present without compromising the ability of future generations to meet their own needs.

Table 14.1

Timeline of Environmental Issues, Action

1938	Trail Smelter case
1946	International Convention for the Regulation of Whaling
1955	UK Clean Air Act to combat "smog" in British cities
1958	International Convention for the Prevention of Pollution of the Sea by Oil
1959	Antarctic Treaty
1962	Rachel Carson publishes *Silent Spring*
1967	*Torrey Canyon* oil tanker disaster
1969	Greenpeace founded
1971	At the Founex meeting in Switzerland, Southern experts formulate a link between environment and development
1972	United Nations Conference on the Human Environment (UNCHE) in Stockholm, United States creates Environmental Protection Agency First Earth Day Establishment of the United Nations Environment Programme (UNEP)
1973	MARPOL Convention on oil pollution from ships Convention on International Trade in Endangered Species (CITES)
1979	Convention on Long-Range Transboundary Air Pollution (LRTAP)
1980	Convention on the Conservation of Antarctic Marine Living Resources
1982	UN Law of the Sea Convention (enters into force in 1994)
1984	Bhopal chemical plant disaster
1985	Vienna Convention for the Protection of the Ozone Layer; Antarctic ozone hole confirmed.
1986	Chernobyl nuclear disaster
1987	Brundtland Commission Report Montreal Protocol on Substances that Deplete the Ozone Layer
1988	Establishment of the Intergovernmental Panel on Climate Change (IPCC)
1989	Basel Convention on the Control of Transboundary Movements of Hazardous Wastes and Their Disposal
1991	Madrid Protocol (to the Antarctic Treaty) on Environmental Protection
1992	United Nations Conference on Environment and Development (UNCED) held at Rio de Janeiro; publication of the Rio Declaration and Agenda 21; United Nations Framework Convention on Climate Change (UNFCCC) and Convention on Biological Diversity (CBD) both signed; establishment of the Commission on Sustainable Development (CSD)
1995	World Trade Organization (WTO) founded
1997	Kyoto Protocol to the UNFCCC
1998	Rotterdam Convention on Hazardous Chemicals and Pesticides Aarhus Convention on Access to Information, Public Participation in Decision-Making, and Access to Justice in Environmental Matters
2000	Cartagena Protocol on Biosafety Millennium Development Goals set out

2001	US President Bush revokes signature of the Kyoto Protocol
2002	World Summit on Sustainable Development (WSSD), Johannesburg; Johannesburg Plan of Implementation
2005	Entry into force of the Kyoto Protocol and introduction of the first international emissions-trading system by the European Union
2006	International discussions commence on the climate change regime after 2012
2007	Fourth Assessment Report of the IPCC
2008	First Commitment Period of Kyoto begins

by a dawning scientific realization that some environmental problems—the thinning of the stratospheric ozone layer and the possibility of climate change—were truly global in scale. The attendant popular concern over such issues, and the relaxation of East-West tension, created the opportunity for a second great UN conference, for which the connection between environment and development had been explicitly drawn through the Brundtland Commission's notion of sustainable development. Though this conference was subject to many subsequent interpretations, its political essence is an accommodation of the environmental concerns of developed states and the development demands of the South, without which there could have been no Earth Summit and no Rio process.

The 1992 UN Conference on Environment and Development (UNCED), or "Earth Summit," was the largest international conference so far held. It raised the profile of the environment as an international issue while concluding several significant documents and agreements, such as Agenda 21 and international conventions on climate change and the preservation of biodiversity. The event's underlying politics were captured in its title—it was a conference on "environment and development," where the most serious arguments concerned aid pledges to finance the environmental improvements under discussion. A process was created at the UN to review the implementation of the Rio agreements, including meetings of the new Commission on Sustainable Development (CSD) and a Special Session of the UNGA in 1997.

On UNCED's tenth anniversary in 2002, the World Summit on Sustainable Development (WSSD) was held in Johannesburg. The change of wording indicated how conceptions of environment and development had shifted since the 1970s. Now discussion was embedded in recognition of the importance of globalization and of the dire state of the African continent. Poverty eradication was clearly emphasized, along with practical progress in providing clean water, sanitation, and agricultural improvements. One controversial element was the role to be played in such provision by private–public sector partnerships.

While the UN conferences marked the stages by which the environment entered the international political mainstream, they also reflected underlying changes

Commercial logging of tropical rainforests has contributed to increased levels of carbon dioxide in the atmosphere. Once the trees are gone, reforestation is often not possible because water erosion removes nutrients in the soil.

in the scope and perception of environmental problems. As scientific understanding expanded, it was becoming a commonplace, by the 1980s, to speak in terms of global environmental change, as most graphically represented by the discovery of the ozone hole and the creeping realization that human activities might be dangerously altering the global climate itself.

Alongside actual environmental degradation and advances in scientific knowledge, the international politics of the environment has responded to the issue-attention cycle in developed countries, peaking at certain moments and then declining. The causes are complex and during the 1960s reflected the countercultural and radical movements of the time, along with wider public reactions to a series of trends and events. The most influential of these was Rachel Carson's book *Silent Spring* (1962), which powerfully conjoined the conservationist and antipollution agendas by bringing to light the damage inflicted on bird life by industrial pesticides like DDT. Well-publicized environmental disasters, such as the 1959 mercury poisoning at Minamata in Japan and the 1967 wreck of the *Torrey Canyon* oil tanker close to beaches in southwestern England, fed public concern. The failure of established political parties to effectively respond to these issues encouraged the birth of several new high-profile NGOs—Friends of the Earth, Greenpeace, and the World Wildlife Fund for Nature—alongside more established pressure groups such as the US Sierra Club and the British Royal Society for the Protection of Birds. The interest in international environmental action and, indeed, most of the NGOs exerting pressure to this end were an almost exclusively developed-world phenomenon. Public attention then receded, until the end of the second Cold War coincided with a new concern over global environmental problems, providing the political impetus for the 1992 Earth Summit. Interest waned again during the ensuing decade, although by 2005–2006 public alarm over the impact of climate change again propelled environmental issues up the political

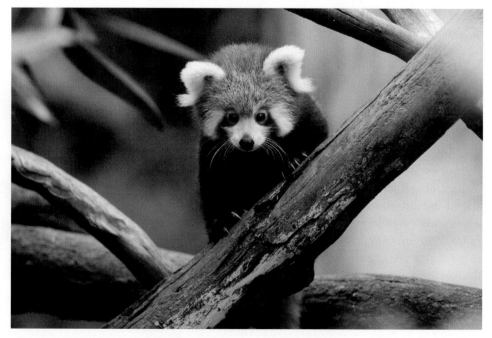

The red panda (*Ailurus fulgens*) is listed on the CITES "endangered list" because of commercial logging in its habitat of Nepal and northern Burma.

The "Doomsday" Seed Vault

One day in February 2008, like a scene out of postapocalyptic science fiction, more than two hundred invited guests hunkered inside puffy parkas at the official opening of the Svalbard Global Seed Vault. The luminaries included Wangari Maathai, Nobel Prize winner for her work in reforestation in Africa, the European Commission president, and several heads of government. Unfortunately dubbed in news media the "Doomsday Vault," the facility is located on an island over six hundred miles north of Norway and about as far from the North Pole. There, at the end of a four-hundred-foot tunnel carved into a mountain and isolated from the outside by a series of air locks, governments will be able to store as many as two billion seeds, representing almost four and a half million species of food plants. It is intended to be the storehouse of last resort for the world's plants.

The seed vault is the idea of a nongovernmental organization based in Rome, Italy, called the Global Crop Diversity Trust. An affiliate of the Food and Agriculture Organization, the trust will administer the facility, which cost more than $9 million. The vault is one response to fears about the long-term effects global warming might have on biodiversity and crop output. It will be a repository for samples of food seeds in the event that a temperature increase will cause plant extinctions. One sign that the host Norwegian government—which covered the entire cost of construction—and Crop Diversity Trust believe the threat of global warming is very real is the location of the tunnel. It is far above the current high tide mark, and also well above where mean high tide will be if the Arctic, Antarctic, and Greenland ice sheets all melt.

Billing itself as "A Foundation for Food Security," the Global Crop Diversity Trust gives grants in support of food-plant research and to maintain gene banks in accordance with the goals of the 1983 International Treaty on Plant Genetic Resources for Food and Agriculture and the 1993 Biodiversity Convention. In addition, the trust seeks to maintain vital food products eaten in the developing world such as bananas, sorghum, barley, cassava, lentils, and several varieties of beans.

There seems to be little not to like about the Svalbard Global Seed Vault, aside from the eminent threat of highly negative effects of global warming. However, the Global Crop Diversity Trust website (www.croptrust.org) FAQ section provides some hints about one possible controversy. The site carefully asserts that it is national governments that will deposit seeds and that each government will retain ownership of its seeds. A look at the donors section of the website suggests an explanation for this statement of seed ownership. There, among a list of donors such as European Union governments, USAID, the Rockefeller Foundation, and the Bill and Melinda Gates Foundation, are the names of two giants of the agribusiness chemical industry: DuPont and Syngenta AG. Many environmentalists remember what Syngenta AG posts in its corporate-history web page: prior to changing its name Syngenta AG in 2001, the chemical firm was known by several names, including Ciba. It was Ciba employees, says the corporate website, who invented both DDT and 2, 4-D. (http://www.syngenta.com/en/about_syngenta/companyhistory.html) The former (DDT) was the villain in Rachel Carson's *Silent Spring*; the latter (2, 4-D) is better known as a component of Agent Orange, an herbicide that United States forces sprayed in uncounted millions of gallons on Vietnam during the 1960s and early 1970s.

As we have seen so far in this book, perspective matters when seeking to understand international politics. Some environmental activists resent the fact that agribusiness seems to be trying to exploit global warming by supporting the Global Crop Diversity Trust, especially because the chemical industry bears some of the guilt for causing the greenhouse-gas problem in the first place. However, as Syngenta AG's website indicates, the company is trying to do its best to save biodiversity. Which side is correct? The answer may be buried under a mountain in the permafrost zone at the end of a tunnel six hundred miles from the North Pole.

The entry corridor to the Global Seed Vault on Svalbard Island.

WHAT'S YOUR WORLDVIEW ❓

The international community seems to understand environmental challenges, but most states seem reluctant to give up sovereignty to solve any global-commons problem. Why?

regimes Sets of implicit or explicit principles, norms, rules, and decision-making procedures around which actors' expectations converge in a given area of international relations. Often simply defined as governing arrangements in a regional or global policy area.

state system The regular patterns of interaction between states, but without implying any shared values between them. This is distinguished from the view of a "society" of states.

capitalism A system of production in which human labor and its products are commodities that are bought and sold in the marketplace.

agenda. The demand was, of course, for international action and governance, but what exactly did this mean?

The Environment and International Relations Theory

Academics who study the international relations of the environment try to understand the circumstances under which potentially effective international cooperation can occur. The later discussion of climate change shows that this question remains important (see "Climate Change" in this chapter, as well as Case Study). Most scholars have used the concept of **regime**. Note, for instance, how the defining characteristics of regimes—principles, norms, rules, and decision-making procedures—can be applied to the environmental cases mentioned in this chapter. Those who try to explain the record of environmental regimes tend to adopt a liberal-institutionalist stance, stressing as a key motivating factor the joint gains arising from cooperative solutions to the problem of providing public goods such as a clean atmosphere (see Chapters 3 and 4). One important addition to the regime literature, made by scholars of environmental politics, points out the importance of scientific knowledge and the roles of NGOs in this area. Whereas orthodox regime approaches assume that behavior is based on the pursuit of power or interest, analysts of international environmental cooperation have noted the independent role played by changes in knowledge (particularly scientific understanding). This cognitive approach appears in studies of the ways in which transnationally organized groups of scientists and policy makers—often referred to as epistemic communities—have influenced the development of environmental regimes.

Liberal-institutionalist analysis of regime creation may still be the predominant approach to global environmental change, but it is not the only one. It makes the important, but often unspoken, assumption that the problem to be solved is how to obtain global governance in a fragmented system of sovereign states. Marxist writers would reject this formulation (see Chapter 4). For them, the **state system** is part of the problem rather than the solution, and the proper object of study is the way global **capitalism** reproduces relationships that are profoundly damaging to the environment. The global spread of neoliberal policies accelerates those features of globalization—consumerism, the relocation of production to the South, and the thoughtless squandering of resources—driving the global ecological crisis (see Chapter 12). Proponents of this view also highlight the incapacity of the state to do anything other than assist such processes. It follows that the international cooperation efforts described here at worst legitimize this state of affairs and at best provide some marginal improvements to the devastation wrought by global capitalism. For example, they would point to how free market concepts are now routinely embedded in discussions of sustainable development and how the WTO rules tend to subordinate attempts to provide environmental regulation of GMOs. This argument is part of a broader debate among political theorists concerning whether the state can ever be "greened." The opposing view would be that within any time frame that is relevant to coping with a threat as large and immediate as climate change, state and international cooperation remain the only plausible mechanisms for providing the necessary global governance, and we shall simply have to do the best we can with existing state and international organizational structures.

With the end of the Cold War, some realist international relations specialists began to apply their ideas about anarchy and war to the study of environmental politics. As a result, they contended that conflict, not cooperation, shaped the issue, and they went looking for proof of this hypothesis. Largely ignoring the many examples of cooperation, like the Antarctic treaty system, they argued that environmental change contributes to the incidence of both internal conflict and even interstate war, even though the causal connections are complex and involve many factors. It is already evident that **desertification** and the degradation of other vital resources are intimately bound up with cycles of poverty, destitution, and war in Africa. But these factors can also be attributed to the effects of European colonization of the continent. However, if we consider such predicted consequences of climate change as mass migrations of populations across international boundaries and acute scarcity of water and other resources, the outlines of potential future conflicts come into sharper focus.

WHAT'S YOUR WORLDVIEW

How do alternative theories like the constructivist, radical-liberal, and some feminist theories of international relations help us to understand environmental problems in ways that traditional theories like realism and liberalism do not?

desertification This is the extreme deterioration of land in arid and dry subhumid areas due to loss of vegetation and soil moisture; desertification results chiefly from manmade activities and is influenced by climatic variations. This condition is principally caused by overgrazing, overdrafting of groundwater, and diversion of water from rivers for human consumption and industrial use—all of these processes fundamentally driven by overpopulation.

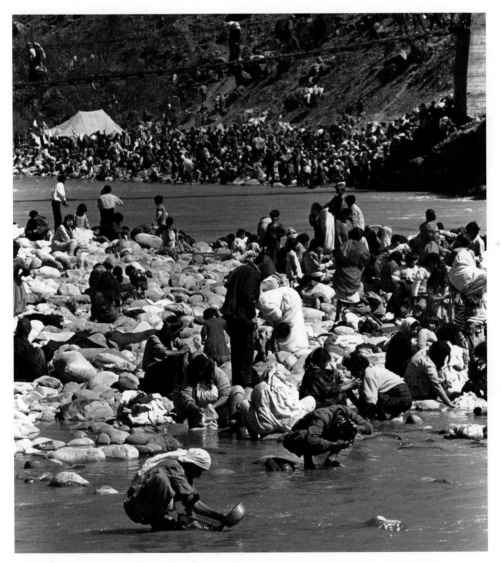

In many developing countries, finding enough water is not the problem: common practices like washing laundry pollute drinking water.

ecosystem A system of interdependent living organisms that share the same habitat, functioning together with all of the physical factors of the environment. Ecosystems can be permanent or temporary. The Convention on Biological Diversity (CBD)—ratified by more than 175 countries—defines the protection of ecosystems as natural habitats and the maintenance of viable populations of species in natural surroundings.

Table 14.2
The Antarctic Treaty Regime

1959 Antarctic Treaty
1972 Convention for the Conservation of Antarctic Seals
1980 Convention on the Conservation of Antarctic Marine Living Resources (CCAMLR)
1988 Convention on the Regulation of Antarctic Mineral Resource Activities (CRAMRA)
1991 Protocol on Environmental Protection to the Antarctic Treaty (Madrid Protocol)

Thus, the more immediate *and* persistent consequence of warfare may very well be the destruction of **ecosystems** that such conflict causes. For example, the list of environmental harm from war and war-related activities is much longer than the atomic bombings of Hiroshima and Nagasaki. During the First World War, artillery shelling devastated farmland along the trench lines in northern France and Belgium, creating eerie moonscapes for years after the war. Similarly, in Vietnam the detrimental environmental effects of United States weapons, including the use of the herbicide Agent Orange (a form of the carcinogenic compound dioxin) and the carpet bombing of wide swaths of jungle and rice paddies, remain visible today. More recently, tank-training exercises in the Mojave Desert of California have increased erosion of the fragile landscape. During both the Gulf Wars, fires set at oil wells sent carcinogenic materials aloft to be carried downwind, where people who breathed the air became sick. In addition, the depleted-uranium antitank bullets fired during those wars put radioactive material into the air and soil. Even the less obvious effects of warfare can have unforeseen, negative impacts: a recent lawsuit filed in the US federal court has charged that US Navy sonar-training exercises can hurt the hearing of migrating whales, causing them to become disoriented.

During the 1991 Gulf War, Iraqi soldiers retreating from Kuwait set fire to oil wells.

Clearly, the environmental degradation caused by wars, and the instruments of war, is impossible to dismiss yet even more difficult to address, since by its very nature warfare is a breakdown of international cooperation. However, when states are not at war and cooperation *is* a viable option, what does it look like and how does it function? Now that we have explored some of the theories surrounding international environmental cooperation, in the next section we will talk more about global mechanisms—or how states and transnational actors attempt to solve environmental issues through formal agreements and cooperative actions.

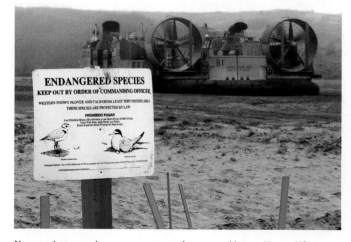

Noncombat exercises can cause environmental harm. Here a US Marine Corps hovercraft tries to avoid a wildlife refuge.

Regime Theory and the Montreal Protocol

Academic advocates of international regime theory discussed in this chapter contend that four factors—context, knowledge, interest, and power—can explain why and when countries decide to create a formal commitment in a given issue area. The same four factors also help to explain what kinds of restraints countries permit on their behaviors. The evolution of international cooperation to protect the ozone layer provides an excellent case on which to test this hypothesis. In brief, if there are significant disagreements about the scientific evidence and one or more countries wants to limit cooperation, then it is unlikely that other countries will be able to establish an effective international regime.

The consequences of the thinning of the stratospheric ozone layer include excessive exposure to UVB radiation, resulting in increased rates of skin cancer for human beings and damage to immune systems. Stratospheric ozone depletion arose from a previously unsuspected source—artificial chemicals containing fluorine, chlorine, and bromine that were involved in chemical reaction with ozone molecules at high altitudes. Most significant were the CFCs (chlorofluorocarbons), which had been developed in the 1920s as "safe" inert industrial gases and which had been blithely produced and used over the next fifty years for a whole variety of purposes from refrigeration to air-conditioning and as propellants for hair spray. Despite growing scientific knowledge, there was no universal agreement on the dangers posed by these chemicals, and production and use continued—except, significantly, where the US Congress decided to ban

some nonessential uses. This meant that the US chemical industry found itself under a costly obligation to find alternatives. Until a US-based chemical company developed an alternative to the harmful CFC compound, the US diplomats blocked serious discussions at the international level. As evidence on the problem began to mount, UNEP acted to convene an international conference in Vienna. It produced a relatively weak "framework convention"—the 1985 Vienna Convention for the Protection of the Ozone Layer—agreeing that international action might be required and that the parties should continue to communicate and to develop and exchange scientific findings. These findings proved to be very persuasive, particularly with the

added public impetus provided by the dramatic discovery of the Antarctic "ozone hole."

Within two years, the Montreal Protocol was negotiated. Some analysts point to a change in US negotiating stance as the reason for the rapid passage of the protocol. Why did this change occur? An American chemical giant found a replacement compound for the ozone-depleting CFCs, seemingly confirming part of the regime-creation hypothesis. In the Montreal Protocol, parties agreed to a regime under which the production and trading of CFCs and other ozone-depleting substances would be progressively phased out. The developed countries achieved this for CFCs by 1996, and Meetings of the Parties (MoP) have

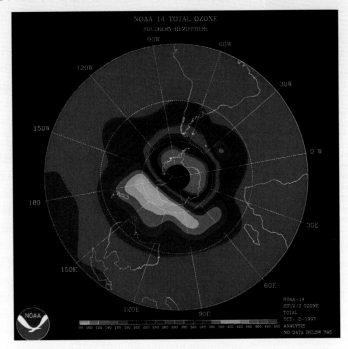

International agreements have reduced the amount of ozone-depleting gases that industries release, but the gases remain a cause of atmospheric damage, as this NASA satellite image shows.

continued

Theory in Practice *continued*

continued to work on the elimination of other substances since that time. There was some initial resistance from European chemical producers, but the US side had a real incentive to ensure international agreement because otherwise its chemical industry would remain at a commercial disadvantage. The other problem faced by the negotiators involved the developing countries, which themselves were manufacturing CFC products. As the Indian delegate put it, it was the developed countries' mess and their responsibility to clear it up! Why should developing countries be forced to change over

to higher-cost CFC alternatives? There were two responses to this. The first was an article in the protocol giving the developing countries a period of grace. The second was a fund, set up in 1990, to finance the provision of alternative non-CFC technologies for the developing world.

Illegal production and smuggling of CFCs was evident in the 1990s. This tested the monitoring and compliance systems of the protocol (which included a possible use of trade sanctions against offenders). Nonetheless, the regime has generally proved to be effective and has continually

widened the scope of its activities to deal with further classes of ozone-depleting chemicals. The damage to the ozone layer will not be repaired until the latter part of the twenty-first century, given the long atmospheric lifetimes of the chemicals involved. However, human behavior has been significantly altered, to the extent that the scientific subsidiary body of the Montreal Protocol has been able to report a measurable reduction in the atmospheric concentration of CFCs. Therefore it seems that the context, knowledge, interest, and power hypothesis is correct.

Legend:
- Tanker operations
- Municipal wastes
- Tanker accidents
- Bilge and fuel oils
- Natural seeps
- Industrial waste
- Urban runoff
- Coastal oil refining
- Offshore oil rigs
- River runoffs
- Other

Sources of Marine Pollution. What do you notice about the top five sources of pollution in this chart? Based on this data and what you have read in this chapter so far, what do you think world governments can do about transboundary pollution? (Note: This data does not include the BP oil-spill in the Gulf of Mexico in 2010.) *Source: Oxford Essential World Atlas, 4th edition.*

The Functions of International Environmental Cooperation

Because environmental issues, such as pollution control, often involve more than one country—or region, or hemisphere—states must establish international governance regimes to regulate these transboundary environmental problems and sustain the global commons. Yet these regimes encompass more than formal agreements between states, although such agreements are very important. Moreover, there are other functions and consequences of international cooperation beyond regime formation, which we will learn about in the following sections.

Transboundary Trade and Pollution Control

When animals, fish, water, or pollution cross national frontiers, the need for international cooperation arises. The regulation of transboundary environmental problems is a long-established function of international cooperation, reflected in hundreds of multilateral, regional, and bilateral agreements providing for joint efforts to manage resources and control pollution.

An important example is provided by the 1979 Convention on Long-Range Transboundary Air Pollution (LRTAP) and its various protocols. They responded to the growing problem of acidification and so-called acid rain by providing mechanisms to study atmospheric pollution problems in Europe and North America and securing commitments by the states involved to control and reduce their emissions. Another set of multilateral environmental agreements (MEAs) regulates the transboundary movement of hazardous wastes and chemicals, in the interest of protecting human health and the environment, and requires that when hazardous chemicals and pesticides are traded, the government from whose territory the exports originate shall obtain the "prior informed consent" of the importing country. (See Table 14.3.)

Table 14.3

Some Environmental Treaties with Weight in International Environmental Law

	Atmospheric Pollution
1985	Convention on Long-Range Transboundary Air Pollution
1988	Protocol on the Reduction of Sulfur Emissions or Their Transboundary Fluxes
1988	Protocol Concerning the Control of Emissions of Nitrogen Oxides
	Stratospheric Ozone Layer
1985	Vienna Convention for the Protection of the Ozone Layer
1987	Montreal Protocol on Substances that Deplete the Ozone Layer
	Hazardous Wastes
1989	Basel Convention on the Control of Transboundary Movements of Hazardous Wastes and Their Disposal
1991	Bamako Convention on the Ban of the Import into Africa and the Control of Transboundary Movement and Management Within Africa of Hazardous Wastes
	Marine Pollution
1969	International Convention on Civil Liability for Oil Pollution Damage
1971	Brussels Convention Relating to Civil Liability in the Field of Maritime Carriage of Nuclear Material
1973/78	International Convention for the Prevention of Pollution from Ships (MARPOL)
1992	London Convention on the Prevention of Marine Pollution by Dumping Wastes and Other Matter
	Wildlife
1971	Ramsar Convention on Wetlands of International Importance Especially as Waterfowl Habitat
1973	International Convention for the Regulation of Whaling
1973	Convention on International Trade in Endangered Species (CITES)
1979	Bonn Convention on the Conservation of Migratory Species of Wild Animals

Controlling, taxing, and even promoting trade has always been one of the more important functions of the state, and trade restrictions can also be used as an instrument for nature conservation. The 1973 Convention on International Trade in Endangered Species (CITES) does this by attempting to monitor, control, or prohibit international trade in species (or products derived from them) whose continued survival might be put at risk by the effects of such trade. Species at risk are "listed" in three appendices to the convention; some six hundred animal and three hundred plant species currently enjoy the highest level of protection (a trade ban) through listing on Appendix I, though decisions on the "up-listing" and "down-listing" of species are sometimes controversial, as in the case of the African elephant, or the northern spotted owl, bald eagle, and gray wolves in the United States.

The use of trade penalties and restrictions by MEAs has been a thorny issue whenever the objective of environmental protection has come into conflict with the rules of the GATT/WTO trade regime (see Chapters 7 and 11). Such a problem arose when the international community attempted to address the controversial question of the new biotechnology and genetically modified organisms (GMOs). There was much resistance to the claims of (primarily American) biotechnology corporations that had made huge investments in developing GMO seed, pharmaceutical, and food products and who argued that these innovations had positive environmental and development potential (through reducing pesticide use and increasing crop yields). European publics, supermarkets, and some developing countries were very wary of GMO technologies on safety and other grounds, which led to pressure for controls on their transboundary movement and to negotiation of the Biosafety Protocol to the Convention on Biological Diversity (CBD) that had been agreed at Rio in 1992. The resulting Cartagena Protocol was signed in 2000 and establishes an advanced informed agreement procedure between governments, to be applied when GMOs are transferred across frontiers for ultimate release into the environment. The criteria to guide decisions on blocking imports reflected a precautionary approach rather than insistence on conclusive scientific evidence of harmfulness. Much of the argument in negotiating the Cartagena Protocol concerned the relationship of these new environmental rules to the requirements of the trade regime and arose from the concern of the United States and other potential GMO exporters that the protocol would permit a disguised form of trade protectionism. Whether the WTO trade rules should take precedence over the emerging biosafety rules was debated at length, until the parties agreed to avoid the issue by providing that the two sets of rules should be mutually supportive.

WHAT'S YOUR WORLDVIEW ?

Which is more important: economic development or environmental protection? Is it possible to achieve both goals? Can we achieve sustainable development?

Norm Creation

norms These specify general standards of behavior and identify the rights and obligations of states. Together, norms and principles define the essential character of a regime, and these cannot be changed without transforming the nature of the regime.

The development of international environmental law and associated **norms** of acceptable behavior has been both rapid and innovative over the last thirty years. Some of the norms mentioned above are in the form of quite technical policy concepts that have been widely disseminated and adopted as a result of international discussion. The precautionary principle has gained increasing but not uncritical currency (see Table 14.4 for other international environmental laws that affect norm creation). Originally coined by German policy makers, the precautionary principle states that where there is a likelihood of environmental damage, banning an activity should not require full and definitive scientific proof. As we saw in the earlier example of GMOs, the latter has tended to be the requirement in trade law (and indeed in UK environmental policy before European Community doctrines on precaution took hold). The norm of "prior informed consent" has also been promoted alongside that of "the polluter pays." In the longer term, one of the key effects of the climate-change regime (dealt with in detail below) may well be the dissemination of new approaches to pollution control, such as emissions trading and joint implementation.

sovereignty The condition of a state having control and authority over its own territory and being free from any higher legal authority. It is related to, but distinct from, the condition of a government being free from any external political constraints.

The UN Earth Summits were important in establishing environmental norms. The 1972 Stockholm Conference produced its "Principle 21," which combines **sovereignty** over national resources with state responsibility for external pollution. This should not be confused with Agenda 21, issued by the 1992 Rio Earth Summit. Agenda 21 was a complex forty-chapter document of some four hundred pages that took two years for members of the United Nations to negotiate in UNCED's Preparatory Committee. Agenda 21 was

Table 14.4
Principles of International Environmental Law that Affect Norm Creation

State Responsibility to Protect Environment
Preventative Action
Good Neighborliness
Sustainable Development
Precautionary Principle
Polluter Pays
Common, Differentiated Responsibility

frequently derided, not least because of its nonbinding character, but this internationally agreed compendium of environmental "best practice" subsequently had a wide impact and remains a point of reference. For example, many local authorities have produced their own "local Agenda 21s." Under the Aarhus Convention (1998), North American and European governments agreed to guarantee to their publics a number of environmental rights, including the right to obtain environmental information held by governments, to participate in policy decisions, and to have access to judicial processes.

Capacity Building

Although not a specific norm of the type dealt with above, sustainable development provides a normative framework built on an underlying deal between developed and developing worlds. Frequent North-South arguments since Rio about the levels of aid and **technology transfer** that would allow developing countries to achieve sustainable development have ended in many disappointments and unfulfilled pledges. In 1991, UNEP, UNDP, and the World Bank created the Global Environmental Facility (GEF) as an international mechanism specifically for funding environmental projects in developing countries. In 2003–2006 it attracted donations of around $3 billion. Most environmental conventions now aim at **capacity building** through arrangements for the transfer of funds, technology, and expertise, because most of their member states simply lack the resources to participate fully in international agreements. The stratospheric-ozone and climate-change regimes aim to build capacity and could not exist in their current form without providing for this function.

Scientific Understanding

International environmental cooperation relies on shared scientific understanding, as evidenced by the form of some important contemporary environmental regimes. An initial framework convention will signal concern and establish mechanisms for developing and sharing new scientific data, thereby providing the basis for taking action in a control protocol. Generating and sharing scientific information has long been a function of international cooperation in public bodies such as the World Meteorological Organization (WMO) and myriad academic organizations such as the International Council for the Exploration of the Seas (ICES) and the International Union for the Conservation of Nature (IUCN). Disseminating scientific information on an international basis makes

technology transfer The process of sharing skills, knowledge, technologies, methods of manufacturing, and facilities among governments and private actors (like corporations) to ensure that scientific and technological developments are accessible to a wider range of users for application in new products, processes, materials, or services.

capacity building Providing the funds and technical training to allow developing countries to participate in global environmental governance.

climate change Represents a change in the statistical distribution of weather over periods of time that range from decades to millions of years. It can be a change in the average weather or a change in the distribution of weather events around an average (for example, greater or fewer extreme weather events). Climate change may be limited to a specific region, or it may occur across the whole Earth.

sense, but it needs funding from governments, because, except in areas like pharmaceutical research, the private sector has no incentive to do the work. International environmental regimes usually have standing scientific committees and subsidiary bodies to support their work. Perhaps the greatest international effort to generate new and authoritative scientific knowledge has been in the area of **climate change**, through the Intergovernmental Panel on Climate Change (IPCC).

Set up in 1988 under the auspices of the World Meteorological Organization (WMO) and UNEP, the Intergovernmental Panel on Climate Charge (IPCC) brings together the majority of the world's climate-change scientists in three working groups: on climate science, impacts, and economic and social dimensions. They have produced assessment reports in 1990, 1995, 2001, and 2007, which are regarded as the authoritative scientific statements on climate change. The reports are carefully and cautiously drafted with the involvement of government representatives and represent a consensus view.

The Fourth Assessment Report, published in February 2007, concluded that "warming of the climate system is unequivocal, as is now evident from observations of increases in global average air and ocean temperatures, widespread melting of snow and ice and rising global sea level" (Intergovernmental Panel on Climate Change 2007, 4). Most of the temperature increase "is *very likely* due to the observed increase in anthropogenic greenhouse gas concentrations" (ibid., 8; original italics). The use of words is significant here, for the IPCC defines *"very likely"* as being more than 90 percent certain. This represents a change from the previous report, which had only estimated that human activity was *"likely,"* or more than 66 percent certain, to be responsible for temperature increases.

Governing the Commons

global commons Areas and resources not under national sovereignty that belong to no single country and are the responsibility of the entire world. The oceans beyond the 200 mile limit, outer space, and Antarctica are global commons areas.

The **global commons** are usually understood as areas and resources not under sovereign jurisdiction—in other words, not owned by anybody. The high seas and the deep ocean floor come within this category (beyond the two-hundred-mile exclusive economic zone that states may claim as their territory created with United National Convention on the Law of the Sea III), as does Antarctica (based on the 1959 Antarctic Treaty.) Outer space is another highly important commons area, its use being vital to modern telecommunications, broadcasting, navigation, and surveillance. Finally, there is the global atmosphere.

The global commons have an environmental dimension, not only as resources but also as a kind of garbage dump for waste products from cities and industry. The fish and whale stocks of the high seas have been relentlessly overexploited, to the point where some species have been wiped out and long-term protein sources for human beings are imperiled. The ocean environment has been polluted by land-based effluent and oil and other discharges from ships. It has been a struggle to maintain the unique wilderness of the Antarctic in the face of increasing pressure from human beings, and even outer space now faces an environmental problem in the form of increasing orbital debris left by decades of satellite launches. Similarly, the global atmosphere has been degraded in a number of highly threatening ways, through damage to the stratospheric ozone layer and, most importantly, by the enhanced greenhouse effect now firmly associated with changes to the Earth's climate. This is often characterized as a "tragedy of the commons." Where there is unrestricted access to a resource owned by no one, there will be an incentive for individuals to grab as much as they can and, if the resource is finite, there will come a time when it is ruined by overexploitation as the short-term interests of individual users overwhelm the longer-run collective interest in sustaining the resource.

Have you ever wondered where your trash goes?

Environmental Regimes

Within the jurisdiction of governments it may be possible to solve the problem by turning the commons into private property or nationalizing them but for the global commons such a solution is, by definition, unavailable. Therefore the function of international cooperation in this context is the very necessary one of providing a substitute for world government, to ensure that global commons are not misused and subject to tragic collapse. Regimes have been created that have enjoyed varying degrees of effectiveness. Many of the functions discussed above can be found in these global-commons regimes, but their central contribution is a framework of rules to ensure mutual agreement between users about acceptable standards of behavior and levels of exploitation, consistent with sustaining commons ecology.

Enforcement poses difficult challenges due to the incentives for users to "free ride" by taking more than a fair share or refusing to be bound by the collective arrangements. Free riding can potentially destroy regimes because other parties will then see no reason to restrain themselves either. In local commons regimes, inquisitive neighbors might deter rule breaking, and a similar role at the international level can be performed by NGOs. However, it is very difficult to enforce compliance by sovereign states—this is a fundamental difficulty for international law and hardly unique to environmental regimes. Mechanisms have been developed to cope with the problem, but how effective they, and the environmental regimes to which they apply, can be is hard to judge, as this involves determining the extent to which governments are in legal and technical compliance with their international obligations. Moreover, it also involves estimating the extent to which state behavior has actually been changed as a result of the international regime concerned. Naturally, the ultimate and most demanding test of the effectiveness of global-commons

> **WHAT'S YOUR WORLDVIEW**
>
> *International relations describes a world of nation-states and sovereignty. How would you convince these states to give up or share sovereignty to address common problems like pollution or climate change?*

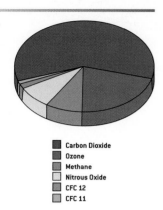

- ■ Carbon Dioxide
- ■ Ozone
- ■ Methane
- □ Nitrous Oxide
- ■ CFC 12
- ■ CFC 11

The Proportions of Greenhouse Gases. This chart combines the potency and volume of major-heat absorbing gases in the atmosphere. Since the Industrial Revolution, Carbon Dioxide concentrations have grown exponentially, from 280 parts per million to 379 ppm in 2005. If nothing is done to curb intensive fossil fuel emissions, what will happen to the average global temperature? What effects might that have? *Source:* Oxford Essential World Atlas, *4th edition.*

regimes is whether or not the resources or ecologies concerned are sustained or even improved.

Some of the first and least successful global-commons regimes were the various fisheries commissions for the Atlantic and elsewhere, which sought agreement on limiting catches in order to preserve stocks. Pollution from ships has been controlled by MARPOL (the 1973 international marine environmental convention—short for "marine pollution"), and there is a patchwork of other treaties to manage such issues as the dumping of radioactive waste at sea. For the Antarctic, a remarkably well-developed set of rules designed to preserve the ecological integrity of this last great wilderness has been devised within the framework of the 1959 treaty. The Antarctic regime is a rather exclusive club: the treaty's "Consultative Parties" include the states that had originally claimed sovereignty over parts of the area, while new members of the club have to demonstrate their involvement in scientific research on the frozen continent. There is a comprehensive agreement on conserving the marine ecosystem around the continent, and in the late 1980s preparations for regulated mineral mining were defeated and replaced by a new 1988 Protocol on Environmental Protection, which included a fifty-year mining ban. The success, with only a minimal level of formal organization, of a restricted group of countries in governing this crucial laboratory for understanding global environmental change demonstrates what can be achieved by international action.

Antarctic science was crucial to the discovery of a problem that resulted in what is perhaps the best example of effective international action to govern the commons. In 1985, a British Antarctic Survey balloon provided definitive evidence of serious thinning of the stratospheric ozone layer. A diminishing ozone layer is a global problem par excellence, because the ozone layer protects the Earth and its inhabitants from the damaging effects of the sun's UVB radiation. A framework convention was signed in 1985, followed in 1987 by its Montreal Protocol imposing international controls over ozone-depleting chemicals. The further evolution of the ozone-layer regime offers the paramount example of how international cooperation can achieve an effective solution to a global environmental problem. The problem's causes were isolated, international support was mobilized, compensatory action was taken to ensure that developing countries participated, and a set of rules and procedures were developed that proved to be effective, at least in reducing the concentration of the offending chemicals in the atmosphere, if not yet fully restoring the stratospheric ozone layer.

Climate Change

Unlike the ozone-layer problem, which was clearly the result of damage caused when people used chlorofluorocarbons (CFCs) in industry, air-conditioning, and personal products like hair spray, climate change and the enhanced greenhouse effect had long been debated among scientists. Only in the late 1980s did sufficient international scientific and political consensus emerge to stimulate action—a clear case of the development and influence of an epistemic community. There were still serious disagreements over the likelihood that human-induced changes in mean temperatures were altering the global climate system. Naturally occurring greenhouse gases (GHGs) in the atmosphere (see Figure 14.2) insulate the Earth's surface by trapping solar radiation. Before the Industrial Revolution, carbon dioxide concentrations in the atmosphere were around 280 parts per million. They have since grown exponentially (to a 2005 figure of 379 ppm) due to burning of fossil fuels and reductions in some of the "sinks" for carbon dioxide—notably forests. Methane emissions have also risen with the growth of agriculture (Intergovernmental Panel on Climate Change 2007, 11). The best predictions of the IPCC are that if nothing is done to curb intensive fossil fuel emissions, there will be a likely rise in mean temperatures on the order of 4.3–11.5 degrees Fahrenheit (or 2.4–6.4 degrees Celsius) by 2099. The exact consequences of this are difficult to predict on the basis of current climate modeling, but sea level rises and turbulent weather are generally expected. According to the EU, to avoid climate catastrophe, it would be necessary to hold temperature increases below 3.6 degrees Fahrenheit (or 2 degrees Celsius) by keeping atmospheric CO^2 concentrations below 550 ppm. In the first decade of the twenty-first century, unusual weather patterns, storm events, and the melting of polar ice sheets have added a dimension of public concern to the fears expressed by the scientific community.

As a common problem, climate change is on a quite different scale from anything that the international system has previously encountered. Climate change is really not a "normal" international environmental problem—it threatens huge changes in living conditions and challenges existing patterns of energy use and security. There is almost no dimension of international relations that it does not actually or potentially affect, and it has already become the subject of "high politics," discussed at G-8 summits and in high-level meetings between political leaders. Indeed, the UK foreign secretary stated in 2006 that climate change and climate security must now be a priority for foreign policy. Although recognizing the importance of this issue for the health of the planet and all living creatures, national leaders could not come to an agreement on next steps at the 2009 Copenhagen Climate Conference.

One way of examining the dimensions of the problem and the steps taken at the international level to respond to the threat is to make a comparison to the stratospheric-ozone problem discussed in the previous section. There are, of course, some similarities.

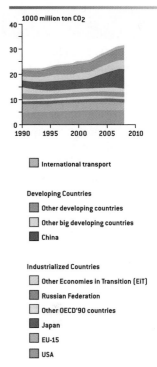

1000 million ton CO_2

International transport

Developing Countries
Other developing countries
Other big developing countries
China

Industrialized Countries
Other Economies in Transition (EIT)
Russian Federation
Other OECD'90 countries
Japan
EU-15
USA

CO^2 Emissions by Region.
Global CO^2 emissions increased from 15.3 billion tons in 1970 to 22.5 billion tons in 1990; by 2008 emissions had increased to 31.5 billion tons. What are governments doing to reverse this trend? What impediments do they face in implementing their plans? *Source: Netherlands Environmental Assessment Agency.*

Global increases of atmospheric temperatures have positive correlation with an increase in glacial ice melting.

WHAT'S YOUR WORLDVIEW ?

When it comes to environmental issues, some nation-states are incrementalists and others are postponers. No one is against the environment. Some want to work slowly toward environmental policy action, others want to postpone any action. They are all pushed by activists who are zealots demanding environmental action. With these different goals among actors, do you think collective action is possible?

CFCs are in themselves greenhouse gases, and the international legal texts on climate change make it clear that controlling them is the responsibility of the Montreal Protocol. The experience with stratospheric ozone and other recent conventions has clearly influenced efforts to build a climate-change regime. At the very start of climate discussions, the same approach was adopted: a framework convention followed by protocols.

The UN Framework Convention on Climate Change (UNFCCC) was signed at the Rio Earth Summit in 1992. It envisaged the reduction of greenhouse-gas emissions and their removal by carbon sequestration, a process through which carbon-based gases are injected into the ground or into peat bogs. The signatories hoped that including a commitment from the developed nations to cut their emissions back to 1990 levels by 2000 could make a start. In a US election year this proved to be impossible, and the parties had to be content with a nonbinding declaration that an attempt would be made. There was a binding commitment, however, for parties to draw up national inventories of sources and sinks. As this included the developing nations, many of whom were ill equipped to fulfill this obligation, there was also funding for capacity building. Most importantly, the convention locked the signatories into holding a continuing series of annual Conferences of Parties (CoPs) to consider possible actions and review the adequacy of existing commitments, supported by regular meetings of the subsidiary scientific and implementation bodies. By the second CoP in Kyoto in 1997, the parties agreed on a "control" measure—the Kyoto Protocol involving emissions reductions by developed countries facilitated by "flexibility mechanisms."

The problem faced by the framers of the Kyoto Protocol was vastly more complex and demanding than that which their counterparts at Montreal had confronted so successfully in 1987. Instead of controlling a single set of industrial gases for which substitutes were available, reducing greenhouse-gas emissions would involve energy, transport, and agriculture—the fundamentals of life in modern societies. This challenges the whole idea of sustainable development. Whether this must involve real sacrifices in living standards and "impossible" political choices is a tough question for governments, although there are potential economic benefits from cutting emissions through the development of alternative-energy technologies. Politicians in Europe have taken the lead in trying to reduce greenhouse-gas emissions. Unfortunately, for most of the 1990s and the first decade of the new millennium, United States politicians—representing one of the worst greenhouse-gas-offending countries by several indicators—were reluctant to make the necessary adjustments.

Yet the 1997 Kyoto Protocol to the UN Framework Convention on Climate Change committed all developed countries to make an average of a 5.2 percent cut in their greenhouse-gas emissions from a 1990 baseline. Within this range, different national targets were negotiated: for example, 7 percent for the United States and 8 percent for the European Union (EU). These targets were to be achieved by the first commitment period—2008–2012. In order to provide flexible ways of achieving these targets, three mechanisms were also agreed on:

1. **Emissions Trading**. This envisages creation of a market in rights to pollute. For example, efficient power plants can sell their permits to emit carbon dioxide to

others, and a long-term reduction in the number of permits available will mean that the price of carbon rises, alternative power sources become more competitive, and the overall amount of carbon dioxide emitted is reduced.

2. **Joint Implementation (JI).** Under this mechanism, a developed country can receive credits against its own emissions-reduction target by financing projects in another developed country. The argument is that a given amount of money is best spent where it can achieve the greatest reduction in world emissions of greenhouse gases. Countries with very efficient power plants will have an incentive to use this scheme.

3. **The Clean Development Mechanism (CDM).** Applies the same principle to relations between developed and developing countries. This has stimulated a good deal of interest in China and elsewhere because it is a source of new funds and technology transfer.

Even with what appeared to be a flexible framework and some useful mechanisms built into the Kyoto Protocol, there was much disagreement and international posturing. Another reason for dissent was that, despite a quite unprecedented international scientific effort in support of the IPCC to establish the causes and consequences of warming, there was not the kind of scientific consensus that had promoted agreement on CFCs—at least not in 1997. At the time, there was disagreement over the significance of human activities and over projections of future change (which has since narrowed dramatically). And there were those who had an economic interest in denying or misrepresenting the science, including fossil fuel interests and producers such as Saudi Arabia. At the other end of the spectrum, the Alliance of Small Island States, some of whose members' territory would simply disappear under projected sea level rises, were desperately concerned that these projections be taken seriously.

There is a further problem in that, even though the effects of climate change are not fully understood, there is enough evidence for some nations to calculate that there might be benefits to them from climatic alterations. Regions of Russia, for example, might become more temperate with rises in mean temperature and more suitable for agricultural production (although one could equally well argue the extremely damaging effects of melting permafrost in Siberia). In North America, variations in rainfall patterns have already begun to disrupt agriculture that replies on irrigation. Snowfall patterns in the major mountain ranges are changing, and some species of frogs and insects—especially honey bees necessary for crop pollination—are slowly disappearing. One generalization that can be made with certainty is that the developing nations, with limited infrastructure and major populations located at sea level, are most vulnerable. In recognition of this, and on the understanding that a certain level of warming is now inevitable, international attention has begun to shift toward the problem of adaptation to the effects of climate change as well as mitigation of its causes. Once again, the comparative simplicity of the stratospheric-ozone problem is evident—the effects of ozone depletion were spread across the globe and affected North Europeans as well as those living in the Southern Hemisphere.

At the heart of the international politics of climate change as a global environmental problem is the structural divide between North and South (see Chapters 6 and 12). For the Montreal Protocol there was a solution available at an acceptable price, delivered through the Multilateral Ozone Fund. Once again, climate change is different. One of the most

WHAT'S YOUR WORLDVIEW

We live in a country that emphasizes individual rights and responsibilities, yet protecting the environment asks us to live collectively and consider the other. Is it possible to change this dominant perspective?

ratification The procedure by which a state approves a convention or protocol that it has signed. There will be rules in the treaty concerning the number of ratifications required before it can enter into force.

significant principles set out in the UNFCCC was that of common but differentiated responsibilities. That is to say that while climate change was the "common concern" of all, it had been produced as a consequence of the development of the old industrialized nations, and it was their responsibility to take the lead in cutting emissions.

The achievement at Kyoto was to bind most of the developed nations to a set of emissions cuts that varied. This accomplished at least part of the objectives of the European Union, but it was soon seen to be wholly inadequate in terms of the projected scale of the global-warming problem. In return, the European Union accepted the US proposal for the Kyoto mechanisms and has since become their enthusiastic champion. However, none of the detail of what was to become a highly complex and innovative agreement had been worked out. It would take a series of difficult CoPs to achieve this, to write the rules for the operation of the protocol, and, above all, to meet the demanding requirements for its **ratification** and entry into force. These were that fifty-five parties had to ratify the agreement and that these parties must also produce over 55 percent of global emissions. It was very evident that the Republican-controlled United States would not ratify Kyoto, so President Clinton did not submit it to the body. When he became president in 2001, George W. Bush actually denounced US signature of the protocol, claiming that it was "fatally flawed" and that the emissions cuts required would be impossibly damaging to the US economy. With a new Obama administration in place, the United States may join Australia, which also initially refused to ratify the agreement but finally did when the Labor Party gained control of the Australian Parliament in 2008. If the United States were to join, that would make it essential for Russia and Japan to ratify the agreement, alongside the European Union. In the meantime, much of the burden of ensuring that Kyoto eventually enters into force has fallen on the EU. The situation has tested the diplomatic capabilities of this new type of international actor and its component member states, in what has become a direct contest with the US government. The EU, meanwhile, has also pioneered the world's first international emissions-trading system, which commenced operation at the beginning of 2005. The hope was not only that it would help to achieve the EU's Kyoto target of an 8 percent reduction in emissions by 2012, but also that it would encourage other countries to join the scheme.

Unfortunately, the success of the climate regime has been complicated by the "free rider" problem. If some countries join together and agree to make cuts that are costly, then others who do not can enjoy the environmental benefits of such action without paying. Thus, proceeding without the United States has been very difficult, not only because it produces around one-quarter of global carbon dioxide emissions, but also because its failure to be involved affects the willingness of others to participate—particularly the fast-developing economies of the global South. There is some hope that the Kyoto targets may be achieved by 2012, but even that is uncertain. Both Bush administrations resolutely opposed Kyoto, but from its entry into force in 2005, discussions have proceeded as to how to construct a new regime involving all of the main industrialized and industrializing countries in collectively making significant cuts in their emissions and adapting to the effects of climate change already becoming evident. There is probably no more urgent or important task for international cooperation. The nation-states participating in the 2009 Copenhagen Conference did not heed this plea for cooperation. Participants made no commitment to a legally binding treaty that would address the need to reduce emissions and keep temperature rises below 2 degrees Celsius.

Common But Differentiated Responsibilities?

A key principle of the climate-change regime, written into the 1992 UNFCCC, was the notion of "common but differentiated responsibilities." This, in effect, meant that although all nations had to accept responsibility for the world's changing climate, it was developed nations that were immediately responsible because they had benefited from the industrialization generally regarded as the source of the excess carbon dioxide emissions (refer to Map 14.1).

Consider the relationship between national carbon dioxide emissions and share of global population. The United States emits around 25 percent of the global total but has only 4.5 percent of the global population. The Chinese figures are 14 percent and over 20 percent of the world's population, while the 35 least developed nations emit under 1 percent and account for over 10 percent of the world's population.

Accordingly, the developed countries were listed in Annex I of the Convention, and it was agreed that they, rather than developing countries, would have to lead the way in making emissions reductions.

This approach was followed in the Kyoto Protocol, where only developed-country parties are committed to make reductions. Even before the protocol was agreed, the US Senate passed the Byrd-Hagel Resolution making it clear that it would not ratify any agreement where developing nations, who were now economic competitors of the United States, did not also have to make emissions reductions.

However, in 2004 the International Energy Agency published projections that underlined how globalization was radically changing the pattern of energy-related carbon dioxide emissions; it estimated that emissions would rise by 62 percent by 2030 but, most significantly, that at some point in the 2020s, developing-world emissions would overtake those of the developed OECD countries.

It therefore became clear that to have any chance of success, the future climate-change regime would have to include emissions reductions by countries such as China and India, but that they in turn would not even consider reductions if the United States remained outside the Kyoto system.

The fundamental question is thus: *On what basis should countries be asked to reduce their emissions?*

The most radical and equitable answer might be to give each individual a fixed carbon allowance, probably allowing rich people to maintain something of their lifestyle by buying the allowances of the poor. A more likely alternative is to find ways of creating and then raising a global carbon price so that alternatives to fossil fuel become economically attractive. Which approach would you support? Why? What alternatives can you imagine?

Global industrial growth has caused an increased demand for power generation, often through the burning of fossil fuels that produce greenhouse gases.

In 2007 the Nobel Prize Committee recognized the IPCC and former vice president Al Gore for their work on the causes and ramifications of global warming.

Conclusion

In this chapter we have seen that cooperation to protect the global environment, though sometimes difficult to achieve, is possible. The determinants of successful cooperation can be found in international-regime theory, beginning with the acceptance of proper norms of behavior, for the costs of not cooperating are potentially too great. Indeed, the environmental issues we are faced with today—global climate change, desertification, and other environmental degradations—can become more severe and less manageable for future generations, as we have seen in our own brief history of the twentieth and early twenty-first century. Solving these issues now requires new perspectives and unprecedented cooperation on a global scale.

Contributors to Chapter 14: John Vogler and Steven L. Lamy.

REVIEW QUESTIONS

1. What are the possible connections, both negative and positive, between globalization and environmental change?
2. Why did environmental issues appear on the international agenda, and what were the key turning points?
3. Summarize the consequences of the 1972 UNCHE and the 1992 UNCED.
4. How would you interpret the meaning of sustainable development?
5. How can regime concepts be applied to the study of international environmental cooperation?
6. Can international trade and environmental protection ever be compatible?
7. Why did the framework convention/control protocol prove useful in the cases of stratospheric ozone depletion and climate change?
8. Analyze the development implications of three of the regimes mentioned in the chapter.
9. How does the "tragedy of the commons" story help to illustrate the need for governance of the global commons?
10. Describe the free rider problem in relation to the climate-change regime.
11. Can "common but differentiated responsibilities" continue to be relevant to the future climate-change regime?
12. Consider the possible security implications of the climate predictions made by the IPCC.

FURTHER READING

Barnett, J. (2001), *The Meaning of Environmental Security: Ecological Politics and Policy in the New Security Era* (London: Zed Books). This lively and critical book is for readers who wish to explore the growing connections between environmental and security issues.

Barry, J., and Eckersley, R. (eds.) (2005), *The State and the Global Ecological Crisis* (Cambridge, MA: MIT Press). A provocative set of essays on the continuing relevance of the state, long forsaken by green activists but still the fundamental unit of global environmental governance.

Birnie, P., and Boyle, A. (2002), *International Law and the Environment* (Oxford: Oxford University Press). An invaluable source of detailed information on formal aspects of international environmental cooperation.

Brenton, T. (1994), *The Greening of Machiavelli: The Evolution of International Environmental Politics* (London: Earthscan). A diplomatic participant's account of the international politics of the environment up to and including the Rio Earth Summit.

Dauvergne, P. (ed.) (2005), *Handbook of Global Environmental Politics* (Cheltenham: Edward Elgar). This very extensive collection of thirty essays covering state governance and security, capitalism, trade and corporations, civil societies, knowledge, and ethics will provide the reader with a more in-depth view of current concerns and controversies in the field.

Dessler, A. E., and Parson, E. A. (2006), *The Science and Politics of Global Climate Change: A Guide to the Debate* (Cambridge: Cambridge University Press). As the title promises, this book presents the essentials of the debate about climate change in an unbiased manner.

DeSombre, E. (2006), *Global Environmental Institutions* (Abingdon: Routledge). Provides a concise introduction within a series on global governance.

Dryzek, J. (1997), *The Politics of the Earth: Environmental Discourses* (Oxford: Oxford University Press). Still extremely useful as a guide to thinking through the different approaches that are applied to the problems of environmental politics and sustainable development.

Elliott, L. (2004), *The Global Politics of the Environment* (Basingstoke: Palgrave). This comprehensive and up-to-date text provides detailed and wide-ranging coverage of the field and of the key international agreements.

Gleick, P. H. (1993), "Water and Conflict: Fresh Water Resources and International Security," *International Security* 18(1): 79–112. Two articles by one of the academic pioneers of the connections between environmental degradation and security risks.

Gleick, P. H. (2003), "Global Freshwater Resources: Soft-Path Solutions for the Twenty-first Century," *Science* (November): 1524–1528. After many years of researching the possibility of war over scarce resources like water, the author offers suggestions to avoid such crises.

Lipschutz, R. D. (2004), *Global Environmental Politics: Power, Perspectives, and Practice* (Washington, DC: CQ Press). Makes innovative and critical connections between global environmental politics and a broad array of relevant political thought and practice.

Paterson, M. (2001), *Understanding Global Environmental Politics: Domination, Accumulation, Resistance* (Basingstoke: Palgrave). As the title suggests, this book provides an alternative critical view of global environmental politics, investigating such problems as the political economy of car use.

Vogler, J. (2000), *The Global Commons: Environmental and Technological Governance* (Chichester: John Wiley). Uses regime analysis to compare and account for the various international arrangements for the ocean, Antarctic, space, and atmospheric commons.

INTERNET RESOURCES

Center for International Earth Science Information Network
www.ciesin.org/TG/PI/TRADE/tradhmpg.html
Information on trade regimes and the environment:

European Environment Agency
www.eea.eu.int
The European Union's supranational agency for monitoring the environment.

International Institute for Sustainable Development
www.iisd.ca
Works to promote environmental sound development practices.

The Biodiversity Convention
www.biodiv.org
An important and reliable source of information on the topic.

UN Environment Program
www.unep.org
Coordinates efforts in this area.

UN Framework Convention on Climate Change Secretariat
www.unfccc.de
An important and reliable source of information on the topic.

World Wildlife Fund
www.panda.org
An NGO working to protect spcies around the world.

For more information, quizzes, case studies, and other study tools, please visit us at **www.oup.com/us/lamy**

THEMATIC
MAPS

BORDERS AND CONFLICT

The potential for peace among established, stable democracies is evident in this map, as are the ravages of colonialism. The dominance of democracy is also clear, though Russia alone is enough to remind us to consider that "trend" with some caution. We can also see how tenuous and conflict-prone transitional governments can be, as well as how contentious borders remain.

MAIN MAP KEY

Types of government

- Multiparty democracy for more than 10 yrs
- Multiparty/transitional democracy within last 10 yrs
- Single-party government
- Military regime
- Theocracy
- Absolute monarchy

Conflicts and international disputes

- Major active territorial or border disputes
- Countries involved in internal conflict
- Active territorial or border disputes and internal conflict

▲ Dates from which current boundaries have existed

- 1990–present
- 1966–1989
- 1946–1965
- 1915–1945
- 1850–1914
- 1800–1849
- Pre-1800

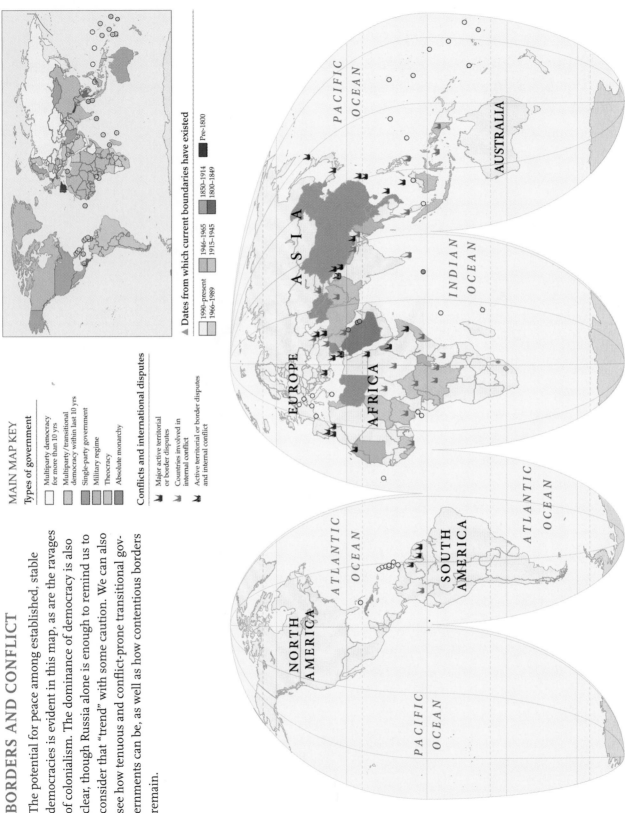

ECONOMIC SYSTEMS

As evident as globalization and interdependence are in this map, so too are the discrepancies in wealth and international financial relationships. Note the disparities in GDP and the sources and endpoints of the various arrows representing foreign direct investment.

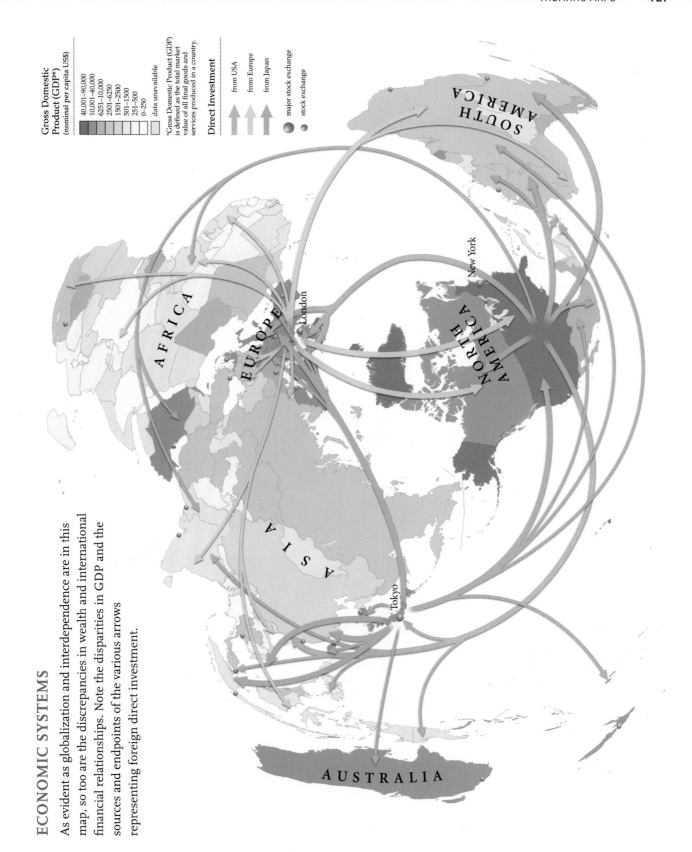

Gross Domestic Product (GDP*)
(nominal per capita US$)

- 40,001–90,000
- 10,001–40,000
- 6251–10,000
- 2501–6250
- 1501–2500
- 501–1500
- 251–500
- 0–250
- data unavailable

*Gross Domestic Product (GDP) is defined as the total market value of all final goods and services produced in a country.

Direct Investment

- from USA
- from Europe
- from Japan

- major stock exchange
- stock exchange

London

New York

Tokyo

SOUTH AMERICA

NORTH AMERICA

AFRICA

EUROPE

ASIA

AUSTRALIA

HEALTH

This map illustrates that people living in the developed world have a higher life expectancy on average than those in the developing world. At almost every stage of life, people in developing countries are more susceptible to health problems than those in richer ones, because poverty, limited access to health care and medication, malnutrition, and poor sanitation contribute to the spread of infectious disease.

MAIN MAP KEY

Life expectancy

- above 80 years
- 75–80 years
- 70–75 years
- 60–70 years
- 50–60 years
- below 50 years

▲ Medical doctors (per 1000 people)

- above 5
- 4–5
- 3–4
- 1–3
- 0.5–1
- below 0.5
- no data

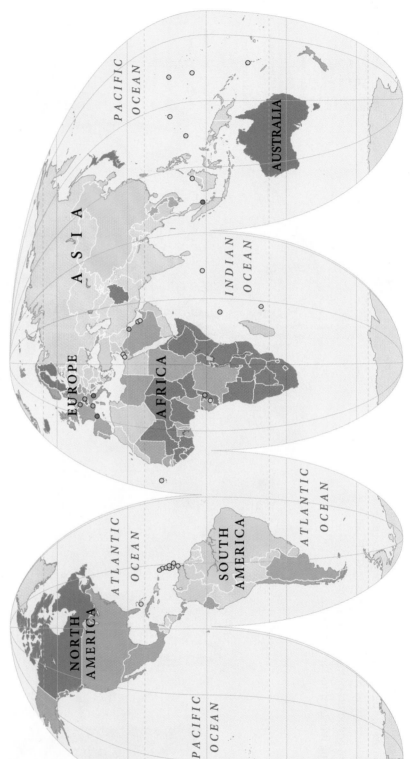

TRAVEL AND COMMUNICATIONS

In an era of globalization, more people are on the move, able to travel and communicate across long distances. As this map shows, however, the patterns of travel and communication vary in different parts of the world. People in the industrialized world travel for business and vacation; people in the developing world usually migrate in search of jobs.

Global transportation

— major road
— major rail

Airline passenger volume
passengers per year

more than 2 million
1.5–2 million
1–1.5 million
0.75–1 million
0.5–0.75 million
● major airport

SOUTH AMERICA

AFRICA

EUROPE

NORTH AMERICA

ASIA

AUSTRALIA

Madrid
London
Paris
Frankfurt
Amsterdam

New York
Philadelphia
Miami
Toronto
Detroit
Chicago
Atlanta
Orlando
Houston
Dallas
Minneapolis
Denver
Phoenix
Las Vegas
Seattle
San Francisco
Los Angeles

Bangkok
Beijing
Hong Kong
Tokyo
Singapore

POPULATION

By 2050, the current world population of more than 6.7 billion people is projected to increase to 9.2 billion. 96 percent of the projected growth will occur in the developing states, where medical advances such as vaccinations have reduced death rates, even as birth rates remain high. Concurrent with this trend is the "graying" of industrialized countries where birth rates have fallen dramatically, leading to older populations.

MAIN MAP KEY
Population density
(persons per sq mile)

- 77–390
- 39–77
- 19–39
- 7–19
- 4–7
- 2–4
- 0.5–2
- 0–0.5

▲ Population growth rate (annual % change)

- above 4%
- 3 to 4%
- 2 to 3%
- 1 to 2%
- 0 to 1%
- -1 to 0%

Source: LandScanTM Global Population Database. Oak Ridge, TN: Oak Ridge National Laboratory. Available at http://www.ornl.gov/landscan/.

WATER RESOURCES

Today, over a billion people lack clean water, and approximately 2.5 billion live without adequate sanitation. Access to safe water is related to a population's health—nearly 80 percent of all cases of disease have been linked to contaminated water. Moreover, the depletion of water has already begun to lead to conflict within and between states.

MAIN MAP KEY

Availability of fresh water
total renewable
(cubic yards/capita/per year)

- less than 1300 (water scarcity)
- 1300–2222 (water stress)
- 2222–3922 (insufficient water)
- 3922–13,078 (relatively sufficient)
- 13,078 or more (plentiful supplies)

major drainage basin

▼ over 50% of water resource originating from outside country

▲ Access to safe
drinking water source
(percentage of population)

- 91%–100%
- 76%–90%
- 50%–75%
- below 50%
- no data

PEOPLE AND THE ENVIRONMENT

The human causes of environmental degradation are usually local, but global in effect, such as deforestation in the Amazon (the conversion of forested land for other uses, such as cropland, or urban and industrial use) and the burning of fossil fuels in Chinese factories and on American highways. For the global public good, solutions must be found, but local politics may stymie such efforts.

MAIN MAP KEY

CO_2 emissions in 2003
(million tons)

- over 4400
- 1100–4400
- 550–1100
- 110–550
- 55–110
- 11–55
- 2.2–11
- 0–2.2
- no data

Kyoto Protocol

- ◁ countries that have reached targets
- ▷ countries that have not reached targets
- ● industrialized countries that have not ratified Kyoto Protocol

▲ Deforestation

- frontier forest
- degraded forest
- frontier forest 8000 years ago

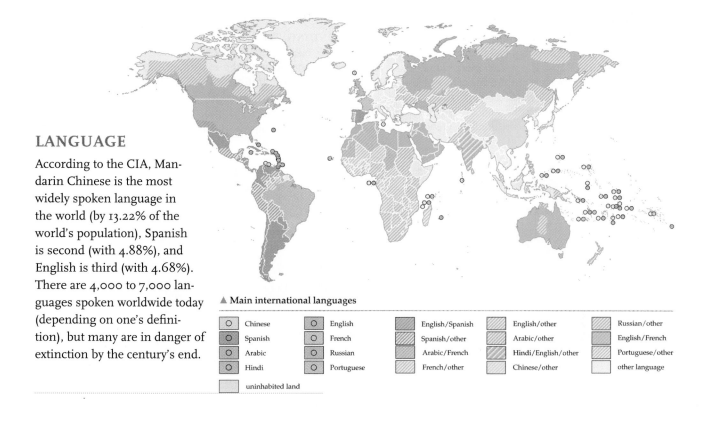

LANGUAGE

According to the CIA, Mandarin Chinese is the most widely spoken language in the world (by 13.22% of the world's population), Spanish is second (with 4.88%), and English is third (with 4.68%). There are 4,000 to 7,000 languages spoken worldwide today (depending on one's definition), but many are in danger of extinction by the century's end.

▲ **Main international languages**

○ Chinese	○ English	English/Spanish
○ Spanish	○ French	Spanish/other
○ Arabic	○ Russian	Arabic/French
○ Hindi	○ Portuguese	French/other
uninhabited land		

English/other	Russian/other
Arabic/other	English/French
Hindi/English/other	Portuguese/other
Chinese/other	other language

RELIGION

The CIA estimates that roughly 85% of the world's population adheres to a religion: Christians 33.32%, Muslims 21.01%, Hindus 13.26%, Buddhists 5.84%, Sikhs 0.35%, Jews 0.23%, Baha'is 0.12%, other religions 11.78%, non-religious 11.77%, atheists 2.32%. Some of the most enduring conflicts involve religion, but religions organizations also often rally people for the public good.

▲ **Majority religions**

○ Protestant Christianity	○ Sunni Islam	○ Mahayana Buddhism
○ Catholic Christianity	○ Hinduism	○ Tibetan Buddhism
○ Orthodox Christianity	○ Judaism	○ other
○ Shi'a Islam	○ Theravada Buddhism	○ Marxism / Maoism

State policy

▲ secular ideologies governing   ● communist states during 20th century   ■ non-pluralist states

MEMBERSHIP OF THE UN

MEMBERSHIP OF THE UN In 1945 there were 51 members; by the end of 2002 membership had increased to 192 following the admission of East Timor and Switzerland. There are 2 independent states which are not members of the UN— Taiwan and the Vatican City. All the successor states of the former USSR had joined by the end of 1992. The official languages of the UN are Chinese, English, French, Russian, Spanish, and Arabic.

FUNDING The UN regular budget for 2010-2011 was US $5.16 billion. Contributions are assessed by the members' ability to pay, with the maximum 22% of the total (USA's share), the minimum 0.01%. The European Union members pay over 37% of the budget.

PEACEKEEPING The UN has been involved in 54 peacekeeping operations worldwide since 1948.

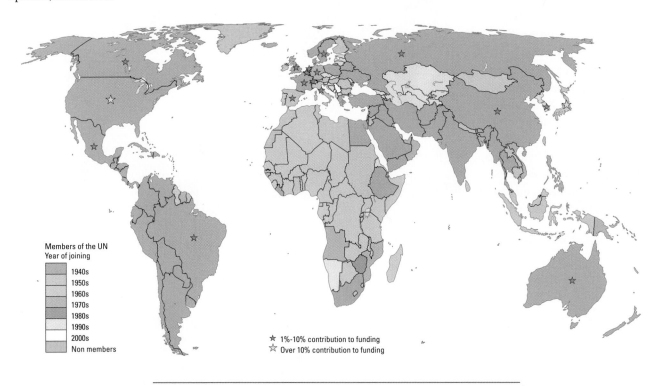

Members of the UN
Year of joining

- 1940s
- 1950s
- 1960s
- 1970s
- 1980s
- 1990s
- 2000s
- Non members

★ 1%-10% contribution to funding
☆ Over 10% contribution to funding

International Organizations

ACP African-Caribbean-Pacific (formed in 1975). The 79 members have economic ties with the EU.

APEC Asia-Pacific Economic Cooperation (formed in 1989). It aims to enhance economic growth and prosperity for the region and to strengthen the Asia-Pacific community. APEC is the only intergovernmental grouping in the world operating on the basis of non-binding commitments, open dialogue, and equal respect for the views of all participants. There are 21 member economies.

ARAB LEAGUE (formed in 1945). The League's aim is to promote economic, social, political, and military cooperation. There are 22 member-states.

ASEAN Association of Southeast Asian Nations (formed in 1967). Cambodia joined in 1999.

AU The African Union replaced the Organization of African Unity (formed in 1963) in 2002. Its 53 members represent over 94% of Africa's population. Arabic, French, Portuguese, and English are recognized as working languages.

COLOMBO PLAN (formed in 1951). Its 26 members aim to promote economic and social development in Asia and the Pacific.

COMMONWEALTH The Commonwealth of Nations evolved from the British Empire. Zimbabwe left the Commonwealth in December 2003. It now comprises of 54 member states.

EU European Union (evolved from the European Community in 1993). The 26 member-states aim to integrate economies, coordinate social developments, and bring about political union of Europe.

LAIA Latin American Integration Association (1980). Its aim is to promote freer regional trade.

NATO North Atlantic Treaty Organization (formed in 1949). It continues after 1991 despite the winding up of the Warsaw Pact. Bulgaria, Estonia, Latvia, Lithuania, Romania, the Slovak Republic, and Slovenia became members in 2004.

OAS Organization of American States (formed in 1948). It aims to promote social and economic cooperation between developed countries of North America and developing nations of Latin America.

OECD Organization for Economic Cooperation and Development (formed in 1961). It comprises 30 major free-market economies. Poland, Hungary, and South Korea joined in 1996, and the Slovak Republic in 2000. "G8" is its "inner group" of leading industrial nations, comprising Canada, France, Germany, Italy, Japan, Russia, UK, and USA.

OPEC Organization of Petroleum Exporting Countries (formed in 1960). It controls about three-quarters of the world's oil supply. Gabon left the organization in 1996.

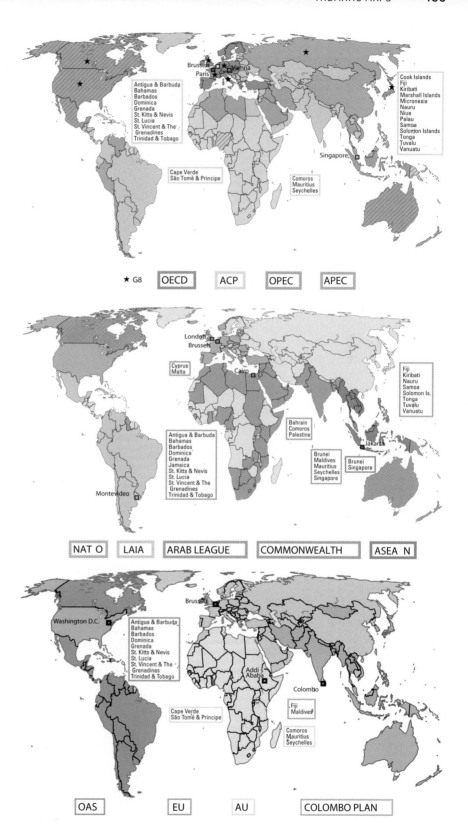

Glossary

Absolute gains All states seek to gain more power and influence in the system to secure their national interests. This is absolute gain. Offensive neorealists are also concerned with increasing power relative to other states. One must have enough power to secure interests and more power than any other state in the system—friend or foe.

Adaptation strategies A foreign policy based on reacting to international events and adjusting national goals to conform to the effects of events external to that state.

Advocacy networks Groups of regional, national, and international NGOs bound together by shared values. They coordinate activity to frame political debate and to influence policy outcomes.

Al Qaeda Most commonly associated with Osama bin Laden, "The Base" (as it means in Arabic) is a religious-based group whose fighters swear an oath of fealty to bin Laden.

Americanization The spread of American values, practices, popular culture, and way of life.

Anarchic system A realist description of the international system that suggests there is no common power or central governing structure.

Anarchy A system operating in the absence of any central government. It does not imply chaos but, in realist theory, the absence of political authority.

Appeasement A policy of making concessions to a revanchist (or otherwise territorially acquisitive) state in the hope that settlement of more modest claims will assuage that state's expansionist appetites. Appeasement remains most (in)famously associated with British prime minister Neville Chamberlain's acquiescence to Hitler's incursions into Austria and then Czechoslovakia, culminating in the Munich Agreement of September 1938. Since then, appeasement has generally been seen as synonymous with a craven collapse before the demands of dictators—encouraging, not disarming, their aggressive designs.

Armistice A cease-fire agreement between enemies in wartime. In the case of World War I, the armistice began at 11:00 a.m., on November 11, 1918.

Arms embargo Similar to economic sanctions, an arms embargo stops the flow of arms from one country to another.

Arms race This is a central concept in realist thought. As states build up their military to address real or perceived threats to their national security, they may create insecurity in other states. These states, in turn, develop their military capacities and thus begin an arms race. This never-ending pursuit of security creates the condition we know as a security dilemma.

Association of Southeast Asian Nations (ASEAN) A geopolitical and economic organization of several countries located in Southeast Asia. Initially formed as a display of solidarity against communism, it has since redefined its aims and broadened to include the acceleration of economic growth and the promotion of regional peace. By 2005 the ASEAN countries had a combined GDP of about $884 billion.

Asymmetric conflict In symmetrical warfare, armies with comparable weapons, tactics, and organizational structures do battle. Wars are fought on near-equal terms. When stakes are high and those actors in conflict are not equal in terms of weapons and technology, the weaker side adopts asymmetrical tactics. These include guerrilla warfare, roadside bombs, attacks on civilians, and other terrorist tactics.

Autarchy The mercantilist recommendation that states strive for economic self-sufficiency by using trade protectionism or policies of complete isolation.

Balance of power In realist theory, this refers to an equilibrium between states; historical realists regard it as the product of diplomacy (contrived balance), whereas structural realists regard the system as having a tendency towards a natural equilibrium (fortuitous balance). It is a doctrine and an arrangement whereby the power of one state (or group of states) is checked by the countervailing power of other states.

Bipolar A term to describe an international political order in which two states dominate all others. It is often used to describe the nature of the international system when the two superpowers, the USSR and the US, were dominant powers during the Cold War.

Blitzkrieg The German term for "lightning war." This was an offensive strategy that used the combination of mechanized forces—especially tanks—and aircraft as mobile artillery to exploit breaches in an enemy's front line. The irony was that in 1940 the French army had more tanks than the German army. The French tanks, however, were spread among units along the front line, while the German commanders concentrated their tanks in a few units.

Bretton Woods System The name given to the three institutions that comprise the post-Second World War international political economic system. It is called Bretton Woods after the hamlet in northern New Hampshire where the leaders from the United States, the United Kingdom, and forty-two other countries met in July 1944.

Capacity building Providing the funds and technical training to allow developing countries to participate in global environmental governance.

Capital controls This is the monetary policy device that a government uses to regulate the flows into and out of a country's capital account, i.e., the flows of investment-oriented money into and out of a country or currency.

Capitalism A system of production in which human labor and its products are commodities that are bought and sold in the marketplace.

Charter rights Civil liberties guaranteed in a written document such as a constitution.

Civil society (1) The totality of all individuals and groups in a society who are not acting as participants in any government institutions, or (2) all individuals and groups who are neither participants in government nor acting in the interests of commercial companies.

Civilization The broadest construction of cultural identity to which individuals may subscribe. A number of broad cultures have emerged from world history, including the Western, Islamic, and Chinese civilizations.

Clandestine or **"sleeper" cell** Usually a group of people, sent by an intelligence organization or terrorist network, that remains dormant in a target country until activated by a message to carry out a mission, which could include prearranged attacks.

Class A social group that in Marxism is identified by its relationship with the means of production and the distribution of societal resources. Thus, we have the bourgeoisie, or the owners or upper classes, and the proletariat, or workers.

Climate change A convention on climate was agreed to at the Rio Conference in 1992. Climate change represents a change in the statistical distribution of weather over periods of time that range from decades to millions of years. It can be a change in the average weather or a change in the distribution of weather events around an average (for example, greater or fewer extreme weather events). Climate change may be limited to a specific region, or it may occur across the whole Earth.

Coercive diplomacy The use of diplomatic and military methods that force a state to concede to another state. These methods may include the threat of force and the actual mobilization of military forces so as to gradually "turn the screw" but exclude the actual use of force. The implication is that war is the next step if diplomacy fails.

Collective security Refers to an arrangement where "each state in the system accepts that the security of one is the concern of all, and agrees to join in a collective response to aggression" (Roberts and Kingsbury 1993, 30).

Common security At times called "cooperative security," it stresses noncompetitive approaches and cooperative approaches through which states—both friends and foes—can achieve security. Sometimes expressed as until all people are secure from threats of war, no one is secure.

Community A human association in which members share common symbols and wish to cooperate to realize common objectives.

Concert of Europe Five great powers (Austria, Britain, France, Prussia, and Russia) created an informal institution and agreed on "rules of the game," including controlling revolutionary forces, managing the balance of power, and accepting interventions to keep current leaders in power. This system kept the peace in Europe from 1815 until WWI.

Conditionality When regional or international lending agencies require that recipient national governments accept certain policy conditions in order to receive a loan or some form of economic assistance.

Congress of Berlin A 1885 meeting of the European states that had an interest in colonizing Africa. The Berlin conference redrew the existing political map of Africa, with a goal to avoid conflict between the Europeans in Africa.

Congress of Vienna A meeting of major European leaders (1814–1815) that redrew the political map of Europe after the end of the Napoleonic Wars. The congress was an attempt to restore a conservative political order in the continent.

Constructivism An approach to international politics that concerns itself with the centrality of ideas and human consciousness. As constructivists have examined world politics they have been broadly interested in how the structure constructs the actors' identities and interests, how their interactions are organized and constrained by that structure, and how their very interaction serves to either reproduce or transform that structure.

Containment American political strategy for resisting perceived Soviet expansion, first publicly espoused by an American diplomat, George Kennan, in 1947 and aimed at limiting Soviet expansion in Europe. Containment became a powerful factor in American policy towards the Soviet Union for the next forty years and a self-image of Western policy makers. However, Kennan's view of containment did not include the aggressive militarization that brought the world closer to the brink of nuclear destruction.

Coordination A form of cooperation requiring parties to pursue a common strategy in order to avoid the mutually undesirable outcome arising from the pursuit of divergent strategies.

Cosmopolitan culture A pattern of relations within which people share the same goals and aspirations, generally to improve that culture for all members.

Cosmopolitan democracy A condition in which international organizations, transnational corporations, and global markets are accountable to the peoples of the world.

Critical theory Theories that are critical of the status quo and reject the idea that things can be fixed under the present system. These theories challenge core assumptions of the dominant paradigm and argue for transformation and not just reform.

Democratic deficit Leaders have created many policy-making institutions at the global, regional, and national levels with policy-making power led by individuals who are appointed and not elected. Thus policy decisions are not subject to review by citizens.

Democratic peace A central plank of liberal-internationalist thought, the democratic-peace thesis makes two claims first, liberal polities exhibit restraint in their relations with other liberal polities (the so-called separate peace), but, second, they are imprudent in relations with authoritarian states. The validity of the democratic-peace thesis has been fiercely debated in the international relations literature.

Dependency theory The world capitalist system divides the world into core, semiperiphery, and periphery states. The core states control both the economic and the political system and exploit the people and resources in the periphery and semiperiphery. The capitalist system is seen as impossible to reform, and only by withdrawing from the system can poor states break this dependency.

Deregulation The removal of all regulation so that market forces, not government policy, control economic developments.

Desertification This is the extreme deterioration of land in arid and dry subhumid areas due to loss of vegetation and soil moisture; desertification results chiefly from manmade activities and is influenced by climatic variations. This condition is principally caused by over-grazing, overdrafting of groundwater, and diversion of water from rivers for human consumption and industrial use—all of these processes fundamentally driven by overpopulation.

Détente Relaxation of tension between East and West; Soviet–American détente lasted from the late 1960s to the late 1970s, and was characterized by negotiations and nuclear arms control agreements.

Deterrence The threat or use of force to prevent an actor from doing something the actor would otherwise do.

Development In the orthodox view, top-down; reliance on "expert knowledge," usually Western and definitely external; large capital investments in large projects; advanced technology; expansion of the private sphere. In the alternative view, bottom-up; participatory; reliance on appropriate (often local) knowledge and technology; small investments in small-scale projects; protection of the commons.

Diplomacy The process by which international actors communicate as they seek to resolve conflicts without going to war and find solutions to complex global problems.

Dollar standard By 1947, the British pound and gold could no longer serve as the world's money. The only currency strong enough to be used to meet the demands for international liquidity was the US dollar. For both political and economic reasons, the US government was willing to become the world's central bank and use dollars for the key currency in the international monetary system.

Ecological footprint Used to demonstrate the load placed on the Earth's carrying capacity by individuals or nations. It does this by estimating the area of productive land and water system required to sustain a population at its specified standard of living.

Ecologies Communities of plants and animals in an environment that supplies raw materials for all living things.

Economic base The substructure of the society is the relationship between owners and workers. Capitalists own the means of production and control technology and resources. The workers are employed by the capitalists, and they are alienated, exploited, and estranged from their work and their society.

Economic sanctions A tool of statecraft that seeks to get a state to behave by coercion of a monetary kind, for example, freeing banking assets, cutting aid programs, or banning trade.

Economic shock An event that produces a significant change within an economy, despite occurring outside of it. Economic shocks are unpredictable and typically impact supply or demand throughout the markets. A sudden rise in commodity process and a devaluation of a currency are two examples of shocks that would hurt economic actors.

Ecosystem A system of interdependent living organisms that share the same habitat, functioning together with all of the physical factors of the environment. Ecosystems can be permanent or temporary. The Convention on Biological Diversity (CBD)—ratified by more than 175 countries—defines the protection of ecosystems as natural habitats and the maintenance of viable populations of species in natural surroundings.

Electronic commerce The buying and selling of products and services over the telephone or Internet. E-Bay and Amazon are examples of leaders in this area of commerce.

Elite nationalism The use of nationalist ideology to encourage unity within an existing state. This is often a tactic that state-strengthening nationalists use.

Empire A distinct type of political entity, which may or may not be a state, possessing both a home territory and foreign territories. This may include conquered nations and colonies.

Enlightenment Associated with rationalist thinkers of the eighteenth century. Key ideas (which some would argue remain mottoes for our age) include secularism, progress, reason, science, knowledge, and freedom. The motto of the Enlightenment is *"Sapere aude!"* (Have courage to know!) (Kant 1991, 54).

Epistemic community A knowledge-based transnational community of experts and policy activists.

Equity Also called "stock" or "share"; a number of equal portions in the nominal capital of a company; the shareholder thereby owns part of the enterprise.

Ethic of responsibility For historical realists, an ethic of responsibility represents the limits of ethics in international politics; it involves the weighing up of consequences and the realization that positive outcomes may result from amoral actions.

European Union (EU) The EU was formally created in 1992 following the signing of the Maastricht Treaty. However, the origins of the EU can be traced back to 1951 and the creation of the European Coal and Steel Community, followed in 1957 with a broader customs union (the Treaty of Rome, 1958). Originally a grouping of six countries in 1957, "Europe" grew by adding new members in 1973, 1981, and 1986. Since the fall of the planned economies in Eastern Europe in 1989, Europe has grown and now includes twenty-seven member states.

Exceptionalism The belief that a country has a unique set of domestic and foreign policy traditions. An implica-

tion is that other countries should embrace the same set of policies.

Export-led growth An outward-oriented economy that is based on exploiting its own comparative advantages, such as cheap labor or resources, to capture a share of the world market in a given industry. Many of the countries in Asia took advantage of cheap labor to gain control of industries like electronics and textiles and thereby to control most of the exports to the world.

Extraterritoriality When one government attempts to use domestic legal authority to control the global activities of its citizens or TNCs.

Failed (or failing) state A state that does not command the primary loyalty of its citizens or subjects. These states have no monopoly of force at home and lack complete control over their own territory.

Feminism A political project to understand so as to change women's inequality, liberation, or oppression. For some, the aim is to move beyond gender, so that it no longer matters; for others, to validate women's interests, experiences, and choices; for others, to work for more equal and inclusive social relations overall. Feminist theories tend to be critical of the biases of the discipline. Many focus their research on the areas where women are excluded from the analysis of major international issues and concerns.

Fixed exchange rate The price a currency will earn in a hard currency. Here a government is committed to keep it at a specific value.

Floating exchange rate The market decides what the actual value of a currency is compared to other currencies.

Foreign direct investment (FDI) Capital speculation by citizens or organizations of one country into markets or industries in another country.

Foreign policy The articulation of national interests and the means chosen to secure those interests, both material and ideational, in the international arena.

Foreign policy style Often shaped by a state's political culture, history, and traditions, this describes how a country deals with other states and how it approaches any decision-making situation. For example, does it act unilaterally or multilaterally; does it seek consensus on an agreement or does it go with majority rule?

Foreign policy tradition A tradition includes national beliefs about how the world works and a list of national interests and priorities based on these beliefs. It also refers to past actions or significant historical events that act as analogs and give guidance to leaders about what strategy would best secure their national interests.

Fourteen Points President Woodrow Wilson's vision of international society, first articulated in January 1918, included the principle of self-determination, the conduct of diplomacy on an open (not secret) basis, and the establishment of an association of nation-states to provide guarantees of independence and territorial integrity. Wilson's ideas exerted an important influence on the Paris Peace Conference, though the principle of self-determination was only selectively pursued when it came to American colonial interests.

Free market A market ruled by the forces of supply and demand, where all buying and selling is not constrained by government regulations or interventions.

Free trade An essential element of capitalism that argues for no barriers or minimal barriers to the exchange of goods, services, and investments between states.

Functionalism An idea formulated by early proponents of European integration that suggests that cooperation should begin with efforts aimed at resolving specific regional or transnational problems. It is assumed that resolution of these problems will lead to cooperation, or spillover, in other policy areas.

Futures Derivatives that oblige a buyer and seller to complete a transaction at a predetermined time in the future at a price agreed on today. Futures are also known as "forwards."

G-8 (Group of Eight) Established in 1975 as the G-5 (France, Germany, Japan, the UK, and the US); subsequently expanded as the G-7 to include Canada and Italy; and since 1998 the G-8, to include the Russian Federation. The G-8 conducts semiformal collaboration on world economic problems. Government leaders meet in annual G-8 summits, while finance ministers or their leading officials periodically hold other consultations. See further www.g8online.org.

Game theory A branch of mathematics that explores strategic interaction.

Genocide Deliberate and systematic extermination of an ethnic, national, tribal, or religious group.

Glasnost Policy of greater openness pursued by Soviet leader Mikhail Gorbachev from 1985, involving greater toleration of internal dissent and criticism.

Global capital markets These are banks, investment companies, insurance companies, trusts, hedge funds, and stock exchanges that transfer funds to industries and other commercial enterprises globally.

Global commons Areas and resources not under national sovereignty that belong to no single country and are the responsibility of the entire world. The oceans beyond the 200 mile limit, outer space, and Antarctica are global commons areas.

Global environmental governance Governance is the performance of regulative functions, often in the absence of a central government authority. Global environmental governance usually refers to the structure of international agreements and organizations but can also involve governance by the private sector or NGOs.

Global goods Products that are made for a global market and are available across the world.

Global governance Involves the regulation and coordination of transnational issue areas by nation-states, international and regional organizations, and private agencies through the establishment of international regimes. These regimes may focus on problem-solving or the simple enforcement of rules and regulations.

Global politics The politics of global social relations in which the pursuit of power, interests, order, and justice transcends regions and continents.

Global polity The collective structures and processes by which "interests are articulated and aggregated, decisions are made, values allocated and policies conducted through international or transnational political processes" (Ougaard 2004, 5).

Global sourcing Obtaining goods and services across geopolitical boundaries. Usually the goal is to find the least expensive labor and raw material costs and the lowest taxes and tariffs.

Globalization A historical process involving a fundamental shift or transformation in the spatial scale of human social organization that links distant communities and expands the reach of power relations across regions and continents.

Government The people and agencies that have the power and legitimate authority to determine who gets what, when, where, and how within a given territory.

Great Depression A byword for the global economic collapse that ensued following the US Wall Street stock market crash in October 1929. Economic shockwaves soon rippled around a world already densely interconnected by webs of trade and foreign direct investment, with the result that the events of October 1929 were felt in countries as distant as Brazil and Japan.

Great power State that has the political, economic, and military resources to shape the world beyond its borders. In most cases such a state has the will and capacity to define the rules of the international system.

Gross domestic product (GDP) The sum of all economic activity that takes place within a country.

Guerrilla wars Conflicts or insurgencies that involve irregular forces. Fighters in these wars use unconventional methods of warfare, such as sabotage, ambushes, roadside bombs, and sniping.

Hard power The material threats and inducements leaders employ to achieve the goals of their state.

Hegemony A system regulated by a dominant leader, or political (and/or economic) domination of a region. It is also means power and control exercised by a leading state over other states.

Holocaust The term used to describe the attempts by the Nazis to murder the Jewish population of Europe. Some 6 million Jewish people were killed in concentration camps, along with a further million that included Soviet prisoners, Roma, Poles, communists, homosexuals, and the physically or mentally disabled.

Horizontal proliferation An increase in the number of actors who possess nuclear weapons.

Human development The notion that it is possible to improve the lives of people. Basically, it is about increasing the number of choices people have. These may include living a long and healthy life, access to education, and a better standard of living.

Human security The security of people, including their physical safety, their economic and social well-being, respect for their dignity, and the protection of their human rights. Simply put, it is freedom from fear and freedom from want.

Humanitarian intervention The use of military force by external actors to end a threat to people within a sovereign state.

Hybrid international organizations Organizations that provide full membership and equality of status both to governmental actors and to transnational actors. They create policy to govern specific areas of international relations.

Hyperpower A term meant to describe the situation of the United States after the Cold War ended. With the Soviet Union's military might greatly diminished and China having primarily only regional power-projecting capability, the United States was unchallenged in the world.

Idealism Referred to by realists as utopianism since it underestimates the logic of power politics and the constraints this imposes on political action. Idealism as a substantive theory of international relations is generally associated with the claim that it is possible to create a world of peace. Some idealists seek to apply liberal thinking in domestic politics to international relations—in other words, to institutionalize the rule of law.

Ideational This refers to ideas like democracy, capitalism, peace, and social justice.

Ideational/ideal interest The psychological, moral, and ethical goals of a state as it sets foreign and domestic policy.

Identity The understanding of the self in relationship to an "other." Identities are social and thus always formed in relationship to others. Constructivists generally hold that identities shape interests; we cannot know what we want unless we know who we are. But because identities are social and produced through interactions, identities can change.

Immigration controls When a government controls the number of people who may work, study, or relocate to its country. It may also include quotas for certain national groups for immigration.

Imperialism The practice of foreign conquest and rule in the context of global relations of hierarchy and subordination. It can lead to the establishment of an empire.

Improvised explosive device (IED) This is usually a homemade device or a crude booby trap, designed to cause death or injury, that can be made of a variety of explosive materials.

Integration A process of ever-closer union between states, in a regional or international context. The process often begins with cooperation to solve technical problems.

Intellectual property rights Rules that protect the owners of content through copyright, patents, trademarks, and trade secrets. The World Intellectual Property Organization (WIPO) is the forum where states (184 members in 2010) discuss this issue.

Intercontinental Ballistic Missiles (ICBMs) Weapons system the USA and USSR developed to threaten each other with destruction. The thirty- to forty-minute flight times of the missiles created a situation that is sometimes called "Mutually Assured Destruction (MAD)" or "the Balance of Terror."

Interdependence A condition where states (or peoples) are affected by decisions taken by others. Interdependence can be symmetric, i.e., both sets of actors are affected equally, or it can be asymmetric, where the impact varies between actors. If political or economic costs of interdependence are high, a state is in a vulnerable position. If costs are low, it is a situation of sensitivity interdependence.

Intergovernmental organization (IGO) A formal, legally constituted organization established by states to handle common problems or issues; membership and decision-making authority is limited to governments.

International law The formal rules of conduct that states acknowledge or contract between themselves.

International nongovernmental organization (INGO) A formal international organization, with transnational members from at least three countries. There are many different types, with membership from national NGOs, local NGOs, companies, political parties, or individual people. A few have other INGOs as members, and some have mixed membership structures.

International order The normative and the institutional pattern in the relationship between states. The elements of this may be thought to include such things as sovereignty, the forms of diplomacy, international law, the role of the great powers, and the codes circumscribing the use of force. It is a shared value and condition of stability and predictability in the relations of states.

International organization Any institution with formal procedures and formal membership from three or more countries. The minimum number of countries is set at three, rather than two, because multilateral relationships have significantly greater complexity than bilateral relationships.

International relations In a traditional sense, this is the study of the interactions of states in the international system. It was initially considered a part of diplomatic history or political science. Today, departments of international relations include concentrations in international security, political economy, foreign policy, human rights, global governance, and environmental issues. The field now includes the study of other actors, including corporations and NGOs, and a wide variety of issues, such as culture, identity, and ethics.

Interparadigm debate This is the debate between the two main theoretical approaches in the field of global politics realism versus liberalism. Some present this debate as one between neorealism and neoliberalism. Critics argue that this is no real debate because the two theoretical approaches share many assumptions.

Intervention Direct involvement within a state by an outside actor to achieve an outcome preferred by the intervening agency without the consent of the host state.

Intrafirm trade International trade from one branch of a TNC to an affiliate of the same company in a different country.

Intransigent foreign policy A foreign policy that challenges the rules established by the great powers or rule-making states.

Invisible hand The concept found in the eighteenth-century writing of Adam Smith that proposed governments leave trade and financial sectors alone.

Jihad In Arabic, *jihad* simply means "struggle." Jihad can refer to a purely internal struggle to be a better Muslim, or a struggle to make society more closely align with the teachings of the Koran.

League of Nations The first permanent collective international security organization aimed at preventing future wars and resolving global problems. The League failed due to the failure of the US to join and the inability of its members to commit to a real international community.

Legitimacy A legitimate authority is respected and recognized by those it rules and by other rulers or leaders of other states. The source of legitimacy can be laws or a constitution and the support of the society.

Liberal Account of Rights The belief that humans have inherent rights that the state has a responsibility to protect.

Liberal democracy States with democratic or representative governments and capitalist economies that are promoters of multilateralism and free trade. Domestic interests, values, and institutions shape foreign policy.

Liberal feminism A position that advocates equal rights for women but also supports a more progressive policy agenda that would include social justice, peace, economic well-being, and ecological balance.

Liberal internationalism A perspective that seeks to transform international relations to emphasize peace, individual freedom, and prosperity, and to replicate domestic models of liberal democracy at the international level.

Liberalism According to Michael Doyle (1997, 207), liberalism includes the following four claims. First, all citizens are juridically equal and have equal rights to education, access to a free press, and religious toleration. Second, the legislative assembly of the state possesses only the authority invested in it by the people, whose basic rights it is not permitted to abuse. Third, a key dimension of the liberty of the individual is the right to own property, including productive forces. Fourth, liberalism contends that the most effective system of economic exchange is one that is largely market driven and not one that is subordinate to bureaucratic regulation and control.

Liberalism of privilege Developed democratic states have a responsibility to spread liberal values for the benefit of all peoples of the earth.

Liberalization Describes government policies that reduce the role of the state in the economy, such as the dismantling of trade tariffs and barriers, the deregulation and opening of the financial sector to foreign investors, and the privatization of state enterprises.

Market democracies See "liberal democracies."

Marshall Plan Officially known as the European Recovery Program, it was a program of financial and other economic aid for Europe after WWII. Proposed by Secretary of State George Marshall in 1948, it was offered to all European states, including the Soviet Union, and these funds played a critical role in European recovery.

Marxism A theory critical of the status quo or dominant paradigm. It is a critique of the capitalist political economy from the view of the revolutionary proletariat, or workers. The relations of production, or the relationship between workers and owners, is the determining factor in political relations. Marxists believe that those who own the means of production also control the political system. In capitalist systems, workers are exploited and thus alienated from both the economic and political systems. Marxists' ideal is a stateless and classless society.

Mass nationalism The use of nationalist ideology to encourage separation from an existing state. This is a tactic often employed with secessionist nationalism.

Material This refers to things that we can see, measure, consume, and use, such as military forces, oil, and currency.

Material interest The tangible physical goals of state officials as they set foreign and domestic policy.

Material structure An arrangement based on economic, political, and military resources.

Materialism In this context materialism means the spreading of a global consumer culture and popular-culture artifacts like music, books, and movies. Christopher Lasch called this the "ceaseless translation of luxuries into necessities." These elements are seen as undermining traditional cultural values and norms.

Middle powers These states, because of their position and past roles in international affairs, have very distinctive interests in the future order. Middle powers are activists in international and regional forums, and they are confirmed multilateralists in most issue areas. They support an equitable and pluralistic rule-based system. They are, for the most part, trading states and thus favor a relatively open and stable world market. Since stability is so important to them, most middle powers see themselves as global problem solvers, mediators, and moderators in international disputes (Wood 1998 and Holbraad 1984).

Modern state Political unit within which citizens identify with the state and see the state as legitimate. This state has a monopoly over the use of force and is able to provide citizens with key services.

Monopoly capitalism A term introduced by Lenin that suggested that competitive capitalism had been replaced by large corporations that control the market in specific sectors.

Most favored nation status This is the status granted to most trading partners that says trade rules with that country will be the same as those given to their most favored trading partner.

Multilateralism The process by which states work together to solve a common problem.

Multinational corporations or enterprises (MNCs/MNEs) A business or firm with administration, production, distribution, and marketing located in countries around the world. Such a business moves money, goods, services, and technology around the world depending upon where the firm can make the most profit.

Nation An community of people who share a common sense of identity, which may be derived from language, culture, or ethnicity; this community may be a minority within a single country or live in more than one country.

Nation-state A political community in which the state claims legitimacy on the grounds that it represents the nation.

National interest The combination of material and ideal goals that comprise the goals of the government of a state.

National liberation This was a doctrine promoted by the Soviet Union that encouraged anticolonial or anti-Western insurgencies in the developing world.

National security A fundamental value in the foreign policy of states secured by a variety of tools of statecraft including military actions, diplomacy, economic resources, and international agreements and alliances. It also depends on a stable and productive domestic society.

Nationalism The *idea* that the world is divided into nations that provide the overriding focus of political identity and loyalty, which in turn should be the basis for defining the population of states. Nationalism also can refer to this idea in the form of a strong sense of identity (*sentiment*) or organizations and movements seeking to realize this idea (*politics*).

National self-determination The right or desire of distinct national groups to become states and to rule themselves.

Natural law The idea that humans have an essential nature, which dictates that certain kinds of human goods are always and everywhere desired; because of this, there are common moral standards that govern all human relations, and these common standards can be discerned by the application of reason to human affairs.

Neoclassical realism A version of realism that combines both structural factors such as the distribution of power and unit-level factors such as the interests of states.

Neoliberalism Shaped by the ideas of commercial, republican, sociological, and institutional liberalism. Neoliberals see the international system as anarchic but believe relations can be managed by the establishment of international regimes and institutions. Neoliberals think that actors with common interests will try to maximize absolute gains.

New wars Wars of identity between different ethnic communities or nations, and wars that are caused by the collapse of states or the fragmentation of multiethnic states. Most of these new wars are internal or civil wars.

New world order This refers to the post–Cold War rhetoric of President George Herbert Walker Bush, who called for a new world order based on neoliberal values of democracy, capitalism, and the rule of law. After periods of turmoil or war, the victors often call for a new world order based on their values, beliefs, and interests.

Niche diplomacy Every state has its national interests and its areas of comparative advantage over other international actors. This is their area of expertise and where they have the greatest interests. Hence, this is where the state concentrates its foreign policy resources.

Noncompliance The failure of states or other actors to abide by treaties or rules supported by international regimes.

Nongovernmental organization (NGO) An organization, usually a grassroots one, with policy goals, but not governmental in makeup. An NGO is any group of people relating to each other regularly in some formal manner and engaging in collective action, provided the activities are noncommercial and nonviolent and are not on behalf of a government.

Nonintervention The principle that external powers should not intervene in the domestic affairs of sovereign states.

Non-nuclear weapons state (NNWS) A state that is party to the Treaty on the Nonproliferation of Nuclear Weapons, meaning that it does not possess nuclear weapons.

Nonpolar An international system in which power is not concentrated in a few states but is diffused among a variety of state and nonstate actors.

Nonpolar world A world in which there are many power centers and many of them are not nation-states. Power is diffused and is in many hands in many policy areas.

Nonstate actor Any participant in global politics that is neither acting in the name of government nor created and served by government. NGOs, terrorist networks, global crime syndicates, and multinational corporations are examples.

Normative orientation In foreign policy this means promoting certain norms and values and being prescriptive in one's foreign policy goals.

Normative theory Systematic analyses of the ethical, moral, and political principles that either govern or ought to govern the organization or conduct of global politics. The belief that theories should be concerned with what ought to be, rather than merely diagnosing what is.

Norms These specify general standards of behavior and identify the rights and obligations of states. Together, norms and principles define the essential character of

a regime, and these cannot be changed without transforming the nature of the regime.

North Atlantic Treaty Organization (NATO) Organization established by treaty in April 1949 comprising twelve (later sixteen) countries from Western Europe and North America. The most important aspect of the NATO alliance was the American commitment to the defense of Western Europe. Today NATO has twenty-eight member states.

Nuclear deterrence Defined by nuclear strategists as the possession of sufficient power to inflict unacceptable damage on a potential adversary. Nuclear deterrence must involve explicit threats in order to effectively prevent a state from using weapons. These threats must be seen as credible and must be clearly communicated.

Nuclear terrorism The use of or threat to use nuclear weapons or nuclear materials to achieve the goals of rogue states or revolutionary or radical organizations.

Nuclear weapon state (NWS) A state that is party to the Nonproliferation Treaty and has tested a nuclear weapon or other nuclear explosive device before January 1, 1967.

Offensive realism A structural theory of realism that views states as security maximizers.

Offshore finance centers Extraterritorial banks that investors use for a range of reasons, including the desire to avoid domestic taxes, regulations, and law enforcement agencies.

Oligarchs A term from ancient Greece to describe a political system in which a few people control a state.

Options Derivatives that give parties a right (without obligation) to buy or sell at a specific price for a stipulated period of time up to the contract's expiry date.

Ostpolitik The West German government's "Eastern Policy" of the mid- to late 1960s, designed to develop relations between West Germany and members of the Warsaw Pact.

Paradigm A model, or example. In the case of international relations theory, the term is a rough synonym for "academic perspective." A paradigm provides the essential basis for a theory. It presents a comprehensive framework for the identification of factors that are referenced in the construction of theory. It tells us what is real and significant in a given area. Research questions fall within the paradigm. It provides a means of selecting what will be the object of theory.

Paradox An absurd or self-contradictory statement.

Parsimony A word that can mean "miserliness," in political science it refers to attempts to develop a paradigm or theory that explains events in the simplest way possible.

Patriarchy A persistent society-wide structure within which gender relations are defined by male dominance and female subordination.

Peace dividend The misplaced belief that the end of the Cold War would bring about a fundamental change in international relations and provide funds for domestic programs or even result in a reduction in taxes.

Peace enforcement Designed to bring hostile parties to agreement and may occur without the consent of the parties.

Peace of Utrecht, 1713 The agreement that ended the War of the Spanish Succession and helped to consolidate the link between sovereign authority and territorial boundaries in Europe. This treaty refined the territorial scope of sovereign rights of states.

Peace of Westphalia, 1648 The treaties of Osnabrück and Münster, which together form the Peace of Westphalia, ended the Thirty Years' War and were crucial in delimiting the political rights and authority of European monarchs.

Peace Treaty of Versailles, 1919 The Treaty of Versailles formally ended the First World War (1914–1918). The treaty established the League of Nations, specified the rights and obligations of the victorious and defeated powers (including the notorious regime of reparations on Germany), and created the "Mandate" system under which "advanced nation-states" were given legal tutelage over colonial peoples.

Peacekeeping The interposition of third-party military personnel to keep warring parties apart.

Peacemaking Active diplomatic efforts to seek a resolution to an international dispute that has already escalated.

Perestroika Gorbachev's policy of restructuring, pursued in tandem with glasnost, and intended to modernize the Soviet political and economic system.

Pluralism The political theory of pluralism holds that political power and influence in society does not belong just to the citizens, nor to elite groups in various sectors of society, but is distributed among a wide number of groups in the society. It can also mean a recognition of ethnic, racial, and cultural diversity.

Political-economy approach The study of the interactions between states or public actors and the market at domestic and international levels.

Positivism and postpositivism Positivists (social scientists) and postpositivists (critical and constitutive theorists) form the basis for fierce debates among scholars. At the core lies a disagreement about whether or not social science theory can be value free. Positivists believe we can explain the social world as effectively as natural and physical scientists explain their phenomena. Postpositivists believe we cannot possibly be objective—value free—observers since we are actively or passively a part of the events and issues unfolding before us.

Positivists Analysts who use the scientific method to structure their research.

Post-conflict peace building Activities launched after a conflict has ended that seek to end the condition that caused the conflict.

Post–Washington Consensus A slightly modified version of the Washington Consensus, promoting economic growth through trade liberalization coupled with pro-poor growth and poverty-reduction policies.

Postmodern or new terrorists Groups and individuals subscribing to millennial and apocalyptic ideologies and system-level goals. Most value destruction for its own sake, unlike most terrorists in the past, who had specific goals, usually tied to a territory.

Postmodern state A political unit within which citizens are less nationalistic and more cosmopolitan in their outlook on both domestic and foreign policy. Policy-making authority for this kind of state is shared with a variety of actors at the local, national, regional, and international levels.

Postmodernity The postmodern international system is one where domestic and international affairs are intertwined, national borders are permeable, and states have rejected the use of force for resolving conflict. The European Union is seen as an example of the evolution of the state-centric system (Cooper 2003).

Poverty In the orthodox view, a situation suffered by people who do not have the money to buy food and satisfy other basic material needs. In the alternative view, a situation suffered by people who are not able to meet their material and nonmaterial needs through their own effort.

Premodern state A state within which the primary identity of citizens or subjects is to national, religious, or ethnic communities. People think of themselves as members of the subnational group first, rather than the state.

Preventive diplomacy Measures that states take to keep a disagreement from escalating.

Preventive war Launching a war to eliminate a perceived threat from another country, often started prior to the escalation of a crisis or before the enemy is itself prepared to attack.

Problem-solving theory Realism and liberalism are problem-solving theories that address issues and questions within the dominant paradigm or the present system. How can we fix capitalism? How can we make a society more democratic? These are problem-solving questions that assume nothing is wrong with the core elements of the system.

Promotive foreign policy A foreign policy that promotes the values and interests of a state and seeks to create an international system based on these values.

Protectionism Not an economic policy but a variety of political actions taken to protect domestic industries from more-efficient foreign producers. Usually this means the use of tariffs, nontariff barriers, and subsidies to protect domestic interests.

Protestant Reformation A social movement in reaction to the widespread perception that the Catholic Church had become corrupt and had lost its moral compass.

Public diplomacy The use of media, the Internet, and other social culture outlets to communicate the message of a state.

Radical liberalism This is the utopian side of liberalism best exemplified by the academic community called the World Order Models Project (WOMP). These scholars advocated a world in which states promote values like social justice, economic well being, peace, and ecological balance. These scholars see the liberal order as predatory and clearly in need of transformation.

Rapprochement Reestablishment of more friendly relations between the People's Republic of China and the United States in the early 1970s.

Ratification The procedure by which a state approves a convention or protocol that it has signed. There will be rules in the treaty concerning the number of ratifications required before it can enter into force.

Realism The theoretical approach that analyzes all international relations as the relation of states engaged in the pursuit of power. Realists see the international system as anarchic or without a common power, and they believe conflict is endemic in the international system.

Realpolitik First used to describe the foreign policy of Bismarck in Prussia, it describes the practice of diplomacy based on the assessment of power, territory, and material interests, with little concern for ethical realities.

Reciprocity A form of statecraft that employs retaliatory strategy, only cooperating if others do likewise.

Regimes Sets of implicit or explicit principles, norms, rules, and decision-making procedures around which actors' expectations converge in a given area of international relations. Often simply defined as governing arrangements in a regional or global policy area.

Regional diversity Each region of the world has experienced economic development differently based on traditions, culture, historical development, and even geographic location.

Regulatory arbitrage In the world of banking, the process of moving funds or business activity from one country to another in order to increase profits by escaping the constraints imposed by government regulations. By analogy, the term can be applied to any transfer of economic activity by any company in response to government policy.

Relative gains One of the factors that realists argue constrain the willingness of states to cooperate. States are less concerned about whether everyone benefits (absolute gains) and more concerned about whether someone may benefit more than someone else.

Responsibility to Protect The 2001 final report of the International Commission on Intervention and State Sovereignty; a UN publication that asserted the moral obligation for states to intervene in a state when that state violates the human rights of people living there.

Revolution in military affairs (RMA) This is the effect generated by the marriage of advanced communications and information processing with state-of-the-art weapons and delivery systems. It is a means of overcoming the uncertainty and confusion that are part of any battle in war.

Risk culture A pattern of relations within which people share the same perils.

Secessionist nationalism The use of nationalist ideology to create a new state, often by seceding from an existing multiethnic state.

Security Measures taken by states to ensure the safety of their citizens, the protection of their way of life, and the survival of their nation-state. Security can also mean the ownership of property that gives an individual the ability to secure the enjoyment or enforcement of a right or a basic human need.

Security community A regional group of countries that have the same guiding philosophic ideals—usually liberal-democratic principles, norms, and ethics—and tend to have the same style of political systems.

Security dilemma In an anarchic international system, one with no common central power, when one state seeks to improve its security it creates insecurity in other states.

Self-help In realist theory, in an anarchical environment, states cannot assume other states will come to their defense even if they are allies. *Each state must take care of itself.*

September 11, 2001 The day when Islamic terrorists in the United States hijacked four aircraft—two of which destroyed the World Trade Center in New York, one partially destroyed the Pentagon, and a fourth crash-landed in a field in Pennsylvania (see also "9/11").

Sex and gender "Sex" is biological difference, born male or female; the sex act; sexual difference. "Gender" is what it means to be male or female in a particular place or time; the social construction of sexual difference.

Sharia law Traditional Islamic law of the Koran ("al Qur'an") and the "Sunna," which are the interpretations of the life of the Prophet Muhammad.

Skyjacking The takeover of a commercial airplane for the purpose of taking hostages and using these hostages to bargain for a particular political or economic goal.

Social movement People with a diffuse sense of collective identity, solidarity, and common purpose that usually leads to collective political behavior. The concept covers all the different NGOs and networks, plus all their members and all the other individuals who share the common value(s). Thus, the women's movement and the environmental movement are much more than the specific NGOs that provide leadership and focus the desire for social change.

Social structure An arrangement based on ideas, norms, values, and shared beliefs. According to constructivists, the social domain does not exist in nature but is constructed through processes of interaction and the sharing of meaning.

Society of states An association of sovereign states based on their common interests, values, and norms.

Soft power Influence and authority deriving from the attraction that a country's political, social, and economic ideas, beliefs, and practices have for people living in other countries.

Sovereign equality The idea that all countries have the same rights, including the right of noninterference in their internal affairs.

Sovereignty The condition of a state having control and authority over its own territory and being free from any higher legal authority. It is related to, but distinct from, the condition of a government being free from any external political constraints.

Special Drawing Right (SDR) IMF members have the right to borrow this asset from the organization up to the amount that the country has invested in the IMF. The SDR is based on the value of a "basket" of the world's leading currencies: British pound, euro, Japanese yen, and US dollar.

Specialized agencies International institutions that have a special relationship with the central system of the United Nations but are constitutionally independent, having their own assessed budgets, executive heads and committees, and assemblies of the representatives of all state members.

Standard operating procedures (SOPs) The prepared-response patterns that organizations create to react to general categories of events, crises, and actions.

Standards of civilization A nineteenth-century European discourse about which values and norms made a country "civilized," or "barbaric" and "uncivilized." The conclusion was that civilized countries should colonize barbaric regions for the latter's benefit.

State A legal territorial entity composed of a stable population and a government; it possesses a monopoly over the legitimate use of force; its sovereignty is recognized by other states in the international system.

State sovereignty The concept that all countries are equal under international law and that they are protected from outside interference; this is the basis on which the UN and other international and regional organizations operate.

State-strengthening nationalism The use of nationalist ideology to bolster or reform a government or seek to regain territory at the expense of other states.

State system The regular patterns of interaction between states, but without implying any shared values between them. This is distinguished from the view of a "society" of states.

Statecraft The methods and tools that national leaders use to achieve the national interests of a state.

Strategic Arms Reductions Treaty (START) Negotiations began in 1982 and progressed at a very slow pace over eight years. The US and the USSR debated these issues in twelve rounds of formal negotiations, thirteen foreign ministers' meetings, and six summit conferences. In May 1990, George H. W. Bush and Gorbachev agreed to a framework for arms reduction. A treaty was signed in Moscow in July 1991. This treaty reversed a forty-five-year-old strategic nuclear arms race. The treaty broke new ground because it called for a reduction of nuclear arms rather than just a limit on the growth of these weapons.

Strategic Defense Initiative (SDI) A controversial strategic policy advocated by some conservative politicians and nuclear physicists such as Edward Teller, who helped to create the hydrogen bomb. SDI was embraced by the Reagan administration. The plan called for a defensive missile shield that would make Soviet offensive missiles ineffective by destroying them in flight. This defensive posture was to replace the US strategy of mutually assured destruction. Reagan wanted to make nuclear weapons impotent and obsolete. The plan is often derisively called "Star Wars," after the movies that were popular at the time.

Summit diplomacy A direct meeting between heads of government (of the superpowers in particular) to resolve major problems. The "summit" became a regular mode of contact during the Cold War.

Superstructure This is the government or political structure that is controlled by those who own the means of production.

Supranational global organization An authoritative international organization that operates above the national state.

Supraterratoriality Social, economic, cultural, and political connections that transcend territorial geography.

Survival In this context it is the survival of the person by the provision of adequate food, clean water, clothing, shelter, medical care, and protection from violence and crime.

Sustainable development This has been defined as development that meets the needs of the present without compromising the ability of future generations to meet their own needs.

Tactics The conduct and management of military capabilities in or near the battle area.

Technology transfer The process of sharing skills, knowledge, technologies, methods of manufacturing, and facilities among governments and private actors (like corporations) to ensure that scientific and technological developments are accessible to a wider range of users for application in new products, processes, materials, or services.

Terrorism The use of violence by nonstate groups or, in some cases, states to inspire fear, by attacking civilians and/or symbolic targets, and eliminating opposition groups. This is done for purposes such as drawing widespread attention to a grievance, provoking a severe response, or wearing down an opponent's moral resolve, to effect political change.

Theocracy A state based on religion.

Theory A proposed explanation of an event or behavior of an actor in the real world. Definitions range from "an unproven assumption" to "a working hypothesis that proposes an explanation for an action or behavior." In international relations we have intuitive theories, empirical theories, and normative theories.

Third-tier states Sometimes called the "less-developed states" or the "premodern states." These countries fail to provide the basics, such as border protection, law and order, and maintenance of a functioning economy.

Thirty Years' War The last of the great wars in Europe nominally for religion. Some historians believe that political leaders cynically used religious differences as an excuse to extend their kingdoms.

Trade liberalization The removal or reduction of barriers to free trade such as tariffs or quotas on the trading of specific goods.

Transborder Economic, political, social, or cultural activities crossing or extending across a border.

Transnational actor Any nongovernmental actor, such as a multinational corporation or one country's religious humanitarian organization, that has relations with any actor from another country or with an international organization.

Transnational company/corporation (TNC) A company that has affiliates in a foreign country. The affiliates may be branches of the parent company, separately incorporated subsidiaries, or associates with large minority shareholdings.

Transnational nonstate actor Any nonstate or nongovernmental actor from one country that has relations with any actor from another country or with an international organization.

Transnational terrorist networks Terrorists use existing global or transnational economic, transportation, and communication systems to manage and maintain terrorist organizations around the world. These networks facilitate the movement of followers and material to locations around the world.

Trench warfare From 1914 to 1918 the two sides in the war dug elaborate defensive fortifications in the ground. Because of the power of weapons like machine guns and rapid-fire cannons, trenches often gave the advantage in battle to the defenders.

Triangulation This occurs when trade or communication between two countries is routed indirectly via a third country. For example, in the early 1980s, neither the Argentine government nor the British government permitted trade between the two countries, but some companies simply sent their exports via Brazil or Western Europe.

Truman Doctrine Statement made by US president Harry Truman in March 1947 that it "must be the policy of the United States to support free people who are resisting attempted subjugation by armed minorities or by outside pressures." Intended to persuade Congress to support limited aid to Turkey and Greece, the doctrine came to underpin the policy of containment and American economic and political support for its allies.

United Nations Charter (1945) The charter of the United Nations is the legal regime that created the United Nations as the world's only "supranational" organization. The charter defines the structure of the United Nations, the powers of its constitutive agencies, and the rights and obligations of sovereign states party to the charter. Among other things, the charter is the key legal document limiting the use of force to instances of self-defense and collective peace enforcement endorsed by the United Nations Security Council.

Vertical proliferation An increase in the number of nuclear weapons a state possesses and in other technologies used for delivery of weapons. Recently, concerns were raised about the production of tactical nuclear weapons like bunker busters that could be used to destroy caves and underground facilities in Afghanistan.

Veto power The right of the five permanent members of the Security Council (United States, Russia, China, France, and Great Britain) to forbid any action by the United Nations.

Virtual jihad academy The use of the Internet to plan, promote, and propagate physical and cyber attacks as well as train and educate future followers or jihadists.

Warsaw Pact The Warsaw Pact was created in May 1955 in response to West Germany's rearmament and entry into NATO. It comprised the USSR and seven communist states (though Albania withdrew support in 1961). The organization was officially dissolved in July 1991.

Washington Consensus The belief of key opinion-formers in Washington that global welfare would be maximized by the universal application of neoclassical economic policies that favor a minimalist state and an enhanced role for the market.

Weapons of mass destruction A category defined by the United Nations in 1948 to include "atomic explosive weapons, radioactive material weapons, lethal chemical and biological weapons, and any weapons developed in the future which have characteristics comparable in destructive effects to those of the atomic bomb or other weapons mentioned above."

Widening school of international security Sometimes called the Copenhagen School, this refers to authors who extend the definition of security to include economic, political, societal, and environmental policy areas.

World Bank Group A collection of five agencies, the first established in 1945, with head offices in Washington, DC. The WBG promotes development in medium- and low-income countries with project loans, structural-adjustment programs, and various advisory services.

World order This is a wider category of order than the "international." It takes as its units of order not states, but individual human beings, and assesses the degree of order on the basis of the delivery of certain kinds of goods (be they security, human rights, basic needs, or justice) for humanity as a whole.

World Trade Organization (WTO) Established in 1995 with headquarters in Geneva. Membership (2010) of 153 states. The WTO is a permanent institution to replace the provisional GATT. It has a wider agenda, covering services, intellectual property, and investment issues as well as merchandise trade. The WTO also has greater powers of enforcement through its dispute-settlement mechanism. The organization's Trade Policy Review Body conducts surveillance of members' commercial measures.

Zero-sum world A pessimistic view of any interaction that suggests that another's gains are your losses.

References

Acharya, A. 2004. A holistic paradigm. *Security Dialogue* 35: 355–56.

——. 2007. *Promoting human security: Ethical, normative and educational frameworks in south east Asia.* Paris: United Nations Scientific, Cultural and Educational Organization.

Adler, E. 1992. The emergence of cooperation: National epistemic communities and the international evolution of the idea of nuclear arms control. *International Organization* 46: 101–45.

Allison, G. 1971. The impact of globalization on national and international security. In *Governance in a globalizing world*, ed. J. S. Nye and J. D. Donahue, 72–85. Washington, DC: Brookings Institution.

Armstrong, D. 1993. *Revolution and world order: The revolutionary state in international society.* Oxford: Clarendon Press.

Aron, R. 1966. *The century of total war.* New York: Garden City.

Axworthy, L. 2003. *Navigating a new world.* Toronto: Alfred Knopf Canada.

Bacevich, A. 2008. Introduction. In *The irony of American history*, R. Niebuhr. Chicago: The University of Chicago Press.

Bakker, E. 2006. *Jihadi terrorists in Europe, their characteristics and the circumstances in which they joined the jihad: An exploratory study.* Clingendael: Netherlands Institute of International Relations.

Barraclough, G. (ed.). 1984. *The Times atlas of world history.* London: Times Books.

Beitz, C. 1979. *Political theory and international relations.* Princeton, NJ: Princeton University Press.

Bellamy, A. J. 2002. *Kosovo and international society.* Basingstoke, UK: Palgrave.

Bello, W. 1994. *Dark victory: The United States, structural adjustment and global poverty.* London: Pluto Press.

Bennett, J., and S. George. 1987. *The hunger machine.* Cambridge: Polity Press.

Bethell, L. 1970. *The abolition of the Brazilian slave trade: Britain, Brazil and the slave trade question 1807–1869.* Cambridge: Cambridge University Press.

BIS. 1996. *International banking and financial market developments.* Basle: Bank for International Settlements.

——. 2006. Semiannual OTC derivatives statistics at end-June 2006. www.bis.org/statistics (accessed June 25, 2007).

Bloom, M. 2005. *Dying to win: The allure of suicide terror.* New York: Columbia University Press.

Booth, K. 1999. Three tyrannies. In *Human rights in global politics*, ed. T. Dunne and N. J. Wheeler. Cambridge: Cambridge University Press.

——. ed. 2004. *Critical security studies in world politics.* Boulder, CO: Lynne Rienner.

Booth, K. and T. Dunne. 1999. Learning beyond frontiers. In *human rights in global politics*, ed. T. Dunne and N. J. Wheeler, 303–28. Cambridge: Cambridge University Press.

Braun, L. 1987. *Selected writings on feminism and socialism.* Bloomington: Indiana University Press.

Breman, J. G. 2001. The ears of the hippopotamus: Manifestations, determinants, and estimates of the malaria burden. *American Journal of Tropical Medicine and Hygiene* 64(1/2): 1–11. http://www.ajtmh.org/cgi/reprint/64/1_suppl/1-c (accessed June 25, 2007).

Brewer, A. 1990. *Marxist theories of imperialism: A critical survey,* 2nd edn. London: Routledge.

Brittan, A. 1989. *Masculinity and power.* Oxford: Basil Blackwell.

Brocklehurst, H. 2007. Children and war. In *Contemporary Security Studies*, ed. A. Collins, 367–82. Oxford: Oxford University Press.

Brodie, B., ed. 1946. *The absolute weapon: Atomic power and world order.* New York: Harcourt Brace.

Brown, D. 2006. Study claims Iraq's "excess" death toll has reached 655,000. *Washington Post*, October 11, A12.

Brown, L. R., and H. Kane. 1995. *Full house: Reassessing the earth's population carrying capacity.* London: Earthscan.

Brundtland, G. H., *et al.* 1987. *Our common future: Report of the world commission on environment and development.* The Brundtland Report. Oxford: Oxford University Press.

Bull, H. 1977. *The anarchical society: A study of order in world politics.* London: Macmillan.

Buvinic, M. 1997. Women in poverty: A new global underclass. *Foreign Policy*: 38–53.

Cammack, P. 2002. The mother of all governments: The World Bank's matrix for global governance. In *Global governance: Critical perspectives*, ed. R. Wilkinson and S. Hughes. London: Routledge.

Carver, T. 1996. *Gender is not a synonym for women.* Boulder, CO: Lynne Rienner.

Castells, M. 2005. Global governance and global politics. *PS* (January): 9–16.

Centers for Disease Control. 2005. Fact sheet: Tuberculosis in the United States (March 17, 2005), http://www.cdc.gov/tb/pubs/TBfactsheets.htm (accessed June 25, 2007).

Chalk, P. 1996. *West European terrorism and counter-terrorism: The evolving dynamic.* New York: St Martin's Press.

Ching, F. 1999. Social impact of the regional financial crisis. In *The Asian economic crisis: Policy choices, social consequences and the Phillipine case*, Linda Y. C. Lim, F. Ching, and Bernardo M. Villegas. New York: Asia Society. http://www.asiasociety.org/publications/update_crisis_ching.html (accessed June 25, 2007).

Christensen, T., K. E. Jørgensen, and A. Wiener, eds. 2001. *The social construction of Europe.* London: Sage.

Clark, I. 1980. *Reform and resistance in the international order.* Cambridge: Cambridge University Press.

——. 1989. *The hierarchy of states: Reform and resistance in the international order.* Cambridge: Cambridge University Press.

Coglianese, C. 2000. Globalization and the design of international institutions. In *Governance in a globalizing world*, ed. J. S. Nye and J. D. Donahue, 297–318. Washington, D.C.: Brookings Institution Press.

Cohn, C. 1987. Sex and death in the rational world of defense. *Signs* Vol. 12, No. 4: 687–718.

Connell, R. W. 1995. *Masculinities*. London: Routledge.

Cooper, R. 2003. *The breaking of nations: Order and chaos in the 21st century*. New York: Atlantic Monthly Press.

Cooper, A., R. Higgott, and K. R. Nossal. 1993. *Relocating middle powers*. Vancouver: UBC Press.

Cooper, R. 2003. *The breaking of nations: Order and chaos in the 21st century*. New York: Atlantic Monthly Press.

Cox, R. 1981. Social forces, states and world orders: Beyond international relations theory. *Millennium Journal of International Studies* 10(2): 126–55.

Cox, R. 1989. Middlepowermanship, Japan, and the future world order. *International Journal* 44(4): 823–62.

Crenshaw, M., ed. 1983. *Terrorism, legitimacy, and power*. Middletown, CT: Wesleyan University Press.

Cronin, A. K. 2002/3. Behind the curve: Globalization and international terrorism. *International Security* 27(3): 30–58.

Davis, Z. S., and B. Frankel, eds. 1993. *The proliferation puzzle: Why nuclear weapons spread and what results*. London: Frank Cass.

Department for International Development. 2005. *Fighting poverty to build a safer world*. London: HMSO. http://www.dfid.gov.uk/pubs/files/securityforall.pdf (accessed June 25, 2007).

——. 2006. *Eliminating world poverty: Making governance work for the poor*, Cm 6876. London: HMSO. http://www.dfid.gov.uk/pubs/files/whitepaper2006/wp2006section3.pdf, (accessed June 25, 2007).

Doyle, M. W. 1986. Liberalism and world politics. *American Political Science Review* 80(4): 1151–69.

——. 1997. *Ways of war and peace: Realism, liberalism, and socialism*. New York: W. W. Norton.

Easterly, W. 2002. How did heavily indebted poor countries become heavily indebted? Reviewing two decades of debt relief. *World Development* 30(10): 1677–96.

Ekins, P. 1992. *A new world order: Grassroots movements for global change*. London: Routledge.

Elshtain, J. B. 1987. *Women and war*. New York: Basic Books.

Elshtain, J. B. and S. Tobias, eds. 1990. *Women, militarism, and war: Essays in history, politics, and social theory*. Totowa, NJ: Rowman & Littlefield.

Enloe, C. 1989. *Bananas, beaches and bases: Making feminist sense of international politics*. London: Pandora Books.

——. 1993. *The morning after: Sexual politics at the end of the cold war*. Berkeley: University of California Press.

——. 2000. *Maneuvers: The international politics of militarizing women's lives*. Berkeley: University of California Press.

Environmental Degradation and Conflict in Darfur: A Workshop Organized by the University of Peace of the United Nations and the Peace Research Institute, University of Khartoum, Khartoum, 15/16 December 2004.

Falk, R. 1995a. Liberalism at the global level: The last of the independent commissions. *Millennium Special Issue: The Globalization of Liberalism?* 24(3): 563–76.

——. 1995b. *On humane governance: Toward a new global politics*. Cambridge: Polity Press.

Fanon, F. 1967b; reissued 1990. *The wretched of the earth*. Harmondsworth: Penguin.

Fausto-Sterling, A. 1992. *Myths of gender: Biological theories about women and men*. New York: Basic Books.

——. 2000. *Sexing the body: Gender politics and the construction of sexuality*. New York: Basic Books.

Finnemore, M. 1996a. Norms, culture, and world politics: Insights from sociology's institutionalism. *International Organization* 50(2): 325–47.

——. 1996b. *National interests in international society*. Ithaca, NY: Cornell University Press.

Finnemore, M. and K. Sikkink. 1998. International norm dynamics and political change. *International Organization* 52 (Oct.): 887–918.

Finnis, J. 1980. *Natural law and natural rights*. Oxford: Clarendon Press.

Forsythe, D. P. 1988. The United Nations and human rights. In *Politics in the United Nations System*, ed. L. S. Finkelstein. Durham, NC, and London: Duke University Press.

Fox-Keller, E. 1985. *Reflections on gender and science*. New Haven, CT: Yale University Press.

Frank, A. G. 1967. *Capitalism and underdevelopment in Latin America*. New York: Monthly Review Press.

Friedman, J., ed. 2003. *Globalization, the state and violence*. Oxford: AltaMira Press.

Fukuyama, F. 1989. The end of history. *The National Interest* 16.

Gaddis, J. L. 2004. *Surprise, security and the American experience*. Cambridge, MA: Harvard University Press.

Gardner, G. T. 1994. *Nuclear nonproliferation: a primer*. London and Boulder, CO: Lynne Rienner.

Gendering human security: From marginalisation to the integration of women in peace-building. Oslo: Norwegian Institute of International Affairs and Fafo Forum on Gender Relations in Post-Conflict Transitions, 2001. http://www.fafo.no/pub/rapp/352/352.pdf (accessed June 25, 2007).

George, A. 1991. *Forceful Persuasion*. Washington, DC: USIP.

Gioseffi, D., ed. 2003. *Women on war: an international anthology of women's writings from antiquity to the present*, 2nd edn. New York: Feminist Press at the City University of New York.

Glendon, M. A. 2002. *A world made new: Eleanor Roosevelt and the Universal Declaration of Human Rights*. New York: Random House.

Gong, G. W. 1984. *The standard of 'civilization' in international society*. Oxford: Clarendon Press.

Goodman, D., and M. Redclift. 1991. *Refashioning nature: food, ecology and culture*. London: Routledge.

Gottlieb, R. S., ed. 1989. *An anthology of western Marxism: from Lukacs and Gramsci to socialist-feminism*. Oxford: Oxford University Press.

Gowa, J. 1983. *Closing the cold window: Domestic politics and the end of Bretton Woods*. Ithaca, NY: Cornell University Press.

Grace, C. S. 1994. *Nuclear weapons: Principles, effects and survivability*. London: Brassey's.

Gray, C. S. 1996. The second nuclear age: insecurity, proliferation, and the control of arms. In *The Brassey's Mershon American defense annual, 1995–1996: The United States and the emerging strategic environment*, ed. W. Murray, 135-54. Washington, DC: Brassey's.

——. 1999b. Clausewitz rules, OK? The future is the past—with GPS. *Review of International Studies* 25: 161–82.

Green, D. 1995. *Silent revolution: The rise of market economics in Latin America*. London: Latin America Bureau.

Greenwood, B. M., K. Bojang, C. J. Whitty, and G. A. Targett. 2005. Malaria. *The Lancet* 365 (9469): 1487–98.

Gunaratna, R. 2002. *Inside Al Qaeda: Global network of terror*. New York: Columbia University Press.

Hass, R. 2008. The age of nonpolarity. *Foreign Affairs*. 44–66.

Haraway, D. 1989. *Primate visions: Gender, race, and nature in the world of modern science*. New York: Routledge.

——. 1991. *Symians, cyborgs and women: The re-invention of nature*. New York: Routledge.

Harrington, M. 1989. *Socialism past and future*. New York: Arcade Publishing.

Hartsock, N. 1998. *The feminist standpoint revisited and other essays*. Boulder, CO: Westview Press.

Held, D. 1993. Democracy: From city-states to a cosmopolitan order? In *Prospects for democracy: North, south, east, west*, ed. D. Held, 13–52. Cambridge: Polity Press.

——. 1995. *Democracy and the global order: From the modern state to cosmopolitan governance*. Cambridge: Polity Press.

Held, D. and A. McGrew. 2002. *Globalization/anti-globalization*. Cambridge: Polity Press; 2nd edn, 2007.

Henderson J., K. Jackson, and R. Kennaway, eds. 1980. *Beyond New Zealand: The foreign policy of a small state*. Auckland, NZ: Methuen

Hennessy, R., and C. Ingraham, eds. 1997. *Materialist feminism: A reader in class, difference, and women's lives*. London: Routledge.

Hettne, B. 1999. Globalization and the new regionalism: The second great transformation. In *Globalism and the New Regionalism*, ed. B. Hettne, A. Intoai, and O. Sunkel. Basingstoke, UK: Macmillan.

Higgins, R. 1994. *Problems and process: International law and how we use it*. Oxford: Oxford University Press.

Hill, C. 2003. *The changing politics of foreign policy*. Houndmills, Basingstoke, UK: Palgrave Macmillan.

Hirst, P., and G. Thompson. 1996; 2nd edn, 1999. *Globalization in question: The international economy and the possibilities of governance*. Cambridge: Polity Press.

Holbraad, C. 1984. *Middle powers in international politics*. London: Macmillan.

Holsti, K. 1991. *Peace and war: Armed conflicts and international order 1648–1989*. Cambridge: Cambridge University Press.

Homer-Dixon, T. 1991. On the threshold: Environmental changes as causes of acute conflict. *International Security* 16: 76–116.

——. 1994. Environmental scarcities and violent conflict: Evidence from cases. *International Security* 19(1): 5–40.

Humphreys, M., and A. Varshney. 2004. Violent conflict and the millennium development: Goals: Diagnosis and recommendations. CGSD Working Paper No. 19, Center on Globalization and Sustainable Development, The Earth Institute at Columbia University. http://www.earthinstitute.columbia.edu/cgsd/documents/humphreys_conflict_and_MDG.pdf (accessed June 25, 2007).

Huntington, S. 1993. The clash of civilizations. *Foreign Affairs* 72(3): 22–169.

——. 1996. *The clash of civilizations and the remaking of the world order*. New York: Simon & Schuster.

Huntington, S. and N. Woods. 1995. Globalization and Inequality. *Millennium* 24(3): 447–70.

Hymans, J. E. 2006. *The psychology of nucleas proliferation*. Cambridge: Cambridge University Press.

ICPF (International Commission on Peace and Food). 1994. *Uncommon opportunities: An agenda for peace and equitable development*. London: Zed.

Ikenberry, G. J. 1999. Liberal hegemony and the future of American post-war order. In *International order and the future of world politics*, ed. T. V. Paul and J. A. Hall, 123–45. Cambridge: Cambridge University Press.

Ingebritsen, C., I. Neumann, S. Gstohl, and J. Beyer. 2006. *Small states in international relations*. Seattle: University of Washington Press.

Intergovernmental Panel on Climate Change (IPCC). 2007. *Climate change 2007: The physical science BASIS*. Contribution of Working Group 1 to the Fourth Assessment Report of the Intergovernmental Panel on Climate Change, www.ipcc.ch.

Jolly, R., and D. B. Ray. 2006. *National human development reports and the human security framework: A review of analysis and experience*. Brighton: Institute of Development Studies.

Junaid, S. 2005. *Terrorism and global power systems*. Oxford: Oxford University Press.

Kant, I. 1991. *Political writings*. Ed. Hans Reiss. Cambridge: Cambridge University Press.

Karp, A. 1995. *Ballistic missile proliferation: The politics and technics*. Oxford: Oxford University Press for Stockholm International Peace Research Institute.

Keck, M., and K. Sikkink. 1998. *Activists beyond borders: Transnational advocacy networks in international politics*. Ithaca, NY: Cornell University Press.

Keohane, R. 1984. *After hegemony: cooperation and discord in the world political economy*. Princeton, NJ: Princeton University Press.

——. ed. 1989a. *International institutions and state power: Essays in international relations theory*. Boulder, CO: Westview Press.

——. 1989b. Theory of world politics: Structural realism and beyond. In *International institutions and state power: Essays in international relations theory*, ed. R. Keohane. Boulder, CO: Westview Press.

——. 2002*a*. The globalization of informal violence, theories of world politics, and the "liberalism of fear." In *Power and governance in a partially globalized world*, ed. R. Keohane, 272-87. London: Routledge.

——. 2002*b*. The public delegitimation of terrorism and coalitional politics. In *Worlds in collision: Terror and the future of global order*, ed. K. Booth and T. Dunne, 141–51. London: Palgrave Macmillan.

Keohane, R. and J. Nye, eds. 1972. *Transnational relations and world politics*. Cambridge, MA: Harvard University Press.

Kinsella, H. M. 2003. For a careful reading: The conservativism of gender constructivism. *International Studies Review* 5: 294–7.

——. 2005*a*. Discourses of difference: Civilians, combatants, and compliance with the laws of war. *Review of International Studies*, Special Issue: 163–85.

——. 2005*b*. Securing the civilian: Sex and gender and laws of war. In *Power in global governance*, ed. M. Barnett and R. Duvall, 249–72. Cambridge: Cambridge University Press.

——. 2006. Gendering grotius: Sex and sex difference in the laws of war. *Political Theory* 34(2): 161–91.

Kirkpatrick, J. 1979. Dictatorships and double standards. *Commentary* 68.

Kissinger, H. A. 1977. *American foreign policy*, 3rd edn. New York: W. W. Norton.

Koehler, S. 2007. Professor explains continuous threat from land mines. Ozarks Local News, 7 February, available online at: http://www.banminesusa.org (accessed June 25, 2007).

Krause, K., and M. C. Williams, eds. 1997. *Critical security studies: Concepts and cases*. London: UCL Press.

Laqueur, W. 1996. Post-modern terrorism. *Foreign Affairs* 75(5): 24–37.

Lavoy, P. 1995. The strategic consequences of nuclear proliferation: A review essay. *Security Studies* 4(4): 695–753.

Leventhal, P., and Y. Alexander, eds. 1987. *Preventing nuclear terrorism*. Lexington, MA, and Toronto: Lexington Books.

Little, R. 1996. The growing relevance of pluralism? In *International theory: Positivism and beyond*, ed. S. Smith, K. Booth, and M. Zalewski, 66–86. Cambridge: Cambridge University Press.

Longino, H. E. 1990. *Science as social knowledge: Values and objectivity in scientific inquiry*. Princeton, NJ: Princeton University Press.

Luard, E., ed. 1992. *Basic texts in international relations*. London: Macmillan.

MacFarlane, N., and Khong Yuen Foong. 2006. *Human security and the UN: A critical history*. Bloomington: Indiana University Press.

Mackinnon, C. 1993. Crimes of war, crimes of peace. In *On human rights*, ed. S. Shute and S. Hurley. New York: Basic Books.

Marx, K. 1992. *Capital: student edition*. ed. C. J. Arthur. London: Lawrence & Wishart. First published 1867.

——. 1888. Theses on Feuerbach. In *Selected Works*, K. Marx and F. Engels, 28-30. London: Lawrence and Wishart, 1968.

Marx, K., and F. Engels. 1848. *The communist manifesto*, intr. by E. Hobsbawm. London: Verso, 1998.

Mathews, J. 1997. Power shift. *Foreign Affairs*. 76(1): 50–66.

Mead, W. R. 2001. *Special providence: American foreign policy and how it changed the world*. New York: Knopf.

Meadows, D. H., D. L. Meadows, and J. Randers. 1972. *The limits to growth*. London: Earth Island.

Mearsheimer, J. 1994/5. The false promise of international institutions. *International Security* 19(3): 5–49.

——. 2001. *The tragedy of great power politics*. New York: W. W. Norton.

Metz, S. 2004. *Armed conflict in the 21st century: the information revolution and post modern warfare*. Honolulu, HI: University Press of the Pacific.

Meyer, S. M. 1984. *The dynamics of nuclear proliferation*. Chicago: University of Chicago Press.

Milner, H. V. 1988. *Resisting protectionism: Global industries and the politics of international trade*. Princeton, NJ: Princeton University Press.

Mingst, K. 2004. *Essentials of international relations*. New York: W. W. Norton.

Mitrany, D. 1943. *A working peace system*. London: RIIA.

Morgenthau, H. J. [1948] 1955, 1962, 1978. *Politics among nations: The struggle for power and peace*, 2nd edn. New York: Knopf.

——. 1952. *American foreign policy: A critical examination*. London: Methuen (also published as *In Defence of the National Interest*).

——. 1960. *Politics among nations*. New York: Knopf.

——. 1985. *Politics among nations*, 6th edn. New York: McGraw-Hill.

Mousseau, F., and A. Mittal. 2006. Free market famine: Foreign policy in focus commentary, October 26, www.fpif.org/pdf/gac/0610famine.pdf (accessed June 25, 2007).

Naisbitt, J. 1994. *Global paradox: The bigger the world-economy, the more powerful its smallest players*. London: Brealey.

Nardin, T. 1983. *Law, morality and the relations of states*. Princeton, NJ: Princeton University Press.

National Counter Terrorism Center. 2005. *NCTC fact sheet and observations related to 2005 terrorist incidents*, www.NCTC.gov (accessed June 25, 2007).

NSS. 2001, 2002. *National security strategy of the United States of America*. Washington, DC: US Government Printing Office.

Nussbaum, M. 1996. *For love of country: Debating the limits of patriotism*. Boston: Beacon Press.

Nye, J. S. 2004. *Soft power*. New York: Public Affairs.

O'Brien, R. 1992. *Global financial integration: The end of geography*. London: Pinter.

Office of the Director of National Intelligence. 2005. Letter from Al-Zawahiri to Al-Zarqawi. October 11.

Ogilvie-White, T. 1996. Is there a theory of nuclear proliferation? *The Nonproliferation Review* 4(1): 43–60.

Ogilvie-White, T., and J. Simpson. 2003. The NPT and its prepcom session: A regime in need of intensive care. *The Nonproliferation Review* 10(1): 40–58.

Olson, J. S., ed. 1988. *Dictionary of the Vietnam War*. New York: Greenwood Press.

Onwudiwe, I. D. 2001. *The globalization of terror*. Burlington, VT: Ashgate.

Ougaard, M. 2004. *Political globalization—state, power and social forces*. London: Palgrave.

Owens, P. 2007. *Between war and politics: International relations and the thought of Hannah Arendt*. Oxford: Oxford University Press.

Oxfam. 2003. Boxing match in agricultural trade. Briefing Paper No. 32, www.oxfam.org (accessed June 25, 2007).

——. 2006. Grounds for change: Creating a voice for small farmers and farm workers with next international coffee agreement, http://www.oxfam.org/en/policy/briefingnotes/bn0604_coffee_groundsforchange (accessed June 25, 2007).

Palme Commission. 1982. Common security: A programme for disarmament. The report of the Palme Commission. London: Pan Books.

Panofsky, W. K. H. 1998. Dismantling the concept of "weapons of mass destruction." *Arms Control Today* 28(3): 3–8.

Pape, R. 2005. *Dying to win: The strategic logic of suicide terrorism*. New York: Random House.

Pastor, R. 1999. *A century's journey: How the great powers shape the world*. New York: Basic Boooks.

Pearson, R. 2000. Rethinking gender matters in development. In *Poverty and development into the twenty-first century*, ed. T. Allen and A. Thomas, 383–402. Oxford: Oxford University Press.

Pendergrast, M. 1993. *For God, country and Coca-Cola: The unauthorized history of the great American soft drink and the company that makes it*. London: Weidenfeld & Nicolson.

Peters, J. S., and A. Wolper, eds. 1995. *Women's rights, human rights: International feminist perspectives*. New York: Routledge.

Petzold-Bradley, E., A. Carius, and A. Vincze, eds. 2001. *Responding to environmental conflicts: Implications for theory and practice*. Dordrecht, Neth.: Kluwer Academic.

Pogge, T. 2002. *World poverty and human rights: Cosmopolitan responsibilities and reforms*. Cambridge: Polity Press.

Power and Interest News Report. 2006. Asia's coming water wars. August 22, http://www.pinr.com (accessed June 25, 2007).

Price, R. 1998. Reversing the gun sights: Transnational civil society targets land mines. *International Organization* 52(3).

Price, R., and N. Tannenwald. 1996. Norms and deterrence: The nuclear and chemical weapons taboos. In *The culture of national security: Norms and identity in world politics*, ed. P. J. Katzenstein, 114–52. New York: Columbia University Press.

Pugh, M. 2001. Peacekeeping and humanitarian intervention. In *Issues in world politics*, 2nd edn, ed. B. White, R. Little, and M. Smith. London: Palgrave.

Rabasa, A., P. Chalk, et al. 2006. *Beyond al-Qaeda: Part 2, the outer rings of the terrorist universe*. Santa Monica, CA: RAND.

Rapley, J. 1996. *Understanding Development*. Boulder, CO: Lynne Rienner.

Rehn, E., and E. J. Sirleaf. 2002. *Women, war, peace: The independent experts' assessment on the impact of armed conflict on women and women's role in peace-building*, http://www.unifem.org/resources/item_detail.php?ProductID;eq17 (accessed June 25, 2007).

Reus-Smit, C. 1999. *The moral purpose of the state*. Princeton, NJ: Princeton University Press.

——. 2001a. The strange death of liberal international theory. *European Journal of International Law* 12(3): 573–93.

Rhodes, E. 2003. The imperial logic of Bush's liberal agenda. *Survival* 45: 131–54.

Rice, S. 2006. The threat of global poverty. *The National Interest*: 76–82.

Richardson, J. L. 1997. Contending liberalisms: Past and present. *European Journal of International Relations* 3(1): 5–33.

Rischard, J. F. 2002. *High noon: Twenty global problems, twenty years to solve them*. New York: Basic Books.

Roberts, A. 1996. The United Nations: Variants of collective security. In *Explaining international relations since 1945*, ed. N. Woods, 309–36. Oxford: Oxford University Press.

Roberts, A., and B. Kingsbury. 1993. Introduction: The UN's roles in international society since 1945. In *United Nations, divided world*, ed. A. Roberts and B. Kingsbury. Oxford: Clarendon Press.

Roberts, G. 1984. *Questioning development*. London: Returned Volunteer Action.

Roberts, S. 1994. Fictitious capital, fictitious spaces: The geography of offshore financial flows. In *Money, Power and Space*, ed. S. Corbridge et al. Oxford: Blackwell.

Roche, D. 1986. Balance out of kilter in arms/society needs. *The Financial Post*, January 18, p.8.

Rodrik, D. 1999. *The new global economy and developing countries: Making openness work*. Washington, DC: Overseas Development Council, 148.

Rorty, R. 1993. Sentimentality and human rights. In *On human rights*, ed. S. Shute and S. Hurley. New York: Basic Books.

Rosamond, B. 2000. *Theories of European integration*. Basingstoke, UK: Macmillan.

Rose, G. 1998. Neoclassical realism and theories of foreign policy. *World Politics* 51(1): 144–72.

Rosenau, J. 1981. *The study of political adaptation*. London: Pinter Publishers.

Sagan, S. D., and K. N. Waltz. 1995. *The spread of nuclear weapons: A debate*. New York and London: W. W. Norton; 2nd edn, 2003.

Sageman, M. 2004. *Understanding terror networks*. Philadelphia: University of Pennsylvania Press.

Sargent, L., ed. 1981. *Women and revolution: A discussion of the unhappy marriage of Marxism and feminism*. Boston, MA: South End.

Scholte, J. A. 2000. *Globalization: A critical introduction*. Basingstoke, UK: Macmillan; 2nd edn, 2005.

Schwarz, A. 1999. *A nation in waiting: Indonesia's search for stability*. Sydney, Australia: Allen & Unwin.

Schweller, R. L. 1996. Neo-realism's status-quo bias: What security dilemma? *Security Studies* 5: 90–121.

——. 1998. *Deadly imbalances: Tripolarity and Hitler's strategy of world conquest.* New York: Columbia University Press.

Seidler, V. 1989. *Rediscovering masculinity: Reason, language and sexuality.* London: Routledge.

Sen, A. 1981. *Poverty and famines.* Oxford: Clarendon Press.

——. 1983. The food problem: Theory and policy. In *South–south strategy,* ed. A. Gauhar. London: Zed.

——. 1999. *Development as freedom.* Oxford: Oxford University Press.

Shue, H. 1996. *Basic rights,* 2nd edn. Princeton, NJ: Princeton University Press.

Smith, K. E., and M. Light, eds. 2001. *Ethics and foreign policy.* Cambridge: Cambridge University Press.

Smith, M. J. 1986. *Realist thought from Weber to Kissinger.* Baton Rouge, LA: Louisiana State University Press.

——. 2002. On thin ice: First steps for the ballistic missile code of conduct. *Arms Control Today* 32(6): 9–13.

Smith, S. 1999. The increasing insecurity of security studies: Conceptualising security in the last twenty years. *Contemporary Security Policy* 20(3).

Spivak, G. C. 1988. Can the subaltern speak? In *Marxism and the Interpretation of Culture,* ed. C. Nelson and L. Grossberg. Basingstoke, UK: Macmillan.

Steans, J. 1998. *Gender and international relations: an introduction.* Cambridge: Polity Press.

Suhrke, A. 2004. A stalled initiative. *Security Dialogue* 35(3): 365.

Tang, J. H., ed. 1994. *Human rights and international relations in the Asia-Pacific region.* London: Pinter.

Thomas, A., et al. 1994. *Third world atlas,* 2nd edn. Milton Keynes, UK: Open University Press.

Thomas, C. 2000. *Global governance, development and human security.* London: Pluto.

Thomas, C., and P. Wilkin. 2004. Still waiting after all these years: The third world on the periphery of international relations. *British Journal of Politics and International Relations,* 6: 223–40.

Thucydides. [1954] 1972. *The Peloponnesian war.* Trans. R. Warner. London: Penguin.

Tickner, J. A. 1992. *Gender in international relations: Feminist perspectives on achieving global security.* New York: Columbia University Press.

Tow, W. T., and R. Trood. 2000. Linkages between traditional security and human security. In *Asia's Emerging Regional Order,* ed. W. T. Tow, R. Thakur, and In-Taek Hyun, 14. New York: United Nations University Press.

UN. 2002. *Women, peace and security: Study submitted by the secretary-general pursuant to security council resolution 1325 (2000).* New York: United Nations, http://www.un.org/womenwatch/feature/wps/ (accessed June 25, 2007).

——. 2004. *A more secure world.* UN Secretary-General's High-Level Panel on Threats, Challenges and Change, http://www.un.org/secureworld.

——. 2005. *In larger freedom: Towards development, security and human rights for all: Report of the Secretary-General,* March.

UNCTAD, Division on Transnational Corporations and Investment. 1996. *Transnational corporations and world development.* London: International Thomson Business Press.

——. 2006a. *Trade and development report.* Geneva: United Nations Conference on Trade and Development.

——. 2006b. *World investment report 2006.* Geneva: United Nations Conference on Trade and Development.

UNDP. 1994. *United Nations human development report.* New York: Oxford University Press.

——. 1997. *United Nations human development report 1997.* New York: United Nations Development Programme.

——. 1998. *United Nations human development report 1998.* Oxford: Oxford University Press.

——. 2003. *United Nations human development report.* New York: United Nations Development Programme.

——. 2005. *Human Development report 2005: International cooperation at a crossroads* New York: United Nations Development Programme.

United Nations Inter-Agency Committee on Women and Gender Equality. 1999. *Final communiqué, women's empowerment in the context of human security* (7–8 December 1999, ESCAP, Bangkok, Thailand), http://www.un.org/womenwatch/ianwge/collaboration/finalcomm1999.htm (accessed June 25, 2007).

University of British Columbia, Human Security Center. 2005. *Human security report 2005: War and peace in the 21st century.* New York: Oxford University Press.

——. 2006. *The human security brief 2006,* http://www.humansecuritybrief.info/, (accessed June 25, 2007).

US Department of State. 2003. *Country reports on human rights practices, Burma.* March 31 2003, http://www.state.gov/g/drl/rls/hrrpt/2002/18237.htm (accessed June 25, 2007).

Vincent, R. J. 1974. *Nonintervention and international order.* Princeton, NJ: Princeton University Press.

Wallerstein, I. 1979. *The capitalist world-economy.* Cambridge: Cambridge University Press.

Walt, S. 2002., The enduring relevance of the realist tradition. In *Political science: The state of the discipline,* ed. I. Katznelson and H. V. Milner. New York: W. W. Norton.

Waltz, K. 1959. *Man, the state and war.* New York: Columbia University Press.

——. 1979. *Theory of international politics.* Reading, MA: Addison-Wesley.

——. 1989. The origins of war in neorealist theory. In *The origin and prevention of major wars,* ed. R. I. Rotberg and T. K. Rabb, 39–52. Cambridge: Cambridge University Press.

Walzer, M. 1977. *Just and unjust wars: a moral argument with historical illustration* Harmondsworth, UK: Penguin and New York: Basic Books.

——. 1994. *Thick and thin: Moral argument at home and abroad.* Notre Dame, IN: University of Notre Dame Press.

——. 1995. The politics of rescue. *Dissent.* Winter.

Weaver, O., B. Buzan, M. Kelstrup, and P. Lemaitre. 1993. *Identity, migration and the new security agenda in Europe.* London: Pinter.

Weber, H. 2002. Global governance and poverty reduction. In *Global governance: Critical perspectives*, ed. S. Hughes and R. Wilkinson. London: Palgrave.

Weber, M. 1949. *The methodology of the social sciences*. Ed. E. Shils and H. Finch. New York: Free Press.

Weiss, T. G. 2004. The sunset of humanitarian intervention? The responsibility to protect in a unipolar era. *Security Dialogue* 35(2):135–53.

Wendt, A. 1992. Anarchy is what states make of it: The social construction of power politics. *International Organisation* 46(2): 391–425.

——. 1995. Constructing international politics. *International Security* 20(1).

——. 1999. *Social theory of international politics*. Cambridge: Cambridge University Press.

Wessel, I., and G. Wimhofer, eds. 2001. *Violence in Indonesia*. Hamburg: Abera-Verl.

Weston, B. H., R. Falk, and A. D'Amato. 1990. *Basic documents in international law*, 2nd edn. St Paul, MN: West Publishing.

Wheeler, N. J. and K. Booth. 1992. The security dilemma. In *Dilemmas of world politics: International issues in a changing world*, ed. J. Baylis and N. J. Rengger. Oxford: Oxford University Press.

Wiener, A., and T. Diez, eds. 2004. *European integration theory*. Oxford: Oxford University Press.

Wilkinson, P. 2003. Implications of the attacks of 9/11 for the future of terrorism. In *Global responses to terrorism*, ed. M. Buckley and R. Fawn. London: Routledge.

Wood, B. 1998. *The middle powers and the general interest*. Ottawa: North-South Institute.

World Health Organization (n.d.). *Roll back malaria: The economic costs of malaria* Geneva: WHO, http://www.rbm.who.int/cmc_upload/0/000/015/363/RBMInfosheet_10.htm (accessed June 25, 2007).

——. 2006. *Avian influenza ("bird flu")—fact sheet*. February 2006, www.who.int/mediacentre/factsheets/avian_influenza/en/ (accessed June 25, 2007).

World Trade Organization. 1995. *International trade: Trends and statistics*. Geneva: WTO.

Wright, R. 1986. *Sacred rage: The wrath of militant Islam*. New York: Simon & Schuster.

Yale University Cambodian Genocide Program. http://www.yale.edu/cgp.

Zakaria, F. 1998. *From wealth to power: The unusual origins of America's world role*. Princeton, NJ: Princeton University Press.

Zalewski, M. 1993. Feminist standpoint theory meets international relations theory: A feminist version of David and Goliath. *Fletcher Forum of World Affairs* 17(2).

Zalewski, M., and J. Parpart, eds. 1998. *The "man" question in international relations*. Boulder, CO: Westview Press.

Zevin, R. 1992. Are world financial markets more open? If so, why and with what effects? In *Financial openness and national autonomy: Opportunities and constraints*, ed. T. Banuri and J. B. Schor. Oxford: Clarendon Press.

Credits

PHOTO CREDITS

Chapter 1
p. 1: AP Photo/Kirsty Wigglesworth; p. 2: AP Photo/Mark Lennihan; p. 6: AP Photo/Jin Lee; p. 8: AP Photo/Kirsty Wigglesworth; p. 10: AP Photo/Rafiq Maqbool; p. 10: AP Photo/Obed Zilwa; p. 11: Glow Images/Getty Images; p. 12: AP Photo/Hideyuki Yamamoto; p. 13: AP Photo/Joerg Sarbach; p. 18: AP Photo/Ben Curtis, File; p. 19: AP Photo/Brennan Linsley; p. 20: Steve Parsons/PA Wire URN: 8058612 (Press Association via AP Images)

Chapter 2
p. 24: AP Photo/File; p. 28: Le Sueur Brothers/Getty Images; p. 31: AP Photo; p. 32: AP Photo; p. 33: AP Photo; p. 39: SuperStock/Getty Images; p. 43: AP Photo/Thomas Kienzle; p. 45: AP Photo/Greg Gibson; p. 47: AP Photo/U.S.M.C., Sgt. Don L. Maes, File; p. 49: AP Photo Bjorn Sigurdson/Scanpix Norway, Pool; p. 51: AP Photo/ Boris Yurchenko; p. 53: AP Photo/APTN; p. 56: AP Photo/J. Scott Applewhite; p. 57: AP Photo/John Moore

Chapter 3
p. 61: Comstock Images/Getty Images; p. 62: Chung Sung-Jun/ Getty Images; p. 65: AP Photo/Tom Pennington; p. 68: AP Photo/ Kamran Jebreili; P. 70: AP Photo, RIA Novosti, Alexei Druzhinin, pool; P. 75: STR/AFP/Getty Images; p. 81: AP Photo/Pablo Martinez Monsivais; p. 82: Time Life Pictures/US Army Signal Corps/Time Life Pictures/Getty Images; p. 85: AP Photo/Lee Jin-man; p. 87: AP Photo/Glenna Gordon; Pool

Chapter 4
p. 92: AP Photo/Kirsty Wigglesworth; p. 97: AP Photo/Herbert Knosowski; p. 101: Imaginechina via AP Images; p. 105: Milos Bicanski/Getty Images; p. 109: AP Photo/Gero Breloer; p. 111: Comstock Images/Getty Images

Chapter 5
p. 115: M. Llorden/Getty Images; p. 116: Junko Kimura/Getty Images; p. 120: AP Photo/Rafiq Maqbool; p. 121: Imaginechina via AP Images; p. 124: AP Photo/Lakruwan Wanniarachchi, Pool; p. 127: AP Photo/Manu Fernandez; p. 131 AP Photo/Kin Cheung; p. 134: Ian Hitchcock/Getty Images; p. 135: AP Photo/Mary Altaffer; p. 138: AP Photo/RIA Novosti, Dmitry Astakhov; p. 141: Andrew Harrer/ Bloomberg via Getty Images; p. 143: AP Photo/Esteban Felix; p. 146: AP Photo/Eraldo Peres, File; p. 147: THE CANADIAN PRESS/Sean Kilpatrick; p. 149: AP Photo/Eraldo Peres; p. 153: Cynthia Johnson/ Time Life Pictures/Getty Images; p. 155: AP Photo/Richard Drew, File

Chapter 6
p. 158: AP Photo/Susan Walsh; p. 160: AP Photo/Mary Altaffer; p. 163: AP Photo/Keystone, Salvatore Di Nolfi; p. 166: AP Photo/ Ahn Young-joon; p. 169: AP Photo; p. 173: AP Photo/Alfred de Montesquiou; p. 177: Comstock Images/Getty Images; p. 179: AP Photo/Mohammed Zaatari; p. 182: Mario Tama/Getty Images; p. 183: AP Photo/Manish Swarup, File; p. 185: AP Photo/Keystone, Sandro Campardo; p. 188: M. Llorden/Getty Images

Chapter 7
p. 194: MIKE CLARKE/AFP/Getty Images; p. 197: Jeoffrey Maitem/ Getty Images; p. 201: AP Photo/Burhan Ozbilici; p. 203: AP Photo/ Greg Baker; p. 205: AP Photo, File; p. 207: JIM WATSON/AFP/ Getty Images; p. 211: GALI TIBBON/AFP/Getty Images; p. 215: AP Photo/Eduardo Verdugo; p. 216: AP Photo/Yahya Ahmed; p. 219: MANPREET ROMANA/AFP/Getty Images

Chapter 8
p. 221: AP Photo/Karel Prinsloo; p. 222: AP Photo/Mikhail Metzel; p. 226: AP Photo/Ramon Espinosa; p. 228: AP Photo/U.S. Marine Corps/Sgt. L.A. Salinas; p. 229: AP Photo/Yves Logghe; p. 232: AP Photo/Don Mell; p. 234: AP Photo/Karel Prinsloo; p. 235: AP Photo/ DoD photo by Master Sgt. Val Gempis, U.S. Air Force; p. 237: Logan Mock-Bunting/Getty Images; p. 241: AP Photo/Ross D. Franklin; p. 243: AP Photo/Department of State/HO; p. 244: PIUS OTOMI EKPEI/AFP/Getty Images; p. 247: AP Photo/Fars News Agency, Vahid Reza Alaei, file; p. 251: AP Photo/Hans Punz; p. 253: AP Photo/Adam Butler

Chapter 9
p. 258: Hazel Thompson/The New York Times/Redux; p. 261: AP Photo/Mark Lennihan; p. 264: AP Photo/Basque Television; p. 266: AP Photo/Greg Baker; p. 267: AP Photo/Chao Soi Cheong/FILE; p. 270: AP Photo/Laurent Rebours; p. 272: The White House/ Getty Images; p. 276: AP Photo/NHK; p. 278: AP Photo; p. 279: AP Photo/Andres Leighton; p. 280: AP Photo/Elaine Thompson

Chapter 10
p. 282: AP Photo/Sven Kaestner; p. 286: AP Photo/David Longstreath; p. 290: AP Photo/Bullit Marquez; p. 291: AP Photo/ Sakchai Lalit; p. 293: AP Photo/Joao Silva; p. 295: AP Photo/Bullit Marquez; p. 296: AP Photo/Bas Czerwinski; p. 300: AP Photo/ Shakh Aivazov, File; p. 306: AP Photo/Schalk van Zuydam; p. 309: George Rose/Getty Images; p. 310: AP Photo/John Stillwell; p. 312: AP Photo/Firdia Lisnawati

Chapter 11
p. 315: Imaginechina via AP Images; p. 316: Press Association via AP Images; p. 319: AP Photo; p. 321: AP Photo/Keystone/Salvatore Di Nolfi; p. 324: AP Photo/Srdjan Ilic; p. 329: AP Photo/Mike Alquinto; p. 332: Imaginechina via AP Images; p. 337: Mario Tama/Getty Images

Chapter 12
p. 340: AP Photo/Richard Drew, File; p. 344: Imaginechina via AP Images; p. 349: AP Photo/Doug Mills; p. 353: Imaginechina via AP Images; p. 355: Michel Delsol/Time Life Pictures/Getty Images; p. 357: Imaginechina via AP Images; p. 365: AP Photo/Keystone/ Martial Trezzini; p. 366: AP Photo/Lefteris Pitarakis, file

Chapter 13
p. 368: JOHN D MCHUGH/AFP/Getty Images; p. 370: ROMEO GACAD/AFP/Getty Images; p. 373: Spencer Platt/Getty Images; p. 375: AP Photo/Al Behrman; p. 381: ALEXANDER JOE/AFP/Getty Images; p. 384: AP Photo/Mike Alquinto; p. 386: Bryan Bedder/ Getty Images for IMG; p. 388: AP Photo/Christine Nesbitt; p. 390: SIMON MAINA/AFP/Getty Images; p. 392: ROBERTO SCHMIDT/ AFP/Getty Images

Chapter 14
p. 396: AP photo/Nasa; p. 399: AP Photo/Romas Dabrukas; p. 399: AP Photo/Dennis Cook; p. 403: AP Photo/Achmad Ibrahim; p. 404: AP Photo/Mark Baker; p. 405: AP Photo/John McConnico;

Index